ORGANIZATIONAL INFLUENCE PROCESSES

ORGANIZATIONAL INFLUENCE PROCESSES

— SECOND EDITION —

**LYMAN W. PORTER,
HAROLD L. ANGLE,
ROBERT W. ALLEN**

EDITORS

M.E.Sharpe
Armonk, New York
London, England

Library of Congress Cataloging-in-Publication Data

Organizational influence processes / edited by Lyman W. Porter, Harold L. Angle, and Robert
W. Allen.—2nd ed.
      p. cm.
    Includes bibliographical references and index.
      ISBN 0-7656-1134-1 (alk. paper) — ISBN 0-7656-0999-1 (pbk.: alk. paper)
        1. Organizational behavior. 2. Power (Social sciences) I. Porter, Lyman W. II. Angle,
Harold L. III. Allen, Robert W., 1931–

HD58.7 .O737 2003
302.3'5—dc21   2002030891

Printed in the United States of America

The paper used in this publication meets the minimum requirements of
American National Standard for Information Sciences
Permanence of Paper for Printed Library Materials,
ANSI Z 39.48-1984.

BM (c)   10   9   8   7   6   5   4   3   2
BM (p)   10   9   8   7   6   5   4   3   2

CONTENTS

LIST OF ILLUSTRATIONS

Tables

Figures

PREFACE

The first edition of this book, published some two decades ago, grew out of a research project (that included our then-colleagues Patty Renwick Lawler, Dan Madison, and Tom Mayes) that dealt with the study of organizational politics. The two authors of that first edition, the late Robert W. Allen (RWA) and Lyman W. Porter (LWP), decided to make a comprehensive review and analysis of not only the literature on organizational politics but also the literature on the more general topic of organizational influence processes. The culmination of that review was the publication of the first edition.

The two authors of the original book subsequently became involved with a number of other intellectual and professional activities over the following years that precluded turning their attention to the preparation of a second edition. Finally, several years ago it was possible to return to the long-intended objective of developing an updated revision. Work in reviewing a large number of articles for possible inclusion proceeded apace. Unfortunately, however, during this time RWA developed a serious illness and passed away. In the months that followed, LWP invited Harold L. Angle (HLA), also a former member of the organizational politics research team, to work with him on finishing the tasks of article review and selection and the drafting of the introduction to the second edition and the introductory essays that lead off each section of the book. Thus, the final product of this second edition is the work of LWP and HLA.

In selecting the articles for this edition, as with the first edition, we were guided by several key criteria: relevance to the topic of organizational influence processes; substance (i.e., "does the article make a relatively significant contribution?"); interest and appeal (i.e., "do we ourselves enjoy reading it and find its contents stimulating?"); and recency. However, the latter criterion requires additional explanation: Consistent with our policy in the first edition, we occasionally have deliberately violated the objective of recency by choosing to include several articles that are more than a decade or so old. In these instances, we believe that the selections have a certain "timelessness" that make them still appropriate for inclusion. We should also note that we found a number of other appropriate and recent articles that could have been included if there were no constraints on the length of the book. However, as is frequently the case in attempting to exercise influence, we were forced to make choices.

In conclusion, we dedicate this second edition to our late colleague, Bob Allen, who influenced us in many positive ways both as an academic colleague and as a person.

LWP
HLA

INTRODUCTION

As suggested several years ago by Chester Barnard (1938), an organization is basically a *cooperative system*—a social system comprised of individuals and groups who join together and collaborate in the pursuit of one or more common goals. The formal structure of an organization provides a rational framework to facilitate the collaborative efforts of the various individuals and groups who make up that organization. Yet, this formal structure is not enough to ensure all of the necessary collaboration. *Social influence* is necessary to accomplish what formal structure, by itself, cannot accomplish.

ORGANIZATIONAL STRUCTURE AND SOCIAL INFLUENCE PROCESSES

At a very basic level, organizational structure consists of a matrix of vertical and horizontal differentiation—a demarcation of levels of hierarchical authority and responsibility and functional areas of expertise required for goal attainment. A complementary function of organizational structure is to provide a rational basis for coordinating or integrating the differentiated parts of the organization. Policies, procedures, operating practices, information systems, and established working relationships are typical examples of integrative devices. This mutually supportive system of differentiation and integration is what makes an organization work—the necessary tasks and responsibilities are allocated to those persons and entities most appropriate for their accomplishment, and the many individual contributions of the members are recombined into a unified whole so that the organization's purposes may be realized.

That having been said, we believe there is much wisdom in that old adage "The devil is in the details." Although at some superordinate level the members of the organization are ostensibly pursuing shared (or at least compatible) objectives, there may also be many lower-level (i.e., individual and subunit) goals that are not entirely mutually consistent, either with each other or with the larger goals of the organization. Moreover, even for the attainment of agreed-upon ends, there may be widely divergent views regarding the best *means* for their attainment. Finally, even under circumstances where there is agreement on both means and ends, there is still no assurance that every member of the system will always spontaneously exhibit the necessary behaviors, without being influenced to do so by someone else such as a supervisor or a colleague. For these and similar reasons, organization members often use various social influence tactics in an attempt to induce others to behave in ways seen as necessary for goal attainment.

This book is about the many varieties of social influence attempts—some successful, some not—that take place when individuals and groups come together in an organization. The daily life of almost any organization is filled with instances of people or groups of people attempting to influence the attitudes and/or behaviors of other people or groups. We believe that such interpersonal and interunit influence processes are among the most pervasive and important activities that take place in just about any organization.

Although social influence has long been a topic of interest to scholars in the social and behavioral sciences, it has not always received the attention it merits in the literatures of organization theory and organizational behavior. This is not to claim that the topic has been ignored altogether in the organizational sciences—only that the perspectives on influence processes have been unduly narrow until fairly recently. Although downward influence, generally in the guise of *leadership*, has been a well-established topic for study for many years (Stogdill 1981), other important social influence processes—that is, those aimed laterally or upward in the organization—have not received nearly as much attention in the past.

The situation has been improving. Since about the time the first edition of this book was published (1983), there has been a marked increase in the attention paid to social influence processes of all types in organizations. This is evident in the proliferation of scholarly publications on organizational politics, power and influence, and related subjects, over the past twenty years or so (Kacmar and Baron 1999). Indeed, a basic purpose of this second edition of *Organizational Influence Processes* is to bring the reader up to date on trends and perspectives that have emerged since the first edition.

This is not to say, however, that everything in the book is new since the first edition. Although most of the readings in this book are new, about 20 percent of the second edition comprises material that appeared in the first edition, some of which has attained "classic" status in the intervening years. We strongly believe that the articles we have carried forward to the second edition are essential to an appreciation of the dynamics of organizational influence—particularly for the reader who is a relative newcomer to the field.

TRENDS AND DEVELOPMENTS SINCE THE FIRST EDITION

It would be difficult to overstate how much the world of organizations has evolved over the past two decades. Profound change has taken place both inside modern organizations and in the environments in which those organizations reside. Many of these changes have greatly increased the importance of the topic of organizational influence processes. This is because so many of the changes have led us toward organizational situations that are much more complex, more ambiguous, more fluid or temporary, and more uncertain—all preconditions for an increase in the role of influence processes, including political behavior.

It would be beyond the scope of this discussion to attempt to catalogue all of the ways in which organizations and their environments have been changing. For example, there are very few people these days who would be surprised to learn that the world has become a virtual global village, or that the demographic makeup of organizations has become much more diverse ethnically, racially, and by gender composition than was the case a generation ago. Such trends certainly have implications for organizational influence processes; however, we believe there has been a cluster of changes taking place that has had even more fundamental impacts on the topic of this book, which is organizational influence processes. This group of changes is essentially a syndrome comprised of several interrelated trends. Although there does not seem currently to be a summary term to describe this syndrome, a term that we believe comes close to capturing most of the more important aspects is *organizational destructuring*.

As we have suggested, organizational destructuring is not simply one type of change but a set of related trends whose effects all point in the same general direction. Perhaps at the center of this cluster of trends is the ongoing trend toward greater *complexity* both inside organizations themselves and in their environments. This almost automatically leads to decentralization of authority because no individual or subunit can know enough to cope with the various contingencies facing the organization. As complexity reaches very high levels, organizations tend to reorient their structure from the vertical dimension (i.e., the chain of authority) to the horizontal. Rather than relying on established hierarchical prerogatives and procedural rules, organizations then tend to make more decisions based on peer-to-peer negotiation. Thus, organizational choices based on policies or rules are rendered relatively ineffective and must be supplanted by people influencing other people.

Another closely related aspect of the syndrome we are describing is the increasingly rapid pace of events in today's organizations, that is, the general rate of change. The effect of this intense pace is much the same as the effect of complexity. At some point, it becomes impractical or impossible to centralize decision prerogatives because a centralized decision-making entity is unable to keep up with the speed of the unfolding demands and signals from the environment. Once again, it becomes necessary to decentralize authority to "where the action is," in order to keep pace with and manage the various contingencies the organizations must deal with. Once again, the ultimate effect is to create a network of parties or stakeholders who must attempt to influence the activities of other stakeholders.

The effects of this escalating pace of events are probably exacerbated by recent technological innovations in communication, such as e-mail. It has become possible to communicate fairly effortlessly and quite rapidly, even across great distances. This capability opens up many new possibilities for its use in influencing others in the organizational milieu.

Many other examples come to mind, but we believe that the basic point has been made. The sum total of developments that make decentralization necessary for organizational survival, let alone organizational success, has created circumstances under which organizational influence processes are even more important than they have been in the past. We do not see any evidence of this trend reversing, in the foreseeable future. On the contrary, we strongly assert that the subject matter of this book has become firmly established as one of the most central and important topic areas within the field of organization science.

PURPOSE AND ORGANIZATION OF THE BOOK

The purpose of this book is to enhance the reader's understanding of social influence processes—both formal and informal—in organizational settings. Organizational influence attempts occur in many guises, and recognition of this complexity may be the beginning of wisdom in the serious study of organizational dynamics. We have often noted that the inexperienced student will make the tacit assumption that the "important" influence in organizations is exerted by legitimate authority figures, in a downward direction (i.e., along the organization's formal authority chain). In this book, we take a decidedly contrary approach and suggest that this type of influence may be in the *minority* of actual influence events in the typical organization. Put in another way, that old cliché, "tip of the iceberg," may apply quite nicely to organizational influence processes. The legitimate-formal-downward type of influence would be analogous to the visible (and relatively small) part of an iceberg, while the underwater part of the iceberg (to continue the analogy, the less formal influence that is often exerted laterally or upward) is not only larger—we believe it is also often more interesting.

In keeping with that view, we have organized this book on organizational influence processes by separating influences into those that are directed downward, those that are directed laterally, and, finally, those that are aimed in an upward direction. We view this directionality-of-influence framework as variations on a theme (a concept we borrow from the field of musical composition). That is, each influence direction has certain unique aspects, but all share certain underlying and fundamental foundations. For this reason, the first section of the book will address general issues of power and influence (i.e., the theme) and Parts 2 through 4 will emphasize the variations—downward, lateral, and upward influence processes.

A carefully selected set of readings is presented in the four sections that follow. Part 1 of the book concentrates on the general concepts of power and influence, providing a broad framework for considering the process of influencing others at various levels in organizations. Here, the emphasis is on general aspects of influence that are not necessarily specific to the direction of influence. This section provides a basic grounding in the literature of power and influence that will serve as background information for the material in the three sections to follow.

In Part 2 we focus on downward influence processes in organizations. A distinguishing characteristic of downward influence is that the influence source is at a higher level in the organizational hierarchy and thereby possesses more organizational power than the influence target. With downward influence, interdependence is usually not symmetrical. That is, usually (but not always), lower-level individuals are more dependent upon higher-level individuals than vice versa. In many instances, the influence agent has ability to formally reward or punish subordinates for complying or not complying with the influence attempt.

Typically, then, the influence source in downward influence has *means control* as well as the formal authority to compel compliance. Even so, formal authority alone may be insufficient to influence subordinates to behave as the superior intends. In some instances, authority of a superior may be resisted by lower-level individuals, rendering it relatively ineffective. That is why the superior must be skillful in choosing methods of influence that are appropriate to the situation and to the nature of the interdependence in the relationship between the superior and the subordinate.

In Part 3 our emphasis shifts to lateral influence. The focus here is on organizational influence processes that are exclusively outside the direct superior-subordinate "chain of command." The target of lateral influence may be within the same department, or in another department or division of the organization. The influence source and the target may be at different hierarchical levels in the organization, but we consider the influence direction to be lateral where the influence source does not possess any formal authority over the target. For our purposes, the influence source and the influence target may generally be regarded as peers, under such circumstances, regardless of whether there is a difference in the value or level of the specialty that they perform. For example, a senior engineer may attempt to influence a quality control analyst. There may be a significant difference between these two positions from a compensation level perspective; however, if no formal authority exists in the relationship, we consider any influence attempt to be lateral.

The fourth and final section of the text deals with the upward influence process in organizations. The distinguishing characteristic of upward influence is that the target of influence actually possesses more formal authority than the influence source, so from a formal authority perspective the influence source would appear to be at a disadvantage. However, as will be seen in Part 4, so-called lower level participants (Mechanic 1962) are not without influence means.

Taken as a whole, the readings in the four sections of the book provide both solid grounding on classic material on organizational influence processes and newer material that reflects the kinds of changes that have occurred since publication of the first edition—changes, that is, in the environments of organizations, in organizations themselves, and in the field of organization studies. For example, in these readings we see an emphasis on issues of influence-without-authority, self-management and team-based organization, which have become more important as organizations have become more "lateral" in their orientation, as we have discussed above. The readings also reflect an emerging recognition of the importance of individual differences (e.g., emotional intelligence) and a shift in the leadership literature toward charismatic or transformational forms.

As the book goes to press, it is interesting to attempt to predict what a review of new literature on organizational influence processes is apt to discover ten or twenty years from now. What we would hope to find would be a much richer literature grounded in the kinds of changes in organizations and their environments that we alluded to above. Specifically, we would hope to find much more research on issues of cross-cultural and cross-national variations on organizational influence processes than we were able to identify for inclusion in the second edition of this book. Although this topic is represented in the book (Ralston, Giacalone, and Terpstra 1994), we found much less published material than we had hoped on cross-cultural aspects of power and influence.

Time will tell. In the meantime, we believe that the present collection of readings provides an accurate map of today's state of the art in this important field of study. We hope you will enjoy the exploration.

REFERENCES

Barnard, C.I. (1938). *The Functions of the Executive*. Cambridge, MA: Harvard University Press.

Kacmar, K.M., and Baron, R.A. (1999). Organizational politics: The state of the field, links to related processes, and an agenda for future research. In G. Ferris (ed.), *Research in Personnel and Human Resource Management*. Greenwich, CT: JAI Press.

Mechanic, D. (1962). Sources of power of lower participants in complex organizations. *Administrative Science Quarterly* 7(3): 349–364.

Ralston, David A., Giacalone, Robert. A., and Terpstra, Robert H. (1994). Ethical perceptions of organizational politics: A comparative evaluation of American and Hong Kong managers. *Journal of Business Ethics* 13(12): 989–999.

Stogdill, R.M. (1981). *Stogdill's Handbook of Leadership: A Survey of Theory and Research*. New York: Free Press.

ORGANIZATIONAL INFLUENCE PROCESSES

PART 1

Influence, Power, and Politics in Organizational Settings

Social influence is a fundamental aspect of life in organizations. Indeed, it is unlikely that organizations could function at all without it. Almost all organizational members engage in influencing others—or at least they attempt to do so—and, in turn, virtually everyone in any organization is subject to the social influence of others. Moreover, this assertion holds true for every type of organization, whether large or small, public sector or private sector. Engineers, social workers, salespeople, union members, and, of course, managers and supervisors all attempt to get others to engage in behaviors that meet the objectives of the influence agent. This is not meant to imply, however, that all influence processes are overt and intentional. It is important to recognize that it is possible to influence others unintentionally, and it is possible to be influenced without conscious awareness of having been influenced.

Part 1 begins with a review of such topics as power, influence, and organizational politics, and it provides an overview of the study of these constructs, as that study has evolved. The readings in this section cite much of the most important literature on power and influence that has appeared over the past few decades and thus provide the interested reader with many worthwhile leads for further study. In these readings, there is a focus on factors that affect people's choice of influence strategies. Also emphasized is the rather difficult cognitive challenge faced by someone who must analyze a situation in order to choose an appropriate influence strategy.

Because Part 1 will provide a theoretical and historical basis for better understanding the material which will comprise the subject matter of Parts 2 through 4, we recommend that Part 1 be read before any of those sections. Before discussing the readings in any more detail, we offer some background on the study of power and influence in organizations.

POWER AND INFLUENCE

Power and influence are closely related concepts, but they are by no means synonymous. Power can be portrayed as a resource—a sort of reservoir of force—that can be used by an agent to change the behavior of another. The actual application of that force is what we mean by "influence." Through the application of power, A has the capacity to influence B to behave in ways that s/he would otherwise not behave. As Hardy (1995, p. xiii) has pointed out, this rather simple notion has been "challenged, amended, critiqued, extended and rebuffed over the years, but nevertheless remains the starting point for a remarkably diverse body of literature."

The diversity in the literature to which Hardy refers extends well beyond the field of organization and management into sociology, political science, and the like. For our present purposes, however, we shall limit our treatment of power and organizational influence processes to literature sources that have been directed at an audience of managers and management scholars. Thus, the readings in this book have all been taken from journals and books that are primarily intended for a management audience.

Even though power is a well-known reality in organizational life—for instance, Salancik and Pfeffer (1977) observed that managers asked to describe power distribution in organizations seem to have little trouble doing so—it tends to be a "messy" and elusive concept. While many aspects of power seem rational and public, there are also aspects that are more-or-less hidden beneath the visible surface. That is, along with the overt aspects of power and power relationships, there are some rather covert or symbolic aspects that do not, at first, meet the eye (Frost 1987).

Early work in management literature tended to distinguish power from authority. The latter was "legitimate" power bestowed by the hierarchy and embedded in the formal system; the former was considered "illegitimate" and tended to be excluded from organizational research. Hardy (1995) argues that this dualistic perspective continues to characterize management literature on power and that the management approach to the topic pursues a *functionalist perspective* in which power and politics are viewed as illegitimate activities that are contrary to the established order. We believe, however, that the readings in this book paint a somewhat different picture—one in which power and legitimate authority are treated as inseparable facets of the same underlying construct.

POWER AND DEPENDENCE

Key to the idea of power, is the notion of *dependence*. The more B is dependent on A, the greater the power that A exerts over B. In order to exert power over B, A must control resources:

(1) that are important to B,
(2) that are relatively scarce, and
(3) that B cannot obtain without A (or that B cannot easily replace by substitute resources).

This set of criteria is consistent with the basic framework for the *strategic contingencies theory* of power, suggested by the Aston Group around thirty years ago (Hickson, Hinings, Lee, Schneck, and Pennings 1971), and elaborated by Salancik and Pfeffer (1977) in their *resource dependence* model. This general way of thinking about power relationships recurs throughout the literature on power and influence. In the most general sense, *dependence* is a function of three, somewhat overlapping, elements: *importance, scarcity* and *nonsubstitutability.*

Importance

Individuals (and organizations) must cope with many uncertainties or problems, and they must be able to obtain scarce and needed resources that they do not possess. Some, of course, are deemed more essential than others (hence the Aston Group's use of the term *strategic contingencies*). If A controls resources or the solution to problems that B needs, A has power over B. The amount of that power is proportional to the relative importance that B places on the missing resources or solutions—that is, the extent of the need. These are what Salancik and Pfeffer (1977) refer to as the "critical contingencies." As they noted, the idea of importance may be obvious but that does not diminish its significance.

Scarcity

It has been said that the term "scarce resources" is a tautology. It is difficult to conceive of any resource that is limitless. Still, some resources are clearly in shorter supply than others. Following the example above, A's power over B is proportional to the scarcity of the resources that B needs and that A controls.

Nonsubstitutability

Here, we mean that neither the source for obtaining the resource nor the resource, per se, is subject to substitution. In the former context, even if a needed resource is both important and scarce, A's power over B would be reduced or even nullified if B were able to go to C or D to obtain it. The more alternative sources that exist, the lower that power of any individual provider. In the latter context, the same dilution effect would exist if the resource, itself, could be substituted for by alternative resources that would solve the critical problem facing B. Thus, either substitution of supplier or substitution of resource would have an equivalent suppressing effect on A's power over B.

It should also be readily apparent that the dependence of B on A would be considerably attenuated if A were also dependent on B for some (presumably other) important, scarce, and nonsubstitutable resource. In such a case, dependence becomes *inter*dependence and each party is in a position to "make a deal" for the needed resources, rather than simply having to yield to influence.

POWER BASES

As we know, not every influence attempt is successful. The efficacy of any influence attempt depends upon the influence agent's ability to apply one or more effective bases of power, as well as to utilize appropriate influence tactics. Regarding bases of power, we who study organizations probably owe our earliest conception of power bases to the work of French and Raven (1959) whose original framework consisted of five categories: *reward* power, *coercive* power, *legitimate* power, *referent* power, and *expert* power.

In the years that followed, French and Raven's original five-category framework has been criticized for being too simplistic and for missing some important bases of power in addition to those suggested. Sources of power that are difficult to categorize under the French and Raven framework (e.g., persuasion, advice, attractiveness) are noted by Bell, Walker, and Willer (2000). Raven (1999) added a sixth category, *information* (both direct and indirect), to French and Raven's original five, and he also increased the explanatory power of the original power bases by dividing each of them into more definitive subcategories. Kotter's classic article "Power, Dependence, and Effective Management" (1977), which is included as a reading in Part 2, noted that it is possible to exert influence over another by capitalizing on the other's perceived sense of obligation, and that many influence tactics are not nearly as direct as implied by the French and Raven framework. Rather, there are several indirect methods available—in general, by manipulating the environment of the target person, rather than by exerting direct influence. Clegg and Hardy (1996) went so far as to assert that one can never achieve closure on what the bases of power are—they might be anything under the appropriate circumstances.

Despite its rudimentary nature, French and Raven's framework provides an appropriately straightforward beginning for our understanding of the variety of power sources that may be available for exerting influence. As a sort of bonus contribution, their framework also emphasizes an aspect of power that is crucially important to our understanding of power and influence—power tends to be a relative concept. It is the *relationship* between the parties (influence agent and target) that determines the power that one party has over the other.

Let us, then, consider each of French and Raven's original categories as background material for newer and more elaborate schemes that will appear in this book. As a convenience, we subdivide their five bases of power into two subsets: *position power* and *personal power*.

Position Power

Position power includes those bases of power that accrue to an individual whose position in an organization or network provides access to, or control over, resources that can be used for rewards or punishments. It also includes power that results from legitimation, by the system, of the right to direct the behavior of others on the basis of position, per se. What these sources of power have in common is their relative impersonality—none depend to any great extent on characteristics of the individual. Instead, as role incumbents are replaced by their successors, most of the position power tends to be transferred to the replacement. First, let us consider the two position-power bases that Kelman (1958) referred to as "means control"—that is, reward power and coercive power.

Reward Power

Reward power is the ability to offer tangible rewards in exchange for a target person's compliance (for example, the offer of an increase in pay, or a promotion). As with other power bases, this ability to reward is largely a matter of the target person's perceptions. In other words, in order to have force, reward power must be credible.

Coercive Power

Coercive power is the power to punish. The effectiveness of this base of power depends on credible threat—that is, the target person believes that the influence agent possesses the means and will employ them to punish him or her, if s/he does not comply.

At first blush, reward power and coercive power might appear to be functionally redundant, i.e., extremes on a continuum. In fact, some scholars have lumped the two together under the general term, "sanctions" (that is, rewards as positive sanctions and punishments as negative sanctions). Clearly, they do have much in common—both depend on credibility of the threats or promises, and on the fit between what is offered (or threatened) and the specific target's needs (or vulnerabilities). Both are based on a quid pro quo exchange, of the if-then or either-or form. Neither is self-sustaining without surveillance; that is, the influence agent must monitor the target's compliance or noncompliance in order to administer outcomes (this is probably relatively more important for coercive power than for reward power). Nevertheless, there is at least one important difference that justifies treating them as separate power bases—they tend to affect the future relationship between the parties differently. Repeated use of punishment is apt to decrease the attractiveness of the influence agent in the eyes of the target, whereas repeated rewards may have the opposite effect. In general, the potentially negative side effects that may accompany punishment seem to have few if any parallels for the use of rewards.

The remaining type of position power to be considered is *legitimate* power, which is often defined in terms of the *authority* that has been conferred on the individual.

Legitimate Power

Legitimate power is based on the target's belief that the influence agent has the *right* to issue directives that the target is obligated to accept. This is usually related to some official position that the influence agent has in the system. It is important to recognize, however, that the right to issue orders is not without limit. Instead, each recipient of orders appears to have an acceptable domain within which orders will be accepted without question. Chester Barnard (1938) termed this range the *zone of indifference*, and Herbert Simon (1997) used the term *zone of acceptance* to describe this range of compliance to legitimate authority.

For most scholars, formal *authority* and legitimate power are seen as generally synonymous. Because this power base is based on position in the system, rather than any personal attributes of the individual, it is considered among the *impersonal* sources of power.

Personal Power

Personal power, as opposed to position power, depends almost entirely on individual attributes and is therefore relatively (but not entirely) transportable from role to role. The two personal-power bases we find within French and Raven's original typology are *referent power* and *expert power.*

Referent Power

Referent power is decidedly personal in its foundation. French and Raven asserted that its basis lies in the psychological *identification* of the target with the agent of influence. Although, unlike means control, referent power does not depend upon surveillance, it is not altogether self-sustaining. Referent power will be in force only so long as the identification relationship between the parties is maintained. If there is a falling-out, or a negative reevaluation of the relationship, referent power may quickly dissipate.

An extension of the concept of referent power is seen in the literature on charisma or charismatic leadership (e.g., Beyer 1999; Jacobson and House 2001). Charismatic leadership will be addressed in Part 2 of this book, in which we emphasize downward influence processes.

Expert Power

Expert power is based on the target's perception that the influence agent possesses sufficient expertise or experience, within an area of knowledge, so that the target willingly subordinates her or his judgment to that of the influence agent. Like legitimate power, expert power appears to operate only within the constraints of a limited zone or domain. That is, expertise is not an all-purpose resource, but it is limited to subject matter that appears to lie within some finite range. Expert power is based on credibility, and is thus somewhat perishable. If the influence agent's credibility is eroded, so is the influence agent's expert power. Expert power may also be perishable in another sense. As knowledge becomes more widely distributed in a network, then it can become less useful as an exclusive source of power that is held close by the original powerholder. This is admittedly a controversial point, and one which will probably continue to be debated for a long time to come.

If we can, for the moment, accept the French and Raven typology as a useful and parsimonious (if incomplete) categorization of the more important forms of power, we may be led to ask, "Under what circumstances might we expect each of these bases of power to emerge?" It will be a recurring theme in this book that *context* is of the essence in answering such questions. What is the prior relationship between the parties? What concerns exist regarding the future relationship? What are the behavioral styles of the key actors? . . . and so forth. Such aspects of micro-context are undoubtedly influential in shaping the choice of influence methods or the power base(s) that the influence agent will attempt to tap. In addition to the micro-context, we should not neglect some equally important *macro* aspects of context, for example, the structural aspects of the organization.

ORGANIZATION STRUCTURE AND THE BASES OF POWER

The work of Henry Mintzberg (1984) illustrates how organization structure and the bases of power are interrelated. His work suggests that, as an organization evolves over time, certain concomitant changes occur in the distribution of power. Basically, organizations tend to evolve to certain prototypical forms. The organizational form to which the organization evolves is a function of which subunits are positioned to solve the organization's strategic contingencies. As these subunits become central to the organization's functioning and purpose, the types of power that the subunits possess become prevalent.

To cite but one example, where a "professionalized" form of organization has evolved (i.e., the skills and knowledge of technical experts are most critical to meeting the organization's most important contingencies) one might expect *expert power* to become preeminent. In such an instance, experts on the organization's core technology or technologies would acquire power in the organization. In such an organization, personal (e.g., charisma or referent power) and bureaucratic (e.g., formal authority) aspects of control would be discouraged because they are incompatible with a strong system of expertise. This is but one example of how organization structure can influence power relationships. For a more complete treatment of these ideas, the reader is referred to Mintzberg (1983, 1984). We must move on, at this point, to more basic matters.

THE READINGS IN PART 1

Ensuing sections of this book will be devoted to each of the three influence directions—downward, lateral, and upward—that constitute the organizing framework for this book. However, we must address first things first, namely, those aspects of power and influence that have more general applicability, regardless of the primary direction of the influence attempt. This is the purpose of Part 1—to examine power and influence in the most general sense.

In the initial article in Part 1, "Developing and Exercising Power and Influence," Jeffrey Pfeffer opens by arguing that, given the general changes that have taken place in organizations, informal influence is both more important and more prevalent in organizations than it was in times past. These changes have ostensibly deemphasized hierarchy in favor of self-management and team-based organizational processes. At least as important has been the very rapid escalation of complexity in organizational environments. This complexity has made it increasingly difficult for any individual to accomplish very much (or even understand very much) without becoming highly dependent on others in the organization.

Pfeffer goes on to chronicle the history of power as a rather unpopular concept in the organizational literature—a concept that has tended to be "conspicuous by its absence," having often been omitted entirely from university curricula. Power—not to mention that even more pejorative notion, politics—has been so tainted, according to Pfeffer, that managers tend to admit only grudgingly of its existence in their organizational experience.

Citing James March, Pfeffer cautions against defining power so broadly that it loses usefulness as a construct, and he asserts that we must take care to distinguish power per se from its use and from its results. He stresses the inherently situational nature of the actual application or utilization of power, and he argues that selection of (effective) tactics is not at all a matter of happenstance, but is tightly coupled to situational factors.

In "Power Politics in Organizational Life," Gilbert W. Fairholm extends Pfeffer's argument of the centrality of power and influence in organizational life, making the point that very little of real importance happens in organizational behavior that does not involve the application of power in order to achieve interpersonal influence. Fairholm's discussion begins with a review of the more organizationally legitimate aspects of power relationships, namely, the place of power in organizational leadership or what has been termed "administrative behavior" in the general organizational literature.

Fairholm then moves beyond the administrative-behavior perspective to raise the issue of what many consider to be the "darker" side of organizational influence processes—*organizational politics*. Although the previously mentioned reading by Pfeffer had broached the issue of organizational politics as an aspect of organizational influence, Pfeffer did not clearly differentiate organizational politics from power and influence in the broader sense. Fairholm is more explicit in the distinction. Here, he draws on the work of several students of organizational politics to differentiate organizational politics from administrative behavior, as well as to argue for the ubiquity of politics in organizations. Rather than attempting to argue that politics is a "bad" form of organizational influence, Fairholm simply treats it as an inevitable aspect of organizational functioning—one which can have positive as well as negative impacts. We will take up the issue of organizational politics in considerable depth in Part 4 of this book. For now, Fairholm provides a useful introduction and overview of the topic.

The third reading, "The Use of Power," by David Kipnis, carries forward the idea that the use of power to attain influence is highly context-dependent. Kipnis argues that availability and selection of influence tactics are affected both by the setting in which the tactics are to be exercised, and by the history of influence attempts between the parties. In the latter respect, he points out that the use of one type of influence attempt may constrain the later use of other modes of influence.

In order to sustain a focus on the tactics-selection process per se, Kipnis makes some simplifying assumptions. Perhaps most important among these is that, in diagnosing the situation, it is the influence agent's *own perceptions* that matter, rather than objective reality (which may in some instances be counter to those perceptions). He argues for the importance of both rational/cognitive processes and affective/emotional considerations in the choice of influence tactics. Overall, he portrays the selection of an influence tactic as anything but simple and straightforward. Given the complexity of the diagnostic challenge, Kipnis grants that misdiagnosis is always a possibility.

The issue of misdiagnosis is picked up in the fourth reading, "Illusions of Influence," by Jeffrey Pfeffer and Robert Cialdini. Here, a specific aspect of misdiagnosis is highlighted, namely, an overestimation of one's own power. As with the preceding reading by Kipnis, this contribution draws upon the attribution-theory literature—specifically, the literature on *self*-attribution. As Pfeffer and Cialdini's title implies, an influence agent often overestimates the amount of influence or control he or she actually has over events. In many such instances, the problem stems from a common error in self-attribution, often referred to as the *self-enhancement bias*.

Pfeffer and Cialdini are careful to acknowledge the cultural specificity of the self-enhancement bias. In the United States and most Western nations, possessing influence is seen as socially desirable, so one way to enhance the self would be to overestimate one's own influence and power. This may be much less the case in countries such as China, where people have more often been socialized not to overcredit themselves for successes. On the other hand, within certain U.S. subcultures (e.g., students in elite business schools) the self-enhancement effect may actually be inflated, and the reading offers some preliminary data that appear to be consistent with this notion. The reading provides a cogent review of these and other factors that can lead to such "illusions" of control, as well as the dysfunctional effects of such illusions.

Clearly, the data reported by Pfeffer and Cialdini are preliminary, and are more suggestive than conclusive. Still, they raise an important point regarding organizational influence processes. The effectiveness of any influence attempt is constrained by the accuracy of one's diagnosis of the situation. Overestimation of one's own power to exert control appears to be a common antecedent of misdiagnosis, at least in Western, managerial culture.

The next reading, "Human Resource Department Power and Influence Through Symbolic Action," by Maria Galang and Gerald Ferris, reminds us that the acquisition of power and influence in organizations is not limited to individuals. Organizational subunits also concern themselves with acquiring power. In this reading, we see the example of one type of subunit—the human resource (HR) department—as a case in point regarding the politics of influence gathering. Although the focus of this reading is necessarily couched in the language of HR and its functional concerns, we believe that most of the discussion is clearly generalizable to many different types of organizational subunits.

This reading also addresses a central issue in the domain of organizational influence processes that constitutes a challenge that many individuals and groups face in organizations, namely, the need to influence without authority. Here, the HR department serves as a useful prototype for this dilemma. Despite much recent literature that argues that HR has finally attained equal status with historically more influential departments, the likely reality is that, in many if not most of today's organizations, HR still has a long way to go.

This reading makes salient the idea that power acquisition often involves the possession of "real" resources and means, but it can involve more symbolic or impressionistic "resources" as well. To the extent that a subunit is deficient in its control over more tangible means, it may well be faced with the necessity to attempt to make up for such deficits through impression-management and similar tactics. (It should be noted, that the data presented in this reading are not very supportive of the efficacy of symbolic action.)

One additional aspect of the Galang and Ferris reading bears mention. The authors make a cogent argument that gaining an understanding of the dynamics of power requires us to find some consensual definition of the power construct. Without that, the task of building a coherent and informative stream of research on power becomes the proverbial exercise in futility. As the authors point out, the recent state of scholarship on power has simply not yielded a consensus in this respect. Further, the authors' own research data, in which they analyze the antecedents of five different components of power, lends further emphasis to the point that what we know about power—and therefore organizational influence processes—depends on how we conceive of power in the first place.

The final offering in Part 1 is "Consequences of Influence Tactics Used with Subordinates, Peers, and the Boss," by Gary Yukl and J. Bruce Tracey. The reading extends our consideration of the gamut of influence tactics to a specific focus on the *effectiveness* of the various tactics. The article presents a research study in which managers' use of nine different influence tactics were related to the influence targets' task commitment, as well as to measures of managerial effectiveness. These nine tactics (*rational persuasion, inspirational appeal, consultation, ingratiation, exchange, personal appeal, coalition, legitimating,* and *pressure*) were selected based on a synthesis of the literature on influence. Collectively, these tactics map a wide range of choices from the potential arsenal of influence mechanisms and appear to represent the broader body of literature on influence tactics very well.

A secondary goal of the research was to extend what we know about differences in the relative frequency of the nine influence tactics, when they are exerted in a downward, lateral, or upward direction. Although the influence methods were moderately intercorrelated, most had unique patterns of directional differences. For example, inspirational appeal, pressure, and ingratiation tended to be used most often in downward influence attempts; coalition was used most frequently in lateral influence; and rational persuasion was the method of choice for upward influence. The Yukl and Tracey reading, which concludes Part 1, serves as a prelude to Parts 2 through 4 of the book.

Taken as a whole, the readings in this section make a compelling case for the ubiquity and centrality of organizational influence processes—political and otherwise—in the functioning of nearly every kind of organization. The readings in this section serve as foundation material for the three sections to follow, in which downward, lateral, and upward influence processes, in turn, will be emphasized. We hope you will enjoy the journey.

REFERENCES

Barnard, C.I. (1938). *The Functions of the Executive.* Cambridge, MA: Harvard University Press.

Bell, R., Walker, H.A., and Willer, D. (2000). Power, influence, and legitimacy in organizations: Implications of three theoretical research programs. In S.B. Bacharach, E.J. Lawler, and D. Torres (eds.), *Research in the Sociology of Organizations* (pp. 131–177). Greenwich, CT: JAI.

Beyer, J.M. (1999). Two approaches to studying charismatic leadership: Competing or complementary? *Leadership Quarterly* 10(4): 575–588.

Clegg, S., and Hardy, C. (1996). Some dare call it power. In S. Clegg, C. Hardy, and W. Nord (eds.), *Handbook of Organization Studies* (pp. 622–641). London: Sage.

French, J.R.P., and Raven, B.H. (1959). The bases of social power. In D. Cartwright (ed.), *Studies in Social Power.* Ann Arbor, MI: Institute for Social Research.

Frost, P.J. (1987). Power, politics, and influence. In F.M. Jablin, L.L. Putnam, and E.T.A.L. (eds.), *Handbook of Organizational Communication: An Interdisciplinary Perspective* (pp. 503–548). Thousand Oaks, CA: Sage.

Hardy, C. (1995). *Power and Politics in Organizations.* Aldershot, UK: Dartmouth.

Hickson, D., Hinings, C., Lee, C., Schneck, R., and Pennings, J. (1971). A strategic contingencies theory of interorganization power. *Administrative Science Quarterly* 16(2): 216–229.

Jacobsen, C., and House, R.J. (2001). Dynamics of charismatic leadership: A process theory, simulation model, and tests. *Leadership Quarterly* 12(1): 75–112.

Kelman, H.C. (1958). Compliance, identification, and internalization: Three processes of attitude change. *Journal of Conflict Resolution* 2: 51–60.

Mintzberg, H. (1983). *Power in and Around Organizations.* Englewood Cliffs, NJ: Prentice-Hall.

———. (1984). Power and organization life cycles. *Academy of Management Review* 9(2): 207–224.

Raven, B.H. (1999). Reflections on interpersonal influence and social power in experimental social psychology. In A. Rodrigues and R.V. Levine (eds.), *Reflections on 100 Years of Experimental Social Psychology* (pp. 114–134). New York: Basic Books.

Salancik, G.R., and Pfeffer, J. (1977). Who gets power—and how they hold on to it. *Organizational Dynamics* 5(3): 2–21.

Simon, H.A. (1997). *Administrative Behavior* (4th ed.). New York: Free Press.

Thompson, J.D. (1967). *Organizations in Action: Social Science Bases of Administrative Theory.* New York: McGraw-Hill.

1

Developing and Exercising Power and Influence

Jeffrey Pfeffer

Social control is often, although not invariably, embedded in a hierarchical process. Certainly leadership, the use of rewards and sanctions, and the development of an organizational culture all convey the implication of some central authority that is setting up the reward system, appointing the leaders, and establishing the corporate culture. For those living and working in organizations but not necessarily in the most senior positions, social control takes on another connotation—how to develop informal influence and power to achieve what one wants and needs for task accomplishment as well as for individual benefit.

The exercise of informal influence is important not only because of individual agendas, however. Changes in organizations have made lateral, nonhierarchical influence comparatively more important. Organizations have flattened their hierarchies, taking out levels of management as well as leagues of middle managers. There is simply less hierarchy left. The increasing emphasis on high-commitment or high-involvement work practices and the concomitant emphasis on self-managing teams (e.g., Katzenbach and Smith 1993) means that the exercise of formal, hierarchical control is less consistent with organizational values and ways of organizing.

This deemphasis on formal authority has been hastened by the increasingly rapid pace of technological, social, and market change, with the corresponding requirement for organizations to reduce the time it takes to make decisions, design products or services, and bring them to market. The emphasis on speed means that few organizations can afford having decisions and information move up and down formal hierarchies of authority. As a result of these trends, there is increasing managerial and research interest in less formal ways of getting things done; these less formal methods rely more on power and influence, leverage individuals' positions in social networks, and entail ongoing negotiations among organizational participants. Consequently, the subjects of power and influence and the biases and problems that beset negotiations have drawn increasing scholarly attention.

POWER AND INFLUENCE

Power has had a bad name in social science research and is most often conspicuous by its absence from the literature. It is not just Williamson (e.g., Williamson and Ouchi 1981) who has critiqued the concept and argued that it was neither necessary nor useful for understanding organizations. Courses about power and influence in schools of administration started only in the late 1970s and still exist in comparatively few institutions. A perusal of management texts at that time and even later reveals that power was often omitted entirely from consideration. When it was discussed, the emphasis was on a relatively simple conception of interpersonal power—French and Raven's (1968) bases of power (expert, reward, sanction, and so forth). Perrow noted that "the literature on power in organizations is generally . . . preoccupied with interpersonal or intergroup phenomena . . . or else it takes as the major dimension of power the relative and absolute power of levels in the hierarchy" (1970, p. 60). Kipnis, Schmidt, and Wilkinson wrote that "organizational psychologists have not been particularly interested in studying the ways in which people at work influence their colleagues and superiors to obtain personal benefits or to satisfy organizational goals" (1980, p. 440). Although power may have always been important and certainly is becoming more so as hierarchical bases of authority erode under the environmental changes described above, power as an idea does not fit very well with either our conception of organizations and individuals as being rational utility and efficiency maximizers or with our social values that emphasize cooperation and deemphasize inequality in the access to social resources.

We are profoundly ambivalent about power (Pfeffer 1992) and that ambivalence has led to recurrent questioning of the concept and its definition. Illustrating the pervasiveness of the ambivalence, Kanter noted, "Power is America's last dirty word. It is easier to talk about money—and much easier to talk about sex than it is to talk about power" (1977, p. 65). John Gardner wrote, "In this country . . . power has such a bad name that many good people persuade themselves they want nothing to do with it" (1990, p. 55). Gandz and Murray, from a survey of 428 managers, provided empirical evidence of the ambivalence: although the managers overwhelmingly agreed with the statements "the existence of workplace politics is common to most organizations" and "successful executives must be good politicians," they also thought that "organizations free of politics are happier than those where there are a lot of politics" and "politics in organizations are detrimental to efficiency" (1980, p. 244).

After first considering the definition of power and issues of its measurement, we address three fundamental questions concerning power in organizations: (1) under what circumstances are power and influence more important in organizational decision making, and under what circumstances are political skills less critical for getting things done? (2) what are the important sources of power? and (3) what are the strategies and tactics through which interpersonal influence is developed and exercised and power gets employed?

THE DEFINITION AND CRITIQUE OF THE CONCEPT OF POWER

Wrong defined power as the "intentional and effective control by particular agents" (1968, p. 676), a definition closely related to that offered by Russell: "the production of intended effects by some men on other men" (1938, p. 25). There are three key elements in the definition: the influence of some over others, the fact that power is not relegated to relations between superiors and subordinates but includes interactions among equals as well, and the idea that this influence is conscious and intended. Because of the concept of intent, Wrong saw power as narrower in its definition than the broader idea of social control: "When social controls have been internalized, the concept of power is clearly inapplicable. . . . We must distinguish the diffuse controls exercised by the group over socialized individuals from direct, intentional efforts by a specific person or group to control another" (1968, p. 676).

Power is also sometimes distinguished from authority. Authority is authorized or legitimated power. The vesting of control in authorities not only makes the exercise of power appear less arbitrary and visible, it also reduces the costs of exercising power (Pfeffer 1981a, p. 4). The exercise of authority is expected—that is why the authority is vested in certain roles and individuals in the first place. The exercise of power may not always be so welcomed.

In order to demonstrate influence or control, most definitions of power include the idea of overcoming resistance. Dahl (1957, pp. 202–203) defined power as a relation among actors in which one can get another to do something that the other would not otherwise have done. Emerson wrote, "The power of an actor A over actor B is the amount of resistance on the part of B which can be potentially overcome by A" (1962, p. 32).

There are also important distinctions made between power as a capacity and power as actually employed. Wrong noted, "power is usually defined as a capacity to control others. . . . The evidence that a person or group possesses the capacity to control others may be the frequency with which successful acts of control have been carried out in the past" (1968, p. 77). March also maintained that "there seems to be general consensus that . . . potential power is different from actually exerted power" (1966, p. 57). He wrote about what he termed activation models, which assume that "power is a potential and that the exercise of power involves some mechanism of activation" (p. 57).

The measurement of the concept of power, then, requires providing evidence of intentional effects on outcomes of importance and the ability to overcome resistance. As March has noted, this may be more difficult to do than first imagined. He contrasted power with models relying on chance:

> Suppose we imagine that each power encounter occurs between just two people chosen at random from the total population. . . . Further, assume that at each encounter we will decide who prevails by flipping a coin. If the total number of encounters per person is relatively small and the total number of persons relatively large, such a process will yield a few people who are successful in their encounters virtually all of the time, others who are successful most of the time, and so on.

... All of the chance models generate power distributions. They are spurious distributions in the sense that power, as we usually mean it, had nothing to do with what happened. But we can still apply our measures of power to the systems involved. (1966, pp. 51–52)

March noted that to distinguish power from chance, one needed to assess (1) whether power was stable over time, (2) whether power was stable over subject matter, (3) whether power was correlated with other personal attributes, and (4) whether power was susceptible to experimental manipulation. He argued that there was evidence for the presence of all of these conditions, and since that time in particular an extensive experimental literature on power (e.g., Cook et al. 1983) has emerged.

Nevertheless, March was concerned about the overuse of the concept of power in analyzing social decision situations. Because power was so ubiquitous and obvious in conversations about everyday life, there is a tendency "to assume that it is real and meaningful. . . . However . . . we run the risk of treating the social validation of power as more compelling than it is simply because the social conditioning to a simple force model is so pervasive" (1966, pp. 68–69). He also was concerned that because of the obviousness of power, it would come to be used as a residual category for explanation— a name for the unobserved variance in research studies. As Dahl noted, "a Thing to which people attach many labels with subtly or grossly different meanings in many different cultures and times is probably not a Thing at all but many Things" (1957, p. 201). Unless considered and studied quite carefully, the force activation model of power is quite difficult to disprove:

It is clear from a consideration both of the formal properties of activation models and of the problems observers have had with such models that they suffer from their excessive *a posteriori* explanatory power. If we observe that power exists and is stable and if we observe that sometimes weak people seem to triumph over strong people, we are tempted to rely on an activation hypothesis to explain the discrepancy. (March, 1966, p. 61)

In studies of power, it is essential to measure power separate from its use and results and to define and measure power before the analysis of the social choice rather than after. Again, however, since these initial concerns, a number of studies have been reasonably successful in overcoming these empirical and theoretical difficulties. Nonetheless, it is wise to keep them in mind in evaluating the literature on power.

There is an alternative perspective that maintains that the very ability of respondents to so quickly identify power and to discuss it provides evidence of the validity of the concept. Perrow has argued forcefully for this position:

Power is a preoccupation of the managers in the firms, as evidenced by the interview data. . . . Given the nature of the concept and the "reality," I am not disturbed that the term "power" has different meanings. . . . A single, consistent meaning of power, or decomposition of the concept into various types, might be preferable, but I doubt it. The annual production of new typologies and distinctions . . . has been intellectually stimulating, but operationally a nightmare. . . . To tie respondents to only one meaning would violate their own perceptions of the complexity, as well as the reality, of power. (1970, pp. 83–84)

Concepts are defined in fact by their operationalization, and consequently it is useful to consider how power has been measured. One approach has been to rely on reputation, with the presumption being that informants as individuals are both willing and able to provide information on the power of social units. Perrow's (1970) study of power in twelve organizations asked respondents to rank each of the four groups (sales, production, research and development, and staff services, including accounting and finance) in terms of how much power they had. This procedure defines power as zero-sum through the measurement process. Perrow noted that such a simple question "does not reflect the complexity of the concept . . . Yet . . . the internal consistency of subgroup perspectives suggests that the bald term 'power' does have some consistent meaning" (p. 63). A study of the power of subunits in breweries in Canada (Hinings et al. 1974) also relied on interviews and questionnaires to assess power. Studies of resource allocations in universities (Pfeffer and Salancik 1974; Pfeffer and Moore 1980) assessed power, in part, by asking each department head to rate all the departments as to how much power they thought the departments possessed. In these latter cases, since ratings rather than rankings were used, power was not defined so as to be zero-sum.

The evidence is compelling that individuals understand the question and, moreover, that reputational indicators of power produce information that is highly correlated across respondents:

> In the University of Illinois study, department heads were asked to rate, on a seven-point scale, the power of all of the departments being studied. Only one department head even asked for a definition of what was meant by the concept of power. . . . No department that was judged, overall, to be in the top third of the departments in terms of power was rated by a single individual as being lower than the top third. Similarly, no department that, overall, was rated in the bottom third in terms of power was rated by a single person as being higher than the bottom third. (Pfeffer 1992, p. 55)

In part to overcome problems with reactivity and to be able to study power historically, which is obviously not possible if one relies solely on the reports of informants, other indicators of power have been developed. The studies of power in universities, for instance, assessed what were key committees in the university and then examined departmental representation on these committees as a measure of departmental power. The evidence indicated that this representational measure was significantly correlated with the measure of departmental power based on respondent reports, with a correlation of .61 at Illinois and .57 at the University of California (Pfeffer 1981b, p. 59).

In corporations, power of various subunits can be similarly assessed by examining the functional backgrounds of senior-level executives such as the CEO or inside directors. For instance, the timing of the rise of attorneys to power at Pacific Gas and Electric can be ascertained by their representation in officer—and manager—level positions, where they increased from four in 1960 to eighteen by 1980 (Pfeffer 1992, p. 58). Another measure of the power of attorneys in corporations is provided in a cross-cultural study by Miyazawa of U.S. based subsidiaries of Japanese firms. He measured the power and prominence of the legal department by its degree of professionalization, defined as "the employment of U.S. licensed lawyers as in-house lawyers and . . . the placing of a U.S. in-house lawyer at the head of the legal department" (1986, p. 100). In the typical Japanese corporation, the legal department is part of a general affairs department and tends to have lay people working on legal-related matters, so that using licensed attorneys represented a shift in the power of the department.

There are also suggestions in the literature that a reliable way to assess power is by examining its consequences (Pfeffer 1992)—for instance, the salaries paid to people at comparable levels in different divisions, growth in budget, and so forth. As long as the assessment of power using one set of indicators, including effects of power on resource allocations, is used solely to predict other, distinct outcomes, there is no problem with this procedure. If power has been measured in a valid and reliable way, the various indicators should correlate with each other and should operate as theoretically expected in studies of power (e.g., the measures of power should be predicted by theoretically developed determinants of power and should explain outcomes that are presumably affected by power).

Finkelstein provided one of the most comprehensive evaluations of the measurement of power in corporations, albeit he was focusing on the power of individuals in the top management team. Many of his measures, however, could be generalized to other levels of analysis such as organizational subunits. He developed four separate indices of power. The first measured structural power, which "is related to the distribution of formal positions within an organization" (1992, p. 512). His indicators of structural power were the percentage of individuals in a top management team with higher titles than the given individual (for the CEO this number is 0), the total cash compensation received, and the number of official titles a manager held. The second power index measured ownership power. The indicators were (1) the percentage of a firm's shares owned by an executive, (2) the percentage of the firm's shares owned by the executive's family, and (3) whether or not the manager was the founder of the firm or was related to the founder and whether or not the manager was related to other senior managers. The third dimension of power assessed expert power. The measures were the number of different functional areas a manager had worked in, the number of different positions a manager had held in the firm, and whether or not the manager's functional background matched the requirements of the environment for particular expertise. The final overall indicator of power was called prestige power and "is related to a manager's ability to absorb uncertainty from the institutional environment" (p. 515). The four indicators of this dimension of power were (1) the total number of corporate boards a manager sat on; (2) the number of non-profit boards a manager sat on; (3) the financial standing of the corporate boards of which an executive was a member; and (4) whether or not the manager had an elite education.

Finkelstein tested his measures of power on a sample of 1,763 top managers from

102 firms in three industries over a five-year period. A factor analysis of indicators reproduced the four scales. Cronbach's alphas for each of the sc. ..ere reasonably high, ranging from .67 for prestige power to .83 for structural power. A second study that asked for the perceived power of individuals revealed that perceived power was most strongly correlated with structural power and prestige power and was not statistically significantly correlated with expert power and was only weakly correlated with ownership power. Finally, Finkelstein reported that the consideration of the power of senior managers permitted better predictions of diversification strategies than models that did not include the power indicators.

CONDITIONS AFFECTING THE USE OF POWER

Because of the inherent appeal of force activation conceptions of power, it is important to understand the conditions under which power is more likely to be employed. Salancik and Pfeffer (1974) argued that power and influence would be employed under conditions of resource scarcity and for critical resources or important decisions. If resources weren't scarce, there was little or no allocation problem and no need to mobilize power. Similarly, if the decision did not concern critical issues, there was little need to expend power resources on its determination. Their study of allocations of a number of different resources at the University of Illinois found evidence consistent with these predictions, although resource criticality and scarcity were too highly correlated for the items they studied to assess separate effects. For instance, the most critical and scarce resource, graduate fellowships, was correlated .44 with departmental representation on important committees, while the least critical and scarce resource, summer faculty fellowships, was correlated only .01 with that measure of power (p. 468).

A subsequent study of resource allocations to departments on two University of California campuses that varied in the scarcity of resources confronted again found support for the idea that power was used more under conditions of scarcity (Pfeffer and Moore 1980). Studying 295 management units in forty-six divisions of a large organization to explore the determinants of interunit influence attempts, Gresov and Stephens also found that resource constraints increased the likelihood of a unit's attempting to exercise influence. They noted that "proactive attempts to influence other units may lead to an alteration of work and information flows . . . that will change the extent and nature of demands on unit members and existing structures" (1993, p. 256), so that influence activity within a set of related units is one possible response to resource constraints and organizational design problems. They reported that interunit influence attempts were also more likely the lower the commitment to the status quo, the lower the managerial tenure, and the greater the managerial dissatisfaction with unit performance.

A somewhat different view of the relationship between slack and power behavior comes from V. E. Schein (1979). She distinguished between power-acquisition strategies and tactics related to the process of getting the work done and power processes "designed to promote the self-oriented objectives of the individuals. Objectives such as promotion or increased status are related far more to individual self-aggrandizement than they are to work-related objectives" (p. 290). She argued:

> it is proposed that the ratio of personal to work-related power acquisition behaviors is in favor of personal power . . . in high-slack systems, whereas the reverse is true in low-slack systems. . . . Vigorous competition in the environment will prevent managers from tailoring their activities to achieve their own personal end and will require more work-related behaviors. . . . The absence of such competitive conditions permits managers to pursue their own goals without obvious disruption of the system. (p. 290)

Schein's article did not provide any evidence for the claim that efficiency considerations would drive out at least some forms of power behavior—the most self-serving—and this remains an important empirical question. There is the problem with this argument that the very definition of how much slack or how much environmental pressure there is, the question of what is the most appropriate response, and the issue of which individuals or units are best suited to coping with the problem are all settled at least in part through a political process. Surveys of managers by Gandz and Murray (1980) and Madison et al. (1980) asking what levels, functions, and decisions in organizations seemed to most involve the use of power revealed that power was used more in major decisions, such as reorganizations or personnel changes, and was used more at senior organizational levels, which also presumably deal with more important decisions. Their results also indicated that power was used more in areas in which there was more uncertainty and in which performance was harder to assess (e.g., staff rather than line production operations).

This idea that power would be used more under conditions of uncertainty or ambiguity has been examined in a number of studies focusing on science and academia. The basic idea came from a typology of decision situations developed by Thompson and Tuden (1959). They categorized decision situations according to whether or not there was agreement about goals or preferences and whether or not there was agreement about technology—the connections between actions and their consequences. A summary of their typology noted:

> computational decision making procedures involved in rational choice are used in decision making only when there is agreement both on the goals and on the connections between actions and outcomes. When there is no agreement on goals, compromise is required to reach a decision. When there is no agreement on technology, judgment is necessary to determine the best course in achieving consensually shared goals. And when there is neither agreement on goals nor on technology, an unstructured, highly politicized form of decision making is likely to occur. (Pfeffer 1981b, p. 71)

The operationalization of the operation of power in these studies has typically been to examine the extent to which resources are allocated to individuals who share an important social affiliation under varying conditions of uncertainty—for instance, to what extent do National Science Foundation grant allocations match the composition of the review panel, controlling for other factors, under varying degrees of uncertainty? The presumption in this research is that allocations based on social similarity or on shared social connections reflect the operation of influence and politics. In a series of studies that equated the degree of uncertainty with the extent to which a scientific field was paradigmatically developed (Lodahl and Gordon 1972), it was shown that the greater the degree of uncertainty (or the lower the level of paradigm development characterizing a field), the greater the effect of politics on National Science Foundation grant allocations (Pfeffer, Salancik, and Leblebici 1976), the choice of editorial board members (Yoels 1974), and the publishing of articles (Pfeffer, Leong, and Strehl 1977).

Pfeffer (1992) has also argued that power is used more when there are differences in point of view or disagreements that must be resolved. And social influence and politics will be used more when interdependence among subunits is higher, requiring more coordination of behavior and increasing the interdependence of that behavior.

SOURCES OF POWER

Research has identified numerous sources of power for both individuals and organizational subunits. Some sources of power are personal characteristics. R. W. Allen et al. (1979) interviewed eighty-seven managers, including thirty chief executives, in southern California electronics firms to assess their beliefs about the personal characteristics associated with being powerful and being effective in the use of organizational politics. The characteristics mentioned most frequently were: articulate, sensitive, socially adept, competent, and popular. The study raises two issues. First, in relating personal characteristics to power, one needs to be careful that the characteristics associated with power (for example, self-confidence or being popular) are not a consequence of power rather than its source. It is reasonable to argue that one will be more socially adept and popular to the extent one has power—these characteristics may be both products and sources of power. The characteristics may also not be independent of each other—articulate and sensitive people may be more popular as a result. Second, there is the question of the extent to which these characteristics are relatively fixed or are malleable. Some, such as sensitivity and articulateness, can presumably be affected by training in clinical skills and public speaking, respectively.

Other sources of power are structural, deriving from one's position in the division of labor or one's location in the network of communication. As Perrow noted, "the preoccupation with interpersonal power has led us to neglect one of the most obvious aspects of this subject: in complex organizations, tasks are divided up between a few major departments or Subunits, and all of these Subunits are not likely to be equally powerful" (1970, p. 59). One structural source of power is the ability to cope with the uncertainty an organization faces (Hickson et al. 1971; Hinings et al. 1974). Since the form and amount of uncertainty can vary, depending on the particular decision and situation, so too do the characteristics associated with having power.

For instance, a study of 304 professionals in a research and development laboratory (Tushman and Romanelli, 1983) found that the type of person who had the most influence depended on the type of project—in applied research units, individuals who spanned boundaries were the most influential, while in technical service projects, with less uncertainty, those most central in the internal communication structure had more power. Booker (1989), examining the power of subunits in semiconductor firms, discovered that founding conditions and the background of the entrepreneur that started the company affected relative power and the perceived importance of different functional units. Miyazawa's study of the status and professionalization of legal departments in thirty-six of the largest Japanese subsidiaries operating in the United States found that this varied by "the industrial specialization of the subsidiary" (1986, p. 152). Although the trading subsidiaries were the largest, they were among the least professionalized. By contrast, subsidiaries in the field of transportation equipment had comparatively larger legal staffs with higher-status personnel, because there were more legal risks, particularly pertaining to product liability and antitrust.

Another important source of power is the ability to provide resources for the organization. Studies of universities (Salancik and Pfeffer 1974; Pfeffer and Moore 1980) found that those departments that brought in the most grants and contracts, with their associated overhead, had the most power. J. D. Hackman (1985) has referred to the ability to obtain critical resources needed by the institution as environmental power and found this to be related to university departments' power.

The ability to cope with uncertainty or to bring in resources is not enough—it is also important that the individual or work unit be central in the workflow and communication structure to develop and exercise influence. Pettigrew's (1972, 1973) case study of a computer purchase decision illustrated how a manager who sat astride the flow of communication was able to substantially influence the final decision through his ability to filter and selectively present information. Ibarra, investigating the effects of individual attributes, formal position, and network centrality on the exercise of influence, reported that centrality was more important for administrative innovation roles and was equal to formal position in its effects on exercising influence in technical innovation roles. She concluded that "an organization's informal structure may be more critical than its formal structure when the exercise of power requires extensive boundary spanning" (1993, p. 471). Brass and Burkhardt (1993) also found that an individual's network centrality was significantly related to others' perceptions of that individual's power.

Power accrues to those who can more accurately assess the social landscape. Krackhardt (1990) studied a small entrepreneurial firm and compared perceptions of the friendship and advice network to the actual networks, as empirically assessed. Those with more accurate perceptions of the existing advice network were rated as being more powerful by others in the organization, although accurate perceptions of the friendship network were unrelated to perceived power.

Because power is used to obtain resources (Pfeffer and Salancik 1974; Pfeffer and Moore 1980), power becomes self-perpetuating through the effective use of the resources so acquired. Boeker (1989) found that the power distribution established at the time of a firm's founding tended to persist in his sample of semiconductor firms. Studying subunits in health care clinics, Lachman (1989) observed that previous power position was the best predictor of subsequent power. One way in which power is self-perpetuating is through the impact of the effective use of power on an individual's reputation, which then becomes a source of power: "Most observers would agree that present reputations for power are at least in part a function of the results of past encounters. . . . Most observers would probably also agree that power reputation, in turn, affects the results of encounters" (March 1966, p. 57).

Power also derives from formal position or authority. Brass and Burkhardt (1993) reported that level in the organizational hierarchy was significantly related to others' perceptions of a focal individual's power. Sometimes that formal position can be used to protect the powerholder from the consequences of poor performance. Becker (1992) studied sixty-seven organizations over a twenty-two-year period and asked what happened to chief executives when organizational performance was poor. He found that powerful chief executives were able to survive performance downturns by displacing the blame onto their subordinates, who tended to be replaced when performance suffered. By contrast, less powerful chief executives, who had less power because they owned less of the company's stock and there were more outsiders on the board of directors, were not able to displace poor performance and fire their subordinates; rather, they were replaced themselves.

Power is built by doing favors for others. Studies of the power of chief executives and its effects consistently find that the higher the proportion of outside directors the CEO has appointed, the more favorably that individual is treated. The argument is that being appointed to the board by someone activates a norm of reciprocity, and one is tied to the individual who did the appointing. Wade, O'Reilly, and Chandratat (1990) noted that there was a higher incidence of the provision of golden parachutes—contracts that pay off executives if they lose their jobs because of a change in control of the corporation, through a takeover, for instance—for CEOs who had been able to appoint more outsiders to their boards.

STRATEGIES AND TACTICS FOR USING POWER

Studies of how power is actually employed are scarcer than studies of the determinants of power or the conditions under which it is used in organizations, for the simple reason that the empirical obstacles to conducting such analyses are greater. Pfeffer (1992) has proposed a number of tactics for exercising power: (1) those having to do with timing, including delay, waiting, and moving first; (2) interpersonal influence strategies such as social proof, liking, commitment, contrast, reciprocity, and scarcity (Cialdini 1988); (3) strategic presentation of information and analysis and selective use of data to buttress one's case; (4) reorganization to consolidate power or to break up the ability of one's opponents to coalesce; (5) use of evocative, emotion-producing language to mobilize support or quiet opposition; and (6) use of task forces and committees to co-opt opposition. Most of these techniques were illustrated with examples, but a few have some systematic empirical study behind them.

An insightful article by Schwartz (1974) analyzed waiting and delay as both indicators of power and as ways of exercising power. Schwartz provided anecdotal examples to illustrate the general theoretical point:

> Waiting is patterned by the distribution of power in a social system. This assertion hinges on the assumption that power is directly associated with an individual's scarcity as a social resource and, thereby, with his value as a member of a social unit. . . . The person who desires a valued service generally cannot gain immediate access to its dispenser, but must instead wait until others are accommodated. . . . To be able to make a person wait is, above all, to possess the capacity to modify his conduct in a manner congruent with one's own interests. To be delayed is . . . to be dependent upon the disposition of the one whom one is waiting for. The latter . . . by virtue of this dependency . . . finds himself further confirmed in his position of power. (pp. 843–844)

Schwartz noted that waiting is a form of investment and, like other forms of investment and commitment, increases the value of the object being sought. If one did not think the person waited for was important or valuable, then one would have engaged in a senseless activity. Conversely, the more one waits, the more important and valuable must be that which is waited for, to make sense of one's own behavior:

> if we regard waiting for a scarce service as an investment or sacrifice in return for a gain, we may measure part of the value of the gain by assessing the degree of sacrifice occasioned on its behalf. . . . The subjective value of the gain is therefore given not only by the objective value of the service but also by the amount of time invested in its attainment. . . . The other's service becomes valuable (and he becomes powerful) precisely because he is waited for. (1974, p. 857)

These initial insights on the relationship between time, waiting, and power have not been extensively pursued in subsequent empirical study. This seems a shame, because, as Schwartz noted, "queuing for resources is . . . a fundamental practice of social organization" (1974, p. 842). Much could be learned about power distributions by examining patterns of waiting time, and the use of delay or waiting to create or ratify power remains to be empirically explored, particularly as to the boundaries beyond which this strategy may backfire.

In an attempt to systematically understand influence tactics, Kipnis, Schmidt, and Wilkinson (1980) developed a fifty-eight-item questionnaire focused on various targets of influence (peers, superiors, and subordinates) that was factor analyzed to extract eight dimensions of influence: assertiveness, ingratiation, rationality, sanctions, exchange, upward appeals, blocking, and coalitions. They found that the use of these influence tactics varied systematically with the context in which they were attempted. The higher the status of the target person, the greater the reliance on rationality tactics (e.g., writing a memo, using logic, or making a plan). Assertiveness was used more with lower-status targets, and exchange was used most frequently with co-workers. The reasons for exercising influence also affected the choice of tactics: personal assistance prompted the use of ingratiation, while efforts to improve a target individual's performance tended to rely on assertiveness and rationality. Kipnis et al. found that "respondents showed the least variation in choice of tactics when attempting to influence their subordinates. No matter what the reason for influencing subordinates, the use of assertiveness . . . accounted for the most variance for each reason" (1980, p. 450). The study found no effect of gender on the choice of influence tactics. Brass and Burkhardt (1993), studying how others perceive an individual's power, found that some behavioral tactics, such as the use of assertiveness, ingratiation, exchange, and forming coalitions with others, were significantly related to perceptions of power, and this effect was independent of structural position.

Kipnis and Schmidt (1988) explored how the influence tactics used by subordinates on their superiors affected their salaries, evaluations, and tension or stress. Based on responses to six scales, four types of influence styles were identified: (1) shotgun, typified by individuals who tended to use all of the influence strategies almost indiscriminately, and were particularly high on the use of assertiveness; (2) ingratiator, typified by individuals who scored high on friendliness and had average scores on the other scales; (3) bystander, typified by individuals who scored low on their use of all of the influence strategies, and (4) tactician, typified by individuals who scored high on the reason (or rationality) strategy and had average scores on the other scales. They found that men and women who used a shotgun style received lower performance ratings. For men, the style that worked best was the tactician. In a study of CEO salaries, Kipnis and Schmidt (1988) found that those that employed the tactician strategy earned more than those using other approaches. The shotgun style was associated with the most stress and tension. This study complements the earlier study of Kipnis and his colleagues that investigated the correlates of the use of different influence approaches by showing that different influence styles have different levels of effectiveness. One issue with all of the Kipnis studies is that they rely on self-reports of influence behavior, which may not be completely accurate. However, there is no reason to believe that the errors are systematically related to the effects being studied.

Gargiulo (1993) studied the use of co-optation to overcome political constraint in a cooperative agribusiness in South America. He found that, consistent with resource dependence (Pfeffer and Salancik, 1978) predictions, leaders tended to build ties of interpersonal obligation with people who directly affected their performance in the organization. When, however, such direct ties could not be built, because of interpersonal friction or fundamental differences about policy, effective leaders used a two-step process in which they built co-optive relations with others who could affect the behavior of the person on whom they depended. Pfeffer and Salancik (1977), in their study of resource allocations at the University of Illinois, discovered that department heads that (1) knew their department's comparative position along a set of possible criteria for resource allocation and (2) advocated those criteria in decision making were able to obtain more resources for their departments, even controlling for the power of the department.

Power is accomplished through talk. In an interesting analysis of some testimony from the Watergate hearings, Molotch and Boden investigated "the ways people invoke routine conversational procedures to accomplish power" (1985, p. 273). They noted that there were three faces of power:

> The first face of power is the capacity to prevail in explicit contests. . . . A second face of power (somewhat less visible) is the ability to set agendas, to determine the issues over which there will be any explicit contest at all. . . . Our third face of power is the most basic of all: it is the ability to determine the very grounds of the interactions through which agendas are set and outcomes determined; it is the struggle over the linguistic premises upon which the legitimacy of accounts will be judged. (p. 273)

Their focus was on Senator Gurney's attempts to discredit the very damaging testimony of John Dean. Gurney was a Republican and a partisan defender of President Nixon; John Dean had been the president's legal counsel and provided evidence concerning Nixon's role in the Watergate cover-up. Gurney's strategy was to demand the literal truth, free of any interpretive context—to demand just the facts. When Dean could not provide this "literal truth" and sought to explain the circumstances of a particular conversation, Gurney used this as a way to discredit Dean's account. As Molotch and Boden noted, "if all accounts are potentially vulnerable to the challenge that they are not really objective, then any conversationalist is open—at all times—to the charge of interactive incompetence" (p. 274). They concluded by noting that "demands for 'just the facts,' the simple answers, the forced-choice response, preclude the 'whole story' that contains another's truth" (p. 285). Gurney was able to translate his potential power advantage, derived from being a U.S. senator, the questioner in the proceedings, and Dean's admission of personal culpability in the events, into an interactional advantage through the use of a conversational ploy of asking only for the literal truth. In addition to providing a specific example of a conversational strategy used for exercising power, the Molotch and Boden study illustrates the potential for this line of analysis to illuminate other situations in which talk is part and parcel of how power is accomplished.

Emotion is, along with language, another important way in which influence is exercised in organizational settings. As Rafaeli and Sutton wrote, "The view that organization members routinely use expressed positive emotions as tools of social influence is ubiquitous in organizational behavior" (1991, p. 749). Expressed negative emotion can also be a potent influencer. Sutton's (1991) study of bill collectors found that negative emotions could be part of an influence strategy of negative reinforcement—when the debtor paid (or at least promised to pay), the anger and disapproval expressed by the bill collector stopped. Thus, the debtor was reinforced (a noxious external stimulus was removed) for agreeing to pay. "Bill collectors believe that expressed emotions such as anger, irritation, and mild disapproval serve as tools of social influence when such conveyed feelings induce anxiety in debtors, and debtors construe that escape from such anxiety will be the consequence of complying with the collectors' demands" (Rafaeli and Sutton 1991, p. 750).

In an ethnographic study of bill collectors and Israeli police interrogators, Rafaeli and Sutton explored the use of emotional contrast strategies as tools of social influence. The principle is that "stimuli that are presented before, during, or after a given stimulus shape its meaning" (1991, p. 750), so that what is nice or noxious behavior is very much affected by the context in which that behavior occurs. Thus, for instance, Kipnis and Vanderveer (1971) found that subjects in the role of supervisor were more likely to give larger pay raises and higher performance evaluations to subordinates attempting influence through ingratiation when a hostile co-worker was present as contrasted to situations in which that hostile co-worker was not present. The Rafaeli and Sutton data suggested that five emotional contrast strategies were employed: "(1) sequential good cop, bad cop, (2) simultaneous good cop, bad cop, (3) one person playing both roles, (4) good cop in contrast to hypothetical bad cop, and (5) good cop in contrast to expectations of bad cop" (1991, p. 758). They argued that the presence (or threatened presence) of both styles of behavior made the good cop behavior appear nicer and the bad cop behavior appear nastier than if either were presented alone. They concluded that there were three mechanisms through which the perceived amplification of expressed emotion, accomplished by using emotional contrast strategies, worked:

> First, target persons may experience accentuated anxiety in response to bad cops and accentuated relief in response to good cops when there is a contrast. . . . They may acquiesce with requests for compliance in order to escape from the anxiety or fear. . . . Second, the contrast may accentuate the targets' perceptions that good cops are kind and helpful. As a result, the targets may feel pressure to reciprocate the kindness by complying with the good cops' wishes. Third, accentuated feeling of relief in response to good cops . . . may lead target people to develop trust in the good cops. (pp. 764–766)

Our understanding of power and influence processes has advanced substantially through research using multiple methods. What that work has not done yet is to explore the scope conditions for the various influence strategies and sources of power. We know less than we might about how strategies of social influence fail, about when theoretically predicted determinants of power don't predict actual power, and about when power is used in situations either more or less than predicted by the context. Consequently, some important research remains to be done.

CONCLUSION

The topic of power illustrates many of the issues that characterize and influence the development of organization studies. The topic is more likely to be comfortably located in a sociology or political science department than in a business school, with its emphasis on the economic model of behavior and on rational decision making. Thus, one might speculate that one consequence of the changing locus of organization studies has been less emphasis on power and influence than there might otherwise be, given the importance of the subject for understanding organizations.

Moreover, the study of power was particularly vigorous in the early 1970s—a time at which both the strategic contingencies (Hickson et al. 1971) and resource dependence (Pfeffer and Salancik 1978) perspectives developed. The 1970s was a particularly political period, comprising both the end of the Vietnam War and the associated political protests and the resignation of Richard Nixon as a consequence of the Watergate scandal. The 1980s and 1990s have been much more politically quiescent; this fact, coupled with a sometimes difficult job market, may also have made power and influence less likely to be subjects of as much research attention.

Power as a topic also suffers from the problem of being politically incorrect. As noted in the discussion of views of control, we prefer a voluntaristic, choice-based conception of action. Considerations of domination and force, of getting one's way against opposition—which is, after all, a part of most definitions of power—perhaps are better left out of sight or discussion. The field's increasing embeddedness in an economic, rational conception of behavior is nicely coupled with its renewed emphasis on the individual as contrasted with the situation. Both rationality and a focus on the individual in isolation more easily permit neglect of issues of interpersonal influence.

REFERENCES

Allen, R.W., D.L. Madison, L.W. Porter, P.A. Renwick, and B.T. Mayes. (1979). Organizational politics: Tactics and characteristics of its actors. *California Management Review* 22: 77–83.

Becker, W. (1992). Power and managerial dismissal: Scapegoating at the top. *Administrative Science Quarterly* 37: 400–421.

Brass, D.J., and M.E. Burkhardt. (1993). Potential power and power use: An investigation of structure and behavior. *Academy of Management Journal* 36: 441–470.

Cialdini, R.B. (1988). *Influence: Science and practice.* Glenview, IL: Scott, Foresman.

Cook, K.S., R.M. Emerson, M.R. Gillinore, and T. Yamagishi. (1983). The distribution of power in exchange networks: Theory and experimental results. *American Journal of Sociology* 89, 275–305.

Dahl, R.A. (1957). The concept of power. *Behavioral Science* 2: 201–215.

Emerson, R.M. (1962). Power-dependence relations. *American Sociological Review* 27: 31–41.

Finkelstein, S. (1992). Power in top management teams: Dimension, measurement, and validation. *Academy of Management Journal* 35: 505–538.

French, J.R.P., Jr., and B. Raven. (1968). The bases of social power. In D. Cartwright and A. Zander (eds.), *Group Dynamics*, 3rd ed., 259–269. New York: Harper and Row.

Gandz, J., and V.V. Murray. (1980). The experience of workplace politics. *Academy of Management Journal* 23: 237–251.

Gardner, J.W. (1990). *On Leadership.* New York: Free Press.

Gargiulo, M. (1993). Two-step leverage: Managing constraint in organizational politics. *Administrative Science Quarterly* 38: 1–19.

Gresov, C., and C. Stephens. (1993). The context of interunit influence attempts. *Administrative Science Quarterly* 38: 252–276.

Hackman, J.D. (1985). Power and centrality in the allocation of resources in colleges and universities. *Administrative Science Quarterly* 30: 61–77.

Hickson, D.J., C.R. Hinings, C.A. Lee, R.E. Schneck, and J.M. Pennings. (1971). A strategic contingencies theory of intraorganizational power. *Administrative Science Quarterly* 16: 216–229.

Hinings, C.R., D.J. Hickson, J.M. Pennings, and R.E. Schneck. (1974). Structural conditions of intraorganizational power. *Administrative Science Quarterly* 19: 22–44.

Ibarra, H. (1993). Network centrality, power, and innovation involvement: Determinants of technical and administrative roles. *Academy of Management Journal* 36: 471–501.

Kanter, R.M. (1977). *Men and Women of the Corporation.* New York: Basic.

Katzenbach, J.R., and D.K. Smith. (1993). *The Wisdom of Teams.* New York: HarperCollins.

Kipnis, D., S.M. Schmidt, and I. Wilkinson (1980). Intraorganizational influence tactics: Explorations in getting one's way. *Journal of Applied Psychology* 65: 440–452.

Kipnis, D., and R. Vanderveer. (1971). Ingratiation and the use of power. *Journal of Personality and Social Psychology* 17: 280–286.

Krackhardt, D. (1990). Assessing the political landscape: Structure, cognitions, and power in organizations. *Administrative Science Quarterly* 35: 342–369.

Lachman, R. (1989). Power from what? A reexamination of its relationships with structural conditions. *Administrative Science Quarterly* 34: 231–251.

Lodahl, J., and G. Gordon. (1972). The structure of scientific fields and the functioning of university graduate departments. *American Sociological Review* 37: 57–72.

Madison, D.L., R.W. Allen, L.W. Porter, P.A. Renwick, and B.T. Mayes. (1980). Organizational politics: An exploration of managers' perceptions. *Human Relations* 33: 79–100.

March, J.G. (1966). The power of power. In D. Easton (ed.), *Varieties of Political Theory,* 39–70. Englewood Cliffs, NJ: Prentice-Hall.

Miyazawa, S. (1986). Legal departments of Japanese corporations in the United States: A study on organizational adaptation to multiple environments. *Kobe University Law Review* 20: 97–162.

Molotch, H.L., and D. Boden. (1985). Talking social structure: Discourse, domination, and the Watergate hearings. *American Sociological Review* 50: 273–288.

Perrow, C. (1970). Departmental power and perspectives in industrial firms. In M.N. Zald (ed.), *Power in Organizations,* 59–89. Nashville: Vanderbilt University Press.

Pettigrew, A.M. (1972). Information control as a power resource. *Sociology* 6: 187–204.

———. (1973). *Politics of Organizational Decision-Making.* London: Tavistock.

Pfeffer, J. (1981a). Management as symbolic action: The creation and maintenance of organizational paradigms. In L.L. Cummings and B.M. Staw (eds.), *Research in Organizational Behavior* 3: 1–52. Greenwich, CT: JAI Press.

———. (1981b). Power in Organizations. Marshfield, MA: Pitman.

———. (1992). *Managing with Power: Politics and Influence in Organizations.* Boston: Harvard Business School Press.

Pfeffer, J., A. Leong, and K. Strehl. (1977). Paradigm, development, and particularism: Journal publication in three scientific disciplines. *Social Forces* 55: 938–951.

Pfeffer, J., and W.L. Moore. (1980). Power in university budgeting: A replication and extension. *Administrative Science Quarterly* 25: 637–653.

Pfeffer, J., and G.R. Salancik. (1974). Organizational decision making as a political process: The case of a university budget. *Administrative Science Quarterly* 19: 135–151.

———. (1977). Administrator effectiveness: The effects of advocacy and information on resource allocations. *Human Relations* 30: 641–656.

———. (1978). *The External Control of Organizations: A Resource Dependence Perspective.* New York: Harper and Row.

Pfeffer, J., G.R. Salancik, and H. Leblebici. (1976). The effect of uncertainty on the use of social influence in organizational decision making. *Administrative Science Quarterly* 21: 227–245.

Rafaeli, A., and R. Sutton. (1991). Emotional contrast strategies as means of social influence: Lessons from criminal interrogators and bill collectors. *Academy of Management Journal* 34: 749–775.

Salancik, G.R., and J. Pfeffer. (1974). The bases and uses of power in organizational decision making: The case of a university. *Administrative Science Quarterly* 19: 453–473.

Schein, V.E. (1979). Examining an illusion: The role of deceptive behaviors in organizations. *Human Relations* 32: 287–295.

Schwartz, B. (1974). Waiting, exchange, and power: The distribution of time in social systems. *American Journal of Sociology* 79: 841–870.

Thompson, J.D., and A. Tuden (1959). Strategies, structures, and processes of organizational decision. In J.D. Thompson, P.B. Hammond, R.W. Hawkes, B.H. Junker, and A. Tuden (eds.), *Comparative Studies in Administration,* 195–216. Pittsburgh: University of Pittsburgh Press.

Tushman, M.L., and E. Romanelli. (1983). Uncertainty, social location, and influence in decision making: A sociometric analysis. *Management Science* 29: 12–23.

Wade, J., C.A. O'Reilly, and I. Chandratat. (1990). Golden parachutes: CEOs and the exercise of social influence. *Administrative Science Quarterly* 35: 587–603.

Williamson, O.E., and W.G. Ouchi (1981). The markets and hierarchies program of research: Origins, implications, prospects. In A.H. Van de Ven and W.F. Joyce (eds.), *Perspectives on Organizational Design and Behavior,* 347–370. New York: Wiley.

Wrong, D.H. (1968). Some problems in defining social power. *American Journal of Sociology* 73: 673–681.

2

Power Politics in Organizational Life: Tactics in Organizational Leadership

Gilbert W. Fairholm

In many ways power is a unifying thread by which we can connect and rationalize the history of mankind. Of course other, more traditional perspectives like economic events, wars, ideology, and religion provide important and needed perspectives on our evolution as a society. But, certainly understanding how leaders as well as followers used power will help in understanding our history. It will be equally useful in helping us determine how people will relate to each other in the twenty-first century.

Viewing our leaders, our literature, our government, our philosophy, and our religion in power terms helps us understand each other better. These social systems record our history of competition, conflict, struggle, violence, and war. In a word, they record our fascination with power (Winter 1973) and the politics of power use. Perhaps there is no single concept of human relationship of more gut importance than how we get our way in the group. It is central to both who and what we are as individuals and as group members.

We engage in power activity in group (that is, political) settings. It is logical, therefore, that psychology, political science, anthropology, and the rest of the social disciplines should have interest in power. Each has something to add to our understanding of power and its use. Each discipline, almost each writer, has added specific definitions to the lexicon of power. The resulting confusion has done little to clarify concepts, or to reduce the trauma many feel when someone introduces the word power into a discussion.

The study of power dates from the earliest efforts to define a social science.

However, most of the modern work on power in organizational contexts had its beginnings in the 1930s. Since then, the focus of research has varied widely. Some focus on sociological underpinnings (Russell 1938; Cartright 1965; Follett 1942; May 1972;

and Crozier 1964). Some see power as political (Mills 1957; Dahl 1957; and Hunter 1959). Others give it a behavioral twist (Weber 1968; Homans 1950; French and Raven 1959; Cartright 1965, Thibaut and Kelley 1959; and many others). A few researchers give power a psychological thrust (McClelland 1975, and Winter 1973). And finally, some discuss power in organizational and structural terms (Etzioni 1961; Smith and Tannenbaum 1963; Crozier 1964; McKinney and Howard 1979; and Pfeffer 1981).

Power continues to be a difficult subject to surround. Disciplinary foci have helped, but have left about as much confusion as they have added insight into the subject. Analytical studies, while relatively few, have helped to clarify elements of power, its sources, and constituent parts. This work has added needed insights into specific dimensions of power, but has not delimited the central essence of power. Indeed, most work on power adds to the ambiguity rather than diminishes it.

Power is a part of life. It is manifestly a part of interpersonal behavior in most social situations. People are always interacting in group settings to secure goals and desired results. All interactive communication is purposeful, and to achieve this purpose, the individual engages in power activity. Because of the ambiguity of the power concept in life, it is not hard to understand the existence of its multiple definitions.

For the purposes of this book I define power as the individual capacity to gain your own aims in interrelationship with others, even in the face of their opposition. I believe this definition captures the essence of power as we use it in group and organizational life. It becomes the foundation for the following discussion about power in formal organizations and in other issues raised hereafter.

POWER IN FORMAL ORGANIZATIONS

When analyzed from the perspective of the individual in a structured organizational setting, we see some interesting insights on power. Achieving desired organizational results is dependent on our capacity to influence others to our point of view. The mechanism often is one of offering desired rewards to followers as inducement to desired behavior. In effect, we say, if you do what I want (i.e., behave in a manner useful to me), I will provide you with physical or psychological results that will meet your needs or be instrumental in achieving one or more of your desires. In this sense power use is a kind of political exchange transaction. It is instrumental to task accomplishment.

Power is also a process by which we induce change in another's behavior or attitudes (Grimes 1978). It is in this sense, then, that one can define power as the basis of all organized action. As a social structure of human interrelationships (Gouldner 1960), the organization controls the action of individuals; and control over others is power. We organize for power (Follett 1942). Control in the organization rests on power. Delegation is a power relationship. Negotiation is an exercise in power. Leadership is power in action (Zaleznik 1963).

Organizationally, we can describe power as the ability to make something happen— the essence of the causal relationship. Power defined in these terms becomes the basis of the "power relationship." Power relationships are interactive, interpersonal processes where one gets power from and uses it in interaction with others in the group.

POWER AND FORMAL AUTHORITY

The literature equates the opportunity to progress within the group with a getting of more authority (position power) than other group members. We see it in action when the group places more of the total so-called group power on one individual (a formal manager or informal leader). Authority (only one of several forms of power) is a divisible commodity that managers ration among themselves via the process of delegation. In this sense it is the basis for organizational order, logic, and control. It is the basis of status and hierarchy in the organization (Barnard 1948).

A view of power in authority terms connotes a system of dependencies; and, in this situation, distribution is the key issue. Each member of the organization relates to others in a power role relationship that constrains each member (Molm 1990). If one gains power, it is at the expense of others in the group. If one gains, others lose. Mary Parker Follett (1942) defined this "face" of power as "power over" others (as opposed to "power with" others).

POWER AND SELF-ESTEEM

Power is central to defining individual self-esteem within the organization. It is part of the pursuit of personal goals (Grimes 1978). Gaining power allows the individual to place himself in the group context in specific terms, in a specific relationship to others. Adler says that power does much to explain the behavior of exceptional people. He claims that it, more than the sex drive propounded by Freud, is the dominant determinant of personality (1956). Weber also ascribes to power a dominant role in social organization (1968).

The word "power" derives from the same root as the word possibility. The Roman root "possess" literally means "I can." The Latin verb "potere" means "to be able." Both words connote the central function of affecting something or someone. The word power entered the English language from this Roman/Latin foundation at the time of the Norman conquest of England (Hunter 1959). Over time, power has come to connote personal capacity in our English heritage. Power is a capacity, a talent, a skill resident in all of us, but held in larger quantities by specific individuals.

Power is the ability or capacity to induce others to behave in desired ways (McKinney and Howard 1979) in human interaction. All individuals can control or influence other people and, in turn, can be under another's influence. Power is part of all organized group activity that results in enhancement or limitation of our ability to do. Thus, power is a part of concepts like organization, authority, control, direction, competition, conflict, coordination, planning, budgeting, staffing, or other administrative functions.

POWER IN LEADERSHIP

Power is the essence of leadership. It is the extra element in interpersonal relations that allows the leader to affect others and secure their willing compliance. Rollo May (1972) defines power as the ability to cause or prevent change. Kaplin (1964) calls it the process of affecting the policies of others. Bertrand Russell (1938) defines it as the "production of intended effects." Power allows people to alter the behavior of others in ways they—the power users—want. Power lets anyone be a leader. The source may (and does) vary but the object appears universal. Power allows the individual to affect, to sway, others' behavior in desired ways; in a word, to lead them.

At one level, all interpersonal relationships are leader-follower relationships. We are constantly moving from a directive position to a follower one in our contacts with others. At times we engage in persuading others to do something we want them to do. It may be to follow our orders, to get us something, to laugh at our jokes, or to understand and respect our ideas and values. At other times—often in the same conversation—we persuade them to laugh, or induce them to do something that we want them to do. We see power in leadership contexts in a much larger dimension. It is a personal, rather than merely a positional, concept. The operative characteristic of leadership is its intimacy. It is a personal power relationship between one leader and one follower reiterated in a series of one-to-one relationships. These power relationships are constituent parts of organizational (and all) life.

POWER IN USE IN ORGANIZATIONAL CONTEXTS

Few ideas are more basic to the study of organizations than power. It is an important and active reality in all dimensions of organizational life. Indeed, power interactivity is, perhaps, humankind's most pervasive dimension. We experience the result of power use at all levels in the organization and by all participants. It is a constituent part of informal as well as formal organization. As Dahl (1961) said, it is as "ancient and ubiquitous as any (concept) that social theory can boast." Power is central to both leadership theory and practice. It is a core element of human interaction.

Organization and management of the environment predate recorded history (Hodgkinson, 1978). It is a primary activity of human organization. Administration and the desire to order our immediate situation have inspired the classics in literature. Certainly, we must count Machiavelli's *The Prince* and Plato's *Republic* among those classics. They typify a literature that carry our search for order and organization of our immediate environment into everyday life.

Power is central to man's continuing concern for administration and organization. How people organize and relate to each other to get planned goals accomplished is central to organization and administrative theory. The overreaching problem of organization life is securing follower compliance. This compliance, however, must come without losing the long-term amicable relationship between the person desiring compliance and the person whose behavior change we seek. And this must be done with an eye on conserving scarce resources.

Machiavelli's *The Prince* provides extensive advice to rulers (read, "leaders") on how to extend and combine their power and capacity to direct compliance. Similarly the libraries of the world are full of books to help us to influence subordinates, raise our children, make friends, and influence others.

Few concepts are more crucial or more central to the understanding of behavior in organizations. We may treat it as a prime aim or as instrumental to other, strategic aims. Nevertheless, power is a necessary part of the interaction of people. Power is a cornerstone of both leadership and management theory and practice. It is the essence of leader behavior. It is central to subordinate-to-superior interaction. It helps explain the myriad relationships we experience with the many peers and external contacts that make up the fabric of organizational interaction.

On another dimension, most organization members influence others and are, in turn, influenced by them. Power use dominates not only management and leadership perspectives, but those of ordinary workers, suppliers, consumers, and other stakeholders also. People in all kinds of work or in any social or hierarchical relationship share the goal of getting others to behave in ways they want them to. We want others to like us, to work for us, to think the way we want them to think. We want them to go where we think they ought to go, to be what we think they ought to be. Seen in this light, power is a political transaction process.

In agrarian societies our power usage was more personal, immediate, and limited in scope and domain. In industrial societies, complexity has affected power use as well as other elements of life. Power use now is more impersonal, anonymous, and institutionalized. In real ways it is the primary measure of our value to the group—be it the work organization or the social group. Hobbes, as early as the seventeenth century, listed power as the measure of our social status. Today, power is in many ways the measure of position. Money or possessions, while instrumental, are less significant in assessing social position than is power. We are a power-oriented society: one particularized by institutions (i.e., organizational, hierarchical representations).

Using these ideas, we can see that many managerial and leadership concepts have power connotations. For example, we can define authority as a manifestation of power characterized by position and relationship within the formal, hierarchical system. Authority connotes the legitimate right of the holder to command, decide, or determine the way the organization will go. It is an obvious manifestation of power, one connoting the formally granted rights inherent in the organizational position held.

Personal influence, an integral part of leadership, is a form power takes. Influence is a form of power, often subtle and indirect, by which we impact the situations and behaviors of others. We can understand influence best as a mechanism of attitude change. It uses esteem and respect to accomplish the task of changing the behavior of another.

Using a power connotation helps us interpret competition and its companion concept, conflict. In competition settings both participants exercise power in trying to achieve their purpose at the expense of the other person. Competition becomes conflict when we include emotions. Conflict, too, is a power relationship.

Power has a direct connection to many of the underlying functions of management. For example, power is a constituent part of organizational control systems. As individuals exert energy toward activating others to behave in organizationally useful ways (that is, to achieve organizational goals), they are exercising power. Direction, control, planning, coordination, and correlation are all manifestations of power used in organizations to accomplish intended results. The process is an impact one; the capacity is power (Handy 1976).

In fact, we can understand all of a manager's tasks—execution of authority, personal interaction, control, direction, planning, conflict resolution, and so on—better from a power perspective. While often masked, ignored, and even denied, power is central in understanding organizational participant behavior. In budgeting, planning, staffing, controlling, and directing, individuals constantly engage in power relationships and power exchanges. They negotiate schedules, compromise goals, marshal support, and compete for available resources. Implicit in each of these traditionally accepted managerial activities is an element of power use, of producing intended behaviors in others. Every act of interpersonal behavior directed toward goal accomplishment results in actual or potential power use.

Using power allows us to affect another's behavior in ways we want. This effect can result regardless of the will of the target of power. Leadership implies the inducement of followers to do something that the follower would not do without the leader's intervention. At some levels, at some times, for some leaders, the operative words may be persuasion, opening of opportunity, or facilitation of the work of followers. At other times the focus may be on coercion, force, or control. Whether the connotation is positive or negative, we are in the business of getting others to do what they would not have done if left alone.

ORGANIZATIONAL POLITICS

An obvious conclusion from this analysis is that management is a political (power-centered) activity. It involves us in all interactions aimed at reserving resources to our special needs. Much of existing literature on management and organizations, in fact, describes aspects of power acquisition, legitimization, and maintenance functions (Rubinoff 1968). Even limited experience in organizational life will leave us with a realization of the importance of political negotiation in organizational systems. Our organizational laws, rules, standards, policy, and regulations are manifestations of political influence—that is, power. Power is at the heart of what Mayes and Allen (1977) call the "management of influence" throughout the organization.

Organizational politics has been a largely undiscussed phenomenon in organization and management theory and practice. It has only recently found its way into the formal literature of organizational behavior (Allen and Porter 1983). Earlier writers also have made significant contributions to our understanding. Hobbes, over 300 years ago, helped distinguish political power (Kaplin 1964). He pointed out that the power of the subject impacts the sovereign as well. Since then, the debate has ranged from concern with the instrumental nature of power to its resource qualities to its operating impacts in group situations.

Definitions of organizational politics typically include several factors. Organizational politics involve (a) actions taken by individuals throughout the organization (Mayes and Allen 1977) and (b) any influence of one actor toward another (Gandz and Murray 1980). It includes (c) effort by one party to promote self-interest over that of another and, therefore, threaten the second party's self-interest (Rosen and Lippitt 1961). It also includes (d) actions typically not sanctioned by the host organization or results sought that it does not sanction (Plott and Levine 1978). That is, organizational politics involve (e) some kind of exchange process with a zero-sum outcome (Frost and Hayes 1979). Much of the literature suggests that organizational politics concerns itself with influence and control relationships of this kind.

Many definitions place organizational politics in this kind of control-of-others light. Pfeffer (1981) suggests that many definitions ascribe "sinfulness" or "illegality" to this social phenomenon. Porter, Allen, and Angle (1981) see organizational politics in self-interest terms (also negatively connoted). Martin and Sims (1974) tie organizational politics to control.

We also can see another construction of organizational politics. Operationally, organizational politics is a ubiquitous fact of organizational life. Allen, Madison, Porter, Renwick, and Mayes (1979) suggest that it is an important social influence process. It has a potential of being both functional and dysfunctional to organizations and individuals. Organizational politics is a solid part of organizational life. Its use conforms with current research suggesting that all group interaction has specific change purposes. Organizational politics is, therefore, a part of social interaction. Its positive or negative face is dependent on factors other than the mere fact of interaction for influence purposes. Our experience with power places it in the center of all social intercourse. Organizational politics is merely a structured, purposeful, organized group version of this universal social practice.

An operationally useful definition of organization politics may include elements that Mayes and Allen (1977) called the management of influence. For them, organizational politics is a process that involves formulating political goals, decision strategies, and tactics. It entails executing those tactics and setting up feedback loops to ensure effective results. Organizational power politics is also defined in terms of a process of change (Coenen and Hofstra 1988). Defined in this way we can say that organizational politics is the essence of leadership.

Organizational politics therefore includes actions taken to gain and use power to control organizational resources to achieve our preferred results instead of those of others. This definition places organizational politics in the classroom when a teacher "teaches." It is in the home as a father asks his child to do something. It is in the office as the subordinate "manages" his or her boss by couching interaction upward in ways calculated to induce the boss to respond favorably. And it is present when the manager orders employees to adopt a new procedure.

David Bell emphasizes the "talk" aspect of organizational politics (1975). He says traditional definitions of politics as who gets what, when, where, and how is not helpful. Getting control over needed resources can be, and often is, an intensely personal and private (even solitary) affair, not a public one. Talk, on the other hand, always involves others and more consistently conforms to the definition of politics. Talk affects others (Duke 1976), and to that extent it is power. To the widest extent possible, organizational politics concerns how people affect each other.

Political Behavior

Given our definition of organizational politics, it is a commonplace activity in organizations. Research by Madison (1980) and others supports the idea that organizational politics is fully a part of organizational life. Sixty percent of managers he surveyed averred that it was "frequently" or "very frequently" a part of organizational life. Most managers see organizational politics as a part of work life at the middle and upper management levels and less so at the lower levels.

Engaging in the politics of the organization may be helpful to the individual. Madison's research reports that 95 percent of respondents agreed that office politics is necessary in achieving individual goals. They also were unanimous in saying that it could harm them. For Madison, engaging in organizational politics is a "crucial path" to success in the organization (Madison 1980).

We use political action in the organization in situations of uncertainty, importance, and salience to either the individual or the unit concerned (Madison 1980). It is an old and hoary behavior pattern in groups. People in groups interact in a power struggle and to limit the exercise of power in others (Frost, Mitchell, and Nord 1982).

Individuals behave politically in all facets of organizational life. They use power to secure promotion, salary increases, or job transfers. It is part of the interplay of activity involved in resource allocation and delegation of authority and responsibility. It is intrinsic to policy development and policy change, performance appraisal, grievances, and intraorganizational coordination. Politics is part of the process of rule making and decision making in all aspects of organizational activity.

Gandz and Murray (1980) ranked perceptions of political action of various common organizational activities and concluded that politics was instrumental in determining interdepartmental harmony. Other areas of organizational activity where politics was a significant factor included promotions and transfers, delegation of authority, facilities and equipment allocation, and work appraisals. Less significant arenas for the exercise of organizational politics were such activities as assessing penalties, hiring, employee development, policy making, setting pay rates, and budgeting. Analysis of these data suggests that people use organizational politics most often in areas where individuals have some discretion in the actions open to them. We see less political behavior in those activity areas where formalized rules and systems are commonly in place.

Madison and others (1980) explored the positive or negative impacts of the use of organizational politics. His research illustrates that organizational politics can be useful in helping the organization reach its goals and cope with survival and organizational health concerns. It confirms also that organizational politics is helpful in coordinating staff and units, developing esprit de corps, and decision making. It is useful in organizational goal achievement. It can result in inappropriate use of scarce resources, cause divisiveness, create tension, allow less fully qualified people to advance, and reduce communication flows. And, finally, it can damage the image of the organization and sully its reputation.

Madison also assessed the positive and negative impacts of the use of organizational politics on the individuals concerned. Engaging in organizational politics can aid significantly in career advancement, getting recognition, and status in the organization, and increasing our power position. It also helps us accomplish personal goals and is helpful in allowing us to get our jobs done. Engaging in organizational politics can help individuals feel positive about their achievement and their ability to be in control of their organizational life.

There are risks involved, however. Engaging in political activity may result in reducing perceived or actual power in the group. It can result in removal from the organization (that is, loss of job). It can accentuate negative feelings about us by others. And, political activity can result in loss of promotion or increased feelings of guilt and interference with job performance.

Political activity can have both positive and negative results. Its use, however, is not in doubt. It is a ubiquitous part of organizational life. Older group members use it more than those newly inducted into the organization. This is the case also with middle and upper levels of the organization. They engage in organizational politics more than do those in lower-level positions. It is beyond doubt an instrument for securing organizational rewards.

Allen, Madison, Porter, Renwick, and Mayes (1979) assessed personal skills and traits common to politically active people in organizations. They conclude that effective political actors (be they chief executive officers, staff managers, or workers), all share some common characteristics. They are articulate, sensitive, and socially adept. They are competent, popular, extroverted, and self-confident. They exhibit aggressive tendencies, are ambitious, can be devious, and are clearly "organization men." They are also "highly intelligent and logical people." The politically adept individual in the organization is outgoing, competent, and effective in interacting with others. They are seeking, energetic advocates of their desired results. They are willing to engage others in competition for available resources and for the dominance of their ideas and ideologies.

Political Behavior Versus Administrative Behavior

We can distinguish organizational politics from administrative behavior in several significant dimensions. Most view administrative behavior by organizational participants as consensus behavior (Frost, Mitchell, and Nord 1982). Group members agree that the behavior in question is legitimate, that it flows from recognized "right," and that it fits the terms of the exchange. On the other hand, people resist political action and behaviors, if power targets recognize their intent. There is a consensus feeling that such behavior is illegitimate.

All members of the organization participate in power use. Senior executives, middle managers, informal leaders, and rank and file employees all use power. Madison's work shows that politics is more in the superior's mind and actions than in that of lower-level employees. While this may be true, it does not lessen the fact that all employees have some power. No one is powerless, even if it is only the power to withhold talent or energy. They use power to secure their desired results in the same ways that higher-level participants use their capacities.

It is a thesis of this book that power politics is a central activity of life. We can define much of life activity as the exercise of power (Krech and Crutchfield, 1948). Our success, in part, is a function of our ability to use power in our interrelationships. Success requires that we develop power skills along with, or perhaps in preference to, functional and task skills. Power is basic to effective living in the same way that energy is basic to physics (Mueller, 1970). It is a foundation element of human interaction. Power is the ability to activate human and material resources to get work done (Homans 1950).

REFERENCES

Allen, Robert W., and Porter, Lyman W. 1983. *Organizational Influence Processes.* New York: Scott, Foresman.

Bell, David V.J. 1975. *Power, Influence, and Authority: An Essay in Political Linguistics.* New York: Oxford University Press.

Cartright, D. 1965. "Influence, Leadership, Control." In J.G. March, ed., *Handbook of Organizations.* Chicago: Rand-McNally.

Coenen, L., and Hofstra, N.A. 1988. "Informational Choice: The Development of Systems-Related Power in Organizations." *Sociological Abstracts,* association paper.

Crozier, Michael. 1964. *The Bureaucratic Phenomenon.* Chicago: University of Chicago Press.

Dahl, Robert A. 1957. "The Concept of Power." *Behavioral Science* 2: 201–215.

———. 1961. *Who Governs.* New Haven, CT: Yale University Press.

Duke, James T. *Conflict and Power in Social Life.* 1976. Provo, UT: Brigham Young University Press.

Etzioni, Amitai. 1961. *A Comprehensive Analysis of Complex Organizations.* New York: Free Press.

Follett, Mary Parker. 1942. *Dynamic Administration: The Collected Papers of Mary Parker Follett.* Henry C. Metcalf and L. Urwick, eds. New York: Harper and Brothers.

French, John R.P., and Raven, Bertram. 1959. *Studies in Social Power.* Dorwin Cartwright, ed. Ann Arbor: Institute for Social Research, University of Michigan, 150–65.

Frost, P.J., Mitchell, V.E., and Nord, W.R. 1982. *Organizational Reality: Reports from the Firing Line.* New York: Scott, Foresman.

Gandz, Jeffrey, and Murray, Victor V. 1980. "The Experience of Workplace Politics." *Academy of Management Journal* 23, no. 2: 237–51, 440–54.

Gouldner, A.W. 1960. "The Norm of Reciprocity: A Preliminary Statement." *American Sociological Review* 25: 161–78.

Grimes, A.J. 1978. "Authority, Power, Influence and Social Control: A Theoretical Synthesis." *Academy of Management Review* (October): 724–35.

Handy, Charles B. 1976. *Understanding Organizations*. Middlesex, England: Penguin.

Hodgkinson, Christopher. 1978. *Toward a Philosophy of Administration*. New York: St. Martin's.

Homans, G.C. 1950. *The Human Group*. New York: Harcourt, Brace.

———. 1958. "Social Behavior as Exchange." *American Journal of Sociology* 63: 597–606.

Hunter, Floyd. 1959. *Top Leadership, USA*. Chapel Hill: University of North Carolina Press.

Kaplan, Abraham. 1964. *Power and Conflict in Organizations*. New York: Basic Books.

Krech, D., and Crutchfield, R.S. 1948. *Theory and Problems of Social Psychology*. New York: McGraw-Hill.

Madison, Dan L., Allen, Robert W., Porter, Lyman W., Renwick, Patricia A., and Mayes, Bronston T. 1980. Organizational Politics: An Exploration of Managers' Perceptions. *Human Relations*, 33, no. 2: 79–100.

Martin, N.H., and Sims, J.H. 1974. "Power Tactics." In D.A. Kolb, I.M. Rubin, and J.M. McIntire, eds., *Organizational Psychology: A Book of Readings*. Englewood Cliffs, NJ: Prentice-Hall, 177–83.

May, Rollo. 1972. *Power and Innocence*. New York: W.W. Norton.

Mayes, Bronston T., and Allen, Robert W. 1977. "Toward a Definition of Organizational Politics." *Academy of Management Review* 2, no. 4: 672–78.

McClelland, David C. 1975. *Power, The Inner Experience*. New York: Irvington.

McKinney, J.B., and Howard, L.C. 1979. *Public Administration: Balancing Power and Accountability*. Oak Park, IL: More.

Mills, C. Wright. 1957. *The Power Elite*. New York: Oxford University Press.

Molm, Linda D. 1990. "Structure, Action, and Outcomes: The Dynamics of Power in Social Exchange." *American Sociological Review* 55, no. 3 (June): 427–47.

Pfeffer, Jeffrey. 1981. *Power in Organizations*. Marshfield, MA: Pittman.

Plott, Charles R., and Levine, Michael E. 1978. "A Model of Agenda Influence on Committee Decisions." *American Economic Review* 68: 146–60.

Porter, Lyman W., Allen, Robert W., and Angle, Harold L. 1981. "The Politics of Upward Influence in Organizations." L.L. Cummings and Barry M. Staw, eds., *Research in Organizational Behavior*, vol. 3, 408–22.

Rosen, S., Levinger, G., and Lippitt, R. 1961. "Perceived Sources of Social Power." *Journal of Abnormal Social Psychology* 62: 439–41.

Russell, Bertrand. 1938. *Power: A New Social Analysis*. New York: W.W. Norton.

Smith, C.G., and Tannenbaum, A.S. 1963. "Organizational Control Structure and Member Consensus." *Human Relations* 16: 265–72.

Thibaut, J.W., and Kelley, H.H. 1959. *The Social Psychology of Group*. New York: Wiley.

Weber, Max. 1968. *On Charisma and Institution Building*. Chicago: University of Chicago Press.

Winter, David G. 1973. *The Power Motive*. New York: Free Press.

Zaleznik, Abraham. 1963. "The Human Dilemma of Leadership." *Harvard Business Review* (July/August): 49–55.

3

The Use of Power

David Kipnis

Once a person has gained control of resources that are given weight by others he must consider how best to use these resources. Statesmen must decide when to offer to negotiate, and when threats will produce the advantageous outcome. Parents must similarly decide how to convince their children to eat their food, to dress properly, and to study.

And so it goes—for all levels of society the perplexing problem is how to gain compliance without losing the long-term affection of the target person, and yet use one's resources economically. In the face of these uncertainties, it is not surprising that there is a continual demand for books that promise to give advice on these matters. Niccolò Machiavelli in *The Prince* provides extensive advice to rulers on how to extend and consolidate their power. Similarly, books on leadership provide advice to managers on the best way to influence subordinates, and books on child psychology are continual best-sellers among parents groping their way from one "identity crisis" of their children to the next.

Rather than offering advice on how best to exert influence, I shall more prudently limit myself to the question of what influences a powerholder's selection of influence tactics, regardless of whether the consequences of this choice lead to favorable or unfavorable outcomes.

The reader should be aware that I have adopted the perspective of the powerholder in discussing the particular means of influence that are used. That is, if the powerholder believes he is offering to reward the target for compliance, I will accept this belief as valid, even though the target may view the offer as an insult and an outside observer may see the same promise of reward as a threat. This kind of relativity exists in defining power relationships, since they represent social acts rather than processes that are invariant with respect to who is doing the observing (Tedeschi, Smith, and Brown, 1972; Bachrach and Baratz 1963). Hence different observers may disagree sharply on the benefit and meaning of any social exchange.

INSTINCTS AND POWER USAGE

One possible answer to the question of what determines the choice of means of influence comes from social philosophers who stress man's inherent enjoyment in exercising power in order to inflict harm on others. Freud, writing in *Civilization and Its Discontent,* described man's destructive impulses this way:

> Men are not gentle, friendly creatures wishing for love, who simply defend themselves if they are attacked . . . a powerful measure of desire for aggression has to be reckoned as part of their intrinsic, instinctual endowment. The result is that their neighbor is to them not only a possible helper or sexual outlet, but also someone who tempts them to satisfy their aggressiveness on him, to exploit his capacity for work without compensation, to use him sexually without his consent, to seize his possessions, to humiliate him, to cause him pain, to torture, and to kill him. Homo homini lupus. Who in the face of all his experience of life and history will have the courage to dispute this assertion?
>
> As a rule this cruel aggressiveness waits for some provocation or puts itself at the service of some other purpose, whose goal might also have been reached by milder methods. In circumstances that are favorable to it, when the mental counterforces which ordinarily inhibit it are out of action, it also manifests itself spontaneously and reveals man as a savage beast to whom consideration to its own kind is something alien. . . . The existence of this inclination to aggression, which we can detect in ourselves and justly presume to be in others, is the factor which disturbs our relations with our neighbors and which makes it necessary for culture to institute its highest demands.

Here we have Freud enumerating various coercive means by which man may harass his neighbor, and for no other reason than to satisfy primitive aggressive instincts that make up his natural endowment. If we are to take Freud seriously on this matter, the decision as to what particular means of influence to use will depend primarily on the presence or absence of societal restraining forces. In their absence, the powerholder will choose the cruellest means available. In this way he may satisfy both the manifest reason for exerting influence and the instinctual reason relating to the gratifications achieved by inflicting harm on others.

Freud's assumptions, however, are not easily verified when we examine the day-to-day behaviors of powerholders in the process of exerting influence. Except under special circumstances of intense anger we find that most powerholders tend to reject the immediate use of coercive means of influence. There is a preference for using less harsh means that will preserve a friendly relationship if possible. And if friendship is impossible, means of influence are sought that will at least allow civil intercourse between the powerholder and the target.

A study by Michener and Schwertfeger (1972) illustrates how the choice of destructive modes of influence are reserved for those persons we dislike to begin with, rather than being used indiscriminately. These investigators reported that, in conflict with a landlord over a rent increase, tenants who liked the landlord either attempted to change his decision through persuasion or by offering to move into a cheaper apartment in the same building complex. Tenants who disliked the landlord, however, appeared to follow the destructive pattern described by Freud, in that their choice of influence tactics were more likely to cause pain to the landlord. That is, tenants who initially disliked the landlord favored either forming a tenant's union to militantly resist the landlord's demands for higher rent or threatened to move elsewhere, thus depriving the landlord of any rent at all. It is mainly when strong antipathy is felt toward a target person that we appear to deliberately make our first choice of influence coercive rather than gentle.

INSTITUTIONAL SETTINGS GUIDE THE CHOICE OF INFLUENCE TACTICS

Any discussion of decisions concerning how power is used, whether benignly or with malevolent application, properly begins with the setting in which the influence is to be exercised. Each formal grouping in our society possesses some unique repertoire of influence means that are considered proper to use in that setting. This repertoire exists to provide persons directly responsible for goal achievement with the means to coordinate and guide the behavior of other participants, and so to achieve the setting's goals. In business organizations, Pelz (1951) and Godfrey, Fiedler, and Hall (1959) have found that when appointed leaders were deprived of power usually associated with their positions (by superiors not supporting their decisions), the appointed leaders were less able to influence their employees. Few of the employees listened when they realized that their supervisor's opinions about their work no longer counted. Clearly, personal charm may have only limited value for inducing behavior in settings that traditionally rely on institutionally based means of influence.

Table 3.1 shows the kinds of coercive means of influence that were found to be available to powerholders in three different settings—marriage, work, and custodial mental hospitals. These means of influence were gathered by the writer and his colleagues while interviewing marriage partners, first-line supervisors, and psychiatric aides. The targets of influence were the respondent's spouse, the employee, and the mental patient.

One of the first impressions gained from examining these listings is that the coercive power in each of these settings directs itself toward different values and needs within the target person. In marriage the coercive means of influence are based upon the ability of one spouse to withdraw emotional support and services from the other. The threat is to "move away" from the other partner. Further in the marriage setting, one has an impression that the threats used are vague and do not precisely specify exact consequences for noncompliance. In the mental hospitals, however, the threats appear to be quite precise. Also, the coercive means tend to be directed at the physical well-being of the patient. Rather than withdrawing emotional support and "moving away" from the target, psychiatric aides may threaten to "move against" the patient if compliance is not forthcoming. Among first-line supervisors the threats are directed toward withholding economic support or toward reducing the employee's self-esteem.

Another impression that is gained from examining Table 3.1 is that the first-line supervisors appear to control a wider range of coercive influence means than do marital

Table 3.1
Coercive Means of Influence Available in Three Settings

Marriage
1. I act cold and say very little to him/her.
2. I make the other person miserable by doing things he or she does not like.
3. I get angry and demand that he/she give in.
4. I threaten to use physical force.
5. I threaten to separate or seek a divorce.

Work
1. I chewed him out.
2. I gave him a verbal warning.
3. I threatened to give him a written warning.
4. I ignored him while being friendly with everyone else.
5. I kept riding him.
6. I scheduled him to work hours he didn't like.
7. I gave him work he didn't like.
8. I put him in a work area he didn't like.
9. I put him in an area of lower premium pay.
10. I gave him a written warning.
11. I took steps to suspend him.
12. I recommended that he be brought before the disciplinary committee.
13. He was suspended from work.
14. He was fired.

Custodial Mental Hospital
1. Warn the patient of loss of privileges (passes, cigarettes).
2. Put the patient in isolation.
3. Scold the patient.
4. Physically control the patient (restraints, etc.).
5. Give medicine to the patient (to sedate).
6. Discipline the patient by removing things or privileges that the patient wants.

partners or psychiatric aides. That is, supervisors appear to control "low keyed" threats for minor forms of resistance and massive threats (firings or suspensions) for strong forms of resistance. Having access to this range of influence means should make the first-line supervisors far more flexible in their attempts to influence employees than either marital partners or psychiatric aides, who may have to choose threats that are inappropriate for the kinds of opposition being encountered from their spouses or patients.

A good deal can be learned about the attempts of powerholders to influence others from simply tabulating the means of influence available to them in each setting. Can rewards be given out freely? What types of punishments may be threatened for noncompliance? Can the target person's environment be altered? If the answer to most of these questions is "no," one can suspect that the influence potential of the individual will be low, regardless of his personality, loquacity, or personal charm.

Suppose we observe two persons attempting to influence target persons. The first adopts a pleasant, democratic style in which mild requests for compliance predominate. The second person adopts a brusque, demanding tone with little concern for the feelings of the target person. If asked to explain these differences, we might guess that the first person is rather timid, while the second has an authoritarian personality. However, we would probably alter our interpretation if we were told that the first person was the president of the local Parent-Teacher Association interacting with one of the members, while the second person was a business manager talking with a subordinate. Rather than resulting from personality differences, the two styles of influence can at least in part be attributed to the fact that the PTA president has no formal sanctions available to induce compliance, while the business manager has such sanctions available.

As a general rule, one should look for increased assertiveness in powerholders as the number of ways in which they can influence others increases. Support for this general rule can be found in several studies by psychologists of the relationship between the availability of means of influence and the assertiveness of the powerholder. In one study by Columbia University psychologists Morton Deutsch and Robert Krauss (1960) it was found that persons running a simulated business game who were given the power to threaten their rivals became far more demanding and less willing to compromise with their business rivals. Seemingly, the added power encouraged the development of a belief system: "We're stronger—we deserve more."

Somewhat similar findings were also obtained by the present writer (1972) in an experimental study in which managers ran a simulated business. The job of manager required the supervision of the work of four employees. There were two conditions in the study. In the first, managers were provided with a number of different ways of influencing the employees; that is, the managers were allowed, if they chose to do so, to give pay raises, pay deductions, to shift their employees from one job to another, to train their employees, or to fire them. In a second condition, the managers were not provided with any of these means of influence. Instead they had to rely on their personal ability to persuade their employees, or on their legitimate rights as managers to issue orders.

The results of this study were that managers who controlled a broad range of ways of influencing were far more assertive and demanding in their relations with their employees than were managers who were not provided with this range of influence. Managers with many institutional powers made twice as many demands upon their employees to work harder as did managers with no institutional powers.

It seems clear, then, that as we move individuals into settings that provide additional ways of influencing others, these individuals will respond by making far more demands upon the world.

There is also a hint in the experimental literature that the kinds of demands made upon others will vary with the kinds of means of influence that are available. In a study of how two people make concessions when bargaining with each other, Schlenker and Tedeschi (1972) provided some participants with the power to reward their opponents if the opponents complied, other participants with the power to punish noncompliance, and still other participants with both the power to reward compliance and to punish noncompliance. The finding of considerable interest was that the type of power available had important effects on the behavior of the powerholders.

Powerholders sent more threats, and actually invoked coercive power more frequently when they possessed only coercive power than when they possessed both coercive and reward power. Thus persons acted more aggressively when they could only punish to gain compliance than when they could choose to either punish or reward. Further, powerholders promised fewer rewards when they possessed only reward power than when they possessed both reward and coercive power. These findings suggest that users of power will be less benevolent and more coercive in situations where they can only reward, or only punish, as compared to situations where they control the power to both reward and punish. Perhaps the power of prison guards to threaten and coerce should be augmented with the power to provide genuine rewards to prisoners in exchange for compliance. One wonders if by this means we could reduce the number of prison-abuse incidents that occur. For if the only way we have to get our way is to threaten and bully, it seems clear from everyday observation that most of us, sooner or later, will get used to the idea of threatening and bullying.

THE INFLUENCE OF STATUS ON THE CHOICE OF MEANS

So far we have stated that simply tabulating the number and kinds of means of influence available to a powerholder in a given setting will tell us a good deal about how the powerholder is likely to behave. Here we wish to consider the implication of this statement as it relates to a person's status within the setting. To state an obvious fact, persons with high status tend to have available a wide variety of means to influence. There are also few restraints on their use of these means as compared to the restraints on persons of lower status. Children can only beg, ask, plead, or whine in order to influence their parents. Parents can legitimately punish, reward, and train their children—that is, bring strong means of influence to bear on their children.

Within institutional settings individuals with high status and great office may have unlimited access to resources, while those with less status, such as supervisors or teachers, will have only limited access to the institution's resources. A study of role conflict among business managers by Robert Kahn and his associates at the University of Michigan (1964) nicely illustrates how access to influence varies with the person's work status in the organization. In this study managers were asked the extent to which they could use a variety of means to influence various target persons with whom they worked. The respondent was either a superior, peer, or subordinate of the target person.

Table 3.2 shows these responses in terms of average rating by each respondent of his ability to use four means of influence: legitimate power, reward power, coercive power, and expert power. Quite clearly, top supervisors reported that they had greater latitude to use legitimate, reward, and coercive powers than did subordinates. It may also be seen that all persons in the organization, regardless of level, felt that they could use their expert power to influence a target person.

This indicates that powers derived purely from participation in the organization, such

Table 3.2
Ability to Use Various Means of Influence at Differing Organizational Levels

	Top Supervisor	Immediate Supervisor	Peer	Subordinate
Legitimate power	4.6	4.3	2.3	1.6
Reward power	4.0	3.7	2.2	1.5
Coercive power	4.1	3.6	1.3	1.3
Expert power	4.1	4.1	4.1	4.1

Note: The higher the score, the greater the ability to use the given power.
*Estimated from text's statement that all respondents averaged above 4.0 on a scale of 1 to 5 (Kahn et al. [1964], p. 200).

as the power to reward and punish, are closely linked with level in the organization. High-status persons have a wider range of influence to choose from than low-status persons. On the other hand, when the means of influence depend upon the individual's own abilities, such as his expert knowledge, we are more likely to find persons at all levels using such means. Thus first-line supervisors can change their superiors' behavior by using professional knowledge. However, first-line supervisors will hardly ever attempt to change this behavior by promising to raise their bosses' pay, that is, by using reward power. This latter power tactic is reserved for those with higher status.

CALCULATION AND THE CHOICE OF INFLUENCE

The previous two sections pointed out that powerholders' willingness to assert themselves is closely tied to the kinds and amount of power bases that are available to them. Assume now that a powerholder does possess a suitable position and an array of means of influence that can be freely used. That is, assume the powerholder can choose to do whatever he wants to make the target person comply. In these circumstances, what determines the powerholder's particular choice of influence from this array? Why does he use one particular means of influence in one situation but not in another? Why in one instance does a teacher use flattery to encourage a student to study but flatly order a second student to engage in similar behavior? Why does a supervisor in one instance spend long hours training an incompetent worker to reach acceptable levels of performance but in another instance threaten to fire an equally incompetent worker? Is the answer, as Freud suggests, simply that powerholders select the means liable to do the most harm, so long as they are not punished themselves? Or are more rational processes involved?

All evidence indicates that more rational processes are almost always involved in decisions concerning tactics of influence. As Raven (1974) points out: "On the assumption that man is rational we would expect him to use the base of power which would most likely lead to successful influence" (p. 192). Raven goes on to point out that if the goal of the powerholder was to produce long-lasting changes in the behavior of the target person, then the powerholder would probably avoid coercive means of influence and perhaps attempt to influence through providing the target person with new information. If long-lasting compliance was not an issue, however, then the powerholder might decide to obtain immediate satisfaction by invoking strong sanctions.

Planning and rationality can almost always be found when powerholders are deciding which of several means of influence should be used in a given situation. This does not mean of course that emotions and feelings do not affect the powerholder's decisions. Such emotional feelings, however, appear to act by narrowing or expanding the range of influence means that the powerholder is likely to believe effective in that situation.

Gamson (1968) illustrates how emotions serve to guide the powerholder's choice of influence means. When the powerholder trusts the target person, persuasion is most likely to be used to convince the target person. Because of this trusting relationship, the powerholder is willing to allow the target person the freedom to make up his own mind, confident that the target person will freely do what the powerholder has requested. If the powerholder does not trust the target person, then it is quite likely that he will decide to invoke threats and punishments. The assumption here is that one cannot rely on influence means that allow the target person freedom of choice (such as persuasion), because with freedom the distrusted target person will probably do exactly the opposite of what the powerholder wants him to do. As Gamson notes: "Since the probability of favorable outcomes is already very low . . . , it is hardly necessary to worry about [the target's feelings]. The attitude then that 'the only thing they understand is force' is a perfect manifestation of this trust orientation" (p. 169).

CHOICE OF INFLUENCE—A TWO-STAGE PROCESS

If we assume that powerholders act rationally when choosing how best to influence a target person, then it follows that there must be at least two stages involved in the choice of a particular means of influence. First the powerholder must diagnose the reasons for the target's refusal to comply with his request. Is the reason for the target's refusal due to the target's dislike of the powerholder, or is it because the target person does not possess the ability to do what the powerholder wants? Perhaps it is because a lack of trust exists between the two parties so that the target person will refuse any suggestion made by the powerholder, no matter how beneficial the suggestion is to both parties. Clearly, there is no end to the number of possible reasons why the target person has offered resistance.

Yet if the powerholder does not understand the reason for this resistance, he will be forced to flail about until by chance he discovers the one influence means that will produce compliance. Given this time-consuming alternative, the rational powerholder, before taking further action, prefers to spend some time analyzing why the target person has refused his request.

Frequently this stage in the decision-making process is complicated by the lack of open communication between the powerholder and the target person. The target person may lie about his reasons or sullenly refuse to talk, since once the causes of resistance have been discovered the powerholder may attempt to overcome the resistance.

Further, the powerholder can make mistakes in his diagnosis. He is in the position of the sixteenth-century physician who possessed only the crudest of diagnostic tools with which to decide what was bothering his patient. As mistakes were common then among physicians, so too are they today among powerholders. The history of modern international negotiations contains many examples where signals of one nation were misperceived by another nation, which saw hostility where in fact peace overtures were intended. We have no X-ray devices available to peer into the mind of the target person and discern there the reasons for his refusal to comply with our request. Our closest approach to such a device is perhaps the consumer surveys that seek to discover the cause of citizen antipathy toward consumer products, or toward politicians, so that precise campaigns can be planned to overcome these resistances. For most powerholders, however, diagnosing the causes of the target persons' resistance remains a subtle art based upon past encounters with the target person, hunches, and the powerholder's own perceptiveness.

Once the diagnosis is reached, regardless of whether it is correct, we reach the second stage of the decision-making process, which involves the actual choice of means of influence. Assuming that the powerholder is acting rationally, this stage is almost completely dependent upon the powerholder's initial diagnosis of the cause of the target's resistance. As the powerholder's diagnosis of the reasons for the target's lack of cooperation varies, so too will his choice of tactics vary.

This two-stage process has an analogy in the practice of medical diagnosis and treatment. When a patient appears at a physician's office and complains of feeling sick, the physician must first decide what is causing these complaints. It is only after the diagnosis has been made that the physician can select a particular mode of treatment. Furthermore, the treatment that is selected must be the one that holds the highest promise of cure. If the physician ignores this treatment in favor of another, his action tends to be viewed as a breach of medical ethics. The concept of "treatment of choice" in medicine refers to this general rule that the treatment with the highest probability of cure must be used before any other is tried. Once the diagnosis has been made, one can predict with almost complete certainty the kinds of treatments the physician will use.

There is also a "treatment of choice" rule associated with the selection of means of influence. We have found that if powerholders agree on the reason for a target person's resistance to their influence, they will also agree on the proper means of influence to use. This two-stage process can be illustrated by studies done by myself and my colleagues William Lane and Joseph Consentino (1962, 1969) among Navy and industrial supervisors.

The purpose of these studies was to determine how appointed leaders used their delegated powers to influence the performance of their subordinates. At the beginning of the studies we had no particular preconceived ideas as to how power would be used.

Rather it was hoped to catalogue the range of means of influence that were relied upon, and to get some idea of when each means was used.

Our procedure consisted of asking supervisors in both the Navy and in various business organizations to describe a recent incident in which they had to correct the behavior of one of their subordinates. We asked the supervisors to describe the problem they faced and what they or someone else did about it. In telling us what they did, the supervisors were in effect telling us about the kinds of influence they had the authority to use.

The reason for these influence attempts did not arise from any particularly sinister motives. Rather they arose from the supervisors' involvement in their work. As part of this work there were obligations to make sure that employees performed at acceptable levels and to force changes if this level was not reached.

The nature of the employee problems that disturbed the supervisors in the first place was also tabulated. Basically the problems could be diagnosed as those caused by an inability of the employee to do his work or by a lack of motivation to do the work or by problems of discipline, in which company rules were violated (such as the problem of habitual lateness). Sometimes a supervisor would describe a subordinate whose poor performance was due to a combination of these problems. These employees were described as manifesting "complex" problems.

Next we looked at the ways in which the supervisors said they attempted to correct their employees' performance. Their attempts involved the use of a variety of institutional means of influence, which we classified as follows: (a) coercive power—threatening or actually demoting the subordinate or assigning him to less pleasant or lower-paying work, or reducing his responsibilities, or sending him an official letter of warning, or suspending or firing him; (b) ecological control, in which the subordinate was shifted to a new job, work shift, or a new job location but not for the purpose of punishment; (c) expert power, in which new information or new skills were shown the worker; (d) legitimate power expressed in terms of direct requests or orders for change.

In addition to these institutional means of influence, supervisors also relied upon their personal powers of persuasion convincing subordinates to change by praising, reprimanding, and encouraging them to expend additional efforts. Readers who adopt a historic or cultural perspective on these kinds of findings will be quick to see how bound by time and space such attempts at influence are. That is, no supervisors mentioned physically striking their employees, as would have been done prior to the twentieth century, and no supervisors mentioned using appeals based upon family and company loyalty, as is still done in some Japanese industries.

One of the strongest findings that emerged from these studies was the discovery that there was a "treatment of choice" rule associated with the selection of means of influence. That is, the kinds of influence invoked by the supervisors were found to vary systematically with the nature of the subordinate's problem as diagnosed by the supervisor. Without any particular instruction in the use of power, most of the supervisors converged on the selection of a given means of influence for a given type of problem. These findings are summarized in Table 3.3.

Table 3.3
Diagnosis of Subordinate Resistance and the Means of Influence Used to Overcome It

| | Diagnosed Cause of Poor Work | | | |
| | Simple Problems | | Complex Problems | |
Means of Influence	Employee Lacks Motivation	Employee Lacks Ability	Employee Lacks Discipline	Combinations of Poor Attitudes, Discipline, and/or Lack of Ability
Discussion	Yes	No	Yes	Yes
Extra training (expert power)	No	Yes	No	Yes
Ecological control	No	No	No	Yes
Legitimate power	Yes	Yes	Yes	Yes
Coercion	Yes	No	Yes	Yes

It can be seen that, as the supervisor's diagnosis of what was causing the subordinate's poor performance changed, so too did the means of influence that were used. For instance, when the supervisor believed that the employee's problem was due to poor attitudes, the supervisor used persuasion and informational modes of influence. The supervisor's concern was to find out the reasons for the subordinate's poor attitudes and, if possible, to persuade him to change. If, however, the supervisor attributed the subordinate's poor performance to a lack of ability, then persuasion was rarely mentioned. Rather, the supervisor invoked his expert powers and devoted time to retraining his subordinate.

If the problem shown by a subordinate was complex, with elements of lack of ability and discipline and poor attitudes, then supervisors increased the number of different means of influence directed toward the subordinate. Apparently, when the supervisors believed that several factors were causing the employee's poor performance ("He could never learn to do the simplest jobs, and on top of that he was always shooting off his mouth"), then the problem was considered more difficult to deal with. Accordingly, more powers were invoked to overcome this added resistance. For instance, 76 percent of a sample of Navy supervisors invoked two or more means of influence (e.g., increased training and change of jobs) when their subordinates manifested complex problems. When the subordinate evidenced a simple problem, however, only 41 percent of the Navy supervisors invoked two or more means of influence. This difference was statistically reliable beyond the .01 level.

A further finding was that, when faced with complex problems, supervisors exercised power by ecological control. That is, significantly more workers were moved to a new job or work shift when their problems were complex rather than simple. The supervisors apparently reasoned: "If he's causing so much fuss on this job, let's try him somewhere else." A moment's reflection will convince the reader that this means of exercising power is not limited to harassed supervisors facing strong resistance. In schools, pupils who are considered intractable by teachers are transferred out of class, while ecological control is exerted over criminals by sending them to prison. In all instances the diagnosis of being hard to influence leads to the temptation to shift the person to a new environment considered more likely to overcome these resistances.

Here we have evidence that powerholders adjusted the kinds of influence they brought to bear to fit what they believed to be the reason for the target's resistance. If the target's resistance was seen as caused by poor attitudes, then persuasion was one of the favored means (coercion was also favored in such cases). If the resistance was seen as caused by a lack of ability, then expert power was used and little time was wasted trying to persuade the target to improve his performance. If the target was seen as manifesting a variety of problems simultaneously, then the powerholder increased the pressure for change by invoking several different kinds of influence. Simply put, as resistance increased, additional means of influence were brought to bear on the target person. And among these was an attempt to move the target person from his present environment.

These findings are consistent with the notion that the use of power involves an active cognitive search which consists of two stages. First, we see that the powerholder diagnoses the causes of the resistance. He says to himself, "The reason X is acting so badly is that. . . ." Second, the powerholder searches for the best means of influence available to him for dealing with this resistance. That is, he says, "Well, if that's why he is doing so poorly, then I'd better do this."

While this process has been illustrated in terms of work settings, it is not difficult to see how a similar search pattern might operate elsewhere. Thus, a parent whose child gets into continual mischief during the summer vacation must decide whether to promise him some benefit for good behavior, sit down and reason with him, send him to summer camp, appeal to his love for his parents, or threaten some kind of punishment. The process of choice will be actively guided by what the parent decides is causing the mischief in the first place.

LIMITATIONS TO RATIONAL CALCULATIONS

There are several reasons why powerholders may not be able to select the best means of influencing a target person. Most obviously, the powerholder may not have available the proper means of influence. For example, a supervisor may not have the authority to promise a pay raise, despite his recognition that he will be able to influence his employees to produce more if such means are used. Related to this reason is the problem that arises when the use of one means of influence may prevent the powerholder from using a second means, despite the powerholder's recognition that the use of the second means would be more appropriate. Thus for example, if one uses coercion on occasion, it becomes difficult then to switch to the use of persuasion. Researchers who have studied the use of power in penal systems point out that therapy programs in prison tend to be unsuccessful because the prisoners tend to be coerced into entering such programs.

The inhibiting effect that the use of one means of influence has upon the use of a second means is also illustrated in the complaints of social caseworkers that their control of the power to grant or withhold welfare money tends to weaken their ability to provide counseling and guidance to their poverty clients. In effect the poor are unwilling to communicate socioemotional problems to a caseworker because of the possibility that some careless revelation about themselves may cause the caseworker to withdraw funds. While many caseworkers would prefer to influence their clients through counseling, they are unable to do so because they also influence the same clients through the use of money. Similar problems have been noted by supervisors in industry who are expected to influence both task attitudes and socioemotional attitudes of their employees. It has been reported (Reed 1962) that subordinates are not willing to openly communicate problems to the supervisors because of the employees' fears that revealing negative information about themselves will reduce their chances for promotion. In both of these instances, the possession of strong economic means prevents the powerholder from using other means despite his recognition of their usefulness for exercising influence.

A second limitation to choosing the appropriate means of influence occurs when a powerholder simply misdiagnoses the causes of the target's resistance and applies the wrong means of influence. Thus, a teacher might threaten to discipline an inattentive student unless the student's behavior improved. The same teacher would rapidly change tactics if it were discovered that the cause of the student's inattention was a hearing loss. Then, perhaps, the student would be moved to the front of the class as a means of improving his attention.

Still another limitation occurs when the powerholder does not consider a particular means of influence as appropriate. For example, open expressions of love as a means of influencing a wife or child are rejected by some men who believe that such expressions are not consistent with their conceived role of manhood. In a different context, Dartmouth College political scientist David Baldwin (1974) has discussed this limitation in terms of the reluctance of government foreign-policy planners to seriously consider other nations in any terms but coercive military power. He points out that:

> students of international politics are so preoccupied with negative sanctions, threat systems, and military force that they have painted themselves into a conceptual corner which has little room for non-military factors, positive sanctions and promise systems. It is not surprising, therefore, that the recent *International Encyclopedia of the Social Sciences* included an article on military power potential but none on economic power potential. At a time when military power is losing utility in international politics and economic power is gaining utility, this omission is especially unfortunate. (p. 395)

LACK OF ABILITY OR LACK OF MOTIVATION?

Powerholders usually diagnose the causes of a target person's resistance into one of two groupings. Either the resistance is attributed to the fact that the target person is inept and lacks ability, or to the fact that the target person has deliberately chosen to refuse to comply. In this second instance, the label of "poor attitude" or "lack of motivation" is used. Thus resistance is attributed by powerholders to either the fact that external forces are controlling the target person ("He wants to help but simply doesn't know how") or to internal forces within the target person ("That s.o.b. could do it if he wanted to help out"). The distinction between internal or external forces tends to be critical for understanding the powerholder's choice of influence tactics.

Here I wish to consider briefly the question of what kinds of information powerholders use when deciding that the target's resistance is due to either internal or external forces.

University of Wisconsin social psychologist H. Andrew Michener and his colleagues (John Fleishman, Gregory Elliot, and Joel Skolnick [1976]) have used concepts derived from attribution theory to help explain this decision. Michener et al. have proposed that the powerholder's judgment is based upon four bits of information: (a) the difficulty of the demands placed upon the target person; (b) the known ability of the target person; (c) the extent to which the target person seems to be trying; and (d) whether the target person's performance improves or not. In a test of this proposal, Michener found that powerholders attributed a target person's poor performance on an experimental task (solving anagrams) to external forces or, lack of ability, when the task was known to be difficult for most people, when the target person had a prior history of ineptness in solving anagrams, when the target person signaled that he was trying as hard as he could, and when the target person's performance improved over time, even though it never quite reached the level expected by the powerholder. Powerholders attributed the target person's poor performance to a lack of motivation when the opposite of the above four bits of information were communicated to the powerholder.

In short, the process by which powerholders diagnose the causes of a target person's resistance to influence has its own logic. Basically the powerholder attempts to reach a diagnosis by comparing the target person's current behavior with past behavior. Inconsistencies between current and past behavior are considered due to deliberate resistance when the powerholder knows that what has been requested is within the capabilities of the target person. Under these circumstances it is not unusual to hear powerholders justifying their selection of influence tactics in terms of the target person's poor attitude, hostility, or lack of motivation.

SUMMARY

This chapter has examined how powerholders convert inert resources into actual influence. The basic proposal is that the decision to convert resources into influence is guided by an active cognitive search for the best means of making this conversion. This search involves two distinct stages. In the first the reasons for the target person's refusal to comply are diagnosed. The second stage involves selecting that means of influence considered by the powerholder as most likely to overcome the diagnosed causes of resistance.

It has also been suggested that there are stable linkages between the diagnosed causes of a target person's resistance and the particular means of influence that are chosen. If powerholders attribute the target person's resistance to external forces over which the target person has no control ("I'm trying, but I just can't seem to do it"), then the influence techniques chosen involve training and expert knowledge. In essence these techniques serve to restore self-control to the target person so that he can comply in future interactions.

When powerholders attribute the target person's resistance to internal forces under the control of the target person ("I refuse"), then the influence techniques chosen involve discussion and persuasion, at least initially. If, however, discussion fails, then power-holders are tempted to invoke stronger means of influence to overcome what they believe to be deliberate resistance. These stronger means of influence involve the use of both rewards and punishments.

Finally the chapter has briefly surveyed sources that restrict the powerholder's selection of the appropriate means of influence. These sources include the fact that often influence tactics are not available to a given powerholder because of his position in an organization, because he does not recognize that it is legitimate to use some influence tactic, or because he has misdiagnosed the reasons for the target person's refusal and simply has chosen the wrong means of influence.

REFERENCES

Baldwin, D.A. 1974. Internation influence revisited. *Journal of Conflict Resolution* 15: 471–86.

Deutsch, M. 1969. Conflicts: Productive and destructive. *Journal of Social Issues* 25: 7–41.

Gamson, W.A. 1968. *Power and Discontent.* Homewood, IL: Dorsey.

Godfrey, E.P., Fiedler, F.E., and Hall, D.M. 1959. *Boards, Management and Company Success.* Danville, IL: Interstate.

Kahn, R.L., Wolfe, D.M., Quinn, R.P., and Snoek, J.D. 1964. *Organizational Stress.* New York: Wiley.

Kipnis, D. 1972. Does power corrupt? *Journal of Personality and Social Psychology* 24: 33–41.

Kipnis, D., and Consentino, J. 1969. Use of leadership powers in industry. *Journal of Applied Psychology* 53: 460–66.

Kipnis, D., and Lane, W.P. 1962. Self-confidence and leadership. *Journal of Applied Psychology* 46: 291–95.

Michener, A., Fleishman, J., Elliot, G., and Skolnick, J. 1976. Influence use and target attributes. *Journal of Personality and Social Psychology.*

Michener, A., and Schwertfeger, M. 1972. Liking as a determinant of power tactic preference. *Sociometry* 35: 190–202.

Pelz, D.C. 1951. Leadership within a hierarchical organization. *Journal of Social Issues* 7: 49–55.

Raven, B.H. 1974. The comparative analysis of power and influence. In J. T. Tedeschi, ed., *Perspectives on Social Power.* Chicago: Aldine.

Reed, W.H. 1962. Upward communication in industrial hierarchies. *Human Relations* 15: 3–15.

Schlenker, B., and Tedeschi, J.T. 1972. Interpersonal attraction and the use of reward and coercive power. *Human Relations* 25: 427–40.

4

Illusions of Influence

Jeffrey Pfeffer and Robert B. Cialdini

The idea of influence is ubiquitous in organizational analysis. Efforts to understand the causes of organizational actions and outcomes inevitably lead to concern with the causal factors responsible for those outcomes—who or what has influence in the situation. Some of the relevant literature pursues the direction set by the demonstration of the fundamental attribution error (Ross 1977) and explores when observers attribute influence to persons, for instance, in leadership roles in contrast to situational factors. Thus, some research asks the question: In what circumstances do observers attribute influence over events and outcomes to individual leadership (Calder 1977; Pfeffer 1977)? Meindl, Ehrlich, and Dukerich (1985) argued that leadership effects would be attributed more under conditions of organizational performance extremes—either very good or very poor performance—and when economic stress was high because of poor macroeconomic conditions. In other literature, the following question is asked: What do individuals do to acquire actual influence over situations? This focus on how individuals develop influence is evident, for instance, in the literature on leadership (House and Baetz 1979) and interpersonal power (Cialdini 1988; Pfeffer 1992).

This chapter focuses on inferences about influence made not by observers but by those who are actually in managerial or supervisorial—in other words, potentially influential—roles. The attributional approach taken in some, although not all, of the relevant literature implies that both actors and observers are engaged in a process of inferring causality (Kelley 1971) and potentially taking subsequent actions based on these attributions. Observers' attributions of influence and causality, the focus of much of the existing literature, are interesting and relevant for understanding individual causal schema and interpersonal perception. The attributions about personal influence developed by the actors themselves, however, are possibly even more consequential because these individuals are likely to act on the basis of their beliefs and thereby affect both themselves and others through their actions.

To the extent that attributional processes are involved in inferring who or what has influence over events and outcomes and how much influence various parties possess, it is possible and perhaps even inevitable that attribution errors will occur. The fundamental attribution error (Ross 1977) is one example of an error in causal reasoning in which outcomes are overattributed to individual characteristics such as personality while the effects of situational constraints are erroneously underestimated. This error in causal reasoning, however, is not the only, or perhaps even the most consequential, error in understanding organizational dynamics. Another possible inference error involves an illusion of influence—the belief that one has influence over a behavior or outcome even when one does not or, at a minimum, overestimating one's degree of influence and control in a particular setting or situation. For example, the literature on the illusion of control (Langer 1983) shows that people come to believe they actually have influence over chance events. When people are more actively involved in the activity and therefore both committed and behaving as though they might have influence, they are likely to believe that they have causal control over random outcomes. Thus, individuals who throw dice or draw colored balls out of urns rather than just watching someone else do these things, thereby having more involvement in the situation, are willing to bet more on the outcome because they feel they have more control over it.

The illusion of influence is probably quite widespread in organizations, with important effects on both those who harbor these illusions and the organizations in which they work. This chapter seeks to understand the factors that can produce an illusion of influence and some of the effects of such illusions. We then discuss possible ways of overcoming illusions of influence in organizational settings under the presumption that by so doing, some of the dysfunctional consequences of influence illusions can be avoided.

WHERE DOES THE ILLUSION OF INFLUENCE COME FROM?

There are a number of psychological factors that would cause someone to believe he or she had influence over a situation in which there was little or none or to overestimate the amount of influence possessed. One such factor is the motivational bias for individuals to want to see themselves in the most favorable light possible, the so-called self-enhancement bias. Myers (1996) has reviewed the extensive literature documenting the tendency of individuals to regard themselves as more intelligent, skilled, ethical, honest, persistent, original, friendly, reliable, attractive, fair-minded, and even better drivers than others. In the negotiations literature, this self-enhancement effect has been shown to lead to overconfidence—for instance, in a situation of final-offer arbitration, the individuals involved thought their offer had a 68 percent chance of winning (Bazerman and Neale 1982). This overconfidence often hinders the willingness to make concessions (Neale and Bazerman 1985), find integrative solutions, or negotiate rationally (Neale and Bazerman 1991).

Unrealistic and ego-enhancing self-perceptions can be maintained by selectively processing and interpreting information in ways that promote the person's self-concept.

Thus, people (and organizations) are more likely to attribute success to internal factors, such as hard work and intelligence, and poor outcomes to factors such as chance or environmental perturbations over which they had no control (Brown and Rogers 1991; Fletcher and Ward 1988). Studies of the accounts for organizational performance provided in annual reports have consistently observed this effect—poor performance is attributed to general economic or industry conditions, whereas good performance is credited to management and other internal organizational factors (Salancik and Meindl 1984, p. 246). Individuals may believe that tests on which they have done well are more valid (Shepperd 1993). Also, people believe that others who accept rather than resist their persuasive arguments are more intelligent (Cialdini, Braver, and Lewis 1974; Cialdini and Mirels 1976).

Possessing influence is, at least in the United States and most other Western countries, seen as something that is desirable. Being powerful rather than powerless, being influential, and being efficacious are all valued and complimentary appellations. Consequently, one way for individuals to engage in self-enhancement is to overestimate their influence and power—to believe that they have more control over others and situations than they actually do. Indeed, the preoccupation with leadership, training in leadership, becoming a leader, and so forth leads to a heightened veneration of those in influential positions. Thus, it is reasonable to expect that, as part of a process of self-enhancement motivated by the desire to have as favorable a self-concept as possible, individuals will overestimate not only their leadership abilities but also the results of their attempts to act as a leader and to influence others.

There are experimental data consistent with these self-enhancement arguments. Pfeffer, Cialdini, Hanna, and Knopoff (in press) conducted an experiment using Stanford MBA students, all of whom have had work experience and some of whom have had supervisory experience—in other words, a reasonably sophisticated subject pool. In the experiment, subjects were told that they would be randomly assigned to one of two roles—either someone given the task of preparing a draft advertisement for a new watch or someone in the position of overseeing that other person's efforts. In actuality, all subjects were in the role of the manager, and the materials they received that were supposedly "prepared" by their colleague in the other room were actually supplied by the experimenters. In the lowest involvement and control condition, subjects spent the time filling out personality questionnaires, were told that, as is often the case, they were too busy to closely oversee the work of their subordinate, and saw only a final advertisement. In an intermediate condition, subjects saw a rough draft of the advertisement and filled out a feedback form (to ensure that they spent time thinking about it) but were told that, again as is the case in the real world, the subordinate would not be able to receive the feedback because of time limitations. In the highest involvement condition, subjects saw the identical rough draft, filled out the feedback form, and believed that the person working on the advertising campaign had seen their advice.

All subjects rated the identical final advertisement on four dimensions: its creativity and originality, its demonstrated business sense, its interest level, and overall quality of the final advertisement. These four items were used to construct an index measuring the overall quality of the advertisement as assessed by the various subjects. Subjects also provided other ratings, such as for the competence of the person doing the work and their own effectiveness as a manager, and answered other questions about the study. The study results were dramatic. The greater the degree of perceived control and involvement, the more highly subjects rated the advertisement. The differences were substantial: The subjects in the highest involvement condition rated the advertisement about twice as favorably (on a seven-point scale) as those in the lowest involvement and control condition. Moreover, the study found that merely being involved in the experiment tended to inflate evaluations of the work. A control group that simply saw the advertisement rated it the least favorable of all. These results are shown in Figure 4.1.

Moreover, in addition to evaluating the advertisement more favorably, subjects evaluated their own managerial effectiveness substantially more favorably to the extent that they were more involved in the activity of supervising and, therefore, felt that they had more control over the final outcome. Also, it is striking how easy it was for a subject population with some work and in many cases actual supervisory experience to come to believe that they had influence over an outcome for which there was minimal supervision and actually no effect on the final product. The results of the experimental manipulations on subjects' ratings of their own managerial effectiveness are shown in Figure 4.2.

To the extent that the illusion of influence is fostered by a motivation for self-enhancement, conditions that affect either the content of what is self-enhancing or the motivational importance of self-enhancement would be expected to affect the magnitude of the influence illusion. Cultural values and beliefs are one such moderating condition (Markus and Kitayama 1991; Triandis 1989). As Heine and Lehman (1995, p. 595) noted, "Evidence suggests that self-enhancing tendencies can be culturally variant; they may, in fact, be less prominent in the motivational repertoire of people from cultures outside of North America." Their study, which compared levels of unrealistic optimism—"The tendency for people to believe that they are more likely to experience positive events, and less likely to experience negative events, than similar others" (p. 596)—between samples of Canadians and Japanese, found that the Canadians showed higher levels of unrealistic optimism.

The idea of individual, compared to group or collective, influence and efficacy is a particularly Western idea. Singelis (1994), in developing a scale measuring independent versus interdependent construals of the self, wrote,

> People in the West hold an independent view of the self that emphasizes the separateness, internal attributes, and uniqueness of individuals (the independent self-construal) and . . . many non-Western peoples hold an interdependent image of self stressing connectedness, social context, and relationships (the interdependent self-construal). (p. 580)

As Morris and Peng (1994) have demonstrated, Chinese are much less likely to make causal attributions to the individual, in part because they have been culturally conditioned to more often subordinate themselves to the group and to view the group as

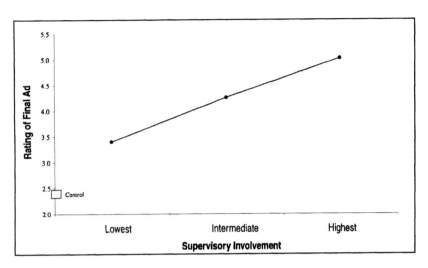

Figure 4.1. **Rating of the Final Ad**

being a more focal social unit. Other cultural distinctions in addition to the Western/ non-Western distinction are relevant, including organizational cultures that also obviously vary in the extent to which they emphasize individual as opposed to more collective bases and causes of action. We expect that there is less tendency to observe people holding illusions of individual influence, and therefore overrating themselves and what they are associated with producing, in more collectivist organizational or national cultures. Since collectivist orientations vary across individuals even within cultures, this argument suggests that measures of collective versus individual orientation (such as those developed by Hofstede 1980, or Singelis 1994) could be useful in studies exploring this idea.

When we described results of our Stanford study to colleagues, a frequent response was the following:

> Of course your student subjects saw both their effectiveness and the quality of the work product as being better the more they were apparently involved in the process that produced the advertisement. After all, they are students in an elite MBA program in which they are learning both how to manage and that, by their very selection into the school, they have managerial skills and talents.

It is certainly plausible to believe that one consequence of going to business school or going through any form of management training is to heighten the importance of being an effective and efficacious manager for an individual's self-concept. After all, the very behavior of investing time and other resources in training means that the individual's self-concept is more closely linked with and committed to being an effective manager.

If this line of argument is correct, it suggests that the illusion of influence, in which

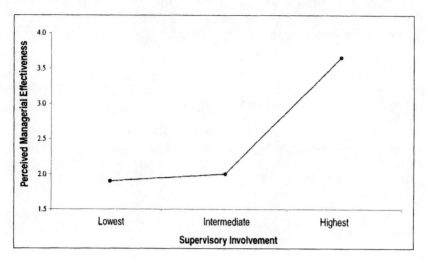

Figure 4.2. **Perceived Managerial Effectiveness**

one inflates one's own effectiveness and the quality of work that one has been involved in producing, should be greater among business students or, for that matter, managers than in a population with a self-concept less directly tied to being an effective leader. Moreover, it is reasonable to hypothesize that one important consequence of going to business school or going through other forms of management training is to increase the likelihood that the person will see himself or herself as effective and influential. The more such training one has, the more one's self-concept is tied with being a "good manager," which at least in Western cultures means being able to get things done and having influence.

Although our subject population was too small for definitive tests, trends in the data are consistent with these arguments. When the same study was conducted using Arizona State University undergraduates as subjects, the effects were somewhat attenuated. Also, there is evidence that the longer the MBA subjects had been in business school at the time of the experiment, the more they tended to view the advertisement as being better and their own management competence as being better in the high-involvement condition.

We have argued that any circumstance that increases the importance of being influential to the self-concept should increase the strength of the illusion of influence and the corresponding inflation of both the perceived quality of the work product and one's own self-evaluation of effectiveness as a manager. Factors that can increase the importance of being influential to the self-concept include anything that elevates a person's status in an organizational hierarchy and, as a consequence, implicates the person's sense of self with his or her success in that hierarchy. Such status markers include increased salary differentials across organizational levels, formal office arrangements that connote status, and job titles—indeed, even the title manager or supervisor. Each of these would be expected to increase the motivation for self-enhancement and, consequently, the strength of the illusion of influence. In this sense, many of the arrangements that rank individuals hierarchically—differences in offices, wages, and job titles—become self-reinforcing in that they produce behavior motivated to enhance the self by believing that one's own actions are important and effective. Consequently, it is not surprising that many high-commitment workplaces and organizations that have implemented total quality management approaches have attempted to do away with, at least to some degree, these status markers (Pfeffer 1994, 1998). With the status distinctions in place, the motivation for self-enhancement is increased and, as a result, the tendency to credit or even involve others or view them as being important in affecting the work process is diminished.

Regarding this point, we have argued that a motivation for self-enhancement leads to the development of an illusion of influence, and this motivation is particularly strong under conditions in which the self-concept is highly implicated—when the individual is a manager, has gone through some sacrifice or behavioral commitment to become one, and has other status distinctions that both make being influential important and create markers that signify influence. Individual motivation for self-enhancement, although important, is not likely to be the only factor involved in the illusion of influence. After all, one of the most reliable findings of social psychology concerns the potency of social influences, including informational social influence (Cialdini 1988; Deutsch and Gerard 1955; Festinger 1954; Salancik and Pfeffer 1978). As briefly mentioned, people in different social environments vary in their beliefs about the efficacy and importance of individual leadership and personal (compared with more social or group) efficacy (Morris and Peng 1994; Triandis 1989).

As the research by Meindl and colleagues (1985) indicates, not only do socially constructed beliefs about the efficacy and potency of individual leaders vary across broad cultural contexts but also these beliefs vary across time and may vary across organizations or even organizational subunits at a single point in time within a single national culture. The research by Meindl et al. suggests that illusions of influence are likely to be particularly potent at times of extreme performance—when the unit or organization is doing either very well or very poorly. Recently, an article in the *Wall Street Journal* noted the rise of the chief executive in U.S. firms as a public figure. In contrast to the situation in, perhaps, the 1950s and 1960s, currently executives write books, are focal in news stories, and have become almost cultural icons (e.g., Bill Gates of Microsoft, Andrew Grove of Intel, and Steve Jobs of Apple and Pixar). When a business newspaper finds the veneration and visibility of executives worthy of comment, something of social importance is occurring. Part of the explanation lies in the exceptional economic performance, as reflected in the stock market, of the past half decade and the apparent attribution of this exceptional performance to the skills of senior business leaders (as contrasted, for instance, with the environment). Part of the explanation must also lie in the fact that senior executive salaries and executive wealth have increased disproportionately, which also makes these individuals more visible, focal, and noteworthy.

It is important to note, however, that the executives and their organizations can either emphasize or deemphasize their individual influence, and by so doing cause others to ascribe more or less influence to them as individuals. Toyota Motors has certainly been among the most successful and admired companies in the world, but its chief executive officer receives limited media attention. In the United States, there are successful organizations, such as USAA in finance and insurance, MBNA in credit cards and banking, Norwest in banking, AES in the production of electric power, and numerous others, in which there is less of an emphasis on the efficacy of individual leadership and, we predict, as a consequence less of a tendency to observe illusions of influence. Our prediction is straightforward. There is a social contagion effect such that persons placed in an information environment in which self-enhancing motivation is emphasized and the independent, rather than the interdependent, self-construal is dominant will over time exhibit more tendency to demonstrate illusions of influence—overvaluing things they have had more ostensible involvement in or control over and overvaluing their own efficacy as leaders or managers.

SOME CONSEQUENCES OF THE ILLUSION OF INFLUENCE

We have already discussed one important consequence of the illusion of influence— the inflated evaluation of work output produced under more supervisory involvement and the more positive self-evaluation of the person's managerial competence and ability. It is implicit that this inflated evaluation of the quality of work produced under more supervisory control is more likely to occur to the extent that the work product itself has some uncertainty or ambiguity associated with it. Allison, Messick, and Goethals (1989), in a study of positive illusions, found smaller effects for ratings of intelligence than morality. They argued that this was because of "the greater publicity, specificity, and/or objectivity of behaviors signaling intelligence than of behaviors indicating morality" (p. 289). In the experiment described previously, evaluating an advertisement for a new watch inherently involves taste and judgment as opposed to the simple application of a formula. Situations of ambiguity and uncertainty are not infrequent in organizations and are particularly prominent the higher one rises in the hierarchy and in staff rather than line positions.

The following question was also addressed in the experimental study: What was the consequence of the illusion of influence for the rating of the presumed subordinate doing the work? There are two different predictions that can be made. Some research (Kipnis 1972; Strickland 1958) would predict that the competence of the subordinate would not be rated highly. Kipnis found that the more someone had power over others, the less likely that person was to want to interact with those others and they were less favorably evaluated. Strickland described the supervisor's dilemma: If someone works under supervision, how can the supervisor know whether or not the person can be trusted or is competent because there is no opportunity in such circumstances to observe the subordinate's trustworthiness or skill at working without direction?

Using the concepts of commitment and consistency, the opposite prediction can be made. If the subjects evaluate the advertisement more favorably with increasing involvement, then a halo or consistency effect (Heider 1958) to maintain cognitive balance should indicate that they also evaluate the person producing that work more favorably. Moreover, more involvement is more committing, and research shows that the more involvement a person has—in this instance, in making the decision to hire someone—the more favorable will be the evaluation of that individual because of the person's commitment (Bazerman, Beekun, and Schoorman 1982; Schoorman 1988).

In the Pfeffer et al. (in press) study, the data supported the consistency prediction. Not only did the degree of supervisory involvement relate to the rating of the advertisement and the self-evaluation of managerial competency but also it significantly related to the evaluation of the subordinate doing the work, with the greater the level of supervisory involvement and control, the more favorable the evaluation of the subordinate's competence (Figure 4.3). Given the absence of actual interpersonal interaction in the experimental situation, it is perhaps not surprising that the consistency effect predominated. In other contexts, interaction can produce self-fulfilling cycles of behavior (Snyder 1982) in which subordinate competence may be devalued over time, which could not happen in this instance.

There are important implications of this result and from the studies by Schoorman for the performance appraisal or evaluation process. If supervisorial involvement in a task inflates the supervisor's opinion not only of the work product but also of the subordinates, there should be serious concern about the extent to which such appraisals will be fair or the likelihood that this bias will encourage decentralization and delegation of decision making. Evaluations that entail obtaining information from peers and subordinates as well as from supervisors—so-called 360-degree feedback—would be preferable because they reduce the effect of supervisory bias while maintaining the involvement of the manager in the evaluation and appraisal process—necessary for maintaining commitment.

The illusion of influence may have other, even more profound, consequences and implications. The following question motivated the Pfeffer et al. (in press) experiment: Given the documented positive effects of participation on organizational performance, why is it that true empowerment (through the use of things such as self-managed teams) is so rare? The study provides one answer: If work produced under more control is evaluated more favorably, the person supervising the work has an enhanced opinion of himself or herself, and the supervisor also rates the subordinate more favorably, there is little in the situation to induce delegation. Control brings its own reward in a more favorable view of almost all aspects of the work setting.

The illusion of influence produces a false sense of self-confidence and security in work produced with one's direct involvement and a corresponding diminished confidence in work produced without one's involvement. Both effects may be harmful to organizations. As one observes organizations making mistakes that seem obvious to outsiders—for instance, airlines' pursuing low-service strategies that result from too fierce cost-cutting, companies foregoing investment in and development of new product technologies as in the case of a number of computer firms that missed the personal computer revolution, and so forth—what is striking is not just the initial judgmental

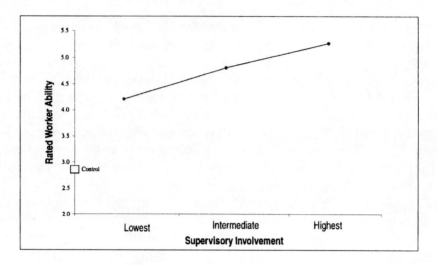

Figure 4.3. **Rating of Employee Ability**

error but also the persistence in seemingly failing decisions. This phenomenon has typically been described as an example of escalating commitment to a failing course of action, with the commitment arising because of the failure and the need, therefore, to justify one's initial decision by investing more resources (Ross and Staw 1993; Staw 1976). The illusion of influence perspective offers a complementary view of the same observed phenomenon. There is persistence with flawed decisions not simply as a way of justifying one's previous commitments but also because, given the level of involvement in the decision-making process, the decision maker does not accurately perceive the outcomes and therefore never really apprehends the true extent of the problem or failure. What appears to be escalating commitment to the outside observer may appear to be persistence with a successful course of action to the decision maker, who is subject to self-enhancement-induced motivations to see decision outcomes as more favorable than they are in reality.

By the same token, the readiness to see problems in work produced without the manager's direct involvement leads to a derogation of the abilities of subordinates that makes delegation difficult. Moreover, the subordinates must certainly learn about the illusion of influence over time from a trial-and-error process. When they do work on their own, the work is not evaluated nearly as favorably as when they involve their supervisor or at least cause that individual to believe that he or she has had control over the work process. Therefore, over time, people will look up the hierarchy for supervision, and supervisors will wonder why they cannot get their subordinates to accept responsibility, thus creating a self-reinforcing, albeit less than healthy, cycle of behavior.

There are two sides to the illusion of influence. Writing about self-enhancing illusions more generally, Taylor and Brown (1988, p. 193) noted that such illusions "can serve a wide variety of cognitive, affective, and social functions." Tyler and Hastie (1991) have also noted that some motivationally based forms of self-enhancement may be good for the individual's mental health as well as for stimulating more effort directed toward achievement. The illusion of influence is associated with inflated evaluations of work that one is involved with, and this very overconfidence may be useful in stimulating entrepreneurial decision making. Many organizational decisions, and certainly decisions associated with starting a new business or launching a new product, are inherently risky and there are limits as to how much data and analysis can reduce that uncertainty. Without some perhaps unjustified sense of control and influence over events, decisions that are required for launching new activities would be more difficult to make and it is less likely that decision makers would get beyond the risk and uncertainty to make these decisions.

A prominent and successful South Korean graduate of Stanford Business School was asked about his experience at the school and what he learned. After graduating, this individual worked at a family-owned company and expanded its scope dramatically, with a particularly bold and successful expansion into financial services. He said that what he had gained most from business school was a sense of self-confidence and, as a consequence, the willingness and ability to take prudent business risks and to lead the firm on a much more aggressive expansion path than it had followed in the past. Therefore, on the one hand, the illusion of influence produces the overconfidence that makes everything one is involved in look better. On the other hand, that same illusion of influence encourages entrepreneurial decision making that might be less evident if one had a more realistic sense of one's own abilities and influence over decisions and outcomes.

REDUCING THE ILLUSION OF INFLUENCE

What does our research suggest about how to ameliorate some of the negative effects of the illusion of influence while not losing some of the positive consequences? In other words, how can organizations reduce the biasing effects of the influence illusion without undermining the commitment of managers to the organization's tasks and performance? Because we were interested in understanding how to overcome some of the resistance to delegation, in the Pfeffer et al. (in press) experiment we ran the same three conditions of increasing involvement, altering the managerial orientation through a simple change in language. In the hierarchical managerial orientation, subjects were consistently referred to as "manager" or "supervisor" and were told that they would be "responsible for supervising while the other person prepares a solution." In a team-based managerial orientation, subjects were told that the company stressed a team approach; they were called "team leaders," and the other person was called a "team member" throughout the experiment. Furthermore, their instructions stated that they were "responsible for assisting while the other person prepares a solution."

This is a relatively subtle manipulation of orientation because in neither case was there any actual contact between the subject and the person presumably preparing the advertisement—people in the "team" orientation did not, in fact, work in teams. Previous research, however, has shown that assigning controlling labels, such as "managing director" or "group supervisor," to people with oversight responsibilities produced more self-oriented behavior than assigning less controlling labels, such as "group leader" (Messe, Kerr, and Sattler 1992; Samuelson and Allison 1994).

In the experiment we conducted, the tendency for the advertisement to be rated more positively under conditions of more supervisory involvement was reduced under the team-based managerial orientation, with this effect being observed primarily for the condition of greatest involvement. This is not surprising because it is only under some degree of involvement in the activity that self-enhancement motivations would be activated.

Although our research does not provide conclusive evidence on the mechanisms explaining why simply invoking a team orientation through a fairly subtle language manipulation had an effect, there are a number of plausible reasons for this result. The term team, particularly when used with a subject population that is itself involved in management training and education, probably conjures up a set of associations and cognitive scripts about what it means to be part of a team compared with being a supervisor, even if the objective differences in the experimental conditions are fairly minor. Being on a team has implications for who gets credit for the work—the team as a whole rather than just a single individual—as well as implications for who is responsible and accountable for the work—once again, the team as a whole rather than the manager or supervisor. One of the most reliable findings in social psychology concerns the effects of expectations on behavior (Eden 1990; Jones 1977). Simply using the term team changes people's orientations, expectations, and, thus, their behavior, including the behavior of overvaluing work and holding an illusion of influence. Language and terminology make some behaviors and expectations comparatively more salient, and what is salient and prominent in consciousness directs behavior.

Salience, although very important in directing and affecting behavior, is fragile and readily altered. This implies that in organizations in which there are multiple sources of information, multiple labels, and multiple messages on an ongoing basis, for one to observe the effects of the team idea in overcoming the illusion of influence, the team concept must be pervasive in all aspects of the organization and its operations. Simply using the term team without also changing rewards, measurements and evaluations, social interactions, and work organization to reinforce the concept is unlikely to be effective, as many organizations have learned through experience. Compensation schemes that do not isolate and reward individual performance but instead reward group performance should reduce the overvaluation and biasing effects of the illusion of influence. More social events attended by people at different levels and functions in the organization should have much the same effect, as would physical design that deemphasizes status distinctions and, instead, reinforces a common social identity. To maintain the team concept, particularly in Western cultures that emphasize the individual, requires maintaining the idea on a chronic basis and ensuring that virtually all the environmental cues are consistent with a team-based orientation.

In the Pfeffer et al. (in press) study, although the team-based managerial orientation did reduce the inflated evaluation of the quality of the advertisement, the orientation did not undermine subjects' estimate of their managerial effectiveness. This is an important result because it is crucial to be able to overcome the illusion of influence, thereby encouraging delegation and participation, without undermining managers' feeling of commitment or efficacy. What one wants is leaders committed to the organization or the group rather than to individual efforts. There is evidence that this is accomplished in a team-based orientation, in which subjects feel effective but that undermines their belief in the efficacy of personal, individual control, and involvement.

CONCLUSION

Much of the research on decentralization and delegation has examined the effects of these management practices on people exposed to them. Much of the research based on attribution theory has explored how observers make attributions about causality. Much of the research on power has taken a similar, outside-in approach, asking what factors and behaviors create power and influence. The premise of this chapter and our research is that although each of these perspectives is useful and important, each omits certain significant social psychological processes.

To understand why decentralization and delegation of decision-making authority has diffused so slowly and with such great difficulty, it is important to explore its effects on supervisors and managers, not just those exposed to that type of management. Managerial centralization and involvement are consistent with beliefs about the potency and efficacy of management and, significantly, lead to an overvaluation of the work produced under tighter managerial control. In a similar fashion, it is important to understand the factors that tend to cause individuals in managerial positions to develop illusions of influence and control, and why and how they see more personal efficacy in situations than may be warranted.

Once one understands the social and social psychological factors that produce illusions of influence, one can begin to develop strategies for mitigating some undesirable consequences while still maintaining commitment and involvement. Our research has suggested that team-based managerial orientations, and elements in the management system that reinforce a team-based orientation, can be helpful in this regard.

Much research remains to be done, however. Although the findings of our experiment and the arguments mustered may be persuasive, they are incomplete as an empirical foundation on which to rest either a complete theory of how illusions of influence develop or the managerial implications of this phenomena. This particular area of inquiry seems to be one in which cultural issues loom large because the independent and interdependent conceptions of the self vary dramatically across contexts. As such, the questions and issues posed in this chapter would particularly benefit from a comparative frame and program of research.

REFERENCES

Allison, S.T., Messick, D.M., and Goethals, G.R. (1989). On being better but not smarter than others: The Muhammad Ali effect. *Social Cognition* 7: 275–296.

Bazerman, M.H., Beekun, R.I., and Schoorman, F.D. (1982). Performance evaluation in a dynamic context: A laboratory study of the impact of prior commitment to the ratee. *Journal of Applied Psychology* 67: 873–876.

Bazerman, M.H., and Neale, M.A. (1982). Improving negotiator effectiveness under final offer arbitration: The role of selection and training. *Journal of Applied Psychology* 67: 543–548.

Brown, J.D., and Rogers, R.J. (1991). Self-serving attributions: The role of physiological arousal. *Personality and Social Psychology Bulletin* 17: 501–506.

Calder, B.J. (1977). An attribution theory of leadership. In B.M. Staw and G.R. Salancik (eds.), *New Directions in Organizational Behavior* (pp. 179–204). Chicago: St. Clair.

Cialdini, R.B. (1988). *Influence: Science and Practice*. Glenview, IL: Scott, Foresman.

Cialdini, R.B., Braver, S.L., and Lewis, S.K. (1974). Attributional bias and the easily persuaded other. *Journal of Personality and Social Psychology* 30: 631–637.

Cialdini, R.B., and Mirels, H.L. (1976). Sense of personal control and attributions about yielding and resisting persuasion targets. *Journal of Personality and Social Psychology* 33: 395–402.

Deutsch, M., and Gerard, H. (1955). A study of normative and informational social influences on individual judgment. *Journal of Abnormal and Social Psychology* 51: 629–636.

Eden, D. (1990). *Pygmalion in Management: Productivity as a Self-fulfilling Prophecy*. Lexington, MA: Lexington Books.

Festinger, L. (1954). A theory of social comparison processes. *Human Relations* 7: 117–140.

Fletcher, G.J.O., and Ward, C. (1988). Attribution processes: A cross-cultural perspective. In M.H. Bond (Ed.), *The Cross-Cultural Challenge to Social Psychology* (pp. 230–244). Newbury Park, CA: Sage.

Heider, F. (1958). *The Psychology of Interpersonal Relations*. New York: Wiley.

Heine, S.J., and Lehman, D.R. (1995). Cultural variation in unrealistic optimism: Does the West feel more invulnerable than the East? *Journal of Personality and Social Psychology* 68: 595–607.

Hofstede, G. (1980). *Culture's Consequences*. Beverly Hills, CA: Sage.

House, R.J., and Baetz, M.L. (1979). Leadership: Some generalizations and new research directions. *Research in Organizational Behavior* 1: 341–423.

Jones, R.A. (1977). *Self-fulfilling Prophecies: Social, Psychological, and Physiological Effects of Expectancies*. Hillsdale, NJ: Lawrence Erlbaum.

Kelley, H.H. (1971). *Attribution in Social Interaction*. Morristown, NJ: General Learning Press.

Kipnis, D. (1972). Does power corrupt? *Journal of Personality and Social Psychology* 24: 33–41.

Langer, E.J. (1983). *The Psychology of Control*. Beverly Hills, CA: Sage.

Markus, H.R., and Kitayama, S. (1991). Culture and the self: Implications for cognition, emotion, and motivation. *Psychological Review* 98: 224–253.

Meindl, J.R., Ehrlich, S.B., and Dukerich, J.M. (1985). The romance of leadership. *Administrative Science Quarterly* 30: 78–102.

Messe, L.A., Kerr, L., and Sattler, D.N. (1992). "But some animals are more equal than others": The supervisor as a privileged status in group contexts. In S. Worchel, W. Wood, & J.A. Simpson (eds.), *Group Processes and Productivity*. Newbury Park, CA: Sage.

Morris, M.W., and Peng, K. (1994). Culture and cause: American and Chinese attributions for social and physical events. *Journal of Personality and Social Psychology* 67: 949–971.

Myers, D.G. (1996). *Social Psychology*. New York: McGraw-Hill.

Neale, M.A., and Bazerman, M.A. (1985). The effects of framing and negotiator overconfidence on bargainer behavior. *Academy of Management Journal* 28: 34–49.

———. (1991). *Cognition and Rationality in Negotiation*. New York: Free Press.

Pfeffer, J. (1977). The ambiguity of leadership. *Academy of Management Review* 2: 104–112.

———. (1992). *Managing with Power*. Boston: Harvard Business School Press.

———. (1994). *Competitive Advantage Through People*. Boston: Harvard Business School Press.

———. (1998). *The Human Equation: Building Profits by Putting People First*. Boston: Harvard Business School Press.

Pfeffer, J., Cialdini, R.B., Hanna, B., and Knopoff, K. (in press). Faith in supervision and the self-enhancement bias: Two psychological reasons why managers don't empower workers. *Basic and Applied Social Psychology* 20.

Ross, J., and Staw, B.M. (1993). Organizational escalation and exit: Lessons from the Shoreham nuclear power plant. *Academy of Management Journal* 36: 701–732.

Ross, L.D. (1977). The intuitive psychologist and his shortcomings: Distortions in the attribution process. In L. Berkowitz (ed.), *Advances in Experimental and Social Psychology*, vol. 10 (pp. 173–220). New York: Random House.

Salancik, G.R., and Meindl, J.R. (1984). Corporate attributions as strategic illusions of management control. *Administrative Science Quarterly* 29: 238–254.

Salancik, G.R., and Pfeffer, J. (1978). A social information processing approach to job attitudes and task design. *Administrative Science Quarterly* 23: 224–253.

Samuelson, C.D., and Allison, S.T. (1994). Cognitive factors affecting the use of social decision heuristics in resource-sharing tasks. *Organizational Behavior and Human Decision Processes* 58: 1–27.

Schoorman, F.D. (1988). Escalation bias in performance appraisals: An unintended consequence of supervisor participation in hiring decisions. *Journal of Applied Psychology* 73: 58–62.

Shepperd, J.A. (1993). Student derogation of the Scholastic Aptitude Test: Biases in perceptions and presentations of college board scores. *Basic and Applied Social Psychology* 14: 455–473.

Singelis, T.M. (1994). The measurement of independent and interdependent self-construals. *Personality and Social Psychology Bulletin* 5: 580–591.

Snyder, M. (1982). Self-fulfilling stereotypes. *Psychology Today* 16 (July): 60–68.

Staw, B.M. (1976). Knee deep in the big muddy: A study of escalating commitment to a chosen course of action. *Organizational Behavior and Human Performance* 16: 27–44.

Strickland, L.H. (1958). Surveillance and trust. *Journal of Personality* 26: 200–215.

Taylor, S.E., and Brown, J.D. (1988). Illusion and well-being: A social psychological perspective on mental health. *Psychological Bulletin* 103: 193–210.

Triandis, H.C. (1989). The self and social behavior in differing cultural contexts. *Psychological Review* 96: 506–520.

Tyler, T., and Hastie, R. (1991). The social consequences of cognitive illusions. In M.H. Bazerman, R.J. Lewicki, and B.H. Sheppard (eds.), *Research in Negotiation in Organizations*, vol. 3. Greenwich, CT: JAI.

5

Human Resource Department Power and Influence Through Symbolic Action

Maria C. Galang and Gerald R. Ferris

INTRODUCTION

Commentaries have been made on the increasing importance of human resource management (HRM) in organizations in the past decade (Baron, Dobbin, and Jennings 1986; Huselid 1995; Kalleberg and Moody 1994; Kochan, Katz, and McKersie 1986). With the human resources (HR) department as a central figure, the question that naturally follows is the role and influence of the HR department in this development. While historical accounts (e.g., Baron et al. 1986) have noted the rise in power of HR specialists in organizations, no empirical work has specifically studied the determinants or sources of power for the HR department. Virtually all research conducted on subunit or departmental power has focused on functional units other than HR (e.g., Crozier 1964; Hackman 1985; Hinings, Hickson, Pennings, and Schneck 1974; Moore and Pfeffer 1980; Perrow 1970; Salancik and Pfeffer 1974), despite the increased attention devoted to the power and politics of the human resources function (Ferris, Galang, Thornton, and Wayne 1995; Ferris and Judge 1991; Frost 1989). Further, no research accounting for differences in the power of HR departments across organizations (e.g., McDonough 1986) has been conducted to date.

The present study seeks to address this research gap by investigating the role of symbolic actions in the determination of HR department power. HR departments are cast in the position of influencing without authority, and in demonstrating effectiveness without the benefit of objective criterion measures. Therefore, we propose that their power in organizations is largely a function of how effectively they manage impressions and structure reality through symbolic actions.

POWER, POLITICS, AND SYMBOLIC ACTION

The power and politics approach recently employed to examine I
has largely concentrated on the micro level, that is, focusing on ii
employees on HRM decisions affecting their individual interests, \ ...ormance
evaluation, selection, salaries, and rewards (Bartol and Martin 1990; Ferris, Judge, Rowland, and Fitzgibbons 1994; Ferris and King 1991; Gilmore and Ferris 1989; Kipnis
and Schmidt 1988; Wayne and Ferris 1990). Nevertheless, Ferris and Judge (1991)
urged that an organizational level of analysis from the political perspective of HRM is
needed, arguing that the organizational context contributes to shaping the interpersonal
level of influence processes. In a subsequent paper, Ferris et al. (1995) further elaborated
on how power and politics involved in the organization's adoption of HRM practices
might influence and in turn be influenced by power and politics occurring in interpersonal interactions.

Several studies have indeed addressed the determination of the organizational context,
particularly of the HRM practices that are adopted by the organization. Taking the
political approach, these studies have focused on the influence of various interest groups
on hiring standards and practices, promotion practices, wage structures, training programs, manpower planning, creation of job titles, employment equity policies and practices, to name a few (e.g., Baron and Bielby 1986; Baron, Davis-Blake, and Bielby
1986; Cohen and Pfeffer 1986; Dimick and Murray 1978; Edelman 1992; Pfeffer and
Cohen 1984; Pfeffer and Davis-Blake 1987). As expected, HR departments are among
the interest groups that have been investigated, but only insofar as it is present or absent
in the organization. Not surprisingly a positive and significant relation between the
presence of HR departments, or at the very least a full-time individual responsible for
the HR function, and many of the HRM practices has been found.

However, organizational members do not remain passive members, but actively engage in influencing events in organizations in pursuit of their own interests and preferences, be they personal or work-related (Pfeffer 1981b, 1982). In particular, HR
practitioners have been urged to use power and politics lest the potential benefits from
HRM not be realized by the organization (Frost 1989; Schein 1983; Watson 1977).
Given that other organizational members have their own interests that may be in conflict
with HR departments, mere presence alone cannot suffice. It may be that those HR
units that are more actively engaged in influencing events are more likely to have more
power in their respective organizations. The question remains then of how HR departments are able to influence and thus gain power within the organization.

So far, only Tsui (1990) has investigated the use of two possible strategies by HR
units at the operating level but in relation to influencing effectiveness assessments made
by different constituencies. Cooptation was found to be related to the satisfaction of
managers with the performance of the HR unit, while responsiveness was the relevant
variable for employees' satisfaction. The study also found a positive relation between
executive satisfaction and budget in terms of personnel ratio, and executives rated the
HR unit the most favorably. As noted by Tsui (1990), both these findings seem to

support the resource dependence theory (Pfeffer and Salancik 1978), which would predict that an organization would tend to satisfy those constituencies that have control over valued resources.

Other than Tsui's (1990) study, Legge and Exley (1975; Legge 1978) identified two strategies used by personnel specialists in gaining more influence, namely, conformist innovation and deviant innovation, differing in terms of values pursued or espoused. The effectiveness of either strategy is dependent on the economic environment faced by the organization. The conformist innovation strategy is more effective where the economic environment is adverse, whereas a deviant innovation strategy is more effective when resource slack allows more experimentation. This argument is reflected in the current prescriptions for HR specialists to be more management- or business-oriented because of the highly competitive environment facing organizations at present (e.g., Schuler 1993).

Although few, there have been studies of political skills and strategies as a determinant of subunit power. Equally rare are studies that compared functionally similar subunits across organizations. Two studies have found significance for political skills, emphasizing that what an organizational actor does is a potential source of power. Jansson and Simmons (1984) found that political strategies account for the differences in power among social work departments across fifty hospitals, measured in terms of their size and the variety and complexity of their roles in their respective host hospitals. Hackman's (1985) study also supported the influence of resource negotiation strategies on departmental power, with the nature of such strategies varying with respect to the degree of concurrence between the unit's purposes and the central mission of the organization. This is consistent with Enz's (1988) finding that top management's perceptions of value congruity with the focal subunit related to the subunit's power.

One of the most accepted explanations of subunit power is its ability to control strategic contingencies faced by the organization (Hickson, Hinings, Lee, Schneck, and Pennings 1971). However, as Hambrick (1981) had pointed out, the Hickson et al. (1971) theory is silent as to how those strategic contingencies are determined. Hambrick (1981) thus suggested that requirements from the organization's strategy and environment determined its strategic contingencies. What is interesting about Hambrick's (1981) study though is the finding that by engaging in environmental scanning behaviors, an executive is still able to acquire power even when his/her functional responsibility does not deal with the critical contingencies defined objectively by the organization's strategic and environmental requirements. Russ and Galang (1994) similarly argued that boundary spanners whose functions no longer represent critical contingencies for the organization discover new "threats" that they can control and cope with, citing as an example the case of HR departments whose increased involvement in boundary spanning activities accounts for its increased influence in organizations.

The notion of socially constructed reality (Berger and Luckmann 1966) suggests an alternative use of political skill that allows the possibility of having power even when situational conditions indicate otherwise. Through the use of language and symbolic actions, organizational actors influence definitions of "reality," and it is on the basis of this constructed reality, rather than the objective or materially concrete reality, that organizational members act (Pfeffer 1981a, 1982). One "reality" defined by organizational actors is what contingencies or resources are critical for the organization (Pfeffer and Salancik 1978).

The strategic contingencies theory (Hickson et al. 1971), in fact, lends itself to the notion of a socially constructed reality. Its components of ability to cope with uncertainties and nonsubstitutability suggest that one needs to be able to demonstrate and call attention to the fact that not only has one dealt successfully with these critical contingencies, but that one has the sole and requisite expertise to handle such affairs and deliver the expected results. A similar argument can be extended to resource dependence, the other dominant theory of intraorganizational power (Pfeffer and Salancik 1978).

Political language and symbols can be utilized not only to directly influence definitions of what contingencies and resources are important, but also to shape the evaluative frame, particularly the values and norms used by organizational actors in judging and making choices (Frost 1989; Griffin, Skivington, and Moorhead 1987). Frost (1989), for example, wrote about three fundamental issues that need to be considered in understanding and utilizing politics in HRM. These interrelated issues, addressing the questions of "doing things right," "doing the right things," and "what is right," involve values and norms of various organizational actors who influence the resolution to these questions. Empirical support for Frost's (1989) argument comes from Enz's (1988) finding that top management's perception of value similarity was the strongest predictor of departmental power.

Hence, while political strategies can rely on sources of power which objectively exist (i.e., those determined by characteristics of the organization and its environment), political influence behaviors can also operate within the interpretive paradigm via the notion of socially constructed reality (e.g., Pondy 1977). However, not much empirical work on managing meanings to acquire power has been conducted. Most of the studies on intraorganizational power fall under the functionalist perspective, which relies on objective conditions or sources of power (Bradshaw-Camball and Murray 1991).

Hypotheses

On the macro level, the power and politics perspective has centered on the influence of various interest groups on the organization's HR function. However, little attention has been given to what determines the influence of these various groups, particularly that of the HR department. In this regard, the literature with respect to the HR function was also examined to unearth aspects unique to the power of the HR department that have not been identified from prior studies of subunit power, and thus help specify the actions that the HR department needs to undertake.

Symbolic Actions

Given the foregoing literature on subunit power, symbolic actions of the HR department which create and maintain the perception that the HR function is a critical and strategic concern become important in determining its power within the organization. The term *symbolic* is used as a descriptive because the actions being considered are those that enable the HR department to acquire power despite the absence of favorable conditions found in the context or situation within which it is operating. This notion is similar to social influence theory (Tedeschi and Melburg 1984), which argues that where the influencer does not possess objective characteristics, he/she needs to engage in various impression management behaviors to create the image that otherwise would have been created by those objective characteristics. Mostly these behaviors pertain to actions that try to communicate certain messages regardless of whether such messages have some basis in fact. They serve to create an image, a reality that is favorable to the actor, so that the same ends are achieved as when favorable conditions actually exist.

In summary, the literature indicates that actions taken by the HR department to influence perceptions also need to deal with several inherent obstacles that tend to reduce the HR department's power, and these concern values, effectiveness, decentralization, and routinization.

The HR function has been described as primarily ceremonial, being an embodiment within the organization of desirable social values, such as social justice, employee welfare, and industrial democracy (Trice, Belasco, and Alutto 1969). Thus, while the HR function may not necessarily contribute to efficiency goals, it may even conflict with such goals of the organization. Literature on professions also suggests the possibility of conflict between managerial values and those represented and pursued by HR professionals (e.g., Golden, Dukerich, and Hauge 1993). It is, in fact, this shifting of HR professionals' values toward managerial goals that has led some scholars to be extremely critical of the profession as currently being practiced (e.g., Hart 1993). The two strategies of HR professionals that Legge and Exley (1975; Legge 1978) pointed to differed primarily with respect to the values being espoused. One strategy adheres to managerial values, while the other attempts to shape what those values should be. While Legge and Exley (1975; Legge 1978) suggested that the effectiveness of these strategies depended on the economic situation of the organization, studies have shown that espousing values in line with managerial interests would be more successful in gaining power (Enz 1988; Hackman 1985; Mumby 1987). Ferris, King, Judge, and Kacmar (1991) also discussed how individuals in organizations engage in tactics to manage shared meaning. One such tactic is to espouse attitudes and values similar to those in power to manage the impression of similarity or agreement in order to gain benefits, regardless of whether such values are actually believed. Consideration of values to espouse therefore is an important issue for the HR department in its claims for power.

Another is the question of effectiveness, or more precisely, assessing the contributions of the HR function to organizational performance. The difficulty in demonstrating means-ends relationships for the HR function has been pointed out as one reason for the lack of authority typically given to HR departments (Legge 1978). For example, many organizational outcomes (e.g., absenteeism and productivity) are determined by a host of factors other than how human resources are managed, or efforts of the department tasked with such function (Tsui 1984). If they were to serve as a source of power for the HR department, symbolic actions should deal with the question of the impact of HRM.

Two other factors tend to reduce the power of the HR department: the trend toward decentralization of the HR function and the tendency toward its routinization. The HR function is unique in that it can be performed by other managers and not necessarily by a specialist department. The ensuing results are a lack of direct control by the HR department, and an impression that HRM is not a truly specialist activity requiring unique knowledge and skills, thus reducing the department's nonsubstitutability, a source of power in organizations (Hickson et al. 1971). Finally, the inherent paradox in the power of the HR department is indicated in its tendency to routinize in order to cope with problems and uncertainties (Goldner 1970; Peterson 1970). Routinization leads to lesser power because it either reduces uncertainty, or increases substitutability (Hickson et al. 1971). Thus, symbolic actions likewise need to address these factors if they can usefully serve the purpose of providing the HR department with sources of power.

The symbolic actions used by the HR department are therefore designed to create and maintain the perception that HRM is a critical and strategic concern of the organization, because it deals with an important component of its operations (e.g., human resources) and because it presents problems to which the organization must attend. In addition, symbolic actions serve to influence interpretive frames, which include not only the use of norms and values to evaluate HRM effectiveness, but also information with regards to one's sole capability to cope with these concerns. Referred to as "niche creation" by Pondy (1977), such information influences perceptions of nonsubstitutability. Finally, the HR department's symbolic actions must address the factors tending to reduce its powers, such as decentralization and routinization.

These symbolic actions become more effective when used persistently. As Peters stated, "senior managers are signal transmitters, and signals take on meaning as they are reiterated" (1978, pp. 11–12). An action repeated often enough gives truth to the message being conveyed (Pfeffer 1981b). In addition, Pfeffer (1981a) indicated that the concurrent use of a variety of actions sending a consistent message provides more potency. Thus, frequency, variety, and consistency are important dimensions to consider.

Hypothesis 1: The more frequently the HR department engages in symbolic actions, the more likely it is able to gain power in the organization.

As used here, power is conceptualized as the ability to acquire organizational resources, authority, and support, reflected eventually in what it is able to do in the organization (Jansson and Simmons 1984; Legge 1978; Watson 1977). Legge argued that "the exercise of power may perhaps be more easily identified through an examination of implicit and explicit policy formulation and implementation" (1978, p. 35), because of the difficulties of observing the use of power in the decision-making process, and in relying on retrospective reports of the process. In a study of social work units within hospitals, Jansson and Simmons (1984) utilized complexity of its various roles, as well as size of the subunit (number of staff) as a ratio of organizational size (number of beds), as measures of its power within the organization.

Pfeffer (1981b) and Provan (1980) pointed out the disadvantages of the various measures of power, which may account for inconsistent findings, and the difficulties in interpreting such results. For example, while unit size may be a reflection of the organizational resources that it is able to acquire and hence an indication of its power, Purcell and Ahlstrand (1994; Purcell 1988) found that in the case of corporate-level HR units, size did not correlate with its influence in strategic business decisions, but did affect the degree of autonomy of the HR units in the lower levels of the multidivisional enterprise. In the case of division-level HR units, size was positively associated with strategic decisions but only in areas requiring employee compliance or where jobs are at stake. Thus, Pfeffer (1981b) suggested that a combination of measures of power be used, and Provan's (1980) conceptual distinction between potential and enacted power serves as a useful guideline in the measures to use. Potential power is the capacity to exert influence, and includes such determinants as formal authority or membership in key decision-making groups, while enacted power refers to the actual use of that power, as in the demonstrated ability to influence organizational outcomes like allocation of resources. As such the present study does not rely on only one measure of power, but several that underscore the HR department's capability or ability to exercise power in the organization, as well as the resources bestowed upon it by the organization.

Other Influencing Factors

While the present study subscribes to the interpretive perspective of intraorganizational power, by showing that engaging in influence behaviors provides sources of power (Bradshaw-Camball and Murray 1991), other factors representing objective situational conditions need to be tested to support the notion of symbolic actions.

The HR department is not the only interest group when it comes to HRM, and indeed prior studies have found that unions not only are another interest group, but may have preferences that are in conflict with the HR department. For example, Cohen and Pfeffer (1986) found that presence of an HR department was significantly related to pre-employment testing, while unionization rate was negatively related. Purcell and Ahlstrand (1994; Purcell 1988) also observed that unionization tended to decrease the influence of the corporate-level HR unit on strategic decisions. Thus, it is likely that HR departments in organizations with more unionized employees may find it more difficult to acquire power.

Power as conceptualized in this study may be construed as a reward for a job well done. Competent HR departments are given more resources, authority, and responsibility (in essence, more power) within the organization. The self-perpetuating cycle of powerlessness that Legge (1978) finds as a typical situation for personnel departments lends support to this notion. The cycle depicts the inability of the department to address human resource problems effectively as stemming from the lack of power that it has been given, which in turn only reinforces the withholding of power from it. Conversely, a department that is able to manage human resource problems well will be able to acquire power which feeds into its ability to be effective. Empirical support is provided by Tsui's (1990) study, which found a positive relation between executive satisfaction and budget in terms of personnel ratio. One explanation offered by Tsui is that " 'satisfied' executives may have awarded the HR subunit a large budget, implying that effectiveness leads to resources" (1990, p. 478). In an earlier investigation, Tsui (1987) found that one of the objective criteria used to assess the effectiveness of HR departments is turnover rate. Turnover rate also has the advantage of usefulness for comparing organizations as this data is likely to be commonly collected.

Top management may have favorable attitudes toward HRM, independent of the HR department's attempts to influence these beliefs. The relevant attitudes of top management pertain to whether human resource management is critical and problematic to the organization, whether human resource management contributes to organizational performance, and whether the human resource department is competent to perform such a vital task.

Hypothesis 2: Unionization, HR performance, and top management attitudes are related to the HR department's power within the organization.

METHOD

Sample

Considering that HR units exist at various levels, the unit at the division or operating level was selected as the study's focus. Units at this level may have wider involvement in HRM systems, from policy formulation to implementation, and therefore would be a more appropriate focus for the study since the measure of department power includes both policy formulation and implementation. In addition, HR units at the operating or division level would be more comparable with organizations with only one HR unit, a practical consideration when available sampling frames do not provide information on number of HR units present. Nevertheless, because the presence of a corporate-level HR unit may have an influence on the lower-level unit, and thus be different from one-unit organizations, the possibility of such influence is statistically controlled.

To ensure that the organizations selected have an HR unit, the sample was drawn from the membership roster of the Society of Human Resource Management (SHRM), the major association for the human resource profession in the United States, comprising more than 50,000 individual members. Compared to the total population of establishments in the United States, SHRM members are biased toward large manufacturing

Table 5.1
Comparison of SHRM Members[a] and Total Establishments,[b] by Industry and Employment Size

	SHRM		Total (1989)	
	N	%	N[c]	%
Industry				
Agriculture/forestry/fisheries	350	0.7	79	1.3
Manufacturing	14,579	29.6	363	5.9
Transportation/other public utilities	3313	6.7	228	3.7
Construction/mining	664	1.3	577	9.5
Wholesale/retail trade	2853	5.8	1955	32
Finance/insurance/real estate	5976	12.1	529	8.7
Services	10,402	21.1	1977	32.4
Health	4043	8.2	—	—
Government	1803	3.7	—	—
Library—corporate/public/academic	59	0.1	—	—
Others	5293	10.7	399	6.5
Total	49,335	99.9	6107	100
Number of employees				
Under 100	6246	12.6	5973	97.8
100–499	14,625	29.6	119	1.9
500–999	6384	12.6	9	0.1
1000–2499	7114	4.4		
2500–4999	4252	8.6	5	0.1
5000 and above	10,762	21.8		
Total	49,383	99.9	6107	99.9

[a]*Source:* Mal Dunn Associates.
[b]*Source:* U.S. Bureau of Census, 1992.

[c]Unit = 1000.

establishments, while heavily underrepresenting service and wholesale and retail trade establishments (see Table 5.1). This is not surprising, considering that these two sectors typically comprise small establishments, which are less likely to have full-time HR staff, and hence less likely to affiliate with SHRM.

Only members at the plant or division level (representing 19.2 percent of total membership), with titles of manager and above, but excluding presidents (82.3%), and whose functions were of a generalist rather than of a specialist nature, were considered. With the further exclusion of members from nonprofit organizations and government organizations (7.5%), a total of 5,159 SHRM members comprised the population from which 1,000 names from different organizations were randomly selected. Considering a response rate of 20–30 percent that can reasonably be expected from survey research, the target number of 1,000 was deemed sufficient to meet the minimum sample size required for data analysis (Cohen 1977).

Profile of Respondents

Of the 1,000 questionnaires mailed out initially, 242 completed questionnaires were returned, resulting in a 24.7 percent net response rate (i.e., less 21 undelivered by the Postal Service). This rate is higher than the 18.7–21.2 percent obtained in previous surveys of similar respondents (Dowling 1988; Jackson, Schuler, and Rivero 1989; Reavlin 1990). Atypical of previous surveys, returns were much slower initially, with only 61 responses received after the initial mailing, surging with an additional 150 (62% of all 242 responses) after the second follow-up sent six weeks after initial mailing. Analysis between early and late respondents did not show any significant differences on all variables.

Most of the 242 responding organizations are from the manufacturing sector ($n = 174$, 71.9%), are nonunionized ($n = 165$. 68.1%), and have a higher-level HR unit ($n = 167$, 69.0%). Employment size ranged from 400 to 20,000, with 74 percent having less than 500 employees. Mean size of the HR department is 5.6 staff members, ranging from 1 to 78.

Comparison with SHRM members is possible only in terms of industry sector and employment size. Respondents are biased toward small manufacturing organizations (Table 5.2). Thus, one must be cautioned about generalizing the findings from this study to total SHRM membership. Nevertheless, the total of 242 exceeded the minimum sample size needed to detect medium effect size of 0.15 at power of 0.80, so that the alternative explanation of any nonsignificant findings as being due to small sample size can be ruled out.

Not all HR managers who returned their questionnaires named a top line manager to whom the second questionnaire was sent. Those who provided names of a top line manager were not significantly different on all variables from those who did not; 195, or 80.6 percent of 242, provided names. Of the 195 top line managers sent the questionnaire, 138 responded, representing a 70.8 percent net response rate, with one returned undelivered by the Postal Service for incomplete address. These results compare favorably with the 68.5 percent and 80 percent, respectively, obtained by Jackson et al. (1989) who used the same procedure. Mean comparisons between respondents and nonrespondents on the second questionnaire for the present study show no significant differences on all variables.

Procedure

Response from a mail survey was the primary source of information on the organizations chosen for the study. For each organization, two respondents were selected to answer different questionnaires, namely, the HR manager, and a top line manager from the same organization, whose name was obtained from the HR person (Jackson et al. 1989).

The questionnaire sent to the HR manager included items involving characteristics of the organization as well as those of the HR department. The questionnaire subse-

Table 5.2
Comparison of Respondents to SHRM Membership

	SHRM	Respondents	
	%	N	%
Industry			
Agriculture/forestry/fisheries	0.7	2	0.9
Manufacturing	29.6	174	76.0
Transportation/other public utilities	6.7	11	4.8
Construction/mining	1.3	3	1.3
Wholesale/retail trade	5.8	9	3.9
Finance/insurance/real estate	12.1	8	3.5
Services	21.1	14	6.1
Health	8.2	8	3.5
Government	3.7	none	
Library—corporate/public/academic	0.1	none	
Others	10.7	none	
Number of employees			
Under 100	12.6	17	7.1
100–499	29.6	160	66.9
500–999	12.9	33	13.8
1000–2499	14.4	17	7.1
2500–4999	8.6	7	2.9
5000 and above	21.8	5	2.1

quently sent to the top line manager consisted of items on top management's perceptions and beliefs of the importance of HRM.

Questionnaire Development

The initial questionnaires that were constructed were further refined after an in-depth interview with an HR executive, and subsequently, were pretested with HR managers and line managers from local organizations, who did not participate in the study. This developmental phase was intended to ensure that both form and content of the questionnaire would yield valid and reliable results, and to minimize nonresponse.

Variables

HR Department Power

There has been considerable controversy with regard to the conceptual definition of "power" as well as with its measurement, and a review of the literature reveals that this controversy has not been resolved (Bacharach and Lawler 1980; Brass and Burkhardt 1993; Cobb 1984; Dahl 1957; Pfeffer 1981b; Provan 1980). Earlier theorists (e.g., Dahl

1957) suggested that the concept be defined by empirical researchers within the context and concerns of their particular research, and that approach is followed here. Thus, consistent with the concern of the present research, HR department power is here defined in terms of what the department is eventually able to do in the organization, and is reflected in the organizational resources and formal authority allocated to the department (Jansson and Simmons 1984; Legge 1978; Watson 1977). Consequently, the measure used for HR department power is a composite index consisting of department staff ratio, department budget, hierarchical level of the highest ranking HR person, scope of HR activities, and involvement in business strategic planning. The power index was calculated by standardizing scores on these indicators and computing their mean.

Department staff ratio was computed over the total number of regular employees of the organization. Department budget is the percentage of HR department budget to the total budget of the organization. Hierarchical level refers to number of hierarchical levels between the rank of the HR department head and the highest level in the organization, which in this case refers to the plant or division, and was reverse-scored. Scope of activities is a measure of the range or number of activities or programs in which the department engages, and the extent of exempt and nonexempt employees covered. The listing of twenty-two activities is based on Tsui's (1987) empirical study of activities of the HR department. A composite score was computed by weighting each item by the proportion of exempt and nonexempt employees covered, and averaging across all items (Huselid 1995). The exempt and nonexempt categories in the United States distinguish which employees are legally entitled to overtime pay, with those in professional, executive, and administrative jobs typically included in the exempt category. A five-point scale was developed to measure strategic planning involvement, following the strategic human resource management framework of Butler, Ferris, and Napier (1991). The scale ranged from no consideration of the organization's business strategy in the HR department's plans, to full and influential participation of the HR department in the organization's strategic planning group.

Symbolic Actions of the HR Department

None of the few empirical studies that have utilized the interpretive paradigm has focused on the use of symbolic actions by the HR department. Therefore, the symbolic actions that the HR department might use were drawn mostly from the works of Peters (1978), Pfeffer (1981a,b), Trice and colleagues (1985; Trice et al. 1969; Trice and Ritzer 1972), Tedeschi and Melburg (1984), and Watson (1977), as well as the first author's experience as an HR manager and the existing literature on HR department power. These actions refer to the less direct, more subtle and therefore less obtrusive behaviors, in contrast to overt and direct means of influence (Conrad and Ryan 1985; Kipnis, Schmidt, and Wilkinson 1980; Yukl and Falbe 1990). Symbolic actions target perceptions in situations where there really are no goods and services that can be exchanged, and thus serve as a basis for claiming power (Pfeffer 1981b). The source of power then becomes acceptance of one's construction of reality.

Of the existing instruments of influence behaviors, the Wayne and Ferris (1990) scale, particularly those items labeled job-focused tactics, comes closest to the symbolic actions conceptualized here, where the concern is with substance rather than form. The Wayne and Ferris (1990) job-focused tactics, however, only measure individual behaviors influencing a superior's assessment of the subordinate's job performance. Of interest here are actions that influence not only perceptions of competence in performing the job ("doing the job right"), but also the importance of the job being performed for the organization ("doing the right job").

While information on symbolic actions can be gathered from other sources, such as archival data (Martinko 1991; Russ 1991), accessibility to such sources for the HR department might prove to be difficult. Relevant records such as employee publications, policy manuals, or other documents may not exist, or may not be made available to outsiders. Likewise, observational data present accessibility problems, as well as resource constraints. Therefore, a 28-item measure was developed, and respondents were asked to indicate the frequency that the HR department engages in the specified action, on a 5-point scale ($\alpha = .86$). Item scores were summed, and the over-all total computed as a measure of the frequency of the HR department's symbolic actions, with higher scores indicating higher frequency.

The items were initially generated from a survey of the literature and personal experience, and the choice of items was guided by the concern for applicability across organizations. An in-depth interview with an HR executive and pretesting among a select group of HR managers were undertaken to determine content validity, as well as trimming down the scale to a more manageable length to encourage more responses. Examples of items include "is concerned with how reports/documents look as much as with what they contain"; "uses such terms as 'competitive advantage,' 'bottom line,' 'efficiency,' 'organizational goals,' 'value-added,' 'productivity,' 'assets,' and the like"; "releases only positive information about the performance of the HR department in official/formal reports"; "relates stories or anecdotes that portray the importance of HRM to the organization"; "displays certificates in office area attesting to the HR staff's training and professional affiliations."

Union Membership Rate

Respondents were asked the percentage of employees who are union members as of a certain cut-off date.

Turnover Rate

Respondents were asked the average annual turnover rate as of the previous year.

Management's Perception of HRM Importance

A twelve-item questionnaire using a five-point scale was used to measure perception and beliefs of top management on the importance of human resources and the contri-

Table 5.3
Descriptives and Correlations of Variables

	Mean	SD	1	2	3	4	5	6
1. Actions of the HR department	71.2	12.4						
2. Union membership rate	19.7	31.7	−.01					
3. Turnover rate	11.2	15.5	−.02	−.07				
4. Management perception of HRM importance	25.7	4.9	.03	−.02	.01			
5. Total number of employees	603.0	1650.0	.09	.08	.36**	.06		
6. Autonomy from higher HR unit	1.6	1.3	−.09	−.01	.03	.07	−.04	
7. Power index	−.004	.5	.43**	−.14*	−.10	−.05	.00	−.05

$*p < .05.$ $** p < .001.$

butions of the HR department. An example of the items reflecting the importance of human resources is "Our employees give us the competitive edge," while that of the contributions of the HR unit is "The HR department in our plant has done a lot to improve the productivity of the employees." This questionnaire was answered by a top line manager within the unit.

Control Variables

Because the respondents vary in organizational size, and comprise both division or operating units of larger organizations as well as stand-alone organizations, two variables are included as control: total number of employees in the organization, and degree of autonomy from a higher-level HR unit, measured on a 5-point scale.

RESULTS

Zero-Order Correlations

Table 5.3 shows the zero-order correlations among all variables, as well as their respective means and standard deviations. In general, the magnitude of the intercorrelations are moderate. Except for one case, the magnitude of correlations among the predictor variables does not exceed .30.

Test of the Hypotheses

Results of a hierarchical regression analysis show that, controlling for total number of employees and autonomy from a higher HR unit, a significant portion of variance (R^2 = .22, $p < .001$) is explained in the criterion variable, HR department power (Table 5.4). Among the hypothesized predictors, actions of the HR department was the strongest predictor ($\beta = .424$, $p < .001$), with union membership rate coming second and the only other significant predictor ($\beta = −.154$, $p < .01$). Hypothesis 1 is therefore supported, whereas Hypothesis 2 is partially supported. Considering that power consists

Table 5.4
Results of Hierarchical Regression Analysis of Power

	β coefficient
Step 1	
Total number of employees	.001
Autonomy from higher HR unit	−.061
R^2 change	.004
Step 2	
Actions of the HR department	.424**
Union membership rate (%)	−.154*
Turnover rate (%)	−.104
Management perception of HRM importance	−.079
Overall R^2	.220**

$*p < .01.$ $**p < .001.$

of different facets, we decided to investigate the possibility of differential effects of the predictors on the various components of our HR power index. Table 5.5 shows the results of the hierarchical regression analysis conducted for the five components of power. Actions of the HR department are significantly and positively related to two components of power (involvement in strategic planning and scope of HR activities), while union membership rate is significant only for one component (scope of HR activities).

DISCUSSION

Overall, symbolic actions taken by the HR department to portray its importance matter most in determinations of HR department power. The more frequently the department engages in such actions, the more likely it is to acquire organizational resources that eventually enables it to perform a wider scope of HR activities and programs. Hence, merely being present in an organization is not enough; taking an active role may differentiate the more influential HR departments from those who enjoy less power. One likely explanation is that organizations consist of various interest groups that may compete in acquiring organizational resources. In the case of HR departments, a significant interest group is unions, and the present study presents further confirmation of previous findings that unions have opposite interests from those of HR departments (e.g., Cohen and Pfeffer 1986; Dimick and Murray 1978).

One might think that unionization could be argued to present the organization with a critical concern that needs to be addressed. In a previous study by Goldner (1970), the union threat was used by industrial relations departments to acquire power within the organization, supporting the strategic contingencies theory (Hickson et al. 1971). Rather, it is the notion of competing interests recognized by political models of organizations that appears to be a more robust explanation, given the negative direction of

Table 5.5
Results of Hierarchical Regression Analysis for Components of Power

	β				
	Planning[a]	Scope[b]	Level[c]	Staff[d]	Budget[e]
Step 1					
Total number of employees	.05	−.04	.12	−.08	−.04
Autonomy from higher HR unit	−.05	.03	.04	−.12	−.12
R^2 change	.01	.00	.02	.02	.02
Step 2					
Actions of the HR department	.46**	.45**	−.09	.11	.09
Union membership rate (%)	−.07	−.18*	.08	−.09	−.16
Turnover rate (%)	−.01	−.12	−.05	−.04	−.11
Management perception of HRM importance	−.03	.04	−.01	−.08	−.12
Overall R^2	.22**	.26**	.03	.05	.06

[a]Involvement in strategic planning.
[b]Scope of HR activities.
[c]Hierarchical level of HR unit head.
[d]Ratio of HR staff to total number of regular employees.
[e]Budget of HR unit.
*$p < .01$. **$p < .001$.

the correlation between unionization and HR department power. However, since political models imply that organizational members are actively engaged in influencing events, and the current study did not use more active measures of union influence, the findings with respect to unionization rate may also be explained from the competence-reward notion. Unionization indicates poor performance on the part of the HR department and hence is being "punished" for it by withholding organizational resources. This explanation is less likely however when considering that turnover rate, a criteria used in evaluating department performance (Tsui 1987), did not turn out to be significantly related.

The nonsignificant findings for turnover rate, however, might also reflect that turnover has both positive and negative consequences (Mobley 1982). For example, Dalton, Todor, and Krackhardt (1982) pointed to the departure of employees who have been evaluated by the organization as poor performers as functional turnover. Furthermore, some amount of turnover enables the organization to replenish its stock with new blood. Turnover might also be related to the downsizing strategy of the organization. We did not distinguish among these different "types" of turnover, and this may have accounted for the nonsignificant results. Moreover, turnover is influenced by both internal and external factors (Hulin, Roznowski, and Hachiya 1985), many of which are beyond the control of the HR department. Internally, organizational outcomes affected by HRM cannot be attributed solely to the work of the HR department (Tsui and Gomez-Mejia 1988).

Management's perceptions of HRM importance did not turn out to be correlated to

HR department power, nor to any of the variables in the study. However, we did not speculate on the possible determinants of such perceptions, but only acknowledged the possibility that management may have attitudes and beliefs about HRM that are independent of the HR department's influence behaviors. The nonsignificant findings related to management's perceptions might be attributed to methodological problems. The scale's low reliability ($\alpha = .60$) might have contributed to the problem. Data was also gathered from only one source who may not represent the views of management. On the other hand, it might be that regardless of how management feels toward HRM or the HR department, it is the views of other constituencies that are more critical. Granting resources, authority, and support to the HR department might signify a symbolic gesture to appease stakeholders whom management considers important. Or it may be that the relevant management group that makes decisions on allocating resources and authority on the plant-level HR unit level is that above the operating or division level that was the focus of this study. It should be noted, too, that unlike Tsui's (1990) use of executive satisfaction, our scale used both satisfaction items with respect to the HR department's performance, as well as beliefs toward the importance of human resources to the organization.

Analysis conducted for each of the components of the power index suggests that the question of power cannot simply be answered; it would depend on what is meant by power, or to which aspect of power is being referred. The HR department's actions are more important for measures like strategic planning involvement and scope of activities, and less important for the more objective measures of department size, HR budget, and hierarchical level. However, in retrospect, this does not appear to be totally surprising when considering the size and structural changes going on in many organizations today. For example, a unit's budget may be partially a function of its power and influence, but it is also influenced by its size. With the current trend toward downsizing of organizations, including the size of HR departments, and doing more with less, budget size may not be an accurate reflection of HR department power. Similarly, much of the downsizing efforts have been focused on both middle management and on staff positions, with a particular sensitivity to reducing the staff to total employment ratios. In fact, many large firms that have downsized recently do so with a targeted staff-total employee ratio of 1:100. Therefore, with such non-power-related issues driving such decisions, the staff to total employment ratios would not appear to be good measures of HR power.

Limitations

As had been pointed out earlier, the sample of respondents may not be representative of the SHRM membership from whence it was drawn, or even of the total population of organizations. Also, the question of how nonresponse might affect the findings remains speculative and hence debatable, as it often does because as Groves (1989) had pointed out, by definition, salient information on nonrespondents cannot be obtained. Current knowledge on nonresponse from social psychological experiments and empirical studies of demographic correlates is likewise inadequate in providing theoretical understanding.

While the present study has established the relationship between symbolic actions and department power, longitudinal studies need to be undertaken to confirm direction of causality.

Directions for Future Research

Future research should investigate further substantive issues regarding subunit power, in particular that of the HR department. One question that is raised is what determines whether a separate HR unit is established initially? How would a political explanation fare against a rational explanation, and if it is also a question of power, whose power becomes the dominant influence and why?

Another is the consequence of power of the HR department. The assumption that a powerful HR department would enhance the benefits that organizations gain from HR programs was not directly tested by the present study. However, the present study does show that an HR department which engages in influence behaviors is likely to perform a wider scope of activities and be more involved in strategic planning. Together with previous studies that have empirically shown the positive organizational impact of many of the HRM activities included in the present study (e.g., Huselid 1995), empirical support for the connection between powerful HR departments and organizational benefits is likely to be found. An interesting specific consequence of HR department power that needs to be investigated, both for its practical implications and its theoretical contributions to macro-micro linkages, is that of its effect on power and politics at the interpersonal level as Ferris et al. (1995) had suggested.

The result with respect to management's perceptions of HRM raises some interesting questions. Which aspect of management's views would be more relevant in decisions to allot more power to the HR unit-satisfaction with the HR unit's competence, other constituencies' satisfaction with the HR unit's performance, or significance of an organization's human resources and how they are managed?

Last, as Bradshaw-Camball and Murray (1991) had urged, simultaneous testing of the different perspectives of intraorganizational power should be conducted for further theoretical development. The present study is one such effort, and needs to be applied to other organizational subunits.

REFERENCES

Bacharach, S.B., and Lawler, E.J. 1980. *Power and Politics in Organizations.* San Francisco: Jossey-Bass.

Baron, J., Dobbin, E., and Jennings, P.D. 1986. War and peace: The evolution of modern personnel administration in U.S. industry. *American Journal of Sociology* 92: 350–383.

Baron, J.N., and Bielby, W.T. 1986. The proliferation of job titles in organizations. *Administrative Science Quarterly* 31: 561–586.

Baron, J.N., Davis-Blake, A., and Bielby, W.T. 1986. The structure of opportunity: How promotion ladders vary within and among organizations. *Administrative Science Quarterly* 31: 248–273.

Bartol, K.M., and Martin, D.C. 1990. When politics pays: Factors influencing managerial compensation decisions. *Personnel Psychology* 43: 599–614.

Berger, P.L., and Luckmann, T. 1966. *The Social Construction of Reality.* New York: Doubleday.

Bradshaw-Camball, Y., and Murray, V.V. 1991. Illusions and other games: A trifocal view of organizational politics. *Organization Science* 2: 379–398.

Brass, D.J., and Burkhardt, M.E. 1993. Potential power and power use: An investigation of structure and behavior. *Academy of Management Journal* 36: 1–29.

Butler, J.E., Ferris, G.R., and Napier, N.K. 1991. *Strategy and Human Resource Management.* Cincinnati: South-Western.

Cobb, A.T. 1984. An episodic model of power: Toward an integration of theory and research. *Academy of Management Review* 9: 482–493.

Cohen, J. 1977. *Statistical Power Analysis for the Behavioral Sciences.* New York: Academic Press.

Cohen, Y., and Pfeffer, J. 1986. Organizational hiring; standards. *Administrative Science Quarterly* 31: 1–24.

Conrad, C., and Ryan, M. 1985. Power, praxis, and self in organizational communication theory. In R.D. McPhee and P.K. Tompkins (eds.), *Organizational Communication: Traditional Theories and New Direction.* Beverly Hills: Sage, pp. 235–257.

Crozier, M. 1964. *The Bureaucratic Phenomenon.* London: Tavistock.

Dahl, R.A. 1957. The concept of power. *Behavioral Science* 2: 201–215.

Dalton, D.R., Todor, W.D., and Krackhardt, D.M. 1982. Turnover overstated: A functional taxonomy. *Academy of Management Review* 7: 117–123,

Dimick, D.E., and Murray, V.V. 1978. Correlates of substantive policy decisions in organizations: The case of human resource management. *Academy of Management Journal* 21: 611–623.

Dowling, P.J. 1988. International HRM. In L. Dyer (ed.), *Human Resource Management: Evolving Roles and Responsibilities.* Washington, DC: Bureau of National Affairs.

Edelman, L.B. 1992. Legal ambiguity and symbolic structures: Organizational mediation of civil rights law. *American Journal of Sociology* 97: 1531–1576.

Enz, C.A. 1988. The role of value congruity in intraorganizational power. *Administrative Science Quarterly* 33: 284–304.

Ferris, G.R., Galang, M.C.. Thornton, M.I., and Wayne, S.J. 1995. A power and politics perspective on human resources management. In G.R. Ferris, S.D. Rosen, and D.T. Barnum (eds.), *Handbook of Human Resources Management.* Oxford, UK: Blackwell, pp. 100–113.

Ferris, G.R., and Judge, T.A. 1991. Personnel/human resources management: A political influence perspective. *Journal of Management* 17: 447–488.

Ferris, G.R., Judge, T.A., Rowland, K.M., and Fitzgibbons, D.E. 1994. Subordinate influence and the performance evaluation process: Test of a model. *Organizational Behavior and Human Decision Processes* 58: 101–135.

Ferris, G.R., and King, T.R. 1991. Politics in human resources decisions: A walk on the dark side. *Organizational Dynamics* 20: 59–71.

Ferris, G.R., King, T.R., Judge, T.A., and Kacmar, K.M. 1991. The management of shared meaning in organizations: Opportunism in the reflection of attitudes, beliefs, and values. In R.A. Giacalone and P. Rosenfeld (eds.), *Applied Impression Management: How Image-Making Affects Managerial Decisions.* Newbury Park, CA: Sage, pp. 41–64.

Frost, P.J. 1989. The role of organizational power and politics in human resource management. In A.N.B. Nedd, G.R. Ferris, and K.M. Rowland (eds.). *Research in Personnel and Human Resources Management* (Supplement 1). Greenwich, CT: JAI, pp. 1–21.

Gilmore, D.C., and Ferris, G.R. 1989. The politics of the employment interview. In R.W. Eder and G.R. Ferris (eds.), *The Employment Interview: Theory, Research, and Practice.* Newbury Park, CA: Sage, pp. 195–203.

Golden, B.R., Dukerich, J.M., and Hauge, E.E. 1993. *The Effects of Values and Issue Interpretation on the Resolution of Ethical Dilemmas in Professional Organizations*. Paper presented at the Annual Meeting of the Academy of Management, Atlanta, Georgia.

Goldner, E.H. 1970. The division of labor: Process and power. In M.N. Zald (ed.), *Power in Organizations*. Nashville, TN: Vanderbilt University Press, pp. 97–143.

Griffin, R.W., Skivington, K.D., and Moorhead, G. 1987. Symbolic and international perspectives on leadership: An integrative framework. *Human Relations* 40: 199–218.

Groves, R.M. 1989. *Survey Errors and Survey Costs*. New York: Wiley.

Hackman, J.D. 1985. Power and centrality in the allocation of resources in colleges and universities. *Administrative Science Quarterly* 30: 61–77.

Hambrick, D.C. 1981. Environment, strategy, and power within top management teams. *Administrative Science Quarterly* 26: 253–276.

Hart, T.J. 1993. Human resource management: Time to exorcise the militant tendency. *Employee Relations* 15: 29–36.

Hickson, D.J., Hinings, C.R., Lee, C.A., Schneck, R.E., and Pennings, J.M. 1971. A strategic contingencies theory of intraorganizational power. *Administrative Science Quarterly* 16: 216–229.

Hinings, C.R., Hickson, D.J., Pennings, J.M., and Schneck, R.E. 1974. Structural conditions of intraorganizational power. *Administrative Science Quarterly* 19: 22–44.

Hulin, C.L., Roznowski, M., and Hachiya, D. 1985. Alternative opportunities and withdrawal decisions: Empirical and theoretical discrepancies and an integration. *Psychological Bulletin* 97: 233–250.

Huselid, M.A. 1995. The impact of human resource management practices on turnover, productivity, and corporate financial performance. *Academy of Management Journal* 38: 635–672.

Jackson, S.E., Schuler, R.S., and Rivero, J.C. 1989. Organizational characteristics as predictors of personnel practices. *Personnel Psychology* 42: 727–786.

Jansson, B.S., and Simmons, J. 1984. Building departmental or unit power within human service organizations: Empirical findings and theory building. *Administration in Social Work* 8: 41–56.

Kalleberg, A.L., and Moody, J.W. 1994. Human resource management and organizational performance. *American Behavioral Scientist* 37: 948–962.

Kipnis, D., and Schmidt, S.M. 1988. Upward-influence styles: Relationships with performance evaluations, salary and stress. *Administrative Science Quarterly* 33: 528–542.

Kipnis, D., Schmidt, S.M., and Wilkinson, I. 1980. Intraorganizational influence tactics: Explorations in getting one's way. *Journal of Applied Psychology* 65: 440–452.

Kochan, T.A., Katz, H.C., and McKersie, R.B. 1986. *The Transformation of American Industrial Relations*. New York: Basic Books.

Legge, K. 1978. *Power, Innovation, and Problem-Solving in Personnel Management*. London: McGraw-Hill.

Legge, K., and Exley, M. 1975. Authority, ambiguity and adaption: The personnel specialist's dilemma. *Industrial Relations Journal* 6: 51–65.

Martinko, M.J. 1991. Future directions: Toward a model for applying impression management strategies in the workplace. In R.A. Giacalone and P. Rosenfeld (eds.), *Applied Impression Management: How Image-Making Affects Managerial Decisions*. Newbury Park, CA: Sage, pp. 259–277.

McDonough, E.F. 1986. How much power does HR have, and what can it do to win more? *Personnel* 63: 18–25.

Mobley, W.H. 1982. Some unanswered questions in turnover and withdrawal research. *Academy of Management Review* 7: 111–116.

Moore, W.L., and Pfeffer, J. 1980. The relationship between departmental power and faculty careers on two campuses: The case for structural effects on faculty salaries. *Research in Higher Education* 13: 291–306.

Mumby, D.K. 1987. The political function of narrative in organizations. *Communication Monographs* 5-1: 113–127.

Perrow, C. 1970. Departmental power and perspective in industrial firms. In M.N. Zald (ed.), *Power in Organizations*. Nashville, TN: Vanderbilt University Press, pp. 59–85.

Peters, T.J. 1978. Symbols, patterns, and settings: An optimistic case for getting things done. *Organizational Dynamics* 7: 3–23.

Peterson, R.A. 1970. Some consequences of differentiation. In M.N. Zald (ed.), *Power in Organizations.* Nashville, TN: Vanderbilt University Press, pp. 144–149.

Pfeffer, J. 1981a. Management as symbolic action: The creation and maintenance of organizational paradigms. In L.L. Cummings and B.M. Staw (eds.), *Research in Organizational Behavior* (vol. 3). Greenwich, CT: JAI, pp. 1–52.

———. 1981b. *Power in Organizations.* Marshfield, MA: Pitman.

———. 1982. *Organizations and Organization Theory.* Cambridge, MA: Ballinger.

Pfeffer, J., and Cohen, Y. 1984. Determinants of internal labor markets in organizations. *Administrative Science Quarterly* 29: 550–572.

Pfeffer, J., and Davis-Blake, A. 1987. Understanding organizational wage structures: A resource dependence approach. *Academy of Management Journal* 30: 437–455.

Pfeffer, J., and Salancik, G.R. 1978. *The External Control of Organizations: A Resource Dependence Perspective.* New York: Harper and Row.

Pondy, L.R. 1977. The other hand clapping: An information-processing approach to organizational power. In T.H. Hammer and B. Bacharach (eds.), *Reward Systems and Power Distribution in Organizations: Searching for Solutions.* Ithaca, NY: Cornell University Press, School of Industrial and Labor Relations, pp. 56–91.

Provan, K.G. 1980. Recognizing, measuring, and interpreting the potential/enacted power distinction in organizational research. *Academy of Management Review* 5: 549–559.

Purcell, J. 1988. The structure and function of personnel management. In P. Marginson, P.K. Edwards, R. Martin, J. Purcell, and K. Sisson (eds.), *Beyond the Workplace.* Oxford: Basil Blackwell, pp. 51–79.

Purcell, J., and Ahlstrand, B. 1994. *Human Resource Management in the Multi-divisional Company.* Oxford: Oxford University Press, 1994.

Reavlin, L.D. 1990. The effect of demographic change on firms' human resource policies. Unpublished dissertation, University of Illinois at Urbana-Champaign.

Russ, G., and Galang, M.C. 1994. Power and influence of organizational subunits through boundary spanning and information management: The case of the human resources function. Working paper, Southern Illinois University, 1994.

Russ, G.S. 1991. Symbolic communication and image management in organizations. In R.A. Giacalone and E. Rosenfeld (eds.), *Applied Impression Management: How Image-Making Affects Managerial Decisions.* Newbury Park, CA: Sage, pp. 219–240.

Salancik, G.R., and Pfeffer, J. 1974. The bases and use of power in organizational decision making: The case of a university. *Administrative Science Quarterly* 19: 453–473.

Schein, V.E. 1983. Strategic management and the politics of power. *Personnel Administrator* (October): 55–58.

Schuler, R.S. 1993. World class H.R. departments: Six critical issues. *The Singapore Accounting and Business Review.*

Tedeschi, J.T., and Melburg, V. 1984. Impression management and influence in the organization. In S.B. Bacharach and E.J. Lawler (eds.). *Research in the Sociology of Organizations* (vol. 3). Greenwich, CT: JAI, pp. 31–58.

Trice, H.M. 1985. Rites and ceremonials in organizational cultures. In S.B. Bacharach and S.M. Mitchell (eds.), *Research in the Sociology of Organizations* (vol. 4). Greenwich, CT: JAI, pp. 221–270.

Trice, H.M., Belasco, J., and Alutto, J.A. 1969. The role of ceremonials in organizational behavior. *Industrial and Labor Relations Review* 23: 40–51.

Trice, H.M., and Ritzer, G. 1972. The personnel manager and his self image. *Personnel Administrator* (January/February): 46–51.

Tsui, A.S. 1984. Personnel department effectiveness: A tripartite approach. *Industrial Relations* 23: 184–197.

———. 1987. Defining the activities and effectiveness of the human resource department: A multiple constituency approach. *Human Resource Management* 26: 35–69.

———. 1990. A multiple-constituency model of effectiveness: An empirical examination at the human resource subunit level. *Administrative Science Quarterly* 35: 458–483.

Tsui, A.S., and Gomez-Mejia, L.R. 1988. Evaluating human resource effectiveness. In L. Dyer and G.W. Holder (eds.), *Human Resource Management: Evolving Roles and Responsibilities*. Washington, DC: Bureau of National Affairs.

U.S. Bureau of Census. 1992. *Statistical Abstract of the U.S.*

Watson, T.J. 1977. *The Personnel Managers: A Study in the Sociology of Work and Employment*. London: Routledge and Kegan Paul.

Wayne, S.J., and Ferris, G.R. 1990. Influence tactics, affect and exchange quality in supervisor-subordinate interactions: A laboratory experiment and field study. *Journal of Applied Psychology* 75: 487–499.

Yukl, G., and Falbe, C.M. 1990. Influence tactics and objectives in upward, downward, and lateral influence attempts. *Journal of Applied Psychology* 75: 132–140.

6

Consequences of Influence Tactics Used with Subordinates, Peers, and the Boss

Gary Yukl and J. Bruce Tracey

One of the most important determinants of managerial effectiveness is success in influencing people and developing their commitment to task objectives (Yukl 1989). Despite the obvious importance of this subject, there has not been much empirical research on the influence behavior of managers. Several studies have examined issues such as how often various influence tactics are used by managers with different targets and for different influence objectives (Ansari and Kapoor 1987; Erez and Rim 1982; Erez, Rim, and Keider 1986; Kipnis, Schmidt, and Wilkinson 1980; Schmidt and Kipnis 1984; Yukl and Falbe 1990). Only a handful of studies have considered the relative effectiveness of different influence tactics.

Mowday (1978) investigated the relationship between the self-rated use of five influence tactics by elementary school principals and ratings made by the immediate superior of each principal on the principal's overall effectiveness in exercising influence. Only one tactic (information distortion) discriminated significantly between more and less effective principals.

Kipnis and Schmidt (1988) used profiles of scale scores on their self-report influence questionnaire to cluster managers into four influencer types, which were then compared with regard to performance evaluations. Kipnis and Schmidt found that shotgun managers (with high scores on assertiveness, appeal to higher authority, and coalition) received the lowest performance ratings and that tacticians (who used rational persuasion more than other tactics) received the highest performance ratings; ingratiators (who used ingratiation more than other tactics) received only a moderate performance rating.

Schilit and Locke (1982) had students interview managers to obtain descriptions of successful or unsuccessful upward influence attempts, either from the perspective of the agent (subordinate) or from the perspective of the target (boss). The influence tactics used in each incident were coded into 18 categories, and the frequency of use for each tactic was compared for successful and unsuccessful influence attempts. Few significant differences were found, and the results for these tactics were not consistent across the two samples.

A series of three studies compared successful and unsuccessful influence incidents obtained by students from interviews with managers. Influence behavior was coded into twenty-one tactics in a study of upward incidents (Case, Dosier, Murkinson, and Keys 1988), seventeen tactics in a study of downward incidents (Dosier, Case, and Keys 1988), and eleven tactics in a study of lateral incidents (Keys, Case, Miller, Curran, and Jones 1987). Despite the large number of comparisons of successful and unsuccessful incidents in the three studies, only two differences were significant at a traditional 5 percent level.

Overall, previous research provides only limited insight into the relative effectiveness of different tactics. Few findings were significant, and results were not consistent across studies. The lack of strong, consistent results from prior research on influence outcomes may be due to a number of reasons. Most of the studies examined only upward influence, in which the utility of some tactics is limited and the agent's influence is likely to be smallest. The selection and measurement of influence tactics differed substantially from study to study, as did the criteria used to evaluate tactics. None of the correlational studies used an immediate outcome, such as the target's task commitment, which is likely to be affected more by an agent's influence behavior than is a criterion such as ratings of overall agent performance. The critical incident studies used an immediate outcome but measured it in terms of a simple dichotomy (i.e., successful versus unsuccessful), which reduced the likelihood of finding any effect of influence tactics on outcomes.

The current study had two research objectives. The primary objective was to investigate the effectiveness of different influence tactics for influencing subordinates, peers, and superiors. Our research attempts to overcome the limitations of earlier research on tactic effectiveness by examining all three directions of influence, by including task commitment as an immediate criterion of influence success in addition to performance ratings, and by comparing a wide variety of potentially relevant influence tactics in the same study.

A secondary objective was to clarify and extend what is known about directional differences in how often various, influence tactics are used with subordinates, peers, and superiors. Three prior studies (Erez et al. 1986; Kipnis et al. 1980; Yukl and Falbe 1990) examined directional differences in the use of influence tactics. Fairly consistent results were found for pressure and exchange, but results were inconsistent across studies for other tactics. In the current study, we used a matched design with a large number of respondents to provide a more powerful test of directional differences than was possible in the earlier research involving a random groups design. Directional differences in tactic effectiveness and frequency of use were examined together for the first time in the same study in an attempt to integrate these previously separate lines of research.

TACTICS AND MODEL

The study reported in this article deals with the nine influence tactics defined in Table 6.1. These tactics are based on results from factor analysis of questionnaires and other types of construct validation research, such as Q sorts by subject-matter experts, inter-rater agreement in the coding of critical incidents, analysis of content validity, and analysis of discriminant validity (Schriesheim and Hinkin 1990; Yukl and Falbe 1990; Yukl, Lepsinger, and Lucia, in press). The nine tactics cover a wide variety of proactive influence behaviors likely to be relevant to a manager's effectiveness in influencing others. These influence tactics have been used in prior research on influence effectiveness, but none of the prior studies included all nine of the tactics.

In our preliminary model, the following interrelated factors determine how frequently an influence tactic is used in a particular direction: (a) consistency with prevailing social norms and role expectations about use of the tactic in that context, (b) agent possession of an appropriate power base for use of the tactic in that context, (c) appropriateness for the objective of the influence attempt, (d) level of target resistance encountered or anticipated, and (e) costs of using the tactic in relation to likely benefits. The underlying assumption is that most agents will prefer to use tactics that are socially acceptable, that are feasible in terms of the agent's position and personal power in relation to the target, that are not costly (in terms of time, effort, loss of resources, or alienation of the target), and that are likely to be effective for a particular objective given the antic-ipated level of resistance by the target. We used the model to derive specific hypotheses about directional differences in the frequency of use of the nine tactics. For example, tactics such as legitimating, exchange, pressure, and ingratiation are more consistent with the power base and role expectations for a boss in relation to a subordinate than for a subordinate in relation to a boss.

In our preliminary model, the following factors determine the effectiveness of an influence tactic used by a particular agent in a particular context: (a) consistency with prevailing social norms and role expectations about the use of the tactic in that context, (b) the agent's possession of an appropriate power base for use of the tactic in that context, (c) potential of the tactic to influence the target's attitudes about the desirability of the requested action, (d) the agent's skill in using the tactic, and (e) the amount of intrinsic resistance by the target due to the nature of the request. The underlying as-sumption is that a tactic is more likely to be successful if the target perceives it to be a socially acceptable form of influence behavior, if the agent has sufficient position and personal power to use the tactic, if the tactic has the capability to affect the target's attitudes about the desirability of the request, if the tactic is used in a skillful way, and if it is used for a request that is legitimate and consistent with the target's values and needs. The model is used to derive specific hypotheses about the effectiveness of the nine tactics for influencing target commitment in a downward, lateral, or upward di-rection. For example, according to Kelman's (1958) theory of influence processes, tac-tics that are likely to cause internalization of favorable attitudes about the request (e.g., consultation, inspirational appeal, and rational persuasion) ought to be more successful

Table 6.1
Nine Influence Tactics

Tactic	Definition
Rational persuasion	The person uses logical arguments and factual evidence to persuade you that a proposal of request is viable and likely to result in the attainment of task objectives.
Inspirational appeal	The person makes a request or proposal that arouses enthusiasm by appealing to your values, ideals, and aspirations or by increasing your confidence that you can do it.
Consultation	The person seeks your participation in planning a strategy, activity, or change for which your support and assistance are desired, or the person is willing to modify a proposal to deal with your concerns and suggestions.
Ingratiation	The person seeks to get you in a good mood or to think favorably of him or her before asking you to do something.
Exchange	The person offers an exchange of favors, indicates willingness to reciprocate at a later time, or promises you a share of the benefits if you help accomplish a task.
Personal appeal	The person appeals to your feelings of loyalty and friendship toward him or her before asking you to do something.
Coalition	The person seeks the aid of others to persuade you to do something or uses the support of others as a reason for you to agree also.
Legitimating	The person seeks to establish the legitimacy of a request by claiming the authority or right to make it or by verifying that it is consistent with organizational, policies, rules, practices, or traditions.
Pressure	The person uses demands, threats, or persistent reminders to influence you to do what he or she wants.

than tactics that cause behavioral compliance without changing the target's attitudes. Tactics involving coercion and manipulation (e.g., pressure, legitimating, and some forms of coalition) are less socially acceptable than tactics that appeal to the target's informed judgment or to the target's friendship and identification with the agent. This set of tactics is least likely to result in target commitment.

HYPOTHESES

Hypotheses about the use and effectiveness of each tactic for influencing target task commitment are presented next, along with a rationale for each hypothesis that is based on our preliminary model and on prior research. Formal hypotheses were not made for ratings of a manager's overall effectiveness because this criterion can be affected by many things besides a manager's use of influence tactics.

Hypothesis 1a: Rational persuasion is used more in an upward direction than in a downward or lateral direction.

Hypothesis 1b: Rational persuasion increases task commitment in all three directions.

Rational persuasion involves the use of logical arguments and factual information to convince a target that the agent's request or proposal is feasible and consistent with shared objectives (Eagly and Chaiken 1984). This is a flexible tactic that can be used for influence attempts in any direction. Nevertheless, rational persuasion is likely to be used more in an upward direction than in other directions, because in an upward direction a manager is limited by a weaker power base and role expectations that discourage the use of some tactics (see discussion of other hypotheses). Directional differences for the use of rational persuasion were not consistent in three prior studies conducted with questionnaires (Erez et al. 1986; Kipnis et al. 1980; Yukl and Falbe 1990). Agents reported greater use of this tactic in upward influence attempts, but directional differences were not found for targets.

Results for the consequences of using rational persuasion have been inconsistent also. In the questionnaire study by Kipnis and Schmidt (1988), managers who received the highest performance ratings had a profile in which rational persuasion was the dominant tactic for upward influence attempts. However, rational persuasion was not related to successful upward influence in the questionnaire study by Mowday (1978). Likewise, tactics involving aspects of rational persuasion were not related to outcome success in the four critical incident studies described earlier.

Hypothesis 2a: Inspirational appeals are used more in a downward direction than in a lateral or upward direction.

Hypothesis 2b: Inspirational appeals increase task commitment in all three directions.

Inspirational appeals use the target's values, ideals, aspirations, and emotions as a basis for gaining commitment to a request or proposal (Yukl 1990). Inspirational appeals appear feasible for influence attempts made in any direction, but this tactic is especially appropriate for gaining the commitment of someone to work on a new task or project. Influence attempts involving task assignments occur most often in a downward direction and least often in an upward direction (Erez et al. 1986; Kipnis et al. 1980; Yukl and Falbe 1990). Thus, managers have more opportunity to use inspirational appeals with subordinates than with peers or superiors. In the only prior study to examine directional differences for inspirational appeals, Yukl and Falbe (1990) found that inspirational appeals were used more in downward influence attempts than in lateral or upward influence attempts.

There is little evidence about the likely effectiveness of inspirational appeals, and this research deals only with the downward influence of leaders over subordinates. Descriptive studies of charismatic and transformational leadership (Bass 1985; Conger 1989; Tichy and Devanna 1986) have found that managers who motivate exceptional effort by subordinates present a clear and inspiring vision, which is one type of inspirational appeal.

Hypothesis 3a: Consultation is used more in a downward direction than in a lateral or upward direction.

Hypothesis 3b: Consultation increases task commitment in all three directions.

When people gain a sense of ownership of a project, strategy, or change after participating in planning how to implement it, they are likely to be more committed to making the project, strategy, or change successful (Yukl 1989). This influence tactic can be used in any direction, but it appears especially appropriate in the situation in which an agent has the authority to plan a task or project but relies on the target to help implement the plans. Because authority to assign work and make changes in work procedures is mostly downward, a manager probably has more opportunity to use consultation to influence subordinates than to influence peers or superiors (Yukl and Falbe 1990). Only one study examined directional differences in frequency of use for consultation (Yukl and Falbe 1990), and results were mixed. Agents reported greater use of consultation in a downward direction, but directional differences were not significant for target reports.

Evidence on the likely effectiveness of consultation as an influence tactic is limited and inconsistent. Schilit and Locke (1982) found that a consultation tactic (using the target as a platform to present ideas) was likely to be effective in upward incidents reported by targets, but the results were not significant for upward incidents reported by agents in that study or in the study by Case et al. (1988). In the study by Dosier et al. (1988) of downward incidents reported by agents, results for consultation tactics (listening, soliciting ideas) were not significant. Indirect evidence comes from research on leadership, which finds that consultation with individual subordinates is effective for increasing decision acceptance in some situations but not in others (see Vroom and Jago 1988).

Hypothesis 4a: Ingratiation is used more in a downward and lateral direction than in an upward direction.

Hypothesis 4b: Ingratiation has a stronger positive effect on task commitment in a downward and lateral direction than in an upward direction.

The basis for influence in ingratiation is an increase in the target's feeling of positive regard toward the agent. Flattery, praise, expression of acceptance, and expression of agreement are used to increase the agent's attractiveness to the target (Liden and Mitchell 1988; Tedeschi and Melburg 1984). A target is more likely to cooperate with an agent for whom the target has feelings of positive regard. Compliments and flattery are more credible when the status and power of the agent is greater than that of the target (Wortman and Linsenmeier 1977). Thus, ingratiation is most likely to increase positive regard and influence target cooperation when the agent is a superior, and it is least likely to do so when the agent is a subordinate.

Findings on directional differences in the use of ingratiation are somewhat inconsistent. In the studies by Kipnis et al. (1980) and Yukl and Falbe (1990), agents reported that ingratiation was used more in downward and lateral influence attempts than in upward influence attempts. No significant directional differences were found for target reports in the study by Yukl and Falbe (1990), and no clear pattern emerged for agent and target reports in the study by Erez et al. (1986).

Only two studies have examined the consequences of using ingratiation as a proactive influence tactic. In their questionnaire study of upward influence, Kipnis and Schmidt (1988) found that male managers whose influence profile involved a relatively high use of ingratiation received only moderate performance ratings but that female ingratiators received higher performance ratings. Outcome success was not significantly affected by ingratiation tactics (using courtesy, kind manners, or friendliness) in lateral incidents described by agents in the study by Keys et al. (1987).

Hypothesis 5a: Exchange is used more in a downward and lateral direction than in an upward direction.

Hypothesis 5b: Exchange has a stronger positive effect on task commitment in a downward and lateral direction than in an upward direction.

Exchange tactics involve explicit or implicit offers by an agent to provide a favor or benefit to the target in return for doing what the agent requests. To be effective, the agent must offer something the target considers desirable and appropriate (Yukl 1990). Managers usually have considerable control over resources and rewards desired by subordinates. The potential for exchange with peers depends on the amount of lateral task interdependence and a manager's control over resources desired by peers. Descriptive studies have found that exchange is often used to obtain support and assistance from peers (see A. Cohen and Bradford 1989; Kaplan 1986). Managers have little control over resources desired by superiors, and it is awkward to initiate an exchange of tangible benefits with them because it is not consistent with role expectations. Thus, there is more opportunity to use exchange with subordinates and peers than with superiors. Three prior studies (Erez et al. 1986; Kipnis et al. 1980; Yukl and Falbe 1990) found that exchange was used more in downward and lateral influence attempts than in upward influence attempts.

Results for the consequences of using exchange are not as clear or consistent. Schilit and Locke (1982) found that exchange (trading job-related benefits) was more likely to be successful than unsuccessful in upward critical incidents described by targets, but results for this tactic were not significant in upward incidents described by agents. No significant effects of exchange tactics (offering to trade favors or concessions) were found in the study of upward incidents by Case et al. (1988), in the study of lateral incidents by Keys et al. (1987), or in the questionnaire study by Mowday (1978) of upward influence.

Hypothesis 6a: Personal appeals are used more in a lateral direction than in a downward or upward direction.

Hypothesis 6b: Personal appeals increase task commitment in all three directions.

Personal appeals are based on referent power already possessed by the agent (Yukl 1990). When a target has strong feelings of friendship toward the agent, it is more likely that the agent can appeal successfully to the target to do something unusual or extra as a special favor (e.g., do some of my work, make a change to accommodate me, help me deal with a problem). This tactic appears to be most appropriate for influence attempts with peers, because managers often need to ask for favors from peers but lack the authority to ensure compliance with a formal request (Kotter 1982). However, no prior research has been conducted on directional differences in the use of personal appeals.

Only three studies have directly examined the effectiveness of personal appeals as an influence tactic. In the critical incident study by Schilit and Locke (1982), personal appeals (asking for favors or pity) were not related to success in upward influence attempts. Likewise, in the critical incidents study by Case et al. (1988), personal appeals (pleading, begging, or asking favors) were not related to the success of upward influence attempts. In the critical incidents study by Keys et al. (1987), personal appeals (appealing to sympathy of target) were not related to the success of lateral influence attempts. Some indirect evidence is provided by a study that found a positive correlation between a manager's referent power and the task commitment of subordinates and peers (Yukl and Falbe 1991). Other power studies (see Podsakoff and Schriesheim 1985) have found a positive correlation between a manager's referent power and measures of subordinate satisfaction and performance.

Hypothesis 7a: Coalition tactics are used more in a lateral and upward direction than in a downward direction.

Hypothesis 7b: Coalition tactics are negatively related to task commitment in all three directions.

With coalition tactics, an agent enlists the aid or endorsement of other people to influence a target to do what the agent wants (Stevenson, Pearce, and Porter 1985). There is evidence from descriptive research that managers use coalitions to influence peers and superiors to support changes, innovations, and new projects (Kanter 1983; Kotter 1982). Yukl and Falbe (1990) proposed that coalitions are less likely to be used in downward influence attempts, because managers usually have substantial power over subordinates, and having to ask for help to influence a subordinate may reflect unfavorably on the competence of the manager. In a study by Erez et al. (1986), agents reported that coalitions were used most often in a lateral direction. However, in two other studies with agent reports (Kipnis et al. 1980; Yukl and Falbe 1990) and in two studies with target reports (Erez et al. 1986; Yukl and Falbe 1990), no significant directional differences were found for use of coalition tactics.

Coalitions are used most often as a follow-up tactic after the target has already resisted a direct influence attempt by the agent (Yukl and Falbe 1992). Thus, use of this tactic often indicates a type of request or proposal for which target commitment is especially difficult to attain. Moreover, this tactic is likely to be viewed as manipulative by a target who is aware that the agent is using it. The most offensive form of coalition may be an upward appeal to the target's superior to pressure the target to comply with the agent's request.

Studies on the consequences of using coalition tactics have yielded inconsistent results. In the questionnaire study by Kipnis and Schmidt (1988), self-reported use of coalitions in upward influence was part of the profile for managers who received the lowest performance ratings. Only one of four critical incident studies found evidence that coalition tactics are effective. In a study by Keys et al. (1987), a lateral influence attempt was more likely to be successful when the agent used a coalition tactic (gain support of several peers to influence target). In the critical incident study by Schilit and Locke (1982), coalition tactics (using group or peer support) were not significantly related to outcome success in upward influence attempts. Likewise, outcome success was not significantly related to use of a coalition tactic (soliciting assistance of peers) in the study of downward incidents by Dosier et al. (1988) or to use of coalition tactics (developing and showing support of peers, subordinates, or outsiders) in the study of upward incidents by Case et al. (1988).

Hypothesis 8a: Legitimating tactics are used more in a lateral direction than in a downward or upward direction.

Hypothesis 8b: Legitimating tactics are negatively related to task commitment in all three directions.

Legitimating tactics involve efforts to verify the legitimacy of a request and the agent's authority or right to make it. This tactic is most appropriate for a request that is unusual and of doubtful legitimacy to the target person (Yukl 1990). Legitimating tactics are needed most in a lateral direction because ambiguity about authority relationships and task responsibilities is greatest in this direction. Legitimating tactics are rarely needed in a downward direction, because most managers have considerable authority to direct the work activities of subordinates. Legitimating tactics are seldom needed in an upward direction, and they are difficult to use in this direction because of the limited basis for claiming a right to dictate the actions of a person with higher authority. Directional differences in use of legitimating tactics were not examined in prior research.

Legitimating tactics may induce the target to comply with a request if the target is convinced the request is within the agent's scope of authority and consistent with organizational rules and policies. Yukl and Falbe (1991) found that the most frequent reason reported by managers for complying with a request made by a superior or peer was the legitimacy of the request. However, there is little reason to expect legitimating tactics to increase task commitment, and a negative reaction by the target may occur if this kind of tactic is used in an arrogant and demanding manner (Yukl 1989). Only a few studies have examined the consequences of using legitimating tactics. In Mowday's (1978) questionnaire study of upward influence, legitimating tactics were not correlated significantly with influence success. In the study by Schilit and Locke (1982), legitimating tactics (using organizational rules) were not related significantly to outcome success in upward influence incidents. In the study by Keys et al. (1987), legitimating tactics (calling on company policies, procedures, or rules) were not related significantly to outcome success in lateral influence incidents.

Hypothesis 9a: Pressure tactics are used more in a downward direction than in a lateral or upward direction.

Hypothesis 9b: Pressure tactics are negatively related to task commitment in all three directions.

Many pressure tactics involve the use of a manager's coercive power, which is greater in relation to subordinates than in relation to peers or superiors. Previous studies consistently find greater use of pressure in a downward direction (Erez et al. 1986; Kipnis et al. 1980; Yukl and Falbe 1990). Pressure may elicit reluctant compliance from a target, but it is unlikely to result in commitment. Research with critical incidents indicates that pressure is used most often as a follow-up tactic after an initial influence attempt has already failed (Yukl, Falbe, and Youn, in press). Thus, use of this tactic often indicates a type of request or proposal for which target commitment or even compliance is difficult to attain. Moreover, in many situations pressure is viewed as an inappropriate form of influence behavior, and target resentment about an agent's use of coercion is likely to result in target resistance.

Most studies on the consequences of influence tactics have found either a negative or nonsignificant correlation between pressure and the success of an influence attempt. In the study by Kipnis and Schmidt (1988), self-reported use of pressure was a key part of the profile for managers who received the lowest performance ratings. In the study by Schilit and Locke (1982), targets reported that some pressure tactics used in upward influence attempts (threatening to go over target's head, challenging the power of the target) were likely to be unsuccessful. In the same study, agents reported that another pressure tactic (threatening to resign) was likely to be unsuccessful. In the study by Case et al. (1988), an upward influence attempt was likely to be unsuccessful when the agent used a pressure tactic (telling or arguing without support). In the study by Dosier et al. (1988) of downward critical incidents, there was a marginally significant ($p < .10$) negative relationship between pressure tactics (threatening, warning, reprimanding, or embarrassing) and the success of an influence attempt. In two other studies (Keys et al. 1987; Mowday 1978) results for the effects of pressure were not significant. Research on the use of coercive power by managers (see Podsakoff and Schriesheim 1985; Yukl and Falbe 1991) provides indirect evidence that pressure tactics are unlikely to result in target commitment.

METHOD

Sample

The study was conducted with respondents from five large companies: a pharmaceuticals company, a chemicals and manufacturing company, a financial services company, and two insurance companies. Each manager who volunteered to participate in a management development workshop conducted by a consulting company was asked several weeks before the workshop to distribute questionnaires (with a cover letter) to his or her boss and 10 other people (peers and subordinates) who had known the manager for at least 6 months. Because questionnaire data would be used to provide feedback to the managers in the workshop, they were encouraged to select a representative set of subordinates and several peers with whom they interacted frequently.

Subordinate and peer respondents were anonymous. They were assured that their individual responses would remain confidential and that only a composite summary of the influence tactic scores based on their responses would be seen by the managers participating in the workshops. The boss of each focal manager was informed that his or her responses to the influence tactics questionnaire would be seen by the manager and would not be anonymous. All respondents were informed that the ratings of task commitment and effectiveness were for research purposes only and would not be seen by the manager or anyone else in the company. Each respondent returned the questionnaire directly to the consulting company in a self-addressed, stamped envelope provided for that purpose. Demographic information was obtained directly from the focal managers with a supplementary questionnaire administered prior to the workshop.

A manager was included in the final data set only if questionnaires were received from the manager's boss and at least three peers and three subordinates. This requirement was imposed to avoid using managers who may have selected only a few close friends who they knew would provide especially favorable ratings. The final sample included 128 managers and the people who rated them on the questionnaires. The respondents included 526 subordinates, 543 peers, and 128 superiors. The number of subordinate and peer respondents describing each manager ranged from 6 to 10, with a median of 8. Half of the managers were in manufacturing companies, and half were in service companies. Looking at the distribution by management level, 24 percent were upper level managers, 62 percent were middle managers or managers of professionals, and 14 percent were supervisors. The median span of control was 6 subordinates (direct reports). The average age of the managers was forty years, and 71 percent of the managers were men. Most of the managers (68%) had been in their current job longer than a year. Demographic information was not available for the target respondents because questions that could be used to identify individual subordinates and peers were not asked in order to guarantee anonymity.

MEASURES

Influence tactics were measured with the 1990 version of the Influence Behavior Questionnaire (IBQ) developed by Yukl and his colleagues (Yukl et al., in press). The IBQ has scales measuring the nine influence tactics listed in Table 6.1. Each scale had from three to six items with the following response choices:

1. I cannot remember him/her ever using this tactic with me.
2. He/she very seldom uses this tactic with me.

3. He/she uses this tactic occasionally with me.
4. He/she uses this tactic moderately often with me.
5. He/she uses this tactic very often with me.

Sample items and a description of the developmental research can be found in the report by Yukl et al. (in press).

The questionnaire also included two items measuring conceptually distinct but important criteria for evaluating the influence behavior of a manager. One item asked how many influence attempts by the agent resulted in complete commitment by the target respondent (i.e., strong enthusiasm and special effort beyond what is normally expected). There were seven response choices:

1. None of them.
2. A few of them.
3. Some (less than half).
4. About half of them.
5. More than half of them.
6. Most of them.
7. All of them.

A second item asked the respondent to rate the overall effectiveness of the influence agent (manager) in carrying out his or her job responsibilities. This item had nine response choices:

1. The least effective manager I have known.
2. Well below average, in the bottom 10 percent.
3. Moderately below average, in the bottom 40 percent.
4. A little below average, in the bottom 40 percent.
5. About average in effectiveness.
6. A little above average, in the top 40 percent.
7. Moderately above average, in the top 25 percent.
8. Well above average, in the top 10 percent.
9. The most effective manager I have ever known.

RESULTS

The data analyses and results are described in four separate sections: reliability and validity of measures, directional differences in use of tactics, relation of tactics to task commitment, and relation of tactics to effectiveness ratings.

Reliability and Validity of Measures

As in the earlier study by Yukl and Falbe (1990), internal consistency was satisfactory for most of the IBQ scales. The alpha coefficients for the combined sample of all respondents are shown in Table 6.2. Results were similar when calculated separately for subordinates, peers, and bosses. Internal consistency was lowest for the two scales with only three items (Personal Appeal and Ingratiation).

Table 6.2
Intercorrelation of Influence Tactics

Tactic	1	2	3	4	5	6	7	8	9
1. Rational persuasion	(.78)								
2. Inspirational appeal	.55	(.83)							
3. Consultation	.60	.58	(.85)						
4. Ingratiation	.33	.54	.48	(.65)					
5. Exchange	.31	.42	.33	.50	(.76)				
6. Personal appeal	.29	.41	.32	.54	.55	(.55)			
7. Coalition	.27	.17	.16	.26	.44	.46	(.68)		
8. Legitimating	.16	.08	.02	.27	.35	.42	.63	(.78)	
9. Pressure	.04	.07	−.03	.11	.19	.33	.41	.44	(.89)

Note: Alpha coefficients are in parentheses.

Some of the IBQ scale scores were moderately correlated for the sample used in the current study (see Table 6.2). Factor analyses of data from this sample and earlier studies suggest that the nine tactics are distinct forms of influence behavior. Research with critical incidents (Yukl et al., in press) revealed that some tactics (e.g., rational persuasion and consultation) are used together in the same influence attempt fairly often, which may account for the moderate correlation among the IBQ scales measuring these tactics. Nevertheless, the descriptive research also indicates that each of the tactics is used alone in some influence attempts, supporting our decision to treat them as distinct forms of behavior.

There was a moderate degree of interrater agreement among sets of respondents describing the same manager. A one-way analysis of variance for the 128 managers yielded eta coefficients ranging from .59 to .71 for subordinates and from .54 to .65 for peers. Stability for all of the scales was found to be moderately high in previous validation research by Yukl et al. (in press).

Internal consistency could not be assessed for the single-item criterion measures, but stability for the two items was found to be high in a pilot study of forty-five master's-level students in business administration who had regular day jobs. Respondents were anonymous but provided a code number to allow matching of the two sets of ratings. Over a five-week interval, the test-retest correlation was .74 for task commitment and .90 for managerial effectiveness. Additional evidence for the validity of the effectiveness ratings is provided by the moderately high level of interrater agreement; the rating made by a manager's boss correlated .54 with the composite rating obtained from the manager's peers and subordinates.

Directional Differences in Use of Tactics

Directional differences in the use of the influence tactics were evaluated with a multivariate analysis of variance (MANOVA). The MANOVA for the nine tactics yielded highly significant results on Wilks's lambda test, $F(18, 2356) = 24.5$, $p < .01$. The

Table 6.3
Means and Standard Deviations of Influence Tactics, Broken Down by Direction

Tactic	Direction			F (2, 1195)	η^2
	Downward	Lateral	Upward		
Rational persuasion					
M	3.19_c	3.31_b	3.72_a	30.5**	.05
SD	0.72	0.71	0.63		
Inspirational appeal					
M	3.05_a	2.83_b	2.82_b	9.3**	0.2
SD	0.87	0.87	0.83		
Consultation					
M	3.37	3.25	3.34	2.9	.00
SD	0.82	0.84	0.76		
Ingratiation					
M	2.77_a	2.67_b	2.28_c	15.23**	.03
SD	0.93	0.91	0.90		
Exchange					
M	1.55_b	1.71_a	1.41_c	17.7**	.03
SD	0.59	0.62	0.53		
Personal appeal					
M	2.10_b	2.23_a	1.97_c	8.4**	.01
SD	0.75	0.78	0.80		
Coalition					
M	1.75_c	2.08_a	1.93_b	33.6**	.05
SD	0.58	0.73	0.64		
Legitimating					
M	2.31_b	2.43_a	2.31_b	3.2*	.01
SD	0.83	0.87	0.91		
Pressure					
M	2.10_a	1.84_b	1.85_b	16.2**	.03
SD	0.82	0.78	0.80		

Note: Within rows, different subscripts indicate significant pairwise differences for means on Duncan's multiple-range test.
*$p < .05$.
**$p < .01$.

means and standard deviations for the tactics are shown in Table 6.3, along with the results of the univariate F tests. Significant directional differences were found for eight of the nine tactics. Despite the moderate intercorrelation among some tactics, most of these tactics had a unique pattern of directional differences, which supports our decision to treat the nine tactics as distinct forms of influence behavior.

Pairwise comparisons were assessed with Duncan's multiple-range test. Complete or partial support was found for all of the directional hypotheses except Hypothesis 3a (involving consultation). Consistent with Hypothesis 1a, rational persuasion was used most in an upward direction. Consistent with Hypotheses 2a and 9a, inspirational appeal and pressure were used most in a downward direction. Consistent with Hypothesis 4a, ingratiation was used less in an upward direction than in a lateral or downward direction. Partially consistent with Hypothesis 5a, exchange was used most in a lateral direction and least in an upward direction. Consistent with Hypothesis 7a, coalition was used least in a downward direction. The current study is the first to examine directional differences for personal appeal and legitimating tactics, and consistent with Hypotheses 6a and 8a, these tactics were used most in a lateral direction. The squared eta values in Table 6.3 indicate that direction of influence accounted for a relatively small percentage of the variance in use of tactics.

Relation of Tactics to Task Commitment

The correlation of each influence tactic with the target's task commitment is shown in Table 6.4. For this criterion, all analyses were conducted at the individual level because data on the predictors and criterion were from the same respondents. Because of the large number of variables and the much greater number of subordinate and peer respondents than of boss respondents, a conservative .01 significance level was used for testing the significance of correlations in the two large samples. Hypothesized directional differences in tactic effectiveness were evaluated by making pairwise comparisons of the correlation coefficients for the relevant subsamples. The difference between each pair of correlations was evaluated with Fisher's Z transformation (Cohen and Cohen 1983).

Consistent with Hypotheses 1b, 2b, and 3b, rational persuasion, inspirational appeal, and consultation by the agent were correlated significantly with target's task commitment in all three directions. Consistent with Hypotheses 4b and 5b, agent ingratiation and exchange correlated significantly with task commitment for subordinates and peers, and each of these correlations was significantly larger ($p < .01$) than the corresponding (nonsignificant) correlation for upward influence. Hypothesis 6b was partially supported; personal appeal correlated significantly with task commitment for subordinates and peers but not for superiors. No directional differences were expected for personal appeal, and the pairwise differences among correlations were not significant for this tactic. Hypothesis 7b was not supported, but the results are consistent with the interpretation that coalition tactics were not effective for influencing task commitment in any direction. Partial support was found for Hypothesis 8b; legitimating tactics correlated negatively with task commitment for peers. Partial support was found for Hypothesis 9b; pressure was negatively correlated with task commitment for subordinates and peers. Directional differences were not expected for legitimating tactics or pressure, and the pairwise differences in correlations were not significant for these two tactics.

Interpretation of the results is complicated by the moderately high correlation among some tactics. A multiple regression analysis was conducted to examine the relationship between each tactic and task commitment after controlling for correlations among the tactics. For downward influence, the tactics of inspirational appeal, consultation, and pressure had significant beta weights (the beta for pressure was negative), and together these three tactics accounted for 33 percent of the variance in the task commitment of

Table 6.4
Correlation of Influence Tactics with Targets' Task Commitment and Ratings of the Agent's Managerial Effectiveness

	Targets' task commitment			Effectiveness rating		
Tactic	Downward ($n = 526$)	Lateral ($n = 543$)	Upward ($n = 128$)	Downward ($n = 128$)	Lateral ($n = 128$)	Upward ($n = 128$)
Rational persuasion	.38**	.43**	.50**	.39**	.33**	.44**
Inspirational appeal	.51**	.52**	.33**	.20*	.19*	.29**
Consultation	.42**	.47**	.26**	.26**	.24**	.21*
Ingratiation	.34**	.31**	−.01	−.01	.08	−.05
Exchange	.26**	.25**	−.04	.10	.07	−.09
Personal appeal	.15**	.19**	.00	.03	.01	−.13
Coalition	.00	−.09	−.03	.04	.03	−.17
Legitimating	−.05	−.17**	−.14	−.08	−.01	−.25**
Pressure	−.23**	−.12**	−.06	−.20*	−.08	−.17

Note: The significance level for correlations was set at .01 (two-tailed test) for the larger samples and at .05 for the smaller samples.
* $p < .05$. ** $p < .01$.

subordinates ($R = .58$), $F(9,504) = 27.9$, $p < .01$. For lateral influence, the tactics of inspirational appeal, consultation, rational persuasion, exchange, coalition, and legitimating had significant beta weights (those for coalition and legitimating were negative), and together these six tactics accounted for 36 percent of the variance in the task commitment of peers ($R = .61$), $F(9,523) = 34.6$, $p < .01$. For upward influence, the tactics of rational persuasion and inspirational appeal had significant beta weights, and these two tactics accounted for 33 percent of the variance in the task commitment of superiors ($R = .58$), $F(9,119) = 6.4$, $p < .01$.

The multiple regression analyses showed that even the most highly intercorrelated tactics may account for unique variance in target commitment, and this finding provides additional support for our assumption that the nine tactics are distinct forms of influence behavior. The results varied more across the three samples for the regression analyses than for the simple correlations, but in general the most effective tactics were still rational persuasion, inspirational appeal, and consultation, and the least effective tactics were still coalition, pressure, and legitimating. Compared with results from the correlational analyses, results in the multiple regression analyses were weaker for ingratiation, exchange, and personal appeal.

Relation of Tactics to Effectiveness Ratings

The correlations between influence tactics and the ratings of effectiveness made by a manager's boss are also shown in Table 6.4. For analyses involving upward influence, data on influence tactics and managerial effectiveness were obtained from the same source, namely, the manager's boss. For downward influence, the group mean score on each influence tactic was computed for a manager's subordinates and correlated with the effectiveness rating made by the manager's boss. For lateral influence, the group mean score on each influence tactic was computed for a manager's peers and correlated with the effectiveness rating made by the manager's boss. Use of group-level analysis is consistent with the moderately high level of interrater agreement found for each tactic within the subordinate sample and the peer sample. Results for the correlations were similar in all three directions. Effectiveness ratings were correlated positively with a manager's use of rational persuasion, inspirational appeal, and consultation. Correlations for the remaining tactics were negative or nonsignificant.

As was done for task commitment, a multiple regression analysis was conducted for each sample. Only rational persuasion had a significant beta weight in the regression analyses for subordinates and peers. A manager's use of rational persuasion with subordinates accounted for 15 percent of the variance in boss ratings of the manager's effectiveness ($R = .43$), $F(9,119) = 3.0$, $p < .01$. A manager's use of rational persuasion with peers accounted for 15 percent of the variance in effectiveness ratings made by the manager's boss ($R = .39$), $F(9,119) = 2.4$, $p < .05$. For the sample of boss respondents, a manager's use of rational persuasion and inspirational appeals accounted for 34 percent of the variance in effectiveness ratings ($R = .59$), $F(9,119) = 6.9$, $p < .01$.

DISCUSSION

Previous research provides no clear indication of the tactics likely to be effective for influencing subordinates, peers, and managers. The current study yielded stronger results, and these results appear consistent with theory and behavioral research in other topic areas, such as leadership, motivation, attitude change, and conflict resolution. The results supported most of the hypotheses about the likely effectiveness of each tactic for influencing target task commitment.

In general, consultation, inspirational appeal, and rational persuasion were moderately effective for influencing task commitment, regardless of direction. These three tactics all involve an attempt to change the target's attitude about the desirability of the request, and the tactics are likely to be viewed as socially acceptable for influence attempts in all three directions.

Pressure, coalition, and legitimating were usually ineffective. The negative correlations between these tactics and target commitment probably reflects their frequent use in influence attempts when resistance is anticipated or has already occurred in an earlier influence attempt. In addition, these tactics are likely to be viewed as socially undesirable forms of influence behavior in many situations, and the target may become resentful or angry with the agent for trying to coerce or manipulate him or her.

Ingratiation and exchange were moderately effective for influencing subordinates and peers, but these two tactics were ineffective for influencing superiors. Agents have a weak power base from which to use these tactics in an upward direction, and they are likely to be viewed as manipulative in this context. Ingratiation is more effective when used as part of a long-term strategy for improving upward relations, rather than as a tactic for immediately influencing a superior.

Personal appeals also appeared to be moderately effective for influencing subordinates and peers, but the results for this tactic were weak and difficult to interpret. The weak results may reflect the relatively low reliability of this scale in the current study. The questionnaire will be revised in subsequent research to increase the number of items for personal appeals and ingratiation.

Fewer tactics were correlated significantly with ratings of managerial effectiveness than with task commitment, but the three tactics that correlated most strongly with task commitment also correlated consistently with effectiveness ratings. Regardless of direction, rational persuasion was clearly the best predictor of effectiveness ratings made by a manager's boss. The strong correlation between rational persuasion and effectiveness ratings may be due to a close association between a manager's skillful use of rational persuasion and rater perception of manager expertise. Because perception of a manager's expertise is a strong predictor of effectiveness ratings (Podsakoff and Schriesheim, 1985; Yukl and Falbe, 1991), it is not surprising that skillful use of rational persuasion (which requires considerable expertise) also correlated strongly with effectiveness ratings.

In general, the findings in the current study are consistent with the explanation proposed earlier for weak and inconsistent findings in the six prior studies, namely, the focus on upward influence and the use of weak criteria. Results for most tactics were weaker for upward influence attempts than for downward or lateral influence attempts. Likewise, most of our results were weaker when the criterion was a rating of managerial effectiveness rather than task commitment. We expected to find stronger results for target task commitment than for effectiveness ratings because the latter criterion is determined by many factors besides agent influence behavior. However, another possible explanation of stronger results for task commitment is use of the same respondent to provide information about the predictors and the criterion. The results for task commitment (and for effectiveness ratings in an upward direction) may be inflated somewhat by respondent biases or attributions.

Directional differences in frequency of use were found for all of the tactics except consultation. The directional differences were consistent with hypotheses based on an analysis of working relationships that exist in most organizations for managers and their subordinates, peers, and bosses. The greater number of significant directional differences found in this study than in the study by Yukl and Falbe (1990) is probably due to our use of large samples and a matched design in which the same focal managers were described by subordinates, peers, and bosses. In earlier studies on directional differences, each sample of respondents described a different set of focal managers, and only Kipnis et al. (1980) used a large sample.

Even though most directional differences were significant, they accounted for only a small proportion of the variance in the measure of tactics. As Yukl and Falbe (1990) found, the relative frequency of use for the tactics was similar in all three directions. Thus, direction does not appear to be a very important determinant of tactic selection in comparison with other factors. Overall, there was a moderate correspondence between effectiveness and frequency of use; effective tactics tended to be used more often in all directions. The reasons why managers select particular tactics should be examined more closely in future research.

Our study has some limitations that need to be acknowledged. First, because influence behavior was not manipulated, causality can only be inferred from the results. The correlations may have been influenced by a variety of extraneous factors, such as differences in measurement accuracy among tactics, reverse causality, and respondent biases and attributions. Second, descriptions of an agent's influence behavior by targets may be insensitive to subtle forms of influence (e.g., use of deception or information distortion, some forms of coalition) that are successful only if the target is not aware they are being used. Third, results for directional differences may be biased by differences in target sensitivity to agent use of tactics that are inconsistent with role expectations (e.g., a manager may be more likely to notice and remember the use of pressure by a subordinate than by a superior). Fourth, the sampling of respondents was not random because the focal managers selected the peers and subordinates who would describe their influence behavior. However, the large number of respondents who described each manager was expected to minimize any problems due to possible bias in respondent selection. Fifth, the use of task commitment as the only immediate criterion of influence effectiveness precluded evaluation of the extent to which pressure, coalition, and legitimating may be useful for eliciting compliance. Sometimes compliance is all that is needed to accomplish a task objective (Yukl 1989).

Our research findings have implications for improving managerial effectiveness because it is an advantage for a manager to know which tactics have the highest likelihood of success for influencing a subordinate, peer, or superior. However, because of the limitations of the study, caution is needed in offering guidelines until the results are verified in follow-up research with different methods and samples. The findings indicate that some tactics are more likely to be successful, but the results do not suggest that these tactics will always result in task commitment. The outcome of any particular influence attempt is determined by many factors besides influence tactics, and any tactic can result in target resistance if it is not appropriate for the situation or is used in an unskillful manner.

In summary, the findings provide some important insights into the effective use of influence tactics by managers, but additional research is needed to verify and extend the findings. More developmental research is needed to refine the IBQ scales and improve reliability and discriminant validity. In future research, it is desirable to identify when the various tactics are likely to result in target compliance rather than commitment. The scope of the research should be extended beyond examination of individual tactics to identify the effects of using multiple tactics at the same time and in different sequences. The contextual determinants of tactic selection and tactic outcomes in our preliminary model need to be investigated more directly. Finally, research with experimental designs is needed to verify the effect of influence tactics on outcomes.

REFERENCES

Ansari, M.A., and Kapoor, A. (1987). Organizational context and upward influence tactics. *Organizational Behavior and Human Decision Processes* 40: 39–49.

Bass, B.M. (1985). *Leadership and Performance Beyond Expectations*. New York: Free Press.

Case, T., Dosier, L., Murkinson, G., and Keys, B. (1988). How managers influence superiors: A study of upward influence tactics. *Leadership and Organizational Development Journal* 9(4): 25–31.

Cohen, A., and Bradford, D. (1989). Influence without authority: The use of alliances, reciprocity, and exchange to accomplish work. *Organizational Dynamics* 17: 5–17.

Cohen, J., and Cohen, P. (1983). *Applied Multiple Regression/Correlation Analysis for the Behavioral Sciences*. Hillsdale, NJ: Erlbaum.

Conger, J.A. (1989). *The Charismatic Leader: Behind the Mystique of Exceptional Leadership*. San Francisco, CA: Jossey-Bass.

Dosier, L., Case, T., and Keys, B. (1988). How managers influence subordinates: An empirical study of downward influence tactics. *Leadership and Organizational Development Journal* 9(5): 22–28.

Eagly, A., and Chaiken, S. (1984). Cognitive theories of persuasion. In L. Berkowitz (ed.), *Advances in Experimental Social Psychology* (vol. 17, pp. 267–359). San Diego, CA: Academic Press.

Erez, M., and Rim, Y. (1982). The relationship between goals, influence tactics, and personal and organizational variables. *Human Relations* 35: 877–878.

Erez, M., Rim, Y., and Keider, L. (1986). The two sides of the tactics of influence: Agent vs. target. *Journal of Occupational Psychology* 59: 25–39.

Kanter, R.M. (1983). *The Change Masters*. New York: Simon and Schuster.

Kaplan, R.E. (1986). Trade routes: The manager's network of relationships. *Organizational Dynamics* (Spring): 37–52.

Kelman, H.C. (1958). Compliance, identification, and internalization: Three processes of attitude change. *Journal of Conflict Resolution* 2: 51–60.

Keys, B., Case, T., Miller, T., Curran, K.E., and Jones, C. (1987). Lateral influence in organizations. *International Journal of Management* 4: 425–431.

Kipnis, D., and Schmidt, S.M. (1988). Upward influence styles: Relationship with performance evaluations, salary, and stress. *Administrative Science Quarterly* 33: 528–542.

Kipnis, D., Schmidt, S.M., and Wilkinson, I. (1980). Intraorganizational influence tactics: Explorations in getting one's way. *Journal of Applied Psychology* 65: 440–452.

Kotter, J.P. (1982). *The General Managers*. New York: Free Press.

Liden, R.C., and Mitchell, T.R. (1988). Ingratiatory behaviors in organizational settings. *Academy of Management Review* 13: 572–587.

Mowday, R.T. (1978). The exercise of upward influence in organizations. *Administrative Science Quarterly* 23: 137–156.

Podsakoff, P., and Schriesheim, C. (1985). Field studies of French and Raven's bases of power: Critique, reanalysis, and suggestions for future research. *Psychological Bulletin* 97: 387–411.

Schilit, W.K., and Locke, E. (1982). A study of upward influence in organizations. *Administrative Science Quarterly* 27: 304–316.

Schmidt, S.M., and Kipnis, D. (1984). Manager's pursuit of individual and organizational goals. *Human Relations* 37: 781–794.

Schriesheim, C., and Hinkin, T.R. (1990). Influence tactics used by subordinates: A theoretical and empirical analysis and refinement of the Kipnis, Schmidt, and Wilkinson subscales. *Journal of Applied Psychology* 75: 246–257.

Stevenson, W., Pearce, J., and Porter, L. (1985). The concept of "coalition" in organization theory and research. *Academy of Management Review* 10: 256–268.

Tedeschi, J.T., and Melburg, V. (1984). Impression management and influence in the organization. In S.B.

Bacharach and E.J. Lawler (eds.), *Research in the Sociology of Organizations* (vol. 3, pp. 31–58). Greenwich, CT: JAI.

Tichy, N.M., and Devanna, M.A. (1986). *The Transformational Leader.* New York: Wiley.

Vroom, V.H., and Jago, A.G. (1988). *The New Leadership: Managing Participation in Organizations.* Englewood Cliffs, NJ: Prentice-Hall.

Wortman, C.B., and Linsenmeier, J.A. (1977). Interpersonal attraction and techniques of ingratiation in organizational settings. In B.M. Staw and G.R. Salancik (eds.), *New Directions in Organizational Behavior* (pp. 133–178). Chicago: St. Clair Press.

Yukl, G. (1989). *Leadership in Organizations.* Englewood Cliffs, NJ: Prentice-Hall.

———. (1990). *Skills for Managers and Leaders.* Englewood Cliffs, NJ: Prentice-Hall.

Yukl, G., and Falbe, C.M. (1990). Influence tactics in upward, down ward, and lateral influence attempts. *Journal of Applied Psychology* 75: 132–140.

———. (1991). The importance of different power sources in downward and lateral relations. *Journal of Applied Psychology* 76: 416–423.

Yukl, G., Falbe, C.M., and Youn, J.Y (in press). Patterns of influence behavior for managers. *Group and Organization Management.*

Yukl, G., Lepsinger, R., and Lucia, T. (in press). Preliminary report on the development and validation of the Influence Behavior Questionnaire. In K. Clark and M. Clark (eds.), *The Impact of Leadership.* Greensboro, NC: Center for Creative Leadership.

PART 2

Downward Influence

When the average person thinks about influence existing in organizations, the first thing that usually comes to mind is influence that flows from upper levels to lower levels. Although, as we emphasize throughout this book, downward influence is only one of the directions of influence in organizations, it is the direction that has received the most attention. Even in today's typically flatter and leaner organizations, downward influence remains a center of attention. One only has to read a daily or weekly business publication to realize that no matter how much organizations have changed over the past several decades, downward influence has not lost its prominence. For this reason, it is the first direction of influence that is dealt with in this book.

Here in Part 2, we first discuss the nature and characteristics of downward influence, its relationship to the topic of leadership, and factors that can impinge on its effectiveness in organizational settings. The readings in this part cover a range of topics related to downward influence, including: its connection with the use of power; various difficulties involved in putting it into practice; some positive actions that supervisors and leaders can take to try to be more effective in attempting to exercise this kind of influence; and the nature and challenges of a particular approach to leadership—charismatic and transformational leadership.

THE NATURE OF DOWNWARD INFLUENCE

In organizational situations involving downward influence, someone is attempting to affect the behavior of another individual or group of individuals at a lower level in the formal organizational hierarchy. Thus, in downward influence, the superior is the initiator of the influence attempt; the subordinates are the recipients of the attempt. Of course, the terms "superior" and "subordinate" used here refer to *relative* positions in the organizational hierarchy, and not necessarily to two positions at immediately adjacent levels. For instance, an example of a downward influence attempt could involve a vice president of sales trying to influence a sales representative who is several levels below the vice president. The key defining feature of downward influence is that, regardless of how close or far apart their positions are in the hierarchy, the influencer is at a relatively higher organizational level than the (potential) influencee. Thus, the only individuals who could *not* engage in downward influence attempts, as we use the term, are those who are at the lowest operative level within the organization.

The most important characteristic of downward influence is the fact that the influencer has more formal authority than the target of the influence attempt. In fact, it is this element that makes downward influence an especially fascinating topic. This is because it is how the person with this kind of power chooses to deploy it that tends to determine whether successful influence has occurred. In many cases in organizations, the person with the greater formal authority misuses that source of power and thus produces little influence or even generates active resistance to influence. On the other hand, when formal authority is effectively and adroitly employed it can serve as a major tool for generating influence with the target. This issue—of how, and how well, those in higher-level positions in organizations use the formal authority granted to them—will receive considerable attention in several of the articles appearing in Part 2.

The point to be made for the moment, however, is to emphasize that the influence agent has this tool available, and typically both the influencer and the intended recipients of downward influence attempts will be acutely aware of this reality.

Although in downward influence situations the hierarchical superior has formal authority available, it must also be kept in mind that she or he also has all of the additional bases of person power (expertise, charisma, etc.) potentially available to anyone in the organization. The formal authority differential is simply an "extra" not available when lateral or upward influence is attempted. When formal authority is utilized together with one or more person-related powers, this can result in an especially potent force for downward influence.

There is another important consideration to keep in mind when analyzing downward influence situations. Typically, though not universally, the lower-level target recipient will be relatively more dependent on the higher-level person for rewards than vice versa. (See the Introduction to Part 4 for a detailed discussion of this issue and the options available to those in lower positions.) This means that ordinarily the recipient of a downward influence attempt will be more motivated to please the initiator than would likely be the case with a recipient in lateral or upward influence situations. Indeed, that is the major challenge for the influence agent in those situations: how to have an impact on someone who is not dependent on the influencing agent for rewards, or, for that matter, subject to credible threats or punishments. However, to reemphasize a point made earlier, in downward influence situations the existence of the typical dependency relationship does not guarantee that it is an easy task for the higher-level manager to use rewards effectively in bringing about influence. In fact, the imbalanced dependency relationship may add an element of complexity and difficulty to the circumstances surrounding the influence attempt. Nevertheless, in downward situations, the person attempting influence starts with the *potential* advantage of having the influence target be in a relatively more dependent position and thus initially predisposed to respond as the influence agent intends.

One reason that downward influence is the direction of influence that has received the most attention to date in the scholarly literature on organizations is because of its close relationship with the topic of leadership. While leadership—interpersonal attempts to influence other people in attaining some goal—can be exercised by anyone in an organization, irrespective of how high or low their formal position, it is an influence process most often associated with those occupying positions possessing some degree of formal authority. Thus, people in positions that are labeled managerial or supervisory have opportunities to exert leadership influence in a downward direction, and the higher the position usually the greater the opportunity. This does not mean, of course, that downward-directed leadership attempts will always be successful. It only means that some people are in positions to make that a possibility.

EFFECTIVE AND INEFFECTIVE DOWNWARD INFLUENCE

The effectiveness of downward influence, indeed influence in any direction, is a function of three critical factors: the influencer, or in this case, the person in the relatively higher-level position; the targets or persons in lower positions; and the nature of the situation that surrounds specific influence attempts. These three components interact to determine whether influence takes place. The person initiating downward influence brings certain skills and abilities to bear on the process. These can be categorized into three major types: conceptual (cognitive ability), technical (specialized knowledge), and interpersonal (e.g., sensitivity, empathy). When all three of these skills and abilities are high, the probability of successful downward influence is increased. When one or more of the three types of skills is not at a high level, the outcome will be more problematic. In this case, it is their relative importance to each other that matters, and that is the focus of one of the articles, by Goleman, later in this Part.

The second critical factor in downward influence attempts, the target(s), possess their own amounts of these skills and also bring along their attitudes and values that affect how much influence will actually occur. In addition, as research over the past several decades has demonstrated, the nature of the relationship between the higher-level initiator and the lower-level target of the influence attempt—the leader-follower relationship in leadership terms—will have considerable impact on the target's reaction and subsequent behavior (Dansereau, Graen and Haga 1975; Graen and Uhl-Bien 1995; Gerstner and Day 1997; Schriesheim, Castro and Cogliser 1999).

Finally, the characteristics and features of the organizational situation that surround the downward influence attempt will also have a major bearing on how successful or unsuccessful the attempt turns out—that is, whether the target is influenced or not. Three of the most important variables of the situation are the nature of the work being performed, the immediate and larger organizational context, and the specific circumstances occurring at the time of influence attempts. Different types of work or tasks being carried out by the influence targets often will affect their reactions to attempted influence by organizational superiors. Thus, whether work is relatively structured or unstructured and whether it involves high or low levels of discretion appears to make a difference in the relative effectiveness of such influence (Turner and Lawrence 1965; Griffin 1982; Hackman and Oldham 1980). The more unstructured the work and the more it involves a high level of discretion, the more likely an over-reliance on formal authority in downward influence attempts will result in reduced effectiveness.

The organizational context for downward influence attempts includes both the immediate work group and the larger organization. A target's immediate work colleagues can affect the downward influence process by the degree to which the target is sensitive to their attitudes and reactions, especially if the target is a member of a highly cohesive work group (Druckman and Swets 1988; Shaw 1981). In other words, in groups that are relatively highly cohesive, an individual member's reaction to downward influence is likely to be consistent with that of the group. If the other members of the group react positively to the influence, the individual is likely to respond in that direction; likewise, if the other members of the group react negatively, the individual could be expected to respond in a similar fashion.

Particularly important with respect to the effects of the larger context on downward influence is the fundamental culture of the organization—its history, traditions, and norms. Downward influence attempts that appear to violate these traditions and norms are probably more likely to face opposition and noncompliance. Of course, that does not mean that attempts that are consistent with norms will necessarily succeed. It only implies that the larger context of the organization's culture and traditions probably will play a role in the degree of success of different approaches to downward influence.

In addition to the nature of work being performed and the organizational context, the specific circumstances occurring at the time of any given influence attempt can be highly significant in determining the type response received from the target. As just one example, a crisis atmosphere would be almost certain to produce different kinds of results than a placid, low-key atmosphere. Whether the influence attempt would be more or less successful would depend on how those specific circumstances interact with other important variables we have already mentioned.

THE READINGS IN PART 2

The articles in Part 2, collectively, examine a number of facets of the downward influence process. We begin with an article by John P. Kotter that serves as a sort of bridge between Part 1 and Part 2 because it places the issue of power at the front and center of the practice of management. Although the article is over twenty years old, it still carries important messages for managers engaging in downward influence. In this article, Kotter focuses on how effective managers both acquire and use power in relating to others in the organization, particularly those below them in the hierarchy. He begins by noting that, if managers are to do a good job, they must recognize that they are dependent on others in the organization—even though the degree of relative dependence is greater from subordinate to superior than vice versa. To state the obvious, managers cannot accomplish their goals by themselves. Therefore, in Kotter's analysis, managers must learn how to establish power in their relationships with others. He identifies four means of creating power: developing a sense of obligation to the manager; developing a sense of belief in the manager's expertise; enhancing subordinates' tendencies for identification with the manager; and making salient to the subordinates their dependence on the manager. Kotter concludes with a discussion of characteristics that are common to managers who are able to generate and utilize power successfully.

The next four articles that follow in Part 2 discuss various problems or difficulties that can occur in downward influence processes. The first of these, "On the Folly of Rewarding A, While Hoping for B," by Steven Kerr, is an updated version of an article that was published in 1975 and which subsequently has become a "classic" in the organizational and management academic literature. The reason is that it was one of the first articles to identify an almost universal phenomenon that occurs frequently in organizations but which had previously received little attention: how attempts by organizations and managers to exert downward influence can easily end up rewarding and reinforcing behaviors of the target that are not what was intended. In this updated 1995 version of the original article, Kerr provides numerous examples of such misguided downward influence occurring in many areas of society—in politics, in war, in medicine, in universities, in government, and, of course, in business. He then proceeds to analyze the causes of this widespread but seemingly paradoxical behavior exhibited by those having the power to influence those in lower organizational positions. Among those causes: "fascination with an 'objective' criterion" of performance, "overemphasis on highly visible behaviors," and sometimes even a certain degree of "hypocrisy." To overcome or reduce these tendencies, the author suggests that managers need to pay more attention to what types of behavior are being rewarded and then to consider altering the reward, or "payoff," system in order to increase the ratio of desired to undesired behaviors. However, this solution is one that is often very difficult for upper-level managers to accept. In a postscript, though, Kerr notes that in our nonorganizational daily lives most of us demonstrate that we already understand the principles involved in practicing successful reinforcement behavior and know how to implement rewards effectively—at least some of the time! So, it is definitely possible to do so on a more consistent basis, whether in or outside of organizations.

The next article dealing with the difficulties involved in exercising downward influence, or the "dark side" of the process, one might say, focuses on the "petty tyrant"—a person who "lords his or her power over others." In reviewing this article, by Blake Ashforth, the reader might want to consider whether any examples from present or past experience come readily to mind. Those who have had some amount of organizational work experience will probably recognize that this is not a rare phenomenon. The article describes petty tyranny in behavioral terms, identifies a set of antecedents or causes of such behavior, and discusses the effects that such behavior has on subordinates. Characteristics of the petty tyrant include such behaviors as: excessively close supervision, distrust and suspicion, rigidity and inflexibility, and an undue emphasis on status and authority differences. As the author notes, the addition of the word "petty" to the tyrant label is meant to "underscore the theme of arbitrariness and small-mindedness" in this pattern of behaviors. In his analysis of the antecedents, Ashforth categorizes them into "personal predispositions" and "situational"/organizational factors. Effects of petty tyranny on subordinates, in the author's analysis, include frustration, feelings of helplessness and work alienation, and the possible undermining of work unit cohesiveness. These and other effects can, in turn, in a sort of vicious cycle reinforce and increase tyrannical tendencies on the part of the higher level wielder of downward influence.

The following article by Charles C. Manz and Harold L. Angle illustrates another potential misuse of downward influence powers. The authors describe a case study of an executive who introduces self-managing work teams in a large office of an insurance company. The teams proceeded to establish rules and procedures to try to increase the efficiency of their operational procedures. However, the teams' emphasis on procedures caused decreased feelings of autonomy on the part of many of the individual team members and also had the effect of reducing customer service on smaller accounts. The net result of the creation of the self-managing teams was that the superior actually ended up gaining greater control than had existed before. The authors conclude their article with some lessons drawn from the case study, and they particularly emphasize that the agendas of upper-level managers are critical in determining how much actual power and influence is transferred, or not transferred at all, to lower-levels.

The article that follows, by Susan S. White and Edwin A. Locke, deals with an interesting finding that has been observed and studied in the psychological literature for over thirty years. First discovered and identified in an experiment in a school classroom setting, the finding was termed the "Pygmalion Effect," after the famous Greek mythology story of the sculptor who fell in love with his statue (Rosenthal and Jacobson 1968). In their study, the researchers found that when elementary school teachers were told at the beginning of the school year that certain of their students had been identified by intelligence tests as "late bloomers" who will probably do much better than expected during the coming year, the students who had been so identified actually did score significantly higher on a second administration of the test at the end of the year compared to an equivalent group of students who had not received this label. This occurred despite the fact that the teachers of the "later bloomers" were unaware that they had treated those students any differently from the other students.

Translated into managerial terms, the Pygmalion Effect is defined as "leader expectations for subordinate performance [that] can subconsciously affect leader behavior and subordinate performance," and is the subject of the White and Locke article. The authors call into question how extensively this effect can be used as a useful and practical influence approach by leaders. After briefly reviewing the history of Pygmalion research in a variety of organizational settings, White and Locke proceed to identify a set of factors that they believe may limit the widespread applicability of this self-fulfilling prophecy approach. These include such factors as whether the approach works equally well when used by leaders of either gender with subordinates of either gender, whether the approach is ethical, whether leaders can be trained to use the approach effectively, and whether it works as well with subordinates already acquainted with the leader as with subordinates who are not. In raising these issues, the authors do not dismiss the possible utility of the Pygmalion Effect; rather, they cast a skeptical eye and suggest possible ways to make it more generally useful. They conclude their article with the trenchant observation that "the basic attitude of managers should be that all employees can improve their skills and performance."

The following two articles in this section focus on positive steps supervisors and leaders can take to influence subordinates in an effective manner. The first of these articles, by L. Alan Witt, analyzes how supervisors can take actions to reduce the level of office politics and some of the possible negative effects of undue political behavior. (See the introduction to Part 4 concerning the issue of whether organizational politics is always negative for the welfare of the organization and for individual members.) Witt identifies several dimensions of what he terms "workplace politics" and some of the possible effects of those politics. The balance of the article is devoted to discussing four supervisory practices that can lessen subordinates' exposure to possible negative effects: providing increased opportunities for subordinate participation in decision-making, attempts to align subordinates' personal priorities with those of the larger organization, making sure that subordinates are not punished or discouraged from reporting unfavorable news or developments, and being receptive to subordinates' feedback and likewise providing as much feedback to them as possible. The reader of this article will need to assess the difficulties involved in using these downward influence processes to reduce any deleterious effects of organizational politics and also to assess the likelihood that those in downward influence positions will be successful in doing so.

The next article, "What Makes a Leader?" by Daniel Goleman, focuses more broadly on the leader as a source of positive downward influence and is probably one of the most important articles in this entire book. Its central theme is that most effective leaders have "a high degree of what has come to be known as 'emotional intelligence.' " Based on his extensive research, Goleman posits that while high cognitive intelligence (i.e., high IQ) and technical skills are important, they basically function as "threshold capabilities" for being able to attain high level positions in organizations. It is, he contends, "emotional intelligence [that] is the sine qua non of leadership." He proposes, again based on his and others' research, that emotional intelligence consists of five components: self-awareness, self-regulation, motivation, empathy, and social skill. He elaborates on each of these five components and shows how they contribute to the overall level of emotional intelligence. Goleman argues persuasively that any person can develop and increase the amount of their emotional intelligence, a capability that appears to be critical to being able to exercise significant downward influence.

The final two readings in Part 2 address a leadership topic that has received considerable attention in the leadership research literature in the past decade or so: charismatic/transformational leadership (e.g., Bass 1985; Sashkin 1988; Tichy and Devanna 1990; Shamir, House, and Arthur 1993). Both terms, "charismatic leadership" and "transformational leadership," have been used to describe an essentially similar type of leadership: leadership that motivates followers to make major changes or achieve at an extraordinary level. The word *charisma* derives from the Greek word for "gift." It literally means "divinely conferred gift," and was first used in the organizational literature early in the twentieth century by the world-famous sociologist, Max Weber. He described the charismatic leader as someone who influences others based on the inspirational qualities of the leader rather than on that person's formal power or position. Thus, when charismatic leadership is being exercised, followers (subordinates) are assumed to identify with the leader because of his or her exceptional qualities (gifts). This characterization of leadership has been used frequently in the political sphere to describe those leaders who are unusually influential with large numbers of people, including such historical figures as Joan of Arc, Mahatma Gandhi, Winston Churchill, Martin Luther King and John F. Kennedy. As we have indicated, the concept of "transformational leadership" is very similar to "charismatic leadership." Probably the primary difference in emphasis between the two closely related concepts is that the charismatic label highlights what the leader is like as a person, whereas the transformational label gives relatively more attention to what leaders actually do. Nevertheless, the two terms in the organizational literature are much more similar than they are different.

The first of the two readings on the charismatic/transformational leadership topic is by Jay A. Conger and Rabindra N. Kanungo and presents (in an excerpt from their coauthored book) a "behavioral model of charismatic leadership." As they stress, the model "builds on the idea that charismatic leadership is an attribution based on followers' perceptions of their leader's behavior." Essentially, they view leadership as a process that involves moving organizational members "away from the status quo toward the achievement of desired longer-term goals." They conceptualize this process as involving three stages: critical evaluation of the status quo, the formulation and articulation of goals, and demonstration by the leader of how these goals can be achieved by the organization. What distinguishes the charismatic leader from the noncharismatic leader, in the authors' analysis, is how they deal with each of the three stages of the process. Thus, charismatic leaders in Stage 1 are especially sensitive to deficiencies in the status quo, in Stage 2 are particularly adept at formulating and articulating a compelling vision of an idealized future, and in Stage 3 use "innovative and unconventional means" to influence followers to achieve that vision. The Conger and Kanungo reading pays particular attention to the nature of the downward influence process involved in charismatic leadership and the interrelated nature of the behavioral components that comprise this kind of leadership. The last section of the reading compares the authors' model of charismatic leadership to other models of charismatic and transformational leadership.

The final article in Part 2, by Lyman W. Porter and Gregory A. Bigley, raises a set of cautionary issues regarding the potential motivational effects of transformational and charismatic leadership. In particular, the authors stress the importance of considering the organizational context as a major condition in determining how well such leadership will work, in practice, in influencing the motivation of those lower in the organizational hierarchy. Specifically, they discuss the possible impacts of three context factors: the situation that exists if there are multiple transformational leaders within the same organization, the risk of unintended organizational consequences of transformational leaders' behavior, and the degree to which such leadership in organizations can sustain a high level of motivation over long periods. The authors conclude their analysis with a discussion of implications of fostering this approach to leadership in organizations, and they also provide some suggestions for needed future research on the topic to help us understand the organizational implications more fully.

Collectively, the nine readings in Part 2 amply serve to demonstrate that there is more to downward influence than meets the eye. Exercising influence in this direction clearly is not as simple and straightforward as it might appear on the surface. In downward influence, the condition of having considerable formal authority brings with it a corresponding set of considerable potential pitfalls. The challenge for the influence agent, as we have seen from the readings in this Part, is to be able to wield this source of power in such a way as to increase influence and decrease the likelihood of encountering those pitfalls. Definitely possible, but not always easy. In the next section, the nature of the challenge changes: Exercising influence when the target has roughly the same amount of formal authority as the influence agent.

REFERENCES

Bass, B.M. (1985). *Leadership and performance beyond expectations*. New York: Free Press.

Dansereau, F., Jr., Graen, G., and Haga, W.J. (1975). A vertical dyad linkage approach to leadership within formal organizations: A longitudinal investigation of the role making process. *Organizational Behavior and Human Performance*, 13: 46–78.

Druckman, D., and Swets, J.A. (eds.) (1988). *Enhancing human performance: Issues, theories and techniques*. Washington, DC: National Academy Press.

Gerstner, C.R., and Day, D.V. (1997). Meta-analytic review of leader-member exchange theory: Correlates and construct ideas. *Journal of Applied Psychology* 82: 827–844.

Graen, G.B., and Uhl-Bien, M. (1995). Development of leader-member exchange (LMX) theory of leadership over 25 years: Applying a multi-level-multi-domain perspective. *Leadership Quarterly* 6: 219–247.

Griffin, R.W. (1982). *Task design: An integrative approach*. Glenview, IL: Scott, Foresman.

Hackman, J.R., and Oldham, G.R. (1980). *Work Redesign*. Reading, MA: Addison-Wesley.

Rosenthal, R., and Jacobson, L. (1968). *Pygmalion in the classroom: Teacher expectation and pupils' intellectual development*. New York: Holt, Rinehart and Winston.

Sashkin, M. (1988). The visionary leader. In J.A. Conger and R.N. Kanungo (eds.), *Charismatic leadership: The elusive factor in organizational effectiveness*. San Francisco: Jossey-Bass.

Schriesheim, C.A., Castro, S.L., and Cogliser, C.C. (1999). Leader-member exchange (LMX) research: A comprehensive review of theory, measurement, and data-analytic practices. *Leadership Quarterly* 10: 63–113.

Shamir, B., House, R.J., and Arthur, M.B. (1993). The motivational effects of charismatic leadership: A self-concept based theory. *Organization Science*, 4: 1–17.

Shaw, M.E. (1981). *Group dynamics: The psychology of small group behavior* (3rd ed). New York: McGraw-Hill.

Tichy, N.M., and Devanna, M.A. (1990). *The transformational leader*. New York: Wiley.

Turner, A.N., and Lawrence, P.R. (1965). *Industrial jobs and the worker*. Boston: Harvard University, School of Business Administration.

7

Power, Dependence, and Effective Management

John P. Kotter

Americans, as a rule, are not very comfortable with power or with its dynamics. We often distrust and question the motives of people who we think actively seek power. We have a certain fear of being manipulated. Even those people who think the dynamics of power are inevitable and needed often feel somewhat guilty when they themselves mobilize and use power. Simply put, the overall attitude and feeling toward power, which can easily be traced to the nation's very birth, is negative. In his enormously popular *Greening of America,* Charles Reich reflects the views of many when he writes, "It is not the misuse of power that is evil; the very existence of power is evil."[1]

One of the many consequences of this attitude is that power as a topic for rational study and dialogue has not received much attention, even in managerial circles. If the reader doubts this, all he or she need do is flip through some textbooks, journals, or advanced management course descriptions. The word power rarely appears.

This lack of attention to the subject of power merely adds to the already enormous confusion and misunderstanding surrounding the topic of power and management. And this misunderstanding is becoming increasingly burdensome because in today's large and complex organizations the effective performance of most managerial jobs requires one to be skilled at the acquisition and use of power.

From my own observations, I suspect that a large number of managers—especially the young, well-educated ones—perform significantly below their potential because they do not understand the dynamics of power and because they have not nurtured and developed the instincts needed to effectively acquire and use power.

In this article I hope to clear up some of the confusion regarding power and managerial work by providing tentative answers to three questions:

1. Why are the dynamics of power necessarily an important part of managerial processes?
2. How do effective managers acquire power?
3. How and for what purposes do effective managers use power?

I will not address questions related to the misuse of power, but not because I think they are unimportant. The fact that some managers, some of the time, acquire and use power mostly for their own aggrandizement is obviously a very important issue that deserves attention and careful study. But that is a complex topic unto itself and one that has already received more attention than the subject of this article.

RECOGNIZING DEPENDENCE IN THE MANAGER'S JOB

One of the distinguishing characteristics of a typical manager is how dependent he is on the activities of a variety of other people to perform his job effectively.[2] Unlike doctors and mathematicians, whose performance is more directly dependent on their own talents and efforts, a manager can be dependent in varying degrees on superiors, subordinates, peers in other parts of the organization, the subordinates of peers, outside suppliers, customers, competitors, unions, regulating agencies, and many others.

These dependency relationships are an inherent part of managerial jobs because of two organizational facts of life: division of labor and limited resources. Because the work in organizations is divided into specialized divisions, departments, and jobs, managers are made directly or indirectly dependent on many others for information, staff services, and cooperation in general. Because of their organization's limited resources, managers are also dependent on their external environments for support. Without some minimal cooperation from suppliers, competitors, unions, regulatory agencies, and customers, managers cannot help their organizations survive and achieve their objectives.

Dealing with these dependencies and the manager's subsequent vulnerability is an important and difficult part of a manager's job because, while it is theoretically possible that all of these people and organizations would automatically act in just the manner that a manager wants and needs, such is almost never the case in reality. All the people on whom a manager is dependent have limited time, energy, and talent, for which there are competing demands.

Some people may be uncooperative because they are too busy elsewhere, and some because they are not really capable of helping. Others may well have goals, values, and beliefs that are quite different and in conflict with the manager's and may therefore have no desire whatsoever to help or cooperate. This is obviously true of a competing company and sometimes of a union, but it can also apply to a boss who is feeling threatened by a manager's career progress or to a peer whose objectives clash with the manager's.

Indeed, managers often find themselves dependent on many people [and things] whom they do not directly control and who are not "cooperating." This is the key to one of the biggest frustrations managers feel in their jobs, even in the top ones, which the following example illustrates:

After nearly a year of rumors, it was finally announced in May 1974 that the president of ABC Corporation had been elected chairman of the board and that Jim Franklin, the vice president of finance, would replace him as president. While everyone at ABC was aware that a shift would take place soon, it was not at all clear before the announcement who would be the next president. Most people had guessed it would be Phil Cook, the marketing vice president.

Nine months into his job as chief executive officer, Franklin found that Phil Cook [still the marketing vice president] seemed to be fighting him in small and subtle ways. There was never anything blatant, but Cook just did not cooperate with Franklin as the other vice presidents did. Shortly after being elected, Franklin had tried to bypass what he saw as a potential conflict with Cook by telling him that he would understand if Cook would prefer to move somewhere else where he could be a CEO also. Franklin said that it would be a big loss to the company but that he would be willing to help Cook in a number of ways if he wanted to look for a presidential opportunity elsewhere. Cook had thanked him but had said that family and community commitments would prevent him from relocating, and all CEO opportunities were bound to be in a different city.

Since the situation did not improve after the tenth and eleventh months, Franklin seriously considered forcing Cook out. When he thought about the consequences of such a move, Franklin became more and more aware of just how dependent he was on Cook. Marketing and sales were generally the keys to success in their industry, and the company's sales force was one of the best, if not the best, in the industry. Cook had been with the company for twenty-five years. He had built a strong personal relationship with many of the people in the sales force and was universally popular. A mass exodus just might occur if Cook were fired. The loss of a large number of salesmen, or even a lot of turmoil in the department, could have a serious effect on the company's performance.

After one year as chief executive officer, Franklin found that the situation between Cook and himself had not improved and had become a constant source of frustration.

As a person gains more formal authority in an organization, the areas in which he or she is vulnerable increase and become more complex rather than the reverse. As the previous example suggests, it is not at all unusual for the president of an organization to be in a highly dependent position, a fact often not apparent to either the outsider or to the lower level manager who covets the president's job.

A considerable amount of the behavior of highly successful managers that seems inexplicable in light of what management texts usually tell us managers do becomes understandable when one considers a manager's need for, and efforts at, managing his or her relationships with others.[3] To be able to plan, organize, budget, staff, control, and evaluate, managers need some control over the many people on whom they are dependent. Trying to control others solely by directing them and on the basis of the power associated with one's position simply will not work—first, because managers are always dependent on some people over whom they have no formal authority, and second, because virtually no one in modern organizations will passively accept and completely obey a constant stream of orders from someone just because he or she is the "boss."

Trying to influence others by means of persuasion alone will not work either. Although it is very powerful and possibly the single most important method of influence, persuasion has some serious drawbacks too. To make it work requires time [often lots of it], skill, and information on the part of the persuader. And persuasion can fail simply because the other person chooses not to listen or does not listen carefully.

This is not to say that directing people on the basis of the formal power of one's position and persuasion are not important means by which successful managers cope. They obviously are. But, even taken together, they are not usually enough.

Successful managers cope with their dependence on others by being sensitive to it, by eliminating or avoiding unnecessary dependence, and by establishing power over those others. Good managers then use that power to help them plan, organize, staff, budget, evaluate, and so on. In other words, it is primarily because of the dependence inherent in managerial jobs that the dynamics of power necessarily form an important part of a manager's processes.

An argument that took place during a middle management training seminar I participated in a few years ago helps illustrate further this important relationship between a manager's need for power and the degree of his or her dependence on others:

Two participants, both managers in their thirties, got into a heated disagreement regarding the acquisition and use of power by managers. One took the position that power was absolutely central to managerial work, while the other argued that it was virtually irrelevant. In support of their positions, each described a very "successful" manager with whom he worked. In one of these examples, the manager seemed to be constantly developing and using power, while in the other, such behavior was rare. Subsequently, both seminar participants were asked to describe their successful managers' jobs in terms of the dependence inherent in those jobs.

The young manager who felt power was unimportant described a staff vice president in a small company who was dependent only on his immediate subordinates, his peers, and his boss. This person, Joe Phillips, had to depend on his subordinates to do their jobs appropriately, but, if necessary, he could fill in for any of them or secure replacement for them rather easily. He also had considerable formal authority over them; that is, he could give them raises and new assignments, recommend promotions, and fire them. He was moderately dependent on the other four vice presidents in the company for information and cooperation. They were likewise dependent on him. The president had considerable formal authority over Phillips but was also moderately dependent on him for help, expert advice, the service his staff performed, other information, and general cooperation.

The second young manager—the one who felt power was very important—described a service department manager, Sam Weller, in a large, complex, and growing company who was in quite a different position. Weller was dependent not only on his boss for rewards and information, but also on thirty other individuals who made up the divisional and corporate top management. And while his boss, like Phillips's was moderately dependent on him too, most of the top managers were not. Because Weller's subordinates, unlike Phillips's, had people reporting to them, Weller was dependent not only on his subordinates but also on his subordinates' subordinates. Because he could not himself easily replace or do most of their technical jobs, unlike Phillips, he was very dependent on all these people.

In addition, for critical supplies, Weller was dependent on two other department managers in the division. Without their timely help, it was impossible for his department to do its job. These departments, however, did not have similar needs for Weller's help and cooperation. Weller was also dependent on local labor union officials and on a federal agency that regulated the division's industry. Both could shut his division down if they wanted.

Finally, Weller was dependent on two outside suppliers of key materials. Because of the volume of his department's purchase relative to the size of these two companies, he had little power over them.

Under these circumstances, it is hardly surprising that Sam Weller had to spend considerable time and effort acquiring and using power to manage his many dependencies, while Joe Phillips did not.

As this example also illustrates, not all management jobs require an incumbent to be able to provide the same amount of successful power-oriented behavior. But most management jobs today are more like Weller's than Phillips's. And, perhaps more important, the trend over the past two or three decades is away from jobs like Phillips's and toward jobs like Weller's. So long as our technologies continue to become more complex, the average organization continues to grow larger, and the average industry continues to become more competitive and regulated, that trend will continue; as it does so, the effective acquisition and use of power by managers will become even more important.

ESTABLISHING POWER IN RELATIONSHIPS

To help cope with the dependency relationships inherent in their jobs, effective managers create, increase, or maintain four different types of power over others.[4] Having power based in these areas puts the manager in a position both to influence those people on whom he or she is dependent when necessary and to avoid being hurt by any of them.

Sense of Obligation

One of the ways that successful managers generate power in their relationships with others is to create a sense of obligation in those others. When the manager is successful, the others feel that they should—rightly—allow the manager to influence them within certain limits.

Successful managers often go out of their way to do favors for people who they expect will feel an obligation to return those favors. As can be seen in the following description of a manager by one of his subordinates, some people are very skilled at identifying opportunities for doing favors that cost them very little but that others appreciate very much:

> Most of the people here would walk over hot coals in their bare feet if my boss asked them to. He has an incredible capacity to do little things that mean a lot to people. Today, for example, in his junk mail he came across an advertisement for something that one of my subordinates had in passing once mentioned that he was shopping for. So my boss routed it to him. That probably took 15 seconds of his time, and yet my subordinate really appreciated it. To give you another example, two weeks ago he somehow learned that the purchasing manager's mother had died. On his way home that night, he stopped off at the funeral parlor. Our purchasing manager was, of course, there at the time. I bet he'll remember that brief visit for quite a while. Recognizing that most people believe that friendship carries with it certain obligations ("A friend in need. . . ."), successful managers often try to develop true friendships with those on whom they are dependent. They will also make formal and informal deals in which they give something up in exchange for certain future obligations.

Belief in a Manager's Expertise

A second way successful managers gain power is by building reputations as "experts" in certain matters. Believing in the manager's expertise, others will often defer to the manager on those matters. Managers usually establish this type of power through visible achievement. The larger the achievement and the more visible it is, the more power the manager tends to develop.

One of the reasons that managers display concern about their "professional reputations" and their "track records" is that they have an impact on others' beliefs about their expertise. These factors become particularly important in large settings, where most people have only secondhand information about most other people's professional competence, as the following shows:

> Herb Randley and Bert Mine were both 35-year-old vice presidents in a large research and development organization. According to their closest associates, they were equally bright and competent in their technical fields and as managers. Yet

Randley had a much stronger professional reputation in most parts of the company, and his ideas generally carried much more weight. Close friends and associates claim the reason that Randley is so much more powerful is related to a number of tactics that he has used more than Mine has.

Randley has published more scientific papers and managerial articles than Mine. Randley has been more selective in the assignments he has worked on, choosing those that are visible and that require his strong suits. He has given more speeches and presentations on projects that are his own achievements. And in meetings in general, he is allegedly forceful in areas where he has expertise and silent in those where he does not.

Identification with a Manager

A third method by which managers gain power is by fostering others' unconscious identification with them or with ideas they "stand for." Sigmund Freud was the first to describe this phenomenon, which is most clearly seen in the way people look up to "charismatic" leaders. Generally, the more a person finds a manager both consciously and (more important) unconsciously an ideal person, the more he or she will defer to that manager.

Managers develop power based on others' idealized views of them in a number of ways. They try to look and behave in ways that others respect. They go out of their way to be visible to their employees and to give speeches about their organizational goals, values, and ideals. They even consider, while making hiring and promotion decisions, whether they will be able to develop this type of power over the candidates:

> One vice president of sales in a moderate-size manufacturing company was reputed to be so much in control of his sales force that he could get them to respond to new and different marketing programs in a third of the time taken by the company's best competitors. His power over his employees was based primarily on their strong identification with him and what he stood for. Emigrating to the United States at age seventeen, this person worked his way up "from nothing." When made a sales manager in 1965, he began recruiting other young immigrants and sons of immigrants from his former country. When made vice president of sales in 1970, he continued to do so. In 1975, 85 percent of his sales force was made up of people whom he hired directly or who were hired by others he brought in.

Perceived Dependence on a Manager

The final way that an effective manager often gains power is by feeding others' beliefs that they are dependent on the manager either for help or for not being hurt. The more they perceive they are dependent, the more most people will be inclined to cooperate with such a manager.

There are two methods that successful managers often use to create perceived dependence.

Finding and Acquiring Resources

In the first, the manager identifies and secures (if necessary) resources that another person requires to perform his job, that he does not possess, and that are not readily available elsewhere. These resources include such things as authority to make certain decisions; control of money, equipment, and office space; access to important people; information and control of information channels; and subordinates. Then the manager takes action so that the other person correctly perceives that the manager has such resources and is willing and ready to use them to help (or hinder) the other person. Consider the following extreme—but true—example.

> When young Tim Babcock was put in charge of a division of a large manufac-
> turing company and told to "turn it around," he spent the first few weeks studying
> it from afar. He decided that the division was in disastrous shape and that he
> would need to take many large steps quickly to save it. To be able to do that, he
> realized he needed to develop considerable power fast over most of the division's
> management and staff. He did the following:
>
>   1. He gave the division's management two hours' notice of his arrival.
>   2. He arrived in a limousine with six assistants.
>   3. He immediately called a meeting of the forty top managers.
>   4. He outlined briefly his assessment of the situation, his commitment to turn things
>   around, and the basic direction he wanted things to move in.
>   5. He then fired the four top managers in the room and told them that they had to be out
>   of the building in two hours.
>   6. He then said he would personally dedicate himself to sabotaging the career of anyone
>   who tried to block his efforts to save the division.
>   7. He ended the 60-minute meeting by announcing that his assistants would set up ap-
>   pointments for him with each of them starting at 7:00 the next morning.

Throughout the critical six-month period that followed, those who remained at the division generally cooperated energetically with Mr. Babcock.

Affecting Perceptions of Resources

A second way effective managers gain these types of power is by influencing other persons' perceptions of the manager's resources.[5] In settings where many people are involved and where the manager does not interact continuously with those he or she is dependent on, those people will seldom possess "hard facts" regarding what relevant resources the manager commands directly or indirectly (through others), what resources he will command in the future, or how prepared he is to use those resources to help or hinder them. They will be forced to make their own judgments.

Insofar as a manager can influence people's judgments, he can generate much more power than one would generally ascribe to him in light of the reality of his resources.

In trying to influence people's judgments, managers pay considerable attention to the "trappings" of power and to their own reputations and images. Among other actions, they sometimes carefully select, decorate, and arrange their offices in ways that give signs of power. They associate with people or organizations that are known to be powerful or that others perceive as powerful. Managers selectively foster rumors concerning their own power. Indeed, those who are particularly skilled at creating power in this way tend to be very sensitive to the impressions that all their actions might have on others.

Formal Authority

Before discussing how managers use their power to influence others, it is useful to see how formal authority relates to power. By formal authority, I mean those elements that automatically come with a managerial job—perhaps a title, an office, a budget, the right to make certain decisions, a set of subordinates, a reporting relationship, and so on.

Effective managers use the elements of formal authority as resources to help them develop any or all of the four types of power previously discussed, just as they use other resources (such as their education). Two managers with the same formal authority can have very different amounts of power entirely because of the way they have used that authority. For example:

1. By sitting down with employees who are new or with people who are starting new projects and clearly specifying who has the formal authority to do what, one manager creates a strong sense of obligation in others to defer to his authority later.
2. By selectively withholding or giving the high-quality service his department can provide other departments, one manager makes other managers clearly perceive that they are dependent on him.

On its own, then, formal authority does not guarantee a certain amount of power; it is only a resource that managers can use to generate power in their relationships.

EXERCISING POWER TO INFLUENCE OTHERS

Successful managers use the power they develop in their relationships, along with persuasion, to influence people on whom they are dependent to behave in ways that make it possible for the managers to get their jobs done effectively. They use their power to influence others directly, face to face, and in more indirect ways. (See Table 7.1.)

Table 7.1
Methods of Influence

Face-to-face methods	What they can influence	Advantages	Drawbacks
Exercise obligation-based power.	Behavior within zone that the other perceives as legitimate in light of the obligation.	Quick. Requires no outlay of tangible resources.	If the request is outside the acceptable zone, it will fail; if it is too far outside, others might see it as illegitimate.
Exercise power based on perceived expertise.	Attitudes and behavior within the zone of perceived expertise.	Quick. Requires no outlay of tangible resources.	If the request is outside the acceptable zone, it will fail; if it is too far outside, others might see it as illegitimate.
Exercise power based on identification with a manager.	Attitudes and behavior that are not in conflict with the ideals that underlie the identification.	Quick. Requires no expenditure of limited resources.	Restricted to influence attempts that are not in conflict with the ideals that underlie the identification.
Exercise power based on perceived dependence.	Wide range of behavior that can be monitored.	Quick. Can often succeed when other methods fail.	Repeated influence attempts encourage the other to gain power over the influencer.
Coercively exercise power based on perceived dependence.	Wide range of behavior that can be easily monitored.	Quick. Can often succeed when other methods fail.	Invites retaliation. Very risky.
Use persuasion.	Very wide range of attitudes and behavior.	Can produce internalized motivation that does not require monitoring. Requires no power or outlay of scarce material resources.	Can be very time-consuming. Requires other person to listen.
Combine these methods.	Depends on the exact combination.	Can be more potent and less risky than using a single method.	More costly than using a single method.

Indirect methods	What they can influence	Advantages	Drawbacks
Manipulate the other's environment by using any or all of the face-to-face methods.	Wide range of behavior and attitudes.	Can succeed when face-to-face methods fail.	Can be time-consuming. Is complex to implement; is very risky, especially if used frequently.
Change the forces that continuously act on the individual: Formal organizational arrangements. Informal social arrangements. Technology. Resources available. Statement of organizational goals.	Wide range of behavior and attitudes on a continuous basis.	Has continuous influence, not just a one-shot effect. Can have a very powerful impact.	Often requires a considerable power outlay to achieve.

Face-to-Face Influence

The chief advantage of influencing others directly by exercising any of the types of power is speed. If the power exists and the manager correctly understands the nature and strength of it, he can influence the other person with nothing more than a brief request or command:

- Jones thinks Smith feels obliged to him for past favors. Furthermore, Jones thinks that his request to speed up a project by two days probably falls within a zone that Smith would consider legitimate in light of his own definition of his obligation to Jones. So Jones simply calls Smith and makes his request. Smith pauses for only a second and says yes, he'll do it.
- Manager Johnson has some power based on perceived dependence over manager Baker. When Johnson tells Baker that he wants a report done in twenty-four hours, Baker grudgingly considers the costs of compliance, of noncompliance, and of complaining to higher authorities. He decides that doing the report is the least costly action and tells Johnson he will do it.
- Young Porter identifies strongly with Marquette, an older manager who is not his boss. Porter thinks Marquette is the epitome of a great manager and tries to model himself after him. When Marquette asks Porter to work on a special project "that could be very valuable in improving the company's ability to meet new competitive products," Porter agrees without hesitation, and works fifteen hours per week above and beyond his normal hours to get the project done and done well.

When used to influence others, each of the four types of power has different advantages and drawbacks. For example, power based on perceived expertise or on identification with a manager can often be used to influence attitudes as well as someone's immediate behavior and thus can have a lasting impact. It is very difficult to influence attitudes by using power based on perceived dependence, but if it can be done, it usually has the advantage of being able to influence a much broader range of behavior than the other methods do. When exercising power based on perceived expertise, for example, one can only influence attitudes and behavior within that narrow zone defined by the "expertise."

The drawbacks associated with the use of power based on perceived dependence are particularly important to recognize. A person who feels dependent on a manager for rewards (or lack of punishments) might quickly agree to a request from the manager 2but then not follow through, especially if the manager cannot easily find out if the person has obeyed or not. Repeated influence attempts based on perceived dependence also seem to encourage the other person to try to gain some power to balance the manager's. And perhaps most important, using power based on perceived dependence in a coercive way is very risky. Coercion invites retaliation.

For instance, in the example in which Tim Babcock took such extreme steps to save the division he was assigned to "turn around," his development and use of power based on perceived dependence could have led to mass resignation and the collapse of the division. Babcock fully recognized this risk, however, and behaved as he did because he felt there was simply no other way that he could gain the very large amount of quick cooperation needed to save the division.

Effective managers will often draw on more than one form of power to influence someone, or they will combine power with persuasion. In general, they do so because a combination can be more potent and less risky than any single method, as the following description shows:

> One of the best managers we have in the company has lots of power based on one thing or another over most people. But he seldom if ever just tells or asks someone to do something. He almost always takes a few minutes to try to persuade them. The power he has over people generally induces them to listen carefully and certainly disposes them to be influenced. That, of course, makes the persuasion process go quickly and easily. And he never risks getting the other person mad or upset by making what that person thinks is an unfair request or command.

It is also common for managers not to coercively exercise power based on perceived dependence by itself, but to combine it with other methods to reduce the risk of retaliation. In this way, managers are able to have a large impact without leaving the bitter aftertaste of punishment alone.

Indirect Influence Methods

Effective managers also rely on two types of less direct methods to influence those on whom they are dependent. In the first way, they use any or all of the face-to-face methods to influence other people, who in turn have some specific impact on a desired person.

Product manager Stein needed plant manager Billings to "sign off" on a new product idea (Product X) which Billings thought was terrible. Stein decided that there was no way he could logically persuade Billings because Billings just would not listen to him. With time, Stein felt, he could have broken through that barrier. But he did not have that time. Stein also realized that Billings would never, just because of some deal or favor, sign off on a product he did not believe in. Stein also felt it not worth the risk of trying to force Billings to sign off, so here is what he did:

> On Monday, Stein got Reynolds, a person Billings respected, to send Billings two market research studies that were very favorable to Product X, with a note attached saying, "Have you seen this? I found them rather surprising. I am not sure if I entirely believe them, but still. . . .

> On Tuesday, Stein got a representative of one of the company's biggest customers to mention casually to Billings on the phone that he had heard a rumor about

Product X being introduced soon and was "glad to see you guys are on your toes as usual."

On Wednesday, Stein had two industrial engineers stand about three feet away from Billings as they waited for a meeting to begin and talk about the favorable test results on Product X.

On Thursday, Stein set up a meeting to talk about Product X with Billings and invited only people whom Billings liked or respected and who also felt favorably about Product X.

On Friday, Stein went to see Billings and asked him if he was willing to sign off on Product X. He was.

This type of manipulation of the environments of others can influence both behavior and attitudes and can often succeed when other influence methods fail. But it has a number of serious drawbacks. It takes considerable time and energy, and it is quite risky. Many people think it is wrong to try to influence others in this way, even people who, without consciously recognizing it, use this technique themselves. If they think someone is trying, or has tried, to manipulate them, they may retaliate. Furthermore, people who gain the reputation of being manipulators seriously undermine their own capacities for developing power and for influencing others. Almost no one, for example, will want to identify with a manipulator. And virtually no one accepts, at face value, a manipulator's sincere attempts at persuasion. In extreme cases, a reputation as a manipulator can completely ruin a manager's career.

A second way in which managers indirectly influence others is by making permanent changes in an individual's or a group's environment. They change job descriptions, the formal systems that measure performance, the extrinsic incentives available, the tools, people, and other resources that the people or groups work with, the architecture, the norms or values of work groups, and so on. If the manager is successful in making the changes, and the changes have the desired effect on the individual or group, that effect will be sustained over time.

Effective managers recognize that changes in the forces that surround a person can have great impact on that person's behavior. Unlike many of the other influence methods, this one doesn't require a large expenditure of limited resources or effort on the part of the manager on an ongoing basis. Once such a change has been successfully made, it works independently of the manager.

This method of influence is used by all managers to some degree. Many, however, use it sparingly simply because they do not have the power to change the forces acting on the person they wish to influence. In many organizations, only the top managers have the power to change the formal measurement systems, the extrinsic incentives available, the architecture, and so on.

GENERATING AND USING POWER SUCCESSFULLY

Managers who are successful at acquiring considerable power and using it to manage their dependence on others tend to share a number of common characteristics:

1. They are sensitive to what others consider to be legitimate behavior in acquiring and using power. They recognize that the four types of power carry with them certain "obligations" regarding their acquisition and use. A person who gains a considerable amount of power based on his perceived expertise is generally expected to be an expert in certain areas. If it ever becomes publicly known that the person is clearly not an expert in those areas, such a person will probably be labeled a "fraud" and will not only lose his power but will suffer other reprimands too.

    A person with whom a number of people identify is expected to act like an ideal leader. If he clearly lets people down, he will not only lose that power, he will also suffer the righteous anger of his ex-followers. Many managers who have created or used power based on perceived dependence in ways that their employees have felt unfair, such as in requesting overtime work, have ended up with unions.

2. They have good intuitive understanding of the various types of power and methods of influence. They are sensitive to what types of power are easiest to develop with different types of people. They recognize, for example, that professionals tend to be more influenced by perceived expertise than by other forms of power. They also have a grasp of all the various methods of influence and what each can accomplish, at what costs, and with what risks. (See Table 7.1.) They are good at recognizing the specific conditions in any situation and then at selecting an influence method that is compatible with those conditions.

3. They tend to develop all the types of power, to some degree, and they use all the influence methods mentioned in the exhibit. Unlike managers who are not very good at influencing people, effective managers usually do not think that only some of the methods are useful or that only some of the methods are moral. They recognize that any of the methods, used under the right circumstances, can help contribute to organizational effectiveness with few dysfunctional consequences. At the same time, they generally try to avoid those methods that are more risky than others and those that may have dysfunctional consequences. For example, they manipulate the environment of others only when absolutely necessary.

4. They establish career goals and seek out managerial positions that allow them to successfully develop and use power. They look for jobs, for example, that use their backgrounds and skills to control or manage some critically important problem or environmental contingency that an organization faces. They recognize that success in that type of job makes others dependent on them and increases their own perceived expertise. They also seek jobs that do not demand a type or a volume of power that is inconsistent with their own skills.

5. They use all of their resources, formal authority, and power to develop still more power. To borrow Edward Banfield's metaphor, they actually look for ways to "invest" their power where they might secure a high positive return.[6] For example, by asking a person to do him two important favors, a manager might be able to finish his construction program one day ahead of schedule. That request may cost him most of the obligation-based power he has over that person, but in return he may significantly increase his perceived expertise as a manager of construction projects in the eyes of everyone in his organization.

Just as in investing money, there is always some risk involved in using power this way; it is possible to get a zero return for a sizable investment, even for the most powerful manager. Effective managers do not try to avoid risks. Instead, they look for prudent risks, just as they do when investing capital.

6. Effective managers engage in power-oriented behavior in ways that are tempered by maturity and self-control.[7] They seldom, if ever, develop and use power in impulsive ways or for their own aggrandizement.

7. Finally, they also recognize and accept as legitimate that, in using these methods, they clearly influence other people's behavior and lives. Unlike many less effective managers, they are reasonably comfortable in using power to influence people. They recognize, often only intuitively, what this article is all about—that their attempts to establish power and use it are an absolutely necessary part of the successful fulfillment of their difficult managerial role.

NOTES

1. Charles A. Reich, *The Greening of America: How the Youth Revolution Is Trying to Make America Liveable* (New York: Random House, 1970).

2. See Leonard R. Sayles, *Managerial Behavior: Administration in Complex Organization* (New York: McGraw-Hill, 1964) as well as Rosemary Stewart, *Managers and Their Jobs* (London: Macmillan, 1967) and *Contrasts in Management* (London: McGraw-Hill, 1976).

3. I am talking about the type of inexplicable differences that Henry Mintzberg has found; see his article "The Manager's Job: Folklore and Fact," *HBR*, July–August 1975, p. 49.

4. These categories closely resemble the five developed by John R. P. French and Bertram Raven; see "The Base of Social Power" in *Group Dynamics: Research and Theory*, Dorwin Cartwright and Alvin Zander, eds. (New York: Harper & Row, 1968), chapter 20. Three of the categories are similar to the types of "authority"-based power described by Max Weber in *The Theory of Social and Economic Organization* (New York: Free Press, 1947).

5. For an excellent discussion of this method, see Richard E. Neustadt, *Presidential Power* (New York: Wiley, 1960).

6. See Edward C. Banfield, *Political Influence* (New York: Free Press, 1965), chapter 11.

7. See David C. McClelland and David H. Burnham, "Power Is the Great Motivator," *HBR*, March–April 1976, p. 100.

8

On the Folly of Rewarding A, While Hoping for B[1]

Steven Kerr

Whether dealing with monkeys, rats, or human beings, it is hardly controversial to state that most organisms seek information concerning what activities are rewarded, and then seek to do (or at least pretend to do) those things, often to the virtual exclusion of activities not rewarded. The extent to which this occurs of course will depend on the perceived attractiveness of the rewards offered, but neither operant nor expectancy theorists would quarrel with the essence of this notion.

Nevertheless, numerous examples exist of reward systems that are fouled up in that the types of behavior rewarded are those which the rewarder is trying to discourage, while the behavior desired is not being rewarded at all.

FOULED-UP SYSTEMS

In Politics

Official goals are "purposely vague and general and do not indicate . . . the host of decisions that must be made among alternative ways of achieving official goals and the priority of multiple goals. . . ."[2] They usually may be relied on to offend absolutely no one, and in this sense can be considered high acceptance, low quality goals. An example might be "All Americans are entitled to health care." Operative goals are higher in quality but lower in acceptance, since they specify where the money will come from, and what alternative goals will be ignored.

The American citizenry supposedly wants its candidates for public office to set forth operative goals, making their proposed programs clear, and specifying sources and uses of funds. However, since operative goals are lower in acceptance, and since aspirants to public office need acceptance (from at least 50.1 percent of the people), most politicians prefer to speak only of official goals, at least until after the election. They of course would agree to speak at the operative level if "punished" for not doing so. The electorate could do this by refusing to support candidates who do not speak at the operative level. Instead, however, the American voter typically punishes (withholds support from) candidates who frankly discuss where the money will come from, rewards politicians who speak only of official goals, but hopes that candidates (despite the reward system) will discuss the issues operatively.

In War

If some oversimplification may be permitted, let it be assumed that the primary goal of the organization (Pentagon, Luftwaffe, or whatever) is to win. Let it be assumed further that the primary goal of most individuals on the front lines is to get home alive. Then there appears to be an important conflict in goals—personally rational behavior by those at the bottom will endanger goal attainment by those at the top.

But not necessarily! It depends on how the reward system is set up. The Vietnam war was indeed a study of disobedience and rebellion, with terms such as "fragging" (killing one's own commanding officer) and "search and evade" becoming part of the military vocabulary. The difference in subordinates' acceptance of authority between World War II and Vietnam is reported to be considerable, and veterans of the Second World War were often quoted as being outraged at the mutinous actions of many American soldiers in Vietnam. Consider, however, some critical differences in the reward system in use during the two conflicts. What did the GI in World War II want? To go home. And when did he get to go home? When the war was won! If he disobeyed the orders to clean out the trenches and take the hills, the war would not be won and he would not go home. Furthermore, what were his chances of attaining his goal (getting home alive) if he obeyed the orders compared to his chances if he did not? What is being suggested is that the rational soldier in World War II, whether patriotic or not, probably found it expedient to obey.

Consider the reward system in use in Vietnam. What did the soldier at the bottom want? To go home. And when did he get to go home? When his tour of duty was over! This was the case whether or not the war was won. Furthermore, concerning the relative chance of getting home alive by obeying orders compared to the chance if they were disobeyed, it is worth noting that a mutineer in Vietnam was far more likely to be assigned rest and rehabilitation (on the assumption that fatigue was the cause) than he was to suffer any negative consequence.

In his description of the "zone of indifference," Barnard stated that "a person can and will accept a communication as authoritative only when . . . at the time of his decision, he believes it to be compatible with his personal interests as a whole."[3] In light of the reward system used in Vietnam, wouldn't it have been personally irrational for some orders to have been obeyed? Was not the military implementing a system which rewarded disobedience, while hoping that soldiers (despite the reward system) would obey orders?

In Medicine

Theoretically, physicians can make either of two types of error, and intuitively one seems as bad as the other. Doctors can pronounce patients sick when they are actually well (a type 1 error), thus causing them needless anxiety and expense, curtailment of enjoyable foods and activities, and even physical danger by subjecting them to needless medication and surgery. Alternately, a doctor can label a sick person well (a type 2 error), and thus avoid treating what may be a serious, even fatal ailment. It might be natural to conclude that physicians seek to minimize both types of error.

Such a conclusion would be wrong. It has been estimated that numerous Americans have been afflicted with iatrogenic (physician caused) illnesses.[4] This occurs when the doctor is approached by someone complaining of a few stray symptoms. The doctor classifies and organizes these symptoms, gives them a name, and obligingly tells the patient what further symptoms may be expected. This information often acts as a self-fulfilling prophecy, with the result that from that day on the patient for all practical purposes is sick.

Why does this happen? Why are physicians so reluctant to sustain a type 2 error (pronouncing a sick person well) that they will tolerate many type 1 errors? Again, a look at the reward system is needed. The punishments for a type 2 error are real: guilt, embarrassment, and the threat of a malpractice suit. On the other hand, a type 1 error (labeling a well person sick) is a much safer and conservative approach to medicine in today's litigious society. Type 1 errors also are likely to generate increased income and a stream of steady customers who, being well in a limited physiological sense, will not embarrass the doctor by dying abruptly. Fellow physicians and the general public therefore are really rewarding type 1 errors while hoping fervently that doctors will try not to make them.

A current example of rewarding type 1 errors is provided by Broward County, Florida, where an elderly or disabled person facing a competency hearing is evaluated by three court-appointed experts who get paid much more for the same examination if the person is ruled to be incompetent. For example, psychiatrists are paid $325 if they judge someone to be incapacitated, but earn only $125 if the person is judged competent. Court-appointed attorneys in Broward also earn more—$325 as opposed to $175—if their clients lose than if they win. Are you surprised to learn that, of 598 incapacity proceedings initiated and completed in the county in 1993, 570 ended with a verdict of incapacitation?[5]

In Universities

Society hopes that professors will not neglect their teaching responsibilities but rewards them almost entirely for research and publications. This is most true at the large and prestigious universities. Clichés such as "good research and good teaching go together" notwithstanding, professors often find that they must choose between teaching and research-oriented activities when allocating their time. Rewards for good teaching are usually limited to outstanding teacher awards, which are given to only a small percentage of good teachers and usually bestow little money and fleeting prestige. Punishments for poor teaching are also rare.

Rewards for research and publications, on the other hand, and punishments for failure to accomplish these, are common. Furthermore, publication-oriented resumes usually will be well-received at other universities, whereas teaching credentials, harder to document and quantify, are much less transferable. Consequently it is rational for university professors to concentrate on research, even to the detriment of teaching and at the expense of their students.

By the same token, it is rational for students to act based upon the goal displacement[6] which has occurred within universities concerning what they are rewarded for. If it is assumed that a primary goal of a university is to transfer knowledge from teacher to student, then grades become identifiable as a means toward that goal, serving as motivational, control, and feedback devices to expedite the knowledge transfer. Instead, however, the grades themselves have become much more important for entrance to graduate school, successful employment, tuition refunds, and parental respect, than the knowledge or lack of knowledge they are supposed to signify.

It therefore should come as no surprise that we find fraternity files for examinations, term paper writing services, and plagiarism. Such activities constitute a personally rational response to a reward system which pays off for grades rather than knowledge. These days, reward systems—specifically, the growing threat of lawsuits—encourage teachers to award students high grades, even if they aren't earned. For example:

> When Andy Hansen brought home a report card with a disappointing C in math, his parents . . . sued his teacher. . . . After a year and six different appeals within the school district, another year's worth of court proceedings, $4000 in legal fees paid by the Hansens, and another $8500 by the district . . . the C stands. Now the student's father, auto dealer Mike Hansen, says he plans to take the case to the State Court of Appeals. . . . "We went in and tried to make a deal: They wanted a C, we wanted an A, so why not compromise on a B?" Mike Hansen said. "But they dug in their heels, and here we are."[7]

In Consulting

It is axiomatic that those who care about a firm's well-being should insist that the organization get fair value for its expenditures. Yet it is commonly known that firms seldom bother to evaluate a new TQM [Total Quality Management], employee empowerment program, or whatever, to see if the company is getting its money's worth. Why? Certainly it is not because people have not pointed out that this situation exists; numerous practitioner-oriented articles are written each year on just this point. One major reason is that the individuals (in human resources, or organization development) who would normally be responsible for conducting such evaluations are the same ones often charged with introducing the change effort in the first place. Having convinced top

management to spend money, say, on outside consultants, they usually are quite ani-
mated afterwards in collecting rigorous vignettes and anecdotes about how successful
the program was. The last thing many desire is a formal, revealing evaluation. Although
members of top management may actually hope for such systematic evaluation, their
reward systems continue to reward ignorance in this area. And if the HR department
abdicates its responsibility, who is to step into the breach? The consultants themselves?
Hardly! They are likely to be too busy collecting anecdotal "evidence" of their own,
for use on their next client.

In Sports

Most coaches disdain to discuss individual accomplishments, preferring to speak of
teamwork, proper attitude, and one-for-all spirit. Usually, however, rewards are distributed according to individual performance. The college basketball player who passes the
ball to teammates instead of shooting will not compile impressive scoring statistics and
is less likely to be drafted by the pros. The ballplayer who hits to right field to advance
the runners will win neither the batting nor home run titles, and will be offered smaller
raises. It therefore is rational for players to think of themselves first, and the team
second.

In Government

Consider the cost-plus contract or its next of kin, the allocation of next year's budget
as a direct function of this years expenditures—a clear-cut example of a fouled up
reward system. It probably is conceivable that those who award such budgets and contracts really hope for economy and prudence in spending. It is obvious, however, that
adopting the proverb "to those who spend shall more be given," rewards not economy,
but spending itself.

In Business

The past reward practices of a group health claims division of a large eastern insurance
company provides another rich illustration. Attempting to measure and reward accuracy
in paying surgical claims, the firm systematically kept track of the number of returned
checks and letters of complaint received from policyholders. However, underpayments
were likely to provoke cries of outrage from the insured, while overpayments often
were accepted in courteous silence. Since it was often impossible to tell from the
physician's statement which of two surgical procedures, with different allowable benefits, was performed, and since writing for clarifications would have interfered with
other standards used by the firm concerning percentage of claims paid within two days
of receipt, the new hire in more than one claims section was soon acquainted with the
informal norm: "When in doubt, pay it out!"

This situation was made even worse by the firm's reward system. The reward system called for annual merit increases to be given to all employees, in one of the following three amounts:

1. If the worker was "outstanding" (a select category, into which no more than two employees per section could be placed): 5 percent.
2. If the worker was "above average" (normally all workers not "outstanding" were so rated): 4 percent.
3. If the worker committed gross acts of negligence and irresponsibility for which he or she might be discharged in many other companies: 3 percent.

Now, since the difference between the five percent theoretically attainable through hard work and the four percent attainable merely by living until the review date is small, many employees were rather indifferent to the possibility of obtaining the extra one percent reward. In addition, since the penalty for error was a loss of only one percent, employees tended to ignore the norm concerning indiscriminant payments.

However, most employees were not indifferent to a rule which stated that, should absences or latenesses total three or more in any six-month period, the entire four or five percent due at the next merit review must be forfeited. In this sense, the firm was hoping for performance, while rewarding attendance. What it got, of course, was attendance. (If the absence/lateness rule appears to the reader to be stringent, it really wasn't. The company counted "times" rather than "days" absent, and a ten-day absence therefore counted the same as one lasting two days. A worker in danger of accumulating a third absence within six months merely had to remain ill—away from work—during a second absence until the first absence was more than six months old. The limiting factor was that at some point salary ceases, and sickness benefits take over. This was usually sufficient to get the younger workers to return, but for those with 20 or more years' service, the company provided sickness benefits of 90 percent of normal salary, tax-free! Therefore . . .).

Thanks to the U.S. government, even the reporting of wrongdoing has been corrupted by an incredibly incompetent reward system that calls for whistleblowing employees to collect up to thirty percent of the amount of a fraud without a stated limit. Thus prospective whistleblowers are encouraged to delay reporting a fraud, even to actively participate in its continuance, in order to run up the total and, thus, their percentage of the take.

I'm quite sure that by now the reader has thought of numerous examples in his or her own experience which qualify as "folly." However, just in case, Table 8.1 presents some additional examples well worth pondering.

CAUSES

Extremely diverse instances of systems which reward behavior A although the rewarder apparently hopes for behavior B have been given. These are useful to illustrate the breadth and magnitude of the phenomenon, but the diversity increases the difficulty of determining commonalities and establishing causes. However, the following four gen-

Table 8.1
Common Management Reward Follies

We hope for . . .	But we often reward . . .
• long-term growth; environmental responsibility	• quarterly earnings
• teamwork	• individual effort
• setting challenging "stretch" objectives	• achieving goals; "making the numbers"
• downsizing; rightsizing; delayering; restructuring	• adding staff; adding budget; adding Hay points
• commitment to total quality	• shipping on schedule, even with defects
• candor; surfacing bad news early	• reporting good news, whether it's true or not; agreeing with the boss, whether or not (s)he's right

eral factors may be pertinent to an explanation of why fouled-up reward systems seem to be so prevalent.

1. Fascination with an "Objective" Criterion	Many managers seek to establish simple, quantifiable standards against which to measure and reward performance. Such efforts may be successful in highly predictable areas within an organization, but are likely to cause goal displacement when applied anywhere else.
2. Overemphasis on Highly Visible Behaviors	Difficulties often stem from the fact that some parts of the task are highly visible while other parts are not. For example, publications are easier to demonstrate than teaching, and scoring baskets and hitting home runs are more readily observable than feeding teammates and advancing base runners. Similarly, the adverse consequences of pronouncing a sick person well are more visible than those sustained by labeling a well person sick. Team-building and creativity are other examples of behaviors which may not be rewarded simply because they are hard to observe.
3. Hyprocrisy	In some of the instances described the rewarder may have been getting the desired behavior, notwithstanding claims that the behavior was not desired. For example, in many jurisdictions within the U.S., judges' campaigns are funded largely by defense attorneys, while prosecutors are legally barred from making contributions. This doesn't do a whole lot to help judges to be "tough on crime" though, ironically, that's what their campaigns inevitably promise.
4. Emphasis on Morality or Equity Rather than Efficiency	Sometimes consideration of other factors prevents the establishment of a system which rewards behavior desired by the rewarder. The felt obligation of many Americans to vote for one candidate or another, for example, may impair their ability

to withhold support from politicians who refuse to discuss the issues. Similarly, the concern for spreading the risks and costs of wartime military service may outweigh the advantage to be obtained by committing personnel to combat until the war is over. The 1994 Clinton health plan, the Americans with Disabilities Act, and many other instances of proposed or recent governmental intervention provide outstanding examples of systems that reward inefficiency, presumably in support of some higher objective.

ALTERING THE REWARD SYSTEM

Managers who complain about lack of motivation in their workers might do well to consider the possibility that the reward systems they have installed are paying off for behavior other than what they are seeking. This, in part, is what happened in Vietnam, and this is what regularly frustrates societal efforts to bring about honest politicians and civic-minded managers.

A first step for such managers might be to explore what types of behavior are currently being rewarded. Chances are excellent that these managers will be surprised by what they find—that their firms are not rewarding what they assume they are. In fact, such undesirable behavior by organizational members as they have observed may be explained largely by the reward systems in use. This is not to say that all organizational behavior is determined by formal rewards and punishments. Certainly it is true that in the absence of formal reinforcement some soldiers will be patriotic, some players will be team oriented, and some employees will care about doing their job well. The point, however, is that in such cases the rewarder is not causing the behavior desired but is only a fortunate bystander. For an organization to act upon its members, the formal reward system should positively reinforce desired behavior, not constitute an obstacle to be overcome.

POSTSCRIPT

An irony about this article's being designated a management classic is that numerous people claim to have read and enjoyed it, but I wonder whether there was much in it that they didn't know. I believe that most readers already knew, and act on in their non-work lives, the principles that underlie this article. For example, when we tell our daughter (who is about to cut her birthday cake) that her brother will select the first piece, or inform our friends before a meal that separate checks will be brought at the end, or tell the neighbor's boy that he will be paid five dollars for cutting the lawn after we inspect the lawn, we are making use of prospective rewards and punishments to cause other people to care about our own objectives. Organizational life may seem to be more complex, but the principles are the same.

Another irony attached to this "classic" is that it almost didn't see the light of day.

It was rejected for presentation at the Eastern Academy of Management and was only published in the *Academy of Management Journal* because Jack Miner, its editor at the time, broke a tie between two reviewers. Nobody denied the relevance of the content, but reviewers were quite disturbed by the tone of the manuscript, and therefore its appropriateness for an academic audience. A compromise was reached whereby I added a bit of the great academic cure-all, data (Table 1 in the original article, condensed and summarized in this update), and a copy editor strangled some of the life from my writing style. In this respect, I would like to acknowledge the extremely competent editorial work performed on this update by John Veiga and his editorial staff. I am grateful to have had the opportunity to revisit the article, and hope the reader has enjoyed it also.

NOTES

1. Originally published in 1975, *Academy of Management Journal* 18: 769–793.

2. Charles Perrow, "The Analysis of Goals in Complex Organizations," in A. Etzioni (ed.), *Readings on Modern Organizations* (Englewood Cliffs, NJ: Prentice-Hall, 1969), 66.

3. Chester I. Barnard, *The Functions of the Executive* (Cambridge, MA: Harvard University Press, 1964), 165.

4. L.H. Garland, "Studies of the Accuracy of Diagnostic Procedures," *American Journal Roentgenological, Radium Therapy Nuclear Medicine* 82 (1959): 25–38; and Thomas J. Scheff, "Decision Rules, Types of Error, and Their Consequences in Medical Diagnosis," in F. Massarik and P. Ratoosh (eds.), *Mathematical Explorations in Behavioral Science* (Homewood, IL: Irwin, 1965).

5. *Miami Herald*, May 8, 1994, 1a, 10a.

6. Goal displacement results when means become ends in themselves and displace the original goals. See Peter M. Blau and W. Richard Scott, *Formal Organizations* (San Francisco, CA: Chandler, 1962).

7. *San Francisco Examiner*, reported in *Fortune*, February 7, 1994, 161.

9

Petty Tyranny in Organizations

Blake Ashforth

INTRODUCTION

The term "petty tyrant" conjures up a host of vivid images. We think of the school teacher who put punctuality and obedience above learning, the bank clerk that insisted we re-do a form because of an insignificant mistake, or the store manager who verbally assaulted a salesperson in front of customers. We think, in short, of an individual who lords his or her power over others.

While the concept appears to be well understood at the intuitive level, there has been surprisingly little research on the nature of petty tyranny in organizations. Although various pathologies of leadership have been identified (e.g., Bennis 1990; Boulding 1990; Kets de Vries 1989), the empirical base is largely anecdotal and impressionistic, and the specific notion of tyranny has seldom been explored. Thus, the purpose of the paper is threefold: (1) to describe managerial petty tyranny in behavioral terms, (2) to propose a set of antecedents of petty tyranny in organizations, and (3) to propose a set of effects that tyrannical management has on subordinates.

Finally, a fourth, underlying purpose is to stimulate interest in the etiologies of ineffective leadership. Most organizational research has focused on the factors associated with effective leadership—with the implicit assumption that ineffective leadership simply reflects the absence of those factors. I maintain that ineffective leadership in general, and petty tyranny in particular, may instead reflect the presence of certain individual and situational factors which foster and sustain the leadership style. Various forms of ineffective leadership, in short, may have their own characteristic etiologies.

THE ORGANIZATIONAL PETTY TYRANT

The management, social psychological, social work, and political science literatures have yielded a host of constructs akin to the notion of petty tyranny. Among others,

From Blake Ashforth, "Petty Tyranny in Organizations," *Human Relations*, vol. 47, no. 7, pp. 755–778. Copyright © 1994 by Sage Publications, Inc. (London). Reprinted by permission of Sage Publications, Inc.

these include the authoritarian personality (Adorno, Frenkel-Brunswik, Levinson, and Sanford 1950; Altemeyer 1988), System 1 manager (Likert 1967), bureaupathic individual (Thompson 1961), abrasive personality (Levinson 1978), dictator (Rubin 1987), wife beater or child abuser (Taubman 1986; Wertsch 1992), and the schoolyard bully (Roberts 1988).

These constructs provide a rich legacy of behavioral descriptions. Recurring elements appear to include: close supervision, distrust and suspicion, cold and impersonal interactions, severe and public criticism of others' character and behavior, condescending and patronizing behavior, emotional outbursts, coercion, and boastful behavior; they suggest an individual who emphasizes authority and status differences, is rigid and inflexible, makes arbitrary decisions, takes credit for the efforts of others and blames them for mistakes, fails to consult with others or keep them informed, discourages informal interaction among subordinates, obstructs their development, and deters initiative and dissent. Pervasive themes in these descriptions are a tendency to overcontrol others and to treat them in an arbitrary, uncaring, and punitive manner. These themes are quite consistent with common definitions of the term "tyrant," such as that offered by *Webster's New Collegiate Dictionary:* "a ruler who exercises absolute power oppressively or brutally." The qualifier "petty" has been added to underscore the theme of arbitrariness and small-mindedness that runs through the various literatures.

As noted, however, the above descriptions have been based largely on observations of cases and events rather than on experimental or systematic survey data. In an effort to remedy this shortcoming, I developed a measure of tyrannical behaviors (Ashforth 1987). Briefly, 562 business students rated their current or most recent manager on an eighty-nine-item scale that incorporated the above descriptions. Forty-five items were derived from existing leadership scales, and forty-four items were generated by the author based in part on a content analysis of the responses of an earlier sample of business students who described actual critical incidents involving a manager they had worked under who had "lorded his or her power." Subsequent factor and item analyses suggested that petty tyranny could be parsimoniously captured by six dimensions (rotated factors), which accounted for 59.4 percent of the variance of the remaining forty-seven items:

1. Arbitrariness and self-aggrandizement (e.g., "Uses authority or position for personal gain," "Administers organizational policies unfairly," " 'Plays favorites' among subordinates").
2. Belittling subordinates (e.g., "Yells at subordinates," "Criticizes subordinates in front of others," "Belittles or embarrasses subordinates").
3. Lack of consideration (e.g., "Is friendly and approachable" [reversed], "Looks out for the personal welfare of group members" [reversed], "Does little things to make it pleasant to be a member of the group" [reversed]).
4. A forcing style of conflict resolution (e.g., "Forces acceptance of his or her point of view," "Demands to get his or her way," "Will not take no for an answer").
5. Discouraging initiative (e.g., "Encourages subordinates to participate in important decisions" [reversed], "Trains subordinates to take on more authority" [reversed], "Encourages initiative in the group members" [reversed]).

6. Noncontingent punishment (e.g., "My supervisor is often displeased with my work for no apparent reason," "I frequently am reprimanded by my supervisor without knowing why," "My supervisor is often critical of my work even when I perform well").

The mean correlation between the dimensions was .58 ($p < .001$). It should be noted that all forty-seven items loaded $> .44$ on the first factor of a principal components analysis. In short, while the six rotated factors speak to the multidimensionality of the construct, the one unrotated factor speaks to a certain coherence among the dimensions.

In a study of tyrannical management, currently in progress, each manager was rated on the forty-seven-item scale by two subordinates. The mean correlation between ratings was $r = .52$ ($p < .01$), which appears comparable to the interrater reliability of other measures of leadership, such as the Leadership Behavior Description Questionnaire (D.R. Day, cited in Bass 1990). Analysis of a multitrait-multimethod matrix (6 dimensions $\times$ 2 subordinates) indicated acceptable convergent and discriminant validity for the measurement of the petty tyrant dimensions.

This preliminary empirical work suggests, then, that the construct of petty tyranny is amenable to survey research methods. While multidimensional, the construct appears to have sufficient integrity for us to speak of organizational petty tyrants. The six dimensions listed above constitute the basis for the subsequent discussion of the antecedents and consequences of petty tyranny in organizations. The proposed model is summarized in Figure 9.1.

A review of the literature suggests that petty tyranny tends to be a joint function of certain individual predispositions and situational facilitators. These factors are discussed sequentially, and then their potential interactions are considered.

Individual Predispositions to Petty Tyranny

The eclectic literature on punitive and arbitrary supervision suggests a host of potential predispositions to tyranny. The predispositions included here are beliefs about the organization (bureaucratic orientation), about subordinates (theory X orientation), about the self (self-esteem), and preferences for action (directiveness, tolerance of ambiguity).

Beliefs About the Organization

Merton's (1968) discussion of the bureaucratic personality and Thompson's (1961) model of the bureaupathic pattern suggest an individual who is domineering, impersonal, inflexible, and insists upon the rights of authority and status. The most frequently used measure of this "bureaucratic orientation" is Gordon's (1973) Work Environment Preference Schedule (WEPS) (see Allinson 1984 for a review). Based on Weber's (1946) description of common bureaucratic characteristics, high scores on the WEPS reflect a willingness to comply with authority, a preference for impersonal and formal relationships with others on the job, a desire for strict adherence to rules and procedures, and a need to identify with the organization and conform to norms. Research on the WEPS has focused on associated personality traits and values rather than on behaviors. Nev-

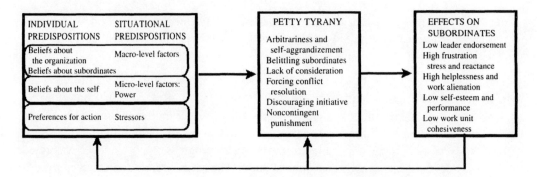

Note: The three ellipses reflect configurations of individual predispositions and situational factors that are
       likely to predict petty tyranny.

       It is not argued that tyrannical behavior fully mediates the impact of the proposed antecedents on the proposed
       effects. It is recognized that certain antecedents may affect certain effects directly or through additional measures.

Figure 9.1. **Proposed Antecedents and Effects of Petty Tyranny**

ertheless, this research is instructive: it suggests that bureaucratically oriented individuals tend to be somewhat insecure, suspicious, authoritarian, dogmatic, and lower in ability, and tend to place a higher value on conformity and order, and a lower value on treating others with consideration (Allinson 1984; Gordon 1973). It should be noted, however, that this research also suggests that such individuals tend to be low on Machiavellianism and dominance, and tend to have an internal locus of control. On balance, it is expected that such an orientation is conducive to overbearing supervision, and thus, is positively associated with tyranny.

Beliefs About Subordinates

McGregor (1960) argues that a certain set of beliefs regarding human nature is widely held by managers. Termed "Theory X," these beliefs include that the average person dislikes work, lacks ambition, avoids responsibility, prefers direction, and is resistant to change. McGregor further argues that managers holding such beliefs often resort to a close, coercive leadership style. In one of the few direct tests of McGregor's arguments, Fiman (1973) found that office supervisors endorsing theory X attitudes were perceived by their subordinates to provide more structure and less consideration. However, these associations held only when theory X endorsement was assessed by subordinates' perceptions rather than by supervisors' self-reports. Following McGregor (1960), it is predicted that such beliefs about subordinates are positively associated with tyrannical supervision.

Beliefs About the Self

Kipnis (1976, p. 120) argues that managers with low self-confidence are less likely to expect "persuasion and other gentle means of influence" to be effective. Consequently, they are more willing to enforce their will through coercive means. This is consistent with the psychodynamic concept of reaction formation, which suggests that individuals may compensate for personal insecurity by overcontrolling others (cf. Kets de Vries and Miller 1984). Thus, Kipnis (1976) found a positive association between managerial self-confidence and expectations of successful influence and a negative association between self-confidence and the endorsement of coercion. Similarly, Raser (1966) contrasted the personalities of totalitarian and democratic political leaders and concluded that totalitarian leaders tend to have lower self-esteem and are more insecure in their private life.

It should be noted, however, that high self-esteem may occasionally contribute to tyrannical behavior. The psychodynamic tendencies of perfectionism, arrogant-vindictiveness, and narcissism are each predicated on unrealistically high self-esteem and frequently lead to such supervisory tendencies as a reliance on fear and intimidation, autocratic and self-centered behavior, and a lack of empathy and consideration (Diamond and Allcorn 1984; Kets de Vries and Miller 1985). It is anticipated, however, that these tendencies are sufficiently rare that they do not materially affect the general, negative association between self-esteem and tyranny.

Preferences for Action

Directiveness is the tendency to impose one's will on others (Ray 1976). Hertzler (1940, p. 167) argues that most political dictators, "dominated by their 'will to be dictator,' have deliberately sought power," and House (1988) argues that individuals high on the need for power experience the acquisition and exercise of power in organizations as more rewarding than do individuals low on the need for power. The construct of directiveness is preferred here because it emerged directly from the classic notion of authoritarianism. As conceived by Adorno et al. (1950), authoritarianism includes a tendency to be dominant toward one's inferiors and submissive toward one's superiors. As Ray (1976) notes, however, authoritarian attitudes (typically measured by variations of the California F-scale) have not consistently predicted submissiveness and there is evidence to suggest that dominance is orthogonal to or even negatively associated with submissiveness (Ray 1981; Ray and Lovejoy 1983; Rigby 1984; however, see Altemeyer 1988). Thus, the concept of directiveness was explicitly formulated to capture "the one irreducible core element in any definition of authoritarianism" (Ray 1981, p. 391). It is predicted that directiveness is positively associated with tyranny.

Tolerance of ambiguity refers to the tendency to perceive an equivocal stimulus as a source of threat (Budner 1962). Equivocality is found in situations characterized by novelty, complexity, or insolubility. Individuals who are intolerant of this equivocality are motivated to impose and preserve a clear and stable order. Thus, intolerance has been associated with rigidity and dogmatism (Feather 1971; Norton 1975). It seems reasonable, then, that intolerance of ambiguity should predict the tendency to over-control subordinates.

Situational Facilitators of Petty Tyranny

The facilitators considered here include macro-level factors (institutionalized values and norms) and micro-level factors (power, stress).

Macro-Level Factors

To some extent, tyrannical behavior may be legitimated by organizational values and norms. "Inmates" in such "total institutions" as prisons, mental hospitals, and army barracks are frequently deindividuated and depersonalized through the use of uniforms, derogatory labels, and other symbols of subordinate status, subjected to debasement and obedience tests and to close, authoritarian supervision, and their activities tend to be tightly regimented (Goffman 1961; Haney, Banks, and Zimbardo 1973). This "institutionalized tyranny" serves to divest inmates of their former identities and to drive home the overriding importance of compliance. Thus, Dyer (1985) notes the " 'good cop-bad cop' manipulation" (p. 113), the punishment for minor rule infractions, and the "constant barrage of abuse and insults" (p. 112) directed at U.S. Marine Corps recruits during basic training. Indeed, Akers (1977) found a high proportion of autocratic and tough inmate leaders in custodial prisons (i.e., closed and punitive), and a high proportion of democratic and benign leaders in treatment-oriented prisons (i.e., open and humane).

To a lesser extent, mechanistic organizations such as auto manufacturers and mechanistic departments such as production may engender tyrannical behavior. Such "machine organizations" (Mintzberg 1989) stress efficient mass production and thus emphasize compliance with centralized decisions and standardized and formalized operating tasks. Accordingly, managers are typically reinforced for exhibiting close, rule-minded supervision. Hofstede (1978) reviewed studies where individuals in control departments were more concerned with the methods of measuring performance than with the content of what was measured, and were less concerned with efficiency and effectiveness than with orderliness and following procedures and schedules. Further, following House (1988), the reliance on hierarchical stratification—coupled with pervasive symbols of status and authority—tends to reduce inhibitions against coercive supervision.

Relatedly, a disproportionate number of "entrepreneurial organizations" (Mintzberg 1989) may evidence tyranny. Kets de Vries (1989) argues that many entrepreneurs are susceptible to: (1) a strong need for independence and control, (2) distrust of others, and (3) a desire for applause. To a certain point, these characteristics help fuel the entrepreneurial spirit.

Past that point, however, these characteristics may induce an entrepreneur to meddle with minute operating details, question the actions and motives of subordinates, hoard information, set others up as scapegoats, and so on. Moreover, given that organizations frequently institutionalize the values and norms of the founder, these tendencies may eventually give way to an institutionalized tyranny that survives the entrepreneur.

In support, Ashforth (1987) found that tyrannical managers were overrepresented in machine and entrepreneurial organizations and underrepresented in Mintzberg's (1989) "professional" and "innovative" organizations.

("Tyrannical managers" were operationalized as individuals falling one standard deviation or more above the mean on the 47-item measure described earlier.) The critical difference between the two sets of organizational types is the degree of centralization: while machine and entrepreneurial organizations tend to be centralized, professional and innovative organizations tend to be decentralized as work is controlled by the experts who comprise the operating cores. Decentralization provides less latitude and tolerance for overbearing supervision. Similarly, Ashforth (1987) also found that at the departmental level, tyrants were overrepresented in such units as production and production support, and branch/office/store/restaurant management. Thus, it appears that tyrannical behavior is disproportionately found in departments and organizations that value compliance with centralized decisions and/or standardized tasks.

It should be noted that the term "institutionalized values and norms" is meant to suggest that organizations often facilitate the emergence of petty tyranny rather than that they actively promote tyranny per se. Except for some extreme cases (such as concentration camps, e.g., Levi 1961), few organizations condone the arbitrary and abusive use of authority inherent in the notion of petty tyranny.

Micro-Level Factors

Powerlessness is defined broadly as an absence of the necessary means—the skills, authority, credibility, autonomy, opportunities for participation, resources, and so forth—to cope with task demands and to influence events that directly affect one. Individuals who perceive that they are relatively powerless often lord what power they do have and put a certain "psychological distance" between themselves and subordinates or others dependent on them (Kanter 1977; Kipnis 1976).

This lording and distancing serve several purposes: (1) given relatively low power, the individual believes that milder forms of influence will not suffice, (2) lording and distancing enhance self-perceptions of superiority and self-efficacy, and (3) distancing affirms the legitimacy of hierarchical control and justifies its use (House 1988; Kipnis 1976). Overcontrol, in short, becomes a tonic for the relatively powerless. Thus, supervisors with low power in a federal bureaucracy were more likely to play favorites and exhibit close and controlling leadership (South, Bonjean, Corder, and Markham 1982), and tyrannical managers from a variety of organizations were perceived by subordinates to have less influence over subordinates and over individuals and issues outside the department (Ashforth 1987). The associations in the latter study, however, were undoubtedly inflated by common method variance since subordinates also provided the tyranny ratings.

Ironically, the opposite conditions may also engender tyranny. Kipnis (1976; Kipnis, Castell, Gergen, and Mauch 1976) argues that the acquisition and successful use of power tends to corrupt the powerholder in several respects: (1) power becomes an end in itself, (2) the powerholder develops an exalted sense of self-worth, (3) power is used increasingly for personal rather than organizational purposes, and (4) the powerholder devalues the worth of others. The greater the power differential and the stronger and more controlling the means of influence (e.g., rewards, coercion), the more inclined is the manager to attribute subordinates' successes to managerial control rather than to the subordinates themselves, and the less inclined are subordinates to openly question the manager. Accordingly, the manager comes to believe that he or she can do no wrong, that he or she should not be bound by the same constraints as others, and that subordinates must be closely supervised.

Thus, the greater one's power, the more assertive and demanding one tends to be (Kipnis 1972). In an experimental simulation of a prison environment, Haney et al. (1973) randomly assigned subjects to the role of either guard or prisoner. During the six-day simulation, Haney et al. found that the guards began—and quickly escalated—harassing and degrading the prisoners "even after most prisoners had ceased resisting and prisoner deterioration had become visibly obvious to them" (p. 92), and appeared to experience this sense of power as "exhilarating" (p. 94). It should be noted, however, that individuals do appear to differ in their predisposition to exercise power coercively (see the following discussion).

Considering the arguments for low and high power simultaneously, it thus appears that tyrannical behavior is associated with power in a U-shaped function, such that petty tyranny tends to be lowest for moderate power. Additionally, these arguments may interact to form a particularly pernicious combination. Following Roberts' (1988) analysis of schoolyard bullies, petty tyranny may be particularly likely where one is relatively powerless with respect to one's superiors but relatively powerful with respect to one's subordinates ("A big fish in a little pond"). One compensates for the former by overcontrolling the latter.

Finally, stressors may also contribute to petty tyranny. Stressors tend to prompt more directive leadership (Bass 1990). First, subordinates under stress tend to look to their managers to provide strong, task-oriented leadership. This is particularly true if the stress is caused by a crisis. Second, managers tend to respond to stressors by becoming more directive. Thus, Mulder, De Jong, Koppelaar, and Verhage (1986) found that the subordinates of bank officers perceived more "forceful" behavior under crisis conditions, but more consultative behavior under noncrisis conditions. This "forcefulness," however, can become excessive. Janis (1982) reports that under stress, decision making tends to become more centralized, hasty, and arbitrary, and Hertzler (1940) concludes that most political dictatorships arise and become entrenched during periods of social disorder and crisis. Similarly, the literature on burnout suggests that individuals subject to chronic stressors often withdraw psychologically from others, treating them more like objects than people (Maslach 1982). Further, one may justify this stance by blaming others ("My subordinates are unable to take the initiative") and developing derogatory stereotypes. Thus, Lee and Ashforth (1993) found that social work managers experiencing emotional exhaustion tended to depersonalize their subordinates and clients. In extreme cases, one may even take perverse pleasure in abusing others.

Interactions of Individual Predispositions and Situational Facilitators

Perhaps the most intriguing issue is the extent to which each of the proposed antecedents is necessary and/or sufficient to prompt petty tyranny. It is likely that each individual and situational factor is capable of prompting at least sporadic instances of tyranny (e.g., a highly stressed manager snaps at her secretary). Thus, each antecedent is argued to constitute a main effect. However, these main effects are likely to be relatively weak as the growing literature on interactionism suggests that no individual or situational factor alone is generally sufficient to sustain ongoing organizational behavior (Mitchell and James 1989)—including tyrannical behavior. Rather, ongoing petty tyranny may be a function of certain configurations of individual and situational factors.

There are, potentially, many such configurations. However, three seem particularly likely to predict tyrannical behavior. First, certain beliefs about the organization and about subordinates may combine with the macro-level factor of institutionalized values and norms to provoke tyranny. Managers who subscribe to a bureaucratic orientation and to a theory X conception of subordinates should find greater acceptance of these beliefs in organizations and departments that value compliance with centralized decisions and standardized tasks. This acceptance may translate into a higher tolerance for tyrannical behavior—indeed, it may even legitimate and normalize such behavior. A prototypical (perhaps stereotypical) example of this configuration is the military drill sergeant (cf. Dyer 1985).

A second potential configuration involves beliefs about the self—perhaps complemented by beliefs about the organization and subordinates—and the micro-level factor of power. As noted, the acquisition and successful use of power may enhance self-perceptions, legitimate one's position, and compensate for a perceived personal inability to influence others. However, McClelland's (1985) work indicates that individuals differ in the degree to which they are psychologically constrained from exercising power in socially undesirable ways. Individuals with low "power inhibition" are more apt to act in a tyrannical manner (House 1988). I would argue that self-esteem is one critical variable that affects this felt inhibition. Following social identity theory (Ashforth and Mael 1989), individuals with high self-esteem may be better able to buffer their personal identity from their social identity as powerholder and thus maintain some psychological distance from the seductive qualities of the latter. Accordingly, consistent with the literature cited earlier, individuals with low self-esteem are likely to find the seductive qualities of power particularly attractive and feel less constrained in their use of power. A prototypical example of a tyrant in this configuration is the martinet who defines himself largely by the work he does (Ashforth and Mael 1992).

A third potential configuration involves preferences for action and the micro-level factor of stressors. As noted, managers tend to respond to stressors by behaving more dictatorially. This tendency may be exacerbated by a predisposition to directiveness and by a low tolerance for ambiguity. Regarding the former, individuals subject to stress tend to rely upon well-learned patterns of behavior (Staw, Sandelands, and Dutton 1981), and, as noted, this particular pattern is to a certain extent functional and normatively expected during troubling times. Regarding the latter, the lower the tolerance for ambiguity, the more likely that a given stressor will be perceived as a threat, and thus, the more likely that one will respond in a controlling manner.

As noted, these three proposed configurations are only a subset of the many possibilities. Given the absence of research on the issue, such interactionist arguments are clearly speculative.

EFFECTS OF PETTY TYRANNY ON SUBORDINATES

Petty tyranny may affect all members of one's role set—clients, peers, subordinates, superiors, and so on—as well as the general interpersonal climate. The following discussion of effects, however, is restricted to subordinates because: (1) they are hierarchically dependent and are thus a frequent target of tyrannical behaviors, and (2) the extent to which petty tyrants display different behaviors to less dependent members of the role set is not clear. A review of the literature suggests five interdependent sets of effects of tyrannical behavior on subordinates: (1) leader endorsement, (2) frustration, stress, and reactance, (3) helplessness and work alienation, (4) self-esteem and performance, and (5) work unit cohesiveness.

Leader Endorsement

Vecchio and Sussmann (1989) report that individuals express lower satisfaction with managers who utilize influence techniques that contravene their preferences. Not surprisingly, then, a litany of field and laboratory studies indicate that the behaviors associated with petty tyranny tend to undermine leader endorsement. Arvey, Davis, and Nelson (1984) found that childish, petty, and inconsistent discipline was negatively associated with supervisor satisfaction among hourly employees in a refinery; in a study of training programs in two wholesaling and retailing firms, Hebden (1986) reports that managers who made unexplained and arbitrary decisions undermined trainees' trust in the managers and their firms; and reviews of laboratory research indicate that inequitable action by a leader reduces the endorsement of the leader (Hollander and Julian 1970; Michener and Lawler 1975).

Two provisos, however, are necessary. First, research on leader-member exchange theory indicates that managers frequently display different patterns of behavior toward different subgroups of subordinates (Dienesch and Liden 1986). This may be particularly true of tyrannical managers since they appear to play favorites and may pursue a divide and conquer strategy. Thus, a petty tyrant may have one or more "lieutenants" who endorse his or her leadership. However, since the relationship between a tyrant and his or her lieutenants tends to be based on a calculated exchange of services—often supported by implicit threat—rather than an affective commitment (Miller, Weiland, and Couch 1978), this endorsement is contingent on the relative power and the respective needs of the parties and is thus inherently fragile.

The second proviso pertains to the psychodynamic notion of "identification with the aggressor" where one assumes the attributes of an aggressor so as to be transformed "from the person threatened into the person who makes the threat" (A. Freud, in Kets de Vries and Miller 1984, p. 140). This defense mechanism protects one from the anxiety caused by the aggressor. Although anecdotal evidence suggests that the process does occur in organizations (e.g., Kets de Vries and Miller 1984), it appears to be a fairly extreme reaction and is more likely to occur in total institutions where one has little or no hope of avoiding the aggressor (e.g., Bettelheim 1943). Thus, it is unlikely to occur to a significant extent in most organizations.

Frustration, Stress, and Reactance

Spector (1978) defines frustration as the interference with goal-oriented activity and goal maintenance. The more complete and persistent the interference, the greater the frustration. Frustration is experienced as a negative emotional state. Motowidlo, Packard, and Manning (1986) define stress in similar terms, that is, as an unpleasant emotional experience associated with elements of fear, anxiety, irritation, and the like. Petty tyranny likely engenders frustration and stress in several respects: (1) arbitrary decisions and noncontingent punishment may create fear and anxiety as well as unpredictability which thwarts planning and goal-directed activity, (2) forcing conflict resolution and discouraging initiative may interfere with subordinates' ability to affect their tasks and work unit, and (3) belittling subordinates and withholding considerate behaviors may create fear and anxiety and threaten the maintenance of self- and social esteem. Indeed, Miller et al. (1978) argue that some tyrants act capriciously and punitively to ensure that subordinates remain uncertain and anxious and thus attentive to the tyrant's every whim.

Field and laboratory research provide support. Myers (1977) found a significant association between coercive and punitive supervisory behavior and the prevalence of fear, anxiety, and anger among subordinates. Nurses reported higher stress when doctors were verbally abusive toward them, became angry at them for something which was not their fault, wasted their time on nonnursing tasks, and publicly criticized them (Motowidlo et al. 1986). In laboratory studies, Shaban and Welling (in Glass and Singer 1972) found that officious and inconsiderate behavior by a laboratory clerk fostered irritation among subjects, and Baron (1988) found that destructive criticism fostered more anger and tension than did constructive criticism.

Further, reactance theory suggests that people react against perceived causes of frustration in either a direct problem-focused manner to regain control or in an indirect nonproblem-focused manner to assert their hegemony (Ashforth 1989). Thus, in a study of production workers, Ashforth (1989) found that the higher the unmet expectations and desires for control and the lower the perceived legitimacy of supervision, the greater the reactance—as operationalized by frequency of complaining, bending or breaking rules, criticizing people, reducing productivity, acting against someone's wishes, arguing, and acting angrily toward others or toward things. Similar behaviors have been reported for subordinates subject to arbitrary and punitive supervision (e.g., Katz, Maccoby, Gurin, and Floor 1951).

It should be noted, however, that reactance is apt to be indirect and covert. Given the tendency of petty tyrants to overcontrol subordinates and to punish deviations, direct and overt reactance against the tyrant is likely to have a high cost and a low probability of success. Thus, Clarke (1985, p. 37) reports that in confrontations with "sadistic managers," the "rebellious employees always lost." Under such conditions, it is not long before employees learn to be more selective in venting their frustration.

Helplessness and Work Alienation

Helplessness is defined as the perception that outcomes are independent of behaviors (Ashforth 1989). Petty tyrants likely foster helplessness in several respects: (1) by discouraging initiative and closely controlling subordinates, tyrants reduce subordinates' autonomy, (2) by restricting communication, tyrants reduce subordinates' opportunities for participation and for understanding the work environment, and (3) through arbitrariness and noncontingent punishment, tyrants render the work environment unpredictable. In the simulated prison environment, Haney et al. (1973) noted a "pathological prisoner syndrome" in response to guards' frequent harassment and capricious behavior. This syndrome "was one of passivity, dependency, depression, helplessness and self-deprecation" (p. 89). Further, helplessness may be exacerbated if the direct reactance discussed above is indeed discovered to be futile. Thus, Ashforth (1989) found a significant association between reactance and helplessness among shopfloor production workers.

Work alienation is defined as a sense of separation of the individual from work and the workplace (Ashforth 1989). The tyrannical elements of overcontrol, arbitrariness, and punitiveness may erode a subordinate's psychological attachment to the job and organization. Clarke (1985) discusses how the subordinates of sadistic managers tended to withdraw either physically in terms of leaving the unit or organization, or psychologically in terms of ceasing to care and becoming passive and less creative. Similarly, Barton (1976) notes how the bossiness of staff in total institutions contributes to an "institutional neurosis," including lack of initiative, disinterest, and general resignation.

Self-Esteem and Performance

Petty tyranny may undermine a subordinate's self-esteem through several mechanisms: (1) belittling a subordinate may chip away at his or her sense of competence and self-worth, (2) discouraging initiative and forcing conflict resolution implicitly devalues a subordinate's contributions, and (3) withholding consideration devalues a subordinate's worth as a unique individual with personal needs and concerns. Indeed, Miller et al. (1978) argue that some tyrants systematically destroy subordinates' self-esteem so as to render them more compliant and less of a potential threat to the tyrant. Thus, Clarke

(1985, p. 37) notes the "plummeting self-confidence" of some subordinates of sadistic managers. Kohli (1985), however, found no association between autocratic and punitive managerial behavior and the job-specific self-esteem of salespeople.

Relatedly, petty tyranny may affect subordinates' task performance. On the one hand, close and punitive supervision may induce defensive conformity to the tyrant's wishes (Ashforth and Lee 1990; Warren 1968), particularly on tasks that are easily observed or verified. In Kelman's (1958) terms, such conformity would reflect the social influence process of compliance rather than identification with the tyrant or internalization of the merit of the demands.

On the other hand, the increasing sense of helplessness and work alienation, and the decreasing sense of self-worth, may reduce subordinates' intrinsic motivation and receptiveness to the tyrant's edicts. Further, some subordinates may choose to reduce performance as an indirect means of reacting against tyrannical management. Also, for complex tasks in particular, the use of noncontingent punishment and arbitrariness and the absence of positive reinforcement and constructive feedback may inhibit task learning. Finally, petty tyranny may reduce the frequency of organizational citizenship behaviors by violating the sense of trust upon which such behaviors are typically predicated (Organ 1988).

Field and laboratory research in fact suggests that tyrannical behavior tends to undermine performance. Field studies indicate that coercive power tends to be negatively related or unrelated to subordinate performance (Podsakoff and Schriesheim 1985). Experimental research found that destructive criticism led to lower self-set goals and performance on a proofreading task (though not on a clerical task) than did constructive criticism (Baron 1988); close and punitive supervision impaired performance on a model building task (Day and Hamblin 1964); and in the previously noted study by Shaban and Welling (in Glass and Singer 1972), the officious and inconsiderate behavior of the laboratory clerk led to more proofreading errors and cheating. On balance, then, it appears that tyrannical behavior is negatively associated with subordinate performance. Note, however, that this research has generally focused on fairly simple tasks rather than on complex tasks or organizational citizenship behaviors.

It should also be noted that the association between petty tyranny and subordinate self-esteem and performance may be partly attributable to differential selection and attrition. First, tyrants may be more inclined to select compliant and mediocre (i.e., nonthreatening) subordinates (e.g., Kets de Vries 1980). Second, high-esteem and high-performing subordinates may chafe more under tyrannical management and have greater mobility than low-esteem or low-performing subordinates. Hamblin (1964) reported that punitive supervision in a manufacturing plant caused the greatest frustration and resentment among workers with a high achievement orientation.

Work Unit Cohesiveness

Finally, petty tyranny may undermine social solidarity. On the one hand, it can be argued that tyrannical behavior may drive subordinates together as a collective defense against the tyrant and to provide a much-needed sense of social support. Van Maanen and Kunda (1989, p. 66) describe how the close and seemingly arbitrary and punitive supervisory practices at an amusement park helped draw ride operators together to "shield one another." However, the literature suggests that managers often utilize punitiveness and tight control deliberately as a wedge to keep subordinates apart. For example, Arendt (1973) and Miller et al. (1978) argue that tyrannical political leaders intentionally sow distrust among subordinates to prevent coalitions from arising and to increase subordinates' dependence on the leader. Additionally, following the notion of "displaced aggression," subordinates may prefer to vent their frustration against one another rather than challenge the more powerful manager. However, an experiment by Day and Hamblin (1964) provided only mixed support for this argument. Finally, tyrannical supervision may foster a negative work unit climate which inhibits the emergence of cohesion. On balance, this suggests that tyrannical behavior is negatively associated with subordinates' cohesion.

A Vicious Circle

Like the proposed antecedents of petty tyranny, the proposed effects on subordinates are obviously somewhat interdependent. For example, frustration and lack of leader endorsement have been linked to reactance, and helplessness has been linked to work alienation (Ashforth 1989; Spector 1978).

Further, as depicted in Figure 9.1, such behavior may trigger a vicious circle such that the effects prompt even greater petty tyranny. First, elaborating on an earlier discussion, the exercise of power often induces a manager to:

(1) attribute subordinates' successes to himself or herself rather than to the subordinates, (2) develop an inflated sense of self-worth, (3) prefer greater psychological distance from subordinates, and (4) view subordinates as objects to be manipulated (Kipnis 1976; Kipnis et al. 1976). Second, as Sunar's (1978) analysis of the dynamics between powerful and powerless groups attests, the various effects of tyranny—helplessness, low commitment, and so forth—may foster or strengthen a negative stereotype of subordinates (e.g., lazy, untrustworthy) which justifies further coercion. Thus, experimental research indicates that leaders encountering low endorsement and high reactance are more likely to use coercion to secure compliance (Zelditch and Walker 1984), and leaders encountering declining subordinate performance are more likely to act in an autocratic and punitive manner (Barrow 1976). To the extent these behaviors further reduce leader endorsement and incite reactance, the vicious circle becomes complete. Indeed, given the often traumatic array of cognitive, affective, and behavioral adjustments caused by petty tyranny, a subordinate's disaffection with the tyrant may generalize to other managers and to the organization as a whole.

This notion of a vicious circle helps explain why a manager may persist with such a patently ineffective leadership style (Ashforth 1991). Supported by defensive attributions and self-fulfilling attitudes and behaviors, he or she may be unable or unwilling to recognize the role that these attitudes and behaviors play in the genesis of the very behaviors he or she is presumably trying to prevent. Further, tyrannical behavior may command at least short-term attentiveness and compliance, which may seduce a manager to discount the longer-term, more disruptive effects—especially if the labor supply is abundant. Finally, once triggered, the initial individual predispositions and situational facilitators may no longer be necessary to sustain the vicious circle. In sum, this process suggests a "tyrant's paradox": the very means used to gain control undermines the viability of that control.

This analysis clearly indicates that, to the extent a manager's overall effectiveness depends on his or her subordinates' effectiveness, tyrannical behaviors will be negatively associated with managerial effectiveness. This conclusion, however, warrants three qualifications. First, insofar as petty tyranny does command compliance, it may be utilized to secure bursts of heightened activity or quick responses to emergent crises. However, given the emphasis on compliance, the utility may be restricted to relatively structured and easily monitored tasks (Warren 1968). Also, given the negative effects on subordinates described earlier, any utility may be restricted to the short run. Second, it remains unclear how petty tyrants behave vis-à-vis their peers, superordinates, and individuals outside the organization (e.g., clients, suppliers). It is quite conceivable that one may act differently—and more effectively—toward these groups than toward one's subordinates, particularly if one has less power over the former. For example, as noted, Adorno et al. (1950) maintain that authoritarian individuals behave differentially toward those in authority. Third, as argued earlier, tyrannical behaviors may be tolerated if not tacitly encouraged in certain institutional settings. Thus, such behaviors may be viewed as effective within the normative framework of the institution. Indeed, the normative framework may include ready justifications for tyrannical behaviors (e.g., employees are unmotivated). This discussion suggests, then, that managers who behave tyrannically toward their subordinates will not necessarily be ineffective in discharging all of their various duties.

DISCUSSION AND CONCLUSION

A petty tyrant was defined as an individual who lords his or her power over others. More specifically, preliminary research suggests an individual who acts in an arbitrary and self-aggrandizing manner, belittles subordinates, evidences lack of consideration, forces conflict resolution, discourages initiative, and utilizes noncontingent punishment.

A model of the antecedents and consequences of petty tyranny was presented. It was argued that tyrannical behavior is a function of individual predispositions, including beliefs about the organization (bureaucratic orientation), about subordinates (theory X orientation), and about the self (self-esteem), and preferences for action (directiveness, tolerance of ambiguity), as well as situational facilitators, including macro-level factors (institutionalized values and norms) and micro-level factors (power, stressors). The effects of petty tyranny on subordinates were argued to include low leader endorsement, self-esteem, and work unit cohesiveness, poor performance, and high frustration, stress, reactance, helplessness, and work alienation. Finally, it was argued that these effects may trigger a vicious circle which sustains the tyrannical behavior and makes it resistant to change.

Research Implications

Given the anecdotal and impressionistic nature of much of the research on petty tyranny in organizations, a more rigorous survey approach appears to be warranted. The model of tyranny presented here is clearly amenable to such an approach. Perhaps the biggest obstacle to survey research is the likelihood that petty tyrants' reports of their behavior and its effects on subordinates will be biased by defensive attributions, social desirability, and so forth. Indeed, as suggested earlier, many tyrants may be unaware of their behavior and its effects. A second major obstacle is common method variance, particularly since perceptions of tyrannical behaviors may strongly color perceptions of both the proposed antecedents and effects of tyranny.

These concerns may be addressed by several methods. One method, currently in progress, would be to sample managers from a diverse range of organizations, departments, and hierarchical levels. This would provide variance in the proposed situational antecedents and some evidence of the general incidence and distribution of petty tyranny in organizations. To counter the obstacles discussed above, each manager could assess the proposed antecedents of tyranny, and one set of his or her subordinates could assess the degree of managerial tyranny while another set could assess the proposed effects. Further, a key issue at this early stage of construct development is the construct validity of the multidimensional measure of petty tyranny. The use of multiple respondents would facilitate the assessment of this or other such measures (Bagozzi, Yi, and Phillips 1991). This method might also incorporate a longitudinal design to capture the feedback loops that are argued to sustain the vicious circle. Finally, given that individuals tend initially to view a given leader in very positive terms (i.e., "honeymoon period," Hollander 1985), such a design could also capture the process of disillusionment that underlies the proposed effects of petty tyranny.

A second method would be to have individuals nominate a set of managers in their organization who lord their power and a set of managers who do not lord their power. This procedure is consistent with Phillips and Lord's (1986) discussion of classification-level accuracy (vs. behavioral-level accuracy) in leadership assessment. They suggest that classifying leaders into categories—in this case, tyrannical and nontyrannical—capitalizes on individuals' propensity to form holistic perceptions of others and on the salience of such categorical perceptions. For each nominated manager, individuals other than the initial nominators could then assess the proposed effects of petty tyranny while the manager and others could assess the proposed antecedents. Discriminant analysis would then be used to ascertain the antecedents and effects that discriminate between the two categories of managers. A similar approach was utilized by Smith (1982) to identify and compare charismatic and noncharismatic managers.

These survey methods could be complemented by other methods, such as participant observation, interviews, and content analyses of published accounts of prominent organizational leaders. Clearly, this does not exhaust the list of possible methods. To increase the likelihood of finding petty tyrants, one could target organizations and positions thought to facilitate the emergence of tyranny, such as machine organizations and retail stores. Of particular interest are the "big fish in a little pond" positions described earlier, where a manager is relatively powerless with respect to superiors but relatively powerful with respect to subordinates.

Additional Research Issues

The discussion of the nature and etiology of petty tyranny in organizations raises numerous questions for future research. Examples include:

1. How do petty tyrants become managers and how do managers become petty tyrants? Are there "early warning signals," or do tyrannical tendencies only become manifest in certain roles? How common is petty tyranny?
2. What role do subordinates play in the dynamics of petty tyranny? Do certain kinds of subordinates encourage or discourage tyrannical behavior? What mechanisms govern the process of identification with the aggressor? To what extent do subordinates mimic the behavior of a tyrannical manager in their dealings with clients or with their own subordinates? How and to what extent do tyrants select favored "lieutenants"?
3. How do petty tyrants interact with their clients, peers, and superiors? Are tyrants deferential toward authority, as Adorno et al.'s (1950) classic formulation of authoritarianism suggests? To what extent is the tyrant aware of his or her behavior, and how comfortable is he or she with it? How does he or she interpret and justify the behavior to themselves and to others?
4. What becomes of the tyrannical manager? What factors moderate and mediate the effectiveness and longevity of a tyrannical career? To what extent do certain organizations tolerate or encourage petty tyranny? What are the mechanisms by which tyranny becomes institutionalized? How might individuals and organizations curb abuses of authority, and how might subordinates cope with tyrannical managers?

CONCLUSION

Incidents involving arbitrary and abusive management are regularly reported in the popular press. This regularity, and the variety of organizations in which the incidents occur, suggests that the "petty tyrant"—one who lords his or her power—is not a rare individual. Yet, the scholarly literature contains only impressionistic accounts of such individuals. It is hoped that this model of the phenomenon of petty tyranny will stimulate interest in the etiologies of ineffective leadership in general, and in this especially pernicious form of leadership in particular.

REFERENCES

Adorno, T.W., Frenkel-Brunswik, E., Levinson, D.J., and Sanford, R.N. 1950. *The Authoritarian Personality.* New York: Harper and Row.

Akers, R.L. 1977. Type of leadership in prison: A structural approach to testing the functional and importation models. *Sociological Quarterly* 18: 378–383.

Allinson, C.W. 1984. *Bureaucratic Personality and Organisation Structure.* Aldershot, England: Gower.

Altemeyer, B. 1988. *Enemies of Freedom: Understanding Right-Wing Authoritarianism.* San Francisco: Jossey-Bass.

Arendt, H. 1973. *The Origins of Totalitarianism* (2nd ed.). New York: Harcourt Brace Jovanovich.

Arvey, R.D., Davis, G.A., and Nelson, S.M. 1984. Use of discipline in an organization: A field study. *Journal of Applied Psychology* 69: 448–460.

Ashforth, B.E. 1987. Organizations and the petty tyrant: An exploratory study. Paper presented at the annual meeting of the Academy of Management, New Orleans, Louisiana, 1987.

———. 1989. The experience of powerlessness in organizations. *Organizational Behavior and Human Decision Processes* 43: 207–242.

———. 1991. The whys and wherefores of organizational Catch-22s: Common types and their implications for organization development. *Public Administration Quarterly* 14: 457–482.

Ashforth, B.E., and Lee, R.T. 1990. Defensive behavior in organizations: A preliminary model. *Human Relations* 43: 621–648.

Ashforth, B.E., and Mael, F. 1989. Social identity theory and the organization. *Academy of Management Review* 14: 20–39.

———. 1992. The dark side of organizational identification. Paper presented at the Annual Meeting of the Academy of Management, Las Vegas, Nevada.

Bagozzi, R.P., Yi, Y., and Phillips, L.W. 1991. Assessing construct validity in organizational research. *Administrative Science Quarterly* 36: 421–458.

Baron, R.A. 1988. Negative effects of destructive criticism: Impact on conflict, self-efficacy, and task performance. *Journal of Applied Psychology* 73: 199–207.

Barrow, J.C. 1976. Worker performance and task complexity as causal determinants of leader behavior style and flexibility. *Journal of Applied Psychology* 61: 433–440.

Barton, R.L. 1976. *Institutional Neurosis* (3d ed.). Bristol, England: Wright.

Bass, B.M. 1990. *Bass and Stogdill's Handbook of Leadership: Theory, Research, and Managerial Applications* (3rd ed). New York: Free Press.

Bennis, W. 1990. *Why Leaders Can't Lead: The Unconscious Conspiracy Continues.* San Francisco: Jossey-Bass.

Bettelheim, B. 1943. Individual and mass behavior in extreme situations. *Journal of Abnormal and Social Psychology* 38: 417–452.

Boulding, K.E. 1990. *Three Faces of Power.* Newbury Park, CA: Sage.

Budner, S. 1962. Intolerance of ambiguity as a personality variable. *Journal of Personality* 30: 29–50.

Clarke, N.K. 1985. The sadistic manager. *Personnel* 62(2): 34–38.

Day, R.C., and Hamblin, R.L. 1964. Some effects of close and punitive styles of supervision. *American Journal of Sociology* 69: 499–510.

Diamond, M.A., and Allcorn, S. 1984. Psychological barriers to personal responsibility. *Organizational Dynamics* 12(4): 66–77.

Dienesch, R.M., and Liden, R.C. 1986. Leader-member exchange model of leadership: A critique and further development. *Academy of Management Review* 11: 618–634.

Dyer, G. 1985. *War.* Toronto: Stoddart.

Feather, N.T. 1971. Value differences in relation to ethnocentrism, intolerance of ambiguity and dogmatism. *Personality* 2: 349–366.

Fiman, B.G. 1973. An investigation of the relationships among supervisory attitudes, behaviors, and outputs: An examination of McGregor's Theory Y. *Personnel Psychology* 26: 95–105.

Glass, D.C., and Singer, J.E. 1972. *Urban Stress: Experiments on Noise and Social Stressors.* New York: Academic Press, 1972.

Goffman, E. 1961. *Asylums: Essays on the Social Situation of Mental Patients and Other Inmates.* Garden City, NY: Anchor Books.

Gordon, L.V. 1973. *Work Environment Preference Schedule: Manual.* New York: The Psychological Corporation.

Hamblin, R.L. 1964. Punitive and nonpunitive supervision. *Social Problems* 11: 345–359.

Haney, C., Banks, C., and Zimbardo, P. 1973. Interpersonal dynamics in a simulated prison. *International Journal of Criminology and Penology* 1: 69–97.

Hebden, J.E. 1986. Adopting an organization's culture: The socialization of graduate trainees. *Organizational Dynamics* 15(1): 54–72.

Hertzler, J.O. 1940. Crises and dictatorships. *American Sociological Review* 5: 157–169.

Hofstede, G. 1978. The poverty of management control philosophy. *Academy of Management Review* 3: 450–461.

Hollander, E.P. 1985. Leadership and power. In G. Lindzey and E. Aronson (eds.), *Handbook of Social Psychology* (3d ed., vol. 2). New York: Random House, pp. 485–537.

Hollander, E.P., and Julian, J.W. 1970. Studies in leader legitimacy, influence, and innovation. In L. Berkowitz (ed.), *Advances in experimental social psychology* (vol. 5). New York: Academic Press, pp. 33–69.

House, R.J. 1988. Power and personality in complex organizations. In B.M. Staw and L.L. Cummings (eds.), *Research in Organizational Behavior* (vol. 10). Greenwich, CT: JAI, pp. 305–357.

Janis, I.L. 1982. Decisionmaking under stress. In L. Goldberger and S. Breznitz (eds.), *Handbook of Stress: Theoretical and Clinical Aspects.* New York: Free Press, pp. 69–87.

Kanter, R.M. 1977. *Men and Women of the Corporation.* New York: Basic Books.

Katz, D., Maccoby, N., Gurin, G., and Floor, L.G. 1951. *Productivity, Supervision and Morale Among Railroad Workers.* Ann Arbor, MI: Institute for Social Research, University of Michigan.

Kelman, H.C. 1958. Compliance, identification, and internalization: Three processes of attitude change. *Journal of Conflict Resolution* 2: 51–60.

Kets de Vries, M.F.R. 1980. *Organizational Paradoxes: Clinical Approaches to Management.* London: Tavistock.

———. 1989. *Prisoners of Leadership.* New York: Wiley.

Kets de Vries, M.F.R., and Miller, D. 1984. *The Neurotic Organization: Diagnosing and Changing Counterproductive Styles of Management.* San Francisco: Jossey-Bass.

———. 1985. Narcissism and leadership: An object relations perspective. *Human Relations* 38: 583–601.

Kipnis, D. 1972. Does power corrupt? *Journal of Personality and Social Psychology* 24: 33–41.

———. 1976. *The Powerholders.* Chicago: University of Chicago Press.

Kipnis, D., Castell, P.J., Gergen, M., and Mauch, D. 1976. Metamorphic effects of power. *Journal of Applied Psychology* 61: 127–135.

Kohli, A.K. 1985. Some unexplored supervisory behaviors and their influence on salespeople's role clarity, specific self-esteem, job satisfaction, and motivation. *Journal of Marketing Research* 22: 424–433.

Lee, R.T., and Ashforth, B.E. 1993. A longitudinal study of burnout among supervisors and managers: Comparisons between the Leiter and Maslach (1988) and Golembiewski et al. (1986) models. *Organizational Behavior and Human Decision Processes* 54: 369–398.

Levi, P. 1961. *Survival in Auschwitz: The Nazi Assault on Humanity* (translated by S. Wolf). New York: Collier.

Levinson, H. 1978. The abrasive personality. *Harvard Business Review* 56(3): 86–94.

Likert, R. 1967. *The Human Organization: Its Management and Value.* New York: McGraw-Hill.

Maslach, C. 1982. *Burnout: The Cost of Caring.* New York: Prentice-Hall.

McClelland, D.C. 1985. *Human Motivation.* Glenview, IL: Scott, Foresman.

McGregor, D. 1960. *The Human Side of Enterprise.* New York: McGraw-Hill.

Merton, R.K. 1968. *Social Theory and Social Structure* (rev. ed.). New York: Free Press.

Michener, H.A., and Lawler, E.J. 1975. Endorsement of formal leaders: An integrative model. *Journal of Personality and Social Psychology* 31: 216–223.

Miller, D.E., Weiland, M.W., and Couch, C.J. 1978. Tyranny. In N.K. Denzin (ed.), *Studies in Symbolic Interaction* (vol. 1). Greenwich, CT: JAI, pp. 267–288.

Mintzberg, H. 1989. *Mintzberg on Management: Inside Our Strange World of Organizations*. New York: Free Press.

Mitchell, T.R., and James, L.R. (eds.) 1989. Theory development forum: Situational versus dispositional factors: Competing explanations of behavior. *Academy of Management Review* 14: 300–407.

Motowidlo, S.J., Packard, J.S., and Manning, M.R. 1986. Occupational stress: Its causes and consequences for job performance. *Journal of Applied Psychology* 71: 618–629.

Mulder, M., De Jong, R.D., Koppelaar, L., and Verhage, J. 1986. Power, situation, and leaders' effectiveness: An organizational field study. *Journal of Applied Psychology* 71: 566–570.

Myers, R.J. 1977. Fear, Anger and Depression in Organizations: A Study of the Emotional Consequences of Power. Unpublished doctoral dissertation, St. John's University, Jamaica, New York.

Norton, R.W. 1975. Measurement of ambiguity tolerance. *Journal of Personality Assessment* 39: 607–619.

Organ, D.W. 1988. *Organizational Citizenship Behavior: The Good Soldier Syndrome*. Lexington, MA: Lexington Books.

Phillips, J.S., and Lord, R.G. 1986. Notes on the practical and theoretical consequences of implicit leadership theories for the future of leadership measurement. *Journal of Management* 12: 31–41.

Podsakoff, P.M., and Schriesheim, C.A. 1985. Field studies of French and Raven's bases of power: Critique, reanalysis, and suggestions for future research. *Psychological Bulletin* 97: 387–411.

Raser, J.R. 1966. Personal characteristics of political decision makers: Peace research and society. *International Papers* 5: 161–181.

Ray, J.J. 1976. Do authoritarians hold authoritarian attitudes? *Human Relations* 29: 307–325.

———. 1981. Authoritarianism, dominance and assertiveness. *Journal of Personality Assessment* 45: 390–397.

Ray, J.J., and Lovejoy, F.H. 1983. The behavioral validity of some recent measures of authoritarianism. *Journal of Social Psychology* 120: 91–99.

Rigby, K. 1984. Acceptance of authority and directiveness as indicators of authoritarianism: A new framework. *Journal of Social Psychology* 122: 171–180.

Roberts, M. 1988. School yard menace. *Psychology Today* 22(2): 52–56.

Rubin, B. 1987. *Modern Dictators: Third World Coup Makers, Strongmen, and Populist Tyrants*. New York: McGraw-Hill.

Smith, B.J. 1982. An initial test of a theory of charismatic leadership based on the responses of subordinates. Unpublished doctoral dissertation, University of Toronto.

South, S.J., Bonjean, C.M., Corder, J., and Markham, W.T. 1982. Sex and power in the federal bureaucracy: A comparative analysis of male and female supervisors. *Work and Occupations* 9: 233–254.

Spector, P.E. 1978. Organizational frustration: A model and review of the literature. *Personnel Psychology* 31: 815–829.

Staw, B.M., Sandelands, L.E., and Dutton, J.E. 1981. Threat-rigidity effects in organizational behavior: A multilevel analysis. *Administrative Science Quarterly* 26: 501–524.

Sunar, D.G. 1978. Stereotypes of the powerless: A social psychological analysis. *Psychological Reports* 43: 511–528.

Taubman, S. 1986. Beyond the bravado: Sex roles and the exploitive male. *Social Work* 31: 12–18.

Thompson, V.A. 1961. *Modem Organization*. New York: Alfred A. Knopf.

Van Maanen, J., and Kunda, G. 1989. "Real feelings": Emotional expression and organizational culture. In L.L. Cummings and B.M. Staw (eds.), *Research in organizational behavior* (vol. 11). Greenwich, CT: JAI, pp. 43–103.

Vecchio, R.P., and Sussmann, M. 1989. Preferences for forms of supervisory social influence. *Journal of Organizational Behavior* 10: 135–143.

Warren, D.I. 1968. Power, visibility, and conformity in formal organizations. *American Sociological Review* 33: 951–970.

Weber, M. 1946. *Essays in Sociology* (translated and edited by H.H. Gerth and C.W. Mills). New York: Oxford University Press.

Wertsch, M.E. 1992. *Military Brats: Legacies of Childhood Inside the Fortress.* New York: Ballantine.

Zelditch, M., Jr., and Walker, H.A. 1984. Legitimacy and the stability of authority. In E.J. Lawler (ed.), *Advances in Group Processes* (vol. 1). Greenwich, CT: JAI, pp. 1–25.

10

The Illusion of Self-Management: Using Teams to Disempower

Charles C. Manz and Harold L. Angle

Self-management and self-managing teams have usually been regarded as the opposite of "boss" control; they are associated with doing business without bosses. This view of self-management, however, has been challenged. Some authors, for example, have suggested that close external supervision is not always inconsistent with self-management.[1] When requirements of a job and the information needed to do it are unclear, some management that defines the job's limits can aid a self-managed employee. In fact, defining the limits of employee discretion can be the primary management task. Nevertheless, these limits can significantly constrain and control self-managed employees. As a result, apparent self-management can sometimes be more of an illusion than a reality.

Such challenges to the conventional view of self-management can enrich our understanding of various degrees of employee self-influence. Perhaps it is unrealistic ever to view self-management as a complete absence of external control. On the contrary, people, behavior, and the external environment influence one another.[2] Furthermore, self-management behavior itself requires some support and reinforcement; it can be very difficult for employees to self-manage without encouragement and incentives from the organization.

The important point is that self-management does not operate in a vacuum. Many external factors foster or constrain the process. One important set of external influences involves the dynamics of work groups within which self-managed employees often find themselves.

This [article] describes an independent insurance firm, specializing in industrial casualty loss coverage, that had recently introduced self-managing work teams. This story is especially interesting because the teams were introduced in an industry that historically has tended to emphasize individual self-management. In this case, however, introducing teams actually placed limits on individual freedom and control. The [article]

From Charles C. Manz and Harold L. Angle, "The Illusion of Self-Management: Using Teams to Disempower," pp. 115–129, in Charles C. Manz and Henry P. Sims Jr., (eds.), *Business Without Bosses*, copyright 1993 by John Wiley & Sons, Inc. This material is used by permission of John Wiley & Sons, Inc.

addresses the question, "In an industry having a deeply ingrained cultural norm of individualism, can team self-management come to represent a loss of personal control?"

THE COMPANY AND THE TEAM SYSTEM

The organization is an independent property and casualty insurance firm that employed 32 people at the time we studied it. The firm was founded in 1941—a time when the independent operation, consisting of one or two agents supported by one or two secretaries, was the industry standard. Typically, even when multiagent organizations were established, these tended to be loose associations of loners, each having a network of highly personal relationships with clients. As a rule, there was little need for coordination, and each account executive operated within a set of rules and procedures, as a relatively independent agent.

In the mid-1970s, changes in the legislative environment led to strong competitive pressures in the insurance industry. Efficiency (e.g., in developing client insurance programs, in collection policies) and synergy (optimizing combined efforts) in the efforts of different persons within an agency became very important. Many of the single-agent establishments were either forced out of business or forced to merge into multiagent organizations. Despite the economic pressures that made such changes necessary, this move was frequently a difficult transition for agents accustomed to autonomy.

Less than a year before we began our research, a recently hired vice president and chief operating officer became acting chief executive officer (CEO). One of his initial acts was to restructure the firm into a set of self-managing work teams. The team philosophy was explained to the employees when the system was introduced, and teams were encouraged to make decisions and solve their problems jointly.

The work system appeared similar to designs used in self-managing team applications in other industries. Within established company guidelines, work teams were expected to be self-managing units that carried out the activities needed for acquiring and servicing accounts cooperatively. The intent of the CEO appeared to be to pass on what were formerly management responsibilities to the teams, with the intended result of more efficient work performance. At the same time, it was apparent that the CEO felt that the company needed to increase its organization and coordination of work efforts. He hoped that the teams would help him achieve efficiencies that would boost the firm's profitability. Thus, although the teams were similar in appearance to self-managing teams found in other work settings (in which team members coordinate their efforts on tasks and work together to solve team problems and make joint decisions), they were apparently implemented with the objective of increasing organizational control from the top—to increase the influence of bosses.

Under the new system, three teams were created. The senior team consisted of the senior, more experienced sales producers (an industry term for agents who bring in premium money), along with administrative assistants (referred to as production assistants) and other support personnel. The junior team was similar in design except that its members were the more junior producers in the firm. Finally, the small accounts team was made up entirely of administrative personnel (no sales producers were included) and handled all small accounts (those that brought in annual premiums less than $500). Our primary focus is on the dynamics that occurred in the senior and junior teams following the introduction of the self-managed team system.

ORGANIZATION THEMES

The Research

Through a series of interviews, two group meetings with team members, a questionnaire, and observing the organization at work, we discovered several themes that reveal how teams were used to disempower employees.

At two group meetings, one for members of the senior team and one for members of the junior team, we asked, "Considering the recent change to the team system, how has the change: (a) helped you, and (b) hindered you in accomplishing what you would like to in your job?" First, team members, independently and silently, generated written lists of answers to the question. After a discussion of the combined ideas generated from all the lists, each individual privately rated each item on a scale ranging from 1 (very important) to 5 (not at all important).

Interviews were conducted with employees at all levels of the organization. First, a series of interviews was conducted with the CEO over a period of about four months. The CEO was very articulate and appeared to be open and candid, as well as highly motivated to provide complete information during the interviews. Each interview session with him lasted about two hours and was kept flexible to focus on issues that emerged during the course of the discussions. Interviews were also conducted with seven members from the senior and junior teams.

Our observations of the work system during each of our visits to the organization led to a better general understanding of the team system and provided valuable insights that helped us to interpret the other information we collected. Finally, we prepared a questionnaire based in part on information obtained from our other study methods. The questionnaire focused on such issues as employees, satisfaction, feelings of autonomy, degree of cooperation, performance, and quality of service to clients. Based on these sources, we discovered four primary themes.

Team Rationale: Self-Management—or Coordination, Efficiency, and Control?

This was the most important theme; the team concept did provide some distinct coordination and efficiency advantages. One junior team member noted that the work system "helps us to be more organized, especially for producers who do not follow procedures." Each team was expected to meet approximately once per week. Initial meetings often focused on company rules and procedures. Junior team members, in particular, told us that these first meetings had been badly needed and were quite productive. Also, given the diversity of job functions on each team (sales producers, production assistants, marketing personnel, and others) meetings provided a forum to discuss and coordinate work flow issues.

The junior team identified several organization and efficiency advantages: clarifying individual responsibility for work, developing a more uniform approach to account handling, facilitating system development and definition and understanding of responsibilities, and designating specific responsibility for special problems. The senior team identified similar issues, including providing more consistent customer service and developing greater knowledge of a smaller number of accounts. Similarly, the questionnaire indicated that the team approach made it clear who was responsible for what.

Efficiency was apparently a high priority of the acting CEO. Senior team members described him as "an efficiency man" and "the most organized man I know. He may be too organized." Junior team members indicated, "He helped me be more organized" and "Before he came, there was a low level of organization in both the people and the firm."

Over time, however, tension emerged concerning this emphasis on efficiency and organization. The agenda of team meetings continued to focus on procedural issues, a tendency apparently fostered by leaders of each team (both team leaders were administrators—a production assistant on the junior team and the marketing specialist on the senior team), whose jobs were made easier when procedures were followed closely by the producers in the team. (The team leaders were selected by the teams, but the acting CEO significantly influenced this process.)

Many individuals expressed frustration with the perceived overemphasis on procedures, indicating on the questionnaire that the new system had resulted in "unnecessary paperwork." An obvious distaste was expressed for the firm's procedural manual, which some team members described as highly detailed ("our bible"). But when we examined this manual, we discovered that it was rather brief—almost an elaborated pamphlet— and limited to a small set of apparently crucial procedural matters. We concluded that overstructuring may be in the eye of the beholder. Perhaps team members' perception of the amount of structure imposed on them was distorted by the frustration they experienced when their expectations and preferences for individual autonomy were violated.

The strong emphasis on rules and procedures in the team system appeared to threaten the sales producers' autonomy and discretion. Team members were pressured to perform a variety of activities dictated by the organization's approach rather than based on their own personal styles. For example, freedom to service small but loyal accounts—a high priority under the old system—was essentially removed. In fact, the questionnaire suggested that producers, particularly on the senior team, felt they had inadequate autonomy. The group meetings, interviews, and questionnaire responses indicated that if the company's procedures were rigidly enforced, individual autonomy for the producers would be very limited. The boundaries placed on self-management would be seen as so restrictive that the remaining area of discretion would be perceived as inconsequential.

In this company, self-managing teams were operating as vehicles for limiting autonomy. One possible conclusion is that these were not self-managing teams at all but merely traditional groups falsely labeled as "self-managing." On the other hand, the external trappings appeared quite similar in design to self-managing teams in other settings. Even so, the process that was unfolding here was in many respects limiting, rather than increasing the freedom for employees to manage themselves. Again, a major reason for this outcome may be the emphasis placed on the small-group process as a means for clarifying and enforcing rules and procedures rather than for empowering employees. Another may be the standard of comparison that the members brought to the teams. An individual's perception of autonomy is largely based on a relative, rather than absolute, standard of comparison. The producers who were members of these teams had been relatively autonomous under the old system, even though the agency itself was somewhat bureaucratic. Each producer, although not explicitly told that he was "self-managed" (all were male), was able to set his own priorities, work schedule, and the like, without first having to reach consensus with others.

Interestingly, the two teams appeared to perceive the external control pressures differently. The senior team members seemed to sense the primary threat to their autonomy as stemming from having to cooperate with other team members. The senior team leader described the situation in this way: "Senior producers are on a constant ego trip. Under the team system we have a democratic ideal. This is hard work. We have several different personalities. These people don't know how to cooperate." A senior producer told us in an interview that if he could change the work system, he would return to a system of independent producers with assigned support staff. He added, "The old system was like a profit center. You could do things."

The junior team seemed to be especially frustrated with the emphasis on rules and procedures. They tended to associate control pressures more with the organization (the work system) and with the personal agenda of their leader than with their team itself. The team was, in fact, viewed more as a source of support than a constraint. One junior producer described his team as providing a place to "compare notes [to share knowledge] with others" and a mechanism for bringing "different types [producers, production assistants and marketing people] together."

The questionnaire (and our other information sources) provided support for this pattern of differences between the two teams. The junior team reported a greater feeling than the senior team of a "pressure to produce results" and "organization conformity pressure." It also reported a slightly lower "team conformity pressure."

Although these perceptual differences between teams are interesting, the primary theme remains the apparent trade-off between the self-managing team system and personal control. Most published studies of self-managing teams have dealt with occupations and situations in which the work prior to the teams was highly structured, so a change to teams caused an increase in autonomy. In many traditional manufacturing and service work settings, introduction of self-managing teams has led to substantial worker autonomy relative to the industry norm. In this organization, by contrast, the change may have been in the opposite direction. Visualize a continuum with one pole representing complete anarchy and the other total control. Somewhere in the middle range is the autonomy interdependence represented by self-managing teams. Whether teams represent autonomy to the participant depends on his or her prior location on the continuum. In this particular setting, to a large degree, team self-management was introducing a loss of personal self-management—the opposite effect of business without bosses.

Reduced Customer Service and Organizational Unity

The emphasis on work teams in the firm had two other significant impacts—a loss of agency identity and reduced customer service on small accounts—both especially troubling to senior team members. Senior team members generally reported that the system promoted team unity, but they felt a sense of agency unity was lost. Outside their team, other sales producers would not possess the knowledge to follow up on a sales producer's accounts if he or she were absent. Team members reported that separation between units caused employees to lose sight of the whole; the system led to a loss of loyalty to the agency; no "young backups" were developed for older producers' accounts; and so forth.

Also, the separation of all small accounts into a third team—one that had no sales producers—troubled senior team members. One member put it this way: "We've lost control and communications on small accounts . . . lost our purpose of serving clients better." A major reason that this bothered some producers was that some small account personal policies were owned by key contacts for large organizational policies. One producer recounted a story in which a policyholder was given notice of cancellation of a personal policy for being a few days overdue on his premium payment. This client also happened to be the company representative on a very large corporate policy (worth hundreds of thousands of dollars). Since the personal policy was handled by administrators in the small accounts team, no special effort was made to provide special service in dealing with this problem.

Team members jointly described the problem in the senior team meeting in the following (composite) way: "The system does not go far enough. It should not split one producer's accounts. Accounts should be divided by producer, not by size. With the system we no longer manage personal accounts as a spinoff from large ones; we lose coordination. We lose brother, sister, aunt, and uncle generated by personal contact." Overall, it was clear (particularly in the senior team) that the self-managing team system was constraining a number of sales producers from servicing small accounts in the way they would if they operated on an individual basis. Here, too, the attempt at achieving efficiency and organization within the system was limiting the discretion and self-management of sales producers.

Education and Training Impacts the Level of Self-Management

Another primary theme concerned the education and training of sales producers. Both the senior and junior teams generally agreed that interaction with others enabled team members to learn from one another, a particularly important benefit for younger, less experienced sales producers. But a disadvantage of the team system was that it created roadblocks between junior producers and senior producers. There was a tendency for team members to be isolated from the activities of other teams.

In the senior team meeting, for example, two of the concerns recorded were "lose benefit of people in the other team . . . cheats inexperienced people of education" and "can't introduce young producers to senior accounts without crossing team lines." Similarly, junior producers were reluctant to go to the other team for help. As one senior producer pointed out, junior producers need "education, guidance, and motivation." His view was that the current system discouraged senior, experienced producers from helping junior people with these needs.

This concern with the education of sales producers is quite consistent with the primary focus of this [article]. The issue of personal freedom involves self-constraints as well as external constraints. The development and learning of the young, inexperienced sales producers is important for providing them with the skills and confidence necessary for effective performance. Sharing ideas and concerns with fellow inexperienced producers in a team setting was viewed as being helpful in this regard. Separation of the senior, more experienced producers, who presumably have the knowledge junior producers need, was considered by many employees to be detrimental.

Leadership Practices

The fourth theme centered on leadership practices within the work system. The issue of team leader assignments was a special concern for the junior team. The acting CEO of the firm had made his desired choice for the position known, and this person was subsequently selected by the team. The team leader was generally respected for her work ability, but her concerns did not reflect those of the majority of team members. Two different sales producers, in separate interviews, said flatly that their team leader's conduct of the meetings focused on "the production assistants' concerns" (procedures). In contrast, the production assistants thought that the team system did provide individual freedom but too little attention to established procedures!

There was a natural conflict of interest between producers and production assistants in this regard. Producers wanted freedom from the red tape of procedures, while production assistants wanted procedures to be carefully followed to reduce their own hassles. The junior team leader apparently chose to focus on this latter concern in meetings, to the dismay of producers. In the team meeting (which included the team leader), one producer said the term of a team leader is too long and should be limited to three months. This was probably as negative a response as could be made in the presence of the team leader. One producer expressed confusion and obvious irritation about how the leader got the position to begin with. Over time, the meetings became shorter and shorter and, in the eyes of most participants, nonproductive. They also became less frequent as, apparently, the incentives for attending were not sufficiently strong.

The acting CEO responded by putting pressure on the teams to be productive and by attending meetings and prodding members to participate—strikingly inconsistent with the principle of self-management and business without bosses. He took pride in his ability to get employees to do what he wanted them to do. For example, he stated, with satisfaction, he could direct his employees to participate in our study. Although he stated that participation in the study should be voluntary, his offer to make it mandatory provided an interesting contrast. Along the same lines, our interviews revealed that the "self-managing" work system itself was instituted without the participation or consent of employees. Our extensive interviews with the acting CEO led us to conclude that he was sincerely committed philosophically to employee participation, but his espoused theory was inconsistent with his theory in use.[3] This contradiction supported our general impressions of the work system: the introduction of work teams was leading to a loss of individual self-management for employees.

As a result, senior producers, who did not need significant moral support from their peers (to develop confidence and skills), were not motivated to support the new system, and junior sales producers, who did need this moral support, were frustrated by their nonrepresentative, procedure-focused team leadership. Eventually team meetings became infrequent and nonproductive, employee skepticism and apathy regarding the team approach rose, and efficiency and coordination plummeted.

The final piece of evidence of employee feelings of reduced autonomy came from answers to our question, "How is the direction of the organization's activities established?" The responses could range from "democratically" to "autocratically." The average response was significantly above the midpoint toward "autocratically."

IMPLICATIONS FOR BUSINESS WITHOUT BOSSES

The story told in this [article] is especially interesting because it examines a setting in which an industry-wide reliance on autonomy and individual self-management is traditional. Our findings suggested a paradox: team self-management can result in a loss of individual control. Leadership practice, group peer pressure, a focus on rigid procedures, and restrictions on junior producers' exposure to experienced role models combined to undermine individual discretion and self-management.

It is important to view this [article] in the light of the uniqueness of the organizational setting. In no way do we mean to suggest that the experience of one service organization indicates that self-managing work teams are inherently threatening to personal self-management and business without bosses. This particular situation contained a number of characteristics specific to this firm and to this industry—one in which individual autonomy has been a norm. As the insurance industry has been forced to examine new ways of organizing to improve efficiency in the face of deregulation, tightening markets, and increasing competition, independent insurance salespersons have been confronted with some new restrictions on their freedom and autonomy. Against this backdrop, self-managing work teams apparently served as a convenient vehicle for increasing control over employees and for gaining some advantages in efficiency—a noteworthy challenge to the universal applicability of conventional wisdom regarding the impact of self-managing teams. In some instances, a "self-managing" team system may serve as a control mechanism that is actually more constraining than the system it replaces.

This story points to a need to understand self-managing teams in work contexts beyond manufacturing settings that have previously emphasized external control. As teams continue to spread through service and white-collar settings, we need answers to several important questions:

1. Under what conditions does the introduction of self-managing teams increase worker autonomy, and under what conditions does it reduce autonomy?
2. How do self-managing teams facilitate employee learning and development, and under what conditions do they limit it?
3. What behaviors are appropriate for self-managing team leaders, and how should their behavior vary according to work setting?
4. What results can be expected from placing self-managing teams in service organizations? How do these results contrast with those found in manufacturing settings?
5. What effect does technological interdependence have on the effectiveness of teams? Does an absence of interdependence suggest that teams may be less useful in certain settings?
6. How does the reward system influence team effectiveness? Are individual incentives inconsistent with a team philosophy?
7. What self-management alternatives capture some of the benefits of employee empowerment without introducing work teams? For example, is individual-based self-management more appropriate in some work settings?[4]
8. How can we ensure that the introduction of self-managing teams advances the objective of business without bosses? What are some key warning signals that a team system is producing more boss control and less self-management?

Some unexpected results can occur when self-managing teams are introduced under nontraditional circumstances. If team members are not involved in establishing team responsibilities, the design of a work system that emphasizes rules and procedures can lead to oppressive boss control of work team members, especially in situations in which employees already possessed a significant amount of autonomy and self-management.

Our final meeting with the CEO (who had become president of the organization) provided a fitting conclusion. We asked if perhaps he had really intended to use the "self-managing" teams to extend and amplify his personal influence and control. He agreed: "Every reason for doing the team system was control." At least in this executive's view, there is no inconsistency in labeling such groups "self-managing"!

The implications of this story are compelling. Depending on the objectives pursued by self-managing teams, the nature of the setting in which they are put in place, and the way that they are implemented and maintained, team-based self-management has the potential for undermining individual discretion, autonomy, and initiative. Business with more boss control, not less, can be the result.

NOTES

This [article] is based in part on material previously published in Charles C. Manz and Harold Angle, "Can Group Self-Management Mean a Loss of Personal Control: Triangulating on a Paradox,"

Group and Organization Studies 11 (1986): 309–334. The original research was partially funded by a grant from the Operations Management Center at the University of Minnesota. The authors are grateful to John Guarino and Rosemarie Orehek for their valuable assistance in data collection. Because of the sensitive nature of the information in this story, the name of the organization is confidential.

1. See, for example, Peter K. Mills, "Self-Management: Its Control and Relationship to Other Organizational Properties," *Academy of Management Review* 8 (1983): 445–453; Peter K. Mills and Barry Z. Posner, "The Relationship Among Self-Supervision, Structure and Technology in Professional Service Organizations," *Academy of Management Journal* 25 (1982): 437–443.

2. See, for example, Albert Bandura, *Social Learning Theory* (Englewood Cliffs, NJ: Prentice-Hall, 1977), and his "The Self-System in Reciprocal Determinism," *American Psychologist* 33 (1978): 344–358.

3. For more information on the tendency for views espoused by managers to be inconsistent with what they actually do, see Chris Argyris, "Leadership, Learning and the Status Quo," *Organizational Dynamics* 9 (1980): 29–43.

4. For more information on individual employee (as well as team-based self-management and self-leadership), see Charles C. Manz, *Mastering Self-Leadership: Empowering Yourself for Personal Excellence* (Englewood Cliffs, NJ: Prentice-Hall, 1992); Charles C. Manz and Henry P. Sims, Jr., *Super Leadership: Leading Others to Lead Themselves* (New York: Berkley, 1990).

11

Problems with the Pygmalion Effect and Some Proposed Solutions

Susan S. White and Edwin A. Locke

In their classic 1968 book, Rosenthal and Jacobson described an experiment in which they told a group of elementary school teachers that an intelligence test had identified some of their students as "late bloomers." The teachers were told to expect that these students would blossom in the coming year. In actuality, the children labeled as late bloomers were chosen at random. At the end of the year, the intelligence test was readministered to the students. Whereas the late bloomers and the control students had the same average score at the beginning of the year, the late bloomers' average score was significantly higher than that of the control group at the second administration of the test. Interestingly, the teachers were unaware of having treated the experimental and control subjects differently. The Pygmalion effect (put in a managerial context) can be defined as the finding that leader expectations for subordinate performance can subconsciously affect leader behavior and subordinate performance.

Although the Pygmalion effect was originally demonstrated in a classroom setting with teachers and pupils, it has also been discussed with respect to therapists and clients (Jenner 1990), nurses and patients (Learman, Avorn, Everitt, and Rosenthal 1990), and managers and employees (Eden 1990). Much of the Pygmalion research that has been directed toward organizational settings has been conducted by Eden and his colleagues. Their careful attention to experimental manipulation and control has led us a long way toward understanding the nature of the Pygmalion effect and its mediators.

This article is primarily concerned with the limitations of the Pygmalion effect in terms of its routine applicability to organizational settings. It has been found that the Pygmalion effect holds less well for female rather than male leaders and for existing rather than newly formed subordinate groups (Jordan 1977; McNatt 1997; Raudenbush 1984). Furthermore, the Pygmalion effect operates subconsciously and is therefore out of conscious control, and the deceptive manipulations that have been used to produce it raise ethical questions when used in organizational settings. Finally, efforts to train managers explicitly to be Pygmalions have largely failed (Eden 1996; Eden et al. in press). Here, we review these problems that limit the application of the Pygmalion effect to the workplace and recommend solutions to them.

It is essential to understand the limitations and boundary conditions of the Pygmalion effect if it is to be applied with routine success in the workplace. The workplace today differs in important ways from the school and military settings from which much of our knowledge of the Pygmalion effect has been derived. Most workplace situations involve mixtures of men and women, as well as experienced and new employees, and the Pygmalion effect may not work equally well for all of these groups. Furthermore, litigation concerning workplace behavior is increasingly placing limits on how employees can be treated (Blodgett and Carlson 1997), raising questions about the wisdom of using deceptive manipulations. Our intent is not to provide a comprehensive review of Pygmalion research since such reviews exist already (e.g., Cooper 1979; Eden 1990, 1992; Jordan 1977). Rather, we provide only a summary of this body of work, expanding previous reviews by focusing on the limitations of the Pygmalion effect.

HISTORY OF PYGMALION RESEARCH

The Rosenthal and Jacobson (1968) study spawned hundreds of demonstrations that teacher expectations could play a measurable role in students' performance (Rosenthal 1994). The results were not accepted unequivocally and criticisms of the research continue to be published today (e.g., Snow 1994). Nonetheless, as Jordan (1977) stated,

> As the dust surrounding this controversy begins to settle, it is becoming increasingly clear that under certain conditions, as yet not completely specified, teacher expectations do serve as self-fulfilling prophecies. (p. 1)

That is, what teachers expect of students can impact the performance of the students—in certain situations. For example, the length of time over which manipulated expectations were operating was cited as a boundary condition on teacher expectation effects.

The Pygmalion effect was tested in organizational settings almost immediately after its introduction to the classroom. Livingston (1969) published a discussion of the implications of the Pygmalion effect for management, arguing that what managers expect from subordinates significantly affects subordinates' performance and careers. Moving into a military setting, Eden and Shani (1982) experimentally verified Livingston's ideas on the Pygmalion effect using trainees and instructors of Israeli Defense Force (IDF) training courses. A random sample of trainees was identified to the training instructors as having exceptionally high command potential, and this group subsequently outperformed the control groups of trainees on four objective exams. Eden and Shani's (1982) replication of the Pygmalion effect was important because of the marked differences between the characteristics of their sample and the typical sample used to demonstrate the Pygmalion effect: adult Israeli soldiers as opposed to American schoolchildren. This suggested that the Pygmalion effect was generalizable beyond the original school setting where it was discovered and replicated.

The finding that a Pygmalion effect could be created in the setting of an IDF training course has since been replicated a number of times (Eden 1990; Eden and Ravid 1982). Furthermore, the Pygmalion effect has been demonstrated in other noneducational settings. For example, nurses and aides in a nursing home were led to believe that some patients would progress more quickly than others with their rehabilitation, and these patients actually exhibited fewer depressive tendencies and were admitted to hospitals less frequently than average-expectancy patients (Learman et al. 1990). (The high-expectancy patients, however, demonstrated less ability than average-expectancy patients in performing activities required for daily living.) The Pygmalion effect has also been discussed in the treatment of alcohol abuse; it has been suggested that if therapists labeled their clients as "motivated," the clients would drop out of treatment less frequently than if they were labeled "unmotivated" (Jenner 1990).

References to the effects of the Pygmalion effect and self-fulfilling prophecies are also ubiquitous in the organizational literature. For example, the labels assigned to work teams early in their lives have been discussed as examples of self-fulfilling prophecies (Saavedra, Cohen, and Denison 1990). Furthermore, assigned goals have been discussed in terms of the expectations that they convey to subordinates (Locke and Latham 1990).

MEDIATORS OF THE PYGMALION EFFECT

Leadership

The Pygmalion effect has been largely explained in terms of two mediators: leadership behavior and self-expectations. The first of these, leadership, was identified by Rosenthal as the mechanism through which teachers' differential expectations for students were subconsciously translated into differential behavior and performance. For example, the teachers tended to create a warmer, friendlier climate for high-expectancy students, displaying behaviors associated with positive emotional attraction (e.g., smiling). In addition, teachers have been shown to give high-expectancy students more challenging assignments, as well as more positive, constructive feedback (Cooper 1979; Harris and Rosenthal 1985; Rosenthal 1994). Eden and Shani (1982) also found leadership to be a mediator of the Pygmalion effect: the overall leadership ratings assigned to instructors by the high command potential trainees were higher than those assigned by the control group trainees. Further discussion of this study in Eden (1990) revealed that the instructors were rated more positively on all four specific dimensions of the Bowers and Seashore (1966) managerial leadership questionnaire. These dimensions capture leaders' efforts (1) to coach subordinates in effective work habits, (2) to stimulate enthusiasm for meeting a goal or achieving excellent performance, (3) to enhance others' feelings of importance and self-worth, and (4) to encourage members to form relationships and work together as a team. Notably, the instructors in the Eden and Shani study were unaware of having treated the trainees differently, even after a debriefing session in which the experimental manipulation was revealed. The finding is consistent with Rosenthal's idea that the special way in which instructors treat high-expectations people is not consciously intended or deliberate.

Missing from Bowers and Seashore's (1966) four factors are aspects of leadership that explicitly convey the managers' expectations to their subordinates. This can involve a myriad of leadership behaviors that Eden describes as Pygmalion leadership style (PLS) (Eden 1990, 1992, 1996). Although leaders in Pygmalion studies have reported being unaware of treating subordinates differently based on expectations (Eden and Shani 1982), PLS appears to include both deliberate and subconscious elements. PLS involves

> ... consistent encouraging, supporting, and reinforcing of high expectations resulting in the adoption, acceptance, or internalization of high expectations on the part of the subordinates. In the simplest and most straightforward instance, it is a manager reassuringly telling a subordinate 'I know you can do this well.' This message can be transmitted in an endless variety of ways. The hallmark of an effective leader is his ability to get this message across convincingly and to inspire high self-confidence among the other persons around him. (Eden 1990, p. 125)

Self-Expectations and the Galatea Effect

The second mediator of the Pygmalion effect is the direct result of PLS: self-expectations (Eden 1990). That is, the leadership behaviors captured by PLS in turn lead subordinates to raise their own expectations for how well they can perform. In a study set in an IDF training course, Eden and Ravid (1982) found that raising instructors' expectations for certain trainees resulted not only in higher performance for those trainees (the Pygmalion effect), but also in those trainees' having higher expectations for themselves. Furthermore, this study found that raising the trainees' expectations directly by telling certain trainees, not their instructors, that they had high potential also resulted in higher performance levels for these trainees.

Eden and Ravid (1982) labeled the effect of directly manipulating subordinates' self-expectations the *Galatea* effect. Examining the Galatea and Pygmalion conditions together, Eden (1990) reported that the experimental manipulations explained 32 percent of the variance in performance scores before controlling for self-expectations, whereas they explained only 6 percent after. Thus, self-expectations are an important mediator of the expectations-raising manipulations, although they do not fully mediate the effect.

Over the years, the definition of the Galatea effect has become blurred. It has essentially been expanded to include almost any situation in which differences in self-expectations result in differences in performance. As mentioned previously, the Galatea effect was originally defined as the result of raising subordinates' self-expectations directly by telling them that they had high potential, but Eden (1990) also described the positive impact of leaders' expectations (conveyed consciously or subconsciously via PLS) on self-expectations as a Galatea effect.

Furthermore, some studies said to demonstrate the Galatea effect focus more on building self-efficacy beliefs through modeling than on directly manipulating expectations. For example, in what they termed a Galatea study, Eden and Aviram (1993) combined behavioral modeling techniques with mastery opportunities and verbal persuasion to significantly increase the self-efficacy levels of a group of unemployed vocational workers. In turn, these workers searched more actively for jobs and found jobs more quickly than control subjects. Furthermore, Eden and Kinnar (1991) used modeling techniques and verbal persuasion to raise the self-efficacy of a group of students for performing in the special forces of the IDF, while a control group was presented with a routine information program. The results showed that the experimental group had a higher volunteer rate than the control group, and the authors labeled this a Galatea effect. In sum, recent demonstrations of the Galatea effect have essentially been exercises in building self-efficacy. The previous discussion indicates that the Galatea effect could be created in a number of different ways. It could occur (a) as an unintended consequence of the classic Pygmalion effect (e.g., as a consequence of nondeliberate but differential treatment by the leader, which affects subordinate expectations) or (b) as a result of deliberate expectancy communications by a third party to the leader-subordinate relationship (e.g., an experimenter telling a subordinate "I know you are good"). The Eden and Ravid (1982) study discussed previously supports both of these conceptualizations of the Galatea effect. In addition, the Galatea effect has been discussed as (c) the result of indirect expectancy communications by the leader. One way of communicating expectancies indirectly would be through role modeling (Eden and Aviram 1993; Eden and Kinnar 1991). Subordinates might develop high expectations for themselves if they are provided with models of high levels of performance for them to follow. Also, expectations might be communicated indirectly through demonstrations of such Bowers and Seashore (1966) leadership behaviors as stimulating enthusiasm for meeting a goal or enhancing feelings of self-worth. As leaders convince subordinates that they can reach certain goals or that they have high self-worth, the subordinates may develop high expectations for themselves as an indirect result of their leaders' behaviors. This is different from the Galatea (b) effect where subordinates are explicitly told that they should have high expectations for themselves.

Finally, with no manipulation from experimenters or leaders, subordinates likely differ in terms of their self-expectations. That is, there might be a trait-like consistency to the expectations that people hold about what they can accomplish across a variety of tasks and situations (Eden 1990). A fourth conceptualization of Galatea, Galatea (d), might therefore describe situations in which performance differences follow trait self-expectation differences independently of the actions and words of the leader. The common thread among the different forms of the Galatea effect is, of course, the subordinate's belief that he or she will do well. There is an element of controversy as to whether Galatea should be considered part of the Pygmalion phenomenon as Eden

(1990) suggests. Since the classic Pygmalion effect is subconscious or nonintentional, we would argue that the Galatea effect should only be considered a part of the Pygmalion phenomenon when it arises as a by-product of raising leaders' expectations [Galatea (a)]. Communicating expectations for subordinates to subordinates, either directly [Galatea (b)] or indirectly [Galatea (c)], represents attempts to raise self-efficacy deliberately and consciously and should not be considered part of the subconscious Pygmalion effect. Finally, Galatea (d) involves the effect of existing differences in self-expectations and is divorced from leadership altogether.

Theoretical Ties

Pure Pygmalion, to the extent that it is focused on subconscious mechanisms, is unique in the leadership literature. However, considering both the Pygmalion effect (including Pygmalion behaviors) and the many versions of Galatea effect together, there are clear ties to other leadership and motivation theories. For example, the theory of transformational leadership describes leaders who inspire their followers to adopt and pursue a common vision, and models of transformational leadership have recognized the importance of leaders' deliberately demonstrating confidence in the abilities of subordinates (Bass 1985). However, Eden notes that although the transformational leadership and Pygmalion theories both recognize the importance of leader expectations in motivating subordinates, "the Pygmalion model is unique in its emphasis on raising leader expectations as a means of initiating a more effective leadership process" (Eden 1992, p. 293).

Furthermore, as mentioned previously, self-expectations have been identified as a mediator of the Pygmalion effect, and this mediator links the Pygmalion effect to expectancy theories of motivation (Lawler 1971; Porter and Lawler 1968; Vroom 1964), as well as to social-cognitive theory (Bandura 1986, 1997). Expectancy theories rest, in part, on the idea that people will try harder in performing a task if they have high expectations that their efforts will pay off in terms of increased performance—creating positive links between expectancies, effort, and performance. Thus, when expectations are raised via the Pygmalion effect, higher performance ultimately results.

In addition, the Pygmalion effect ties to social-cognitive theory and its central concept of self-efficacy (i.e., beliefs in one's abilities to orchestrate the actions needed to reach a particular level of performance; Bandura 1997; Eden 1992).[1] Like expectancies, self-efficacy has been positively linked to performance. The Pygmalion research that has been conducted has expanded both expectancy and social-cognitive theories by incorporating the role of leader expectations in affecting subordinate expectations and by focusing on the manipulation of leader expectations. For a more comprehensive treatment of the Pygmalion research, the reader is referred to Eden (1990, 1992). We will now turn to the limitations that affect the application of the Pygmalion effect to the workplace. We will also present ideas for addressing them.

LIMITATIONS IN THE PRACTICAL APPLICATION OF THE PYGMALION EFFECT

The bulk of the Pygmalion work that has been done has been geared toward improving performance. Thus, at its core, the Pygmalion effect has practical implications for workplace settings. However, there are a number of factors that limit the application of the Pygmalion effects to traditional work settings. Below, we address the limitations of gender effects, ethics, the subconscious nature of Pygmalion, and new versus experienced employees. Following a presentation of the problems are some ideas for addressing them. We have summarized the topics we discuss in Table 11.1, to be used as a guide to readers throughout the following pages.

Gender

One serious limitation in applying Pygmalion research to the workplace is that there is some question as to whether the Pygmalion effect works as consistently with women as it does with men. It is important to note that the failure to find the Pygmalion effect for women is limited to Pygmalion in the workplace studies; no systematic gender differences have been found in the classroom (Hall and Briton 1993). It is also necessary to note that the problem does not seem to lie in raising female leaders' expectations for their subordinates; studies by Sutton and Woodman (1989) and Dvir, Eden, and Banjo (1995) have managed to raise the expectations of women leaders. However, the raised expectations of female leaders do not consistently seem to lead to raised subordinate performance as they do with male leaders.

Past Research on Gender

This broad issue of gender and the Pygmalion effect essentially encompasses two questions: (1) Do men and women function equally well as Pygmalions (leaders) and (2) can the Pygmalion effect be created equally well among male and female subordinates? To answer these questions adequately, we need to examine studies of men leading men, men leading women, women leading men, and women leading women. This would allow us to untangle the effects of leader and subordinate gender. Unfortunately, the vast majority of studies reporting on female subordinates have also used female leaders. Of the eight female subordinate studies discussed below, five use female leaders and subordinates, two did not disclose the gender of the leaders, and one study used male leaders. There are no reported studies of female leaders attempting to create a Pygmalion effect among male subordinates. Several studies have failed to find the Pygmalion effect when using a predominantly female subordinate sample. For example, King's 1970 unpublished dissertation (cited in Eden 1990) contained two reports of failed attempts to create the Pygmalion effect, both of which involved primarily female subordinate samples, and Sutton and Woodman (1989) also failed to find a Pygmalion

Table 11.1
Summary of Limitations and Suggestions for Future Research

	Limitation	**Proposed solutions/future research**
Gender	The Pygmalion effect has not been successfully demonstrated for women leading men or women leading a normal population of women. In addition, the Pygmalion effect is weaker among female subordinates than male subordinates.	We suggest focusing on certain follower characteristics to study gender differences in the Pygmalion effect: acceptance of authority, trust in the leader, and affection for the leader. Male and female leaders may engender these characteristics to different extents; they may exist to different extents in male and female subordinates; or their levels may depend on the interaction between leader and subordinate gender.
Ethics/ subconscious operation	The classic Pygmalion manipulation involves deception, which is ethically unacceptable in the workplace. Also, evidence suggests that the Pygmalion effect is subconscious. Since leaders have little control over subconscious processes, we argue that the subconscious nature of the Pygmalion effect is a limitation.	Managers should be trained in developing high expectations for all of their subordinates. Explicitly training managers to be Pygmalions focuses on particular behaviors in which they should engage and brings the effects of the expectations into conscious awareness. In addition, training managers to be Pygmalions eliminates the need for deceptive practices.
Training	The current programs for training Pygmalions have not been very successful. The application of the Pygmalion effect to the workplace is limited in not knowing if the Pygmalion effect can be created through training as opposed to deception.	We believe that the subconscious Pygmalion effect can be made conscious and that leaders can be trained to be Pygmalions. To improve Pygmalion training, we suggest a greater emphasis on using proven techniques to build the self-efficacy of all subordinates. In addition, we recommend instilling a learning orientation in the leaders, as well as training them to display specific leadership behaviors.
New versus established employees	The Pygmalion effect is stronger to the extent that the leader is unacquainted with the subordinates.	The techniques that we recommend for inclusion in Pygmalion training should apply to both new and established employees.

effect among a predominantly female subordinate sample of retail salespersons. (Neither King nor Sutton and Woodman reported the gender of the leaders in their studies.) In addition, Dvir et al. (1995) discussed their own failure to create the Pygmalion effect among female trainees (led by female instructors), as well as an earlier failed attempt to do so by Eden and Ravid (1981, cited in Dvir et al. 1995).

The above studies raise questions about the usefulness of the Pygmalion effect for women, but, as noted previously, they did not allow the gender effects of the leader and the subordinates to be separated. As a partial solution to this problem, Dvir et al. (1995) conducted a study using three samples of IDF soldiers: a group of women led by a woman, a group of men led by a man, and a group of women led by a man. (No sample of men led by a woman was available.) The results showed the usual Pygmalion effect for both groups led by men, including the one with female subordinates. However, significant results were not found for the group of women led by a woman.

Dvir et al. (1995) concluded that although leader expectation effects have been demonstrated for women subordinates, ". . . it remains questionable whether they can be obtained among female leaders" (p. 267). However, more recent work by Eden and Davidson (1997) and Davidson and Eden (1997) has served to shed some light on this issue. In two separate studies, these authors examined female IDF instructors in charge of female trainees who had objectively low potential; these were women who had been selected for training because of substandard mental test scores, limited schooling, or disadvantaged backgrounds. Leaders' normal expectations for such trainees were low, but the experimental manipulation convinced the female leaders of half of the squads that their disadvantaged squads had trainees of higher than average potential for their disadvantaged population. The results from both experiments showed higher squad performance in the experimental group than control group. Thus, in these two cases, the Pygmalion effect was found for a sample of low-potential women led by another woman.

Recent metanalyses of Pygmalion studies have attempted to combine the above studies to address the issue of gender. McNatt (1997) compared the size of the Pygmalion effect created in five female leader–female subordinate studies to the effect size created in nine male leader–male subordinate studies. He found that the effect size was larger for the all male studies, although the difference was not significant at the $p = .05$ level. He stated, nevertheless, that "these meta-analytic results support the existence of a strong effect among men and a somewhat smaller one among women" (p. 31).

Gold and Kierein (1998) also conducted a metanalysis of Pygmalion studies, and they attempted to examine the moderators of leader gender and subordinate gender separately. The authors found no significant difference in the size of the effects created by male and female leaders, but they did find a significantly stronger Pygmalion effect among male subordinates than female ones. However, as noted previously, there has been only one reported male leader–female subordinate study (Dvir et al. 1995), and no reported female leader–male subordinate studies. Because these two combinations are so severely underrepresented, we believe that the efforts to separate the effects of leader gender and subordinate gender may have been premature and the results should be interpreted with caution.

These metanalyses seem to paint a more encouraging picture of women and the Pygmalion effect than has been painted in the past. However, the small number of studies included in these metanalyses limits the conclusions that we can draw from them. The gender effects of both metanalyses are based primarily on two studies that successfully demonstrated the effect with women leading women (Davidson and Eden 1997; Eden and Davidson 1997), and two that did not (Dvir et al. 1995, experiments 1 and 2). (McNatt [1997] also included the Presser sample from King's [1971] report as an all female group.) Furthermore, the analyses did not include the nonpublished studies, such as Eden and Ravid's 1981 study (cited in Dvir et al. 1995), which failed to find the Pygmalion effect for women leaders. McNatt noted that King's 1970 unpublished studies did not contain sufficient information to be included and that efforts to obtain the necessary information were unsuccessful. More definitive conclusions await more studies that examine gender and the Pygmalion effect—particularly those studies in which men lead women and women lead men.

In sum, recent efforts to cast women as Pygmalions have been more successful than in the past (Davidson and Eden 1997; Eden and Davidson 1997), but there is still some doubt that women consistently function as well as male Pygmalions. The Pygmalion effect has yet to be successfully demonstrated in a work setting for a female leader of a normal population. Furthermore, there is some evidence that female subordinates respond less well to the Pygmalion effect than to male ones. Because many organizations today have a substantial number of female managers and subordinates, organizations would probably be hesitant to use a technique that might work less well for some groups than others. Thus, more research must be done on the role of gender in the Pygmalion effect.

Possible Explanations for Gender Differences in the Pygmalion Effect

One possibility for the findings of nonsignificant or weakly significant Pygmalion effects with women leaders in normal populations is leadership competence. Dvir et al. (1995) suggest that women may have to be superior to their male counterparts in order to reach the same leadership positions and may therefore already be naturally exhibiting the PLS toward everyone. Accordingly, the experimental manipulation would not do much to affect their leadership because of a ceiling effect. Because women do not have to compete as hard to become schoolteachers, this explanation would address why the Pygmalion effect is found for teachers in the classroom, but not leaders in the workplace.

However, the explanation that women in positions of leadership achieved such positions by being superior to their male counterparts would imply that groups led by women in the workplace would consistently outperform groups led by men, because the women would be demonstrating PLS. However, there is no evidence to support this implication. In fact, most leadership research seems to indicate that male and female leaders do not produce consistently different results (e.g., Donnell and Hall 1980).

Another explanation for why the Pygmalion effect is not often found for women outside of the classroom is that women may be uneasy about discriminating among their subordinates. Women in organizations have been shown to lead in more participative ways than men (e.g., Eagly and Johnson 1996; Eagly, Makhijani, and Klonsky 1992). That is, women leaders may be more likely to include their subordinates in decision-making processes and make greater efforts to lead in an egalitarian style. Women may accordingly be less willing—either consciously or subconsciously—to treat different subordinates differently. The Pygmalion effect might not work because, although the female leaders hold different expectations for different subordinates, they display the same leadership toward all. However, a disinclination on the part of women to differentiate among their subordinates based on expectations cannot explain why the Pygmalion effect is found for women in the classroom or why the Pygmalion effect is still not found for women leaders when whole groups are assigned to the experimental condition. In whole-group studies, different expectations are induced for entire groups of people, such that the leader in the experimental condition has her expectations raised for all of her subordinates. Thus, finding the Pygmalion effect entails finding differences between entire groups and would not require an individual leader to discriminate among her own subordinates. In addition, the argument that women are more hesitant to discriminate among employees is questionable because there is some indication that women managers do establish different types of relationships with different subordinates (e.g., Fairhurst 1993).

Future Steps to Address Gender Limitations

To our knowledge, Eden and Davidson's (1997) and Davidson and Eden's (1997) studies that found the Pygmalion effect for women leading disadvantaged women are the first studies to find that women can function in leadership roles as Pygmalions. These findings lead to the conclusion that women can be Pygmalions—sometimes. The question that now must be answered is "When?" Dvir et al. (1995) examined moderating variables, such as trait anxiety, generalized self-efficacy, and self-task compatibility (the relationship between a subordinate's perception of her gender role and the gender type of the task at hand) in exploring the relationship between female leaders' expectations and their subordinates' performance. However, none of these moderators was successful in allowing the Pygmalion effect to emerge for the women leaders.

The previous discussion indicates that considerable research has been done on exploring the issue of gender and the Pygmalion effect. However, most of this research has focused on the women leaders and not their subordinates, even though the nature of the subordinate population has been a major difference between successful and unsuccessful attempts to demonstrate the Pygmalion effect among women. The studies finding the Pygmalion effect for women have involved schoolchildren and at-risk populations—vastly different groups than average working-age adults. In recognition of this point, Eden and Davidson (1997) noted that their atypical finding of a Pygmalion effect for women outside of the classroom might be because women may function better as Pygmalions with at-risk populations than with normal populations of adults.

We believe that the most promising avenue for researching gender and the Pygmalion effect is to examine the characteristics of the subordinate population and how these interact with the characteristics of the leaders. For example, a factor worth considering here is Deborah Tannen's (1991) theory about the different ways that men and women communicate. She argues that men communicate in a task-focused way designed to demonstrate knowledge and competence, while women's top priority in communicating is to establish relationships. This is consistent with other arguments that women tend to lead in a more relationship-oriented style than do men (Powell, Butterfield, and

Mainiero 1982; Weider-Hatfield 1989). However, it is possible that the emphasis some women tend to put on relationships might be subordinated to an emphasis on competency and performance under certain circumstances, such as when the need for performance improvement is critical. This would be the case for an at-risk population and could possibly explain why the Pygmalion effect has been found with disadvantaged populations. Thus, we propose that the relationship-versus-performance focus of female leaders may differ depending on the leaders' perceptions of her followers' potential. Of course, there is some debate about whether women actually do lead in a more relationship-oriented style than men (e.g., Eagly and Johnson 1990),[2] but it remains an avenue that future Pygmalion research might explore. The idea of studying gender differences in relationship and task orientations in Pygmalion studies is captured in the following research recommendation.

The levels of relationship and task orientation of female leaders should be examined in the context of a Pygmalion study to determine if the levels shift depending on the leaders' perceptions of the subordinates' potential. Additional support for the idea that more attention should be paid to the subordinates of managers can also be found in the literature on charismatic leadership (Smith-Major 1996). As discussed previously, Eden (1992) explicitly addresses the relationship between the two areas of leadership research, and we elaborate on this relationship here. Primary among the lessons of charismatic leadership for understanding the Pygmalion effect is work that has been done on the followers of charismatic leaders. Leadership researchers are increasingly coming to the conclusion that "charisma resides in the relationship between a leader who has charismatic qualities and those of his or her followers who are open to charisma, within a charisma-conducive environment" (Klein and House 1995, p. 183). Similarly, the Pygmalion effect may not be due to just the actions and behaviors of the leaders, but rather to an interaction between the leader and the followers—and the gender of the leader might substantially affect this interaction. Certain follower attributes have been found to be important in fostering charismatic leadership: acceptance of authority, trust in the leader, values that are congruent with the leader's message, an expressive orientation to work and life, affection for the leader, and a principled orientation to social relationships (Conger and Kanungo 1987; Klein and House 1995; Shamir, House, and Arthur 1993). Extending this work to the realm of the Pygmalion effect, it is possible that any one of these characteristics must be present for the Pygmalion effect to emerge, and it may be that the gender of the leader affects whether these characteristics are present. It is also possible that the gender of subordinates affects the level of these characteristics. For example, the Pygmalion effect may produce weaker effects among female subordinates because they are less susceptible to effects of their leaders' expectations. Thus, it might be a difference in the characteristics of followers that would explain the weaker Pygmalion effects among female subordinates versus male (Gold and Kierein 1998).

In sum, we would argue that Pygmalion researchers should measure the follower characteristics listed above (e.g., acceptance of authority), as well as leadership behaviors, because it may be the interaction between the two that affects performance. In particular, the characteristics of at-risk populations such as the ones that yielded the Pygmalion effect with a woman leader (Davidson and Eden 1997; Eden and Davidson 1997) should be compared with the characteristics of normal populations to determine if these differences can account for differences in finding the Pygmalion effect. For example, female leaders may not engender states such as unquestioning acceptance of their authority in normal populations. However, they may do so in at-risk populations whose disadvantaged backgrounds may have created a more submissive attitude toward authority figures.

With more attention to the characteristics of a leader's followers, and how these interact with characteristics of the leader, we are likely to gain a greater understanding of when and with whom the Pygmalion effect will emerge. Although numerous follower characteristics might affect the functioning of the Pygmalion effect, the following research recommendation highlights a few that might be good starting points for Pygmalion researchers to measure. Future research should examine the follower characteristics of acceptance of authority, trust in the leader, and affection for the leader to determine if their levels affect the emergence of the Pygmalion effect. In addition, research should study whether lower levels of these characteristics occur for female subordinates or in the presence of female leaders.

Ethics

A second issue to address is the deceptive means used to create the Pygmalion effect in organizational settings. What the experimenter tells the leader in Pygmalion experiments to create differential expectations for subordinates is not based on actual facts, but is a deceptive manipulation. Eden has acknowledged the ethical considerations involved in using deceptive practices, but maintains that the improved performance and other positive outcomes that often result from Pygmalion manipulations are worth the price of using deceptive tactics to create them (Eden et al. 2000). He argues that, just as doctors should prescribe placebo drugs to patients if they will improve the patient's health, organizations should willfully create leader expectation effects, using deception if necessary (Eden 1992). However, although deception may be acceptable for the purposes of conducting experiments like those of Eden and his colleagues, we do not believe that they should be used as standard practice in organizational settings. It should be noted that the deception involved here is not in telling managers that higher expectations for subordinates will likely benefit subordinate performance, but in creating the false impression among managers that some of their subordinates have the potential to shine (with the further implication that other subordinates will not) with no actual supporting data.

Consider some of the ramifications of using deceptive practices to create the Pygmalion effect in business settings.

1. Managers would have to be deceived by their own bosses or staff personnel (e.g., Human Resources Management Director). First, it is very unlikely that no one would find out what was happening. Furthermore, when people did find out, organizational trust would likely be severely damaged.

2. It is unclear whether it would be possible to limit the deception to just this one issue. When organizational members find out that deception is officially sanctioned, it is a only small step for others to follow suit on other issues—always, of course, "for a good reason."

3. Serious organizational justice implications emerge when people are treated differently in contradiction of the actual facts of their known potential, and the organizational justice literature suggests that negative consequences result when people think they are being treated unjustly. For example, procedural justice perceptions have been linked to variables such as organizational commitment and trust in supervisors (Konovsky, Folger, and Cropanzano 1987; McFarlin and Sweeney 1992).

4. Finally, the legal implications of such deceptive practices are great, especially in today's litigious climate in which so many play the role of aggrieved victim (often successfully).

The primary ethical issue surrounding the Pygmalion effect is whether it is acceptable to deceive leaders about their subordinates' potential. Although Eden (1990, 1992) has held that it can be justified, we have argued against such a practice and hold that expectations should not be deceptively manipulated in the workplace. We believe that Pygmalion interventions should focus on the capacity that all employees have to upgrade their skills and improve their performance rather than on singling out certain individuals or groups of individuals based on false "data." This last statement, in fact, is the principle behind Eden's (1990) program of Pygmalion Leadership Training. He stated that "supervisors are taught to expect that their subordinates can improve and to expect that they, the supervisors, have the capacity to lead their subordinates to higher levels of performance. . . . In short, Pygmalion Leadership Training gives supervisors reason to believe that all or most of their subordinates can become more productive through the manager's own leadership efforts" (pp. 167–168). It remains, of course, to make such programs successful.

Subconscious Operation

A third factor limiting the application of the Pygmalion effect to the workplace is its subconscious nature. By a "subconscious" process, we are referring to a process that is not in focal awareness. Since only about seven items can be held in focal awareness at any one time, virtually all of our knowledge is stored in the subconscious, where its accessibility through introspection varies. Evidence exists that the results of inducing expectations for others are not easily accessed in that Pygmalions deny treating people differently after the experimental inductions.

Specifically, a common Pygmalion manipulation is for the experimenter (or confederate) to tell leaders of single groups that some of the group members are better than others in some respect or else to tell leaders that their entire group is better than another group. Leaders then develop different expectations for the different group members or the entire group (e.g., Eden 1990; Eden and Ravid 1982; Eden and Shani 1982; King 1971). In turn, subordinates of whom more is expected report receiving better leadership. However, although leaders may be aware of holding different expectations for different subordinates, it appears that the translation of these expectations into leadership behaviors operates at a subconscious level. Leaders are unaware of treating their subordinates differently following a Pygmalion manipulation. Eden and Shani (1982) reported that this unawareness was maintained even after a debriefing session in which the experimental manipulation was revealed to the leaders.

Earlier, we defined the Pygmalion effect as "the finding that leader expectations for subordinate performance can subconsciously affect leader behavior and subordinate performance." The fact that the Pygmalion effect has been found to be subconscious has differentiated Pygmalion from theories entailing direct persuasion effects (e.g., much of social psychology, attitude change research, social cognitive theory, etc.). To the degree that Pygmalion principles are taught and applied deliberately, the distinction between Pygmalion and other theories (e.g., social-cognitive theory advocating direct persuasion as a method of raising self-efficacy in others [Bandura 1986, 1997]) may blur to the point of indistinguishability.

A leadership phenomenon of which the leaders themselves are unaware is difficult to implement reliably in the workplace. One cannot consistently control a psychological phenomenon of which one is not conscious. We believe that the problem of the Pygmalion effect's being subconscious is best addressed by making the process completely conscious and deliberate. That is, we would argue that leaders should be trained to use Pygmalion leadership behaviors (e.g., coaching, stimulating enthusiasm, enhancing others' self-worth, encouraging relationships and teamwork) deliberately. The program would not technically be one in Pygmalion training (as the Pygmalion effect is subconscious), but it would aim to achieve the same results as the Pygmalion effect through the same mediators.

Training

Can leaders be trained (rather than tricked) to have higher expectations for their subordinates and consequently function as Pygmalions? The application of the Pygmalion effect to organizations is limited in that we do not know if leaders can be trained to be Pygmalions. Current training programs have been unable to achieve this goal.

Eden (1996) and Eden et al. (2000) reported seven failed attempts to train managers explicitly to be Pygmalions in a variety of organizations (e.g., IDF instructors, summer camp counselors, factory supervisors, bank managers). An initial report stated, "Although the results were mixed, most of the experiments showed little evidence that the workshops improved participants' leadership or that they aroused any response at all among the followers" (Eden 1996, p. 10). Meta-analytic results supported this conclusion, with an effect size of $r = .13$ ($p < .01$). Despite statistical significance, an r of .13 indicates that the training programs explain only 1.6 percent of the variance in subsequent measures of performance. As Eden points out, this makes it difficult to justify the expense and effort of the current Pygmalion leadership training program (Eden et al. 2000).

What did these failed training programs entail? They were all similar, although they varied in length from a one-day workshop, with a thirty-minute follow-up, to a three-day workshop with a half-day follow-up. All had the same three primary aims: to get the managers involved to believe that their subordinates were capable of better performance, to get the managers to believe that they could lead their subordinates to better performance, and to raise the managers' skills in enacting Pygmalion leadership behaviors (Eden 1994; Eden et al. 2000). Using lectures, demonstrations, role-playing, and video analyses, the training was designed (1) to emphasize the impact that expectations can have on subordinate performance, (2) to help the trainees identify everyday opportunities to apply Pygmalion leadership, and (3) to allow the trainees to rehearse leadership behaviors in a variety of management situations.

Eden et al. (2000) suggest that the training efforts might have failed for several reasons. First, it is possible that leadership training efforts are often unsuccessful, and the authors suggest conducting more meta-analytic studies to determine the effectiveness of leadership training in general. In addition, they posit ideas such as training interventions that are too weak, low statistical power because of group-level analyses, and psychometrically questionable measures. In contrast to these explanations, however, the authors also raise the question of whether the training failed because unawareness of the Pygmalion is essential for its operation, with awareness actually blocking the process. An inability to train Pygmalions and harness the effect would indicate that the Pygmalion effect ". . . lacks 'application validity,' that is, the purposive applicability that would render it an effective tool in the hands of practicing managers" (Eden et al. 2000, p. 42).

Although Eden et al. (in press) raised the possibility that leaders cannot be trained to be Pygmalions, the article also includes a discussion of Eden's plans for future efforts to improve Pygmalion leadership training. This indicates the belief that effective training of Pygmalions is possible. We agree that the idea of training leaders to expect more from their subordinates should not be abandoned. However, since the training program developed by Eden has not been successful in creating Pygmalion-like effects, efforts must be made to identify the elements of an effective training program.

Some hints about how a successful Pygmalion-related training program could be designed come from a study by Crawford, Thomas, and Fink (1980) concerning a group of sailors with historically low performance. In this program, both subordinates and their supervisors went through separate training. The most important aspect of the supervisor training program, from the perspective of the trainers, was teaching the supervisors methods for rewarding desired subordinate actions. The subordinate training focused on (1) personal growth and self-improvement (e.g., the development of life goals and objectives, self-discipline skills), and (2) issues raised by the low performers (e.g., requests to provide them with "reverse psychology" tools to use on the supervisors, reading skills, and vocational guidance). Subsequent measures of overall performance and discipline showed the low performers achieving the same levels as their shipmates.

Thus, this training, which was not explicitly Pygmalion training, did improve subordinate performance. Its success could have been in large part due to its focus on actions rather than on expectations per se. Given that there has been some success in

Pygmalion-like training, we believe that a successful training program can be designed. We will now turn to our suggestions for characteristics of such a program.

Suggestions for Making Pygmalion Training More Effective

Ultimately, the goal of Pygmalion training programs is to improve subordinate performance by training managers to expect more from subordinates and, accordingly, to adopt a Pygmalion leadership style. There are several changes that might be made to the training program developed by Eden that would make the programs more successful. For example, among other suggestions, Eden et al. (in press) discuss the potential benefits of the following: (1) improved participant buy-in for the training program, (2) an increased emphasis on overcoming early failures in transfer of training, (3) more follow-up sessions (including on-site consultations from the Pygmalion trainer), (4) greater attention paid to specific plans for implementing training, and (5) greater involvement and/or support of higher management for the Pygmalion efforts of their subordinates.

Although the changes given by Eden et al. (2000) should benefit Pygmalion training programs, we believe that changing the content of the programs will have more substantial effects on their success in training managers to expect more from their subordinates. An obvious solution to developing a new training program is to work to enhance self-efficacy using methods that have already proven effective in past research and practice (Bandura 1986, 1997). In addition, we believe that training managers to adopt a learning orientation versus a performance one in efforts to improve subordinate performance would be a beneficial addition to Pygmalion leadership training. Finally, explicit types of leadership behaviors identified as mediators of the Pygmalion effect (Cooper 1979; Harris and Rosenthal 1985; Rosenthal 1994) should be taught.

As stated earlier, the goal of these training suggestions is to bring the Pygmalion effect from people's subconscious into consciousness. Given that increased self-efficacy is a central component of the Pygmalion effect, we believe that a focus on Bandura's proven methods of building self-efficacy should benefit Pygmalion leadership training. Furthermore, as will be discussed later, our suggestion to adopt a learning orientation in Pygmalion training reflects a shared focus of these two topics on expecting improvement rather than immediate results. Again, our goal was to take what is known about how the Pygmalion effect operates through subconscious channels and apply what is known about similar—but conscious—effects. In this way, it might be possible to train the Pygmalion effect to be exercised consciously. Our last training suggestion of training people in specific leadership behaviors identified with the Pygmalion effect is also an excellent demonstration of the attempt to bring the Pygmalion effect to conscious levels.

Self-Efficacy

First, we would suggest training managers in building subordinate self-efficacy. As mentioned previously, Eden's Pygmalion Leadership Training adopts an attitude similar to this, holding that managers are trained to develop confidence in their abilities in encouraging improvement from all of their subordinates. However, to improve Pygmalion leadership training, we would argue that the specific techniques developed by Bandura for building self-efficacy should be followed more closely. Recall that we previously described Galatea (a) as the increases in self-efficacy/self-expectations that arise as an unintended consequence of the Pygmalion manipulation and the subsequent performance increases. This earlier discussion highlighted the relationship between self-efficacy and the Pygmalion effect and emphasizes the importance of building self-efficacy for improving performance. That is, we would argue that a focus on the specific actions that have been demonstrated to improve self-efficacy might yield superior results than previous Pygmalion training programs that have not explicitly employed them.

The four techniques identified by Bandura (1986, 1997) for enhancing self-efficacy are as follows: (1) enactive mastery or building skills through practice (which ties well with the competency approach to training; Boyatzis 1982), (2) role modeling or observing the performance of competent others with whom one can identify, (3) verbal persuasion or expressions of encouragement, and (4) interpreting ambiguous states of arousal in positive terms (i.e., encouraging someone to interpret the butterflies in his stomach as excitement rather than fear). Next, we briefly address the first three of the efficacy building approaches mentioned. (The fourth has limited applications in organizational settings.)

Building Self-Efficacy

First, managers should be educated in how to use guided mastery. Guided mastery refers to a procedure that involves training people to perform a particular task by breaking it down into its constituent elements, practicing the elements one at a time with instruction, and gradually reintegrating them into a whole. The goal of this procedure is to build the trainee's sense of self-efficacy through a series of "small wins" (Weick 1984) by starting with easily mastered subtasks and gradually increasing difficulty and complexity until the trainee feels confident of performing the whole task. As Eden (1990) notes, using a small wins technique allows people to achieve challenging goals in the long term by pursuing relatively easy goals in the short term.

Leaders using guided mastery must learn to deliver constructive feedback to subordinates. To be effective, the feedback should specifically refer to progress relative to some standard (Locke and Latham 1990) and provide constructive suggestions for how to improve performance or performance strategies (Bandura 1997). In addition, it is important that the feedback be delivered in an encouraging, nonthreatening manner in order to avoid resentment or discouragement on the part of employees.

Second, modeling is a self-efficacy technique that involves learning to perform a task correctly by observing others (Bandura 1986, 1997). Although modeling is typically thought of in terms of teaching observable behaviors, people can also model cognitive skills by listening to other people report how they think and learning to use those same thinking processes themselves (e.g., Gist 1989). Managers can therefore use modeling to teach their subordinates to replace negative thoughts like "I'm no good, and I'll never be able to do this" with positive ones like "I'm sure I can do this if I keep working at it." Thus, people can learn from models how to demonstrate a healthy thinking process in the face of mistakes, errors, or failures (Bandura 1997).

Managers must be conscious of the fact that many employees use them as models and could even encourage subordinates to use them as such. However, managers should learn what makes a good model (e.g., similarity of age, gender, ability level; Bandura 1997) and realize when they are not the right model for particular subordinates. Thus, an older male manager might help a younger female trainee find a more suitable role model, or a manager of struggling trainees might find them a role model who is also struggling but progressing.

Furthermore, managers should be trained in how to use the technique of positive self-modeling, which involves trainees' watching videotapes of themselves performing a task, with the mistakes removed through editing. Employees find it easy to identify with themselves, and observing a series of successful actions readily builds a sense of efficacy (Bandura 1997). Edited videotapes of other types of models (e.g., managers, other trainees) as they successfully perform the task should also help build subordinate self-efficacy (e.g., Bandura 1997; Gist, Rosen, and Schwoerer 1988; Gist, Schwoerer, and Rosen 1989). It is important to note that the trainees in these kinds of exercises are informed that the videotapes are edited; there is no deception involved in this self-modeling technique.

Managers also should be trained in how to help their subordinates observe models such that they derive the maximum benefit from them (Bandura 1997). They need to ensure that the subordinates are actively attending to the model, mentally organizing what they observe (i.e., identifying principles), practicing what they observe, and being motivated to perform what they have observed. For example, managers could take pains to help the subordinate abstract the essential features of the model's actions (e.g., "Did you notice that when the customer complained about our service, the model did not try to defend the company, but apologized and asked what could be done to correct the problem?").

A third method of building efficacy is persuasive communications. This method (which reflects Eden's original conceptualization of the Galatea effect) is less powerful than enactive mastery or modeling, but it can still be beneficial. The classic form of persuasion is when the coach says "Hang in there; I know you can do it." Although it may seem that doing this should come to people naturally, giving positive feedback is a skill that needs to be trained like any other skill. Such communications are most beneficial if managers reveal why and how they believe that employees can succeed. Telling employees they can succeed without any reasons may seem arbitrary; while the manager is waxing optimistic, they can be thinking "Yeah; that's what you say." Rather, managers should give the reasons why they think the subordinate can succeed (e.g., "You have been well trained" or "You have had relevant experience").

Encouraging statements are more likely to build self-efficacy if they are credible, and giving reasons for the statements lends them this credibility. Telling subordinates how they can succeed pertains mainly to strategy or the method by which they can succeed. For example, a manager could follow an encouraging statement of "I'm sure you can handle this!" with the explanation of "We'll sell this project by having you explain in your presentation its cost benefits. We'll have a dry run on Tuesday to work out the kinks."

Gist and Mitchell (1992) suggest that Bandura's efficacy-building techniques be used to improve both the individual's skills and knowledge of the performance strategies required to perform the task. These strategies should increase self-efficacy directly. The authors proposed that the degree to which the strategies change the self-efficacy beliefs of individuals is influenced by initial levels of self-efficacy (there is little room to improve on high levels), the variability and locus of performance determinants (self-efficacy is most likely to change when determinants are highly variable and internal), and the controllability of the determinants of performance. The techniques of enactive mastery, modeling, and verbal persuasion can be used alone or in combination with each other to build self-efficacy. The overriding goal of the actions taken to build subordinate self-efficacy should be to provide the individual with a thorough under-standing of the attributes, complexity, and environment of the task they are to perform and how they can best control these factors (Gist and Mitchell 1992). As mentioned previously, when subordinates have higher self-efficacy for performance, they are more likely to set challenging goals for themselves or commit to challenging goals that are assigned to them (Bandura 1997). Goal difficulty has, in turn, been associated with higher performance (Locke and Latham 1990). In addition, self-efficacy has a direct positive relationship with performance, and people with high self-efficacy tend to react more positively and constructively to performance setbacks (Bandura 1997). We rec-ommend that future research focus on the following:

> Pygmalion leadership training should focus on building manager self-efficacy for building subor-dinate self-efficacy using Bandura's methods of enactive mastery, role modeling, and verbal persuasion.

Learning Orientation

It is important to emphasize that the focus of Pygmalion training, from both our per-spective and Eden's, is to train managers to expect improvement from subordinates. This focus on improvement bears certain similarities to the idea of adopting a learning orientation toward task goals as opposed to a performance orientation (e.g., Stevens and Gist 1997; VandeWalle, Brown, Cron, and Slocum 1999). Employing a learning orientation could be of particular benefit in Pygmalion training because of a similarity in focus: the message underlying both a learning orientation toward performance and Pygmalion training is to emphasize improvement. A learning orientation reflects the attitude that the pursuit of a goal is a learning process. As efforts are made to achieve a goal, people with learning orientations may devote time to trying to uncover what skills are necessary for performing a task, or what task strategies are most beneficial for reaching a goal. In addition, they are likely to view mistakes or setbacks on the road to reaching a goal as opportunities for learning and development. People with a performance orientation typically stress working on easy tasks to ensure success and getting recognition and praise rather than working on challenging tasks for the pleasure of learning and mastery. Mistakes are viewed in terms of slowing down progress toward the goal rather than as mechanisms for learning.

Past research has found positive relationships between level of learning orientation and performance outcomes (Button, Mathieu, and Zajac 1996; Phillips and Gully 1997), indicating that instilling a learning orientation in people can benefit performance. Furthermore, past research has demonstrated that a learning orientation can be instilled in people as they pursue goals (e.g., improved subordinate performance). Stevens and Gist (1997) implemented two-hour training programs designed to create a mastery (or learning) versus a performance orientation; the mastery orientation training differed from the performance orientation training by including negative, as well as positive, modeling. Thus, participants in the mastery orientation condition were exposed to examples of ineffective uses of behaviors and how these should not be displayed. In addition, participants in the mastery orientation condition were taught the self-management skills of identifying and overcoming obstacles to performance, while the performance orientation training focused on skills of setting performance goals.

We would argue that Pygmalion leadership training should adopt some of the lessons learned from the mastery orientation training sessions and their focus on improvement and overcoming obstacles. Accordingly, we offer the following recommendation for future research:

> Managers should be trained to adopt a learning orientation with their subordinates in pursuing the goal of improved subordinate performance (at least in the early stages of goal pursuit).

Teaching Leadership Behaviors

In addition to Bandura's techniques for raising self-efficacy levels, we would also advocate teaching managers to display some of the behaviors found by Rosenthal to create the Pygmalion effect (Cooper 1979; Harris and Rosenthal 1985; Rosenthal 1994). For example, managers should be urged to establish friendlier climates for their subordinates so that subordinates feel free to approach their supervisors for help when they need it. Based on classroom Pygmalion studies, Cooper (1979) points out that more positive climates can lead to more student (subordinate)-initiated contact with their teachers (managers). In addition, managers should be encouraged to give positive and constructive feedback to all of their subordinates and also to be persistent in pursuing satisfactory conclusions to any performance issues.

New Employees

Another limitation of the Pygmalion effect is that it seems to work best (or only) with new employees/trainees—with people the leaders do not know. Raudenbush (1984) reviewed 18 classroom Pygmalion studies and found that the length of time that the teachers and students had been in contact with each other prior to the induction of the expectancy manipulation was significantly and negatively related to the study's effect size. When the studies were dichotomized into categories of "high contact" (more than two weeks of contact between teachers and students prior to any experimental manipulation of expectations) and "low contact" (two weeks or less of contact), four different meta-analytic computations revealed significant effects of the expectancy manipulation in the low contact category, although none revealed significant effects in the high contact category. In an earlier review, Jordan (1977) had reached the same conclusion, holding that students' IQs were unlikely to be enhanced when teachers' expectations were manipulated in the spring semester—when teachers' natural expectancies were already operating.

In the workplace, Pygmalion with established groups seems not to work because it is difficult to manipulate and change the expectations of managers who know their employees well (Eden 1990). When managers have known their subordinates for some time, they have presumably integrated a great deal of information about them and developed firm expectations of their potential; a short speech by an experimenter that contradicts this information is unlikely to convince them that their own judgment is mistaken (even if it is). If the information is inconsistent with the managers' own expectations, the contradictory information is likely to be disregarded. Even in cases where it is incorporated into the manager's expectations, it is only one piece of information among many, and it is unlikely to be given much weight. However, when managers who are unacquainted with their subordinates are given information by an experimenter, the information conveyed is likely to color their expectations. "Raising expectations" in these instances can be interpreted as having created expectations that were higher than they would have been without the manipulation. If the managers then treat the high expectancy subordinates differently (though unwittingly) from the other subordinates, the resulting effects will serve to confirm the prophecy set in motion by the expectations. Future research might examine the relative importance of information conveyed by an experimenter or a third party for new versus experienced employees. For example, Werner (1994) used a computer simulation to determine the types of information that managers considered in rating the performance of several hypothetical employees. A similar technique could be used here, with managers rating their expectations for both new and experienced employees. A dependent variable of interest could be whether and/or how often a manager chose to review the experimenter-provided information about an employee when rating expectations for an employee. Furthermore, after completing their ratings, managers could rate the impact of the experimenter's information on their expectations. Presumably, a manager would turn to the experimenter's information more often for new versus experienced employees and would rate it as more important.

Most of the time, however, managers deal with employees whom they know and with whom they have worked. Even if employees or managers are transferred, the managers may still know quite a lot about their new subordinates from other sources (e.g., their reputation in the company, their personnel files, their known accomplishments). They may even know something about new hires, because they may have interviewed them personally and/or seen their records. This typical organizational scenario sets a markedly different stage for interventions than does the typical IDF study, where there is a constant stream of new recruits who are all virtually unknown to the leaders. It seems clear that the chances of a brief expectancy manipulation having an effect are much lower in the first case than in the second. This is a severe limitation for the majority of organizations where leaders usually work with people they know. Next, we will discuss how this problem might be resolved.

Possibilities for Applying the Pygmalion Effect to New Employees

The steps listed previously for convincing leaders that all employees have the potential to improve and for training leaders in self-efficacy building techniques should work as well for experienced employees as for new ones. The Pygmalion effect has not worked well with experienced employees because it is difficult to convince leaders to change their expectations for particular subordinates about whom they already have opinions. However, teaching leaders that all employees have the capacity to improve does not require a leader to abandon his or her opinions of particular employees. That is, it does not require a leader to believe a mediocre performer is actually a higher-than-average performer of whom great things should be expected. Rather, it attempts to convince leaders that everyone, even mediocre performers, can improve and do better if they are trained properly and their self-efficacy is enhanced. A recommendation for future research is as follows:

> Managers should be trained to expect improvement from *all* of their subordinates so that Pygmalion-like effects can emerge with both experienced and new employees.

SUMMARY AND CONCLUSIONS

The Pygmalion effect is a useful heuristic for understanding the impact that expectations can have on performance in a multitude of settings, including the workplace. However, there are currently a number of problems that prevent the direct application of the Pygmalion effect to the workplace. We have offered suggestions for how these problems might be better understood. First, we recommended paying more attention to the characteristics and behaviors of subordinates. A better knowledge of the subordinates involved in the Pygmalion effect could explain why studies often fail to find the Pygmalion effect for women leaders. In addition, we have suggested that deception not be used to build subordinate efficacy. We suggest a new focus for Pygmalion training which would entail building the skills and efficacy of all employees using well-established techniques.

Focusing on building subordinates' self-efficacy might circumvent the problems with gender that are associated with the Pygmalion effect. Unlike the Pygmalion effect, the self-efficacy building techniques recommended by Bandura have been found to work equally well for men and women. Although there seem to be gender differences in self-efficacy level for certain areas (e.g., math skills), no gender differences have been reported with respect to self-efficacy building techniques (Bandura 1997). Furthermore, these techniques should work for experienced employees because they do not require changing already formed expectations about employees. The basic attitude of managers should be that all employees can improve their skills and performance. This would at the same time make training more effective, move Pygmalion from the subconscious to the conscious level, and eliminate the need for deceptive manipulations. We encourage future researchers to explore these possibilities.

NOTES

1. Self-efficacy is strongly related to expectancies, but it is a broader concept. It refers to people's beliefs in whether they can perform a task as a whole rather than just whether their efforts affect performance.

2. Eagly and Johnson's (1990) metanalysis found no gender differences in either relationship or task orientation when leaders in actual organizational settings were studied, although women leaders did display a greater degree of relationship orientation when lab studies or assessment studies were considered.

REFERENCES

Bandura, A. (1986). *Social Foundations of Thought and Action: A Social-Cognitive View*. Englewood Cliffs, NJ: Prentice-Hall.

———. (1997). *Self-efficacy: The Exercise of Control*. New York: W.H. Freeman.

Bass, B.M. (1985). *Leadership and Performance Beyond Expectations*. New York: Free Press.

Blodgett, M.S., and Carlson, P.J. (1997). Corporate ethics codes: A practical application of liability prevention. *Journal of Business Ethics* 16: 1363–1369.

Bowers, D.G., and Seashore, S.E. (1966). Predicting organizational effectiveness with a four-factor theory of leadership. *Administrative Science Quarterly* 11: 238–263.

Boyatzis, R.E. (1982). *The Competent Manager*. New York: Wiley.

Button, S., Mathieu, J., and Zajac, D. (1996). Goal orientation in organizational behavior research: A conceptual and empirical foundation. *Organizational Behavior and Human Decisions Processes* 67: 26–48.

Conger, J.A., and Kanungo, R.N. (1987). Toward a behavioral theory of charismatic leadership in organizational settings. *Academy of Management Review* 12(4): 637–647.

Cooper, H.M. (1979). Pygmalion grows up: A model for teacher expectation communication and performance influence. *Review of Educational Research* 49(3): 389–410.

Crawford, K.S., Thomas, E.D., and Fink, J.J. (1980). Pygmalion at sea: Improving the work effectiveness of low performers. *Journal of Applied Behavioral Science* 16: 482–505.

Davidson, O.B., and Eden, D. (1997). Golem effects among underprivileged women: Mediating role of leadership, subordinate expectations, and motivation. Paper presented at the annual meeting of the Academy of Management (Organizational Behavior Division), Boston, MA.

Donnell, S., and Hall, J. (1980). Men and women as managers: A significant case of no significant difference. *Organizational Dynamics* 8: 60–76.

Dvir, T., Eden, D., and Banjo, M.L. (1995). Self-fulfilling prophecy and gender: Can women be Pygmalion and Galatea? *Journal of Applied Psychology* 80(2): 253–270.

Eagly, A., and Johnson, B. (1996). Gender and leadership style: A meta-analysis. In R. Steers, L. Porter, and G. Bigley (eds.), *Motivation and Leadership at Work* (pp. 315–345). New York: McGraw-Hill.

Eagly, A.H., and Johnson, B.T. (1990). Gender and leadership style: A meta-analysis. *Psychological Bulletin* 108: 233–256.

Eagly, A.H., Makhijani, M.G., and Klonsky, B.G. (1992). Gender and the evaluation of leaders: A meta-analysis. *Psychological Bulletin* 111(1): 3–22.

Eden, D. (1990). *Pygmalion in Management: Productivity as a Self-fulfilling Prophecy*. Lexington: D.C. Heath.

———. (1992). Leadership and expectations: Pygmalion effects and other self-fulfilling prophecies in organizations. *Leadership Quarterly* 3(4): 271–305.

———. (1994). Getting managers to be Pygmalions: It's harder to train them than to trick them. Presented at the meeting of the Society of Organizational Behavior, Toronto, October 21–23.

———. (1996). Implanting Pygmalion Leadership Style through training, coaching, and long-term follow-up. Unpublished manuscript.

Eden, D., and Aviram, A. (1993). Self-efficacy training to speed reemployment: Helping people to help themselves. *Journal of Applied Psychology* 78(3): 352–360.

Eden, D., and Davidson, O.B. (1997). Remedial self fulfilling prophecy: Preventing Golem effects among disadvantaged women. Poster session presented at the annual conference of the Society for Industrial and Organizational Psychology, St. Louis, MO.

Eden, D., Geller, D., Gewirtz, A., Gordon-Terner, R., Inbar, I., Liberman, M., Pass, Y., Salomon-Segev, I., and Shalit, M. (2000). Implanting Pygmalion leadership style through workshop training: Seven field experiments. *The Leadership Quarterly* 11: 171–210.

Eden, D., and Kinnar, J. (1991). Modeling Galatea: Boosting self-efficacy to increase volunteering. *Journal of Applied Psychology* 76(6): 770–780.

Eden, D., and Ravid, G. (1982). Pygmalion versus self-expectancy: Effects of instructor- and self-expectancy on trainee performance. *Organizational Behavior and Human Performance* 30: 351–364.

Eden, D., and Shani, A.B. (1982). Pygmalion goes to boot camp: Expectancy, leadership, and trainee performance. *Journal of Applied Psychology* 67: 194–199.

Fairhurst, G.T. (1993). The leader-member exchange patterns of women in industry: A discourse analysis. *Communications Monographs* 60: 321–351.

Gist, M.E. (1989). The influence of training method on self-efficacy and idea generation among managers. *Personnel Psychology* 42: 787–805.

Gist, M.E., and Mitchell, T.R. (1992). Self-efficacy: A theoretical analysis of its determinants and malleability. *Academy of Management Review* 17: 183–211.

Gist, M.E., Rosen, B., and Schwoerer, C. (1988). The influence of training method and trainee age on the acquisition of computer skills. *Personnel Psychology* 41: 255–265.

Gist, M.E., Schwoerer, C., and Rosen, B. (1989). Effects of alternative training methods on self-efficacy and performance in computer software training. *Journal of Applied Psychology* 74: 884–891.

Gold, M., and Kierein, N. (1998). Pygmalion in organizations: A meta-analysis. Poster presented at the annual conference of the Society for Industrial and Organizational Psychology, Dallas, Texas.

Hall, J.A., and Briton, N.J. (1993). Gender, nonverbal behavior, and expectations. In P.D. Blanck (ed.), *Interpersonal Expectations* (pp. 276–295). Cambridge, UK: Cambridge University Press.

Harris, M.J., and Rosenthal, R. (1985). Mediation of interpersonal expectancy effects: 31 meta-analyses. *Psychological Bulletin* 97(3): 363–386.

Jenner, H. (1990). The Pygmalion effect: The importance of expectancies. *Alcoholism Treatment Quarterly* 7(2): 127–133.

Jordan, R. (1977). Teacher expectations and pupil performance: A review of research on the Pygmalion effect. *Catalog of Selected Documents in Psychology* 7(2): 52–53.

King, A. (1971). Self-fulfilling prophecies in training the hard core: Supervisors' expectations and the underprivileged workers' performance. *Social Science Quarterly* 52: 369–378.

Klein, K.J., and House, R.J. (1995). On fire: Charismatic leadership and levels of analysis. *Leadership Quarterly* 6(2): 183–198.

Konovsky, M.A., Folger, R., and Cropanzano, R. (1987). Relative effects of procedural and distributive justice on employee attitudes. *Representative Research in Social Psychology* 17: 15–24.

Lawler, E., III. (1971). *Pay and Organizational Effectiveness: A Psychological View.* New York: McGraw-Hill.

Learman, L.A., Avorn, J., Everitt, D.E., and Rosenthal, R. (1990). Pygmalion in the nursing home: The effects of caregiver expectations on patient outcomes. *Journal of the American Geriatrics Society* 38(7): 797–803.

Livingston, J. (1969). Pygmalion in management. *Harvard Business Review* 47(4): 81–89.

Locke, E.A., and Latham, G.P. (1990). *A Theory of Goal Setting and Task Performance.* Englewood Cliffs, NJ: Prentice Hall.

McFarlin, D., and Sweeney, P. (1992). Distributive and procedural justice as predictors of satisfaction with personal and organizational outcomes. *Academy of Management Journal* 35(3): 626–637.

McNatt, D.B. (1997). Ancient Pygmalion joins contemporary management: A meta-analysis of the result. Paper presented at the annual meeting of the Academy of Management, Boston, MA.

Phillips, J., and Gully, S. (1997). Role of goal orientation, ability, need for achievement, and locus of control in the self-efficacy and goal-setting process. *Journal of Applied Psychology* 82: 792–802.

Porter, L., and Lawler, E. (1968). *Managerial Attitudes and Performance.* Homewood, IL: Richard D. Irwin.

Powell, G., Butterfield, D., and Mainiero, L. (1982). Sex-role identity and sex as predictors of leadership style. *Psychological Reports* 49: 829–830.

Raudenbush, S.W. (1984). Magnitude of teacher expectancy effects on pupil IQ as a function of the credibility of expectancy induction: A synthesis of findings from 18 experiments. *Journal of Educational Psychology* 76(1): 85–97.

Rosenthal, R. (1994). Interpersonal expectancy effects: A 30-year perspective. *Current Directions in Psychological Science* 3(6): 176–179.

Rosenthal, R., and Jacobson, L. (1968). *Pygmalion in the Classroom: Teacher Expectation and Pupils' Intellectual Development.* New York: Holt, Rinehart, and Winston.

Saavedra, R., Cohen, S., and Denison, D. (1990). Summary: Customer service teams. In R. Hackman (ed.), *Groups That Work (and Those That Don't)* (pp. 398–405). San Francisco: Jossey Bass.

Shamir, B., House, R.J., and Arthur, M.B. (1993). The motivational effects of charismatic leadership: A self-concept based theory. *Organization Science* 4: 577–594.

Smith-Major, V. (1996). Have we "harnessed" Pygmalion? An analysis of the Pygmalion effect in the workplace. Unpublished manuscript, University of Maryland.

Snow, R.E. (1994). Pygmalion and intelligence? *Current Directions in Psychological Science* 4(6): 169–171.

Sutton, C., and Woodman, R. (1989). Pygmalion goes to work: The effects of supervisor expectations in a retail setting. *Journal of Applied Psychology* 74(6): 943–950.

Stevens, C., and Gist, M. (1997). Effects of self-efficacy and goal-orientation training on negotiation skill maintenance: What are the mechanisms? *Personnel Psychology* 50: 955–978.

Tannen, D. (1991). *You Just Don't Understand: Women and Men in Conversation.* New York: Ballantine.

VandeWalle, D., Brown, S., Cron, W., and Slocum, J. (1999). The influence of goal orientation and self-regulation on sales performance: A longitudinal field test. *Journal of Applied Psychology* 84: 249–259.

Vroom, V. (1964). *Work and Motivation*. New York: Wiley.

Weick, K.E. (1984). Small wins: Redefining the scale of social problems. *American Psychologist* 39: 40–49.

Weider-Hatfield, D. (1989). Differences in self-reported leadership behavior as a function of biological sex and psychological gender. *Women's Studies in Communication* 10: 1–14.

Werner, J. (1994). Dimensions that make a difference: Examining the impact of in-role and extrarole behaviors on supervisory ratings. *Journal of Applied Psychology* 79: 98–107.

12

Influences of Supervisor Behaviors on the Levels and Effects of Workplace Politics

L. Alan Witt

In 1920, Winston Churchill was overheard to say, "Politics are almost as exciting as war, and quite as dangerous. In war you can be killed only once, but in politics many times." While office workers have long been aware of the dangers of politics at work, substantial, systematic research on office politics began only in the last decade (e.g., Farrell and Peterson 1982; Mintzberg 1985; Narayanan and Fahey 1982; Porter, Allen, and Angle 1983). Evolving from research on perceptions of organizational climate, work has focused on organizational politics and its effects on both individuals and organizations. This [article] presents an argument that efforts to address office politics might be most effectively targeted below the level of the organization, and suggests that even in highly political organizations, individual supervisors can reduce the level of office politics and its effects on their subordinates.

ORGANIZATIONAL CLIMATE

The influence of the organization's "psychological atmosphere" (Pritchard and Karasick 1973) on employee behavior has received considerable attention during the last four decades. Into the mid-1980s, organizational scientists devoted considerable effort to empirically investigating it under the rubric of "organizational climate." Organizational climate was viewed as a molar concept including values, norms, perceptions, and behaviors of an organization's members. Many climate instruments included a multitude of factors that were not clearly distinguished from the organizational situation. Some examined issues that might more appropriately be labeled organizational structure (e.g., size, span of control). James and Jones (1974), however, noted that some aspects of organizations are phenomenological rather than objective (e.g., warmth vs. size). They

From *Organization Politics, Justice and Support*, edited by R.S. Cropanzano and K.M. Kacmar. Copyright 1995 by Quorum Books. Reproduced with permission of Greenwood Publishing Group, Inc.

coined the phrase "psychological climate" to denote the meaning that individuals attach to their work environments (Jones and James 1979). Zohar's (1980, pp. 96–97) definition of climate well represented the thinking of many climate researchers:

> Based on a variety of cues present in their work environment, employees develop coherent sets of perceptions and expectations regarding their behavior-outcome contingencies and behave accordingly. These coherent sets of organizational perceptions, when shared and summarized for individual employees, are defined here as organizational climates.

According to this definition, workers develop perceptual clusters based on their work experiences. These perceptions serve psychological utility as guides for appropriate behavior. The importance of this point cannot be overemphasized. People act on the basis of their perceptions (Lewin 1936). Implicitly agreeing with Koffka's (1935) argument that perceptions of the situation are more appropriate in the understanding of behavior than are objective measures of the situation, organizational climate researchers focused on identifying people's perceptions about the workplace.

Unfortunately, accurately measuring perceptions about the workplace and demonstrating relationships between the perceptions and important organizational outcomes have been problematic for climate researchers. The traditional approach was to use holistic climate measures, such as Litwin and Stringer's (1968) Organizational Climate Questionnaire, assessing a multitude of aspects of the organizational context to predict organizational behaviors. This is analogous to using an omnibus personality measure such as the Minnesota Multiphasic Psychological Inventory to predict job performance or absenteeism. In retrospect, it is not surprising that this approach met with little empirical success.

Schneider and Reichers (1983) argued that an organization consists of a number of distinct psychological climates, each predicting behavioral outcomes which are conceptually relevant. This represented a conceptual revolution in climate research, moving from global climate to "referent" climates. Examples include climate for safety (Zohar 1980) and climate for industrial relations (Dastmalchian, Blyton, and Adamson 1989). Accordingly, much of the recent research on job-related cognitions has examined specific issues, such as perceptions of organizational fairness (e.g., Moorman 1991). However, most researchers have dropped the prefix "climate for" and have focused on individual-level perceptions rather than perceptions aggregated at the work unit or organizational level.

One argument in the organizational science literature is that there is a higher-order "g-factor" of emotional cognition that influences an employee's evaluation of whether the workplace is beneficial or detrimental (James and James 1989; Lazarus 1984). A basic determinant of this g-factor of emotional cognition might be the organization's social climate, simply operationalized for employees as the extent to which they view the organization as "on their side." Eisenberger and others (Eisenberger, Huntington, Hutchison, and Sowa 1986; Eisenberger, Fasolo, and Davis-LaMastro 1990; Shore and Tetrick 1991) have found that employees form global perceptions of an organization's support, which are related to increased organizational commitment and innovation and to reduced absenteeism. Akin to the concepts measured in Litwin and Stringer's (1968) "warmth" and "risk" subscales, the construct of organizational support reflects how the organization values the contributions and addresses the needs of its employees—very much an indicator of "being on one's side." Some evidence suggests that perceptions of organizational support and workplace politics are mirror images of employees' views of the extent to which the organization is on their side (Nye and Witt 1993). The construct of workplace politics refers to phenomena in which organization members attempt either directly or indirectly to influence other members by means not sanctioned by formal standard operating procedures or informal norms in an attempt to achieve personal or group objectives. Consistent with the notion of a g-factor of emotional cognition, perhaps employees see high levels of organizational support as evidence of being on their side and high levels of politics as not on their side. It is difficult to imagine political and support levels being simultaneously high when measured at the same level (e.g., organization or work unit).

From the practical standpoint of managing employees, however, there is an important difference between support and politics: The effects of politics are more pervasive than those of support. Whereas some employees can function well with extremely low levels of organizational support, very few can succeed amidst very high levels of politics. The extent to which perceptions of organizational support have an influence on behavior is largely a function of the individual's "exchange ideology"—reflecting the expected relationship between what the individual gives and receives in the person-organization exchange (Eisenberger, Cotterell, and Marvel 1987). At one end of the exchange ideology continuum are the high maintenance employees who ask "not what you can do for your company but what can your company do for you." These individuals are not likely to work hard when perceiving little organizational support. At the other end, employees act relatively independently from organizational reinforcement; these are the employees who can function well with extremely low levels of organizational support. Empirical evidence has shown that exchange ideology influences the impact of organizational support on absenteeism (Eisenberger et al. 1986) and supervisor-rated organizational citizenship behaviors (Witt 1991).

In contrast, the presence of politically based coalitions that restrict information and resource distribution is likely to affect team, work unit, and/or organizational performance; in such a case, politics can affect most employees. The pervasiveness of workplace politics is such that preventing political behavior from reaching dysfunctional levels should be a priority for management.

WORKPLACE POLITICS DEFINED

Discussed under the conceptual rubric of "organizational politics," political behavior in organizations has received increasing attention since Gandz and Murray (1980) reported finding very little empirical research in a literature review of workplace politics. As noted by Kacmar and Ferris (1991), political behavior in organizations has been described as both omnipresent and elusive. They suggested that its elusiveness is reflective of insufficient conceptual clarity. Indeed, while we may "know it when we see it," a consensually agreed-upon definition of workplace politics has not been developed.

Gandz and Murray (1980) presented two categories of conceptual work on workplace politics. In one, writers have defined organizational politics as an inherent process associated with the use of power revolving around most policy decisions (Eisenhardt and Bourgeois 1988; Pfeffer and Salancik 1974) or specific policy decisions, such as resource allocation (Wildavsky 1964) or executive compensation (Ungson and Steers 1984). In the second category, writers have discussed organizational politics in terms of self-serving behaviors often associated with organizational ineffectiveness (Ashforth and Lee 1990; Cobb 1984; Gray and Ariss 1985; Martin and Sims 1974; Mayes and Allen 1977; Parker, Dipboye, and Jackson 1992; Pettigrew 1973; Robbins 1976, 1983; Schein 1977). With respect to the latter category, Batten and Schwab (1965, p. 13) wrote that individuals "engage in company politics because they believe that they can best achieve what they want in a devious, indirect, and underhanded way." In contrast, Jones (1987) entered a third category when she argued that definitions of organizational politics should include mutual caring, trust, tolerance, and sensitivity to others—what others might consider to fall under the conceptual umbrella of organizational support.

Most definitions of workplace politics fall into the second category and focus on its negative consequences. For example, Vredenburgh and Maurer (1984, p. 50) suggested that political behavior at work: (a) is undertaken by individuals or interest groups to influence directly or indirectly target individuals, roles, or groups toward the actor's personal goals, generally in opposition to others' goals, (b) consists of goals or means either not positively sanctioned by an organization's formal design or positively sanctioned by unofficial norms, and (c) is objective and subjective in nature, involving real organization events as well as perceptual attributions.

Dimensions of Workplace Politics

When are behaviors considered political? Ascertaining the existence of politics relies on a judgment by the individual as to whether or not a perceived behavior is within the parameters of sanctioned behavior. A key to determining whether or not the behavior is political and outside of sanctioned behavior (i.e., not acceptable strategic self-presentation or citizenship behavior) is the attribution of intended self-interest and manipulation (Ferris, Bhawuk, Fedor, and Judge 1994a). Drory and Romm (1990) suggested that the domain of organizational politics should include any organizationally controlled event desirable for the individual. Such an approach would make difficult the operationalization of workplace politics for measurement purposes. In contrast, Kacmar and Ferris (1991) argued that organizational politics may best be conceived as having three elements, namely general political behavior, going along to get ahead, and pay and promotion.

General Political Behavior

General political behavior stems from the development of coalitions based on self-interests rather than on business issues. Membership in such alliances leads to a variety of political behaviors, including directing scarce resources to members of the coalition and making policy changes primarily on their behalf. Others, as identified by Pfeffer (1981), include controlling information, controlling lines of communication, using outside experts, controlling the agenda, and controlling decision parameters.

Going Along to Get Ahead

Employees know when most others in the workplace value unquestioned compliance with the prevailing policy. Not only is compliance valued, but deviation is met with sanction. The employee who asks the CEO an important but embarrassing question in a public forum is later transferred to a remote outpost. Employees learn that creativity and innovation are not the keys to career advancement. Rather, promotional dollars require going along to get ahead.

Pay and Promotion

The criteria for promotion into the management ranks in most organizations implicitly includes popularity. Is the candidate liked by other members of the management team? Will the candidate fit in with the group? Management does not want a troublemaker in the ranks. Given that interpersonal skills are recognized as a key factor in managerial performance, employees expect and accept strategic impression management among future managers jockeying for promotion. At what point are these behaviors considered political? There may be a fine line between using person-culture fit as a promotional criterion and rewarding people for behaving in an underhanded or back-door fashion to get promoted at the expense of others. Decisions on the wrong side of the line promote a political climate in terms of pay and promotion.

EFFECTS OF WORKPLACE POLITICS

In their model of workplace politics, Ferris, Russ, and Fandt (1989) focused primarily on politics as seen and experienced at the level of the individual. If one agrees with Gandz and Murray's (1980, p. 248) view that politics constitute a subjective state in which "organization members perceive themselves or others as intentionally seeking selfish ends in an organizational context when such ends are opposed to those of others," it requires a very short inferential leap to understand their finding that workers feel that office politics are generally bad, unfair, unnecessary, conflictual, and unhealthy. In addition, Gandz and Murray (1980) reported negative effects of politics for individuals in terms of lower job satisfaction, job variety, job autonomy, and promotional opportunity.

However, political behavior can have effects on organizational systems as well as on individuals.

Organizational Systems

Larson and LaFasto (1989) argued that team politics are a significant threat to team effectiveness. Political activity can be dysfunctional for not only teams but also for work units and whole organizations as well. A study by Eisenhardt and Bourgeois (1988) well illustrates the harmful effects of workplace politics on organizational systems. They found that firms with politically active executive teams experienced slow growth and lower profits. Their research focused on general political behaviors, as the executives they studied developed alliances based on political concerns. These politically based coalitions prevented the natural shifting of alliances based on specific issues. This led not only to poor decisions but also to inaccurate, even distorted attributions about the behavior of outgroups. Eisenhardt and Bourgeois (1988) identified two other factors to explain how politics led to poor performance. First, political activity was time-consuming and distracted key executives from their functional responsibilities. Executives resorted to covert coalition-building to accomplish objectives that were not directly related to their primary goals. Second, politics restricted the flow of key information; executives were secretive about information. They also reported that poor firm performance triggered power centralization, which led to increased politics among the executive team. While Eisenhardt and Bourgeois (1988) focused on the impact of political behavior in executive teams on the organization, it is likely that such political norms will have similar effects throughout the organization. The levels of politics, however, may vary across work units or teams.

Safety is another outcome of politics with systemic effects. Hilton, Witt, and Hellman (1994) hypothesized that political behavior might create an atmosphere in which employees fear retaliation for bringing concerns about safety violations or hazards. Thus, management practices that either promote or fail to discourage a norm of "going along to get ahead" might be perceived as reflecting a general desire to avoid problems that do not seem to be of a high priority to management, including safety issues. In such circumstances, workers have little choice but to continue unsafe practices and accept unsafe conditions. Thus, political norms can undermine management's actual support for a company safety program. In a path analytic study of 350 warehouse and repair workers, they found that organizational politics had indirect effects on safety levels mediated by the organization's safety climate.

Individuals

The effects of politics on the individual are important (Kamar and Ghadially 1989). Given the damaging effects of politics on unit and team functioning, it is likely that political behavior can interfere with an individual's ability to acquire resources and get information relevant to one's tasks and career. Such an impact can lead to several damaging outcomes. Ferris et al. (1989b) specified four: job involvement, job anxiety, job satisfaction, and voluntary withdrawal. Job involvement (see Kanungo 1982) reflects an employee's identification with the job, and high levels of political activity are likely to elicit dissonance in this important component of the social identity. Similarly, political activity leads to anxiety, job dissatisfaction, and reduced continuance commitment (e.g., Ferris and Kacmar 1992; Gandz and Murray 1980; Parker, Dipboye, and Jackson 1992).

REDUCING WORKPLACE POLITICS

Surprisingly, organizational scientists paid relatively little attention to workplace politics as a target problem for organizational assessment and intervention until the 1980s (e.g., Bateman 1980; Cobb 1986a 1986b; Cobb and Margulies 1981; Gummer and Edwards 1985). Conceptual and empirical work has largely focused on organizational politics per se rather than team or work group politics. Unfortunately, methodological and practical problems limit the utility of focusing on politics at the level of the organization.

Methodological Limitation

The methodological limitation lies in the assessment of politics. In order to show relationships between organization-level politics and such important organization-level outcomes as performance and turnover, individual-level politics scores must be aggregated at the organization level. This aggregation must meet a satisfactory degree of between-employee agreement (James, Demaree, and Wolf 1984; Kozlowski and Hattrup 1992) in order to justify the label of organizational politics. The inconsistency with which organizational scientists found agreement among employees regarding organization-level norms severely limited the utility of organizational climate research. Given the plethora of factors that affect political norms in organizations and individual differences in what would be perceived as political behavior, it is unlikely that an agreed-upon picture of an organization's politics can be found in large organizations. Attempts to aggregate politics perceptions at the work unit or team level might be more meaningful.

Practical Limitations

The practical problems are twofold. First, such system-wide efforts as the institutionalization of formal human resources management rules and procedures to thwart political norms at the organization level are often limited in impact by the narrow scope of the targeted problems, resistance (i.e., politics about politics), and the considerable time required for changes to reach the field. With the frequency of reorganizations and executive turnover, it is unlikely that change champions would be around long enough for systemic change to occur beyond superficiality.

The second practical problem stems from two demographic trends. The first is the increasing infrequency with which employees remain in organizations for long periods of time. Many workers see themselves as marketable commodities, compensated for their services with pay and other benefits as well as with experience and training that affect their marketability. More so than in the past, workers move from organization to organization in order to find the optimal transaction. The second is the recent change in corporate retention practices. Many private and public sector organizations have downsized, laying off regular, full-time employees and replacing some of them with temporary contract workers. These fundamental changes in the employee-organization relationship have almost made moot over three decades of research (e.g., Mathieu 1991) on organizational commitment. If current trends continue, perhaps few people will be loyal to their employing organizations, and visa versa. In ten years, the expression that IBMers "bleed blue" may have as much salience to young employees as does the patriotic expression "loose lips sink ships" to the post baby-boom generation today. Given that employee social identities (see Ashforth and Mael 1989) will increasingly stray from the organization and move to the supervisor, team, and work unit, it is unlikely that employees would (1) view the organization as making sincere efforts to reduce political norms on their behalf, and (2) act to support such efforts on behalf of the organization per se.

Work Unit and Team Politics

It is likely that a focus on commitment to the supervisor, team, and work group will replace the emphasis on commitment to the organization, because it is at these levels that employees will form the key emotional ties. Similarly, efforts to reduce politics and the negative effects of politics might have the greatest utility when aimed below the level of the organization.

Previous work in the social exchange literature suggests that the supervisor is essentially upper management's representative to nonsupervisors and thus is a significant influence on perceptions of the organization's social climate. Keeley (1988) suggested that organizations be viewed as social contracts. Farh, Podsakoff, and Organ (1990, p. 706) made a case that "much of the evolving contract as seen from the individual's point of view derives from the exchange between the individual and his or her immediate supervisor." Because the supervisor mediates or determines what the organization gives to the subordinate (e.g., training opportunities) and implements the organization's policies and procedures, the subordinate's assessment of the social contract will largely depend on the supervisor's behavior.

Even in corporate cultures that reinforce political behavior, individual supervisors and managers can address politics and its negative effects on their work units, teams, and individual subordinates. Supervisors and managers are positioned to have impact. They can target relevant problems, directly address resistance to his/her efforts, act quickly, and take follow-up action.

SPECIFIC STRATEGIES

How can individual supervisors and managers help their employees cope with work-place politics? Direct attempts by supervisors to reduce political activity at the orga-nization level would be limited in potential for success, because organizational political norms are typically beyond the influences of a single individual or a supervisor-subordinate dyad. While office politics may reflect organization-level norms, the be-havior of the supervisor can have impact on both the experience of workplace politics and its consequences on individuals within their immediate sphere of influence. Indeed, basic supervisory practices reflected in daily interactions with subordinates can reduce uncertainty, increase understanding of organizational events, and, as shared information is to some extent shared power, lead to feelings of control. As pointed out by Ferris et al. (1989b), perceived control and understanding have impacts on the extent to which perceptions of politics affect work behavior.

Four supervisory practices that can reduce the subordinate's experience of politics are discussed here: (1) providing opportunities for subordinates to participate in making decisions on key issues, (2) taking action to ensure that subordinates have similar pri-orities for organizational, work unit, and/or team goals, (3) proactively encouraging subordinates to initiate communication about unfavorable circumstances, and (4) en-couraging and responding appropriately to subordinate feedback in addition to providing subordinates with feedback.

Participation in Decision Making

The outcomes of increased worker participation in decision making (PDM) have been of theoretical and practical interest for several years. Argyris (1964) argued that workers will manifest responsible adult behaviors only when their managers realize that they want to be involved in making decisions. Indeed, "psychological folklore" (Greenberg and Folger 1983) suggests that PDM will generally have positive outcomes. Although empirical investigations of the effects of PDM have yielded mixed results (cf. Cotton, Vollrath, Froggatt, Lengnick-Hall, and Jennings 1988; Kruse 1984; Locke and Schweiger 1979; Strauss 1982; Wagner 1994), a number of positive outcomes have been identified, including improved employee health (Jackson 1983), higher job satis-faction (Smith and Brannick 1990; Vanderslice, Rice, and Julian 1987; Wright 1990), increased organization information-processing capabilities (Castrogiovanni and Macy 1990), and a better understanding of work tasks (Niehoff, Enz, and Grover 1990).

Among the problems with interpreting PDM research has been the difficulty in iden-tifying what it entails (Dachler 1978). Thibaut and Walker (1975) conceptualized two forms of participation: (1) choice or decision control, where the participant has some control over the outcome; and (2) voice or process control, where the participant artic-ulates his/her interest to the decision maker. Voice may include influence over defining the problem, gathering information bearing on the decision, and identifying alternatives, but not making the decision. Cohen (1985) argued that to the extent subordinates can express opinions to the supervisor, they have a "voice."

When subordinates make decisions without discussions with the supervisor, they are acting autonomously and essentially have choice, but they are making decisions without the supervisor's voice. This reflects a low level of PDM. A low level of PDM is also reflected in situations where decisions are made by the supervisor without discussion; as the subordinate has neither choice nor voice. Two moderate levels of PDM occur when: (1) the supervisor usually makes the decisions following discussion, as both have voice but the subordinate usually has little choice; and (2) the subordinate generally makes the decision after discussion, as both have choice and voice (the supervisor has choice, because he/she permitted the subordinate to make the decision). However, it may be likely that the supervisor did not engage the issue if the subordinate usually makes the decision, even if the supervisor has assigned global permission to the subordinate to make decisions. When supervisors and subordinates discuss issues and reach a decision based on consensus (i.e., a collaboration to find resolution), both have optimal voice and choice, which results in a high level of PDM.

Baumgartel (1957) reported that employee performance, job satisfaction, and positive attitudes toward the supervisor were higher among employees whose supervisors engaged in participative decision making, were lowest among employees whose supervisors directed activities with no discussion, and were intermediate among employees whose supervisors took a laissez-faire (subordinate decides) approach.

Evidence (Schaubroeck and Jennings 1991) suggests that the effects of PDM on job satisfaction are mediated by situational perceptions. It is likely that supervisor practices in terms of PDM can reduce the experience of politics and negate the impact of politics, thereby increasing job satisfaction, continuance commitment, and performance. Employees who actively engage in discussions about important issues with their supervisors and, as a result, develop a consensus to resolve the issues might be able to reduce both the level of their experience of office politics and the negative impact of politics on their job attitudes to a greater extent than employees who typically make decisions or whose supervisors make decisions for them.

Four arenas of research support this argument. First, Eisenhardt and Bourgeois (1988) found that levels of political activity among executives were higher in companies whose CEOs centralized power and decision making. Second, researchers have noted that uncertainty is central in the development of political behaviors (Cobb 1986a, 1986b; March and Simon 1958; Tushman 1977). Empirically identified uncertainty-related antecedents of workplace politics include: (1) a disparity between formal authority and actual influence (Dalton 1959), (2) incomplete knowledge about cause and effect (Tushman 1977), (3) the absence of objective performance standards (Pfeffer 1978), (4) rewards based on nonperformance criteria (Robbins 1979), (5) decisions about important issues made in secrecy (Pfeffer 1978), (6) overall uncertainty (Madison, Allen, Porter, Renwick, and Mayes 1980), (7) concerns for career success (Luthans, Hodgetts, and Rosenkrantz 1988), (8) career stage, confidence, and maturity (DuBrin 1978, 1988; Schein 1978), (9) a discussed disagreement over outcomes (Tushman 1977), (10) ambiguous goals (Miles 1980), (11) changing technological and environmental conditions (Miles 1980), and (12) nonprogrammed decisions (Miles 1980). Consensus PDM is likely to reduce uncertainty between the subordinate and supervisor, as the subordinate will have a consensually developed decision and some anticipation of the supervisor's responses to outcomes. Third, individuals select the most defensible course of action when—as perhaps is often the case in political environments (Ferris et al. 1989b)— they anticipate having to justify their decisions or when searching for ways to rationalize past decisions (Staw 1980). Fourth, research on the "self-serving bias" (e.g., Weary-Bradley 1978) suggests that individuals are likely to emphasize their roles in successful decisions but deemphasize their roles in unsuccessful decisions. A concerted decision provides both joint ownership and understanding, which may generate feelings of security and protection in a political environment. As noted by Ferris et al. (1989b, p. 153), "one of the simplest ways of coping in the decision environment is by making decisions that one is reasonably confident will be acceptable to others."

Thus, by making important decisions with the subordinates by consensus, the supervisor is: (1) reducing subordinate uncertainty about how he/she may respond to subsequent decision outcomes, (2) providing subordinates with a defensible course of action with which to justify decisions, and (3) decreasing the probability that he/she will deemphasize his/her role in decisions that led to unfavorable outcomes.

As noted by Witt and Myers (1992), the importance of PDM as an antecedent of organizational outcomes has been empirically identified, yet some managers avoid PDM and sharing information. Some of these managers may do so because they do not know how to collaborate with their workers, while others may explicitly decide to maintain or exercise power and authority to keep their people unaware of goings-on, and others may simply have not thought about alternative management styles. Some managers may also believe that they have more information about a situation than do subordinates and thus do not engage in what they may perceive as needless PDM. Nogradi and Koch (1981) argued that providing additional opportunities for decision making for personnel who are involved in fewer than desired decisions is extremely important from an organizational perspective. They stressed (p. 157) that allowing "individuals to move toward a decisional equilibrium state must be a high priority for the manager." PDM is likely to help reduce general political behaviors.

Goal Congruence

Research on goal-setting theory (e.g., Locke and Latham 1990; Locke, Shaw, Saari, and Latham 1981) has provided substantial evidence of the motivational effects of clear, reachable, and challenging objectives. Supervisors and subordinates working together to establish goals is one of the most important manifestations of PDM. In some organizations, however, subordinates may be either informally discouraged or formally prevented from having input to the goal-setting process. In such environments, the supervisor might be able to reduce the experience of politics for their subordinates by making efforts to ensure that members of the work unit/team hold common objectives.

Both empirical and anecdotal evidence clearly suggest positive outcomes arise from supervisors and subordinates sharing goals for their work unit or team. For example, Vancouver and Schmitt (1991) demonstrated relationships between congruence of non-operational organizational goals and favorable job attitudes.

Witt and Nye (1992) hypothesized that a psychological interpretation of the organization's treatment of employees mediates the relationship between organizational goal congruence and job attitudes. In a path analytic study of 991 federal employees, they reported that organizational goal congruence scores had direct, positive effects on perceptions of organizational support. They suggested that employees whose goals are consistent with those of peers and supervisors may receive more favorable treatment than those whose goals stem from conflicting agendas. Indeed, coworkers and supervisors are unlikely to spend resources to support the work efforts of individuals who have goals different from their own. Rather, they are more likely to support individuals who hold similar goals and agendas. In addition, Witt and Nye (1992) hypothesized that these higher levels of organizational support would have corresponding effects on levels of job satisfaction and organizational commitment. They found that organizational goal congruence scores had indirect, positive effects on job satisfaction and organizational commitment mediated through perceptions of organizational support.

This argument holds for politics as well. At the very least, employees whose goals are inconsistent with those of peers, supervisors, and workers in other organizational units are likely to spend considerable time and idiosyncrasy credits attempting to acquire resources and accomplish objectives. At the most, they face proactive resistance to their efforts. In organizations where goals are not well communicated, employees may not even know that they are operating from a different map. In organizations where both individual-and unit-level goals are explicitly stated and linked with performance appraisal outcomes, employees may act to support only their specific goals to the detriment of the larger system. Supervisor efforts to ensure that members of the work unit appropriately prioritize organizational goals might help the employees reduce their experience of politics in terms of general political behaviors and going along to get ahead, and, in so doing, increase their performance and job effect.

Making Welcome Unwelcome News

Stereotypes suggest that managers in large, bureaucratic organizations seem to dread bad news. However, the desire to keep bad news under the carpet is not unique to large organizations. When political norms suggest silence, workers fear retaliation for speaking up. A supervisor's disapproving receipt of unfavorable news from a subordinate can promote going along to get ahead. Three ways in which this is typically expressed are killing the messenger, silencing the "wave-maker," and nuking the whistleblower. Essentially, leaders are implicitly or explicitly communicating, "do not rock the boat."

Delivering bad news may lead to or be associated with higher levels of productivity by identifying dysfunctional processes. Refusing to receive bad news or making the delivery cost high eventually restricts the flow of vital information. When management teams do not receive accurate data, flawed decisions are inevitable, rework is unavoidable, and costs rise.

Perhaps the most common method of discouraging bad news is killing the messenger. This occurs when the supervisor inflicts damage on subordinates who inform the supervisor about problems. An example: An account executive identifies previously unimagined costs and operational breakdowns. She informs the responsible manager. The manager, who wants to look good in front of senior management, responds angrily, sending a clear message to the account executive—keep your mouth shut and fix it. Eventually, this subordinate and perhaps her peers as well learn to put a positive slant on reports to the supervisor.

Another method is silencing the "wave-maker." Wave-makers are individuals who—because of their role or personal uniqueness—maintain a pattern of delivering news of problems and/or suggesting innovation. The orientation to suggest creative, new ways of thinking about old problems is rare and requires greater cognitive capacity than simply serving as a messenger to report problems. Wave-making can have either direct or indirect effects on unit performance: By questioning strategies and/or tactics, the wave-maker might identify opportunities for improvement or stimulate others to do so. Supervisors who react angrily to, transfer, or even prevent the promotion of wave-makers are sending—either intentionally or unintentionally—a clear signal that bad news and/or innovation is unwelcome.

An example of when an intolerance of wave-making is dysfunctional is well illustrated by a common occurrence in matrix teams. Many organizations have adopted the matrix team approach in recent years. The matrix team strategy brings together workers from different organizational functions (e.g., research and development, engineering, quality assurance, legal, acquisition, users) to work on a common project. Decision making is decentralized to the level of the project/team leader, so that the knowledge relevant to the decision can be collected and outcomes closely monitored (Kolodny 1979). Because team members represent diverse functions, different perspectives are brought to bear on decisions and, in theory, potential problems are likely to be identified and solutions reached. Similarly, cross-functional coordination is enhanced. Political behaviors constitute a problem that could wipe out the advantages of a matrix team structure.

The formal role of team members is to continually represent the interests of their functional department and the project overall; for example, the representative from operations is expected to determine whether or not the project will work when implemented. However, the team leader can discourage inputs or actions that could delay project completion consistent with established deadlines. For example, as team leaders sometimes have input into the performance appraisal of team members via formal communication with the members' supervisors, team members who make waves by constantly throwing wrenches into the deadline-making machinery may face considerable risk. In such situations, members might choose to keep quiet and go along with the team and/or leader's agenda, rather than openly take positions that they perceive to be correct but that might cost them personally. This influence tactic is considered political, as it reflects an attempt to influence other team members by means inconsistent with the objectives of matrix team functioning in an attempt to achieve personal rather than formal team or organizational objectives. An unfortunate result is that deadlines are met, but later the product is delivered with serious problems.

Supervisors or team leaders can reduce the effects of organizational, unit, or team political norms by (1) accepting unfavorable news positively and (2) either proactively promoting or at least tolerating wave-making. In contrast, leaders who balk upon hearing bad news or who are intolerant of wave-makers are likely to exacerbate the political climate.

The third way in which supervisors communicate their intolerance for openness is their response to whistleblowing. Whistleblowing—in which a subordinate communicates very bad news far up or outside the chain of command—typically promotes extreme "CYA" actions simultaneously across many levels of the organization. Thus, there is probably very little a supervisor can do to protect the subordinate once the whistle has sounded; indeed, a study of 161 whistleblowers by Jos, Tompkins, and Hays (1989) indicated that about 80 percent had lost their jobs. Preventive medicine is the key here; one does not want to hear the whistle blow. Miceli and Near (1985) suggested that an individual's decision to blow the whistle is in part based on the assessment of his/her power in the organization and the probability of retaliation. Workers who perceive that they must resort to whistleblowing reflect a symptom that "going along to get head" norms are dominant. Supervisors who experience whistleblowing might serve themselves well by investigating why a subordinate had to go outside the chain of command.

Feedback

Feedback is important. Supervisor-to-subordinate feedback has been identified as a critical element of work design (Hackman and Oldham 1980).

Supervisors who clearly identify the performance expectations of their subordinates and inform them of their degree of conformance to the stated requirements may be providing their subordinates with feelings of control and reducing their feelings of uncertainty (Ferris et al. 1989b). Employees who know that they are acting appropriately within the guidelines set by the boss are likely to feel protected, even in a highly political work climate. In contrast, employees who do not know whether or not their performance has management approval are likely to experience considerable uncertainty. Also, feedback can include information about what employees need to do in order to be promoted—a means for reducing the "pay and promotion" component of politics. Whereas cliques are not difficult to identify and most employees can easily recognize when they need to go along to get ahead, the judgment whether or not promotional decisions are based primarily on popularity or personal relationships is a close call. The explicit clarification of promotional criteria is a potential contributing factor to reducing the experience of politics.

The appropriateness and utility of subordinate-to-supervisor feedback have been issues of practical concern for many years (e.g., Bowers and Franklin 1975) but have not received as much attention as the outcomes of supervisor-to-subordinate feedback. Rosebush and Tallarigo (1991) found that subordinate feedback to the supervisor increased both supervisor and work unit effectiveness. Carroll and Schneier (1982) suggested that subordinate feedback to supervisors has at least three advantages: (1) providing opportunities for employee participation, (2) providing supervisors with useful information that might enhance their effectiveness, and (3) providing a means for team building between subordinates and supervisors. They also noted two disadvantages of subordinate feedback, namely reprisal or apathy from a supervisor upon receiving the feedback results.

Witt and Hellman (1992) hypothesized that subordinate-to-supervisor feedback practices would be related to perceptions of organizational support. They suspected that some subordinate feedback is designed to direct the supervisor's behavior toward facilitating the subordinate's work efforts. Thus, the supervisor's response to feedback can affect the subordinate's view of the support received. They found that favorable subordinate-to-supervisor feedback practices contributed additional variance to the explanation of perceptions of organizational support over and above the variance contributed by PDM, biodata, and personality.

If employees perceive a supervisor to be receptive to their feedback and, when appropriate, to act in a manner consistent with their feedback, they may be likely to perceive lower levels of politics, in contrast to employees who perceive their supervisor as defensive, negative, or apathetic toward feedback. As some of the subordinate's feedback may be designed to direct the supervisor's behavior toward overcoming the political forces inhibiting the subordinate's work efforts, the supervisor's response to the feedback can affect the subordinate's view of the politics. Moreover, supervisors who actively discourage feedback from subordinates or who respond negatively are likely to promote a political climate in which subordinates should go along to get ahead.

CONCLUSION

While there may be a higher order g-factor of emotional cognition reflected in perceptions of the organization's social climate, there is an important difference between perceptions of support and politics. Whereas some employees may work well when receiving little organizational support, few can succeed amidst high levels of politics. For this reason, preventing political behavior from reaching dysfunctional levels should be a priority for management.

Because of demographic factors, workers will decreasingly identify with their employing organization. It is likely that a focus on commitment to the supervisor, team, and work group will replace the emphasis on commitment to the organization, because it is at these levels that employees will form the key emotional ties. Similarly, efforts to reduce politics and the negative effects of politics might have the greatest utility when aimed below the level of the organization, even if the goal is to reduce dysfunctional political behavior that is systemic.

Executives interested in reducing systemic office politics might be served well by a focus on management development, so that the first-line supervisors are equipped with the interpersonal and leadership skills necessary to address politics on behalf of their employees. Adapting different motivational styles to fit the personalities of subordinates is a critical element of managerial performance (Davis, Skube, Hellervik, Gebelein, and Sheard 1992). Thus, a key to a supervisor's success is his/her ability to lead not only the employees who easily adapt to prevailing direction of political winds but also the high maintenance employees with challenging personalities and little awareness of those political winds. Until even more sophisticated models of politics are empirically derived, management development efforts might find utility in focusing on four basic supervisory practices: (1) providing opportunities for subordinates to participate in making decisions on key issues, (2) taking action to ensure that subordinates have similar priorities for organizational, work unit, and/or team goals, (3) proactively encouraging subordinates to initiate communication about unfavorable circumstances, and (4) encouraging and responding appropriately to subordinate feedback in addition to providing subordinates with feedback.

REFERENCES

Argyris, C. (1964). *Integrating the Individual and the Organization*. New York: Wiley.

Ashforth, B.E., and Lee, R.T. (1990). Defensive behavior in organizations: A preliminary model. *Human Relations* 43: 621–648.

Ashforth, B.E., and Mael, F. (1989). Social identity theory and the organization. *Academy of Management Review* 14: 20–39.

Bateman, T.S. (1980). Organizational change and the politics of success. *Group and Organizational Studies* 5: 198–209.

Batten, J.D., and Schwab, J.L. (1965). How to crack down on company politics. *Personnel* 42: 8–20.

Baumgartel, H. (1957). Leadership style as a variable in research administration. *Administrative Science Quarterly* 2: 344–360.

Bowers, D.G., and Franklin, J. (1975). *Survey-Guided Development: Data-Based Organizational Change*. Ann Arbor, MI: University of Michigan, Institute for Social Research.

Carroll, S., and Schneier, C. (1982). *Performance Appraisal and Review Systems: The Identification, Measurement, and Development of Performance in Organizations*. Glenview, IL: Scott, Foresman, and Co.

Castrogiovanni, G.J., and Macy, B.A. (1990). Organizational information processing capabilities and degree of employee participation. *Group and Organizational Studies* 15: 313–336.

Cobb, A.T. (1984). An episodic model of power: Toward an integration of theory and research. *Academy of Management Review* 9: 482–493.

———. (1986a). Informal influence in the formal organization. *Group and Organizational Studies* 11: 229–253.

———. (1986b). Political diagnosis: Applications in organizational development. *Academy of Management Review* 11: 482–496.

Cobb, A.T., and Margulies, N. (1981). Organization development: A political perspective. *Academy of Management Review* 6: 49–59.

Cohen, R.L. (1985). Procedural justice and participation. *Human Relations* 38: 643–663.

Cotton, J.L., Vollrath, D.A., Froggatt, K.L., Lengnick-Hall, M.L., and Jennings, K.R. (1988). Employee participation: Diverse forms and different outcomes. *Academy of Management Review* 13: 8–22.

Dachler, H.P. (1978). The problem nature of participation in organizations: A conceptual evaluation. In B.

King, S. Sweufert, and F.E. Fiedler (eds.), *Managerial Control and Organization Democracy* (pp. 17–29). New York: Wiley.

Dalton, M. (1959). *Men Who Manage.* New York: Wiley.

Dastmalchian, A., Blyton, P., and Adamson, R. (1989). Industrial relations climate: Testing a construct. *Journal of Occupational Psychology* 62: 21–32.

Davis, B.L., Skube, C.J., Hellervik, L.W., Gebelein, S.H., and Sheard, J.L. (1992). *Successful Manager's Handbook.* Minneapolis: Personnel Decisions, Inc.

Drory, A., and Romm, T. (1990). The definition of organizational politics: A review. *Human Relations* 43: 1133–1154.

DuBrin, A.J. (1978). *Winning at Office Politics.* New York: Van Nostrand Reinhold.

———. (1988). Career maturity, organizational rank, and political behavior tendencies: A correlational analysis of organizational politics and career experience. *Psychological Reports* 63: 531–537.

Eisenberger, R., Cotterell, N., and Marvel, J. (1987). Reciprocation ideology. *Journal of Personality and Social Psychology* 53: 743–750.

Eisenberger, R., Fasolo, P., and Davis-LaMastro, V. (1990). Perceived organizational support and employee diligence, commitment, and innovation. *Journal of Applied Psychology* 75: 51–59.

Eisenberger, R., Huntington, R., Hutchison, S., and Sowa, D. (1986). Perceived organizational support. *Journal of Applied Psychology* 71: 500–507.

Eisenhardt, K.M., and Bourgeois, L.J. III (1988). Politics of strategic decision making in high velocity environments: Toward a mid-range theory. *Academy of Management Journal* 31: 737–770.

Farh, J.L., Podsakoff, P.M., and Organ, D.W. (1990). Accounting for organizational citizenship behavior: Leader fairness and task scope versus satisfaction. *Journal of Management* 16: 705–721.

Farrell, D., and Petersen, J.C. (1982). Patterns of political behavior in organizations. *Academy of Management Review* 7: 403–412.

Ferris, G.R., Bhawuk, D.P.S., Fedor, D.B., and Judge, T.A. (1994). Organizational politics and citizenship: Attributions of intentionality and construct definition. In M.J. Martinko (ed.), *Advances in Attribution Theory: An Organizational Perspective.* Delray, FL: St. Lucie Press.

Ferris, G.R., and Kacmar, K.M. (1992). Perceptions of organizational politics. *Journal of Management* 18: 93–116.

Ferris, G.R., Russ, G.S., and Fandt, P.M. (1989). Politics in organizations. In R.A. Giacalone and P. Rosenfeld (eds.), *Impression Management in Organizations* (pp. 143–170). Newbury Park, CA: Sage.

Gandz, J., and Murray, V.V. (1980). The experience of workplace politics. *Academy of Management Journal* 23: 237–251.

Gray, B., and Ariss, S.S. (1985). Politics and strategic change across organizational life cycles. *Academy of Management Review* 10: 707–723.

Greenberg, J., and Folger, R. (1983). Procedural justice, participation, and the fair process effect in groups and organizations. In P. Paulus (ed.), Basic Group Processes (pp. 235–256). New York: Springer-Verlag.

Gummer, B., and Edwards, R.L. (1985). A social worker's guide to organizational politics. *Administration in Social Work* 9: 13–21.

Hackman, J.R., and Oldham, G. (1980). *Work Redesign.* Reading, MA: Addison-Wesley.

Hilton, T.F., Witt, L.A., and Hellman, C.M. (1994). Management influences on perceived safety conditions. Paper presented at the July meeting of the American Psychological Society, Washington, D.C.

Jackson, S.E. (1983). Participation in decision making as a strategy for reducing job-related strain. *Journal of Applied Psychology* 68: 3–19.

James, L.A., and James, L.R. (1989). Integrating work environment perceptions: Explorations into the measurement of meaning. *Journal of Applied Psychology* 74: 739–751.

James, L.R., Demaree, R.G., and Wolf, G. (1984). Estimating within-group interrater reliability with and without response bias. *Journal of Applied Psychology* 69: 85–98.

James, L.R., and Jones, A.P. (1974). Organizational climate: A review of theory and research. *Psychological Bulletin* 81: 1096–1112.

Jones, A.P., and James, L.R. (1979). Psychological climate: Dimensions and relationships of individual and aggregated work environment perceptions. *Organizational Behavior and Human Performance* 23: 201–250.

Jones, S. (1987). Organizational politics: Only the darker side? *Management Education and Development* 18: 116–128.

Jos, P.H., Tompkins, M.E., and Hays, S.W. (1989). In praise of difficult people: A portrait of the committed whistleblower. *Public Administration Review* (November/December): 552–561.

Kacmar, K.M., and Ferris, G.R. (1991). Perceptions of Organizational Politics Scale (POPS): Development and construct validation. *Educational and Psychological Measurement* 51: 193–205.

Kanungo, R.N. (1982). Measurement of job and work involvement. *Journal of Applied Psychology* 67: 341–349.

Keeley, M. (1988). *A Social Contract Theory of Organizations*. Notre Dame, IN: University of Notre Dame Press.

Koffka, K. (1935). *Principles of Gestalt Psychology*. New York: Harcourt and Brace.

Kolodny, H.F. (1979). Evolution of matrix organization. *Academy of Management Review* 4: 543–553.

Kozlowski, S.W.J., and Hattrup, K. (1992). A disagreement about within-group agreement: Disentangling issues of consistency versus consensus. *Journal of Applied Psychology* 77: 161–167.

Kruse, D. (1984). *Employee Ownership and Employee Attitudes*. Norwood, PA: Norwood.

Larson, C.E., and LaFasto, F.M.J. (1989). *Teamwork: What Must Go Right/What Can Go Wrong*. Newbury Park, CA: Sage.

Lazarus, R.S. (1984). On the primacy of cognition. *American Psychologist* 39: 134–129.

Lewin, K. (1936). *Principles of Topological Psychology*. New York: McGraw-Hill.

Litwin, G.H., and Stringer, R.A. (1968). *Motivation and Organizational Climate*. Boston: Harvard Business School.

Locke, E.A., and Latham, G.P. (1990). *A Theory of Goal-Setting and Task Performance*. Englewood Cliffs, NJ: Prentice-Hall.

Locke, E.A., Shaw, K.N., Saari, L.M., and Latham, G.P. (1981). Goal-setting and task performance: 1969–1980. *Psychological Bulletin* 90: 125–152.

Luthans, F., Hodgetts, R.M., and Rosenkrantz, S.A. (1988). *Real Managers*. Cambridge, MA: Ballinger.

Madison, D.L., Allen, R.W., Porter, L.W., Renwick, P.A., and Mayes, B.T. (1980). Organizational politics: An exploration of managers' perceptions. *Human Relations* 33: 79–100.

March, J.G., and Simon, H.A. (1958). *Organizations*. New York: Wiley.

Marks, M.L., Mirvis, P.H., Hackett, E.J., and Grady, J.F., Jr. (1986). Employee participation in a quality circle program: Impact on quality of work life, productivity, and absenteeism. *Journal of Applied Psychology* 71: 61–69.

Martin, J.H., and Sims, H.J. (1974). Power tactics. In D.A. Kolb, I.M. Rubin, and J.M. McIntyre (eds.), *Organizational Psychology: A Book of Readings* (pp. 177–178). Englewood Cliffs, NJ: Prentice-Hall.

Mathieu, J.E. (1991). A cross-level nonrecursive model of the antecedents of organizational commitment and satisfaction. *Journal of Applied Psychology* 76: 607–618.

Mayes, B.T., and Allen, R.W. (1977). Toward a definition of organizational politics. *Academy of Management Review* 2: 672–678.

Miceli, M.P., and Near, J.P. (1985). Characteristics of organizational climate and wrongdoing associated with whistleblowing decisions. *Personnel Psychology* 38: 525–544.

Miles, R.H. (1980). *Macro Organizational Behavior*. Glenview, IL: Scott, Foresman, and Co.

Mintzberg, H. (1985). The organization as political arena. *Journal of Management Studies* 22: 133–154.

Moorman, R.H. (1991). Relationship between organizational justice and organizational citizenship behaviors: Do fairness perceptions influence employee citizenship? *Journal of Applied Psychology* 76: 845–855.

Narayanan, V.K., and Fahey, L. (1982). The micropolitics of strategy formulation. *Academy of Management Review* 7: 25–34.

Niehoff, B.P., Enz, C.A., and Grover, R.A. (1990). The impact of top management actions on employee attitudes and perceptions. *Group and Organizational Studies* 15: 337–352.

Nogradi, G.S., and Koch, S.A. (1981). The relationship between decisional participation and commitment to the organization, community, and profession among municipal recreation administrators. *Leisure Sciences* 4: 143–159.

Nye, L.G., and Witt, L.A. (1993). Dimensionality and construct validity of the perceptions of organizational politics scale (POPS). *Educational and Psychological Measurement* 53: 821–829.

Parker, C.P., Dipboye, R.L., and Jackson, S.L. (1992). Politics perceptions: An investigation of antecedents and consequences. Paper presented at the seventh annual conference of the Society for Industrial and Organizational Psychology, Montreal, May.

Pettigrew, A.M. (1973). *The Politics of Organizational Decision Making*. London: Tavistock.

Pfeffer, J. (1978). *Organizational Design*. Arlington Heights, IL: AHM Publishing.

———. (1981). *Power in Organizations*. Boston: Pitman.

Pfeffer, J., and Salancik, G.R. (1974). Organizational decision making as a political process: The case study of a university budget. *Administrative Science Quarterly* 19: 135–151.

Porter, L.W., Allen, R.W., and Angle, H.L. (1983). The politics of upward influence in organizations. In R.W. Allen and L.W. Porter (eds.), *Organizational Influence Processes* (pp. 408–422). Glenview, IL: Scott, Foresman.

Pritchard, R.D., and Karasick, B.W. (1973). The effect of organizational climate and managerial job performance on managerial job performance and job satisfaction. *Organizational Behavior and Human Performance* 9: 126–146.

Robbins, S.E. (1976). *The Administrative Process: Integrating Theory and Practice*. Englewood Cliffs, NJ: Prentice-Hall.

———. (1983). *Organizational Behavior*. Englewood Cliffs, NJ: Prentice-Hall.

Rosebush, M.A., and Tallarigo, R.S. (1991). Assessments of the usefulness of subordinate survey feedback to supervisors. Paper presented at the Third Annual Meeting of the American Psychological Society, June.

Schaubroeck, J., and Jennings, K.R. (1991). A longitudinal investigation of the factors mediating the participative decision making–job satisfaction linkage. *Multivariate Behavioral Research* 26: 49–68.

Schein, E.H. (1978). *Career Dynamics: Matching Individual and Organizational Needs*. Reading, MA: Addison-Wesley.

Schein, V.E. (1977). Individual power and political behaviors in organizations: An inadequately explored reality. *Academy of Management Review* 2: 64–72.

Schneider, B., and Reichers, A.E. (1983). On the etiology of climates. *Personnel Psychology* 36: 19–39.

Shore, L.M., and Tetrick, L.E. (1991). A construct validity study of the Survey of Perceived Organizational Support. *Journal of Applied Psychology* 76: 637–643.

Smith, C.S., and Brannick, M.T. (1990). A role expectancy model of participation in decision making: A replication and theoretical extension. *Journal of Occupational Behavior* 11: 91–104.

Staw, B.M. (1980). Rationality and justification in organizational life. In B.M. Staw and L.L. Cummings (eds.), *Research in Organizational Behavior* (vol. 2, pp. 45–80). Greenwich, CT: JAI.

Strauss, G. (1982). Workers' participation in management: An international perspective. In B. Staw and L.L. Cummings (eds.), *Research in Organizational Behavior* (vol. 5). Greenwich, CT: JAI Press.

Thibaut, J., and Walker, L. (1975). *Procedural Justice: A Psychological Analysis*. Hillsdale, NJ: Lawrence Erlbaum.

———. (1978). A theory of procedure. *California Law Review* 66: 541–566.

Tushman, M.E. (1977). A political approach to organization: A review and rationale. *Academy of Management Review* 2: 206–216.

Ungson, G.R., and Steers, R.M. (1984). Motivation and politics in executive compensation. *Academy of Management Review* 9: 313–323.

Vancouver, J.B., and Schmitt, N.W. (1991). An exploratory examination of person-organization fit: Organizational goal congruence. *Personnel Psychology* 44: 333–352.

Vanderslice, V.J., Rice, R.W., and Julian, J.W. (1987). The effects of participation in decision making on worker satisfaction and productivity: An organizational simulation. *Journal of Applied Social Psychology* 17: 158–170.

Vredenburgh, D.J., and Maurer, J.G. (1984). A process framework of organizational politics. *Human Relations* 37: 47–66.

Wagner, J.A. III (1994). Participation's effect on performance and satisfaction: A reconsideration of research evidence. *Academy of Management Review* 19: 312–330.

Weary-Bradley, J. (1978). Self-serving bias in the attribution process: A reexamination of the fact or fiction question. *Journal of Personality and Social Psychology* 36: 56–71.

Wildavsky, A. (1964). *The Politics of the Budgeting Process*. New York: Little, Brown.

Witt, L.A. (1991). Exchange ideology as a moderator of job attitudes–organizational citizenship behaviors relationships. *Journal of Applied Social Psychology* 21: 1490–1501.

Witt, L.A., and Hellman, C.M. (1992). Effects of subordinate feedback to the supervisor and participation in decision-making in the prediction of organizational support. In K.A. Vaverek (ed.), *Proceedings of the Southwest Academy of Management* (pp. 191–195). Houston, TX: The Mescon Group.

Witt, L.A., and Myers, J.G. (1992). Perceived environmental uncertainty and participation in decision-making in the prediction of perceptions of the fairness of personnel decisions. *Review of Public Personnel Administration* 12: 49–56.

Witt, L.A., and Nye, L.G. (1992). Organizational goal congruence and job attitudes revisited. Technical report #DOT/FAA/AM-92-8, Washington, DC: Office of Aviation Medicine, Federal Aviation Administration.

Wright, P.L. (1990). Teller job satisfaction and organizational commitment as they relate to career orientations. *Human Relations* 43: 369–381.

Zohar, D. (1980). Safety climate in industrial organizations: Theoretical and applied implications. *Journal of Applied Psychology* 65: 96–102.

13

What Makes a Leader?

Daniel Goleman

Every businessperson knows a story about a highly intelligent, highly skilled executive who was promoted into a leadership position only to fail at the job. And they also know a story about someone with solid—but not extraordinary—intellectual abilities and technical skills who was promoted into a similar position and then soared.

Such anecdotes support the widespread belief that identifying individuals with the "right stuff" to be leaders is more art than science. After all, the personal styles of superb leaders vary: some leaders are subdued and analytical; others shout their manifestos from the mountaintops. And just as important, different situations call for different types of leadership. Most mergers need a sensitive negotiator at the helm, whereas many turnarounds require a more forceful authority.

I have found, however, that the most effective leaders are alike in one crucial way: they all have a high degree of what has come to be known as emotional intelligence. It's not that IQ and technical skills are irrelevant. They do matter, but mainly as "threshold capabilities"; that is, they are the entry-level requirements for executive positions. But my research, along with other recent studies, clearly shows that emotional intelligence is the sine qua non of leadership. Without it, a person can have the best training in the world, an incisive, analytical mind, and an endless supply of smart ideas, but he still won't make a great leader.

In the course of the past year, my colleagues and I have focused on how emotional intelligence operates at work. We have examined the relationship between emotional intelligence and effective performance, especially in leaders. And we have observed how emotional intelligence shows itself on the job. How can you tell if someone has high emotional intelligence, for example, and how can you recognize it in yourself? In the following pages, we'll explore these questions, taking each of the components of emotional intelligence—self-awareness, self-regulation, motivation, empathy, and social skill—in turn.

EVALUATING EMOTIONAL INTELLIGENCE

Most large companies today have employed trained psychologists to develop what are known as "competency models" to aid them in identifying, training, and promoting likely stars in the leadership firmament. The psychologists have also developed such models for lower-level positions. And in recent years, I have analyzed competency models from 188 companies, most of which were large and global and included the likes of Lucent Technologies, British Airways, and Credit Suisse.

In carrying out this work, my objective was to determine which personal capabilities drove outstanding performance within these organizations, and to what degree they did so. I grouped capabilities into three categories: purely technical skills like accounting and business planning; cognitive abilities like analytical reasoning; and competencies demonstrating emotional intelligence such as the ability to work with others and effectiveness in leading change.

To create some of the competency models, psychologists asked senior managers at the companies to identify the capabilities that typified the organization's most outstanding leaders. To create other models, the psychologists used objective criteria such as a division's profitability to differentiate the star performers at senior levels within their organizations from the average ones. Those individuals were then extensively interviewed and tested, and their capabilities were compared. This process resulted in the creation of lists of ingredients for highly effective leaders. The lists ranged in length from seven to fifteen items and included such ingredients as initiative and strategic vision.

When I analyzed all this data, I found dramatic results. To be sure, intellect was a driver of outstanding performance. Cognitive skills such as big-picture thinking and long-term vision were particularly important. But when I calculated the ratio of technical skills, IQ, and emotional intelligence as ingredients of excellent performance, emotional intelligence proved to be twice as important as the others for jobs at all levels.

Moreover, my analysis showed that emotional intelligence played an increasingly important role at the highest levels of the company, where differences in technical skills are of negligible importance. In other words, the higher the rank of a person considered to be a star performer, the more emotional intelligence capabilities showed up as the reason for his or her effectiveness. When I compared star performers with average ones in senior leadership positions, nearly 90% of the difference in their profiles was attributable to emotional intelligence factors rather than cognitive abilities.

Other researchers have confirmed that emotional intelligence not only distinguishes outstanding leaders but can also be linked to strong performance. The findings of the late David McClelland, the renowned researcher in human and organizational behavior, are a good example. In a 1996 study of a global food and beverage company, McClelland found that when senior managers had a critical mass of emotional intelligence capabilities, their divisions outperformed yearly earnings goals by 20%. Meanwhile, division leaders without that critical mass underperformed by almost the same amount.

McClelland's findings, interestingly, held as true in the company's U.S. divisions as in its divisions in Asia and Europe.

In short, the numbers are beginning to tell us a persuasive story about the link between a company's success and the emotional intelligence of its leaders. And just as important, research is also demonstrating that people can, if they take the right approach, develop their emotional intelligence. (See the appendix, "Can Emotional Intelligence Be Learned?")

SELF-AWARENESS

Self-awareness (see Table 13.1) is the first component of emotional intelligence—which makes sense when one considers that the Delphic oracle gave the advice to "know thyself" thousands of years ago. Self-awareness means having a deep understanding of one's emotions, strengths, weaknesses, needs, and drives. People with strong self-awareness are neither overly critical nor unrealistically hopeful. Rather, they are honest—with themselves and with others.

People who have a high degree of self-awareness recognize how their feelings affect them, other people, and their job performance. Thus a self-aware person who knows that tight deadlines bring out the worst in him plans his time carefully and gets his work done well in advance. Another person with high self-awareness will be able to work with a demanding client. She will understand the client's impact on her moods and the deeper reasons for her frustration. "Their trivial demands take us away from the real work that needs to be done," she might explain. And she will go one step further and turn her anger into something constructive.

Self-awareness extends to a person's understanding of his or her values and goals. Someone who is highly self-aware knows where he is headed and why; so, for example, he will be able to be firm in turning down a job offer that is tempting financially but does not fit with his principles or long-term goals. A person who lacks self-awareness is apt to make decisions that bring on inner turmoil by treading on buried values. "The money looked good so I signed on," someone might say two years into a job, "but the work means so little to me that I'm constantly bored." The decisions of self-aware people mesh with their values; consequently, they often find work to be energizing.

How can one recognize self-awareness? First and foremost, it shows itself as candor and an ability to assess oneself realistically. People with high self-awareness are able to speak accurately and openly—although not necessarily effusively or confessionally—about their emotions and the impact they have on their work. For instance, one manager I know of was skeptical about a new personal-shopper service that her company, a major department-store chain, was about to introduce. Without prompting from her team or her boss, she offered them an explanation: "It's hard for me to get behind the rollout of this service," she admitted, "because I really wanted to run the project, but I wasn't selected. Bear with me while I deal with that." The manager did indeed examine her feelings; a week later, she was supporting the project fully.

Such self-knowledge often shows itself in the hiring process. Ask a candidate to

Table 13.1
The Five Components of Emotional Intelligence at Work

	Definition	Hallmarks
Self-Awareness	the ability to recognize and understand your moods, emotions, and drives, as well as their effect on others	self-confidence realistic self-assessment self-deprecating sense of humor
Self-Regulation	the ability to control or redirect disruptive impulses and moods the propensity to suspend judgment—to think before acting	trustworthiness and integrity comfort with ambiguity openness to change
Motivation	a passion to work for reasons that go beyond money or status a propensity to pursue goals with energy and persistence	strong drive to achieve optimism, even in the face of failure organizational commitment
Empathy	the ability to understand the emotional makeup of other people skill in treating people according to their emotional reactions	expertise in building and retaining talent cross-cultural sensitivity service to clients and customers
Social Skill	proficiency in managing relationships and building networks an ability to find common ground and build rapport	effectiveness in leading change persuasiveness expertise in building and leading teams

describe a time he got carried away by his feelings and did something he later regretted. Self-aware candidates will be frank in admitting to failure—and will often tell their tales with a smile. One of the hallmarks of self-awareness is a self-deprecating sense of humor.

Self-awareness can also be identified during performance reviews. Self-aware people know—and are comfortable talking about—their limitations and strengths, and they often demonstrate a thirst for constructive criticism. By contrast, people with low self-awareness interpret the message that they need to improve as a threat or a sign of failure.

Self-aware people can also be recognized by their self-confidence. They have a firm grasp of their capabilities and are less likely to set themselves up to fail by, for example, overstretching on assignments. They know, too, when to ask for help. And the risks they take on the job are calculated. They won't ask for a challenge that they know they can't handle alone. They'll play to their strengths.

Consider the actions of a mid-level employee who was invited to sit in on a strategy meeting with her company's top executives. Although she was the most junior person in the room, she did not sit there quietly, listening in awestruck or fearful silence. She knew she had a head for clear logic and the skill to present ideas persuasively, and she offered cogent suggestions about the company's strategy. At the same time, her self-awareness stopped her from wandering into territory where she knew she was weak.

Despite the value of having self-aware people in the workplace, my research indicates that senior executives don't often give self-awareness the credit it deserves when they look for potential leaders. Many executives mistake candor about feelings for "wimpiness" and fail to give due respect to employees who openly acknowledge their shortcomings. Such people are too readily dismissed as "not tough enough" to lead others.

In fact, the opposite is true. In the first place, people generally admire and respect candor. Further, leaders are constantly required to make judgment calls that require a candid assessment of capabilities—their own and those of others. Do we have the management expertise to acquire a competitor?

Can we launch a new product within six months? People who assess themselves honestly—that is, self-aware people—are well suited to do the same for the organizations they run.

SELF-REGULATION

Biological impulses drive our emotions. We cannot do away with them—but we can do much to manage them. Self-regulation, which is like an ongoing inner conversation, is the component of emotional intelligence that frees us from being prisoners of our feelings. People engaged in such a conversation feel bad moods and emotional impulses just as everyone else does, but they find ways to control them and even to channel them in useful ways. Imagine an executive who has just watched a team of his employees present a botched analysis to the company's board of directors. In the gloom that follows, the executive might find himself tempted to pound on the table in anger or kick over a chair. He could leap up and scream at the group. Or he might maintain a grim silence, glaring at everyone before stalking off.

But if he had a gift for self-regulation, he would choose a different approach. He would pick his words carefully, acknowledging the team's poor performance without rushing to any hasty judgment. He would then step back to consider the reasons for the failure. Are they personal—a lack of effort? Are there any mitigating factors? What was his role in the debacle? After considering these questions, he would call the team together, lay out the incident's consequences, and offer his feelings about it. He would then present his analysis of the problem and a well-considered solution.

Why does self-regulation matter so much for leaders? First of all, people who are in control of their feelings and impulses—that is, people who are reasonable—are able to create an environment of trust and fairness. In such an environment, politics and infighting are sharply reduced and productivity is high. Talented people flock to the organization and aren't tempted to leave. And self-regulation has a trickle-down effect. No one wants to be known as a hothead when the boss is known for her calm approach. Fewer bad moods at the top mean fewer throughout the organization.

Second, self-regulation is important for competitive reasons. Everyone knows that business today is rife with ambiguity and change. Companies merge and break apart regularly. Technology transforms work at a dizzying pace. People who have mastered their emotions are able to roll with the changes. When a new change program is announced, they don't panic; instead, they are able to suspend judgment, seek out information, and listen to executives explain the new program. As the initiative moves forward, they are able to move with it.

Sometimes they even lead the way. Consider the case of a manager at a large manufacturing company. Like her colleagues, she had used a certain software program for five years. The program drove how she collected and reported data and how she thought about the company's strategy. One day, senior executives announced that a new program was to be installed that would radically change how information was gathered and assessed within the organization. While many people in the company complained bitterly about how disruptive the change would be, the manager mulled over the reasons for the new program and was convinced of its potential to improve performance. She eagerly attended training sessions—some of her colleagues refused to do so—and was eventually promoted to run several divisions, in part because she used the new technology so effectively.

I want to push the importance of self-regulation to leadership even further and make the case that it enhances integrity, which is not only a personal virtue but also an organizational strength. Many of the bad things that happen in companies are a function of impulsive behavior. People rarely plan to exaggerate profits, pad expense accounts, dip into the till, or abuse power for selfish ends. Instead, an opportunity presents itself, and people with low impulse control just say yes.

By contrast, consider the behavior of the senior executive at a large food company. The executive was scrupulously honest in his negotiations with local distributors. He would routinely lay out his cost structure in detail, thereby giving the distributors a realistic understanding of the company's pricing. This approach meant the executive couldn't always drive a hard bargain. Now, on occasion, he felt the urge to increase profits by withholding information about the company's costs. But he challenged that impulse—he saw that it made more sense in the long run to counteract it. His emotional self-regulation paid off in strong, lasting relationships with distributors that benefited the company more than any short-term financial gains would have.

The signs of emotional self-regulation, therefore, are not hard to miss: a propensity for reflection and thoughtfulness; comfort with ambiguity and change; and integrity—an ability to say no to impulsive urges.

Like self-awareness, self-regulation often does not get its due. People who can master their emotions are sometimes seen as cold fish—their considered responses are taken as a lack of passion. People with fiery temperaments are frequently thought of as "classic" leaders—their outbursts are considered hallmarks of charisma and power. But when such people make it to the top, their impulsiveness often works against them. In my research, extreme displays of negative emotion have never emerged as a driver of good leadership.

MOTIVATION

If there is one trait that virtually all effective leaders have, it is motivation. They are driven to achieve beyond expectations—their own and everyone else's. The key word here is achieve. Plenty of people are motivated by external factors such as a big salary or the status that comes from having an impressive title or being part of a prestigious company. By contrast, those with leadership potential are motivated by a deeply embedded desire to achieve for the sake of achievement.

If you are looking for leaders, how can you identify people who are motivated by the drive to achieve rather than by external rewards? The first sign is a passion for the work itself—such people seek out creative challenges, love to learn, and take great pride in a job well done. They also display an unflagging energy to do things better. People with such energy often seem restless with the status quo. They are persistent with their questions about why things are done one way rather than another; they are eager to explore new approaches to their work.

A cosmetics company manager, for example, was frustrated that he had to wait two weeks to get sales results from people in the field. He finally tracked down an automated phone system that would beep each of his salespeople at 5 P.M. every day. An automated message then prompted them to punch in their numbers—how many calls and sales they had made that day. The system shortened the feedback time on sales results from weeks to hours.

That story illustrates two other common traits of people who are driven to achieve. They are forever raising the performance bar, and they like to keep score. Take the performance bar first. During performance reviews, people with high levels of motivation might ask to be "stretched" by their superiors. Of course, an employee who combines self-awareness with internal motivation will recognize her limits—but she won't settle for objectives that seem too easy to fulfill.

And it follows naturally that people who are driven to do better also want a way of tracking progress—their own, their team's, and their company's. Whereas people with low achievement motivation are often fuzzy about results, those with high achievement motivation often keep score by tracking such hard measures as profitability or market share. I know of a money manager who starts and ends his day on the Internet, gauging the performance of his stock fund against four industry-set benchmarks.

Interestingly, people with high motivation remain optimistic even when the score is against them. In such cases, self-regulation combines with achievement motivation to overcome the frustration and depression that come after a setback or failure. Take the case of another portfolio manager at a large investment company. After several successful years, her fund tumbled for three consecutive quarters, leading three large institutional clients to shift their business elsewhere.

Some executives would have blamed the nosedive on circumstances outside their control; others might have seen the setback as evidence of personal failure. This portfolio manager, however, saw an opportunity to prove she could lead a turnaround. Two years later, when she was promoted to a very senior level in the company, she described the experience as "the best thing that ever happened to me; I learned so much from it."

Executives trying to recognize high levels of achievement motivation in their people can look for one last piece of evidence: commitment to the organization. When people love their job for the work itself, they often feel committed to the organizations that make that work possible. Committed employees are likely to stay with an organization even when they are pursued by headhunters waving money.

It's not difficult to understand how and why a motivation to achieve translates into strong leadership. If you set the performance bar high for yourself, you will do the same for the organization when you are in a position to do so. Likewise, a drive to surpass goals and an interest in keeping score can be contagious. Leaders with these traits can often build a team of managers around them with the same traits. And of course, optimism and organizational commitment are fundamental to leadership—just try to imagine running a company without them.

EMPATHY

Of all the dimensions of emotional intelligence, empathy is the most easily recognized. We have all felt the empathy of a sensitive teacher or friend; we have all been struck by its absence in an unfeeling coach or boss. But when it comes to business, we rarely hear people praised, let alone rewarded, for their empathy. The very word seems un-businesslike, out of place amid the tough realities of the marketplace.

But empathy doesn't mean a kind of "I'm okay, you're okay" mushiness. For a leader, that is, it doesn't mean adopting other people's emotions as one's own and trying to please everybody. That would be a nightmare—it would make action impossible. Rather, empathy means thoughtfully considering employees' feelings—along with other factors—in the process of making intelligent decisions. For an example of empathy in action, consider what happened when two giant brokerage companies merged, creating redundant jobs in all their divisions. One division manager called his people together and gave a gloomy speech that emphasized the number of people who would soon be fired. The manager of another division gave his people a different kind of speech. He was upfront about his own worry and confusion, and he promised to keep people informed and to treat everyone fairly.

The difference between these two managers was empathy. The first manager was too worried about his own fate to consider the feelings of his anxiety-stricken colleagues. The second knew intuitively what his people were feeling, and he acknowledged their fears with his words. Is it any surprise that the first manager saw his division sink as many demoralized people, especially the most talented, departed? By contrast, the second manager continued to be a strong leader, his best people stayed, and his division remained as productive as ever.

Empathy is particularly important today as a component of leadership for at least three reasons: the increasing use of teams; the rapid pace of globalization; and the growing need to retain talent.

Consider the challenge of leading a team. As anyone who has ever been a part of one can attest, teams are cauldrons of bubbling emotions. They are often charged with reaching a consensus—hard enough with two people and much more difficult as the numbers increase. Even in groups with as few as four or five members, alliances form and clashing agendas get set. A team's leader must be able to sense and understand the viewpoints of everyone around the table.

That's exactly what a marketing manager at a large information technology company was able to do when she was appointed to lead a troubled team. The group was in turmoil, overloaded by work and missing deadlines. Tensions were high among the members. Tinkering with procedures was not enough to bring the group together and make it an effective part of the company.

So the manager took several steps. In a series of one-on-one sessions, she took the time to listen to everyone in the group—what was frustrating them, how they rated their colleagues, whether they felt they had been ignored. And then she directed the team in a way that brought it together: she encouraged people to speak more openly about their frustrations, and she helped people raise constructive complaints during meetings. In short, her empathy allowed her to understand her team's emotional makeup. The result was not just heightened collaboration among members but also added business, as the team was called on for help by a wider range of internal clients.

Globalization is another reason for the rising importance of empathy for business leaders. Cross-cultural dialogue can easily lead to miscues and misunderstandings. Empathy is an antidote. People who have it are attuned to subtleties in body language; they can hear the message beneath the words being spoken. Beyond that, they have a deep understanding of the existence and importance of cultural and ethnic differences.

Consider the case of an American consultant whose team had just pitched a project to a potential Japanese client. In its dealings with Americans, the team was accustomed to being bombarded with questions after such a proposal, but this time it was greeted with a long silence. Other members of the team, taking the silence as disapproval, were ready to pack and leave. The lead consultant gestured them to stop. Although he was not particularly familiar with Japanese culture, he read the client's face and posture and sensed not rejection but interest—even deep consideration. He was right: when the client finally spoke, it was to give the consulting firm the job.

Finally, empathy plays a key role in the retention of talent, particularly in today's information economy. Leaders have always needed empathy to develop and keep good people, but today the stakes are higher. When good people leave, they take the company's knowledge with them.

That's where coaching and mentoring come in. It has repeatedly been shown that coaching and mentoring pay off not just in better performance but also in increased job satisfaction and decreased turnover. But what makes coaching and mentoring work best is the nature of the relationship. Outstanding coaches and mentors get inside the heads of the people they are helping. They sense how to give effective feedback. They know when to push for better performance and when to hold back. In the way they motivate their proteges, they demonstrate empathy in action.

In what is probably sounding like a refrain, let me repeat that empathy doesn't get much respect in business. People wonder how leaders can make hard decisions if they are "feeling" for all the people who will be affected. But leaders with empathy do more than sympathize with people around them: they use their knowledge to improve their companies in subtle but important ways.

SOCIAL SKILL

The first three components of emotional intelligence are all self-management skills. The last two, empathy and social skill, concern a person's ability to manage relationships with others. As a component of emotional intelligence, social skill is not as simple as it sounds. It's not just a matter of friendliness, although people with high levels of social skill are rarely mean-spirited. Social skill, rather, is friendliness with a purpose: moving people in the direction you desire, whether that's agreement on a new marketing strategy or enthusiasm about a new product.

Socially skilled people tend to have a wide circle of acquaintances, and they have a knack for finding common ground with people of all kinds—a knack for building rapport. That doesn't mean they socialize continually; it means they work according to the assumption that nothing important gets done alone. Such people have a network in place when the time for action comes.

Social skill is the culmination of the other dimensions of emotional intelligence. People tend to be very effective at managing relationships when they can understand and control their own emotions and can empathize with the feelings of others. Even motivation contributes to social skill. Remember that people who are driven to achieve tend to be optimistic, even in the face of setbacks or failure. When people are upbeat, their "glow" is cast upon conversations and other social encounters. They are popular, and for good reason.

Because it is the outcome of the other dimensions of emotional intelligence, social skill is recognizable on the job in many ways that will by now sound familiar. Socially skilled people, for instance, are adept at managing teams—that's their empathy at work. Likewise, they are expert persuaders—a manifestation of self-awareness, self-regulation, and empathy combined. Given those skills, good persuaders know when to make an emotional plea, for instance, and when an appeal to reason will work better. And motivation, when publicly visible, makes such people excellent collaborators; their passion for the work spreads to others, and they are driven to find solutions.

But sometimes social skill shows itself in ways the other emotional intelligence components do not. For instance, socially skilled people may at times appear not to be working while at work. They seem to be idly schmoozing—chatting in the hallways with colleagues or joking around with people who are not even connected to their "real" jobs. Socially skilled people, however, don't think it makes sense to arbitrarily limit the scope of their relationships. They build bonds widely because they know that in these fluid times, they may need help someday from people they are just getting to know today.

For example, consider the case of an executive in the strategy department of a global computer manufacturer. By 1993, he was convinced that the company's future lay with the Internet. Over the course of the next year, he found kindred spirits and used his social skill to stitch together a virtual community that cut across levels, divisions, and nations. He then used this de facto team to put up a corporate Web site, among the first by a major company. And, on his own initiative, with no budget or formal status, he signed up the company to participate in an annual Internet industry convention. Calling on his allies and persuading various divisions to donate funds, he recruited more than fifty people from a dozen different units to represent the company at the convention.

Management took notice: within a year of the conference, the executive's team formed the basis for the company's first Internet division, and he was formally put in charge of it. To get there, the executive had ignored conventional boundaries, forging and maintaining connections with people in every corner of the organization.

Is social skill considered a key leadership capability in most companies? The answer is yes, especially when compared with the other components of emotional intelligence. People seem to know intuitively that leaders need to manage relationships effectively; no leader is an island. After all, the leader's task is to get work done through other people, and social skill makes that possible. A leader who cannot express her empathy may as well not have it at all. And a leader's motivation will be useless if he cannot communicate his passion to the organization. Social skill allows leaders to put their emotional intelligence to work.

It would be foolish to assert that good-old-fashioned IQ and technical ability are not important ingredients in strong leadership. But the recipe would not be complete without emotional intelligence. It was once thought that the components of emotional intelligence were "nice to have" in business leaders. But now we know that, for the sake of performance, these are ingredients that leaders "need to have."

It is fortunate, then, that emotional intelligence can be learned. The process is not easy. It takes time and, most of all, commitment. But the benefits that come from having a well-developed emotional intelligence, both for the individual and for the organization, make it worth the effort.

Appendix: Can Emotional Intelligence Be Learned?

For ages, people have debated if leaders are born or made. So too goes the debate about emotional intelligence. Are people born with certain levels of empathy, for example, or do they acquire empathy as a result of life's experiences? The answer is both. Scientific inquiry strongly suggests that there is a genetic component to emotional intelligence. Psychological and developmental research indicates that nurture plays a role as well. How much of each perhaps will never be known, but research and practice clearly demonstrate that emotional intelligence can be learned.

One thing is certain: emotional intelligence increases with age. There is an old-fashioned word for the phenomenon: maturity. Yet even with maturity, some people still need training to enhance their emotional intelligence. Unfortunately, far too many training programs that intend to build leadership skills—including emotional intelligence—are a waste of time and money. The problem is simple: they focus on the wrong part of the brain.

Emotional intelligence is born largely in the neurotransmitters of the brain's limbic system, which governs feelings, impulses, and drives. Research indicates that the limbic system learns best through motivation, extended practice, and feedback. Compare this with the kind of learning that goes on in the neocortex, which governs analytical and technical ability. The neocortex grasps concepts and logic. It is the part of the brain that figures out how to use a computer or make a sales call by reading a book. Not surprisingly—but mistakenly—it is also the part of the brain targeted by most training programs aimed at enhancing emotional intelligence. When such programs take, in effect, a neocortical approach, my research with the Consortium for Research on Emotional Intelligence in Organizations has shown they can even have a negative impact on people's job performance.

To enhance emotional intelligence, organizations must refocus their training to include the limbic system. They must help people break old behavioral habits and establish new ones. That not only takes much more time than conventional training programs, it also requires an individualized approach.

Imagine an executive who is thought to be low on empathy by her colleagues. Part of that deficit shows itself as an inability to listen; she interrupts people and doesn't pay close attention to what they're saying. To fix the problem, the executive needs to be motivated to change, and then she needs practice and feedback from others in the company. A colleague or coach could be tapped to let the executive know when she has been observed failing to listen. She would then have to replay the incident and give a better response; that is, demonstrate her ability to absorb what others are saying. And the executive could be directed to observe certain executives who listen well and to mimic their behavior.

With persistence and practice, such a process can lead to lasting results. I know one Wall Street executive who sought to improve his empathy—specifically his ability to read people's reactions and see their perspectives. Before beginning his quest, the executive's subordinates were terrified of working with him. People even went so far as to hide bad news from him. Naturally, he was shocked when finally confronted with these facts. He went home and told his family but they only confirmed what he had heard at work. When their opinions on any given subject did not mesh with his, they, too, were frightened of him.

Enlisting the help of a coach, the executive went to work to heighten his empathy through practice and feedback. His first step was to take a vacation to a foreign country where he did not speak the language. While there, he monitored his reactions to the unfamiliar and his openness to people who were different from him. When he returned home, humbled by his week abroad, the executive asked his coach to shadow him for parts of the day, several times a week, in order to critique how he treated people with new or different perspectives. At the same time, he consciously used on-the-job interactions as opportunities to practice "hearing" ideas that differed from his. Finally, the executive had himself videotaped in meetings and asked those who worked for and with him to critique his ability to acknowledge and understand the feelings of others. It took several months, but the executive's emotional intelligence did ultimately rise, and the improvement was reflected in his overall performance on the job.

It's important to emphasize that building one's emotional intelligence cannot—will not—happen without sincere desire and concerted effort. A brief seminar won't help; nor can one buy a how-to manual. It is much harder to learn to empathize—to internalize empathy as a natural response to people—than it is to become adept at regression analysis. But it can be done. "Nothing great was ever achieved without enthusiasm," wrote Ralph Waldo Emerson. If your goal is to become a real leader, these words can serve as a guidepost in your efforts to develop high emotional intelligence.

14

A Model of Charismatic Leadership

Jay A. Conger and Rabindra N. Kanungo

CHARISMATIC LEADERSHIP: A BEHAVIORAL MODEL

Most of us carry in our heads a naive theory of what constitutes charismatic leadership. What is needed is a more precise and scientific understanding of the phenomenon. It was toward this end, a decade ago, that we proposed a behavioral theory of charismatic leadership (Conger and Kanungo 1987). In our theory, a leader's charismatic role, like any other type of leadership role (e.g., task, social, participative), is considered an observable behavioral process that can be described and analyzed in terms of a formal model.

Our model builds on the idea that charismatic leadership is an attribution based on followers' perceptions of their leader's behavior. For example, most social psychological theories consider leadership to be a by-product of the interaction between members of a group. As each member works with others to attain group objectives, each begins to realize his or her status in the group as either a leader or a follower. This realization is based on observations of the influence process within a group, which helps members determine their status. The individual who exerts maximum influence over other members is perceived to be filling the leadership role. Leadership is then consensually validated when the membership recognizes and identifies the leader on the basis of their interactions with that person. In other words, leadership qualities are attributed to an individual's influence.

Charismatic leadership is no exception to this process. Thus, charisma must be viewed as an attribution made by followers. This is consistent with the assumption stated earlier that leadership is a relational and attributional phenomenon. The leadership role behaviors displayed by a person make that individual (in the eyes of followers) not only a task leader or a social leader and a participative or directive leader but also a charismatic or noncharismatic leader. The leader's observed behaviors can be interpreted by his or her own followers as expressions of charismatic qualities. Such qualities

Adapted from *Charismatic Leadership in Organizations*, edited by Jay A. Conger and Rabindra N. Kanungo, pp. 35–70, copyright © 1998 by Sage Publications, Inc. Reprinted by permission of Sage Publications, Inc.

are seen as part of the leader's inner disposition or personal style of interacting with followers. These dispositional attributes are inferred from the leader's observed behavior in the same way as other styles of leadership that have been identified previously (Blake and Mouton 1964; Fiedler 1967; Hersey and Blanchard 1977). In this sense, charisma can be considered an additional inferred dimension of leadership behavior or an additional leadership role. As such, it can and should be subjected to the same empirical and behavioral analysis as participative, task, or social dimensions of leadership.

THE BEHAVIORAL COMPONENTS OF CHARISMATIC LEADERSHIP

If a follower's attribution of charisma depends on the observed behavior of the leader, what are the behavioral components responsible for such an attribution? Can these components be identified and operationalized so that we might understand the nature of charisma among organizational leaders? In the following sections, we describe the essential and distinguishable behavioral components of charismatic leadership. These behaviors are interrelated, and the presence and intensity of these characteristics are expressed in varying degrees among different charismatic leaders.

To begin, we can best frame and distinguish these components by examining leadership as a process that involves moving organizational members from an existing present state toward some future state. This dynamic also might be described as a movement away from the status quo toward the achievement of desired longer-term goals.

This process can be conceptualized in a stage model with three specific stages (see Figure 14.1). In the initial stage, the leader must critically evaluate the existing situation or status quo. Deficiencies in the status quo or poorly exploited opportunities in the environment lead to formulations of future goals. Before devising appropriate organizational goals, the leader must assess what resources are available and what constraints stand in the way of realizing future goals. In addition, the leader must assess the inclinations, the abilities, the needs, and the level of satisfaction experienced by followers. This evaluation leads to a second stage: the actual formulation and articulation of goals. Finally, in Stage 3, the leader demonstrates how these goals can be achieved by the organization. It is along these three stages that we can identify behavioral components unique to charismatic leaders.

Before we identify these behaviors, a caveat is in order. In reality, the stages just described do not follow such a simple linear flow. Instead, most organizations face ever-changing environments, and their leadership must constantly revise existing goals and tactics in response to unexpected opportunities or other environmental changes. This model, however, nicely simplifies and approximates this dynamic process and allows us to more effectively contrast the differences between charismatic and noncharismatic leadership. The reader should simply keep in mind that, in reality, a leader is constantly moving back and forth between the stages or engaging in them simultaneously.

Behaviorally, we can distinguish charismatic leaders from noncharismatic leaders in Stage 1 by their sensitivity to environmental constraints and by their ability to identify deficiencies and poorly exploited opportunities in the status quo. In addition, they are

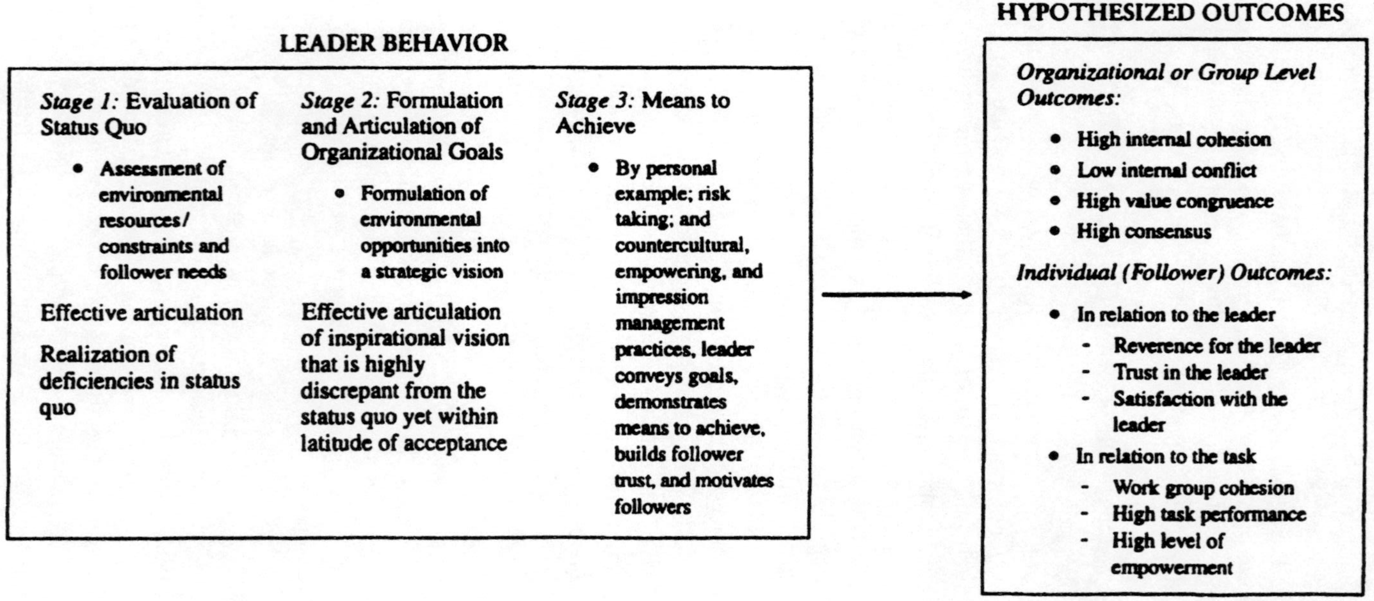

LEADER BEHAVIOR

Stage 1: Evaluation of Status Quo

- Assessment of environmental resources/ constraints and follower needs

Effective articulation

Realization of deficiencies in status quo

Stage 2: Formulation and Articulation of Organizational Goals

- Formulation of environmental opportunities into a strategic vision

Effective articulation of inspirational vision that is highly discrepant from the status quo yet within latitude of acceptance

Stage 3: Means to Achieve

- By personal example; risk taking; and countercultural, empowering, and impression management practices, leader conveys goals, demonstrates means to achieve, builds follower trust, and motivates followers

HYPOTHESIZED OUTCOMES

Organizational or Group Level Outcomes:

- High internal cohesion
- Low internal conflict
- High value congruence
- High consensus

Individual (Follower) Outcomes:

- In relation to the leader
  - Reverence for the leader
  - Trust in the leader
  - Satisfaction with the leader
- In relation to the task
  - Work group cohesion
  - High task performance
  - High level of empowerment

Figure 14.1. A Stage Model of Charismatic Leadership

Table 14.1
Distinguishing Attributes of Charismatic and Noncharismatic Leaders

	Noncharismatic Leaders	Charismatic Leaders
Stage 1		
Environmental sensitivity	Low need for environmental sensitivity to maintain status quo	High need for environmental sensitivity to change the status quo
Relation to status quo	Essentially agrees with status quo and strives to maintain it	Essentially opposes status quo and strives to change it
Stage 2		
Future goals	Goals not too discrepant from status quo	Idealized vision that is highly discrepant from status quo
Likableness	Shared perspective makes him or her likable	Shared perspective and idealized vision make him or her likable and worthy of identification and imitation
Articulation	Weak articulation of goals and motivation to lead	Strong and/or inspirational articulation of future vision and motivation to lead
Stage 3		
Behavior novelty	Conventional, conforming to existing norms	Unconventional or counternormative
Trustworthiness	Disinterested advocacy in persuasion attempts	Passionate advocacy, incurring great personal risk and cost
Expertise	Expert in using available means to achieve goals within the framework of the existing order	Expert in using unconventional means to transcend the existing order
Influence Strategy		
Power base usage	Position power and personal power (based on reward and/or expert power, and liking for a friend who is similar other)	Personal power (based on expert power; respect and admiration for a unique hero)

sensitive to follower abilities and needs. In Stage 2, it is their formulation of an idealized future vision and their extensive use of articulation and impression management skills that sets them apart from other leaders. Finally, in Stage 3, it is their deployment of innovative and unconventional means to achieve their vision and their use of personal power to influence followers that are distinguishing characteristics. Table 14.1 highlights these essential differences. The behavioral components in each of the three stages are discussed in the sections that follow.

Stage 1: Sensitivity to the Environmental Context

Charismatic leaders are very critical of the status quo. They tend to be highly sensitive to both the social and physical environments in which they operate. When a leader fails to assess properly either constraints in the environment or the availability of resources, his or her strategies and actions may not achieve organizational objectives. That leader, in turn, will be labeled ineffective. For this reason, it is important that a leader be able to make realistic assessments of the environmental constraints and resources needed to bring about change within the organization. This is where the knowledge, experience, and expertise of the leader become critical. A leader also must be sensitive to both the abilities and the emotional needs of followers—the most important resources for attaining organizational goals. As Kenny and Zacarro (1983) point out, "Persons who are consistently cast in the leadership role possess the ability to perceive and predict variations in group situations and pattern their own approaches accordingly. Such leaders are highly competent in reading the needs of their constituencies and altering their behaviors to more effectively respond to these needs" (p. 683).

Such assessments, although not a distinguishing feature of charismatic leaders, are nevertheless particularly important for these leaders because they often assume high risks by advocating radical change. Their assessment of environmental resources and constraints then becomes extremely important before planning courses of action. A leader's environmental assessment may dictate that instead of launching a course of action as soon as a vision is formulated, he or she prepare the ground and wait for an appropriate time and place, and/or for the availability of resources. It is presumed that many times charisma has faded because of a lack of sensitivity for the environment.

In the assessment stage, what distinguishes charismatic from noncharismatic leaders is the charismatic leaders' ability to recognize deficiencies in the present context. In other words, they actively search out existing or potential shortcomings in the status quo. For example, the failure of firms to exploit new technologies or new markets might be highlighted as a strategic or tactical opportunity by a charismatic leader. Likewise, a charismatic entrepreneur might more readily perceive marketplace needs and transform them into opportunities for new products or services. In addition, internal organizational deficiencies may be perceived by the charismatic leader as platforms for advocating radical change.

Thus, as noted in Chapter 1, any context that triggers a need for a major change and/or presents unexploited market opportunities is relevant for the emergence of a charismatic leader. In some cases, contextual factors so overwhelmingly favor transformation that a leader can take advantage of them by advocating radical changes for the system. For example, when an organization is dysfunctional or when it faces a crisis, leaders may find it to their advantage to advocate radical changes, thereby increasing the probability of fostering a charismatic image for themselves.

During periods of relative tranquillity, charismatic leaders play a major role in fostering the need for change by creating the deficiencies or exaggerating existing minor ones. They also may anticipate future changes and induce supportive conditions for these. In any case, context can be viewed as a precipitating factor, sometimes facilitating the emergence of certain behaviors in a leader that form the basis of his or her charisma.

Because of their emphasis on deficiencies in the system and their high levels of intolerance for them, charismatic leaders are always seen as organizational reformers or entrepreneurs. In other words, they act as agents of innovative and radical change. The attribution of charisma, however, is dependent not on the outcome of change but simply on the actions taken to bring about change or reform.

From the perspective of managing and fostering change, charismatic leaders need to be distinguished from administrators and supervisors. As mentioned earlier, administrators generally act as caretakers who are responsible for the maintenance of the status quo. They influence others through the power of their positions as sanctioned by the organization. As such, they have little interest in significant organizational change. Supervisors, in their task, social, and participative leadership roles, therefore often act as noncharismatic leaders. Sometimes they act as change agents who may direct or nudge their followers toward established and more traditional goals. Although they may advocate change, it usually is incremental and within the bounds of the status quo. Charismatic leaders, however, seek radical reforms for the achievement of their idealized goals and transform their followers (instead of directing or nudging them). Charisma, then, can never be perceived either in an administrator (caretaker) role or in a supervisory role designed only to nudge the system.

Stage 2: The Future Vision

After assessing the environment, a leader will formulate goals for achieving the organization's objectives. Charismatic leaders can be distinguished from others by the nature of their goals and by the manner in which they articulate them. Charismatic leaders are often characterized by a sense of strategic vision (Bass and Avolio 1993; Berlew 1974; Conger 1985; Dow 1969; House 1995; Marcus 1961; Willner 1984; Zaleznik and Kets de Vries 1975). Here the word vision refers to some idealized goal that the leader wants the organization to achieve in the future. The nature, formulation, articulation, and means for achieving this goal as proposed by the charismatic leader can be distinguished from those advocated by other types of leaders.

Formulating the Vision

The more idealized or utopian the future goal advocated by the leader, the more discrepant it becomes in relation to the status quo. The greater the discrepancy of the goal from the status quo, the more likely is the attribution that the leader has extraordinary vision, not just an ordinary goal. Moreover, by presenting a very discrepant and idealized goal to followers, a leader provides a sense of challenge and a motivating force for change. If we turn to the attitude change literature, it is suggested that a maximum discrepant position within the latitude of acceptance puts the greatest amount of pressure on followers to change their attitudes (Hovland and Pritzker 1957; Petty and Cacioppo 1981). Because the idealized goal is articulated to represent a perspective shared by the followers and promises to meet their hopes and aspirations, it tends to be within this latitude of acceptance in spite of its extreme discrepancy. Leaders then become charismatic as they succeed in changing their followers' attitudes to accept their advocated vision. We argue that leaders are charismatic when their vision represents an embodiment of a perspective shared by followers in an idealized form.

What are the attributes of charismatic leaders that make them successful advocates of their discrepant vision? Research on persuasive communication suggests that to be a successful advocate, one needs to be a credible communicator and that credibility comes from projecting an image of being a likable, trustworthy, and knowledgeable person (Hovland, Janis, and Kelley 1953; Sears, Freedman, and Peplau 1985).

It is the shared perspective of the vision and its potential for satisfying followers' needs that make leaders "likable" persons. Both the perceived similarity and the need satisfaction potential of the leaders form the basis of their attraction (Byrne 1977; Rubin 1973). The idealized (and therefore discrepant) vision, however, also makes such leaders admirable persons deserving of respect and worthy of identification and imitation by the followers. It is this idealized aspect of the vision that makes them charismatic. Charismatic leaders are not just similar others who are generally liked (as popular consensus-seeking people) but similar others who are also distinct because of their idealized vision.

Articulating the Vision

To be charismatic, leaders not only need to have visions and plans for achieving them but also must be able to articulate their visions and strategies for action in effective ways so as to influence their followers. Here, articulation involves two separate processes: articulation of the context and articulation of the leader's motivation to lead. First, charismatic leaders must effectively articulate for followers the following four scenarios representing the context:

1. the nature of the status quo and its shortcomings;
2. a future vision;
3. how the future vision, when realized, will remove existing deficiencies and fulfill the hopes of followers; and
4. the leader's plan of action for realizing the vision.

In articulating the context, the charismatic's verbal messages construct reality such that only the positive features of the future vision and only the negative features of the status quo are emphasized. The status quo usually is presented as intolerable, and the vision is presented in clear, specific terms as the most attractive and attainable alternative. In articulating these elements for subordinates, the leader often constructs several scenarios representing the status quo, goals for the future, needed changes, and the ease or difficulty of achieving goals depending on available resources and constraints. In his or her scenarios, the charismatic leader attempts to create among followers a disenchantment or discontentment with the status quo, a strong identification with future goals, and a compelling desire to be led in the direction of the goal despite environmental hurdles. This process of influencing followers is similar to the path-goal approach to leadership behavior advocated by many theorists (for example, see House 1971).

In addition to verbally describing the status quo, future goals, and the means to achieve them, charismatic leaders also must articulate their own motivation for leading their followers. Using expressive modes of action, both verbal and nonverbal, they manifest their convictions, self-confidence, and dedication to materialize what they advocate. In the use of rhetoric, words are selected to reflect their assertiveness, confidence, expertise, and concern for followers' needs. These same qualities also may be expressed through their dress, their appearance, and their body language. Charismatic leaders' use of rhetoric, high energy, persistence, unconventional and risky behavior, heroic deeds, and personal sacrifices all serve to articulate their high motivation and enthusiasm, which then become contagious among their followers. These behaviors form part of a charismatic leader's impression management.

Stage 3: Achieving the Vision

In the final stage of the leadership process, effective leaders build in followers a sense of trust in their abilities and clearly demonstrate the tactics and behaviors required to achieve the organization's goals. The charismatic leader does this by building trust through personal example and risk taking, as well as through unconventional expertise. It is critical that followers develop a trust in the leader's vision. Generally, leaders are perceived as trustworthy when they advocate their position in a disinterested manner and demonstrate a concern for followers' needs rather than their own self-interest (Walster, Aronson, and Abrahams 1966). To be charismatic, leaders must make these qualities appear extraordinary. They must transform their concern for followers' needs into a total dedication and commitment to a common cause they share, and they must express this in a disinterested and selfless manner. They must engage in exemplary acts that are perceived by followers as involving great personal risk, cost, and energy (Friedland 1964). In this case, personal risk might include the possible loss of personal finances, the possibility of being fired or demoted, and the potential loss of formal or informal status, power, authority, and credibility. Examples of such behaviors entailing risk include Lee Iacocca's reduction of his salary to $1 in his first year at Chrysler (Iacocca and Novak 1984) and John DeLorean's confrontations with the senior management at General Motors (Martin and Siehl 1983). The higher the manifest personal cost or sacrifice for the common goal, the greater is the trustworthiness of a leader. The more leaders are able to demonstrate that they are indefatigable workers prepared to take on high personal risks or incur high personal costs to achieve their shared vision, the more they reflect charisma in the sense of being worthy of complete trust.

Finally, charismatic leaders must appear to be knowledgeable and experts in their areas of influence. Some degree of demonstrated expertise, such as reflected in successes in the past, may be a necessary condition for the attribution of charisma (Conger 1989; Weber 1947). For example, Steven Jobs's success with the Apple I personal computer and Lee Iacocca's responsibility for the Ford Mustang made each more credible with employees. Research by Puffer (1990) has shown that, under conditions of successful outcomes, leaders are in turn credited with greater charisma and expertise. This positive impression may then be used to foster an illusion that the leader has control over uncontrollable events (Meindl et al. 1985). Furthermore, it is hypothesized that the attribution of charisma generally is influenced by the expertise of leaders in two areas. First, charismatic leaders use their expertise in demonstrating the inadequacy of the traditional technology, rules, and regulations of the status quo as a means of achieving the shared vision (Weber 1947). Second, charismatic leaders show an expertise in devising effective but unconventional strategies and plans of action (Conger 1985). We can say that leaders are perceived as charismatic when they reveal expertise in transcending the existing order through the use of unconventional or countercultural means. Iacocca's use of government-backed loans, money back guarantees on cars, union representation on the board, and advertisements featuring himself are examples of unconventional strategic actions in the automobile industry.

The attribution of charisma to leaders also depends on followers' perceptions of their leaders' "revolutionary" and "countercultural" qualities (Berger 1963; Conger 1985; Dow 1969; Friedland 1964; Marcus 1961). The countercultural qualities of leaders are manifested partly in their discrepant idealized visions. More important, charismatic leaders must engage in unconventional, countercultural, and therefore innovative behavior while leading their followers toward the realization of their visions. Martin and Siehl (1983) demonstrated this in their analysis of John DeLorean's countercultural behavior at General Motors. Charismatic leaders are not consensual leaders but active innovators and entrepreneurs. Their plans and strategies for achieving desired changes and their exemplary acts of heroism involving personal risks or self-sacrificing behaviors must be novel and unconventional. Their uncommon behavior, when successful, evokes in their followers emotional responses of surprise and admiration. Such uncommon behavior also leads to a dispositional attribution of charisma.

We now turn to the actual influence process under charismatic leadership.

THE INFLUENCE PROCESS UNDER CHARISMATIC LEADERSHIP

A charismatic leader's behaviors can be viewed as attempts on the part of the leader to influence his or her followers' values, attitudes, and behaviors. The following section describes the psychological underpinnings, or explanations of the influence process involved in charismatic leadership. As mentioned earlier, the leader's role behaviors constitute the "content," or what leaders do, whereas the influence process adopted by the leader constitutes the "process," or how and why the leader's behavior is effective in influencing followers. To further elaborate on the "process" explanation of leadership, one can use Burns's (1978) idea that there are basically two influence processes, or ways of influencing followers, available to leaders. These are (1) the transactional influence processes and (2) the transformational influence processes.

Under transactional influence, the leader ensures that the followers perform the required behaviors through the use of rewards and sanctions. The success of the transactional influence model obviously is limited to the effectiveness of the "life span" of the commodities offered in exchange. In other words, in the transactional influence mode, followers' compliance is governed by the value in exchange of rewards and sanctions. When the major concern of supervisors and managers is to attend to the day-to-day administrative or the operational demands of their organization—that is, to maintain the status quo—they are more likely to use transactional influence to induce compliance in their subordinates. The transactional mode of exercising leadership influence is implicit in the traditional supervisory roles of consideration (or the social role), initiating structure (or the task role), and participation.

The psychological mechanisms and dynamics of the transactional influence process, described in the section on modal orientations, can be explained briefly in terms of a host of resources, under the control of supervisors and managers, that are valued by followers because these resources are instrumental in satisfying the subordinates' salient needs. These resources generally are limited to contingent or noncontingent rewards and punishment and to the authority of an office or a position of power. In their traditional supervising roles, managers can offer these resources to subordinates in exchange for subordinates' compliance with the managers' demands or directives as well as for the subordinates' commitment and loyalty to managers. As demonstrated by the work of Katz and Kahn (1978), the compliance behaviors can be traced to the reward, coercive, and legal power strategies of the manager. This motivational process may be understood best by expectancy theory (Kanungo and Mendonca 1997; Lawler 1973). Subordinates are motivated to perform the behaviors desired by their managers when they can consistently expect certain valued outcomes following their performance behaviors.

On the other hand, the transformational mode of exercising influence is explicit in the charismatic leadership role (see Kanungo and Mendonca [1996] for an extensive treatment of this issue). When managers no longer accept the status quo of their organizations and instead formulate an idealized vision that is discrepant from the status quo and that is shared by subordinates, then such managers move away from being caretakers or administrators and instead function as transformational leaders. In this case, the leader works to bring about a change in the followers' attitudes and values, as he or she moves the organization toward its future goals. This change in followers' attitudes and values essentially is achieved through empowering techniques that increase the self-efficacy beliefs of the followers and affirm that they are capable of achieving the future goals. Followers' compliance is the result of two important factors: (1) their internalization of the leader's vision and (2) an increase in their self-efficacy beliefs. The effects of transformational influence on followers therefore is more enduring and potentially permanent.

To understand the psychological dynamics underlying transformational influence, we draw on social psychological theories of influence processes (notably French and Raven 1959; Kelman 1958) and empowerment (Conger and Kanungo 1988; Thomas and Velthouse 1990). A leader's influence over followers can stem from different bases of power, as suggested by French and Raven (1959). Charismatic influence stems from the leader's personal idiosyncratic power (referent and expert powers) rather than from position power (legal, coercive, and reward powers) determined by organizational rules and regulations. Participative leaders also may use personal power as the basis of their influence. Their personal power, however, is derived from consensus seeking. In addition, some organizational leaders may use personal power through their benevolent but directive behavior. Charismatic leaders, however, are different from both consensual and directive leaders in the use of their personal power. The sources of charismatic leaders' personal power are manifest in their elitist idealized vision, their entrepreneurial advocacy for radical changes, and their depth of knowledge and expertise. In charismatic leaders, all these personal qualities appear extraordinary to followers, and these extraordinary qualities form the basis of both their personal power and their charisma. Although the use of a personal power base (as opposed to a position power base) helps us to understand the charismatics' transformational influence on followers, the leaders' empowerment strategies and the resulting empowering experience of followers are the ingredients critical to the success of the transformational influence process (Kanungo and Mendonca 1996). Also critical to the effectiveness of the transformational influence process is the idealized and shared vision. After leaders formulate an idealized vision, they articulate it by demonstrating their identification with the vision and their commitment to achieve the vision. The leader's identification and commitment, and the exertion of efforts to realize the idealized and shared vision, serve as a model to inspire the followers to undergo a self- or inner transformation consistent with the vision.

Another effect of the leader's formulation and articulation of the vision is to engender in followers a trust in the leader. Followers' trust is earned not only through an inspirational articulation of the vision—although this is a necessary element. It is not developed by a statement of the vision, nor by statements of the leader's expertise in glowing and convincing terms—although these also are necessary. The followers begin to trust their leader when they perceive, beyond a shadow of a doubt, that their leader is unflinchingly dedicated to the vision and is willing to work toward it even at the risk of considerable personal cost and sacrifice.

Here it may be pointed out that the empowerment of followers (building follower self-efficacy and having trust in the leader) is greatly enhanced when charismatic leaders exercise the expert and referent power bases, as mentioned earlier (French and Raven 1959). The leader's expert power is effective in exerting transformational influence because followers perceive their leader to possess the knowledge, abilities, and expertise that followers can draw on and that they see to be necessary for attainment of the vision. The followers' perception that their leader possesses the needed expertise makes the leader credible and trustworthy. Similar to expert power, the leader's referent power also lies in the followers' perception of the leader's commitment to followers' welfare. The leader's transformational influence on followers is derived from the fact that followers perceive their leader's efforts to be selfless and his or her intent to be altruistic. As a result of such perceptions, the followers are attracted to and identify with the leader.

The transformational influence processes in charismatic leadership also can be examined from the viewpoint of attitudinal change processes. According to Kelman (1958), there are three processes of attitude change: compliance, identification, and internalization. We can think of compliance in terms of when "an individual accepts influence . . . [and] adopts the induced behavior not because he believes in its content—but because he expects to gain specific rewards or approval and avoid specific punishments or disapproval by conforming" (Kelman 1958, p. 53). The change in the followers is temporary and superficial; it does not extend to self-transformation of the followers. This type of attitude change is typical of the transactional influence process in supervisory roles.

Identification occurs when "an individual accepts influence because he wants to establish or maintain a satisfying self-defining relationship to another person. . . . The individual actually believes in the responses which he adopts through identification, but their specific content is more or less irrelevant" (Kelman 1958, p. 53). The followers are attracted to the charismatic leader "as a person." That is, the leader's personal qualities and behavior make him or her adorable, like a hero figure or a model to imitate. In the internalization process of attitude change, an individual is willing to accept influence because "the content of the induced behavior—the ideas and actions of which it is composed—is intrinsically rewarding . . . because it is congruent with his value system" (Kelman 1958, p. 53). In the context of the leader-follower interaction, the charismatic leader's articulation of the vision, values, and goals and his or her empowering and tactics bring about profound change in the followers. This change is the transformation of the followers' innermost values and goals resulting from the internalization of the leader's vision. With very rare exceptions, it is unlikely that the identification and internalization processes will occur simultaneously. More likely, the leader's use of empowerment strategies first results in the followers' identification with the leader, and then, over time, in their internalization of the values and the idealized vision professed by the leader.

CHARISMA AS A CONSTELLATION OF BEHAVIORS

Through the leadership roles and influence process models just discussed, we have identified a number of behavioral components that distinguish charismatic from noncharismatic leaders. Although each component, when manifested in a leader's behavior, can contribute to a follower's attribution of charisma to the leader, we consider all these components interrelated because they often appear in a given leader in the form of a constellation rather than in isolation. It is this constellation of behavior components that distinguishes charismatic leaders from other leaders.

Certain features of the components listed under the three stages in Figure 14.1 are critical for the perception of charisma in a leader. It is quite probable that effective and noncharismatic leaders will sometimes exhibit one or more of the behavioral components we have identified. The likelihood of followers attributing charisma to a leader will depend on three major features of these components: the number of these components manifested in a leader's behavior, the level of intensity of each component as expressed in a leader's behavior, and the level of saliency or importance of individual components as determined by the existing situation or organizational context and the level of follower proximity to the leader.

As the number of behavioral components manifested in a leader's behavior increases, the likelihood of a follower's attribution of charisma to the leader also increases. Thus, a leader who is only skillful at detecting deficiencies in the status quo is less likely to be seen as charismatic than is one who not only detects deficiencies but also formulates future visions, articulates them, and devises unconventional means for achieving them.

In addition to differing in the total number of manifested behavioral components, leaders may differ in the magnitude (and/or frequency) of a given behavioral component they exhibit. The higher the manifest intensity or frequency of a behavior, the more likely it is to reflect charisma. Thus, leaders who engage in advocating highly discrepant and idealized visions and use highly unconventional means to achieve these visions are more likely to be perceived as charismatic. Likewise, leaders who express high personal commitment to an objective, who take high personal risk, and who use intense articulation techniques are more likely to be perceived as charismatic.

Followers are more likely to attribute charisma to a leader when they perceive his or her behavior to be contextually appropriate and/or in congruence with their own values. Thus, in a traditional organizational culture that subscribes to conservative modes of behavior among employees and the use of conventional means to achieve organizational objectives, leaders who engage in excessive unconventional behavior may be viewed more as deviants than as charismatic figures. Similarly, a leader whose vision fails to incorporate important values and lacks relevance for the organizational context is unlikely to be perceived as charismatic. Certain behavioral components are more critical and effective sources of charisma in some organizational or cultural contexts, but not in others. For example, in some contexts, unconventionality may be less valued as an attribute of charisma than articulation skills, and in other contexts it may be more valued. The constellation of behaviors and their relative importance as determinants of charisma will differ from one organization to another or from one cultural (or national) context to another. Thus, to develop a charismatic influence, a leader must have an understanding of the appropriateness or importance of the various behavioral components for a given context.

Finally, proximity to the leader may influence the importance of certain behavioral components in attributions of charisma. For example, the components that influence follower attributions of charisma among a close circle of followers having direct contact with the leader may differ from those that influence attributions among a larger group of followers who have no direct contact with the leader. For example, in a recent study, Shamir (1995) showed that rhetorical skills were more frequently attributed as an important characteristic of distant charismatic leaders, whereas being considerate of others and exhibiting unconventional behavior were more important in attributions to close charismatic leaders. Leaders wishing to promote a charismatic influence therefore need an understanding of the relative importance of various behavioral components given their proximity to or distance from followers.

OUTCOMES OF CHARISMATIC LEADERSHIP BEHAVIOR

Our discussion of charismatic leadership in three distinct stages points to a number of ways in which leaders serve their organizations. To ensure the survival and growth of their organizations, they act as status evaluators, constantly monitoring the environment for constraints to overcome and opportunities to utilize. On the basis of their environmental assessment, they act as visionaries and set realistic future task goals for the organization, for work groups, and for individuals. Finally, to achieve these goals, they influence organizational members' beliefs, attitudes, values, and behaviors. The outcomes of these leadership behaviors can be observed either in terms of the end results for the organization, such as the objective indexes of return on investment, units produced, cost per unit, or cost savings, or in terms of follower outcomes, such as changes in follower beliefs, attitudes, and behavior. Earlier in this [article], we argued that the effects on followers are the more appropriate measures of leadership effectiveness, because the objective indexes of end results often depend not only on followers' instrumental behavior but also on other environmental contingencies over which leaders have little control.

Following the above rationale, we postulate that leadership behavior outcomes can be assessed best through followers' attitudes and behaviors and can be identified both at an aggregate (organizational and group level outcomes) and at an individual level. The hypothesized outcomes are presented in Figure 14.1.

At the aggregate level, we hypothesize that charismatic leadership behaviors will result in high internal cohesion, low internal conflict, high value congruence, and high consensus. Under a charismatic leader, there will be a greater degree of sharing of the vision and a greater degree of agreement with respect to the means for achieving the vision.

At the individual level, followers' outcomes can be assessed in two ways: the followers' behaviors and attitudes toward the leader and toward the task. With respect to followers' relations with the charismatic leader, we hypothesize that followers will show a high degree of reverence for the leader, a high degree of trust in the leader, and a high level of satisfaction with the leader. With respect to the followers' relations to the task, we hypothesize that followers will show a high degree of cohesion with the work group, a high level of task performance, and a high level of feeling empowered within the organization to accomplish tasks.

SOME TESTABLE HYPOTHESES ON CHARISMATIC LEADERSHIP

In terms of the charismatic leadership model discussed in the previous sections, it is suggested that the attribution of a charismatic role to people who assume leadership positions is based on a set of leader behaviors. This implies that understanding the phenomenon of charismatic leadership involves an examination of two sides of the same coin: a set of dispositional attributions by followers and a set of leaders' manifest behavior. The two sides are linked in the sense that the leader's behaviors form the basis of followers' attributions. A comprehensive understanding of the charismatic influence process will involve both the identification of the various components of leaders' behavior and assessment of how the components affect the perceptions and attributions of followers.

To validate the behavioral model, we have proposed a set of hypotheses for empirical testing (Conger and Kanungo 1987). This set of testable hypotheses is reproduced in Table 14.2. Evidence in the literature supports the general framework we have suggested here, but the specific predictions listed in Table 14.2 also provide directions for future research.

RELATING TO OTHER BEHAVIORAL APPROACHES TO CHARISMA

The formalized model of charismatic leadership presented in the previous section is often identified as "the attributional theory of charisma" (House 1995, p. 414). This is because the model considers followers' attribution of leadership status to a person as the main reason for the existence of the leadership phenomenon in organizational contexts. As we have asserted, without the followers' attribution of "leadership" to a given person based on their perception of that person's role behaviors, the leadership phenomenon simply would cease to exist.

How can this attributional approach be integrated with other approaches to charismatic leadership? In what ways is the approach similar to or different from other existing charismatic leadership roles? Our review of literature to answer these questions suggests that there are more similarities than differences between the attributional model and other approaches to charismatic leadership. See Table 14.3 for a comparison of the various models.

The attributional model may be compared with three other behavioral approaches that are currently in vogue:

1. the transformational leadership theory advanced by Bass and his associates (Bass 1985; Bass and Avolio 1993),
2. the charismatic leadership theory advanced by House and his associates (House 1995; House and Shamir 1993), and
3. the visionary leadership theory advocated by Sashkin (1988).

These theories can be compared with respect to both the behavioral components identified in charismatic leadership and the nature of the influence process. House and Shamir (1993) compared the behavioral components of charismatic leadership identified in each of these theories and found that there is considerable overlap among the theories, such that differences are marginal. Table 14.3 presents a modified version of the comparison made by House and Shamir. The table shows that both the Bass and House-Shamir models fail to recognize the importance of Stage 1 leader behaviors (evaluation of status quo) in charismatic leadership. As House and Shamir (1993) assert, "While these behaviors have pragmatic value in such circumstances, we see no self-implicating or motive-arousing effects on followers. . . . Thus we do not believe these attributes to be unique to charismatic leaders" (p. 101). This difference between the Conger-

Table 14.2
Some Testable Hypotheses on Charismatic Leadership

Hypotheses on Charisma and Context

1. Charismatic leaders, to foster or retain their charisma, engage in realistic assessments of the environmental resources and constraints involving their visions. They put their innovative strategies into action when they find the environmental resource constraint is favorable to them.

2. Contextual factors that cause potential followers to be disenchanted with the prevailing social order, or that cause followers to experience psychological distress, although not a necessary condition for the emergence of charismatic leaders, facilitate such emergence.

3. Under conditions of relative social tranquility and lack of potential follower psychological distress, the induction of an organizational context by a leader that fosters or supports an attribution of charisma will facilitate the emergence of that leader as a charismatic leader.

4. Charismatic leaders act as reformers or agents of radical changes, and their charisma fades when they act as administrators (caretaker role) or managers (nudging role).

Hypotheses on Charisma and Vision Formulation and Articulation

1. Leaders are charismatic when their vision represents an embodiment of a perspective shared by followers in an idealized form that is highly discrepant from the status quo yet within a latitude of acceptance.

2. Charismatic leaders articulate the status quo as negative or intolerable and the future vision as the most attractive and attainable alternative.

3. Charismatic leaders articulate their motivation to lead through assertive behavior and expression of self-confidence, expertise, unconventionality, and concern for followers' needs.

Hypotheses on Charisma and Achieving the Vision

1. Charismatic leaders take on high personal risks (or incur high costs) and engage in self-sacrificing activities to achieve a shared vision.

2. Charismatic leaders demonstrate expertise in transcending the existing order through the use of unconventional or extraordinary means.

3. Charismatic leaders engage in behaviors that are novel, unconventional, and counternormative, and as such involve high personal risk or high probability of harming their own self-interest.

Kanungo and the House-Shamir and Bass models stems from two sources. First, the Conger-Kanungo approach provides a stage model analysis of charismatic leadership, where Stage 1 behaviors (status quo evaluation) are necessary for the emergence of Stage 2 behaviors (visioning and articulation). Perhaps this is the reason why House and Shamir consider Stage 1 behaviors to have only pragmatic value. Second, House and Shamir suggest that Stage 1 behavior may not have direct motive-arousing effects on followers. In a stage model of analyses, however, status quo evaluation forms the basis of vision formulation and articulation; hence, Stage 1 behaviors affect followers in an indirect manner. Beyond this, the articulation of status quo deficiencies that results from the status quo evaluation does indeed affect followers' attitudes and values toward change in a direct fashion. It may be noted that only through an evaluation of the status quo can the leader present the current situation as either a crisis to overcome or as an opportunity to avail if the vision is pursued.

Table 14.3
Comparison of Behavioral Attributes in Charismatic Leadership Theories

	Conger-Kanungo	Bass	House-Shamir	Sashkin
Stage 1: Evaluation of Status Quo				
Environmental sensitivity to resources and constraints	X			X
Concern for follower needs	X	X		X
Stage 2: Formulation and Articulation of Goals				
Vision:				
Formulation of goals	X	X	X	X
Setting challenging expectations	X		X	
Articulation:				
Inspirational	X	X		
Frame alignment	X		X	
Intellectually stimulating	X	X	X	
Stage 3: Means to Achieve Goals				
Empowering:				
Showing confidence in followers	X	X	X	X
Setting personal examples (role modeling)	X	X	X	X
Displaying competence (role modeling)	X		X	X
Showing self-confidence (role modeling)		X	X	X
Taking risks (establishing trust)	X		X	X
Showing selfless effort (role modeling)	X		X	X
Unconventional tactics to transcend existing order	X		X	X

Furthermore, while comparing the models, House and Shamir (1993) in their analysis failed to notice the presence of frame alignment and the intellectually stimulating articulation of the vision in Stage 2 of the Conger-Kanungo model. Frame alignment implies that communication by the leader should be aligned with followers' attitudes, values, and perspectives. In the Conger-Kanungo model, a leader's vision must represent a perspective shared by followers. In other words, the vision, although discrepant from the status quo, must be within the followers' latitude of acceptance. The Conger-Kanungo model also implicitly recognizes the fact that charismatic leaders engage in intellectually stimulating articulation. When leaders challenge the status quo and formulate their vision in a discrepant and idealized manner, the followers are intellectually challenged to examine their behavior supporting the status quo and to reflect on the idealized vision.

As can be seen in Table 14.3, the greatest overlap is between the Conger-Kanungo, House-Shamir, and Sashkin models. These three models focus more on the behaviors of the leader, whereas the Bass model is more descriptive of the nature of the leadership effects on followers.

The transformational leadership model proposed by Bass and his associates (e.g., Bass and Avolio 1993) claims that charismatic and transformational forms of leadership are distinguishable in organizational contexts. Charismatic leadership is seen as one of the four components in transformational leadership. The four components in transformational leadership are:

1. charisma or idealized influence on followers (sample item measuring the component: "Has my trust in his or her ability to overcome any obstacle"),
2. inspirationally motivating followers (sample item measuring the component: "Uses symbols and images to focus our efforts"),
3. intellectually stimulating followers (sample item measuring the component: "Enables me to think about old problems in new ways"), and
4. individualized consideration of followers (sample item to measure component: "Coaches me if I need it").

The distinction made by Bass between charismatic and transformational leadership is based on a narrow specification of charismatic influence (i.e., limited to formulation of vision or challenging goals). The other three models of charismatic leadership have used the term to include all four components specified in the Bass model. In addition, as we noted in Chapter 1, empirical research on the Bass model consistently shows that the charisma component is the most prominent factor explaining transformational leadership. Research literature on both charismatic and transformational leadership models itself portrays the leader's strategic vision as playing a central role in animating and empowering followers (Bryman 1992).

From our vantage point, what distinguishes transformational from charismatic leadership has little to do with any fundamental differences in leader behavior or tactics but rather with the perspective from which the leadership phenomenon is viewed. The charismatic theories and research have measured leadership from the standpoint of perceived leader behavior, whereas the transformational theories to date have concerned themselves primarily with follower outcomes. In the case of the transformational forms, this was the natural outcome of Burns's (1978) original conceptualization focusing on elevating follower needs and motives to the forefront of the leadership experience. On the other hand, the earlier formulations of charismatic leadership emerging from the fields of sociology and political science were concerned primarily with which leader behaviors and contexts induced follower responses. In essence, the two formulations of charismatic and transformational in the organizational literature are highly complementary and study the same phenomenon, only from different vantage points.

In addition to the overlap of specific behavior components of charismatic leadership identified in various models, there also is an overlap with respect to the nature of the leadership influence process in these models. All four models of charismatic leadership discussed above suggest that leaders use empowerment rather than control strategies to achieve transformational influence over their followers. Conger and Kanungo (1988) have proposed a model of the empowerment process that explains a leader's empowerment strategies (see also Kanungo and Mendonca 1996). During the evaluation of the status quo, the leader identifies organizational and environmental conditions that are alienating followers and hence need to be changed. Such a diagnosis prepares the leader in empowerment strategies such as the idealization of the vision, inspirational articulation, and modeling behavior (personal risk taking and sacrifice) that provide self-efficacy information to the followers. As a result of receiving self-efficacy information from the leader's behaviors, followers strengthen their self-determination belief and feel empowered and self-assured. Such feelings in turn make them more productive and committed to the leader and to the vision.

House and Shamir (1993, p. 88) also suggest that the charismatic leader's behavior influences the self-concept of followers by creating high self-esteem, self-worth, and self-efficacy. This, in turn, results in heightened commitment in followers to a leader and his or her vision.

Bass and Avolio's (1993, p. 56) behavioral indication of transformational leadership clearly has empowering effects on followers. For example, behavioral indicators such as (1) promoting self-development among followers (individualized consideration), (2) convincing followers that they have the ability to achieve high performance levels (inspirational motivation), (3) fostering a readiness for changes in thinking (intellectual stimulation), and (4) modeling through self-sacrifice (idealized influence) do provide self-efficacy information to followers and consequently have empowering effects on them. Recently, Bass (1997) himself has pointed out that "envisioning, enabling, and empowering leadership . . . are central to transformational leadership" (p. 131). In addition, Sashkin (1988) suggests that visionary leaders "boost the sense of self-worth of those around them by expressing unconditional positive regard, paying attention, showing trust, sharing ideas, and making clear how important and valued organization members are" (p. 145).

All these charismatic leadership models advocate the transformational influence of leaders, where the main goal is to change followers' core attitudes, beliefs, and values rather than only to induce compliance behavior in them. Again, all the models agree that charismatic leadership leads to attitude changes among followers, characterized by identification with the leader and the internalization of values embedded in the leader's vision.

Because all the charismatic leadership models discussed above are behavioral models, they agree that the leadership behavior components and their effects on followers can be observed at all levels of the organizations. As Bass and Avolio (1993) point out, however, "Even though transformational leadership behavior has been observed at lower organizational levels, it is likely to occur more frequently at the highest organizational levels" (p. 54) because organizations provide greater scope for visioning (or mission formulation and implementation) behavior at the higher rather than the lower levels.

In conclusion, the Conger-Kanungo model of charismatic leadership is the most comprehensive (across all three leadership stages) of the proposed leadership theories on charismatic and transformational leadership.

NOTE

The "romance of leadership" refers to a school of thought arguing that followers and others exaggerate the importance of a leader in their need to explain events and attribute causality to an individual in a position of authority.

REFERENCES

Bass, B.M. (1985). *Leadership and Performance Beyond Expectations*. New York: Free Press.

———. (1997). Does the transactional-transformational leadership paradigm transcend organizational and national boundaries? *American Psychologist* 52: 130–139.

Bass, B.M., and Avolio, B. (1993). Transformational leadership: A response to critiques. In M. M. Chemers and R. Ayman (eds.), *Leadership theory and research: Perspectives and Directions* (pp. 49–80). New York: Academic Press.

Berger, P.L. (1963). Charisma and religious innovation: The social location of the Israelite Prophecy. *American Sociological Review* 28: 940–950.

Berlew, D.E. (1974). Leadership and organizational excitement. *California Management Review* 17: 21–30.

Blake, R.R., and Mouton, J.S. (1964). *The Managerial Grid*. Houston: Gulf.

Bryman, A. (1992). *Charisma and Leadership in Organizations*. London: Sage.

Burns, J.M. (1978). *Leadership*. New York: Harper and Row.

Byrne, D. (1977). *The Attraction Paradigm*. New York: Academic Press.

Cell, C.P. (1974). Charismatic heads of state: The social context. *Behavioral Science Research* 4: 255–305.

Conger, J.A. (1985). Charismatic leadership in business: An exploration study. Unpublished doctoral dissertation, School of Business Administration, Harvard University.

———. (1989). *The Charismatic Leader: Behind the Mystique of Exceptional Leadership*. San Francisco: Jossey-Bass.

Conger, J.A., and Kanungo, R.N. (1987). Toward a behavioral theory of charismatic leadership in organizational settings. *Academy of Management Review* 12: 637–647.

———. (1988). The empowerment process: Integrating theory and practice. *Academy of Management Review* 13: 471–482.

Dow, T.E. (1969). A theory of charisma. *Social Quarterly* 10: 306–318.

Fiedler, F.E. (1967). *A Theory of Leadership Effectiveness*. New York: McGraw-Hill.

French, J.R., Jr., and Raven, B.H. (1959). The bases of social power. In D. Cartwright (ed.), *Studies in Social Power* (pp. 150–167). Ann Arbor: University of Michigan Press.

Friedland, W.H. (1964). For a sociological concept of charisma. *Social Forces* 43: 18–26.

Hersey, P., and Blanchard, K.H. (1977). *Management of Organizational Behavior* (3d ed.). Englewood Cliffs, NJ: Prentice Hall.

House, R., and Shamir, B. (1993). Toward the integration of transformational, charismatic, and visionary theories. In M. Chemmers and R. Ayman (eds.), *Leadership Theory and Research Perspectives and Directions* (pp. 577–594). Orlando, FL: Academic Press.

House, R.J. (1971). A path-goal theory of leader effectiveness. *Administrative Science Quarterly*, 16: 321–339.

———. (1995). Leadership in the twenty-first century: A speculative inquiry. In A. Howard (ed.), *The Changing Nature of Work* (pp. 411–450). San Francisco: Jossey-Bass.

Hovland, C.I., Janis, I.L., and Kelley, H.H. (1953). *Communication and Persuasion*. New Haven, CT: Yale University Press.

Hovland, C.I., and Pritzker, H.A. (1957). Extent of opinion change as a function of amount of change advocated. *Journal of Abnormal Psychology* 54: 257–261.

Iacocca, L., and Novak, W. (1984). *Iacocca: An Autobiography*. New York: Bantam.

Kanungo, R.N., and Mendonca, M. (1996). *Ethical Dimensions of Leadership*. Thousand Oaks, CA: Sage.

———. (1997). *Fundamentals of Organizational Behavior*. Dubuque, IA: Kendall/Hunt.

Katz, J., and Kahn, R.L. (1978). *The Social Psychology of Organizations*. New York: Wiley.

Kelman, H.C. (1958). Compliance, identification, and internalization: Three processes of attitude change. *Journal of Conflict Resolution* 2: 51–56.

Kenny, P.A., and Zacarro, S.J. (1983). An estimate of variance due to traits in leadership. *Journal of Applied Psychology* 68: 678–685.

Lawler, E.E. (1973). *Motivation in Work Organizations.* Monterey, CA: Brooks/Cole.

Marcus, J.T. (1961, March). Transcendence and charisma. *Western Political Quarterly* 14: 236–241.

Martin, J., and Siehl, C. (1983). Organizational culture and counterculture: An uneasy symbiosis. *Organizational Dynamics* 12(2): 52–64.

Meindl, J.R., Ehrlich, S.B., and Dukerich, J.M. (1985). The romance of leadership. *Administrative Science Quarterly* 30: 521–551.

Petty, R.E., and Cacioppo, J.T. (1981). *Attitudes and Persuasion: Classic and Contemporary Approaches.* Dubuque, IA: Brown.

Puffer, S.M. (1990). Attributions of charismatic leadership: The impact of decision style, outcome, and observer characteristics. *Leadership Quarterly* 1: 177–192.

Rubin, Z. (1973). *Liking and Loving: An Invitation to Social Psychology.* New York: Holt, Rinehart, and Winston.

Sashkin, M. (1988). The visionary leader. In J.A. Conger and R.N. Kanungo (eds.), *Charismatic Leadership: The Elusive Factor in Organizational Effectiveness* (pp. 122–160). San Francisco: Jossey-Bass.

Sears, D.O., Freedman, L., and Peplau, L.A. (1985). *Social Psychology* (5th ed.). Englewood Cliffs, NJ: Prentice Hall.

Shamir, B. (1995). Social distance and charisma: Theoretical notes and an exploratory study. *Leadership Quarterly* 6(1): 19–47.

Thomas, K.W., and Velthouse, B.A. (1990). Cognitive elements of empowerment: An interpretive model of intrinsic task motivation. *Academy of Management Review* 15: 666–681.

Walster, E., Aronson, D., and Abrahams, D. (1966). On increasing the persuasiveness of a low prestige communicator. *Journal of Experimental Social Psychology* 2: 325–342.

Weber, M. (1947). *The Theory of Social and Economic Organizations* (A.M. Henderson and T. Parsons, trans.; T. Parsons, ed.). New York: Free Press.

Willner, A.R. (1984). *The Spellbinders: Charismatic Political Leadership.* New Haven, CT: Yale University Press.

Zaleznik, A., and Kets de Vries, M. (1975). *Power and the Corporate Mind.* Boston: Houghton Mifflin.

15

Motivation and Transformational Leadership: Some Organizational Context Issues

Lyman W. Porter and Gregory A. Bigley

The study of motivation and that of leadership progressed relatively independently of one another for decades during the first half of the twentieth century. More recently, however, an intersection of these areas formed and has been expanding at an increasingly rapid rate, as researchers—especially those in the area of leadership—have specifically emphasized the linkage between the two topics. For example, the path-goal theory connected leader behavior to subordinate satisfaction and effort through an expectancy model of follower motivation (House 1971; House and Dessler 1974). Additionally, scholars who have investigated the emerging and related topics of transformational and charismatic leadership have, in many cases, discussed motivational constructs as central components in their frameworks (e.g., Bass 1985, 1990; Shamir, House, and Arthur 1993). In fact transformational leadership has been explicitly defined in terms of the motivational effects that it has on followers (Bass 1985).

Even though recent scholarship has enlarged somewhat the conceptual area connecting motivation with leadership, it has done so with relatively little consideration for organizational context issues. Conceptual models and empirical studies of transformational leadership have tended to focus narrowly on the leader-follower relationship. Consequently, motivational effects that are revealed when transformational leadership is viewed as a process embedded within an organization have been neglected. The purpose of this paper is to demonstrate that the nature and scope of the linkage between employee motivation and transformational leadership can be more fully understood through an explicit consideration of organizational context factors. After a discussion of some of the motivational underpinnings of transformational leadership, the implications of three situations involving such leadership are explored: (1) the possible effects on followers of multiple transformational leaders, (2) some likely unintended conse-

Originally published in *Work Motivation in the Context of a Globalizing Economy,* edited by M. Erez, U. Kleinbeck, and H. Thierry. Copyright © 2001 by Lawrence Erlbaum Associates.

quences of transformational leadership occurring in one part of an organization, and (3) the potential sustainability of high levels of transformational leadership. The concluding section of this paper highlights some implications for organizations and sets out several suggestions for future research.

MOTIVATION AND TRANSFORMATIONAL LEADERSHIP

A new approach to leadership has become increasingly central in the area of Organizational Behavior over the past two decades. It is characterized by an emphasis on leaders and the leadership processes that appear to have extraordinary effects on followers and, ultimately, on the groups, organizations, or other collectivities to which both the leader(s) and their followers belong (e.g., Bass 1985, 1990; Bennis and Nanus, 1985; Berlew, 1974; Bryman, 1992; Burns 1978; Conger 1989; Conger and Kanungo, 1987, 1988; House 1977; House and Baetz 1979; Howell and Frost 1989; Kouzes and Posner 1987; Nadler and Tushman 1989, 1990; Sashkin 1986, 1988; Sashkin and Burke 1990; Shamir, House, and Arthur 1993; Tichy and Devanna 1990; Trice and Beyer, 1986). Although individual frameworks associated with this new approach have been given numerous labels—such as "visionary," "charismatic," and "transformational" leadership—the expression "transformational leadership" will be used here to refer collectively to these related models, since it seems to be the most all-encompassing of the existing terms.

At the individual level, transformational leadership purportedly alters the motivational basis of individual action, which, in turn, results in a marked increase in follower performance (e.g., followers do more than they originally expected to do) and, possibly, significant personal sacrifices on the part of followers attempting to pursue the leader's mission or vision (Bass 1985, 1990; Conger and Kanungo 1987, 1988; House 1977; House and Baetz 1979; Shamir, House, and Arthur 1993). Explanations for the motivational effects of such leadership tend to emphasize how factors within individuals (e.g., needs, values, self-concepts) are activated or engaged by the leader and then linked to the leader and his or her goals, mission, or vision.

At least four fundamental and interrelated motivational effects of transformational leadership have been set forth in the literature on this topic. First, transformational leadership raises followers' awareness concerning the importance and value of objectives and goals and about ways to reach them (Bass 1985; Burns 1978). Second, such leadership elevates the level of activated needs in followers' psyches from lower to higher orders in Maslow's (or Alderfer's) hierarchy, or it expands followers' needs portfolios at a particular level (Bass 1985; Burns 1978). Third, transformational leadership successfully influences followers to transcend their own self-interests for the sake of the team, organization, or larger polity. Finally, it engages particular elements of followers' self-concepts (e.g., values) in pursuit of the leader's vision or mission (Shamir, House, and Arthur 1993). Supposedly, then, transformational leaders activate certain of their followers' needs or engage particular aspects of their followers' self-concepts, and then present ways for individuals either to fulfill their needs or to express their self-concepts through behaviors that advance the leader's mission or vision.

According to some scholars investigating transformational leadership, the changes in the motivational basis of follower action, such as those described above, are associated with certain types of leader behaviors (Bass 1985, 1990; Conger and Kanungo 1987, 1988; House 1977; House and Baetz 1979; Shamir, House, and Arthur 1993). Perhaps the most widely investigated and empirically supported taxonomy of such behaviors is the one presented by Bass (1985, 1990). In his original formulation, Bass introduced three behavioral categories: charisma, intellectual stimulation, and individualized consideration. A fourth, inspirational motivation (which he originally viewed as a subfactor within charismatic leadership behavior) was added later (Bass 1985; Bass and Avolio 1990). These four behavior types are described briefly below and employed in several examples in subsequent sections.

Bass (1985, p. 39) defined charisma as "an endowment of an extremely high degree of esteem, value, popularity, and/or celebrity-status attributed to others." Charisma is connected with leaders who instill pride in being associated with them, go beyond their self-interests for the good of the group or organization, act in ways that build followers' respect, and display a sense of power and confidence (Bass and Avolio 1995). Inspirational motivation is closely associated with charisma (Bryman 1992). It is characterized as talking optimistically about the future, talking enthusiastically about what needs to be accomplished, articulating a compelling vision of the future, and expressing confidence that goals will be achieved (Bass and Avolio 1995).

Another category of transformational leadership behavior is intellectual stimulation (Bass 1985, 1990). This occurs when leaders encourage their followers to rethink "old" ways of doing things. It entails the leader providing a flow of new ideas to followers, shifting their orientation, or raising their level of consciousness so that followers are induced to reformulate problems that require solutions. Finally, individualized consideration (Bass 1985, 1990) entails the leader showing personal concern for and responding to the needs of individual followers. These four behavior types are purported to directly affect follower motivation. However, we suggest that certain organizational context-related elements may intervene in the leader-follower relationship.

POTENTIAL IMPACTS OF THREE ORGANIZATIONAL CONTEXT FACTORS

In this section, we attempt to demonstrate that the positive motivational effects researchers have attributed to transformational leadership may be enhanced, dampened, or even reversed by organizational context factors. Three examples are provided. First, it is argued that the extent to which transformational leadership behaviors actually result in increased motivation is partly dependent on the distribution of, and coordination among, transformational leaders within the organization's hierarchy. Next, we suggest that transformational leadership taking place in a particular unit may impact the motivation of employees in other units who are neither the intended targets of influence nor the formal subordinates of the transformational leader, and transformational leadership behaviors may trigger group dynamics that could, in turn, have their own (unintended) motivational consequences. Finally, we submit that intense and continuous transformational leadership behaviors may have diminishing motivational effects over time, since individuals cannot be expected to perform at peak levels over extremely prolonged periods.

The Motivational Effects on Organizational Members of Multiple Transformational Leaders

Most of the literature on the topic of transformational leadership deals with cases where individuals are the targets of the influence stemming from only one transformational leader, especially a leader who occupies the highest formal authority position in their followers' group or organization (see Bryman 1992, for a discussion). As a result, most of the extant research has emphasized situations in which transformational leadership flows in a downward direction in line with the organization's formal authority structure. However, most theoretical frameworks do not restrict transformational leadership to these types of circumstances (e.g., Bass 1985, 1990). In fact, transformational leadership has been explicitly conceptualized as an influence process that can spring from almost any point in an organization and may flow in almost any direction (downward, laterally, upward); (cf. Bass 1985; Burns 1978; Yammarino 1994). Consequently, transformational leaders may conceivably be dispersed throughout a particular organization, and a certain employee may be, at one particular time, the target of powerful influence attempts from more than one transformational leader within his or her role set.

A role is typically regarded as an expected pattern or set of behaviors attached to a social position or job within an organization (cf. Katz and Kahn 1978). The expectations connected with a particular role are established and supported primarily by the role occupant and by other people who occupy adjacent organizational roles (e.g., the supervisor, certain peers, subordinates). The extent to which a role may be motivational for employees is partially dependent on the degree to which it is free of ambiguity (i.e., expectations that are not clear to the role occupant) and conflict (e.g., incompatible expectations sent from members of the focal person's role set).

When two or more transformational leaders are present within a focal person's role set, the motivational consequences of transformational leadership are not straightforward. Multiple transformational leaders within a person's role set may increase the focal person's motivation to perform, perhaps even synergistically, if the leaders' behaviors complement or reinforce one another. For example, one such "leader" may establish a direction for a focal person's behavior through the articulation of an appealing vision, another may contribute to helping that individual achieve the vision or mission through compatible intellectual stimulation-type behaviors, and still another may exhibit consistent individualized consideration behaviors toward the focal person. At a more elemental level, transformational leadership behaviors that are consistent with each other will increase motivation by activating the same or complementary needs in employees or by involving the same or complementary aspects of their self-concepts.

In contrast, multiple individuals attempting to exhibit transformational leadership behaviors within an individual's role set may actually decrease the focal person's motivation by increasing his or her role ambiguity or conflict, if the leader behaviors work toward cross purposes. For example, the inspirational message of one transformational leader will increase a focal person's role ambiguity and conflict to the extent that it communicates a mission that is inconsistent with that of other transformational leaders or with that of individuals who occupy higher positions of formal authority.

At a basic motivational level, transformational leader behaviors may activate incompatible needs (perhaps needs at different levels in the hierarchy) that result in conflicts when the individual attempts to satisfy them through role behavior. For example, one transformational leader may activate safety needs in a focal person by emphasizing how tenuous job security is at work. Under this circumstance, the focal person may decide that these types of needs can only be satisfied through a narrow focus on routine task accomplishment. However, another transformational leader may activate self-actualization needs by emphasizing the importance of attempting to realize growth potentials. To fulfill self-actualization needs, the focal person may find that engaging in creative and innovative behavior in the performance of his or her tasks is essential. From this focal person's perspective, safety needs and growth needs cannot be satisfied simultaneously, resulting in conflict.

Unintended Motivational Consequences of a Transformational Leader's Behavior

Previous research has typically focused on the direct relationship between a transformational leader's behaviors and their effects on the followers within his or her own unit (or within the organization as a whole, as in the case of a CEO; for an exception, see Yammarino [1994]). Here, we will discuss how transformational leadership behaviors exhibited by an individual in one unit (e.g., a department) that is one of several or many such units may affect employees' motivation in other units where the employees are neither the subordinates nor the targets of influence of the transformational leader. In addition, it is suggested that organizational processes—specifically, group conflict—can mediate the relationship between transformational leadership behaviors and the motivation of employees, both within the leader's own unit and within other units of the organization.

The extent to which the effects of transformational leadership behaviors taking place in one unit are actually motivational elsewhere in the organization may depend on a variety of context factors. For example, an inspirational message delivered in one department of an organization but experienced by employees in other departments (through formal or informal communication channels) may activate certain needs in those employees. This situation could result in increased motivation to perform at work if the jobs in those other departments allow people to satisfy their activated needs. On the other hand, individualized consideration occurring in one group may result in a decrease in employee motivation in other groups if employees who are not experiencing direct individualized consideration become jealous of those who are and begin to resent their own supervisors for not treating them similarly.

In addition to the potential "spillover" effects of transformational leadership, such leadership occurring within a given organizational unit can conceivably trigger or intensify certain intra- and intergroup dynamics that may, themselves, either increase or decrease employee motivation throughout the organization. For example, transformational leadership may bring about or exacerbate intergroup conflict within an organization by increasing the cohesion among members of a particular group. Further, the heightened conflict could serve as the catalyst for group dynamics that have various motivational consequences, some of which may augment those typically associated with transformational leadership, and others of which may decrease employee motivation in one or more of the conflicting groups. In addition, intergroup conflict may reduce the potential for certain types of transformational leadership behaviors in subsequent time periods.

To illustrate, the literature investigating transformational leaders suggests that such individuals encourage followers to transcend their own self-interests for the welfare of the group or organization by establishing clear group boundaries, by emphasizing common objectives, and by encouraging social identification through the articulation of vision statements and through inspirational talks and emotional appeals (Bass 1985, 1990; House 1977; House and Baetz 1979; Shamir et al. 1993). Group members experiencing transformational leadership, then, are likely to become highly cohesive and focused on goals held in common.

However, other research over many years has acknowledged social identification and the consequent group cohesion as potential antecedents to intergroup discrimination and conflict (Sherif, Harvey, White, Hood, and Sherif 1961; Tajfel 1974, 1981; Tajfel and Turner 1979; Turner 1975, 1987). In fact, intergroup conflict appears to be a natural, though not inevitable, outcome of group member identification and cohesion, and such conflict tends to escalate as cohesion increases. Feelings of solidarity among members within a group can lead to the development of unfavorable attitudes and negative stereotypes of out-group members. Therefore, this research suggests that feelings of hostility and criticism, and subsequent conflict, could exist between two or more groups in an organization, even though the groups may not directly interact or compete with each other for scarce resources.

Any intergroup conflict that is generated appears to have various motivational effects on the employees within the conflicting units (cf. Daft 1983). On the one hand, it may enhance the impact of transformational leadership. For example, group conflict seems to intensify group cohesion. (This suggests that there is a two-way causal effect between cohesion and conflict.) In addition, members of groups in conflict become focused on their own task performance and committed to their own group objectives. On the other hand, group conflict may result in forces that diminish motivation within the organization as a whole. For instance, it may have negative motivational consequences for members of groups that see themselves as losing. In such groups, member cohesion decreases, members experience increased tension among themselves, and they spend time and energy looking for a scapegoat to blame for their failure.

Further, increasing group conflict may result in intra-group dynamics that could discourage leaders from exhibiting certain types of transformational leadership behaviors as conflict increases. For example, in situations of conflict, particularly extreme conflict, autocratic leadership styles are sometimes preferred by group members (Driskell and Salas 1991); consequently, certain behaviors associated with transformational leadership (e.g., individualized consideration and intellectual stimulation) may be resisted by followers because they are viewed as ineffective or too time-consuming.

The Sustainability of High Levels of Motivation Resulting from Transformational Leadership Behaviors

Individuals typically cannot be expected to work at their peak levels indefinitely. Further, most organizations, by their nature, bring people into contact with one another for extended periods. Moreover, once an individual has decided to become a member, much of the contact that he or she has with specific others is determined by the structural features (e.g., roles, policies, procedures, norms) of the organization, and employees may not be able to disengage from relationships (at least, short of quitting the organization) that become, in some respects, uncomfortable. Therefore, since employees may not be able to regulate their own contact with the transformational leaders in their organization who encourage them to perform at peak levels, it will be argued that a high level of continuous transformational leadership can be regarded as a stressor that may, over time, exhibit curvilinear effects on employee motivation. In other words, we will suggest that over prolonged periods of time, particular transformational leadership behaviors may actually reduce motivation as employees become "stressed" or "burned out."

Some of the research reported by Beehr (1995) suggests that high levels of stress can negatively impact employee motivation to perform at work. More specifically, stress appears to be accompanied by anger, anxiety, depression, nervousness, irritability, tension, and boredom (e.g., Gaines and Jermier 1983). High levels of stress experienced at work may lead to what has been termed "burnout," a condition marked by demoralization, frustration, exhaustion, and reduced efficiency (e.g., Beehr 1995; Golembiewski and Munzenrider 1988; Schaufeli, Maslach, and Marek 1993). Under conditions of burnout, the individual can no longer cope with the demands of his or her task environment.

Burnout typically contains three components. Employees experiencing burnout (a) feel emotionally exhausted, (b) depersonalize other individuals that they deal with in their work settings, and (c) feel a sense of low personal accomplishment (Jackson, Schwab, and Schuler 1986; Lee and Ashforth 1990). The types of psychological problems associated with high levels of stress and burnout, in turn, are related to poor job performance, lowered self-esteem (McGrath 1976), resentment of supervision, inability to concentrate and make decisions, and job dissatisfaction (Beehr and Newman 1978). Further, there is some research evidence indicating a positive relationship between stress and absenteeism and turnover (Steers and Rhodes 1978). In addition, some literature suggests that individuals at risk for burnout have several attributes in common, including a tendency to be idealistic and self-motivating achievers and an inclination to seek unattainable goals (Niehouse 1984). These characteristics are similar to the qualities of "transformed" followers of transformational leaders (Bass 1985).

Since transformational leadership can place more of a demand on individuals' psychological and physical capacities to perform than other types of leadership, it potentially represents more of a stressor than other types of leadership. Therefore, although high levels of transformational leadership may lead to higher levels of motivation and performance, this may be only a short-run effect. Such leadership may actually exhibit diminishing (or negative) marginal returns over time. For example, sustained leadership behaviors such as inspirational motivation and intellectual stimulation may have the consequence of increasing motivation and performance initially, but then they may result in diminished motivation and performance as individuals exhaust themselves in their attempts to fulfill the expectations set out by the leader. Although the findings of Seltzer, Numerof, and Bass (1989) suggest that intellectual stimulation is positively associated with charisma and is negatively related to burnout, their study involved a cross-sectional design which could not examine the time dependent nature of the relationships discussed above. It is fair to say that the work to date on transformational leadership has not investigated adequately the effects of high levels of sustained transformational leadership behaviors.

IMPLICATIONS FOR ORGANIZATIONS AND SUGGESTIONS FOR FUTURE RESEARCH

Here we suggest both implications for organizations and directions for future research that follow from the discussion presented in the previous section. It is important to note, however, that in either case we do not intend to present a comprehensive list of issues. Rather, we will set out several salient points that seem to be highlighted by an organizational context perspective.

Implications for Organizations

We have attempted to show that within organizations the relationship between transformational leadership behavior and employee motivation may be more complex than has been commonly assumed. One implication of our argument is that, under certain conditions, managers may be able to raise employee motivation through a reduction in transformational leadership behaviors. For example, in situations where the focal person is the target of influence stemming from two or more individuals displaying conflicting transformational leadership behaviors, such behaviors may cancel each other out, and the focal person's motivation to perform at work may be increased if one of the transformational leaders is removed from the focal person's role set. For another example, a decrease in transformational leadership behaviors may increase overall employee motivation over the long run in situations where the leader's behaviors have been causing unusually high stress for employees.

Another implication pertains to the potential indirect and unintended effects of transformational leadership. For example, a transformational leader may have an additional, and often unintended, impact on employees in other units of the organization. Additionally, motivational effects may not be directly related to transformational-type behaviors. Rather, the relationship between transformational leadership behaviors and employee motivation may be mediated by various processes, e.g., an intergroup conflict dynamic, within the organization.

An organizational context perspective is required to ascertain more accurately the effects of transformational leadership on the motivation of an organization's members. The argument presented above suggests that, depending on the circumstances, members' motivation may be heightened through an increase in transformational leadership, through a redistribution of the transformational leaders within the organization (holding the level of transformational leadership behaviors constant), through a reduction in the level of transformational leadership behaviors, or through some combination of these. Thus, the popular idea that low levels of motivation can be remedied by increased transformational leadership behaviors appears to be overly simplistic where organizations are concerned. Indeed, low levels of employee motivation may be caused by too much transformational leadership behavior in the organization.

Suggestions for Future Research

Several directions for future research follow from our discussion. First, researchers investigating the motivational impact of transformational leadership behaviors within an organization should attempt to ascertain the dispersion pattern of such behaviors within that organization. Since transformational leadership behaviors can emanate from almost any point, and since they may interact in either complementary or conflicting ways, the total effects of such behaviors on employees' motivation may not be determinable without an understanding of how those exhibiting significant transformational leadership behaviors are connected to one another within the organization.

Second, future research may be advanced through investigations of how various transformational leadership behaviors, stemming from different individuals, interact to affect the motivation of a particular target person (or persons) within an organizational setting. It has been suggested that such behaviors may be either complementary or conflicting. In addition, they may interact synergistically, or they may have simply an additive effect.

Third, future research may benefit from attempts to identify organizational processes that can be important mediators between transformational leadership behaviors and employees' motivation. As indicated above, these behaviors may serve as catalysts for organizational dynamics that may have their own motivational effects after they have been activated. The case of intergroup conflict was discussed as one potentially important mediating factor. However, there may be other organizational processes that can act as mediators of transformation leadership behaviors.

Fourth, and following Yammarino (1994), researchers should take a broader view of the potential recipients of a transformational leader's influence within an organization. In most studies of transformational leadership, a leader's direct reports or other specifically intended targets are typically the focus of study. This approach may, however, underestimate the motivational effects of a transformational leader's behavior on the members of the larger organization. As discussed in the preceding section, a transformational leader in one unit of an organization may inadvertently affect employee motivation in other units.

Finally, a longitudinal approach to research on transformational leadership may have particularly high payoffs. It has been suggested that in organizations the relationship between certain types of transformational leadership behaviors and the motivation of employees may be curvilinear across time, because these behaviors may be highly stressful and employees may not be able to regulate their own exposure to them. This type of relationship can be investigated most effectively through research designs involving data collection extending over significant time periods. Longitudinal research can help us answer an important but, as of yet, unaddressed question in the area of transformational leadership: From a motivational standpoint, how much transformational leadership behavior can an organization and its members tolerate?

REFERENCES

Bass, B.M. (1985). *Leadership and Performance Beyond Expectations*. New York: Free Press.

———. (1990). From transactional to transformational leadership: Learning to share the vision. *Organizational Dynamics* 18: 19–31.

Bass, B.M., and Avolio, B.J. (1990). The implications of transactional and transformational leadership for individual, team, and organizational development. *Research in Organizational Change and Development* 4: 231–272.

———. (1995). *The Multifactor Leadership Questionnaire*, 5–45. Binghamton, NY: Center for Leadership Studies.

Beehr, T.A. (1995). *Psychological Stress in the Workplace*. New York: Routledge.

Beehr, T.A., and Newman, J.E. (1978). Job stress, employee health, and organizational effectiveness: A facet analysis, model, and literature review. *Personnel Psychology* (Winter): 665–699.

Bennis, W.G., and Nanus, B. (1985). *Leaders: The Strategies for Taking Charge*. New York: Harper and Row.

Berlew, D.E. (1974). Leadership and organizational excitement. In D.A. Kolb, I.M. Rubin, and J.M. McIntyre (eds.), *Organizational Psychology: A Book of Readings*. Englewood Cliffs, NJ: Prentice-Hall.

Bryman, A. (1992). *Charisma and Leadership in Organizations*. London: Sage.

Burns, J.M. (1978). *Leadership*. New York: Harper and Row.

Conger, J.A. (1989). *The Charismatic Leader: Behind the Mystique of Exceptional Leadership*. San Francisco: Jossey-Bass.

Conger, J.A., and Kanungo, R. (1987). Toward a behavioral theory of charismatic leadership in organizational settings. *Academy of Management Review* 12: 637–647.

————. (1988). Behavioral dimensions of charismatic leadership. In J.A. Conger and R.N. Kanungo (eds.), *Charismatic Leadership: The Elusive Factor in Organizational Effectiveness* (pp. 78–97). San Francisco: Jossey-Bass.

Daft, R.L. (1983). *Organization Theory and Design*. St. Paul, MN: West.

Driskell, J.E., and Salas, E. (1991). Group decision-making under stress. *Journal of Applied Psychology* 76: 473–478.

Gaines, J., and Jermier, J.M. (1983). Emotional exhaustion in high stress organization. *Academy of Management Journal* (December): 567–586.

Golembiewski, R.T., and Munzenrider, R.F. (1988). *Phases of Burnout: Developments in Concepts and Applications*. New York: Praeger.

House, R.J. (1971). A path-goal theory of leader effectiveness. *Administrative Science Quarterly* 16: 321–339.

————. (1977). A 1976 theory of charismatic leadership. In J.G. Hunt and L.L. Larson (eds.), *Leadership: The Cutting Edge* (pp. 189–207). Carbondale: Southern Illinois University Press.

House, R.J., and Baetz, M.L. (1979). Leadership: Some empirical generalizations and new research directions. *Research in Organizational Behavior* 1: 1–14.

House, R.J., and Dessler, G. (1974). The path-goal theory of leadership: Some post hoc and a priori tests. In J. Hunt and L. Larson (eds.), *Contingency Approaches to Leadership*. Carbondale: Southern Illinois University Press.

Howell, J.M., and Frost, P.J. (1989). A laboratory study of charismatic leadership. *Organizational Behavior and Human Decision Processes* 43: 243–269.

Jackson, S.E., Schwab, R.L., and Schuler, R.S. (1986). Toward an understanding of the burnout phenomenon. *Journal of Applied Psychology* 71: 630–640.

Katz, D., and Kahn, R.L. (1978). *The Social Psychology of Organizations* (2d ed.). New York: Wiley.

Kouzes, J.M., and Posner, B.Z. (1987). *The Leadership Challenge*. San Francisco: Jossey-Bass.

Lee, R.T., and Ashforth, B.E. (1990). On the meaning of Maslach's three dimensions of burnout. *Journal of Applied Psychology* 75: 743–747.

McGrath, J.E. (1976). Stress and behavior in organizations. In M.D. Dunnette (ed.), *Handbook of Industrial and Organizational Psychology*. Chicago: Rand McNally.

Nadler, D.A., and Tushman, M.L. (1989). What makes for magic leadership? In W.E. Rosenbach and R.L. Taylor (eds.), *Contemporary Issues in Leadership*. Boulder, CO: Westview.

————. (1990). Beyond the charismatic leader: Leadership and organizational change. *California Management Review* 32: 77–97.

Niehouse, O.I. (1984). Controlling burnout: A leadership guide for managers. *Business Horizons* 27: 80–85.

Sashkin, M. (1986). True vision in leadership. *Training and Development Journal* 40: 58–61.

————. (1988). The visionary leader. In J.A. Conger and R.N. Kanungo (eds.), *Charismatic Leadership: The Elusive Factor in Organizational Effectiveness*. San Francisco: Jossey-Bass.

Sashkin, M., and Burke, W.W. (1990). Understanding and assessing organizational leadership. In K.E. Clark and M.B. Clark (eds.), *Measures of Leadership*. West Orange, NJ: Leadership Library of America.

Schaufeli, W.B., Maslach, C., and Marek, T. (1993). *Professional Burnout: Recent Developments in Theory and Research*. Washington, DC: Taylor and Francis.

Seltzer, J., Numerof, R.E., and Bass, B.M. (1989). Transformational leadership: Is it a source of more burnout and stress? *Journal of Health and Human Resources Administration* 12: 174–185.

Shamir, B., House, R.J., and Arthur, M.B. (1993). The motivational effects of charismatic leadership: A self-concept based theory. *Organization Science* 4: 1–17.

Sherif, M., Harvey, O.J., White, B.J., Hood, W.R., and Sherif, C.W. (1961). *Intergroup Conflict and Cooperation: The Robber's Cave Experiment*. Norman, OK: Institute of Group Relations, University of Oklahoma.

Steers, R.M., and Rhodes, S.R. (1978). Major influences on employee attendance: A process model. *Journal of Applied Psychology* (August): 391–407.

Tajfel, H. (1974). Social identity and intergroup behavior. *Social Science Information* 13: 65–93.

———. (1981). *Human Groups and Social Categories*. Oxford: Blackwell.

Tajfel, H., and Turner, J.C. (1979). An integrative theory of intergroup conflict. In W. Austin and S. Worchel (eds.), *The Social Psychology of Intergroup Relations* (pp. 33–47). Monterey, CA: Brooks/Cole.

Tichy, N.M., and Devanna, M.A. (1990). *The Transformational Leader*. New York: John Wiley.

Trice, H.M., and Beyer, J.M. (1986). Charisma and its routinization in two social movement organizations. In L.L. Cummings and B.M. Staw (eds.), *Research in Organizational Behavior* (vol. 8, pp. 113–164). Greenwich, CT: JAI Press.

Turner, J.C. (1975). Social comparison and social identity: Some prospects for intergroup behavior. *European Journal of Social Psychology* 5: 5–34.

———. (1987). *Rediscovering the Social Group: A Self-categorization Theory*. New York: Basil Blackwell.

Yammarino, F.J. (1994). Indirect leadership: Transformational leadership at a distance. In B.M. Bass and B.J. Avolio (eds.), *Improving Organizational Effectiveness Through Transformational Leadership*. Thousand Oaks, CA: Sage.

PART 3

Lateral Influence

In the "real" world of organizations where work is carried out, the importance of lateral influence is increasing rapidly. One only has to consider the strong contemporary trend toward flatter, less hierarchical organizations; the increasing use of groups to accomplish organizational tasks; and the related emphasis on structuring organizations as interacting sets of networks of units, groups, and individuals that are marked by few, if any, formal status or rank differences. Taken together, these developments point toward the need for greater attention to, and understanding of, how lateral influence works and what factors facilitate or impede its progress in organizational contexts.

It should be noted here at the outset of Part 3 that organizational scholars have not always given this form of influence the amount of attention it deserves. To illustrate this assertion, we can cite the results of a tabulation carried out early in the 1990s by a research assistant of one of the authors. An examination of articles in three relevant academic journals (*Academy of Management Journal*, *Academy of Management Review*, and *Journal of Applied Psychology*) revealed that across the most recent five-year time span articles that dealt with some aspect of the organizational hierarchy were four times as likely to have concerned the vertical dimension exclusively compared to the horizontal or lateral dimension. (That was "progress," however, since a survey of similar journal articles published fifteen years earlier demonstrated a five-to-one vertical to lateral emphasis.) Our conclusion was that "This [kind of] distribution is analogous to developing a city that has many tall buildings but that gives relatively little attention to the transportation infrastructure that connects those buildings" (Porter 1996, p. 265).

In the remainder of this introduction to this section of the book, we discuss the essence of lateral influence, its different types, and the challenges involved in this form of influence for both the agent or initiator and the target. The eight readings that follow the introduction cover a range of illustrations of different kinds of lateral influence in action in organizational settings. The readings also highlight a number of the interesting features of lateral influence, not the least of which is its potential power to affect the attitudes and behavior of organizational participants.

THE NATURE AND TYPES OF LATERAL INFLUENCE

Clearly, it would seem that not only is more scholarly and research emphasis needed on lateral influence processes, but a fairly safe prediction is that this will in fact happen over the next decade. The changing nature of the structures and operations of organizations will be the driving force that will cause this to happen. Even if organizations weren't evolving as rapidly as they are, the simple fact is that a great many organizational relationships have always been of an essentially lateral character. These basic types of lateral influence include the following:

- Socialization: an organization's influence on individuals other than by formal commands or requirements;
- Individualization (or Personalization): the reciprocal process, referring to an individual member's influence on the organization (or a part of it);
- Intergroup influence: a group's influence on another group or groups;
- Group influence: a group's influence on individual group members; and
- Interindividual influence: an organizational or group member's influence on another individual member or members.

For each of these types of lateral relationships, several of which will be illustrated in the articles that follow in this section, the fundamental feature that characterizes the associated influence situations is that the two parties involved do not have a clear and unambiguous hierarchical (vertical) difference between them. Thus, lateral influence does not necessarily require that the amount of power possessed by the two parties be exactly equal—only that one party does not report through the chain of command to the other within the organization. In contrast to vertical influence patterns, neither party is in a position to use formal authority over the other in lateral influence. It is the absence of a formal authority relationship that distinguishes lateral influence from the downward influence process discussed in Part 2.

CHALLENGES FOR THE AGENT OF INFLUENCE

It is precisely this absence of a formal authority relationship that makes lateral influence situations so fascinating. The basic challenge for the agent of influence is how to bring about a positive response or compliance to the influence attempt without having available the considerable leverage of conferred authority. This challenge is amplified in today's organizations compared to those of bygone eras, given the often greater education level of the typical member and the far stronger norm for members to exert their (relative) independence and "voice." Thus, potential influencers are probably more likely to use expert and referent forms of power than in the past. That does not mean, however, that direct or implied rewards and punishments play no role in lateral influence in modern organizations. These remain potentially important sources of power in lateral situations, since either party may have access to them and could at least use them indirectly to affect the other party. In any event, it is up to the influence agent to select an effective form of influence for use in the circumstances of nonvertical relationships. As previously noted, our research-based knowledge of the lateral influence process is, unfortunately, still relatively limited at this point in time. Thus, lateral influence presents a challenge not only for those attempting to exercise influence but also for those who study influence processes in organizations.

CHALLENGES FOR THE TARGET OF INFLUENCE

In analyzing lateral influence processes in organizational settings, one can also take the perspective of the influence target. In many instances, as several of the readings in this section demonstrate, the object of lateral influence frequently seems to be unaware that influence is even taking place. Thus, one key issue is target awareness. Another concerns the range of options available to the target to respond to an influence attempt when it is perceived or noticed. To put it another way, in lateral influence situations the target often has a clear choice about how to respond. This can range from a welcoming or accepting type of response on one end of a continuum to a response of opposition at the other end, and any number of gradations of response in between these two extremes. In effect, this choice gives influence targets a kind of power if they decide to exercise it. In many organizational circumstances, the target of lateral influence is not necessarily a passive target but rather one that can be quite active in supporting or defeating an influence attempt. Here, again, this feature adds to the interesting nature of lateral influence.

THE READINGS IN PART 3

The readings in this section begin with a classic article that examines the process of socialization. In this article, by Edgar H. Schein, the author analyzes some of the basic elements of socialization and the effects of the overall process. He describes socialization as "the process of 'learning the ropes' . . . the process by which a new members learns the value systems, the norms and behavior patterns of the society, organization, or group to which he is entering." Schein particularly emphasizes the dangers of nonconformity or overconformity responses by organizational members to the organization's socialization attempts. It should be noted that socialization in organizational situations happens not only when a person enters an organization, but also can occur when an individual takes a new position or is transferred to a new location. Particularly important in Schein's analysis is his distinction among pivotal, relevant, and peripheral norms, and how each of these relates to several types of potential responses by the individual. These responses include "rebellion," "creative individualism," and "conformity." Schein concludes with an interesting discussion of the potential for conflict between socialization to a profession (as carried out in schools of business and management, for example) and socialization within a specific organization.

The following article, by Solomon E. Asch, is another "classic" in the academic literature relevant to lateral influence. In fact, it was first published over a half-century ago. Nevertheless, its insights are timeless with respect to the amount of influence that a group potentially can have on an individual member. A subject in the set of experiments described in the article was typically led to believe that the other "members" of the group (actually confederates pre-instructed by the experimenter) differed with the subject about their judgments about the perceived length of a small line. Thus, the subject found that his or her opinion was contradicted by that of the majority of the group, and the issue was whether the subject would change to the group's opinion if given a chance. The experiments were designed to understand the social and personal conditions that lead to group influence on individual judgments. Although over fifty years old, the findings of Asch's studies and their implications are as important today as they were at the time the research was carried out. The results convey a number of important, even crucial, messages for anyone attempting to understand this type of lateral influence situation. For example, the findings conclusively demonstrate the enormous effect that a majority opinion can have on the single individual in a group. They also, however, highlight the extent of a large range of individual differences in susceptibility to group influence and the fact that some people are quite resistant to group pressure if they believe that they are correct in their own judgments.

The phenomenon of a group's influence on the individual is also the subject of the next article, by Bertram H. Raven. He takes a retrospective view of a famous concept relating to group influence on individual members put forth some thirty years ago by the late psychologist Irving Janis, namely, "groupthink." Janis had proposed to explain how very intelligent individuals can unintelligently suppress "critical thoughts as a result of internalization of group norms." Subsequent to the publication of his articles and books about the concept of groupthink, there has been considerable critical examination of its explanatory validity by some social scientists. Raven, who, like Janis, is a social psychologist, examines both the concept and the controversy from the vantage point of the late 1990s. He concludes that "by and large, the basic principles of groupthink theory have still held strong."

The following article vividly illustrates group pressure "at work" in an actual work group. In this article, James R. Barker describes a study carried out in a small manufacturing plant. The company in question decided to convert its traditional hierarchical structure that relied on strong and ever-present supervisory control to one that was formed around self-managing work groups with vastly decreased direct supervisory oversight. In the initial phase of the transition, the work teams devoted considerable time to building a consensus on what constituted quality work both for the group as a whole and for the individual member. They also focused on what types of concrete behavior by group members would convert these standards into actual practice. In the next phase of the transition, the groups developed norms that would support the desired behavior. These norms gradually became more formalized and took on the characteristics of rules—rules enforced by the groups. As the researcher concluded, "The teams had now created, in effect, a nearly perfect form of control . . . the team members had become their own masters and their own slaves." The groups had, in effect, become (in the author's term) "iron cages" for their individual members. Obviously, in some circumstances, as this article illustrates, lateral influence in the form of social pressure can, and often does, become more powerful than downward, formal authority influence.

The next article, by Sandra L. Robinson and Anne M. O'Leary-Kelly, provides another example of work group lateral influence, in this case an illustration of the contagion effect of undesirable or negative behaviors in a group. In this well-controlled study the researchers collected data from employees in thirty-five different work groups, ranging in size from 4–10 members, across twenty organizations. The results clearly indicated that an individual working in a group with a higher level of so-called antisocial behavior (e.g., "damaged property belonging to employer," "did work badly, incorrectly or slowly on purpose") was more likely to exhibit such behavior than an employee working in a group with lower levels of this kind of behavior. Furthermore, a group's influence on such behavior by the individual member was stronger the longer the employee had been in the group and the greater the task interdependence required by work procedures. As the researchers concluded, "these findings present a consistent pattern, suggesting that as the richness of the group experience increases, members became more likely to match their level of antisocial behavior to that of the group." It would be interesting to speculate on how much employees were aware of the effect of their work group on their own tendencies to engage in negative behavior of this type. It might be guessed that many workers would deny that such influence effects occurred, even though the data indicate otherwise.

The sixth selection in this section, by Ruth Wageman and Elizabeth A. Mannix, analyzes issues of how those individuals with greater power within groups can use such power for more effective group performance and member satisfaction or, on the other hand, misuse their power to the detriment of the group's performance and satisfaction. Thus, this piece focuses on how an individual—a relatively powerful member, in this analysis—can influence a group. The authors present a number of propositions regarding what kind of behaviors by the (relatively) powerful individual member contribute to positive group responses and which behaviors tend to lead to more negative team reactions. The propositions provide general guidelines for anyone holding a position of relative power within a group, and the discussions of the propositions provide explanations of why and how such power can be used or misused in the process of influencing a group.

The next article, by Allen R. Cohen and David L. Bradford, essentially focuses on peer-to-peer lateral relationships and the problem of "finding ways to develop mutual influence without the formal authority to command." As the authors succinctly put the issue: "Organizational members who want to make things happen often find themselves in this position. . . . They find it necessary to influence colleagues . . . [who] cannot be ordered around because they are under another area's control and can legitimately say no because they have many other valid priorities. They can respond only when they choose to." In their analysis of how such peer-to-peer influence can be accomplished, Bradford and Cohen invoke the "law of reciprocity"—"the almost universal belief that people should be paid back for what they do, that one good (or bad) deed deserves another." The authors argue that influence is possible precisely because "people expect that their actions will be paid back in one form or another. . . ."

An emphasis on the norm of reciprocity to understand how lateral influence can be accomplished without formal authority in turn requires an understanding of exchange process of relationships. For productive exchanges to take place, according to Bradford and Cohen, the two parties need some kind of equivalent "currency"—something to be exchanged that both parties accept as "payment." The article lists some five different types of currencies—the content of the exchange—that could potentially be used to good advantage in this type of lateral influence situation. Not only is exchange content important, of course, but so is the process. In this regard, the authors discuss four features of the exchange process that a potential influencer should consider in order to make the exchange as effective as possible. They conclude by emphasizing that any exchange process is facilitated by a prior development of trust between the parties involved, and that for some situations where there are fundamental differences between the two parties there may be no feasible currencies or effective exchange processes that will achieve the influencer's objectives.

The final article in this section, by Ferris et al., could be placed in any of the latter three Parts of this book because it deals with a topic, "political skill," that is relevant to downward and upward influence as well as lateral influence. However, we place it here at the end of Part 3 because it is centrally involved as an element in the lateral influence process and because the article provides a sort of direct transition to the next Part on "Upward Influence," where the subject of organizational politics has an especially prominent role.

Ferris and his colleagues define political skill as "an interpersonal style construct that combines social astuteness with the ability to relate [to other people] well. . . ." They see it as a "distinct type of social skill" that combines a set of dimensions of other social skills, such as tacit knowledge, emotional intelligence, and social self efficacy, among others. Also, as their definition implies, the authors give special weight to the concept of "style" as a critical component of political skill. They state that this kind of skill "makes . . . influence behavior better," and that it plays an important part in developing an individual's reputation for being effective and successful. Toward the latter part of the article, Ferris et al. make a case for the importance of including the building of this kind of skill in human resource development programs for organizational members, since, in their view, "the use of political skill is becoming increasingly important in organizations as team management and related programs are implemented." To this, the authors of this book couldn't agree more.

Overall, the set of readings presented here in Part 3 serve to emphasize the pervasiveness and variety of types of lateral influence that exist in organizational contexts. Any organizational participant who wants to be effective, and especially anybody in a managerial position, will need to develop a degree of both sensitivity to, and proficiency in, the exercise of lateral influence. Also, as the readings demonstrate, such lateral influence can emanate from individuals, from groups, and from organizations, and, of course, can be directed toward any or all of these different categories of recipients.

Although the process of lateral influence, regardless of the source or the target, can sometimes be less tangible and less visible than vertical influence, it is no less important in organizations.

REFERENCE

Porter, L.W. (1996). Forty years of organization studies: Reflections from a micro perspective. *Administrative Science Quarterly* 41: 262–269.

16

Organizational Socialization and the Profession of Management

Edgar H. Schein

I can define my topic of concern best by reviewing very briefly the kinds of issues upon which I have focused my research over the last several years.[1] In one way or another I have been trying to understand what happens to an individual when he enters and accepts membership in an organization. My interest was originally kindled by studies of the civilian and military prisoners of the Communists during the Korean War. I thought I could discern parallels between the kind of indoctrination to which these prisoners were subjected, and some of the indoctrination which goes on in American corporations when college and business school graduates first go to work for them. My research efforts came to be devoted to learning what sorts of attitudes and values students had when they left school, and what happened to these attitudes and values in the first few years of work. To this end I followed several panels of graduates . . . into their early career.

Organizational socialization is the process of "learning the ropes," the process of being indoctrinated and trained, the process of being taught what is important in an organization or some subunit thereof. This process occurs in school. It occurs again, and perhaps most dramatically, when the graduate enters an organization on his first job. It occurs again when he switches within the organization from one department to another, or from one rank level to another. It occurs all over again if he leaves one organization and enters another. And it occurs again when he goes back to school, and again when he returns to the organization after school.

Indeed, the process is so ubiquitous and we go through it so often during our total career, that it is all too easy to overlook it. Yet it is a process which can make or break a career, and which can make or break organizational systems of manpower planning. The speed and effectiveness of socialization determine employee loyalty, commitment, productivity, and turnover. The basic stability and effectiveness of organizations therefore depends upon their ability to socialize new members.

Let us see whether we can bring the process of socialization to life by describing

Adapted from *Sloan Management Review*, vol. 9, no. 2, "Organizational Socialization and the Profession of Management," pp. 1–16, copyright 1968 by MIT Press. Reprinted with permission from the publisher.

how it occurs. I hope to show you the power of this process, particularly as it occurs within industrial organizations. Having done this, I would like to explore a major dilemma which I see at the interface between organizations and graduate management schools. Schools socialize their students toward a concept of a profession, organizations socialize their new members to be effective members. Do the two processes of socialization supplement each other or conflict? If they conflict, what can we do about it in organizations and in the schools?

SOME BASIC ELEMENTS OF ORGANIZATIONAL SOCIALIZATION

The term socialization has a fairly clear meaning in sociology, but it has been a difficult one to assimilate in the behavioral sciences and in management. To many of my colleagues it implies unnecessary jargon, and to many of my business acquaintances it implies the teaching of socialism—a kiss of death for the concept right there. Yet the concept is most useful because it focuses clearly on the interaction between a stable social system and the new members who enter it. The concept refers to the process by which a new member learns the value system, the norms, and the required behavior patterns of the society, organization, or group which he is entering. It does not include all learning. It includes only the learning of those values, norms, and behavior patterns which, from the organization's point of view or group's point of view, it is necessary for any new member to learn. This learning is defined as the price of membership.

What are such values, norms, and behavior patterns all about? Usually they involve:

1. The basic goals of the organization.
2. The preferred means by which these goals should be attained.
3. The basic responsibilities of the member in the role which is being granted to him by the organization.
4. The behavior patterns which are required for effective performance in the role.
5. A set of rules or principles which pertain to the maintenance of the identity and integrity of the organization.

The new member must learn not to drive Chevrolets if he is working for Ford, not to criticize the organization in public, not to wear the wrong kind of clothes or be seen in the wrong kinds of places. If the organization is a school, beyond learning the content of what is taught, the student must accept the value of education, he must try to learn without cheating, he must accept the authority of the faculty and behave appropriately to the student role. He must not be rude in the classroom or openly disrespectful to the professor.

By what processes does the novice learn the required values and norms? The answer to this question depends in part upon the degree of prior socialization. If the novice has correctly anticipated the norms of the organization he is joining, the socialization process merely involves a reaffirmation of these norms through various communication channels, the personal example of key people in the organization, and direct instructions from supervisors, trainers, and informal coaches.

If, however, the novice comes to the organization with values and behavior patterns which are in varying degrees out of line with those expected by the organization, then the socialization process first involves a destructive or unfreezing phase. This phase serves the function of detaching the person from his former values, of proving to him that his present self is worthless from the point of view of the organization and that he must redefine himself in terms of the new roles which he is to be granted.

The extremes of this process can be seen in initiation rites or novitiates for religious orders. When the novice enters his training period, his old self is symbolically destroyed by loss of clothing, name, often his hair, titles and other self-defining equipment. These are replaced with uniforms, new names and titles, and other self-defining equipment consonant with the new role he is being trained for.

It may be comforting to think of activities like this as being characteristic only of primitive tribes or total institutions like military basic training camps, academies, and religious orders. But even a little examination of areas closer to home will reveal the same processes both in our graduate schools and in the business organizations to which our graduates go.

Perhaps the commonest version of the process in school is the imposition of a tight schedule, of an impossibly heavy reading program, and of the assignment of problems which are likely to be too difficult for the student to solve. Whether these techniques are deliberate or not, they serve effectively to remind the student that he is not as smart or capable as he may have thought he was, and therefore, that there are still things to be learned. . . .

Studies of medical schools and our own observations . . . suggest that the work overload on students leads to the development of a peer culture, a kind of banding together of the students as a defense against the threatening faculty and as a problem-solving device to develop norms of what and how to study. If the group solutions which are developed support the organizational norms, the peer group becomes an effective instrument of socialization. However, from the school's point of view, there is the risk that peer group norms will set up counter-socializing forces and sow the seeds of sabotage, rebellion, or revolution. The positive gains of a supportive peer group generally make it worthwhile to run the risks of rebellion, however, which usually motivates the organization to encourage or actually to facilitate peer group formation. . . .

Let me next illustrate the industrial counterpart of these processes. Many of my panel members, when interviewed about the first six months in their new jobs, told stories of what we finally labeled as "upending experiences." Upending experiences are deliberately planned or accidentally created circumstances which dramatically and unequivocally upset or disconfirm some of the major assumptions which the new man holds about himself, his company, or his job.

One class of such experiences is to receive assignments which are so easy or so trivial that they carry the clear message that the new man is not worthy of being given anything important to do. Another class of such experiences is at the other extreme—

assignments which are so difficult that failure is a certainty, thus proving unequivocally to the new man that he may not be as smart as he thought he was. Giving work which is clearly for practice only, asking for reports which are then unread or not acted upon, protracted periods of training during which the person observes others work, all have the same upending effect.

The most vivid example came from an engineering company where a supervisor had a conscious and deliberate strategy for dealing with what he considered to be unwarranted arrogance on the part of engineers whom they hired. He asked each new man to examine and diagnose a particular complex circuit, which happened to violate a number of textbook principles but actually worked very well. The new man would usually announce with confidence, even after an invitation to double-check, that the circuit could not possibly work. At this point the manager would demonstrate the circuit, tell the new man that they had been selling it for several years without customer complaint, and demand that the new man figure out why it did work. None of the men so far tested were able to do it, but all of them were thoroughly chastened and came to the manager anxious to learn where their knowledge was inadequate and needed supplementing. According to this manager, it was much easier from this point on to establish a good give-and-take relationship with his new man.

It should be noted that the success of such socializing techniques depends upon two factors which are not always under the control of the organization. The first factor is the initial motivation of the entrant to join the organization. If his motivation is high, as in the case of a fraternity pledge, he will tolerate all kinds of uncomfortable socialization experiences, even to extremes of hell week. If his motivation for membership is low, he may well decide to leave the organization rather than tolerate uncomfortable initiation rites. If he leaves, the socialization process has obviously failed.

The second factor is the degree to which the organization can hold the new member captive during the period of socialization. His motivation is obviously one element here, but one finds organizations using other forces as well. In the case of basic training there are legal forces to remain. In the case of many schools one must pay one's tuition in advance, in other words, invest one's self materially so that leaving the system becomes expensive. In the case of religious orders one must make strong initial psychological commitments in the form of vows and the severing of relationships outside the religious order. The situation is defined as one in which one will lose face or be humiliated if one leaves the organization.

In the case of business organizations the pressures are more subtle but nevertheless identifiable. New members are encouraged to get financially committed by joining pension plans, stock option plans, and/or house purchasing plans which would mean material loss if the person decided to leave. Even more subtle is the reminder by the boss that it takes a year or so to learn any new business; therefore, if you leave, you will have to start all over again. Why not suffer it out with the hope that things will look more rosy once the initiation period is over.

Several of my panel members told me at the end of one year at work that they were quite dissatisfied, but were not sure they should leave because they had invested a year of learning in that company. Usually their boss encouraged them to think about staying. Whether or not such pressures will work depends, of course, on the labor market and other factors not under the control of the organization.

Let me summarize thus far. Organizations socialize their new members by creating a series of events which serve the function of undoing old values so that the person will be prepared to learn the new values. This process of undoing or unfreezing is often unpleasant and therefore requires either strong motivation to endure it or strong organizational forces to make the person endure it. The formation of a peer group of novices is often a solution to the problem of defense against the powerful organization, and, at the same time, can strongly enhance the socialization process if peer group norms support organizational norms.

Let us look next at the positive side of the socialization process. Given some readiness to learn, how does the novice acquire his new learning? The answer is that he acquires it from multiple sources—the official literature of the organization; the example set by key models in the organization; the instructions given to him directly by his trainer, coach, or boss; the example of peers who have been in the organization longer and thus serve as big brothers; the rewards and punishments which result from his own efforts at problem solving and experimenting with new values and new behavior.

The instructions and guidelines given by senior members of the organization are probably one of the most potent sources. . . . Similar kinds of lessons can be learned during the course of training programs, in orientation sessions, and through company literature. But the more subtle kinds of values which the organization holds, which indeed may not even be well understood by the senior people, are often communicated through peers operating as helpful big brothers. They can communicate the subtleties of how the boss wants things done, how higher management feels about things, the kinds of things which are considered heroic in the organization, the kinds of things which are taboo.

Of course, sometimes the values of the immediate group into which a new person is hired are partially out of line with the value system of the organization as a whole. If this is the case, the new person will learn the immediate group's values much more quickly than those of the total organization, often to the chagrin of the higher levels of management. This is best exemplified at the level of hourly workers where fellow employees will have much more socializing power than the boss.

An interesting managerial example of this conflict was provided by one recent graduate who was hired into a group whose purpose was to develop cost reduction systems for a large manufacturing operation. His colleagues on the job, however, showed him how to pad his expense account whenever they traveled together. The end result of this kind of conflict was to accept neither the cost reduction values of the company nor the cost inflation values of the peer group. The man left the company in disgust to start up some businesses of his own.

One of the important functions of organizational socialization is to build commitment and loyalty to the organization. How is this accomplished? One mechanism is to invest much effort and time in the new member and thereby build up expectations of being repaid by loyalty, hard work, and rapid learning. Another mechanism is to get the new member to make a series of small behavioral commitments which can only be justified by him through the acceptance and incorporation of company values. He then becomes his own agent of socialization. Both mechanisms involve the subtle manipulation of guilt.

To illustrate the first mechanism, one of our graduates went to a public relations firm which made it clear to him that he had sufficient knowledge and skill to advance, but that his values and attitudes would have to be evaluated for a couple of years before he would be fully accepted. During the first several months he was frequently invited to join high ranking members of the organization at their luncheon meetings in order to learn more about how they thought about things. He was so flattered by the amount of time they spent on him that he worked extra hard to learn their values and became highly committed to the organization. He said that he would have felt guilty at the thought of not learning or of leaving the company. Sending people to expensive training programs, giving them extra perquisites, indeed the whole philosophy of paternalism, is built on the assumption that if you invest in the employee he will repay the company with loyalty and hard work. He would feel guilty if he did not.

The second mechanism, that of getting behavioral commitments, was most beautifully illustrated in Communist techniques of coercive persuasion. The Communists made tremendous efforts to elicit a public confession from a prisoner. One of the key functions of such a public confession, even if the prisoner knew he was making a false confession, was that it committed him publicly. Once he made this commitment, he found himself under strong internal and external pressure to justify why he had confessed. For many people it proved easier to justify the confession by coming to believe in their own crimes than to have to face the fact that they were too weak to withstand the captor's pressure.

In organizations, a similar effect can be achieved by promoting a rebellious person into a position of responsibility. The same values which the new member may have criticized and jeered at from his position at the bottom of the hierarchy suddenly look different when he has subordinates of his own whose commitment he must obtain.

Many of my panel members had very strong moral and ethical standards when they first went to work, and these stood up quite well during their first year at work even in the face of less ethical practices by their peers and superiors. But they reported with considerable shock that some of the practices they had condemned in their bosses were quickly adopted by them once they had themselves been promoted and faced the pressures of the new position. As one man put it very poignantly—"my ethical standards changed so gradually over the first five years of work that I hardly noticed it, but it was a great shock to suddenly realize what my feelings had been five years ago and how much they had changed."

Another version of obtaining commitment is to gain the new member's acceptance of very general ideals like "one must work for the good of the company," or "one must meet the competition." Whenever any counter-organizational behavior occurs one can then point out that the ideal is being violated. The engineer who does not come to work on time is reminded that his behavior indicates lack of concern for the good of the company. The employee who wears the wrong kind of clothes, lives in the wrong neighborhood, or associates with the wrong people can be reminded that he is hurting the company image.

One of my panel members on a product research assignment discovered that an additive which was approved by the Food and Drug Administration might in fact be harmful to consumers. He was strongly encouraged to forget about it. His boss told him that it was the FDA's problem. If the company worried about things like that it might force prices up and thus make it tough to meet the competition.

Many of the upending experiences which new members of organizations endure are justified to them by the unarguable ideal that they should learn how the company really works before expecting a position of real responsibility. Once the new man accepts this ideal it serves to justify all kinds of training and quantities of menial work which others who have been around longer are unwilling to do themselves. This practice is known as "learning the business from the ground up," or "I had to do it when I first joined the company, now it's someone else's turn." There are clear elements of hazing involved not too different from those associated with fraternity initiations and other rites of passage.

The final mechanism to be noted in a socialization process is the transition to full fledged member. The purpose of such transitional events is to help the new member incorporate his new values, attitudes, and norms into his identity so that they become part of him, not merely something to which he pays lip service. Initiation rites which involve severe tests of the novice serve to prove to him that he is capable of fulfilling the new role—that he now is a man, no longer merely a boy.

Organizations usually signal this transition by giving the new man some important responsibility or a position of power which, if mishandled or misused, could genuinely hurt the organization. With this transition often come titles, symbols of status, extra rights or prerogatives, sharing of confidential information or other things which in one way or another indicate that the new member has earned the trust of the organization. Although such events may not always be visible to the outside observer, they are felt strongly by the new member. He knows when he has finally "been accepted," and feels it when he becomes "identified" with the company.

So much for examples of the process of socialization. Let us now look at some of the dilemmas and conflicts which arise within it.

FAILURES OF SOCIALIZATION—NON-CONFORMITY AND OVER-CONFORMITY

Most organizations attach differing amounts of importance to different norms and values. Some are pivotal. Any member of a business organization who does not believe in the value of getting a job done will not survive long. Other pivotal values in most business organizations might be belief in a reasonable profit, belief in the free enterprise system and competition, belief in a hierarchy of authority as a good way to get things done, and so on.

Other values or norms are what may be called relevant. These are norms which it is not absolutely necessary to accept as the price of membership, but which are considered desirable and good to accept. Many of these norms pertain to standards of dress and decorum, not being publicly disloyal to the company, living in the right neighborhood and belonging to the right political party and clubs. In some organizations some of these norms may be pivotal. Organizations vary in this regard. You all know the stereotype of IBM as a company that requires the wearing of white shirts and hats. In some parts of IBM such values are indeed pivotal; in other parts they are only relevant, and in some parts they are quite peripheral. The point is that not all norms to which the new member is exposed are equally important for the organization.

The socialization process operates across the whole range of norms, but the amount of reward and punishment for compliance or non-compliance will vary with the importance of the norm. This variation allows the new member some degrees of freedom in terms of how far to conform and allows the organization some degrees of freedom in how much conformity to demand. The new man can accept none of the values, he can accept only the pivotal values, but carefully remain independent on all those areas not seen as pivotal, or he can accept the whole range of values and norms. He can tune in so completely on what he sees to be the way others are handling themselves that he becomes a carbon copy and sometimes a caricature of them.

These basic responses to socialization can be labeled as follows:

Type 1 Rebellion
Rejection of all values and norms

Type 2 Creative individualism
Acceptance only of pivotal values and norms; rejection of all others

Type 3 Conformity
Acceptance of all values and norms

Most analyses of conformity deal only with the type 1 and 3 cases, failing to note that both can be viewed as socialization failures. The rebellious individual either is expelled from the organization or turns his energies toward defeating its goals. The conforming individual curbs his creativity and thereby moves the organization toward a sterile form of bureaucracy. The trick for most organizations is to create the type 2 response—acceptance of pivotal values and norms, but rejection of all others, a response which I would like to call "creative individualism."

To remain creatively individualistic in an organization is particularly difficult because of the constant resocialization pressures which come with promotion or lateral transfer. Every time the employee learns part of the value system of the particular group to which he is assigned, he may be laying the groundwork for conflict when he is transferred. The engineer has difficulty accepting the values of the sales department, the staff man has difficulty accepting the high pressure ways of the production department, and the line manager has difficulties accepting the service and helping ethic of a staff group. With each transfer, the forces are great toward either conforming or rebelling. It is difficult to keep focused on what is pivotal and retain one's basic individualism.

PROFESSIONAL SOCIALIZATION AND ORGANIZATIONAL SOCIALIZATION

The issue of how to maintain individualism in the face of organizational socialization pressures brings us to the final and most problematical area of concern. In the traditional professions like medicine, law, and teaching, individualism is supported by a set of professional attitudes which serve to immunize the person against some of the forces of the organization. The questions now to be considered are (1) Is management a profession? (2) If so, do professional attitudes develop in managers? and (3) If so, do these support or conflict with organizational norms and values?

Professionalism can be defined by a number of characteristics:

1. Professional decisions are made by means of general principles, theories, or propositions which are independent of the particular case under consideration. For management this would mean that there are certain principles of how to handle people, money, information, etc., independent of any particular company. The fact that we can and do teach general subjects in these areas would support management's claim as a profession.
2. Professional decisions imply knowledge in a specific area in which the person is expert, not a generalized body of wisdom. The professional is an expert only in his profession, not an expert at everything. He has no license to be a "wise man." Does management fit by this criterion? I will let you decide.
3. The professional's relations with his clients are objective and independent of particular sentiments about them. The doctor or lawyer makes his decisions independent of his liking or disliking of his patients or clients. On this criterion we have a real difficulty since, in the first place, it is very difficult to specify an appropriate single client for a manager, and, in the second place, it is not all clear that decisions can or should be made independent of sentiments. What is objectively best for the stockholder may conflict with what is best for the enterprise, which, in turn may conflict with what is best for the customer.
4. A professional achieves his status by accomplishment, not by inherent qualities such as birth order, his relationship to people in power, his race, religion, or color. Industry is increasingly moving toward an acceptance of this principle for managerial selection, but in practice the process of organizational socialization may undermine it by rewarding the conformist and rejecting the individualist whose professional orientation may make him look disloyal to the organization.
5. A professional's decisions are assumed to be on behalf of the client and to be independent of self-interest. Clearly this principle is at best equivocal in manager-customer relations, though again one senses that industry is moving closer to accepting the idea.
6. The professional typically relates to a voluntary association of fellow professionals, and ac-

cepts only the authority of these colleagues as a sanction of his own behavior. The manager is least like the professional in this regard, in that he is expected to accept a principle of hierarchical authority. . . .

7. A professional has sometimes been called someone who knows better what is good for his client than the client. The professional's expertness puts the client into a very vulnerable position. This vulnerability has necessitated the development of strong professional codes and ethics which serve to protect the client. Such codes are enforced through the colleague peer group. One sees relatively few attempts to develop codes of ethics for managers or systems of enforcement.

On several bases, then, management is a profession, but on several others it is clearly not yet a profession.

This long description of what is a profession was motivated by the need to make a very crucial point. I believe that management education . . . is increasingly attempting to train professionals, and in this process is socializing the students to a set of professional values which are, in fact, in severe and direct conflict with typical organizational values.

For example, I see us teaching general principles in the behavioral sciences, economics, and quantitative methods. Our applied subjects like marketing, operations management, and finance are also taught as bodies of knowledge governed by general principles which are applicable to a wide variety of situations. Our students are given very broad concepts which apply to the corporation as a whole, and are taught to see the relationship between the corporation, the community, and the society. They are taught to value the long-range health and survival of economic institutions, not the short-range profit of a particular company. They come to appreciate the necessary interrelationships between government, labor, and management rather than to define these as mutually warring camps. They are taught to look at organizations from the perspective of high ranking management, to solve the basic problems of the enterprise rather than the day-to-day practical problems of staff or line management. Finally, they are taught an ethic of pure rationality and emotional neutrality—analyze the problem and make the decisions independent of feelings about people, the product, the company, or the community. All of these are essentially professional values.

Organizations value many of the same things, in principle. But what is valued in principle by the higher ranking and senior people in the organization often is neither supported by their own behavior, nor even valued lower down in the organization. In fact, the value system which the graduates encounter on their first job is in many respects diametrically opposed to the professional values taught in school. The graduate is immediately expected to develop loyalty and concern for a particular company with all of its particular idiosyncrasies. He is expected to recognize the limitation of his general knowledge and to develop the sort of ad hoc wisdom which the school has taught him to avoid. He is expected to look to his boss for evaluation rather than to some group of colleagues outside the company.

Whereas the professional training tells him that knowledge is power, the graduate now must learn that knowledge by itself is nothing. It is the ability to sell knowledge to other people which is power. Only by being able to sell an application of knowledge to a highly specific, local situation, can the graduate obtain respect for what he knows. Where his education has taught the graduate principles of how to manage others and to take the corporate point of view, his organizational socialization tries to teach him how to be a good subordinate, how to be influenced, and how to sell ideas from a position of low power.

On the one hand, the organization via its recruiters and senior people tells the graduate that it is counting on him to bring fresh points of view and new techniques to bear on its problems. On the other hand, the man's first boss and peers try to socialize him into their traditional mold. A man is hired to introduce linear programming into a production department, but once he is there he is told to lay off because if he succeeds he will make the old supervisors and engineers look bad. Another man is hired for his financial analysis skills but is not permitted access to data worth analyzing because the company does not trust him to keep them confidential. A third man is hired into a large group responsible for developing cost reduction programs in a large defense industry, and is told to ignore the fact that the group is overstaffed, inefficient, and willing to pad its expense accounts. A fourth man, hired for his energy and capability, put it this way as an explanation of why he quit to go into private consulting: "They were quite pleased with work that required only two hours per day; I wasn't." . . .

What seems to happen in the early stages of the managerial career is either a kind of postponement of professional socialization while organizational socialization takes precedence or a rebelling by the graduate against organizational socialization. The young man who submits must first learn to be a good apprentice, a good staff man, a good junior analyst, and perhaps a good low level administrator. He must prove his loyalty to the company by accepting this career path with good graces, before he is trusted enough to be given a position of power. If he has not lost his education by then, he can begin to apply some general principles when he achieves such a position of power. . . .

CONCLUSION

The essence of management is to understand the forces acting in a situation and to gain control over them. It is high time that some of our managerial knowledge and skill be focused on those forces in the organizational environment which derive from the fact that organizations are social systems who do socialize their new members. If we do not learn to analyze and control the forces of organizational socialization, we are abdicating one of our primary managerial responsibilities. Let us not shrink away from a little bit of social engineering and management in this most important area of the human side of the enterprise.

NOTE

1. This paper was presented as the 1967 Douglas McGregor Memorial Lecture in honor of the late Douglas McGregor, Alfred P. Sloan Professor of Management at the Massachusetts Institute of Technology.

BIBLIOGRAPHY

Blau, P.M., and Scott, R.W. *Formal Organizations*. San Francisco: Chandler.

Goffman, E. *Asylums*. Garden City, NY: Doubleday Anchor, 1961.

Schein, E.H. "Management Development as a Process of Influence." *Industrial Management Review* II (1961): 59–77.

———. "Forces Which Undermine Management Development," *California Management Review* V (Summer): 1963.

———. "How to Break in the College Graduate," *Harvard Business Review* XLII (1964).

———. "Training in Industry: Education or Indoctrination," *Industrial Medicine and Surgery* XXXIII (1964).

———. *Organizational Psychology*. Englewood Cliffs, NJ: Prentice-Hall, 1965.

———. "The Problem of Moral Education for the Business Manager," *Industrial Management Review* VIII (1966): 3–14.

———. "Attitude Change During Management Education," *Administrative Science Quarterly* XI (1967): 601–628.

———. "The Wall of Misunderstanding on the First Job," *Journal of College Placement* (February/March): 1967.

Schein, E.H., Schneier, Inge, and Barker, C.H. *Coercive Persuasion*. New York: Norton, 1961.

17

Effects of Group Pressure upon the Modification and Distortion of Judgments

Solomon E. Asch

Our immediate object was to study the social and personal conditions that induce individuals to resist or to yield to group pressures when the latter are perceived to be *contrary to fact.* The issues which this problem raises are of obvious consequence for society; it can be of decisive importance whether or not a group will, under certain conditions, submit to existing pressures. Equally direct are the consequences for individuals and our understanding of them, since it is a decisive fact about a person whether he possesses the freedom to act independently, or whether he characteristically submits to group pressures. . . .

THE EXPERIMENT AND FIRST RESULTS

We developed an experimental technique which has served as the basis for the present series of studies. We employed the procedure of placing an individual in a relation of radical conflict with all the other members of a group, of measuring its effect upon him in quantitative terms, and of describing its psychological consequences. A group of eight individuals was instructed to judge a series of simple, clearly structured perceptual relations—to match the length of a given line with one of three unequal lines. Each member of the group announced his judgments publicly. In the midst of this monotonous "test" one individual found himself suddenly contradicted by the entire group, and this contradiction was repeated again and again in the course of the experiment. The group in question had, with the exception of one member, previously met with the experimenter and received instructions to respond at certain points with wrong—and unanimous—judgments. The errors of the majority were large (ranging between ½ and 1¾ inches) and of an order not encountered under control conditions. The outstanding

Originally published in *Groups, Leadership and Men: Research in Human Relations*, edited by Harold Guetzkow. New York: Russell and Russell, 1963.

person—the critical subject—whom we had placed in the position of a minority of one in the midst of a *unanimous majority*—was the object of investigation. He faced, possibly for the first time in his life, a situation in which a group unanimously contradicted the evidence of his senses.

This procedure was the starting point of the investigation and the point of departure for the study of further problems. Its main features were the following: (1) The critical subject was submitted to two contradictory and irreconcilable forces—the evidence of his own experience of an utterly clear perceptual fact and the unanimous evidence of a group of equals. (2) Both forces were part of the immediate situation; the majority was concretely present, surrounding the subject physically. (3) The critical subject, who was requested together with all others to state his judgments publicly, was obliged to declare himself and to take a definite stand vis-à-vis the group. (4) The situation possessed a self-contained character. The critical subject could not avoid or evade the dilemma by reference to conditions external to the experimental situation. (It may be mentioned at this point that the forces generated by the given conditions acted so quickly upon the critical subjects that instances of suspicion were rare.)

The technique employed permitted a simple quantitative measure of the "majority effect" in terms of the frequency of errors in the direction of the distorted estimates of the majority. At the same time we were concerned from the start to obtain evidence of the ways in which the subjects perceived the group, to establish whether they became doubtful, whether they were tempted to join the majority. Most important, it was our object to establish the grounds of the subject's independence or yielding—whether, for example, the yielding subject was aware of the effect of the majority upon him, whether he abandoned his judgment deliberately or compulsively. To this end we constructed a comprehensive set of questions which served as the basis of an individual interview immediately following the experimental period. Toward the conclusion of the interview each subject was informed fully of the purpose of the experiment, of his role and of that of the majority. The reactions to the disclosure of the purpose of the experiment became in fact an integral part of the procedure. We may state here that the information derived from the interview became an indispensable source of evidence and insight into the psychological structure of the experimental situation, and in particular, of the nature of the individual differences. Also, it is not justified or advisable to allow the subject to leave without giving him a full explanation of the experimental conditions. The experimenter has a responsibility to the subject to clarify his doubts and to state the reasons for placing him in the experimental situation. When this is done most subjects react with interest and many express gratification at having lived through a striking situation which has some bearing on wider human issues.

Both the members of the majority and the critical subjects were male college students. We shall report the results for a total of fifty critical subjects in this experiment. . . .

The quantitative results are clear and unambiguous.

1. There was a marked movement toward the majority. One-third of all estimates in the critical group were errors identical with or in the direction of the distorted estimates of the majority. The significance of this finding becomes clear in the light of the virtual absence of errors in control groups the members of which recorded their estimates in writing. . . .
2. At the same time the effect of the majority was far from complete. The preponderance of estimates in the critical group (68 per cent) was correct despite the pressure of the majority.
3. We found evidence of extreme individual differences. There were in the critical group subjects who remained independent without exception, and there were those who went nearly all the time with the majority. (The maximum possible number of errors was 12, while the actual range of errors was 0–11.) One-fourth of the critical subjects was completely independent; at the other extreme, one-third of the group displaced the estimates toward the majority in one-half or more of the trials.

The differences between the critical subjects in their reactions to the given conditions were equally striking. There were subjects who remained completely confident throughout. At the other extreme were those who became disoriented, doubt-ridden, and experienced a powerful impulse not to appear different from the majority.

For purposes of illustration we include a brief description of one independent and one yielding subject.

Independent. After a few trials he appeared puzzled, hesitant. He announced all disagreeing answers in the form of "Three, sir; two, sir"; not so with the unanimous answers. At trial 4 he answered immediately after the first member of the group, shook his head, blinked, and whispered to his neighbor: "Can't help it, that's one." His later answers came in a whispered voice, accompanied by a deprecating smile. At one point he grinned embarrassedly, and whispered explosively to his neighbor: "I always disagree—darn it!" During the questioning, this subject's constant refrain was: "I called them as I saw them, sir." He insisted that his estimates were right without, however, committing himself as to whether the others were wrong, remarking that "that's the way I see them and that's the way they see them." If he had to make a practical decision under similar circumstances, he declared, "I would follow my own view, though part of my reason would tell me that I might be wrong." Immediately following the experiment the majority engaged this subject in a brief discussion. When they pressed him to say whether the entire group was wrong and he alone right, he turned upon them defiantly, exclaiming: "You're *probably* right, but you may be wrong!" To the disclosure of the experiment this subject reacted with the statement that he felt "exultant and relieved," adding, "I do not deny that at times I had the feeling: 'to heck with it, I'll go along with the rest.' "

Yielding. This subject went with the majority in 11 out of 12 trials. He appeared nervous and somewhat confused, but he did not attempt to evade discussion; on the contrary, he was helpful and tried to answer to the best of his ability. He opened the discussion with the statement: "If I'd been the first I probably would have responded differently"; this was his way of stating that he had adopted the majority estimates. The primary factor in his case was loss of confidence. He perceived the majority as a decided group, acting without hesitation: "If they had been doubtful I probably would have changed, but they answered with such confidence." Certain of his errors, he explained, were due to the doubtful nature of the comparisons; in such instances he went with the majority. When the object of the experiment was explained, the subject volunteered: "I suspected about the middle—but tried to push it out of my mind." It is of interest that his suspicion was not able to restore his confidence and diminish the power of the majority. Equally striking is his report that he assumed the experiment to involve an "illusion" to which the others, but not he, were subject. This assumption too did not help to free him; on the contrary, he acted as if his divergence from the majority was a sign of defect. The principal impression this subject produced was of one so caught up by immediate difficulties that he lost clear reasons for his actions, and could make no reasonable decisions.

A FIRST ANALYSIS OF INDIVIDUAL DIFFERENCES

On the basis of the interview data described earlier, we undertook to differentiate and describe the major forms of reaction to the experimental situation, which we shall now briefly summarize.

Among the *independent* subjects we distinguished the following main categories:

(1) Independence based on *confidence* in one's perception and experience. The most striking characteristic of these subjects is the vigor with which they withstand the group opposition. Though they are sensitive to the group, and experience the conflict, they show a resilience in coping with it, which is expressed in their continuing reliance on their perception and the effectiveness with which they shake off the oppressive group opposition.

(2) Quite different are those subjects who are independent and *withdrawn*. These do not react in a spontaneously emotional way, but rather on the basis of explicit principles concerning the necessity of being an individual.

(3) A third group of independent subjects manifest considerable tension and doubt, but adhere to their judgments on the basis of a felt necessity to deal adequately with the task.

The following were the main categories of reaction among the yielding subjects, or those who were with the majority during one-half or more of the trials.

(1) *Distortion of perception* under the stress of group pressure. In this category belong a very few subjects who yield completely, but are not aware that their estimates have been displaced or distorted by the majority. These subjects report that they came to perceive the majority estimates as correct.

(2) *Distortion of judgment.* Most submitting subjects belong to this category. The factor of greatest importance in this group is a decision the subjects reach that their perceptions are inaccurate, and that those of the majority are correct. These subjects suffer from primary doubt and lack of confidence; on this basis they feel a strong tendency to join the majority.

(3) *Distortion of action.* The subjects in this group do not suffer a modification of perception nor do they conclude that they are wrong. They yield because of an overmastering need not to appear different from or inferior to others, because of an inability to tolerate the appearance of defectiveness in the eyes of the group. These subjects suppress their observations and voice the majority position with awareness of what they are doing.

The results are sufficient to establish that independence and yielding are not psychologically homogeneous, that submission to group pressure (and freedom from pressure) can be the result of different psychological conditions. It should also be noted that the categories described above, being based exclusively on the subjects' reactions to the experimental conditions, are descriptive, not presuming to explain why a given individual responded in one way rather than another. The further exploration of the basis for the individual differences is a separate task upon which we are now at work.

EXPERIMENTAL VARIATIONS

The results described are clearly a joint function of two broadly different sets of conditions. They are determined first by the specific external conditions, by the particular character of the relation between social evidence and one's own experience. Second, the presence of pronounced individual differences points to the important role of personal factors, of factors connected with the individual's character structure. We reasoned that there are group conditions which would produce independence in all subjects, and that there probably are group conditions which would induce intensified yielding in many, though not in all. Accordingly we followed the procedure of experimental variation, systematically altering the quality of social evidence by means of systematic variation of group conditions. Secondly, we deemed it reasonable to assume that behavior under the experimental social pressure is significantly related to certain basic, relatively permanent characteristics of the individual. The investigation has moved in both of these directions. . . . We shall limit the present account to a sketch of the representative experimental variations.

The Effect of Nonunanimous Majorities

Evidence obtained from the basic experiment suggested that the condition of being exposed *alone* to the opposition of a "compact majority" may have played a decisive role in determining the course and strength of the effects observed. Accordingly we undertook to investigate in a series of successive variations the effects of *nonunanimous* majorities. The technical problem of altering the uniformity of a majority is, in terms of our procedure, relatively simple. In most instances we merely directed one or more members of the instructed group to deviate from the majority in prescribed ways. It is obvious that we cannot hope to compare the performance of the same individual in two situations on the assumption that they remain independent of one another. At best we can investigate the effect of an earlier upon a later experimental condition. The comparison of different experimental situations therefore requires the use of different but comparable groups of critical subjects. This is the procedure we have followed. In the variations to be described we have maintained the conditions of the basic experiment (e.g., the sex of the subjects, the size of the majority, the content of the task, and so on) save for the specific factor that was varied. The following were some of the variations we studied:

1. The Presence of a "True Partner"

(a) In the midst of the majority were two naive, critical subjects. The subjects were separated spatially, being seated in the fourth and eighth positions, respectively. Each therefore heard his judgment confirmed by one other person (provided the other person remained independent), one prior to, the other subsequently to announcing his own judgment. In addition, each experienced a break in the unanimity of the majority. There were six pairs of critical subjects. (b) In a further variation the "partner" to the critical subject was a member of the group who had been instructed to respond correctly throughout. This procedure permits the exact control of the partner's responses. The partner was always seated in the fourth position; he therefore announced his estimates in each case before the critical subject.

The results clearly demonstrate that a disturbance of the unanimity of the majority markedly increased the independence of the critical subjects. The frequency of pro-majority errors dropped to 10.4 per cent of the total number of estimates in variation (a), and to 5.5 per cent in variation (b). These results are to be compared with the frequency of yielding to the unanimous majorities in the basic experiment, which was 32 per cent of the total number of estimates. It is clear that the presence in the field of *one* other individual who responded correctly was sufficient to deplete the power of the majority, and in some cases to destroy it. This finding is all the more striking in the light of other variations which demonstrate the effect of even small minorities provided they are unanimous. Indeed, we have been able to show that a unanimous majority of three is, under the given conditions, far more effective than a majority of eight containing one dissenter. That critical subjects will under these conditions free themselves of a majority of seven and join forces with one other person in the minority is, we believe, a result significant for theory. It points to a fundamental psychological difference between the condition of being alone and having a minimum of human support. It further demonstrates that the effects obtained are not the result of a summation of influences proceeding from each member of the group; it is necessary to conceive the results as being relationally determined.

2. Withdrawal of a "True Partner"

What will be the effect of providing the critical subject with a partner who responds correctly and then withdrawing him? The critical subject started with a partner who responded correctly. The partner was a member of the majority who had been instructed to respond correctly and to "desert" to the majority in the middle of the experiment. This procedure permits the observation of the same subject in the course of transition from one condition to another. The withdrawal of the partner produced a powerful and unexpected result. We had assumed that the critical subject, having gone through the experience of opposing the majority with a minimum of support, would maintain his independence when alone. Contrary to this expectation, we found that the experience of having had and then lost a partner restored the majority effect to its full force, the proportion of errors rising to 28.5 per cent of all judgments, in contrast to the preceding level of 5.5 percent. Further experimentation is needed to establish whether the critical subjects were responding to the sheer fact of being alone, or to the fact that the partner abandoned them.

3. Late Arrival of a "True Partner"

The critical subject started as a minority of one in the midst of a unanimous majority. Toward the conclusion of the experiment one member of the majority "broke" away and began announcing correct estimates. This procedure, which reverses the order of conditions of the preceding experiment, permits the observation of the transition from being alone to being a member of a pair against a majority. It is obvious that those critical subjects who were independent when alone would continue to be so when joined by another partner. The variation is therefore of significance primarily for those subjects who yielded during the first phase of the experiment. The appearance of the late partner exerts a freeing effect, reducing the level to 8.7 per cent. Those who had previously yielded also became markedly more independent, but not completely so, continuing to yield more than previously independent subjects. The reports of the subjects do not cast much light on the factors responsible for the result. It is our impression that having once committed himself to yielding, the individual finds it difficult and painful to change his direction. To do so is tantamount to a public admission that he has not acted rightly. He therefore follows the precarious course he has already chosen in order to maintain an outward semblance of consistency and conviction.

4. The Presence of a "Compromise Partner"

The majority was consistently extremist, always matching the standard with the most unequal line. One instructed subject (who, as in the other variations, preceded the critical subject) also responded incorrectly, but his estimates were always intermediate between the truth and the majority position. The critical subject therefore faced an extremist majority whose unanimity was broken by one more moderately erring person. Under these conditions the frequency of errors was reduced but not significantly. However, the lack of unanimity determined in a strikingly consistent way the direction of the errors. The preponderance of the errors, 75.7 per cent of the total, was moderate, whereas in a parallel experiment in which the majority was unanimously extremist (i.e., with the "compromise" partner excluded), the incidence of moderate errors was reduced to 42 per cent of the total. As might be expected, in a unanimously moderate majority, the errors of the critical subjects were without exception moderate.

The Role of Majority Size

To gain further understanding of the majority effect, we varied the size of the majority in several different variations. The majorities, which were in each case unanimous, consisted of 16, 8, 4, 3, and 2 persons, respectively. In addition, we studied the limiting case in which the critical subject was opposed by one instructed subject. . . .

With the opposition reduced to one, the majority effect all but disappeared. When the opposition proceeded from a group of two, it produced a measurable though small distortion, the errors being 12.8 per cent of the total number of estimates. The effect appeared in full force with a majority of three. Larger majorities of four, eight, and sixteen did not produce effects greater than a majority of three.

The effect of a majority is often silent, revealing little of its operation to the subject, and often hiding it from the experimenter. To examine the range of effects it is capable of inducing, decisive variations of conditions are necessary. An indication of one effect is furnished by the following variation in which the conditions of the basic experiment were simply reversed. Here the majority, consisting of a group of sixteen, was naive; in the midst of it we placed a single individual who responded wrongly according to instructions. Under these conditions the members of the naive majority reacted to the lone dissenter with amusement and disdain. Contagious laughter spread through the group at the droll minority of one. Of significance is the fact that the members lack awareness that they draw their strength from the majority, and that their reactions would change radically if they faced the dissenter individually. In fact, the attitude of derision in the majority turns to seriousness and increased respect as soon as the minority is increased to three. These observations demonstrate the role of social support as a source of power and stability, in contrast to the preceding investigations which stressed the effects of withdrawal of social support, or to be more exact, the effects of social opposition. Both aspects must be explicitly considered in a unified formulation of the effects of group conditions on the formation and change of judgments.

The Role of the Stimulus-Situation

It is obviously not possible to divorce the quality and course of the group forces which act upon the individual from the specific stimulus-conditions. Of necessity the structure of the situation moulds the group forces and determines their direction as well as their strength. Indeed, this was the reason that we took pains in the investigations described above to center the issue between the individual and the group around an elementary and fundamental matter of fact. And there can be no doubt that the resulting reactions were directly a function of the contradiction between the objectively grasped relations and the majority position. . . .

One additional dimension we have examined is the magnitude of discrepancies above the threshold. . . . Within the limits of our procedure we find that different magnitudes of discrepancy produce approximately the same amount of yielding. However, the quality of yielding alters: as the majority becomes more extreme, there occurs a significant increase in the frequency of "compromise" errors.

We have also varied systematically the structural clarity of the task, including in separate variations judgments based on mental standards. In agreement with other investigators, we find that the majority effect grows stronger as the situation diminishes in clarity. Concurrently, however, the disturbance of the subjects and the conflict-quality of the situation decrease markedly. We consider it of significance that the majority achieves its most pronounced effect when it acts most painlessly.

SUMMARY

We have investigated the effects upon individuals of majority opinions when the latter were seen to be in a direction contrary to fact. By means of a simple technique we produced a radical divergence between a majority and a minority, and observed the ways in which individuals coped with the resulting difficulty. Despite the stress of the given conditions, a substantial proportion of individuals retained their independence throughout. At the same time a substantial minority yielded, modifying their judgments in accordance with the majority. Independence and yielding are a joint function of the following major factors: (1) The character of the stimulus situation. Variations in structural clarity have a decisive effect: with diminishing clarity of the stimulus-conditions the majority effect increases. (2) The character of the group forces. Individuals are highly sensitive to the structural qualities of group opposition. In particular, we demonstrated the great importance of the factor of unanimity. Also, the majority effect is a function of the size of group opposition. (3) The character of the individual. There were wide, and indeed, striking differences among individuals within the same experimental situation. . . .

BIBLIOGRAPHY

Asch, S.E. Studies in the principles of judgments and attitudes: II. Determination of judgments by group and by ego-standards. *J. Soc. Psychol.*, 1940, 12, 433–465.

———. The doctrine of suggestion, prestige and imitation in social psychology. *Psychol. Rev.*, 1948, 55, 250–276.

Asch, S.E., Block, H., and Hertzman, M. Studies in the principles of judgments and attitudes: 1. Two basic principles of judgment. *J. Psychol.* 1938, 5, 219–251.

Coffin, E.E. Some conditions of suggestion and suggestibility: A study of certain attitudinal and situational factors influencing the process of suggestion. *Psychol. Monogr.*, 1941, 53, No. 4.

Lewis, H.B. Studies in the principle of judgments and attitudes: IV. The operation of prestige suggestion. *J. Soc. Psychol.*, 1941, 14, 229–256.

Lorge, I. Prestige, suggestion, and attitudes. *J. Soc. Psychol.*, 1936, 7, 386–402.

Miller, N.E. and Dollard, J. *Social Learning and Imitation.* New Haven: Yale University Press, 1941.

Moore, H.T. The comparative influence of majority and expert opinion. *Amer. J. Psychol.*, 1921, 32, 16–20.

Sherif, M. A study of some social factors in perception. Arch. Psychol., N.Y., 1935, No. 187.

Thorndike, E.L. *The Psychology of Wants, Interests, and Attitudes.* New York: Appleton-Century, 1935.

18

Groupthink, Bay of Pigs, and Watergate Reconsidered

Bertram H. Raven

OUR OFF-AGAIN-ON-AGAIN LOVE AFFAIR WITH THE GROUP

The period following World War II was one of great optimism, with expectations of positive change throughout the world. As the result of experiences during the war, social psychology benefited especially, and indeed the immediate postwar period led to a golden period in growth of educational programs and research support. One aspect of this period was an on-again-off-again love affair with groups and social influence processes. In social psychology, the term "group dynamics," popularized by Kurt Lewin and his colleagues, became a catchword which quickly spread to the population at large. The importance of group cooperation and group decisions in productivity and effective problem-solving became an important topic of study and application (Lewin 1947, 1952). In order to implement change in working conditions, group discussion and participation was demonstrated in theory, research, and application (Coch and French 1948). However, at the same time, we saw others who questioned and even ridiculed the emphasis on groups and committees. The group discussion and group decision studies, which showed how group norms could contribute to greater productivity, were attacked as simply one more manipulative device whereby management could get workers to work harder and longer without an increase in pay (Gunderson 1950). Groups and committees were often seen as wasteful of time and often resulting in inferior products. C. Northcote Parkinson (1957), with his clever tongue-in-cheek style, illustrated how decisions by groups and committees effectively operated at their lowest common denominator.[1] The controversy continues even to this day. Moscovici (1976) and his colleagues seem to see the group majority as stifling correct creative solutions by the minority member, pointing out how a heroic minority member can (and probably should) overcome the tyranny of the majority though forceful independence. Paicheler

(1988), following this same line, argues that the entire emphasis on group decisions and conformity can be seen as a kind of cultural conspiracy to maintain the status quo against social change. By now the resolution parallels those which follow most such debates: groups can be effective and can have much to contribute in terms of effective decision making, greater productivity, higher morale, and so forth. However, they can also lead to negative and wasteful results, and they can also be manipulated by those who wish to use them for their own purposes. The practical issue boils down to how we can benefit from their positive contributions while minimizing the negative. That would seem to be the very issue that Janis examined in his analysis of what he called groupthink.

THE POWER OF THE ERRONEOUS MAJORITY

I have often thought that the paradigm for what Janis later called the groupthink phenomenon can be seen in a generally forgotten, simple experiment conducted by Norman Maier and Allen Solem (1952). They presented their subjects with a simple problem: "A man bought a horse for $60 and sold it for $70. Then he bought it back for $80 and sold it again for $90. How much money did he make or lose in the horse business?" Subjects, when asked individually, gave a variety of answers: losing $10, breaking even, or making $10, $20, or $30.[2] When the problem was presented to discussion groups of five or six, and a unanimous decision was required, the number of correct answers rose somewhat, in comparison with the individual judgments. (Chalk one up for the pro-group side?) However, this happened only when the majority started out with a correct answer—if the majority held an incorrect answer, then there was an even greater likelihood of group errors. (Anti-group?) However, the number of correct answers increased substantially even in those latter groups, if there was a group leader who encouraged the expression of minority opinions! In a later study, it was found that groups that reached a unanimous decision were more satisfied than those which did not reach a unanimous decision—and this was true even when the unanimous decision was incorrect! (Thomas and Fink 1961).

Despite our ambivalence toward groups, everyday wisdom would argue that it is obvious that in solving complex problems which require a broad range of information, a decision by several people would be superior to a decision by a single person. If "two heads are better than one," what about six, seven, or eight heads? Further, suppose that the group is composed of very intelligent and knowledgeable people; their collective wisdom should be all the better. How then could one account for John F. Kennedy's presidential advisory group, composed of the "best and the brightest" (Halberstam 1972), developing and approving plans for the Bay of Pigs invasion of Cuba, frequently characterized as one of the most militarily disastrous and morally disgraceful ventures in American history. There were many who were bothered by this question, including leading members of the Kennedy team, and even President Kennedy himself.

THE ROOTS OF GROUPTHINK

Irving Janis also thought about this curious phenomenon and suggested it to his daughter, Charlotte, who was looking for an interesting topic for her high school history term paper. As he reviewed her research, Janis became increasingly obsessed and felt compelled to find some answers. For his explanations, he drew on tools with which he was familiar; he reviewed especially the vast literature of theories and research on group behavior. His initial search might have shown all sorts of theories and empirical evidence which would have predicted what general wisdom would have suggested. After all, there is plenty of evidence that groups perform better if they have high morale, high cohesiveness, good leadership, high intelligence, excellent knowledge and experience, and so forth. Then, he also noted how factors which might ordinarily lead to greater effectiveness could also in some circumstances lead to less effective and even disastrous results. He did, in fact, note the very high morale and cohesiveness in the Kennedy team, as the Democrats took control of the presidency after eight years out of office. But he also was aware of studies which indicated that groups tend to conform to a common norm when cohesiveness and morale are high. In such cases, pressures on the deviant members of the group can be tremendous. When the majority is wrong, that can obviously have very deleterious effects. He would have been aware of findings, such as those reported by Muzafer Sherif et al. in the Robber's Cave study (Sherif, Harvey, White, Hood, and Sherif 1961), which showed how a high level of morale could lead to a sense of superiority toward the outgroup. The effects of group norms on polarization and adoption of extreme, often maladaptive, decisions had been demonstrated in various studies, including the research on group polarization and the "risky shift" (e.g., Kogan and Wallach 1967; Stoner 1961; Teger and Pruitt 1967). There is even evidence that group polarization will lead groups to take more extreme positions in evaluating outgroups (Moscovici and Zavalloni 1969). Janis did not document most of these studies in either edition of *Groupthink* (1972, 1982) [he does not even mention Maier and Solem (1952)], but we can assume that he was aware of the basic findings. Further documentation is provided in the very thorough review by Hart (1990) and by Esser (1998), Hart (1998), and McCauley (1998). . . .

THE IMPORTANCE OF GROUP COHESIVENESS

In their article . . . Sally Fuller and Ramon Aldag (1998) boldly assume the role of devil's advocate in criticizing the groupthink analysis offered by Janis. How, they ask, can Janis say that high cohesiveness is the "critical trigger in the groupthink phenomenon" when the "benefits of group cohesion have long been recognized"? They rely on such arguments to say that Janis's theory is inherently inconsistent and empirically not supported. Perhaps the analogy might be the benefits of various forms of fertilizer, which have contributed to human benefit by leading to bumper crops and better life for plants, animals, and humans. When combined in certain combinations, with other elements, they become the destructive force which can destroy all living things, as in the Oklahoma bombing. We can all think of things which are generally beneficial, but which in certain circumstances and in certain combinations can become very destructive. So it is with group cohesiveness. The real genius, then, lies in determining what these circumstances and combinations might be which would lead to deleterious effects. Once one knows this, then recommendations can be made as to how effective leadership might operate to allow for the beneficial effects of group cohesiveness while safeguarding against its stultifying effects in inhibiting expression of minority opinion and against the unrealistic positive evaluation of one's own group and the negative evaluation of opposing groups.

GROUPTHINK IN WATERGATE AND ITS COVER-UP

Just as Janis became infatuated with the mystery of the Bay of Pigs decision making process, several years later, like many of us, I found myself taken by the advisory groups associated with President Nixon, who were involved in the planning activities which resulted in the Watergate fiasco and the cover-up afterward. The Nixon advisory group was also composed of very intelligent and knowledgeable men (yes, again, they were all men). The phenomena which eventually led to the collapse of the Nixon administration were, of course, quite different from those which led to the disaster at the Bay of Pigs. First of all, the "enemy" was different. The Kennedy group had to deal with an external enemy, with Fidel Castro and the government of Cuba. The Nixon group had to deal with a domestic "enemy," the so-called liberal establishment and more specifically the Democratic Party. Also, the activities of the Nixon people actually involved two sets of actions: (a) What have been called the "White House horrors," wherein the executive offices were involved, directly and indirectly, in secret surveillance of opponents, use of the Internal Revenue Service and various governmental agencies to punish the "enemies," and use of burglaries to gain destructive information (including the burglary of the offices of the psychiatrist to scientist and peace activist Daniel Ellsburg, and the final bungling burglary of the Democratic Party headquarters in the Watergate building) and (b) the cover-up activities after the discovery of the White House horrors. There were different planning and advisory groups involved in these two decision-making processes.

I watched many hours of hearings on television, read many transcripts and reports, and then drew on what I knew from the literature from social psychology and group dynamics. Much of what I read, then, led me to find Janis's groupthink theory helpful in my analysis—though I cited a number of other theories as well (Raven 1974). I, of course, felt highly complimented when the second edition of *Groupthink* was published and I found that Janis found my analysis helpful in his updating his analysis of groupthink (Janis 1982).

WAS THE "NIXON GROUP" COHESIVE?

Janis had emphasized the importance of group cohesiveness to the groupthink process. Did high cohesiveness characterize the Nixon group? Not if you think of cohesiveness in terms of the members of the group being having strong positive feelings toward one another. In fact, there is evidence that a number of members of the group strongly disliked and were in active competition with one another. However, group cohesiveness is defined in terms of the resultant forces on individual members to continue their membership in and identification with the group. Back (1951) pointed out that factors other than interpersonal attraction can affect cohesiveness, a point also made by McCauley (1998) in his article. . . . Among the other factors are attraction to the group goal, the prestige and other qualities of membership in the group itself, and attraction toward and dependence upon the leader of the group. What can attract one to a group more than the perception that this group is successful, coupled with the belief that by maintaining significant membership in that group one's own future can be assured? These seemed quite evident in the Nixon group. Certainly after the successful defeat of the Democrats in the 1972 election, they could sense that belonging to that group and association with Nixon and his administration would lead to their personal advancement both politically and otherwise.

INTRAGROUP COMPETITION AND THE "RUNAWAY NORM"

It was this form of "cohesiveness" and its effects in the Nixon group which I found particularly intriguing. The many illusions which Janis had described in his analysis of the Kennedy advisory group were very much present: the sense of invulnerability and superiority (buttressed by prior success), the suppression of personal doubt, conformity to basic norms reinforced by suave leadership. . . . However, there was the additional factor which I called a "runaway norm."[3] The concept is similar to the notion of group polarization. Though we usually think of group norms as operating to lead to pressure to conform to the norm, there are situations in which simply conforming to the norm is not sufficient. In order to maintain one's position in the group, or improve it, one must attempt to exceed the norm. As the members each try to exceed the norm, the norm itself rises, leading to escalation of behavior in the group. This is one explanation which had been offered for the "risky shift" phenomenon—it is sometimes highly desirable to try to be a bit more risky than other group members. In the Nixon group, the norm was to be more aggressive, less inhibited by the usual moral restraints, in taking action against the "enemy," especially as represented in the Democratic party and liberal thinkers. The model for such behavior was the president himself who was known to have successfully utilized unrestrained aggressive techniques throughout his political career.[4] However, in the Nixon group, there were two subgroups, characterized by Theodore White (1973) as "the big team" and "the young team."[5] The individuals in each team were pressed to be more extreme than each of their members, but this was further amplified by pressures on each team to try to exceed the other in aggressiveness.

POLITICAL AND OTHER CONSIDERATIONS IN GROUPTHINK

In this issue and elsewhere there have been discussions of many examples which are relevant to the groupthink theory. In some of these, it appears that the basic features of Janis's theory apply; others do not fit the theory so neatly. It is important for us to keep in mind that in neither of his two books on groupthink did Janis take the position that groupthink was the only factor which accounted for the failures of the group decisions which he describes. In that sense, then, I believe that it is reasonable to assume that Janis would not have had any uneasiness in accepting Rod Kramer's (1998) position that political considerations would enter into the process as well, as indeed they often have. In my discussion here, I have been focusing on the two examples of group decision processes which appear to have gone awry: the Bay of Pigs Fiasco and Watergate and the related cover-up attempts. Obviously, the two examples are quite different in many ways, and I have pointed out some ways in which they differ. In both cases, there were, in fact, political considerations, but these were especially clear, I think, in the Nixon group. The entire process, including the disastrous burglary, was guided by political motivations. The additional difference, as we have noted above, is that Richard Nixon himself loomed large in that entire process. His referent power, furthered by his immense success through lack of usual restraints, was especially powerful. His reward and coercive power were also very salient. To a considerable extent, the competition in the group, the runaway norm, can be seen in terms of who could best emulate him and his immediate followers in giving no quarter to political opponents.

Does Groupthink Necessarily Lead to Failure?

Groupthink, as it is generally defined, suggests a fiasco, a failure of the group in its basic mission. Reviewing recent new information, particularly as revealed in Nixon's White House tapes, suggests that "failure" in its mission need not be a necessary part of the definition of groupthink. While there seems to be a clear deterioration of moral judgment, and a move to extreme uninhibited action in the Nixon group, I think we might recognize the frightening thought that in fact the Nixon team came remarkably close to being successful! The array of weapons which Nixon and his team had developed in dealing with uncooperative liberal Democrats and Republicans, news media, government officials, including the Secret Service, the FBI, the IRS, and other governmental and nongovernmental agencies (burglars, eavesdroppers, spies, etc.), is truly staggering. Did these fail because of the natural deteriorating process of groupthink? Not really. One might contemplate what could have developed were it not for (a) some bungling burglars breaking in to Democratic Party headquarters at the wrong time and leaving some suspicious scotch tape to keep a door unlocked; (b) some observant guards and custodians at the Watergate building who happened to notice lights on at the wrong place at the wrong time and then noting the suspicious tape; (c) Nixon's confidently taping conversations in the Oval Office, and later being reluctant to destroy these tapes. Both Carl Bernstein (1997) and Alexander Haig (1997), as well as others, discussing the Watergate phenomenon on its anniversary, and with the new information recently revealed, have expressed alarm at how close we came to a virtual police state. So we must consider that many of the elements of groupthink which lead to reduction of restraints against extreme measures, and suspension of moral values, might indeed lead to success, but with frightening consequences. It is likely that we can find examples in which such unfortunate outcomes have occurred. Some of the safeguards which Janis suggested might help to avoid such outcomes, but it is likely that even more are needed.

GROUPTHINK: A GENERAL ASSESSMENT

The article by Fuller and Aldag (1998) is quite clever and entertaining. However, in my opinion, they got carried away by their adopted role as devil's advocate. Even if most of us can identify some flaws in the groupthink analysis, we would still give Janis a lot of credit for his careful and scholarly analysis, his relating a broad body of literature on group processes and group dynamics to the understanding of a series of very significant social-political events. Most of the articles in this issue have taken issue with some of his applications and some of his interpretations of the social psychological literature. However, it is bordering on the absurd to see groupthink as in the same category with collective imaginative nonsense such as the foul-smelling "el chupacabra" (goatsucker) or the mythical tale of Tonypandy. There are, of course, many other similar phenomena which they could also have cited. Why not the Abominable Snowman, Sasquatch, the Loch Ness monster, or visiting aliens in their UFOs? Yes, we can accept their point that myths and folk tales will often develop in a community or society. However, can they really believe that that applies to groupthink and to its widespread acceptance? No social scientific theory is perfect, but there is no need to so demean Janis's theories, the care with which he examined the evidence and tried to make sense out of it, his application of a wide range of careful research on group dynamics and social psychology, or the intelligence of the many competent scholars who find them convincing.

Janis goes on to apply the groupthink model not only to the Bay of Pigs fiasco, and Watergate, but also group decisions relating to the Korean War, lack of proper defense of Pearl Harbor, escalation of the Vietnam War, and the more effective decision in the Cuban Missile Crisis. There have been several applications by others (several of which are discussed in this issue): (a) the Space Challenger disaster (Esser 1998; Moorhead, Ference, and Neck 1991), (b) the decision by the Japanese advisory group to bomb Pearl Harbor (Whyte 1998), (c) decision making in self-managing work teams, and top-management teams (Moorhead, Neck, and West 1998; Peterson, Owens, Tetlock, Fan, and Martorana 1998). In practically all of these applications, the authors have found some points in which the phenomenon they studied did not fit Janis's groupthink formulation exactly. Often, these investigators have focused on an additional factor which needed to be considered, which fit that particular investigator's line of research and theory. However, by and large, the basic principles of groupthink theory have still held strong. Clearly, as with any dynamic theory, there will be grounds for modification and improvement. Aside from any inaccuracy in applicability to specific failures or successes in group decision, the impact of Janis's work has been very substantial indeed, particularly in making decision-making bodies aware of the ways in which they may develop policies which lead to disasters, even when the decision-making group is competent, cohesive, and experienced. Even more important, we would hope that work by Janis and his followers will sensitize policy-making and other decision groups about what they might do to counter the effects of groupthink. From reading articles in this issue and other works, I am convinced that in this respect, the work of Irving Janis will continue to be quite substantial in its impact on the ways in which important policy groups make decisions in the future.

NOTES

1. I don't know how many times I have heard a speaker, searching for a humorous introduction, begin his/her presentation by saying that a camel was a horse designed by a committee. I always laugh dutifully, along with the others, but later think, "Wait a minute. Considering the terrain in which it operates, a camel is actually a quite well-designed horse."

2. Of course, the correct answer is $20 profit—the man laid out a total of $140 and received a total of $160. It is always surprising the number of intelligent subjects who don't come out with the correct answer.

3. The concept of "runaway norm" is not original with me. However, I forget who I got it from and therefore regret that I cannot give due credit. The physical analogy would be a thermostat in which someone had altered the element so that as the temperature increased, the thermostat is programmed not to reduce the temperature but to increase it.

4. Richard Nixon, over his political career, despite a few setbacks, appears to have been remarkably successful in using strong, and sometimes Machiavellian, methods to defeat his political opponents, going back to his early defeat of Congressman Jerry Voorhis, in his first congressional campaign, and popular senator Helen Gahagan Douglas a few years later. [See, for example, Brodie (1981), Mazo and Hess (1968); and Wills (1971).] For ambitious politicians who had been recruited to his advisory groups, he would serve as a powerful referent and expert power [source] in affecting their behavior and also the norms of the groups of which they were a part.

5. I was, of course, pleased that Janis (1982) was able to include my analysis in his expansion of his groupthink review in the second edition. In my analysis, I tried to represent the membership of these two competitive teams in diagrams indicating the positive and negative relationships among the members. Janis (1982) takes some issue with exactly who was a member of each team. My representation was based on my reading of White (1973), which, in turn, were his observations of the membership during the 1972 election campaign. Quite possibly there was a change by the time of the meetings on the cover-up following the bungled Watergate burglary. In any case, I would stick by my representation of the essential process.

REFERENCES

Back, K. (1951). Influence through social communication. *Journal of Abnormal and Social Psychology* 46: 9–23.

Bernstein, C. (1997). Charley Rose Interviews. Public Broadcasting Service, June 18, 1997.

Brodie, F.M. (1981). *Richard Nixon: The Shaping of His Character*. New York: Norton.

Coch, L., and French, J.R.P., Jr. (1948). Overcoming resistance to change. *Human Relations* 1: 512–532.

Esser, J.K. (1998). Alive and well after 25 years: A review of groupthink research. *Organizational Behavior and Human Decision Processes* 73: 116–141.

Fuller, S.R., and Aldag, R.J. (1998). Organizational tonypandy: Lessons from a quarter century of the group think phenomenon. *Organizational Behavior and Human Decision Processes* 73: 163–184.

Gunderson, R.G. (1950). Group dynamics—Hope or hoax? *Quarterly Journal of Speech* 36: 34–48.

Haig, A. (1997). *Larry King Live*, CNN, June 17, 1997.

Halberstam, D. (1972). *The Best and the Brightest*. New York: Random House.

Hart, P.T. (1990/1994). *Groupthink in Government: A Study of Small Groups and Policy Failure*. Amsterdam: Swets and Zeitlinger; Baltimore: Johns Hopkins University Press.

———. (1998). Preventing groupthink revisited: Evaluating and reforming groups in government. *Organizational Behavior and Human Decision Processes* 73: 306–326.

Janis, I.L. (1972). *Victims of Groupthink: A Psychological Study of Foreign Policy Decisions and Fiascoes*. Boston: Houghton-Mifflin.

———. (1982). *Groupthink: Psychological Studies of Policy Decisions and Fiascoes*. Boston: Houghton-Mifflin.

Kogan, N., and Wallach, M.A. (1967). Risk-taking as a function of the situation, the person, and the group. In G. Mandler, P. Mussen, N. Kogan, and M.A. Wallach (eds.), *New Directions in Psychology* (vol. 3, pp. 224–266). New York: Holt, Rinehart, and Winston.

Kramer, R.M. (1998). Revisiting the Bay of Pigs and Vietnam decisions: 25 Years later: How well has groupthink hypothesis stood the test of time? *Organizational Behavior and Human Decision Processes* 73: 236–271.

Lewin, K. (1947). Frontiers in group dynamics. I. Concept, method and reality in social science: Social equilibria and social change. *Human Relations* 1: 5–41.

———. (1952). Group decision and social change. In G.E. Swanson, T.M. Newcomb, and E.L. Hartley (eds.), *Readings in Social Psychology* (2d ed., pp. 459–473). New York: Holt, Rinehart, and Winston.

Maier, N.R.F., and Solem, A.R. (1952).The contribution of a discussion leader to the quality of group thinking: The effective use of minority opinions. *Human Relations* 5: 277–288.

Mazo, E., and Hess, S. (1968). *Nixon: A Political Portrait*. New York: Popular Library.

McCauley, C. (1998). Group dynamics in Janis's theory of groupthink: Backward and forward. *Organizational Behavior and Human Decision Processes* 73: 142–162.

Moorhead, G., Ference, R., and Neck, C.P. (1991). Group decision fiascoes continue: Space shuttle Challenger and a revised framework. *Human Relations* 44: 539–550.

Moorhead, G., Neck, C.P., and West, M.S. (1998). The tendency toward defective decision-making within self-managing teams: The relevance of groupthink for the 21st Century. *Organizational Behavior and Human Decision Processes* 73: 327–351.

Moscovici, S. (1976). *Social Influence and Social Change*. New York: Academic Press.

Moscovici, S., and Zavalloni, M. (1969). The group as a polarizer of attitudes. *Journal of Personality and Social Psychology* 16: 125–135.

Paicheler, G. (1988). *The Psychology of Social Influence*. Cambridge: Cambridge University Press.

Parkinson, C.N. (1957). *Parkinson's Law*. Boston: Houghton-Mifflin.

Peterson, R.S., Owens, P.D., Tetlock, P.E., Fan, E.T., and Martorana, P. (1998). Group dynamics in top management teams: Groupthink, vigilence, and alternative models of organizational failure and success. *Organizational Behavior and Human Decision Processes* 73: 272–305.

Raven, B.H. (1974). The Nixon group. *Journal of Social Issues* 30 (Whole no. 4): 297–320.

Sherif, M., Harvey, O.J., White, B.J., Hood, W.R, and Sherif, C.W. (1961). *Intergroup Conflict and Co-operation: The Robbers Cave Experiment.* Norman, OK: Univ. Book Exchange.

Stoner, J.A.F. (1961). A comparison of individual and group decisions, involving risk. Unpublished master's thesis, Sloan School of Management, Massachusetts Institute of Technology, Cambridge, MA.

Teger, A.I., and Pruitt, D.G. (1967). Components of group risk taking. *Journal of Experimental Social Psychology* 3: 189–205.

Thomas, E.J., and Fink, C.F. (1961). Models of group problem-solving. *Journal of Abnormal and Social Psychology* 63: 53–63.

White, T.H. (1973). *The Making of the President.* 1972. New York: Bantam.

Whyte, G. (1998). Recasting Janis's groupthink model: The lead role of collective efficacy in decision fiascoes. *Organizational Behavior and Human Decision Processes* 73: 185–209.

Wills, G. (1971). *Nixon Agonistes.* New York: NAL-Dutton.

19

Tightening the Iron Cage: Concertive Control in Self-Managing Teams

James R. Barker

I don't have to sit there and look for the boss to be around; and if the boss is not around, I can sit there and talk to my neighbor or do what I want. Now the whole team is around me and the whole team is observing what I'm doing.

"Ronald," a technical worker in a small manufacturing company, gave me this account one day while I was observing his work team. Ronald works in what contemporary writers call a postbureaucratic organization, which is not structured as a rule-based hierarchy. He works with a team of peers who are all equally responsible for managing their own work behaviors. But Ronald described an unexpected consequence of this team-based design. With his voice concealed by work noise, Ronald told me that he felt more closely watched now than when he worked under the company's old bureaucratic system. He said that while his old supervisor might tolerate someone coming in a few minutes late, for example, his team had adopted a "no tolerance" policy on tardiness and that members monitored their own behaviors carefully.

Ronald's comments typify life under a new form of organizational control that has prospered in the last decade as a means of avoiding the pitfalls of bureaucracy. This form, called "concertive control," grows out of a substantial consensus about values, high-level coordination, and a degree of self-management by members or workers in an organization. This paper describes and analyzes the development of concertive control after Ronald's company, "ISE Communications," converted to self-managing (or self-directing) teams, a concertive structure that resulted in a form of control more powerful, less apparent, and more difficult to resist than that of the former bureaucracy. The irony of the change in this postbureaucratic organization is that, instead of loosening, the iron cage of rule-based, rational control, as Max Weber called it, actually became tighter.

THE PROBLEM OF CONTROL

Control has been a central concept in organizational theory since the time of Weber and remains perhaps the key issue that shapes and permeates our experiences of organizational life. Barnard (1968: 17) best stated the importance of control when he wrote that a key defining element of any organization was the necessity of individuals to subordinate, to an extent, their own desires to the collective will of the organization. For individuals to achieve larger goals they must actually surrender some autonomy in organizational participation. Because of this basic tension, control is always problematic in any organization.

To work through this problem, an organization's members—managers and workers alike—must engage in ongoing formal and informal "processes of negotiation in which various strategies are developed . . . [that] produce particular outcomes" for the organization (Coombs, Knights, and Willmott 1992: 58). Herein lies the essence of control as it becomes manifest in organizational activity. For any organization to move toward its goals and purposes, its "particular outcomes," its members must interactively negotiate and implement some type of strategy that effectively controls members' activities in a manner functional for the organization.

Edwards' Three Strategies of Control

Edwards (1981) has identified three broad strategies that have evolved from the modern organization's struggle with controlling members' activities. First is "simple control," the direct, authoritarian, and personal control of work and workers by the company's owner or hired bosses, best seen in nineteenth-century factories and in small family-owned companies today. Second is "technological control," in which control emerges from the physical technology of an organization, such as in the assembly line found in traditional manufacturing. And third and most familiar is bureaucratic control, in which control derives from the hierarchically based social relations of the organization and its concomitant sets of systemic rational-legal rules that reward compliance and punish noncompliance.

A pivotal aspect of Edwards' model is that the second and third strategies, technological and bureaucratic control, represent adaptations to the forms of control that preceded them, each intended to counter the disadvantages of the previous form. Technological control resulted not only from technological advances in factories but also from worker alienation and dissatisfaction with the despotism too often possible in simple control. But technological control proved subject to such factors as worker protests, slow-downs, and assembly-line sabotage. The stultifying effects of the assembly line, with workers as just cogs in the machine, still produced worker alienation from the company. The bureaucratic form of control, with its emphasis on methodical, rational-legal rules for direction, hierarchical monitoring, and rewards for compliance such as job security, already existed in the nineteenth century and was further developed to counter the problems inherent in technological control. The bureaucracy and bureaucratic control, which become manifest in a variety of forms (Riggs 1979; Perrow 1986), have matured into the primary strategy available to managers to control work effectively in the modern organization. But, as with its predecessors, this strategy of control, too, is problematic.

Bureaucratic Control and the Iron Cage

Weber articulated the bureaucracy as the dominant form of modern control, in both positive and negative senses. While the bureaucracy offers the fairest and most efficient method of control, its system of rational rules may become troublesome, as seen in the infamous "red tape" that constrains and slows the bureaucracy and makes it unresponsive to environmental changes. Also, as Weber warned us, we, in our desire for organizational order and predictability, tend to focus too much on the rationality of the rules in and of themselves, overintellectualizing the moral and ethical values critical to our organizational lives and making decisions according to the rules, without regard to the people involved (Kalberg 1980: 1158). We become so enmeshed in creating and following a legalistic, rule-based hierarchy that the bureaucracy becomes a subtle but powerful form of domination.

This notion of the inevitable, highly rational, but powerfully oppressive bureaucracy refers to what Weber (1958: 180–181) called the "iron cage." Weber saw the bureaucracy and bureaucratic control as an irresistible force of high rationality that would commandeer and consume all other forms of control. For Weber (1978), we would, out of our desire for order, continually rationalize our bureaucratic relationships, making them less negotiated and more structured. These structures ultimately become immovable objects of control: "Once fully established, bureaucracy is among those social structures which are the hardest to destroy. Bureaucracy is the means of transforming social action into rationally organized action (Weber 1978: 987). As organizational activity increasingly becomes saturated by bureaucratic rationalization processes, it is increasingly constrained by them. A rule requiring a customer service representative to have all refund decisions approved by someone two hierarchical levels above may impede the representative's ability to meet a customer's demands for a quick response. Thus a rule that apparently benefits an organization's effectiveness (getting managerial approval and oversight of refunds) also constrains its effectiveness (slows down response). In Weber's (1978: 987–988) words, the individual organizational actor in a modern bureaucracy "cannot squirm out of the apparatus into which he has been harnessed."

Weber's image of how we become trapped in an iron cage of bureaucratic control suggests that control, as it becomes manifest as organizational activity through Edwards' three strategies, has become less apparent, or not as readily personal, as it has become more imbedded in the social relations of organizational members (Tompkins and Cheney 1985; Barker and Cheney 1994). Control in the bureaucratic organization becomes impersonal because its authority rests ultimately with the system, leaving organization members, in many cases, with what Weber (1958: 182) called "specialists without spirit, sensualists without heart." Whereas the nineteenth-century mill owner overtly controlled workers, ordering, directing, and firing them at will, the bureaucracy's rules are more indirect: They control workers by shaping their knowledge about the "right" ways to act and interact in the organization. A worker seeks supervisory approval for a decision because that is what the worker is supposed to do. The "apparency" of control becomes hidden in the bureaucracy's seemingly natural rules and hierarchy. Thus, bureaucratic control leaves us in a paradoxical situation. The same rational activities that enable collective organizational interaction eventually come to constrain that activity in ways often difficult for us to perceive, much less comprehend, the consequences and ramifications. Our bureaucratic rules ultimately confine us as solidly as if we were in a cage bound by iron bars.

Concertive Control as a Fourth Strategy

Almost since the beginning of modern organizational study, influential theorists have argued that decentralized, participative, and more democratic systems of control offer the most viable alternatives to the bureaucracy's confining routines and rules (e.g., Follett 1941; Lewin 1948). This continual push toward participation and a flat organizational structure has become something of an obsession in managerial literature in the last decade or so (Eccles and Nohria 1992). Contemporary writers have unleashed a flood of literature announcing the "coming demise of bureaucracy and hierarchy" (Kanter 1989: 351) and detailing the dawn of a postbureaucratic age in which control emerges not from rational rules and hierarchy but from the concertive, value-based actions of the organization's members (Soeters 1986; Ogilvy 1990; Parker 1992). Characteristic of this movement are influential business consultants such as Tom Peters (1988) and Peter Drucker (1988) who have urged corporate executives to de-bureaucratize their firms and adopt more ideologically based designs drawn around unimpeded, agile authority structures that grow out of a company's consensual, normative ideology, not from its system of formal rules. By cutting out bureaucratic offices and rules, organizations can flatten hierarchies, cut costs, boost productivity, and increase the speed with which they respond to the changing business world.

Tompkins and Cheney (1985) argued that the numerous variations these authors have offered on the postbureaucratic organization represent a new type of control, "concertive" control, built on Edwards' three traditional control strategies. This form represents a key shift in the locus of control from management to the workers themselves, who collaborate to develop the means of their own control. Workers achieve concertive control by reaching a negotiated consensus on how to shape their behavior according to a set of core values, such as the values found in a corporate vision statement. In a sense, concertive control reflects the adoption of a new substantive rationality, a new set of consensual values, by the organization and its members.

This negotiated consensus creates and re-creates a value-based discourse that workers use to infer "proper" behavioral premises: ideas, norms, or rules that enable them to act in ways functional for the organization. For example, a newly concertive company may have a vision statement that states, "We are a principled organization that values teamwork." This value may lead one of its members to create a discourse that calls out the premise that "To be principled and value teamwork, we all must come to work on time." The actors can then infer a method of acting (coming to work promptly at 7:00 A.M. not at 7:30), without the traditional supervisor's direction, that is functional for the organization. Thus concertive control becomes manifest as the team members act within the parameters of these value systems and the discourses they themselves create. These new collaboratively created, value-laden premises (manifest as ideas, norms, and rules) become the supervisory force that guides activity in the concertive control system. In concertive control, then, the necessary social rules that constitute meaning and sanction modes of social conduct become manifest through the collaborative interactions of the organization's members. Workers in a concertive organization create the meanings that, in turn, structure the system of their own control. Rule generation moves from the traditional supervisor-subordinate relationship to the actors' negotiated consensus about values.

A second and more important difference between the concertive control model and its bureaucratic predecessor lies in the locus of authority. In the concertive organization, the locus of authority, what actors see as the legitimate source of control to which they are willing to submit (Whitley 1977), transfers from the bureaucratic system and its rational-legal constitutive rules to the value consensus of the members and its socially created generative rules system. Under bureaucratic control, employees might ensure that they came to work on time because the employee handbook prescribed it and the supervisor had the legal right to demand it, but in the concertive system, employees might come to work on time because their peers now have the authority to demand the workers' willing compliance. The key question is whether or not the concertive system offers a form of control that conceptually and practically transcends traditional bureaucratic control. I address this question by examining the process through which actors in a concertive organization collaborate to form the rules that structure their day-to-day work and how they give this process legitimate authority. I report on the processes of control that became manifest as a manufacturing organization changed and adapted to a concertive-based structure, in the form of a self-managing, or self-directed team design.

Self-Managing Teams: An Exemplar of Concertive Control

Currently, the most popular planned organizational change to a postbureaucratic structure is the transformation of a traditional, hierarchically based organization to a flat confederation of concertively controlled self-managing teams. Xerox, General Motors, and Coors Brewing have all initiated this kind of change over the last few years. Although self-managing teams have gained much of their popularity in recent years, they are not a new phenomenon. Research and writing on the subject originally dates from Trist's study of self-regulating English coal miners in the 1950s (Trist et al. 1963; Trist 1981) and includes the Scandinavian experience with semiautonomous teams (Bolweg 1976; Katz and Kahn 1978) and early U.S. team experiences, most notably the Gaines

Dog Food plant in Kansas (Walton 1982; Ketchum 1984). The contemporary version of the self-managing team concept draws on both the past experiences with teams in Europe and the United States and the more recent influence of Japanese-inspired quality circles in Western organizations (Sundstrom, De Meuse, and Futrell 1990; Sewell and Wilkinson 1992).

Proponents of self-managing teams have described it as a radical change in the traditional managerial and authority structure of an organization (e.g., Orsburn et al. 1990; Wellins, Byham, and Wilson 1991). In line with the impulse toward postbureau-cratic, concertive-based organizations, they assert that traditional management structures entail inflexible hierarchical and bureaucratic constraints that stifle creativity and in-novation. These rigid organizations are top-heavy with managers and unresponsive to changing, dynamic markets, ultimately reducing their competitive viability. From the proponents' viewpoint, U.S. organizations must radically change their managerial struc-ture by converting to worker-run teams and eliminating unneeded supervisors and other bureaucratic staff (traditional management structures). Proponents argue that self-managing teams make companies more productive and competitive by letting workers manage themselves in small, responsive, highly committed, and highly productive groups. Thus, the self-management perspective proposes a "radical" shift from hierar-chical supervision to hands-off, collaborative worker management.

This change from supervisory to participatory structures means that workers in a self-managing team will experience day-to-day work life in vastly different ways from workers in a traditional management system. Instead of being told what to do by a supervisor, self-managing workers must gather and synthesize information, act on it, and take collective responsibility for those actions. Self-managing team workers gen-erally are organized into teams of 10 to 15 people who take on the responsibilities of their former supervisors. Top management often provides a value-based corporate vision that team members use to infer parameters and premises (norms and rules) that guide their day-to-day actions. Guided by the company's vision, the self-managing team mem-bers direct their own work and coordinate with other areas of the company.

Usually, a self-managing team is responsible for completing a specific, well-defined job function, whether in production or service industries. The team's members are cross-trained to perform any task the work requires and also have the authority and responsibility to make the essential decisions necessary to complete the function. Self-managing teams may build major appliances, process insurance claims, assemble com-ponent parts for computers, or handle food service for a large hospital. Along with performing their work functions, members of a self-managing team set their own work schedules, order the materials they need, and do the necessary coordination with other groups. Besides freeing itself from some of the shackles of bureaucracy and saving the cost of low-level managers, the self-managing company also gains increased employee motivation, productivity, and commitment. The employees, in turn, become committed to the organization and its success (Orsburn et al. 1990; Mumby and Stohl 1991; Wel-lins, Byham, and Wilson 1991). Most current research on self-managing teams concen-trates on the functional or economic outcomes of the change to teams. Another body

of practitioner-oriented writing recounts how self-managing teams increase organizational productivity, profitability, and employee satisfaction, as well as how corporations
deal with problems encountered during the transition to teams (Dumaine 1990; Lewis
1990). Other research on self-managing teams tends toward organizational design issues
that concern implementing the change (Andrasik and Heimberg 1982; Carnall 1982),
attitudinal attributes of teamwork (Cordery, Mueller, and Smith 1991), and leadership
requirements within and outside the team (Manz and Sims 1987). As Sundstrom, De
Meuse, and Futrell (1990) and Hackman (1986) have pointed out, however, we still
have very little empirical knowledge of how self-managing teams construct new and
functional forms of control and how these forms compare with how we have conceptualized control in the past. ISE Communications offered me a useful case for examining
this aspect of organizational control longitudinally.

METHODS

ISE Communications

ISE Communications, a small manufacturing company located in a mountain-state metropolitan area, converted from a traditional manufacturing structure to self-managing
teams in 1988. ISE manufactures voice and data transmission circuit boards for the
telecommunications industry and employs about 150 people, with approximately ninety
in manufacturing. ISE was originally a division of a large telecommunications firm,
and the ISE management team bought it outright in 1984, although the large firm still
remains ISE's largest customer. ISE has the traditional manufacturing, engineering,
sales/marketing, human resources, and executive staffs found in most production companies. ISE pays its manufacturing employees by the hour, while the support staff
members are on salary.

   As expected of a manufacturing company in a large metropolitan area, ISE's production workers represent a cross-section of the local working-class community. Out of
90 manufacturing workers (the worker population when I ended my research in fall
1992), the ratio of females to males fluctuates but tends to stay around two-thirds female
to one-third male. Latino/as, African Americans, and Asian Americans are ISE's main
ethnic groups, making up about 60 percent of the workforce. At any given time, ISE's
manufacturing department employs around 15 percent temporary workers that the company trains in-house. In fact, only one job on the teams, an electronic technician, requires training not provided by ISE.

   Manufacturing circuit boards involves requesting board parts (resistors, potentiometers, transistors, etc.) from the supply room, assembling these parts onto a circuit board,
and soldering the parts to the boards. The workers must then test the boards for electronic problems, trouble-shoot any problems they find, and make any necessary repairs.
This becomes a time-consuming and labor-intensive process. After a board passes the
final tests, the workers must package it and process the necessary shipping paperwork.
Building and testing boards requires repetitive tasks that easily become monotonous.

Unfortunately, the errors that arise from monotony mean costly and lengthy retesting delays or repairs. The work requires close attention to detail and tightly coordinated effort.

Early in my research (spring 1990), ISE was struggling to survive in a highly competitive and innovative marketplace that demanded flexibility, an emphasis on customer service, and increasing productivity. By the time I wrote this paper two and a half years later, ISE had increased both productivity and profitability. ISE's executives believed that the change to teams was a major reason for their company's success.

"Jack Tackett," the manufacturing vice president and one of ISE's founding members, developed and instigated the company's change to self-managing teams. After reading the works of Crosby, Peters, Drucker, and other consultants, studying manufacturing philosophies like "Just In Time" (JIT)—a company-specific manufacturing method that emphasizes low inventories, first-line decision making, and fast, effective employee action—and taking the pulse of ISE's competition, Jack decided that his company's very survival depended on converting to self-management. As he told me:

> I thought that if we did things the same way all the time, we were headed for disaster. We could not meet customer demands anymore. Hierarchy insulates people from the customer. The traditional organization cannot know the customer, they are in the dark about what goes on around them with the manager making all the decisions. You can't succeed with that anymore. The demands of the market are too dynamic for a company to be controlled by a handful of managers. The whole company needs to be focused on customer needs and I needed to marshal the resources of the whole organization, not just a few. . . . You have to look forward and say what will it take to survive. You can't look inwardly all the time. You can't look back and say, "Well, we survived this way." I say that we aren't going to survive if we always consider what we're doing now to be successful for the future.

In 1986, Jack proposed a plan for implementing self-managing teams at ISE to his management staff. Jack actually convinced many of them that the change to teams was absolutely necessary for ISE to survive—which, for some of them, meant giving up their management jobs, although Jack did arrange lateral moves for them within ISE—and recruited them to help him institute the change. Some thought that the change was a "stupid idea." But Jack was adamant that self-management was the way to revitalize the company:

> I had it firmly set in my mind that this was the way we had to go and these guys [the reluctant supervisors] were going to come up to speed or I was gonna get rid of them. And this team process was the natural opportunity to give people the chance to either get on board on their own or to fall by the wayside.

And the change proceeded with surprisingly little managerial turnover.

After more than a year of planning and training in teamwork skills, which included drafting and distributing ISE's vision statement, Jack and his advisory group started one self-managing team on a trial run in early 1988. He planned slowly to convert the entire production department to teams over the course of a year.

After working through some difficulties, the new team soon began to work better than Jack or anyone else had expected, so Jack and his group decided to expedite the complete conversion. First, they increased the pace of employee training in teamwork, self-supervision, and JIT manufacturing. Then, over a weekend in August of that year, Jack had the manufacturing area completely remodeled and set up for three self-managing teams, originally called red, white, and blue teams. His group rearranged machines, worktables, and other equipment to form three distinct and self-sufficient work areas that gave each team all the necessary equipment needed to produce the types of circuit boards that the new teams would build. The work areas had separate sections for circuit board assembly, testing, repair and touch-up, trouble-shooting, and packaging/shipping, all the key tasks required in making a complete circuit board. On Monday, Jack divided the workers into three teams and assigned each team to manufacture or configure two or three particular types of boards (the teams did not make the same types of boards). Table 19.1 summarizes the differences between ISE's operations before and after the change. Jack, the former managers, and the workers now began the difficult process of adjusting to their new work environment. The workers struggled with establishing concertive control, which meant they had to negotiate such supervisory issues as accepting responsibility, making decisions, and setting their own ground rules for doing good work, such as deciding who was going to perform which tasks, whether or not the team needed to work overtime or on weekends, and whether to hire or fire team members. For his part, Jack tried to build a supportive climate for the teams. He put three of the former supervisors into a nonsupervisory support group focused on helping the teams solve technical problems. He also provided new team-building and interpersonal-skill training programs. If a team came to him with a problem, Jack would only offer suggestions, requiring the team to make the decision. Then he would support the decisions that the teams made, right or wrong, as long as the teams learned from their mistakes.

I began my research at ISE during this initial phase of adjustment to self-management, as the new teams were creating the collaborative process that characterizes the dynamics of concertive control.

My interest in self-managing teams came from my own experience with them. Prior to returning to graduate school, I worked as the "leader" of a self-managing team for a large trucking company, which gave me a well-informed perspective on ISE's experience. I first met Jack at a social event in January 1990, where, after finding out about our mutual interest in teams, he invited me to come study what was happening at ISE.

Data Collection

When I first arrived at ISE, Jack introduced me as a researcher from the university interested in writing about self-managing teams and told me to roam around the plant as I wanted. I initially set about meeting people and getting to know the workplace. I

Table 19.1
Structure of ISE Before and After the Change to Teams

Before the change	After the change
1. Three levels of managerial hierarchy between the vice president and the manufacturing workers.	1. Managerial hierarchy extends directly from the manufacturing teams to the vice president.
2. Manufacturing assembly line organizes the plant. Workers manufacture boards according to their individual place on the line.	2. Team work areas organize the plant. Teams are responsible for complete fabrication, testing, and packaging of their assigned circuit boards.
3. Line and shift supervisors form the first managerial link.	3. Teams manage their own affairs, elect one person to coordinate information for them.
4. Workers have little input into work-related decisions. Managers make all decisions and give all directions.	4. Team members make their own decisions within guidelines set by management and the company vision statement. Teams have shared responsibility for their own productivity.
5. Management disciplines workers.	5. Team members discipline themselves.
6. Management interviews and hires all new workers.	6. Team members interview, hire, and fire their own members.

spent my first six months there talking with members of each team and various management and support personnel. I watched workers at different stages of production and asked questions about how and why they were doing various tasks. During this period, I cultivated key informants on each team and developed plans and guides for in-depth worker interviews. During my initial learning phase, I established a schedule of weekly, half-day (four-hour) visits to ISE. I normally alternated between morning and afternoon visits, and I also included some early evening observations of the second shift. I decided on a weekly schedule, mainly because ISE was a 90-minute drive from my residence.

Occasional schedule variations occurred, when key events were happening at ISE and I would visit more than once a week, and when I had academic constraints, which would limit my visits to once every two weeks or so for brief periods. After my first six months, I began an extended process of gathering data, primarily from in-depth interviews, observations, and conversations with key informants, but also from such sources as company memos, flyers, newsletters, and in-house surveys. Then I would withdraw from the setting to analyze the data, write, and develop revised research questions. I would repeat this process by returning to the setting, collecting more data, and then analyzing, writing, and revising again. I also observed and recorded team and company meetings, collected examples of naturally occurring team interactions, and closely followed one team's experiences for four months. In addition, I interviewed nonmanufacturing workers and former ISE employees. When my data collection ended, I had accumulated 275 research hours and conducted 37 in-depth interviews that ranged from as short as 45 minutes to as long as two hours.

In conducting the interviews, I tried as much as possible, given the constraints of voluntary participation, to stratify the interviews roughly across teams, including full-time and temporary employees and crossing ethnic and gender lines. I also interviewed Jack, the team coaches, and a few other members of the management and support staffs. I asked open-ended questions about how the teams made decisions, solved problems, and did day-to-day work. Finally, I probed into their responses for key examples.

During all phases of my data collection, my observer role at ISE did not change. The team members knew that I was studying and writing about their work processes. They were very cooperative and generally accommodated my needs for observation space and interview time. While I would, on occasion, discuss my observations with Jack, I have never filled a formal consulting role, nor has Jack ever asked me to disclose what I considered to be sensitive information about my informants.

Data Analysis

I began my analysis by working from the basic question, "How are the control practices in ISE's new team environment different from the control practices in place prior to the change to teams?" This basic question allowed particular themes about control to emerge from my data that I could compare, revise, and refine as I collected more data and grew more familiar with the case. The particular themes and data analyses I present here emerged from my application to the database of sensitizing concepts (Jorgensen 1989) primarily drawn from Tompkins and Cheney's (1985), Giddens's (1984), and Weber's (1978) theories of value-based control and constitutive rules. For example, I would examine my data by asking such general questions as, "How has a value-consensus occurred in the team's interactions?" or "Have any teams developed new decision premises or rules?" As significant themes emerged from my data, I would ask about them in subsequent interviews, which allowed their interrelated patterns and sub-themes to take shape.

From this analysis I developed an analytical description of the general character of concertive control as it became manifest during ISE's experience with teams, which I present below. To help ensure the validity of this analytical conceptualization and its attendant claims, I cross-checked my interview data with my field notes and observations, interviews with management or support staff, and relevant hard data (team performance results, consultant surveys, human resource data, previous team-training programs). Finally, I reviewed my analysis, claims, and conceptualizations with colleagues not familiar with or participating in the setting (Adler and Adler 1987).

The result of my analysis is a three-part narrative about the three phases of the evolution of concertive control at ISE. The first phase covers the period of consolidation following the turbulence of the change to teams (late 1988–late 1990). In this phase, the teams began to develop and apply concertive consensus about values that allowed them to infer functional decision premises and interact effectively with each other. The second phase (late 1990–late 1991) saw the teams develop strong norms from their value consensus and begin to enforce these norms on each other as a set of rules. The third phase (late 1991 to mid-1992) saw the stabilization and formalization of these new systems of rules. The rules became rationalized and codified and served as a strong controlling force of team actions.

THE DEVELOPMENT OF CONCERTIVE CONTROL

Phase 1: Consolidation and Value Consensus

Phase 1 began with the chaos of Jack's abrupt changing of the manufacturing area to teams over that weekend in August 1988. While the workers knew that the change was coming, they still walked into a whole new experience on Monday morning. Bonnie, an original ISE employee, described the scene for me:

> Well, it was mass confusion. Nobody knew where they were sitting, what team they were on. They had an idea of what was going on at that point and what the team aspect was all about. As far as details, no idea! So, basically, everybody was just kind of like WOW, this is kinda fun! Because everything was different, it was wonderful in a way, the atmosphere had changed. It was fun to see who you were going to be sitting with, what team you were going to be on, what you were going to be doing. For me it was like, what board am I going to be working on? 'Cause before, I had a certain board that I had worked on from the beginning [of her tenure at ISE] and I still wanted to be working on it.

Jack assigned workers to the three new teams by drawing names out of a hat. He also assigned a former manager to coach each of the teams for six to nine months until they got used to managing themselves. Jack directed these coaches, who had themselves been key players (and believers) in the transition to teams, not to direct the teams overtly but to let them learn how to manage themselves. The coaches saw their role primarily as preventing disasters and helping the teams to keep the production flowing.

The challenge for the teams during this first phase was learning how to work together and supervise themselves functionally: They had to learn how to get a customer's order manufactured and out the door. To do this, they had to merge, or consolidate, a variety of differing perspectives on how to do good work. For example, the new team members knew the separate activities involved in circuit board production, but they did not know how to control their individual efforts so that they could complete the whole process themselves. They knew how their former supervisors valued good work, but they lacked a means of articulating this value for themselves. To meet this need, the teams began developing their own value consensus as to what constituted, both collectively and individually, good work for the teams and patterns of behavior that put this consensus into action. Jack had already provided the foundation of this consensus in the vision statement that he had written for his new teams.

When ISE began converting to self-managing teams, Jack, along with ISE's president, crafted a vision statement that articulated a set of core values and goals, which all employees were to use to guide their daily actions. ISE's seven-paragraph vision statement functioned in the consolidation phase as a socially integrating myth that merged basic human values and "day-to-day [employee] behavior with long-run [organizational] meaning and purpose" (Peters and Waterman 1982: 282). Within this context, ISE's vision statement gave Jack a formula for creating his new concertive organization that centered on all the new team members working together in concert under the guidance of shared values rather than the old ISE managerial hierarchy.

The vision's fourth paragraph detailed the essential values that the teams would draw from during the consolidation phase:

We will be an organization where each of us is a self-manager who will:

- initiate action, commit to, and act responsibly in achieving objectives
- be responsible for ISE's performance
- be responsible for the quality of individual and team output
- invite team members to contribute based on experience, knowledge, and ability.

The values expressed here, such as personal initiative, responsibility, commitment to the team, quality of individual and team contributions, along with Jack's directive for all to be self-managers, provided the necessary and legitimated preconditions for the teams to draw their value consensus, essential for concertive control.

Early in my research I saw a framed copy of the vision statement near Jack's desk and asked him what he saw as its purpose. He replied, "The vision provides the company the guiding light for driving day-to-day operations for each of the teams." The goals and values in ISE's vision statement served as the nexus for consolidating the teams' material reality (how work gets done) with their ideational reality (their values) (Jermier et al. 1991: 172). When ISE converted to self-management, Jack distributed copies of the vision statement to all team members, and framed copies appeared in each team's area and in central locations like the break room. This led the new team members to talk with each other separately and at team meetings about the vision, particularly its fourth paragraph, and how it related to their work. Out of this talk came the functional patterns that allowed the teams to work together.

When I first began my research (early 1990), I readily noticed the results of this process. The team members talked openly about initiating action, taking ownership for their team's success, taking responsibility for satisfying ISE's customers' needs, emphasizing team quality, and expecting member contributions. The teams had learned to direct their work through planned and ad-hoc team meetings run by a peer-elected coordinator who did just that—coordinated information, such as production schedules, parts supplies, and companywide memos. All the teams met formally for about 15 minutes at the start of the workday to plan the day and solve any known problems. When serious problems arose during the workday, such as an unknown parts shortage holding up production, the teams would meet briefly and decide how to deal with the problem.

During team meetings workers would spend some time talking in administrative terms about the work they had to do and in abstract terms about values expressed in the vision: responsibility, quality, member contribution, commitment to their team and the company. The most prevalent example of these discussions occurred when team members had to decide whether or not to work overtime to meet their production schedules. My illustration comes from my field notes of one of many such situations the blue-team members found themselves in while I was tracking their decision making during the fall of 1990.

Early Friday afternoon, Lee Ann, the coordinator, was anxiously awaiting word from the stockroom that a shipment of circuit potentiometers had arrived. The vendor, about 800 miles away, had promised the shipment would arrive that morning, and the blue team had to get a customer's board order out that evening. Jim, from the stockroom, came running down to the blue team's area about 12:30 to tell Lee Ann that the potentiometers had just arrived, and she called the other eleven members of the team together for a short meeting.

She looked at the team, "We've got the 'pots' in but it's gonna take us two extra hours to get this done. What do you want to do?"

Larry groaned, "Damn, I've got plans for five-thirty!" Suna spoke up, "My daughter's school play's tonight!" Johnny countered, "But we told Howard Bell [their customer] that we would have these boards out today. It's our responsibility." Tommy followed, "We're gonna have to stay. We have to do this right."

What followed was a process in which the team negotiated which values and needs (individual or team) would take precedence here and how the team would work out this problem. The team decided to work late; members valued their commitment to a quality product delivered on time to their customer more than their individual time. Lee Ann volunteered to coordinate for the late shipment and to tell Jack Tackett that they would be working overtime (they could do this without his approval). Another team member went to arrange for the building to stay open for them. Larry said that he could put off his plans for two hours. The team agreed to let Suna leave, but she promised to work late the next time they were in a bind.

This vignette depicts how the teams concertively reached a value consensus that, in turn, controlled their individual and collective work. They brought the abstract values of the vision statement into concrete terms. The team members agreed on the priority of their commitment to the team's goals and responsibility for customer needs, and they acted based on this value consensus. These points of agreement also set strong precedents for future action. The blue team's agreement to work overtime to meet customer needs was not a one-time quick fix; it became a pattern that team members would follow as similar situations arose. In a conversation some time after the above meeting, Diego described for me the continuing power of the blue team's value consensus about personal responsibility: "I work my best at trying to help our team to get stuff out the door. If it requires overtime, coming in at five o'clock and spending your weekend here, that's what I do."

Although there were slight differences, this value consensus and these decision premises emerged powerfully and with remarkable consistency across the new teams. Early in 1991, I was sitting with Wendy watching her work with the blue team. I asked her how she reacted to missing a customer requirement:

I feel bad, believe it or not. Last Friday we missed a shipment. I feel like I missed the shipment since I'm the last person that sees what goes to ship. But Friday we missed the shipment by two boards and it shouldn't have been missed. But it was and I felt bad because it's me, it's a reflection on me, too, for not getting the boards out the door.

Over time, the teams faced many situations that called for members to reach some sort of value consensus. Other values, not explicitly stated in the vision but influenced by its general thrust, began to appear in the team members' talk and actions. These values helped them unite, learn how to work together, and navigate the turbulence of the change and the possible failure of the company. Team members like Wendy talked about taking ownership of their work, being committed to the success of their team, and viewing ISE as a family and their teammates as family members. Debbie, another original team member, told me about this new feeling of ownership: "Under the old system, who gave a hoot if the boards shipped today or not? We just did our jobs. Now, we have more buy-in by the team members. We feel more personal responsibility for the product." Other values included the need for everyone to contribute fully. The team members called this "saying your piece" at team meetings so that the team's decision would be better (and their consensus stronger). Another part of this value was the need for all team members to learn all the jobs required by the team so that they could fill in and cover for each other. This was also a time when ISE was struggling desperately and almost went under. In mid-1990, layoffs reduced the teams from three to two. The power of their values helped the teams navigate this difficult period. One of my most vivid memories of this time comes from Liz, who became one of my primary key informants. In August 1990, when the workers did not know if ISE would survive the quarter, she told me how she thought of ISE as a family and how she "spends more time with these people than my real family." She told me that if ISE closed down, "I'm gonna turn the lights out. I love this place and these people so much, I've got to be the last one out. I've gotta see the lights go out to believe it."

The teams' value-based talk and action during the consolidation phase created, in Weber's terms, a new substantive rationality. The team members had committed themselves "first and foremost to substantive goals, to an ethic" that overrode all other commitments (Rothschild and Whitt 1986: 22). Substantive rationality, in this context, extends from what Weber called "a unified configuration of values" (Kalberg 1980: 1164) held by a collectivity of people, in this case ISE's team members. This value configuration, or consensus, is intellectually analyzable by the members; they use it to make sense of and guide their everyday interactions. In an organizational situation, a consensus about values informs and influences members' outlooks on and processes of work activity, such as decision making. In doing this, the members place a psychological premium on themselves to act in ethical ways in terms of their values (Weber 1978: 36; Kalberg 1980: 1165). These values, then, are morally binding on the team members because they represent the will of the teams and were arrived at through the democratic participation of the team members (Homans 1950: 125–127; Rothschild and Whitt 1986: 50). The old rationality and ethic of obeying the supervisor had given way to a new substantive rationality, the teams' value consensus, and a new form of ethical rational action, working in ways that supported the teams' values: Wendy's taking personal responsibility for her team's failure, Debbie's buying in to the team's success, Johnny's reminding the team of its customer commitment, and Diego's willingness to come in at 5 A.M. all illustrate this point.

These examples also point out another significant aspect of substantive rationality. The ethical rational action spawned by a value consensus will take on a methodical character (Kalberg 1980: 1164): The teams will develop behavioral norms that put their values into action in consistent patterns applicable to a variety of situations, just as team members applied their norm of working overtime to meet customer demands to a variety of situations requiring extra work. Thus, the teams could turn their value consensus into social norms or rules. The teams had manifested the essential element of concertive control: Their value-based interactions became a social force that controlled their actions, as seen in Larry's willingness to forego his plans in order to work overtime for the team. Authority had transferred from ISE's old supervisory system to the team's value consensus. These norms of ethical action, based in consensual values, penetrate and subjugate other forms of action by the team members. As this occurs, these norms take on a "heightened intensity" (Kalberg 1980: 1167); they become powerful social rules among the team (Hackman and Walton 1986; Hackman 1992). This process played a pivotal role in the next phase of ISE's experience with teams.

There were four key points in the consolidation phase: (1) The teams received ISE's vision statement, which framed a value system for them; (2) the teams began to negotiate value consensus on how to act in accordance with the vision's values; (3) a new substantive rationality emerged among the teams that filled the void left by the former supervisors and the formal rationality associated with following their directives (the teams' values now had authority); and (4) the teams began to form normative rules that brought this rationality into social action. The consolidation phase left ISE with a core group of long-time ISE team workers, committed to the company and to teamwork. The employees had developed a consensus about what values were important to them, what allowed them to do their work, and what gave them pride. And they would guard this consensus closely.

Phase 2: Emergence of Normative Rules

ISE did survive through 1990. In early 1991, the company began to prosper, and a large number of new workers had to be integrated into the teams. These workers were unfamiliar with the teams' value consensus and they posed an immediate challenge to the power relationships the older employees had formed. Further, when ISE began to hire new workers, they hired them on a temporary basis and let the teams decide who to hire on as full-time workers. ISE also added four new teams to the two remaining original teams, for a total of six—red, blue, a new white, and green, silver, and aqua. Jack had to place some of the older, experienced workers on these new teams to help them get organized, and the teams had to integrate their new teammates into their value-based social order. As the team's value consensus and particular work ethic began to penetrate and subjugate the new members' individual work ethics, this process took on a heightened intensity. The substantive rationality of the teams' values gave them authority, which they would exercise at will.

Members of the old teams responded to these changing conditions by discursively turning their value consensus into normative rules that the new workers could readily understand and to which they could subject themselves. By rationalizing their value-based work ethic, the new team members could understand the intent and purpose of their team's values and norms (e.g., why it was important to work overtime to meet a customer need), use the norms to make sense of their daily work experience, and develop methodical patterns of behavior in accordance with the team's values (Miller and O'Leary 1987; Hackman 1992).

The longer-tenured team members expected the new workers to identify with (they called it "buy into") the teams' values and act according to their norms. By doing this, ISE's teams were asserting concertive control over the new workers: The new members began to take part in controlling themselves. Slowly, the value-based norms that everyone on the team once "knew" became objective, rationalized rules that the new members could easily understand and follow. Around March–April 1991, I began to notice that the way the team members talked, both informally and at team meetings, had changed. They did not talk so much about the importance of their teamwork values as they did about the need to "obey" the team's work norms. Team meetings began to have a confrontational tone, and the new workers' attitudes and performance became open topics for team discussion. When the longer-tenured team members saw someone not acting in accordance with their norms, such as not being willing to do whatever it took for the team to be successful, they said something about it. Liz, an original team member, told me of the old team workers' feelings: "We've had occasions where we've had a person say, 'I refuse to sit on the [assembly] line.' And we had to remind him, 'Hey, you are a part of the team and you go where you're needed and you do it.' " Team meetings became a forum for discussing norms and creating new rules. Team members could bring up anybody's behavior for discussion. Again, Liz clarified their feelings: "If you notice that somebody's not getting anything done, then we can bring it up at a meeting, you know, and ask them what the problem is, what's causing them not to be able to get their work done."

The new team members began to feel the heat, and the ones who wanted to be full-time members began to obey the norms. The teams' value-based concertive control began to penetrate and inform the new workers' attitudes and actions. Stephi, who was a temporary employee at the time, told me how she personally tried to conform to the values and norms of her team: "When I first started I really didn't start off on the right foot, so I've been having to re-prove myself as far as a team player. My attitude gets in the way, I let it get in the way too many times and now I've been watching it and hoping they [her team] will see the change in me and I can prove to them that I will make a good ISE employee." Stephi's words indicate that concertive control at ISE now revolved around human dignity. The team members rewarded their teammates who readily conformed to their team's norms by making them feel a part of the team and a participant in the team's success. In turn, they punished teammates who had bad attitudes, like Stephi, with guilt and peer pressure to conform (Hackman and Walton 1986; Mumby and Stohl 1991; Hackman 1992). The power of the team's concertive work ethic had taken on its predicted heightened intensity.

A pivotal occurrence during this phase was the teams' value-based norms changing from a loose system that the workers "knew" to a tighter system of objective rules. This transformation most often occurred when new members were not acting according to the team's work norms, such as coming to work on time. Danny told me how easily this change came about:

> Well we had some disciplinary thing, you know. We had a few certain people who didn't show up on time and made a habit of coming in late. So the team got together and kinda set some guidelines and we told them, you know, "If you come in late the third time and you don't wanna do anything to correct it, you're gone." That was a team decision that this was a guideline that we were gonna follow.

The teams experienced the need to make their normative work ethic easily understandable (and rewardable and punishable), and they responded by making objective guidelines.

The team members' talk turned toward the need to follow their rules, to work effectively in concert with each other. In mid-1991 I found Ronald, a technician and my key informant on the green team, angrily cleaning up a mistake made by a new technician who had not followed the rules: "All this should have been caught three months ago, and I'm just now catching it. And upon looking into it, it was because the tech wasn't taking his responsibility for raising the flag or turning on the red light when he had a problem." Later that day, I was sitting with the silver team when I saw Ryan confront a newer team member who was working on four boards at a time instead of one, which the team had discovered increased the chance for error. Ryan stood above the offender and pointed at him, "Hey quit doing that. You're not allowed to do that. It's against the rules."

By turning their norms into rational rules, the teams could integrate new members and still be functional, getting products out the door on time. The "supervisor" was now not so much the teams' value consensus as it was their rules. You either obeyed the rules and the team welcomed you as a member, or you broke them and risked punishment. This element of concertive control worked well. As Danny, a temporary worker at this time told me, "If you're a new person here, you're going to be watched." Even the coordinator's role and responsibilities became more objectified during this phase. Some teams agreed on five specific tasks for the coordinator to do, other teams had seven. The teams now elected coordinators for six-month periods rather than one month. The coordinator role began to take on the aura of a supervisor. People began to look to coordinators for leadership and direction. Lee Ann, a coordinator at this time, told me one day, "Damn, I feel like a supervisor, I just don't get paid for it."

The second pivotal occurrence during this phase involved how authority worked among the teams. After the consolidation phase, authority had moved from the former supervisory system to the new value consensus of the teams, but during the second phase, the old team members, all full-time employees, were the keepers of this new system. They identified strongly with it and expected new members to demonstrate their worthiness to participate with them in the concertive process. They began to use rewards and punishments to encourage compliance among the team members. Temporary workers either obeyed the rules and became integrated into this system, or they found the door. The teams' interactions left little room for resistance. This placed strong pressure on the temporary workers to conform to their team's rules. Tommy, a temporary worker then, explained the pressure:

> Being temporary, you could come in any day and find out you don't have a job no more. So, that's kind of scary for a lot of people who have, you know, kids and a lot of bills to take care of. So they tend to hold it in, what they want to say, to the point where they can't do it anymore and they just blow up, which causes them to lose their job anyway.

Before the change to teams, the line supervisors would generally tolerate some degree of slackness among the workers and allow someone many chances to screw-up before taking drastic action. But now the team members exercised their newfound authority with much less patience. In mid-1991 I walked into the blue team's area one morning and found the temporary workers very agitated and the full-time workers nowhere around. I asked Katie what was happening. She said that the full-time workers had gone off to fire Joey. Joey was a temporary who worked hard but had a tendency to wander off across the shop and socialize. While he did not do this often, he had the knack of doing it when Martha, the coordinator, or another full-time worker happened to notice his absence. The previous day, Joey had been caught again. That morning, after the team meeting, the full-time workers said that they were going to go to the conference room to talk about Joey's problem. Right before I came to the team's area, they had called him back to the conference room. Katie looked back over her shoulder toward the conference room and sighed, "He's a good worker, but they [the full-time workers] don't see that. They don't know him. Now they're back there, judge, jury, and executioners."

While peer pressure may be essential to the effective work of any team (Walton and Hackman 1986: 186; Larson and Lafasto 1989: 96), the dynamics of ISE's teams during this phase go much deeper. The above episode was not a simple case of the full-timers beating up on the temporaries. What seemed to be peer pressure and power games on the surface was in fact a manifestation of concertive control. Authority here rests in the team's values, norms, and now rules. Team members rewarded themselves for compliance and punished themselves for noncompliance. They had invested their human dignity in the system of their own control (Parker and Slaughter 1988; Mumby and Stohl 1991). As participants in concertive control, the team members had begun a process of functionally constructing both their work activity and their own identities (Cheney 1991).

The second phase represents a natural progression of the value-based substantive rationality the teams had created in phase 1. The teams demystified their value consensus for new members by making it intellectually analyzable. The norms of phase 1 now became guidelines or rules, increasingly objectified and clarified for the team members, which allowed for effective interaction. The values forming the teams' substantive rationality provided the boundaries of action and interest within and among the teams (Kalberg 1980: 1170), but the control of actions and interests in the teams is not stable; it has to be fixed at particular points in time. The emergence of rational rules during the second phase served this function. These rules made concertive control concrete, almost as tangible as their old supervisor's book of job descriptions. It was the locus of authority resting with the teams themselves, however, that gave the rules their power. It empowered the teams to enable certain activity and constrain others. The locus of authority made concertive control work for ISE's teams.

Four key points characterize the development of concertive control at ISE during the second phase: (1) The teams had to bring new members into the particular value-based social systems they had created during phase 1; (2) To meet this need, the teams began to form normative rules for doing good work on the teams, creating what Hackman and Walton (1986: 83) called a team's "core norms." Longer-tenured team members expected the new members to identify and comply with these rules and their underlying values; (3) The rules naturally began to take on a more rationalized character; and (4) Concertive control functioned through the team members themselves sanctioning their own actions. While the influx of new members may have served as a catalyst for the emergence of normative rules on the teams, the rules came about through the natural progression of the team's value consensus into what Weber called a "methodical way of life" on the organizational/team level (Kalberg 1980: 1164). This was how the new members could learn their teams' value consensus and participate in their new form of control. Further, these particular tensions between full-time and temporary workers were not enduring. What did last was the impact of rationalizing the rules and the fact that authority rested with the peer pressure of the teams.

Phase 3: Stabilization and Formalization of the Rules

During this time (late 1991 to mid-1992), the company began to stabilize and turn a profit. A large number of temporary workers had been integrated into the full-time pool during phase 2, which resulted in the number of temporary workers falling from a high of almost 50 percent at times in phase 2 to as few as 10 percent during phase 3. But the stabilization phase also saw the teams' normative rules become more and more rationalized: Their value-based substantive rationality was giving way to rationalization (Cooper and Burrell 1988: 93). What were simple norms in phase 1 (we all need to be at work on time) now became highly objective rules similar to ISE's old bureaucratic structure (if you are more than five minutes late, you're docked a day's pay). On the surface, day-to-day control still looked much different from when ISE had traditional supervisors, but, on a deeper level, this control seemed hauntingly familiar and much more powerful.

The most noticeable change occurred in the coordinator's role. From my first days at ISE, I had tracked a continual pressure to make the coordinator's duties clearer and more specified. Thus, the coordinators' work gradually had become more formalized. If the team members needed something from the human resources department, they would ask the coordinator to get it. If Jack needed information about a team's work, he would ask the coordinator for it. The coordinators began to take on more and more specific tasks: scheduling, tracking production errors, holding regular meetings with each other, and so forth. In early 1992, the role became formalized as a permanent position, now called facilitator. The teams nominated workers for the six positions, and a committee of workers and managers (including Jack) interviewed the nominees and selected the new facilitators. These six workers received a 10 percent boost in their hourly wage to signify their new importance. They also drew up a list of duties for the role, which really just formalized what the old coordinators had already been doing. Lee Ann, who became the blue team's facilitator saw this process, too, as she told me about a month after assuming the new role: "It's more formalized acceptance that somebody is gonna be the one to answer the questions, and you might as well have someone answering the questions of the team and of management. And, I get paid for it, too." The most interesting aspect of the change in the coordinator role for me was that the workers wanted it, not so much to reinvent hierarchy on the teams but because formalizing their work life seemed so natural to them.

Formalizing the aspects of their work appeared to give the teams a sense of stability that would insulate them from the turmoil of the past year, and so rules proliferated in all aspects of the teams' activity. As Brown (1978: 368) suggested, the rules were taking on their own rationality and legitimacy. What was once an abstract value, such as "a team member should be able to do all the work roles on the team," had now became a set of specific guidelines for how long new members had to train for a specific function (assembling, testing, repairing, etc.) and how long a team member would have to work in assembly before rotating to a new team job, such as repair.

During phase 3, I saw the teams' social rules become more and more rigid. The teams seemed to be trying to permanently fix their social rules. Two examples stand out for me. In mid-1992 I was talking with Liz, who had also become a facilitator, about how members directed each other's actions now, as opposed to three years before. Liz told me that her team had been talking about drafting a "code of conduct" for team members that spelled out the behaviors needed to be a good team member. She began to get very excited about the possibilities of making these actions clear and concrete. She said, "If we can just get this written down [emphasis hers]. If we can just get our code of conduct in writing, then everyone will know what to do. We won't have so many problems. If we can just get it written down." I found the second telling example when I visited ISE again two weeks later. I had been following how the teams were dealing with attendance and how their rules for coming into work on time were becoming more specific. A team member who came in five minutes or more late would be charged with an "occurrence" and considered to be absent for the whole day. If a worker accumulated four occurrences in a month, the team facilitator would place a written warning in that person's company file. A worker who came in less than five minutes late received a "tardy," and seven tardies equaled one occurrence. While I knew that all the teams had some kind of attendance policy, what I found this day truly surprised me. When I walked into the red team's area, I saw a new chart on its wall. The chart listed each team member's name down the left-hand side and had across the top a series of columns representing days of the week. Beside each name were color-coded dots that indicated "on time," "tardy," or "occurrence." The team had posted this board in plain sight for all team members to see, and the team updated its board every day. I found a similar chart in use by the other teams.

Three thoughts went through my mind. The first was the powerful insight of Ronald's comment, which opened this paper: "Now the whole team is around me and the whole team is observing what I'm doing." The second was that this policy seemed uncannily similar to something I would have expected to find in the old supervisory system. The third was that the teams had now created, in effect, a nearly perfect form of control. Their attendance behavior (and in a way their human dignity) was on constant display for everyone else on the team to monitor: an essentially total system of control almost impossible to resist (Foucault 1976). The transformation from values to norms to rules had gained even more heightened intensity.

The fact that the teams were creating their own rational rule systems was not lost on all the team members, but they expressed the feeling that these rules were good for them and their work. As Lee Ann told me at this time:

We are making a lot of new rules, but most of them come from, "Well see, because so and so person did such and such, well we're not gonna allow that anymore" [concertive control at work]. But the majority of the rules that we are putting in are coming from what the old rules were [before the change to teams]. They had a purpose. They did stop people from making, like expensive mistakes. . . . With more people on the teams, we have to be more formal. We have seventeen people on my team. That large amount of people moving is what's causing the bureaucracy to come back in. Lee Ann's use of "bureaucracy" perplexed me. Had ISE's teams reinvented a bureaucratic system of control? Certainly the substantive rationality and its focus on value consensus that characterized phase 1 now had become blurred with a new formal rationality that focused on making rules, which appeared to fit with Weber's prediction that "a multiplicity of rationalization processes . . . variously conflict and coalesce with one another at all societal and civilizational levels" (Kalberg 1980: 1147), including among ISE's teams. And certainly much of the pressure toward formalization came from the team's need to be productive and efficient in order for ISE to survive in its competitive market (Kalberg 1980: 1163). But as I later reflected on Lee Ann's comment and my experience at ISE, the nature of this blurring of substantive and formal rationality became clearer.

The progression of the teams' value-based work ethic from norms to rational rules indicated that the workers had created micro-level disciplines that rationalized their work behaviors so to make them purposeful, functional, and controlled (Foucault 1980; Barker and Cheney 1994). Discipline, here, refers to a willingly accepted social force that rationalizes organizational work to ensure normalized and controlled individual and collective action. During phase 3, the teams developed formalized rule systems out of the normative ethics of their original value consensus. These disciplinary systems enabled the teams to work effectively, integrate new members easily, and meet their production demands. The team members willingly accepted these disciplines because they themselves had created them. And these disciplines appeared to work. During phase 3, ISE became profitable again. ISE's top management believed that the change to teams was one of the key reasons (along with other key changes in engineering and marketing) for the company's success. Jack credited the change to teams with cutting his factory costs 25 percent since 1988.

But the teams' formalization of their value system and norms did not mean that they had re-created a bureaucracy. Authority in ISE's concertive system rested with the teams and their interactions with each other. The character of ISE's concertive control was still much different from when it operated under bureaucratic control. As they integrated more temporary workers into the ranks of full-time members, the team members still held authority over each other. They still expected each other to follow the rules and, as evidenced by their attendance charts, still monitored each other's behavior carefully. The team members themselves still rewarded or punished each other's behavior. They did not give this function to the new facilitators: they kept it for themselves.

Close to the end of my data collection, Liz told me of an incident that had occurred a few days before, involving Sharon, a single mother who had some difficulty getting to work at 7 A.M. The team had been sensitive to her needs and had even given her a week off when one of her children was sick. The day before the incident, enough time had passed for Sharon to drop one of her many occurrences. She even announced this to the team by making a joke of it, "I just dropped one occurrence, so that means I can have another." The next morning one of her children was sick again and she was late. And the team remembered her "joke" of the night before.

When Sharon showed up, the team reacted in the same way a shift supervisor in ISE's old system might have. The team confronted Sharon immediately and directly. They told her that they were very upset that she was late. They bluntly told her how much they had suffered from having to work short-handed. Stung by the criticism of her peers, Sharon began to cry. The team's tack shifted to healing the wounds they had caused. They told her that they had not meant to hurt her feelings but that they wanted her to understand how her actions had affected them. They asked her to be certain to contact them immediately when she had a problem. The episode closed with the team telling her, "we really count on you to be here and we really need you here." When I checked a month later, Sharon had not recorded another occurrence.

In phase 3, the team members still kept the authority to control each other's behaviors: concertive control still occurred within the teams. In many ways, the formalization of the team's normative rules made this process easier, as seen in the incident with Sharon. The teams had created an omnipresent "tutelary" eye of the norm, with the team members themselves as the eye, that continually observed their actions, ready either to reward or, more importantly, punish. Being under the constant eye of the norm appeared to me to have an effect on the workers. To a person, the older team workers told me that they felt much more stress in the team environment than they had under the old ISE system. The newer members also complained of the constant strain of self-management. This sense of heightened stress that ISE's workers expressed to me was similar to that found in other team-based organizations (e.g., Grenier 1988; Mumby and Stohl 1991). Parker and Slaughter (1988) even called the self-management concept management by stress.

My key informants also appeared more strained and burdened than in times past. I had watched Liz change from the totally committed team member in 1990, who saw her team as a family and wanted to be the last one to turn out the lights, to a distant, distracted facilitator in 1992, too harried and pressured to take any enjoyment in her team or to think of it as a family. Lee Ann, in a conversation with me in August 1992, expressed the same feelings:

> After you've been here awhile, you're gonna get super-involved, then you're gonna get burned out. I see this with person after person. You get really involved, you take it home with you, you eat with it, you sleep with it. You work 12, 16-hour days and you just burn out. You may step out just a bit, let someone else get super-involved for awhile, then you'll pick it up again. But you won't have that enthusiasm anymore.

The tutelary eye of the norm demanded its observants become super-involved or risk its wrath, and critical to this phase, the eye also demanded that its observants demonstrate this involvement by following its rules, its rational routine. That was work life in the eye of the norm, in ISE's brand of concertive control.

In phase 3, the teams' activity appeared to stabilize around sets of formalized rules that provided a rational and effective routine for their day-to-day actions. As in the previous phases, this formalization did not change the locus of authority in the teams but rather strengthened it. The team members directed and monitored each other's actions. Concertive control still occurred within the teams themselves. Four key points characterize phase 3: (1) The normative rules of phase 2 became more and more objective, creating a new formal rationality among the teams; (2) The teams appeared to "settle in" to the rational routine these formal rules brought to their work. The rules made it easier for them to deal objectively with difficult situations (such as Sharon's coming in late) by establishing a system of work regulation and worker self-control; (3) The team members felt stress from the concertive system, but they accepted this as a natural part of their work. They did not want to give up their feeling of being self-managers, however, no matter how intense the system of control became; and (4) The work life at ISE stabilized into a concertive system that revolved around sets of rational rules, as in the old bureaucracy, but in which the authority to command obedience rested with the team members themselves, in contrast to the old ISE. The team members had become their own masters and their own slaves.

CONSEQUENCES OF CONCERTIVE CONTROL AT ISE

Table 19.2 summarizes and juxtaposes the manifest and latent consequences emerging from the system of concertive control that evolved at ISE between 1988 and 1992. This table depicts how concertive control, in a process akin to Lewin's (1946) model of "unfreezing-moving-refreezing," matured from a loosely held consensus about abstract values to a tightly bound system of rational rules and powerful self-control. ISE's experience with teams and the analysis I have reported here are consistent with other research reports of self-management systems at the level of the worker (e.g., Grenier 1988), which suggests that concertive control has a particular character: Concertive control, as it becomes manifest in organizational interaction, is more powerful and has a greater ability to control than the bureaucratic system it replaces.

Writers on concertive control have warned that this new system could become a stronger force than bureaucratic control. Tompkins and Cheney (1985: 184) asserted that concertive control would increase the strength of control in its system, and Tannenbaum (1968) proposed that if management will give up some of its authority to the workers, it will, in turn, increase the effectiveness of control in the firm. Tannenbaum (1968: 23) wrote that participative (self-managing in this case) organizations could not be productive "unless they have an effective system of control through which the potentially diverse interests and actions of members are integrated in concerted, that is, organized behavior. The relative success of participative approaches, therefore, hinges not on reducing control but on achieving a system of control that is more effective than that of other systems." This "more effective system of control," in terms of self-managing teams, comes from the authority and power teammates exercise on each other as peer managers. Peer management increases the total amount of control in a concertive system through two important dynamics. The first is that concertive workers have created this system through their own shared value consensus, which they enforce on each other. But in doing so, as seen in ISE's experience, the teams necessarily create a system of value-based rational rules, such as their strict attendance policy. They have put themselves under their own eye of the norm, resulting in a powerful system of control.

The second reason for the increased power of concertive control is that the way it becomes manifest is less apparent than bureaucratic control. Team members are relatively unaware of how the system they created actually controls their actions (Tompkins and Cheney 1985). Concertive control is much more subtle than a supervisor telling a group of workers what to do. In a concertive system, as with ISE, the workers create a value-based system of control and then invest themselves in it through their strong identification with the system (Barker and Cheney 1994). Because of this identification, the team members are socially constructed by the system they have created (Mumby and Stohl 1991). When this happens, the team members readily accept that they are controlling their own actions. It seems natural, and they willingly submit to their own control system. ISE's team members felt that developing a very strict and objective attendance policy was a natural occurrence. Likewise, their challenging Sharon's personal dignity when she violated the policy was another natural occurrence. And ISE's

Table 19.2
Manifest and Latent Consequences of ISE's Experience with Concertive Control

Manifest	Latent
1. Teams developed value consensus by drawing from ISE's vision statement.	1. Teams began to form a value-based substantive rationality, which led them to develop a mutually shared sense of ethical rational action at work.
2. Team members identified with their particular value consensus and developed emotional attachments to their shared values.	2. Authority transferred from ISE's old bureaucratic control system to the team's value system. The team members' human dignity became invested in submitting to this authority.
3. Teams formed behavioral norms from the values that enabled them to work effectively, thus put their values into action.	3. The teams became methodical about putting their values into action. Their values began a natural progression toward rationalization, which allowed the values and norms to be intellectually analyzable by all members.
4. Older team members expected new members to identify with the norms and values and act in accordance with these value-based norms.	4. Concertive control became nested in the team. Members themselves took on both superior and subordinate roles, monitoring and directing.
5. The teams' normative rules grew more rationalized. Team members enforced their rules with each other through peer pressure and behavioral sanctions.	5. ISE's concertive system became a powerful force of control. Since they had created it themselves, this control was seemingly natural and unapparent to the team members.
6. Teams further objectified and formalized the rules and shared these rules with each other. The work environment appeared to stabilize.	6. The teams had developed their own disciplines that merged their substantive values with a rule-based formal rationality. These disciplines enabled the teams to work efficiently and effectively. The teams controlled their work through a system of rational rules and the self-monitoring of their own individual and collective actions.

teams work effectively without Jack's constant (i.e., more apparent) monitoring. Thus, ISE's team workers are both under the eye of the norm and in the eye of the norm, but from where they are, in the eye, all seems natural and as it should be. Their system of rational rules winds tighter and tighter about them as the power of their value consensus compels their willful obedience.

ISE's experience with concertive control, then, is consistent with two theoretical predictions about the future of organizational activity. The first, which extends from Weber (1978) to Foucault (1976, 1980), asserts that organizational life will become increasingly rationalized and controlled. The second, which emerges primarily from Tompkins and Cheney (1985), Tannenbaum (1968), and Edwards (1981), posits that organizational control will become less apparent and more powerful.

The development of concertive control at ISE also complements the traditional literature on work-group norms and team development (e.g., Sundstrom, De Meuse, and Futrell 1990; Hackman 1992). ISE's experience with concertive control illuminates the linkages between the emergence of group norms and the broader organizational issues of authority, rationality, power, and control.

ISE's teams developed a concertive system of control that grew from value-laden premises to strong norms, to rational rules for good work in the teams. ISE's system became deeply embedded in the social relations of the members, which served to conceal the character of concertive control. Because of this, the concertive, value-based rules increased the overall force of control in the system, making it more powerful than bureaucratic control had been. Unlike the bureaucratic hierarchy, authority and the possibility of appeal first and finally resided in the peer pressure of the teams.

ISE's experience with concertive control still begs the question: Does the concertive system offer a form of control that conceptually and practically transcends traditional bureaucratic control? My analysis of ISE's experience with teams indicates that, on the one hand, a concertive system creates its own powerful set of rational rules, which resembles the traditional bureaucracy. But, on the other hand, the locus of authority has transferred from the hierarchical system to the teams' values, norms, and rules, which does not resemble the bureaucracy. Concertive control works by blurring substantive and formal rationality into a "communal-rational" system (Barker and Tompkins 1993). Concertive workers create a communal value system that eventually controls their actions through rational rules.

More importantly, however, my analysis suggests that concertive control does not free workers from Weber's iron cage of rational rules, as the culturalist and practitioner-oriented writers on contemporary organizations often argue. Instead, an ironic paradox occurs: The iron cage becomes stronger. The powerful combination of peer pressure and rational rules in the concertive system creates a new iron cage whose bars are almost invisible to the workers it incarcerates. ISE's team workers, as Weber (1978: 988) warned, have harnessed themselves into a rational apparatus out of which they truly cannot squirm. As ISE's experience demonstrates, uncommitted workers do not last in the concertive system. Concertive workers must invest a part of themselves in the team: they must identify strongly with their team's values and goals, its norms and rules. If they want to resist their team's control, they must be willing to risk their human dignity, being made to feel unworthy as a "teammate." Entrapment in the iron cage is the cost of concertive control.

REFERENCES

Adler, Patricia A., and Peter Adler. 1987. *Membership Roles in Field Research.* Beverly Hills, CA: Sage.

Andrasik, Frank, and Judy Stanley Heimberg. 1982. "Self-management procedures." In Lee W. Frederiksen (ed.), *Handbook of Organizational Behavior Management:* 219–247. New York: Wiley.

Barker, James R., and George Cheney. 1994. "The concept and the practices of discipline in contemporary organizational life." *Communication Monographs,* vol. 60 (in press).

Barker, James R., and Phillip K. Tompkins. 1993. "Organizations, teams, control, and identification." Unpublished manuscript, Department of Communication, University of Colorado, Boulder.

Barnard, Chester. 1968. *The Functions of the Executive.* (Originally published in 1938.) Cambridge, MA: Harvard University Press.

Bolweg, Joep F. 1976. *Job Design and Industrial Democracy.* Leiden: Martinus Nijhoff.

Brown, Richard Harvey. 1978. "Bureaucracy as praxis: Toward a political phenomenology of formal organizations." *Administrative Science Quarterly* 23: 365–382.

Carnall, C.A. 1982. "Semi-autonomous work groups and the social structure of the organization." *Journal of Management Studies* 19: 277–294.

Cheney, George. 1991. *Rhetoric in an Organizational Society: Managing Multiple Identities.* Columbia: University of South Carolina Press.

Coombs, Rod, David Knights, and Hugh C. Willmott. 1992. "Culture, control, and competition: Towards a conceptual framework for the study of information technology in organizations." *Organization Studies* 13: 51–72.

Cooper, Robert, and Gibson Burrell. 1988. "Modernism, postmodernism, and organizational analysis: An introduction." *Organization Studies* 9: 91–112.

Cordery, John L., Walter S. Mueller, and Leigh M. Smith. 1991. "Attitudinal and behavioral effects of autonomous group working: A longitudinal field study." *Academy of Management Journal* 34: 464–476.

Drucker, Peter E. 1988. "The coming of the new organizations." *Harvard Business Review* (January–February): 45–53.

Dumaine, Brian. 1990. "Who needs a boss?" *Fortune*, May: 52–60.

Eccles, Robert G., and Nitin Nohria. 1992. *Beyond the Hype: Rediscovering the Essence of Management.* Cambridge, MA: Harvard Business School Press.

Edwards, Richard C. 1981. "The social relations of production at the point of production." In Mary Zey-Ferrell and Michael Aiken (eds.), *Complex Organizations: Critical Perspectives:* 156–182. Glenview, IL: Scott, Foresman.

Follett, Mary Parker. 1941. *Dynamic Administration: The Collected Papers of Mary Parker Follett.* Henry C. Metcalf and L. Urwick, eds. London: Pitman.

Foucault, Michel. 1976. *Discipline and Punish.* New York: Vintage.

———. 1980. *Power/Knowledge.* New York: Pantheon.

Giddens, Anthony. 1984. *The Constitution of Society: Outline of the Theory of Structuration.* Berkeley: University of California Press.

Grenier, Guillermo J. 1988. *Inhuman Relations.* Philadelphia: Temple University Press.

Hackman, J. Richard. 1986. "The psychology of self-management in organizations." In Michael S. Pallak and Robert O. Perloff (eds.). *Psychology and Work: Productivity, Change, and Employment:* 89–136. Washington, DC: American Psychological Association.

———. 1992. "Group influences on individuals in organizations." In Marvin D. Dunnette and Leaetta M. Hough (eds.), *Handbook of Industrial and Organizational Psychology,* 2d ed., 3: 199–267. Palo Alto, CA: Consulting Psychologists Press.

Hackman, J. Richard, and Richard E. Walton. 1986. "Leading groups in organizations." In Paul S. Goodman and Associates (eds.), *Designing Effective Work Groups:* 72–119. San Francisco: Jossey-Bass.

Homans, George C. 1950. *The Human Group.* New York: Harcourt, Brace and World.

Jermier, John M., John W. Slocum, Jr., Louis W. Fry, and Jeannie Gaines. 1991. "Resistance behind the myth and facade of an official culture." *Organization Science* 2: 170–194.

Jorgensen, Danny L. 1989. *Participant Observation: A Methodology for Human Studies.* Newbury Park, CA: Sage.

Kalberg, Stephen. 1980. "Max Weber's types of rationality: Cornerstones for the analysis of rationalization processes in history." *American Journal of Sociology* 85: 1145–1179.

Kanter, Rosabeth Moss. 1989. *When Giants Learn to Dance.* New York: Simon and Schuster.

Katz, Daniel, and Robert L. Kahn. 1978. *The Social Psychology of Organizations.* New York: Wiley.

Ketchum, L.D. 1984. How redesigned plants really work. *National Productivity Review* 3: 246–254.

Larson, Carl E., and Frank M.J. Lafasto. 1989. *Teamwork: What Must Go Right/What Can Go Wrong.* Newbury Park, CA: Sage.

Lewin, Kurt. 1946. "Research on minority problems." *Technology Review* 3: 48.

———. 1948. *Resolving Social Conflicts: Selected Papers on Group Dynamics.* New York: Harper and Row.

Lewis, Betty. 1990. "Team-directed workforce from a worker's view." *Target* (Winter): 23–29.

Manz, Charles C., and Henry P. Sims. 1987. "Leading workers to lead themselves: The external leadership of self-managing work teams." *Administrative Science Quarterly* 32: 106–128.

Miller, P., and T. O'Leary. 1987. "Accounting and the construction of the governable person." *Accounting, Organizations and Society* 12: 235–265.

Mumby, Dennis K., and Cynthia Stohl. 1991. "Power and discourse in organizational studies: Absence and the dialectic of control." *Discourse and Society* 2: 313–332.

Ogilvy, Jack. 1990. "This postmodern business." *Marketing and Research Today* (February): 4–20.

Orsburn, Jack D., Linda Moran, Ed Musselwhite, and John H. Zenger. 1990. *Self-Directed Work Teams: The New American Challenge.* Homewood, IL: Irwin.

Parker, Martin. 1992. "Post-modern organizations or postmodern organizational theory?" *Organization Studies* 13: 1–17.

Parker, Mike, and Jane Slaughter. 1988. *Choosing Sides: Unions and the Team Concept.* Boston: South End Press.

Perrow, Charles. 1986. *Complex Organizations: A Critical Essay.* New York: Random House.

Peters, Thomas J. 1988. *Thriving on Chaos.* New York: Knopf.

Peters, Thomas J., and Richard Waterman, Jr. 1982. *In Search of Excellence: Lessons from America's Best-Run Companies.* New York: Harper & Row.

Riggs, Fred. 1979. "Introduction: Shifting meanings of the term 'bureaucracy'." *International Science Journal* 31: 563–584.

Rothschild, Joyce, and J. Allen Whitt. 1986. *The Cooperative Workplace.* Cambridge: Cambridge University Press.

Sewell, Graham, and Barry Wilkinson. 1992. "Someone to watch over me: Surveillance, discipline and the just-in-time labour process." *Sociology* 26: 271–289.

Simon, Herbert A. 1976. *Administrative Behavior: A Study of Decision-Making Processes in Administrative Organizations,* 3d edition. New York: Free Press.

Soeters, Joseph L. 1986. "Excellent companies as social movements." *Journal of Management Studies* 23: 299–312.

Sundstrom, Eric, Kenneth P. De Meuse, and David Futrell. 1990. "Work teams: Applications and effectiveness." *American Psychologist* 45: 120–133.

Tannenbaum, Arnold S. 1968. *Control in Organizations.* New York: McGraw-Hill.

Tompkins, Phillip K., and George Cheney. 1985. "Communication and unobtrusive control in contemporary organizations." In Robert D. McPhee and Phillip K. Tompkins (eds.), *Organizational Communication: Traditional Themes and New Directions:* 179–210. Newbury Park, CA: Sage.

Trist, Eric L. 1981. "The evolution of socio-technical systems." Occasional Paper No. 2. Toronto: Quality of Working Life Centre.

Trist, Eric L., G. Higgin, H. Murray, and A.B. Pollock. 1963. *Organizational Choice.* London: Tavistock.

Tuckman, Bruce W. 1965. "Development sequences in small groups." *Psychological Bulletin* 63: 384–399.

Walton, Richard E. 1982. "The Topeka work system: Optimistic visions, pessimistic hypothesis, and reality." In Robert Zager and Michael P. Roscow (eds.), *The Innovative Organization:* 260–287. New York: Pergamon.

Walton, Richard E., and J. Richard Hackman. 1986. "Groups under contrasting management strategies." In Paul S. Goodman and associates (eds.), *Designing Effective Work Groups:* 168–201. San Francisco: Jossey-Bass.

Weber, Max. 1958. *The Protestant Ethic and the Spirit of Capitalism.* New York: Scribner's.

———. 1978. *Economy and Society.* Guenther Roth and Klaus Wittich, eds. Berkeley: University of California Press.

Wellins, Richard S., William C. Byham, and Jeanne M. Wilson. 1991. *Empowered Teams: Creating Self-Directed Work Groups That Improve Quality, Productivity, and Participation.* San Francisco: Jossey-Bass.

Whitley, Richard. 1977. "Organizational control and the problem of order." *Social Science Information* 16: 169–189.

20

Monkey See, Monkey Do: The Influence of Work Groups on the Antisocial Behavior of Employees

Sandra L. Robinson and
Anne M. O'Leary-Kelly

The prevention of antisocial actions in organizations is increasingly important to American managers and organizational scholars. Recent estimates suggest there is good reason for both managers and researchers to take a closer look at these actions. Some research reports that as many as 42 percent of women have been victims of sexual harassment at work (Gruber 1990), that as many as 75 percent of employees have stolen from their employers (McGurn 1988), and that 33 to 75 percent of all employees have engaged in behaviors ranging from insubordination to sabotage (Harper 1990). These actions, of course, represent some of the most serious forms of antisocial behavior. Yet we must also note the apparent prevalence of less serious, yet still harmful, actions, such as lying (DePaulo and DePaulo 1989), spreading rumors (Skarlicki and Folger 1997), withholding effort (Kidwell and Bennett 1993), and absenteeism (Johns 1997), that may violate work norms and therefore may be antisocial (Robinson and Bennett 1995).

One of the complexities of initial research in this area has been the use of diverse labels to describe these actions. For example, Robinson and Bennett (1995) used the term "deviant behavior"; O'Leary-Kelly, Griffin, and Glew (1996) described "aggressive work behavior"; and Vardi and Wiener (1996) discussed "organizational misbehavior." In this article, we use the broad term "antisocial behavior" to describe negative behaviors in organizations. We chose this expansive term because, like the well-established and related term "prosocial behavior" (Brief and Motowidlo 1986; George 1990), "antisocial behavior" captures a wide range of actions. In addition, the term captures the harmful nature of these acts, the fact that they have the potential to cause harm to individuals and/or the property of an organization (Giacalone and Greenberg 1996).

Adapted from *Academy of Management Journal* 41, pp. 658–672, copyright 1998 by Academy of Management. Adapted with permission of Academy of Management via Copyright Clearance Center.

This dimension of potential harmfulness is the critical focus of most definitions of related constructs (for a review, see Robinson and Greenberg [1998]).

To date, forms of antisocial behavior in organizations have been examined from various theoretical perspectives. For example, using social learning theory (Bandura 1977), O'Leary-Kelly and colleagues (1996) identified a number of individual and environmental antecedents. Martinko and Zellars (1996) expanded this framework, incorporating attribution theory into the social learning explanation. Other examples include Greenberg's (1990, 1993) work on theft and Skarlicki and Folger's (1997) research on retaliation, both of which used principles of justice theory to explain antisocial employee actions. These approaches, well grounded in established theory, have resulted in important advances in the understanding of why and when employees engage in antisocial behavior.

Although this previous research makes significant contributions, it also is limited because antisocial behaviors have predominately been examined as individual-level phenomena. This focus is reasonable in that decisions to exhibit any behavior, whether antisocial or prosocial, are made by individuals. However, additional insights might be acquired if these behaviors were examined within the social context of work groups. The purpose of this research was to address antisocial behavior as a group-related activity. Specifically, we examined the extent to which individuals' antisocial actions are shaped by the group context within which they work. It should be emphasized that we see this focus as a supplement, not an alternative, to individual-level explanations.

THE INFLUENCE OF GROUPS ON INDIVIDUAL ANTISOCIAL ACTIONS

George (1990; George and James 1993) used a group level of analysis to examine prosocial behaviors in organizations. Her research showed that the levels of positive and negative affectivity within a work group influenced the affective tone of the group and the group's general level of prosocial behaviors. Given the importance of work groups in predicting prosocial actions, it seems appropriate to consider whether and how work groups affect antisocial actions.

A variety of theoretical perspectives support the notion that individuals' work groups will influence the likelihood of their behaving in antisocial ways. In this research, we invoked three: (1) the attraction-selection-attrition perspective, (2) social information processing theory, and (3) social learning theory.

The Attraction-Selection-Attrition Perspective

A basic assumption underlying the attraction-selection-attrition framework is that individuals carefully analyze their work environments and adjust their individual actions accordingly (Schneider 1975). Individuals with antisocial tendencies are more likely to be attracted to, and selected into, the group environments that fit well with those tendencies. In addition, most individuals will likely adapt some of their behaviors, conditions, and attitudes to better fit with the social environment in which they work. Those that adapt well are more likely to remain with the organization, whereas those who do not sufficiently adapt are more likely to leave. Thus, employees within work groups should tend to be relatively homogeneous in terms of their attitudes and behavior regarding antisocial behavior because they are generally similar individuals who are experiencing comparable conditions and are trying to adapt to their common environment (Schneider 1987; Schneider and Reichers 1983). In other words, we would expect a positive relationship between a given individual's level of antisocial behavior and the level of antisocial behavior of his or her coworkers.

Social Information Processing Theory

Social information processing theory would also support the predictions that group-level antisocial behavior will influence the antisocial behavior of individual members and that, over time, individual members will come to have more similar levels of antisocial behavior. According to the social information processing approach, individuals use information from their immediate social environments to interpret events, develop appropriate attitudes, and understand expectations concerning their behavior and its consequences (Salancik and Pfeffer 1978). The social context greatly determines how individuals behave by influencing how they think and feel about aspects of their work environment (Salancik and Pfeffer 1978). Applying this perspective to antisocial behavior suggests that individual group members, working in a shared social environment, will receive similar social cues that convince them that certain types and levels of antisocial behavior are acceptable adaptations to their shared working conditions.

Social Learning Theory

O'Leary-Kelly and colleagues (1996) used Bandura's (1977) social learning perspective to examine factors that encourage antisocial behavior. One such factor was the presence of role models within a work context. They argued that if individuals work in environments that include others who serve as models for antisocial behavior, these individuals are more likely themselves to behave in antisocial ways. When individuals operate within group settings, they are typically able to observe other group members, which creates the opportunity for these members to serve as models. In addition, Bandura's research on disengagement of moral control suggests that diffusion of responsibility, a common outcome in group contexts, can lead individuals to disconnect the self-regulatory systems that typically govern moral conduct (Bandura 1990, 1991; Bandura, Barbaranelli, Caprara, and Pastorelli 1996).

Integrating social learning theory with the attraction-selection-attrition perspective and the social information processing approach, we considered it likely that members of groups who are analyzing their social environments for information regarding the appropriateness of particular beliefs, attitudes, and behaviors would often use other group members as role models. If other group members serve as role models, groups may have a significant influence on individual antisocial behavior through this role-modeling process. Drawing on these three theoretical foundations, we hypothesized the following:

Hypothesis 1:   There will be a positive relationship between the level of antisocial behavior within a group and the level of antisocial behavior of individual group members.

To this point, we have conceptualized social climates as relatively fixed phenomena, as conditions that either exist or do not. A more realistic portrayal, and one more consistent with the attraction-selection-attrition framework (Schneider 1975, 1987; Schneider and Reichers 1983), would represent such environments according to their degree of strength. A group's climate reflects the aggregate perceptions of group members regarding a particular aspect of the work setting, perceptions that influence the types of behaviors that are exhibited within the group. When there is strong similarity in members' perceptions and behaviors, the social context is most potent and thus most capable of having a profound influence on member behavior. Therefore, we expected that the degree of similarity in group members' levels of antisocial behavior would moderate the extent to which a group's general level of antisocial behavior would influence an individual group member's level.

Salancik and Pfeffer's (1978) discussion of social information processing theory is consistent with the above argument. Salancik and Pfeffer posited that the effect of a particular social environment on individual attitudes and behavior depends on the degree to which there are shared beliefs within the social environment. Social learning theory also would be consistent with this moderating effect. As argued above, the antisocial behavior of individual group members may be influenced by the role models they encounter within a group. To the extent that potential role models exhibit similar levels of antisocial behavior, there is a stronger probability that the individual member will choose a role model that reflects the group's norms. For example, if most members of a work group behave in antisocial ways, the likelihood that a new group member might choose a role model who exhibits antisocial behavior is increased, and the chance that the newcomer will develop antisocial actions is also greater. Drawing on these arguments, we predict the following moderated effect:

Hypothesis 2:   The degree of similarity or of variance in antisocial behavior within a group will moderate the relationship between group antisocial behavior and individual members' antisocial behavior in such a way that the greater the similarity (the lower the variance), the stronger the relationship.

The impact of a group on individuals is also likely to be enhanced as the members' time in the group increases. Numerous theoretical frameworks support the existence of this moderating effect. For example, social impact theory (Latane 1981) suggests that the extent of social influence that any individual has over others is a function of, among other factors, the proximity in time and space between the relevant parties, which has been labeled "immediacy." Attraction-selection-attrition theory also supports this argument. Compared to a newcomer, an individual who has been a member of a group for some time is likely to have acquired more accurate perceptions of the group's attributes. This individual is, therefore, in a better position to determine the degree of fit between personal and group attributes. Attraction-selection-attrition principles suggest that this individual will either adjust personal behavior to fit the work environment or leave the organization (Schneider 1975; Schneider and Reichers 1983). The longer a member remains, then, the more likely it is that this person has chosen to remain with the group and to behave in accordance with the group's climate.

Social information processing theory and social learning theory are also consistent with this moderating effect. With the former, the longer an individual retains membership in the group, the greater is the group's ability to provide social information that shapes the individual's beliefs, attitudes, and behaviors (Salancik and Pfeffer 1978). According to social learning theory, individuals determine the utility of modeled actions by watching the model's interactions with the environment (Bandura 1986). Central to the notion of modeling, then, is the assumption that individuals have the opportunity to observe the model. Certainly, the longer an individual's tenure in a work group, the greater his or her opportunity to observe role models and thus, the stronger the impact of antisocial behavior role models.

> *Hypothesis 3:* An individual member's tenure in a group will moderate the effect of the group's antisocial behavior on the individual's antisocial behavior in such a way that the relationship is stronger for members with longer tenure in the group.

In both the attraction-selection-attrition and social information processing theories, the social context is represented as the fundamental determinant of behavior (Salancik and Pfeffer 1978; Schneider 1975). Although the social context is not as explicit in social learning theory, this perspective is also consistent with the notion that interactions between people determine individual behavior. Thus far, we have not addressed the question of how other factors, such as objective characteristics of a work group (for example, its structure and technology), might influence individual behavior. According to Schneider (1987), these factors will influence individual behavior indirectly, through their ability to enhance or limit interactions between people.

One objective organizational characteristic that has a history of importance within group settings is task interdependence, or the degree to which employees in a work group must coordinate their individual efforts. In groups with high task interdependence, individual members are likely to have greater opportunity to interact with others in the group. This enhanced interaction allows members to more easily acquire the social information that will, according to both the attraction-selection-attrition and social information processing frameworks, determine their subsequent behavior. In addition, in line with social learning theory (Bandura 1973, 1977), the higher level of interaction among group members will increase the likelihood that group members will be perceived as relevant comparison others and therefore chosen as role models. Under conditions of high task interdependence, therefore, the influence of a group's antisocial behavior on individual antisocial behavior should be intensified.

> *Hypothesis 4:* A group's level of task interdependence will moderate the relationship between group antisocial behavior and the antisocial behavior of individual members in such a way that the higher the task interdependence, the stronger the relationship.

Each of the three perspectives provides a conceptual explanation of how groups might influence the antisocial behavior of individual members. Only the attraction-selection-attrition perspective, however, deals directly with the issue of how individuals might become alienated from, and ultimately leave, a group. As mentioned previously, the attrition component of the attraction-selection-attrition framework suggests that individuals who do not fit a work environment will wish to leave their organizations (Schneider 1975, 1987; Schneider and Reichers 1983). This lack of fit implies that people perceive themselves to be significantly different on relevant attributes from others in the work environment, feel dissatisfied with the poor fit, and want to withdraw from the setting. One might expect, therefore, that individuals whose behaviors are very different from those of others in their work group would experience dissatisfaction with members of the group and would wish to leave it. With regard to antisocial behavior, it seems quite likely that there will be individuals who find their personal attributes or behavioral tendencies at odds with the attributes or behaviors of a work group that engages in antisocial behavior because such behaviors are, by definition, in violation of generally held (that is, societal level) social mores.

> *Hypothesis 5:* To the extent that individual group members exhibit lower levels of antisocial behavior than their group exhibits, they will report lower satisfaction with group members.
>
> *Hypothesis 6:* To the extent that individual group members exhibit lower levels of antisocial behavior than their group does, they will report greater intentions to leave.

The theories that provide the conceptual foundation for our previous hypotheses are useful for determining how the group environment, with its explicit and implicit pressures and its formal and informal social constraints and sanctions, might affect an individual's antisocial behavior at work. However, given the potentially negative repercussions of antisocial behavior, organizations (that is, the organizational environments that exist beyond immediate work groups) typically have a clear interest in preventing such actions, even if they are explicitly and/or implicitly encouraged by a work group. For example, a work group may ignore employee theft by its members, but organizational managers outside the group want to prevent theft. This contrast presents an interesting dilemma—if the group's climate encourages antisocial behaviors, but these actions are discouraged in the larger environment, will individual group members behave in antisocial ways?

Generally, we expected a group's ability to influence a member's antisocial behavior to depend on the member's perception that such behavior can be engaged in without negative consequences; therefore, conditions that enhance the belief that punishment will follow antisocial behavior should lessen the group's influence. Two techniques that managers often use to deter antisocial behavior are the threat of punishment and close supervision of employees. We expected the group's influence to be limited by these managerial actions and predicted the following:

Hypothesis 7: The likelihood of punishment by management will moderate the relationship between group antisocial behavior and individual antisocial behavior in such a way that the greater the likelihood of punishment, the weaker the relationship.

Hypothesis 8: Closeness of supervision will moderate the relationship between group antisocial behavior and individual antisocial behavior in such a way that the closer the supervision, the weaker the relationship.

METHODS

Overview

Sample

Data were collected from 187 full-time employees. Average tenure within the firm was 5.93 years, and average tenure in the current job was 3.87 years. Occupations and the percentages of respondents in them were as follows: production workers, 24 percent; business consultants, 19 percent; general managers, 18 percent; administrative/ clerical personnel, 10 percent; real estate agents, 8 percent; accountants, 7 percent; human resource professionals, 4 percent; sales personnel, 2 percent; engineers, 2 percent; R and D staff members, 2 percent; paralegals, 2 percent; and other, 2 percent.

Respondents were from 35 work groups in 20 different organizations. The groups ranged in size from 4 to 10 employees, with the average size being 5.34 employees. Industries and the numbers of organizations in them were as follows: consumer products, 7; consulting and accounting, 6; financial services, 2; real estate, 2; social services, 1; insurance, 1; and gambling, 1.

Close to equal numbers of men (52%) and women (48%) participated in the study. Age ranged from 21 to 65 years, with an average of 32. Fifty-one percent were married. Educational level varied: 9.4 percent had high school educations, 29 percent had some college experience, 29.2 percent had bachelor's degrees, and 32.7 percent possessed graduate degrees.

Procedures

Participating organizations were selected from a list of firms recruiting from a large midwestern business school. Thirty-two percent agreed to participate. Organizationally defined boundaries were used to define work groups. Most organizations provided multiple and varied work groups for the study. For example, a manufacturer of aircraft brake linings provided five work groups in administration, engineering, and sales, and an optical and eye care product firm provided work groups in manufacturing, accounting, and administration. We used this sampling procedure because it enabled us to obtain a sample that was more diverse in terms of industries, organizations, and occupational groups. This diversity was valuable in that it enabled us to more confidently generalize our results to the larger employee population. All employees within each work group were asked to participate. They received surveys by mail and were asked to mail completed surveys back to us. Response rates within the work groups ranged from 37 to 100 percent, and the overall response rate was 67 percent.

Design

Our design was cross-level and primarily involved contextual independent and moderating variables and individual-level dependent variables. We measured the contextual variables by asking employees to report on characteristics of their groups and aggregating those reports for each group. Aggregating employee perceptions is a common and valid means by which to assess contextual variables (Rousseau 1985). Aggregation of individual perceptions is more useful than using individual perceptions alone to measure contextual variables because it reduces error by averaging out random individual-level errors and biases.

Where possible, we used a version of a split sample design that allowed us to reduce many of the problems associated with common method bias. Common method bias can pose problems for survey research that relies on self-report data, especially if the data are provided by the same person at the same time (Campbell and Fiske 1959). One important concern in such cases is that common method bias may artificially inflate observed relationships between variables. This problem may be avoided or reduced by using different respondents for reports of the independent and dependent variables. Our split sample design allowed us to do just that.

When analyzing the impact of contextual variables on an individual-level variable such as an employee's antisocial behavior, we excluded the focal employee's report of the independent variable from the aggregation of the contextual variable. We developed a program in SPSS that (1) averaged the employees' reports for each work context variable across each group and (2) assigned, to each employee within a particular group, the average score of each work context variable for that group excluding the employee's own assessment of the work context variable. Hence, the respondents who provided information on the independent variables were different from the respondents who provided information on the dependent variable.

Dependent Variables

Individual Antisocial Behavior

The dependent variable, individual antisocial behavior, was measured with a scale composed of the following items: "damaged property belonging to my employer," "said or did something to purposely hurt someone at work," "did work badly, incorrectly or slowly on purpose," "griped with coworkers," "deliberately bent or broke a rule(s)," "criticized people at work," "did something that harmed my employer or boss," "started an argument with someone at work," and "said rude things about my supervisor or organization."

The behaviors included in this scale were derived from two sources. The primary source was other scales found in the literature that measure similar behaviors (e.g., Robinson and Bennett 1995; Skarlicki and Folger 1997). A secondary source was a survey of fifty employees on the university campus who were asked to provide examples of antisocial behavior at work that they had witnessed. From these two sources, we derived a large pool of behaviors. Five coders who were blind to the purpose of the study independently categorized the behaviors. Inappropriate behaviors and redundant descriptions were removed. Initially, we selected ten behaviors on the basis of their frequency, generalizability, and distinctiveness. Many of the behavior descriptions were then modified to ensure that they were clear, consistent, and not compound. Given the sensitive nature of these behaviors, we modified many descriptions in order to reduce socially desirable response bias; for instance, innocuous-sounding terms were employed where possible.

Respondents used a one-to-five scale to indicate the extent to which they had engaged in each behavior in the year prior to data collection. We used the retrospective time frame of one year to address the expected low base rate of self-reported socially undesirable behaviors (Hulin and Rousseau 1980). A high score indicated a high level of antisocial behavior.

Face Validity Assessment of Individual Antisocial Behavior

We used a sample of 70 evening master of business administration (M.B.A.) students to assess face validity. All worked full-time, and most had at least two years of work experience. Their average age was 28.12 years, and 29.4 percent were women. They were provided with a list of the ten behaviors and asked to indicate whether they perceived each behavior as potentially harmful to an organization and/or its members.

With the exception of one item, the behaviors were indicated to be potentially harmful by the vast majority of respondents. The one behavior that was not perceived as potentially injurious was "used property belonging to my employer for my own benefit," which only 47.1 percent of the sample identified as potentially harmful. Thus, this item was dropped from the scale. For the remaining nine items, 71 to 100 percent of respondents said the behavior described was potentially harmful to organizations and/or their members. In sum, this validity analysis ensured that the items captured in the scale closely reflected our definition. The revised scale was composed of nine items.

Construct Validity Assessment of Individual Antisocial Behavior

We used a sample of 133 full-time employees from the Midwest. Forty-nine percent were women, and their average age was 43.58 years ($s.d. = 10.94$). The education level of the respondents varied; the average years of work experience was 23.52 ($s.d. = 10.57$); and the modal annual income was between \$15,000 and \$30,000.

First, we wanted to examine convergent validity by demonstrating that our measure of antisocial behavior was highly correlated with measures purported to assess similar constructs. Thus, we examined the relationship between our scale and two other scales. Lehman and Simpson's (1992) measure of antagonistic behaviors ($r = .49$, $p < .01$) and Rusbult, Farrell, Rogers, and Mainous's (1988) measure of neglect behaviors. We found that our measure was positively related to the antagonistic behaviors scale ($r = .49$, $p < .01$) and the neglect behaviors scale ($r = .46$, $p < .01$).

A demonstration that a focal measure is moderately correlated with measures of theoretically related constructs in a predicted fashion also provides evidence of convergent validity. Thus, we examined the relationship between our measure of antisocial behavior and two theoretically related constructs: intentions to leave a firm (Rusbult et al. 1988) and lack of job involvement. Those with high scores on these measures should also have high scores on our measure of antisocial behavior at work. The correlations were .30 ($p < .01$) for intentions to leave and .20 ($p < .05$) for job involvement. As expected, these correlations between our antisocial behavior measure and measures of theoretically related constructs were significant and in the predicted direction but not as high as the correlations between our measure of antisocial behavior and measures purporting to assess similar constructs.

We also examined discriminant validity, assessing the relationship between our measure of antisocial behavior and constructs expected to be conceptual opposites of antisocial behavior: consciousness, a type of citizenship or prosocial behavior (Podsakoff, MacKenzie, Moorman, and Fetter 1990), and loyalty behaviors (Rusbult et al. 1988). As expected, our antisocial behavior measure was moderately and negatively related to both the measure of citizenship behavior ($r = -.24$, $p < .05$) and the measure of loyalty ($r = -.46$, $p < .05$).

In summary, the above results lent support to the construct validity of our antisocial behavior measure. The results revealed that the measure was related, in expected ways, to measures purporting to measure similar constructs, to measures of theoretically related constructs, and to measures of conceptually opposing constructs.

Reliability Assessment of Individual Antisocial Behavior

We collected additional data from the sample of 102 evening M.B.A. students. These respondents were asked to complete the above nine-item scale measuring individual antisocial behavior at two points in time two weeks apart. The test-retest reliability for this scale was .87.

The internal reliability (Cronbach's alpha) of this nine-item scale was .68 for the primary respondents used in this study. However, the alphas for the evening M.B.A. students were .75 at time 1 and .81 at time 2.

Other Dependent Variables

Satisfaction with coworkers was measured with one facet of the job Descriptive Index (JDI; Smith, Kendall, and Hulin 1969). Respondents used "yes," "no," or "uncertain" to indicate whether each of 18 different adjectives described different aspects of the people with whom they worked. The higher the score, the higher the satisfaction with coworkers. Reliability for this scale was .84.

We measured employees' intentions to leave their organizations with the following question: "How long do you intend to remain with your company?" Respondents were given an open response format and all responses were converted to years. These were then reverse-coded so that a high value reflected a high level of intentions to leave.

Independent, Moderator, and Control Variables

Group Antisocial Behavior

The self-report scale used to measure the dependent variable individual antisocial behavior was also used to measure group antisocial behavior, a contextual variable. The distinction between these two variables was that the dependent variable, individual antisocial behavior, was each employee's self-report of his or her antisocial behavior, whereas the independent variable, group antisocial behavior, was a value assigned to each person that reflected an aggregation of all employees' self-reports of antisocial behavior across the group, excluding the employee whose antisocial behavior was being predicted.

Moderator Variables

To measure individual tenure in group, we asked respondents to indicate, in years, how long they had worked in the same group.

To measure task interdependence, we used Van de Ven, Delbecq, and Koenig's (1976) index. In this measure diagrams represent tasks as either independent, sequentially dependent, reciprocally dependent, or teamwork. Respondents were asked to indicate the percentages of their work that conformed to each of these types of interdependence. The higher the rating, the greater the degree of task interdependence. Measuring internal reliability was not appropriate for this scale because each item (a diagram) represents an increased level of interdependence. However, Van de Ven and colleagues (1976), using two alternative measures of the construct, reported the correlation between the measures to be .72.

Likelihood of punishment was measured by giving respondents a list of four anti-social behaviors and asking them to use a one-to-five scale to indicate the extent to which they would be rewarded or punished by their superiors for engaging in each behavior. The behaviors were "engaging in destructive activities such as stealing or damaging property belonging to our employer," "doing things that could hurt other people in the organization," "doing things that could hurt the department or the organization we work for," and "doing work badly, slowly or incorrectly on purpose." A high score indicated a greater likelihood of punishment for engaging in these behaviors. Reliability was .73.

To measure close supervision, we used a modified version of Dewar and Werbel's (1979) measure of surveillance and enforcement; this measure primarily reflects the degree to which employees are supervised closely by their superiors. Respondents were asked to indicate, using a one-to-five scale, the extent to which they agreed or disagreed with six statements. Examples of those statements include "We are constantly being watched to see that we obey all rules" and "Our superiors are aware of everything that we do on the job." The higher the score, the closer the supervision. The reliability of this scale was .88.

Control Variables

We controlled for several variables in most of our analyses. These were variables perceived to be common predictors of antisocial behavior in the workplace. To the extent we were able to control for alternative predictors of antisocial behavior, we were able to demonstrate the unique influence of group antisocial behavior on individual antisocial behavior.

First, we controlled for both close supervision and likelihood of punishment, except in direct tests of these variables. In traditional explanatory models of destructive behavior, such behavior has been viewed as largely dependent upon the presence or absence of formal constraints (e.g., Hirschi 1969), such as monitoring employee behavior and applying sanctions (e.g., Tittle 1973). Indeed, a host of research has suggested that the use of monitoring and sanctions can reduce employee deviance (e.g., Hollinger and Clark 1983), workplace theft (e.g., Greenberg and Scott 1996), and cheating (e.g., Covey, Saladin, and Kilen 1989).

We also controlled for level of job satisfaction, including the facets of job satisfaction found within the JDI: pay satisfaction, promotion satisfaction, work satisfaction, and supervisor satisfaction. In another common explanatory model of destructive workplace behavior, such behavior is viewed as emanating from job dissatisfaction, or perceived discrepancies between what has been received and what is desired or expected (Ditton 1977; Merriam 1977). Indeed, a common assumption is that disgruntled employees are the most likely to engage in harmful or vengeful acts (Skarlicki and Folger 1997). A high score on this general satisfaction measure indicated high general satisfaction.

We also controlled for perceived control, since another theoretical explanation for antisocial workplace behavior is that it is the result of a lack of control on the part of an employee. Indeed, some research has suggested that such behavior is an unconventional means by which employees seek to gain more control over their environment when conventional means are unavailable (Bennett 1998; Storms and Spector 1987). This variable was assessed with Ashford, Lee, and Bobko's (1989) three-item measure, which uses a five-point response scale. A high score on this variable indicated high perceived control.

We also controlled for a number of demographic variables, including gender, age, tenure in the organization, and educational level, for several reasons. First, these variables provide distal proxies for an individual predisposition toward antisocial behavior. Second, numerous studies have found demographics to be significant predictors of antisocial behavior. For example, gender has been linked to aggression (Baron and Richardson 1994), absenteeism (Johns 1997), and drug use at work (Hollinger 1988); education has been linked to alcohol and substance abuse on the job (Mensch and Kandel 1988); and age has been associated with absenteeism (Martocchio 1994), substance abuse at work (Steffy and Laker 1991), and organizational theft (Murphy 1993).

Gender was measured with the question "Are you male or female?" (male was coded 1 and female, 0). Age was measured with the open-ended question "How old are you?" Educational level was measured with "What is your educational level?" Respondents could check one of four categories as representing the highest level they had completed: high school (coded 1), bachelor's degree (2), some college or advanced training from a college (3), or graduate degree (4).

RESULTS

Justification of Aggregation

We assessed the appropriateness of aggregating our contextual variables to the group level using two different procedures: between-group analysis of variance (ANOVA) and r_{WG} (James, Demaree, and Wolf 1984, 1993; George and James 1993), a meaningful indicator of within-group agreement (Kozlowski and Hattrup 1992). The results of the ANOVAs indicated that there were significant between-group differences for group antisocial behavior ($F_{34,152} = 1.96$, $p < .01$), task interdependence $F_{34,145} = 3.27$, $p < .01$), close supervision ($F_{34,144} = 1.39$, $p < .09$), and likelihood of punishment ($F_{34,151} = 2.82$, $p < .01$).

The results of r_{WG} analyses (mean r_{WG}'s) using a rectangular uniform null distribution yielded values for all the variables that indicated high levels of within-group agreement. Values above 0.70 are desirable (George 1990; Nunnally 1978). Values for group antisocial behavior ranged from 0.92 to 0.99, with median of 0.98. Values for the measure of task interdependence ranged from 0.80 to 0.97, with a median of 0.89. For the measure of close supervision, values ranged from 0.26 to 0.99, but the median was 0.90, and 86 percent of the groups had values above 0.70. And values for the measure of likelihood of punishment ranged from 0.75 to 1.0, with a median of 0.98.

Tests of Hypotheses

The correlation matrix and descriptive statistics of our variables are presented in Table 1 [*omitted*]. Hypothesis 1 predicted that group antisocial behavior would be positively related to the antisocial behavior of individual group members. To test this hypothesis, we performed hierarchical regression analyses. Table 2 [*omitted*] presents these results. In the first step, only the control variables were entered into the equation: tenure in the organization, age, education, gender, perceived control, general satisfaction, likelihood of punishment, and close supervision. In the second step, group antisocial behavior was added to the equation. Group antisocial behavior significantly predicted individual antisocial behavior ($â = .29, p < .01; F_{9, 125} = 3.36, p < .01; R^2 = .19$). Thus, as predicted, group antisocial behavior explained considerable unique variance in individual antisocial behavior beyond that which was accounted for by the control variables.

Hypotheses 2 through 4 each predicted a moderating effect for the relationship between group antisocial behavior and individual antisocial behavior. We used moderated regression analysis to test these hypotheses; Table 3 [*omitted*] has results. In order to reduce the multicollinearity associated with the use of interaction terms, we centered the independent variables around zero before creating the interaction terms (Aiken and West 1991).

Hypothesis 2 predicted that the degree of similarity in the levels of group members' antisocial behavior would moderate the relationship between group antisocial behavior and individual antisocial behavior in such a way that the more similar the group antisocial behavior (the lower the variance), the stronger the relationship. The interaction of group antisocial behavior and variance in group antisocial behavior was significant ($β = -.48, p < .01; F_{11, 121} = 6.60, p < .01; R^2 = .37$). To interpret the direction of this interaction effect, we followed Aiken and West's (1991) recommendations. First, the regression equation was restructured algebraically to express the regression of individual antisocial behavior on group antisocial behavior at different levels of variance in the group measure. Next, we derived a series of simple regression equations by substituting in three different values of variance, as recommended by Cohen and Cohen (1983). Next, we examined the simple slopes to determine if they differed from zero and each other. The interaction term was found to be in the predicted direction: variance in group antisocial behavior moderated the relationship between group and individual antisocial behavior in such a way that the lower the group variance (the more similar the levels of antisocial behavior in the group), the stronger the relationship. Hence, Hypothesis 2 was supported.

Hypothesis 3 predicted that individual tenure in a work group would moderate the relationship between group and individual antisocial behavior in such a way that the longer an employee has been in his or her group, the stronger the relationship will be. The interaction of group antisocial behavior and individual tenure was significant in the moderated regression analysis ($β = .25, p < .01; F_{11, 121} = 3.54, p < .01; R^2 = .24$). To test the direction of this significant relationship, we performed the same calculus described above and found that the direction of the interaction effect was as predicted. Hence, Hypothesis 3 was supported.

Hypothesis 4 predicted that the greater the task interdependence of a work group's members, the stronger the relationship between group antisocial behavior and individual antisocial behavior. When this interaction term was entered into the equation with the control variables and the main effects, it was significant ($\beta = .20$, $p < .05$; $F_{11, 121} = 3.51$, $p < .01$; $R^2 = .24$) and in the predicted direction. Thus, Hypothesis 4 was supported.

Hypotheses 5 and 6 predicted that to the extent that an individual group member engaged in less antisocial behavior than his or her group, the focal individual's satisfaction with group members would be lower and his or her intentions to leave would be greater. To test this prediction, we created a variable representing the difference between group and individual antisocial behavior; the higher the value of this variable, the higher the level of group antisocial behavior relative to the individual level. Separate hierarchical regression analyses were performed for each of the dependent variables. Table 4 [*omitted*] shows results. In the first step, we entered the control variables age, education, gender, tenure in group, and tenure in organization. In the second step, the variable reflecting the difference between group and individual antisocial behavior was entered. As predicted, the higher the group's antisocial behavior relative to the individual's antisocial behavior, the less satisfied an individual was with his or her coworkers ($\beta = -.25$, $p < .01$; $F_{7,148} = 3.04$, $p < .01$; $R^2 = .13$). However, the difference between group and individual antisocial behavior was not significantly related to intentions to leave ($\beta = -.09$, *n.s.*; $F_{7, 106} = 15.69$, $p < .01$; $R^2 = .51$). Thus, support was found for Hypothesis 5 but not Hypothesis 6.

Finally, we used moderated hierarchical regression analysis to test Hypothesis 7 and Hypothesis 8, which predicted that likelihood of punishment by management and degree of close supervision would moderate the relationship between group and individual antisocial behavior. As Table 5 [*omitted*] shows, when the interaction of group antisocial behavior and likelihood of punishment was entered into the equation, it was significant ($\beta = -.20$, $p < .05$; $F_{10, 124} = 3.76$, $p < .01$; $R^2 = .23$). Following the same procedure previously described, we found that the relationship was in the predicted direction. However, group antisocial behavior by close supervision was not significant when it was entered ($\beta = .02$, *n.s.*; $F_{10, 124} = 3.00$; $p < .01$; $R^2 = .19$). Hence, support was found for Hypothesis 7 but not for Hypothesis 8.

DISCUSSION

In this research, we explored the extent to which work group context influenced the antisocial behavior of individual employees. We found that, even with many other explanatory variables controlled, the antisocial behavior exhibited by a work group was a significant predictor of an individual's antisocial behavior at work. These findings provide preliminary evidence that a group-level focus is appropriate and important for understanding such behavior in work settings.

Our findings also suggest that several conditions moderate this group influence. Con-

sistent with attraction-selection-attrition theory (Schneider 1975, 1987; Schneider and Reichers 1983), groups with stronger antisocial climates appeared to have greater ability to influence individual members' antisocial actions. In addition, we found that the influence of a group's antisocial behavior on an individual's antisocial behavior became stronger as the individual's time in the group increased. Finally, our results indicated that when group members had to rely upon each other for task accomplishment (task interdependence was high), individual behavior was more strongly related to the level of antisocial behavior exhibited by the group. When considered together, these findings present a consistent pattern, suggesting that as the richness of the group experience increases, members become more likely to match their level of antisocial behavior to that of the group.

Another interesting finding of this study is that to the extent that an individual employee exhibited less antisocial behavior than his or her group, he or she was less satisfied with coworkers. This finding is consistent with the attraction-selection-attrition perspective, suggesting that prosocial individuals working in a sea of antisocial individuals may experience discomfort or dissonance that in turn may lead to attrition among those who do not fit. However, contrary to our prediction, we did not find that intentions to leave an organization were higher for those whose antisocial behavior was lower than that of the group. Possibly our single-item measure of intentions to leave was inadequate. Another explanation is that a misfit with one's work group results in attrition through leaving the group (a variable we did not assess in this study) rather than through leaving the organization.

Implications for Future Research

These results have interesting implications for the groups literature, for research on antisocial behavior in organizations, and for practicing managers. In light of the groups literature, the general finding that groups influence their members is not unexpected. Since the time of the Hawthorne studies (Roethlisberger and Dickson 1939), management scholars have noted the effects of work groups on individuals. What has changed over time, however, is the manner in which these effects have been viewed. Early research depicted groups as sources of management problems, but more recent research has conceptualized groups as solutions to many work-related problems (Shea and Guzzo 1987). Of course, in reality group effects are both positive and negative. Our results indicate that groups displaying high levels of antisocial behavior may influence members to perform antisocial actions. The alternative, however, should not be overlooked— that groups displaying high levels of prosocial behavior encourage such behavior by members (George 1990). Therefore, the primary implication of our research is not that groups have negative effects on individuals but, rather, that group effects are significant and should be better understood. The groups literature suggests that the group influences we found were driven by the development of anti-social norms within the studied groups. An important future research direction will be to identify how work group expectations regarding antisocial behavior are developed, communicated, and enforced.

Our results also are informative for the workplace deviance literature. The findings reported here provide preliminary evidence that a group effect does occur, suggesting that future research at the group level will be beneficial to an enhanced understanding of why, when, and how people behave aggressively at work. Previous research on deviance has emphasized the importance of both individual and environmental factors in predicting individuals' antisocial workplace actions (O'Leary-Kelly et al. 1996). To date, however, environmental factors have been described primarily as organization-level phenomena. Of course, the work group itself is also a component of an individual's work environment. However, we would argue that the work group's influence should be conceptualized as more than just an additional environmental variable to be explored. Because of its centrality to the individual-organization interface, an understanding of the group may be critical to an understanding of other antecedents, both environmental and individual.

For example, with regard to environmental antecedents to aggression, previous research has examined factors such as adverse treatment (for instance, an individual's perception that an organization has blocked his or her personal goals; O'Leary-Kelly et al. 1996). Of course, an individual's belief that he or she has been adversely treated by an organization depends on how this term is defined. The individual's definition will be influenced not only by the actual treatment that is received, but also by his or her interpretation of this treatment, with that interpretation being affected by information received from the social environment—for instance, from the work group (Salancik and Pfeffer 1978; Schneider 1987). A strong work group can be conceptualized as a setting that exists at the intersection of the individual and the organization. The group provides a social context that is critical to the individual's interpretation of organization-level systems. This social context, therefore, can have a significant effect on individuals' antisocial behavior.

Implications for Managers

Finally, our research has implications for managers. Perhaps most obviously, it highlights the necessity for strong actions to be taken to counter antisocial behavior in organizations. The group effect we found here might be described more simply as a contagion effect. This effect may help to explain why it appears that acts of aggression seem to spread or occur in clusters within a given industry or organization. The message for managers seems clear—antisocial groups encourage antisocial individual behavior. It is crucial to nip behaviors deemed harmful in the bud so as to avoid a social influence effect. Managers who expect that isolating or ignoring antisocial groups will encourage them to change are probably mistaken.

The findings related to the influence of likelihood of punishment and closeness of supervision also have interesting implications for practice. Although we found that the likelihood of punishment weakened the relationship between group antisocial behavior and individual antisocial behavior, we did not find that closeness of supervision made any difference. This suggests that common forms of deterrence, such as monitoring employee behavior, will not necessarily impact individuals' antisocial behavior if perceptions of punishment are unaffected.

Limitations

As always, limitations of our study should be considered in its interpretation. First, our design was cross-sectional, not longitudinal. Research that assesses the influence of group context over time would provide additional and stronger support for the existence of these effects. Another possible limitation is the sampling method we employed. We obtained a diverse sample of occupational groups from different organizations and industries so that our results would be generalizable to the overall population of employees. This method, however, may have introduced unnecessary noise, deflating our observed relationships. In addition, we could not be certain that we obtained representative groups from each organization. For example, certain types of employees within each group may have been more likely to respond than others, thus biasing our results. However, we contend that our sample is more representative of the overall population of employees than a sample drawn from all employees within only one organization.

Also, we were unable to reduce all common method bias. Our split-sample design was useful in reducing most of the method variance because, for the most part, different respondents were used to assess the dependent and independent variables. Nevertheless, this design cannot eliminate all forms of common method variance. For example, perhaps the observed relationships were somewhat inflated because all of the variables were assessed with survey measures.

Finally, we were unable to control for the role of individual predispositions in explaining antisocial behavior at work. Although our control variables included individual demographic characteristics as proxies for predispositions, ideally we would have more directly measured and controlled for antisocial predispositions, such as prior learning of aggressive behavior, family background, personality, and child-rearing practices. Future researchers should consider this possibility.

CONCLUSION

Despite these limitations, the implications of this study are significant. Antisocial behavior is not simply an individual-level phenomenon. As the results of this study show, the social context of the work group has an extensive influence over whether and when individuals will behave in antisocial ways at work. From a research perspective, these findings suggest numerous useful directions for future investigation. From a managerial perspective, these findings indicate that organizations have both the ability and responsibility to influence antisocial behavior by shaping work group dynamics. Our results confirm that antisocial behavior at work is not only prevalent—it is also contagious.

REFERENCES

Aiken, L.S., and West, S.G. 1991. *Multiple Regression: Testing and Interpreting Interactions*. Thousand Oaks, CA: Sage.

Ashford, S.J., Lee, C., and Bobko, P. 1989. Content, causes, and consequences of job insecurity: A theory-based measure and substantive test. *Organizational Behavior and Human Decision Processes* 43: 207–242.

Bandura, A. 1973. *Aggression: A Social Learning Analysis*. Englewood Cliffs, NJ: Prentice-Hall.

———. 1977. *Social Learning Theory*. Englewood Cliffs, NJ: Prentice-Hall.

———. 1986. *Social Foundations of Thought and Action: A Social Cognitive Theory*. Englewood Cliffs, NJ: Prentice-Hall.

———. 1990. Selective activation and disengagement of moral control. *Journal of Social Issues* 46(1): 27–46.

———. 1991. Social cognitive theory of moral thought and action. In W.M. Kurtines and J.L. Gewirtz (eds.), *Handbook of Moral Behavior and Development: Theory, Research, and Application*, vol. 1: 71–129. Hillsdale, NJ: Erlbaum.

Bandura, A., Barbaranelli, C., Caprara, G.V., and Pastorelli, C. 1996. Mechanism of moral disengagement in the exercise of moral agency. *Journal of Personality and Social Psychology* 71: 364–374.

Baron, R.A., and Richardson, D.R. 1994. *Human Aggression* (2d ed.). New York: Plenum.

Bennett, R. 1998. Perceived powerlessness as a cause for workplace deviance. In R. Griffin, A. O'Leary-Kelly, and J. Collins (eds.), *Dysfunctional behavior in organizations*: 229–240. Greenwich, CT: JAI Press.

Brief, A.P., and Motowidlo, S.J. 1986. Prosocial organizational behaviors. *Academy of Management Review* 11: 710–725.

Campbell, D.T., and Fiske, D.W. 1959. Convergent and discriminant validation by the multitrait-multimethod matrix. *Psychological Bulletin* 56: 81–105.

Cohen, J., and Cohen, P. 1983. *Applied Multiple Regression/Correlation Analyses for the Behavioral Sciences* (2d ed.). Hillsdale, NJ: Erlbaum.

Covey, M.K., Saladin, S., and Kilen, P.J. 1989. Self-monitoring, surveillance, and incentive effects on cheating. *Journal of Social Psychology* 129: 673–679.

DePaulo, P.J., and DePaulo, B.M. 1989. Can deception by salespersons and customers be detected through nonverbal behavioral cues? *Journal of Applied Social Psychology* 19: 1552–1577.

Dewar, R.D., and Werbel, J. 1979. Universalistic and contingency predictions of employee satisfaction and conflict. *Administrative Science Quarterly* 24: 426–448.

Ditton, J. 1977. *Part-time Crime: An Ethnography of Fiddling and Pilferage*. London: Macmillan.

George, J.M. 1990. Personality, affect and behavior in groups. *Journal of Applied Psychology* 75: 107–116.

George, J.M., and James, L.R. 1993. Personality, affect, and behavior in groups revisited: Comment on aggregation, levels of analysis, and a recent application of within and between analysis. *Journal of Applied Psychology* 78: 798–804.

Giacalone, R.A., and Greenberg, J. 1996. *Antisocial Behavior in Organizations*. Thousand Oaks, CA: Sage.

Greenberg, J. 1990. Employee theft as a reaction to underpayment inequity: The hidden cost of pay cuts. *Journal of Applied Psychology* 75: 561–568.

———. 1993. Stealing in the name of justice: Informational and interpersonal moderators of theft reactions to underpayment inequity. *Organizational Behavior and Human Decision Processes* 54: 81–103.

Greenberg, J., and Scott, K.S. 1996. Why do workers bite the hands that feed them? Employee theft as a social exchange process. In B.M. Stow and L.L. Cummings (eds.), *Research in Organizational Behavior*, vol. 18: 111–156. Greenwich, CT: JAI Press.

Gruber, J.E. 1990. How women handle sexual harassment: A literature review. *Social Science Research* 74: 3–9.

Harper, D. 1990. Spotlight abuse-save profits. *Industrial Distribution* 79(3): 47–51.

Hirschi, T. 1969. *Causes of Delinquency*. Berkeley: University of California Press.

Hollinger, R.C. 1988. Working under the influence (WUI): Correlates of employees' use of alcohol and other drugs. *Journal of Applied Behavioral Science* 24: 439–454.

Hollinger, R.C., and Clark, J.P. 1983. Deterrence in the workplace: Perceived certainty, perceived severity, and employee theft. *Social Forces* 62: 398–418.

Hulin, C., and Rousseau, D.M. 1980. Analyzing infrequent events: Once you find them, your troubles begin. In K.H. Roberts and L. Burstein (eds.), *Issues in Aggregation*: 65–75. San Francisco: Jossey-Bass.

James, L.R., Demaree, R.G., and Wolf, G. 1984. Estimating within-group interrater reliability with and without response bias. *Journal of Applied Psychology* 69: 431–444.

———. 1993. r_{wg}: An assessment of within-group interrater agreement. *Journal of Applied Psychology* 78: 306–309.

Johns, G. 1997. Contemporary research on absence from work: Correlates, causes, and consequences. In C.L. Cooper and I.T. Robertson (eds.), *International Review of Industrial and Organizational Psychology*: 115–174. London: Wiley.

Kidwell, R.E., and Bennett, N. 1993. Employee propensity to withhold effort: A conceptual model to intersect three avenues of research. *Academy of Management Review* 18: 429–456.

Kozlowski, S.W., and Hattrup, K. 1992. A disagreement about within-group agreement: Disentangling issues of consistency versus consensus. *Journal of Applied Psychology* 77: 161–167.

Latane, B. 1981. The psychology of social impact. *American Psychologist* 36: 343–356.

Lehman, W., and Simpson, D. 1992. Employee substance abuse and on-the-job behaviors. *Journal of Applied Psychology* 77: 309–321.

Martinko, M.J., and Zellars, K.L. 1996. Toward a theory of workplace violence: A social learning and attributional perspective. Paper presented at the annual meeting of the Academy of Management, Cincinnati.

Martocchio, J.J. 1994. The effects of absence culture on individual absence. *Human Relations* 47: 243–262.

McGurn, M. 1988. Spotting the thieves who work among us. *Wall Street Journal* (March 8): A16.

Mensch, B.S., and Kandel, D.B. 1988. Do job conditions influence the use of drugs? *Journal of Health and Social Behavior* 29: 169–184.

Merriam, D.H. 1977. Employee theft. *Criminal Justice Abstracts* 9: 375–406.

Murphy, K.R. 1993. *Honesty in the workplace*. Belmont, CA: Brooks/Cole.

Nunnally, J.C. 1978. *Psychometric Theory* (2d ed.). New York: McGraw-Hill.

O'Leary-Kelly, A.M., Griffin, R.W., and Glew, D.J. 1996. Organization-motivated aggression: A research framework. *Academy of Management Review* 21: 225–253.

Podsakoff, P.M., MacKenzie, S., Moorman, R.H., and Fetter, R. 1990. Transformational leader behaviors and their effects on followers' trust in leader, satisfaction, and organizational citizenship behaviors. *Leadership Quarterly* 1: 107–142.

Robinson, S.L., and Bennett, R.J. 1995. A typology of deviant workplace behavior: A multidimensional scaling study. *Academy of Management Journal* 38: 555–572.

———. 1997. Workplace deviance: Its nature, its causes, and its manifestations. In R.J. Lewicki, R.J. Bies, and B.H. Sheppard (eds.), *Research on Negotiation in Organizations*, vol. 6: 3–28. Greenwich, CT: JAI.

Robinson, S.L., and Greenberg, J. 1998. Employees behaving badly: Dimensions, determinants and dilemmas in the study of workplace deviance. In D.M. Rousseau and C. Cooper (eds.), *Trends in Organizational Behavior*, vol. 5: Forthcoming. New York: Wiley.

Roethlisberger, F.J., and Dickson, W.J. 1939. *Management and the Worker*. Cambridge, MA: Harvard University Press.

Rousseau, D.M. 1985. Issues of level in organizational research. In L.L. Cummings and B.M. Staw (eds.), *Research in Organizational Behavior*, vol. 7: 1–37. Greenwich, CT: JAI.

Rusbult, C., Farrell, D., Rogers, G., and Mainous, A. 1988. Impact of exchange variables on exit, voice, loyalty, and neglect: An integrative model of responses to declining job satisfaction. *Academy of Management Journal* 31: 599–627.

Salancik, G.J., and Pfeffer, J. 1978. A social information processing approach to job attitudes and task design. *Administrative Science Quarterly* 23: 224–253.

Schneider, B. 1975. Organizational climates: An essay. *Personnel Psychology* 28: 447–480.

———. 1987. The people make the place. *Personnel Psychology* 40: 437–454.

Schneider, B., and Reichers, A.E. 1983. On the etiology of climates. *Personnel Psychology* 36: 19–39.

Shea, G.P., and Guzzo, R.A. 1987. Groups as human resources. In K.M. Rowland and G.R. Ferris (eds.), *Research in Personnel and Human Resources Management*, vol. 5: 323–356. Greenwich, CT: JAI.

Skarlicki, D.P., and Folger, R. 1997. Retaliation in the workplace: The roles of distributive, procedural, and interactional justice. *Journal of Applied Psychology* 82: 416–425.

Smith, P.C., Kendall, L.M., and Hulin, C.L. 1969. *The Measurement of Satisfaction in Work and Retirement*. Chicago: Rand McNally.

Steffy, B.D., and Laker, D.R. 1991. Workplace and personal stresses antecedent to employee's alcohol use. *Journal of Social Behavior and Personality* 6:115–126.

Storms, P., and Spector, P. 1987. Relationships of organizational frustration with reported behavioral reactions: The moderating effect of locus of control. *Journal of Occupational Psychology* 60: 227–234.

Tittle, C.R. 1973. Sanction fear and the maintenance of social order. *Social Forces* 55: 579–596.

Van de Ven, A.H., Delbecq, A.L., and Koenig, R. 1976. Determination of coordination modes within organizations. *American Sociological Review* 41: 322–338.

Vardi, Y., and Wiener, Y. 1996. Misbehavior in organizations: A motivational framework. *Organizational Science* 7: 151–165.

21

Uses and Misuses of Power in Task-Performing Teams

Ruth Wageman and Elizabeth A. Mannix

As organizational researchers have struggled to understand and explain the causes of team effectiveness (or the lack of it), they have drawn on work in social psychology, sociology, and organizational behavior. From this work, several models have emerged on how group behavior influences group performance, and most models include task as well as relational and external functions (Goodman, Ravlin, and Schminke 1987; Hackman 1987). Task functions are directed toward the production or performance of a product or service, the end result of which can potentially be measured or evaluated. In addition, to achieve their common goals, teams must establish and maintain productive internal relationships (Levine and Moreland 1990). Finally, externally directed activities are those that remind us that groups within organizations are not closed systems (Ancona 1990; Goodman et al. 1987).

Research on team functions generally treats such behaviors as if they are enacted by the whole team. We pay closer attention to the issue of who engages in these behaviors. Does it matter for team effectiveness whether particular behavioral functions are fulfilled by the group as a whole or by particular individuals? This question bring us to the focus of this [article]—the intersection of team effectiveness, team member behavior, and power.

THE PHENOMENON

Teams in organizations are frequently composed of individuals who vary in their hierarchical status, competency, resources, and other characteristics that invest that person with power relative to other group members. Thus, in most teams there exists broad potential for particular individuals to exert more influence on team functioning than the average member (Hollander 1958). How powerful members use their power and the influence on team effectiveness of their choices are the central questions we address here. We limit our discussion to complex task-performing teams—that is, we treat only those teams that together produce a product or service and have the authority to determine their work strategies and manage their internal processes. We thus exclude groups that exist primarily or solely for social purposes or those groups that do routinized work and have little or no authority over their process.

We define team effectiveness following Hackman (1990) as the degree to which (a) the team's output meets the standards of quality of the people who receive or review that output, (b) the process enhances the team's ability to work together interdependently and effectively in the future, and (c) the group experience contributes to the personal well-being or satisfaction of the team members. The following examples taken from some real teams illustrate the potential importance of the phenomenon.

During our time in the MBA classroom, we have had opportunity to observe scores of project teams and to learn (via retrospective accounts by team members) about the dynamics in such teams, including their power dynamics. These teams typically are asked to identify, analyze, and make recommendations to solve a pressing management problem in a real-world organization. To that end, teams must find a client organization. Most often, one member of the project group acquires access to an organization of which he or she was a past employee. Thus, at the launch of most of these teams, one team member has control of a critical resource—that is, the team project site and client. Because of this critical resource, this team member has the potential to exert influence over team functioning to a greater extent than those members who do not have any particular power source (Pfeffer 1992).

How do these team members use this particular form of power? Our observations have uncovered at least three different patterns of power use by this team member—patterns that appear to have very different consequences for team outcomes. First is what we label the "overuse" pattern, in which the team member with the client contact uses his or her special status in the group to exert influence over most aspects of group functioning, including task processes (e.g., how the group will collect data), external relations (e.g., what questions the group should raise with the client), and interpersonal processes (e.g., the group operating norms). The individual uses his or her power to dominate team processes in ways that are in the powerholder's best interests or consistent with the powerholder's views of effective task strategies. Our observations suggest that many of these teams perform quite poorly. In addition, these teams are characterized by widespread member dissatisfaction and frustration with the group and with its final product.

The second pattern we label "abdication." In this pattern, we see the team member with client access behaving no differently from any other team member (generally to avoid taking on what is viewed as excessively difficult work), exerting no special influence over task, internal, or external relations processes—not even to the extent of managing the team's entry into the client organization. Our observations suggest that this, too, is a dysfunctional pattern. Such teams tend toward mediocre to poor performance (usually because of limited data from the client). By contrast to the first pattern, however, they tend to show relatively positive affective reactions to each other and to the team's work process.

The third pattern is referred to as "managing the resource." In this pattern, the powerful member influences other team members only in the specific domain of his or her special resource—that is, relations with the client. The powerful team member may influence the team in defining the client's problem, choosing whom in the organization would be good sources of information, and he or she may serve as the main contact who establishes meetings of the team with the client. On the basis of our data, this appears to be the most effective pattern; teams with this pattern of power use perform relatively well and show no particular tendency toward member dissatisfaction.

Thus, we argue that individual powerholders use their power for different ends, and that these different uses of power have differential consequences for team effectiveness—positively influencing some aspects of team effectiveness and negatively influencing others. Throughout this [article], we define a "misuse of power" as an influence attempt by the powerholder that will undermine team effectiveness. We return to the example behaviors at the end of this [article]. We describe a functional view of team behavior in which it is argued that there are functions (task, internal, and external relations) that must be fulfilled for a team to perform effectively. We propose that all teams are better off when these functions are performed by someone; teams will perform best, however, when particular functions are performed by the team, whereas others are executed by a powerful individual. Through our discussion of team functions and power, we derive specific and testable propositions about the uses and misuses of individual power in task-performing teams. Finally, by identifying the critical similarities among functions that represent uses or misuses of individual power, we induce three general propositions that specify the kinds of functions that are best fulfilled by powerful individuals and those that are best fulfilled by the group as a whole. Our aim throughout this discussion is to develop researchable predictions about the consequences for group effectiveness of the arenas in which individual team members use their power.

POWER AND A FUNCTIONAL VIEW OF TEAM BEHAVIOR

In the previous example, we focused on one particular type of power that might be available to individuals in project teams. Of course, individuals come to teams with a variety of backgrounds, experiences, and, often, different levels and sources of power. Power has been defined in several ways, but a simple definition is that with power one party can get the other to do what the latter normally would not do (Dahl 1957; Kotter 1979). Adding to this definition is the view of power as a function of the dependency of others on the focal individual (Emerson 1964; Pfeffer and Salancik 1977; Thibaut and Kelley 1959). In their work on power, French and Raven (1959) identified five major bases of social power: reward power, coercive power, legitimate power, expert power, and referent power. Many contemporary discussions of power are grounded in this typology. Another prominent perspective is resource dependency theory, which defines power as the control over resources, including money, supplies, time, equipment, critical services, human capital, or all these (Pfeffer 1992; Pfeffer and Salancik 1974). Also important is network theory, which defines power by an individual's location in the organizational structure (Burt 1992; Granovetter 1973; Marsden 1983; White 1970). In the network view, issues of centrality, criticality, and weak and strong ties are important determinants of power. Regardless of the power source, one of the important features of the theory of social power is the conceptual feature of "potentiality" (French and Raven 1959). Power bases give individuals the potential to influence. How (and if) powerful individuals use their power to influence or lead the team can vary widely; they might shape task strategies, establish the teams' basic norms and values, allocate resources, coordinate group efforts, or negotiate with outsiders on behalf of the team. This [article] explores the appropriate uses and inappropriate misuses of power—regardless of its source—by team members. We define uses and misuses in terms of the consequences (positive or negative, respectively) for team effectiveness.

As outlined previously, we take a functional view of team behavior—that is, there are functions that must be fulfilled for a team to perform effectively. These team functions can be performed by particular individuals or by the team as a whole. In this view, all teams are better off when these functions are performed by someone; teams will perform best, however, when specific functions are performed by the team, whereas others are executed by a powerful individual. Although there are many functions that teams can perform, we use as examples those behaviors that we, as well as other theorists and researchers, have found to be important influences on team performance. In the following discussion, we break down team functions into two domains: task directed and relations directed. The study of task functions has included developing task strategies and task-related values (Liang, Moreland, and Argote 1995; Wageman 1995), setting team goals (Crowne and Rosse 1995; Mitchell and Silver 1990; Weingart 1992), arriving at decision rules (Guzzo 1982; Miller 1989; Stasser, Kerr, and Davis 1989), and role differentiation and the division of labor (Jackson and Schuler 1985; Moreland and Levine 1982; Turner and Colomy 1988). Relational functions include both internally directed and externally directed behaviors. Internally directed behaviors include managing team boundaries and interpersonal relationships (Hackman 1983, 1990; Mannix, Goins, and Carroll 1996; Moreland 1987), arriving at group values and norms of behavior (Argote 1989; Bettenhausen and Murnighan 1985; O'Reilly and Caldwell 1985), and managing conflict (Ancona, Friedman, and Kolb 1991; Bazerman, Mannix, and Thompson 1988; Gladstein 1984; Jehn 1995). Externally directed behaviors include boundary-spanning and liaison with external parties (Alderfer and Smith 1982; Ancona 1987, 1990; Katz and Tushman 1981; Tushman 1977), follow-through on information and links to clients (Hackman 1990), accessing external information or resources (Pfeffer 1986; Pfeffer and Salancik 1978), and the implementation, recommendation, and review of final team output (Nadler and Tushman 1988).

Although we do not claim that all the previously discussed functional behaviors are essential to all teams at all times, we do argue that each of these functions is useful for the group to achieve a high-quality output and to enhance the satisfaction of group members. In the following sections, we draw on examples of particular behaviors within the two domains to make specific predictions about the connections between these functions, who performs them, and team outcomes.

TASK DOMAIN

As noted previously, research has identified a wide range of task-related behaviors that are observed to varying degrees in teams. Such behaviors include coordinating member activities, assigning specific task roles, and helping other team members. We focus on two particular task-related behaviors to illustrate our arguments: (a) active monitoring of the team's performance and (b) altering task strategies in response to performance decrements or changes in task demands (i.e., problem solving).

Both these basic task functions have been demonstrated to be important influences on team performance. Attending to feedback and actively seeking data about performance have often been identified as essential task functions that differentiate between superior and poor-performing teams (Hackman 1987; Hare 1976; Kolodny and Kiggundu 1980; Nadler 1979; Pearce and Ravlin 1987). Druskat (1995) found, for example, that a tendency to focus attention on the team's strengths and weaknesses and to seek feedback directly from their work outcomes differentiated among superior—and average—performing teams. Similarly, McIntyre and Salas (1995) found that members of effective teams monitor performance and provide other team members with feedback.

By comparison, research is sparse on the devising of appropriate task strategies by teams. Many theorists do emphasize the importance of team strategies (Cohen 1994; Goodman et al. 1987; Guzzo 1982; Hackman 1987; Schwarz 1994; Steiner 1972), and what little research has addressed the devising of task strategies has shown a positive relationship to team performance (Druskat 1995; Wageman 1996). Wageman, for example, showed that superb teams took time out from task execution to discuss different task strategies more often than did poor-performing teams.

Both monitoring performance and devising task strategies are functions that can be initiated and fulfilled by the team as a whole or by particular team members. In each case, we argue that teams that do engage in these behaviors will outperform those that do not. Nevertheless, our central question, unaddressed by any previous research, remains: Are groups better off if these functions are fulfilled by powerful individuals or by the team as a whole?

Previous studies of the effects of performance monitoring (or attention to feedback) have not differentiated between individual and group behavior. That is, the group is assumed to have attended to performance feedback if any individual in the group has done so. Some recent evidence suggests that for monitoring performance, this is a reasonable stance—that is, who does it matters less than whether it is done at all. A field study of 40 self-managing teams (Wageman 1996) assessed via interview and observation the degree to which teams engaged in specific self-managing behaviors. In this study, teams that monitored their own performance regularly strongly outperformed those that did not on a variety of objective performance measures. In some cases, it was not the team as a whole that did the performance monitoring but rather a specific powerful individual (in this case, the "specialist," an individual who became an informal team leader on the basis of his or her technical expertise). This individual used his or her power to collect and interpret performance information and present these data to the team. In other teams, these actions were taken by various team members, and the data were reviewed by the team as a whole.

The data showed that there were no differences in the performance of teams whose specialist did the monitoring compared with teams who reviewed their performance together. Teams in which either the specialist or the team as a whole monitored performance, however, did outperform those teams that did not do it at all.

Thus, the basic function of collecting information and bringing it to the attention of the team can be done by anyone. Why does it not matter who does the monitoring? We suggest that monitoring of team performance requires only attention, a cognitive process that is more naturally an individual than a group process. To be sure, the process of making sense of data can draw effectively on multiple intelligences, but in the studies cited previously the researchers were concerned only with whether or not data were attended to and not how well those data were used. Attention by a single individual and the communication required to convey the data to the rest of the team are functions filled effectively by one person.

Proposition 1: Performance monitoring—drawing performance feedback to the attention of the team—is an appropriate use of individual power.

In contrast to monitoring, strategy design is a creative task influenceable by collective knowledge and skills; moreover, task strategies require execution by the team as a whole. Consequently, the effects of task strategy on team performance depend to a great degree on the capabilities used to design it and the commitment of team members to execute it. Decades of group research attest to the notion that multiple perspectives and sources of expertise enhance group performance. Moreover, research has shown that as groups interact they add knowledge and creativity, increase the understanding and acceptance of ideas, and improve commitment and motivation (Levine and Moreland 1990; Maier 1970; McGrath 1984; McGrath and Kravitz 1982; Shaw 1981; Zander 1979). Both capabilities brought to bear on a choice of task strategy and collective commitment to that strategy are likely to be lower when strategy is determined by one individual.

Data from Wageman (1996) support the view that asserting task strategies is a misuse of power by powerful individuals. First, teams that frequently adapted their task strategies in response to data about performance decrements strongly outperformed those that did not. Groups in which the team as a whole determined strategy changes, however, outperformed those in which the informal team leader did so. Thus, for this team function, groups were better off when the team as a whole determined performance strategies than when a powerful individual used his or her influence to make such a decision for the team.

Proposition 2: Imposing a task strategy for the group is a misuse of individual power.

Before discussing relational functions, it is instructive to note the similarities in the patterns of findings for the two task functions. For both functions, the group performed more effectively when someone in the group engaged in that function than when no one engaged in that function. Although at one level this simply provides supportive evidence for our functional view of team behavior, it also provides a clue about appropriate uses of power by individual team members. Some teams fail to attend to important task-relevant feedback, or fail to adjust their task strategies, to their ultimate detriment. When a group is avoiding a task-relevant issue, one appropriate use of power by an individual member may be to influence the group to attend to that issue.

RELATIONS DOMAIN: INTERNAL

The focus in this [article] is task-performing groups; thus, we are most concerned with the effects of essential functions on task performance. As such, the internal relations in groups are relevant to the extent that they affect the group interaction processes, and group interaction is relevant to the extent that it influences performance. A group composed of individuals who agree on work values and norms, and who are capable of handling conflict productively, should be better equipped to enact task-relevant strategies and goals (Bar-Tal 1989; Jehn 1994; Jehn and Mannix 1996; Schein 1986). When the internal relations break down, the result can be motivation losses such as withdrawal or free riding (Maier 1967; Steiner 1972), opinion conformity (Janis 1982), or destructive emotion-based conflict (Amason 1996; Argyris 1962; Jehn 1995; Kelley 1979). In the following sections, we focus on the internal relations issues of conflict, work values, and norms.

CONFLICT AND TEAM PERFORMANCE

Conflict is defined as an awareness by the parties involved of discrepancies, incompatible wishes, or irreconcilable desires (Boulding 1963). Organizational researchers have recognized both the assets and the liabilities of conflict in group decisions. Some research has shown that conflict is detrimental to organizational functioning, decreases individual satisfaction, and lowers group productivity (Bourgeois 1980; Evan 1965; Gladstein 1984; Schwenk and Crosier 1993). Conversely, other findings show conflict to be beneficial, enhancing decision quality and planning, innovation, and productivity (Coser 1970; Crosier and Rose 1977; Eisenhardt and Bourgeois 1988; Nemeth and Staw 1989; Tjosvold 1991).

It is apparent that the connection between conflict and performance remains less than well understood (Eisenhardt and Zbaracki 1992). One key to unlocking this complex relationship lies in the differentiation of conflict as either relationship or task related (Crosier and Rose 1977; Guetzkow and Gyr 1954; Jehn 1995; Pinkley 1990; Wall and Nolan 1986). Relationship conflict, also called affective conflict, is an awareness of interpersonal incompatibilities. It includes personal and affective components, such as friction, tension, and dislike among group members. Studies show that relationship conflict is detrimental to individual and group performance, member satisfaction, and the likelihood the group will work together in the future (Jehn 1995; Jehn and Mannix 1996; Shah and Jehn 1993). When group members have interpersonal problems or feel friction with one another, they may be distracted from the task, work less cooperatively, and produce suboptimal products (Argyris 1962; Kelley 1979; Roseman, Wiest, and Swartz 1994; Staw, Sandelands, and Dutton 1981).

Task, or cognitive, conflict is an awareness of differences in viewpoints and opinions pertaining to the group's task. In contrast to relationship conflict, moderate levels of task conflict have been shown to be beneficial to group performance in various decision-making and group tasks. Teams performing complex cognitive tasks benefit from differences of opinion about the work being done (Bourgeois 1985; Eisenhardt and Schoonhoven 1990; Jehn 1995; Jehn and Mannix 1996; Shah and Jehn 1993). Task conflict improves decision quality as groups drop old patterns of interaction and adopt new perspectives; the synthesis that emerges from the conflict is generally superior to the individual perspectives themselves (Mason and Mitroff 1981; Schweiger and Sandberg 1989; Schwenk 1990).

The task conflict necessary to produce high-quality outcomes, however, may leave a feeling of negativity among team members (Amason 1996; Schweiger, Sandberg, and Ragan 1986; Schweiger, Sandberg, and Rechner 1989). Critical evaluations, for example, seem to cause negative affective reactions regardless of the outcome (Baron 1990). Negotiation researchers have consistently demonstrated the benefits of open conflict in reaching integrative solutions of high mutual gain in the dyad as well as the group (Ancona et al. 1991); a natural tendency of many negotiators, however, is to avoid the level of conflict necessary to reach optimal solutions (Lewicki and Litterer 1994; Neale and Bazerman 1991; Pruitt 1981). In addition, some theorists have proposed that relationship, or affective, conflict can be the result of task conflict being misperceived as personal criticism (Amason 1996; Brehmer 1976; Deutsch 1969). In other words, some groups develop a pattern of misinterpreting task conflict as relationship conflict resulting in performance loss rather than gain. If this pattern is set, it is likely to continue (Bettenhausen and Murnighan 1985), resulting in high overall levels of relationship conflict and reducing the performance of the group.

Thus, there are many complexities associated with the effective use of conflict within groups. What role might powerful individuals play in influencing the nature and handling of conflict to the team's benefit? Given research evidence that task conflict enhances whereas relational conflict undermines team performance, combined with the natural tendency in teams toward conflict avoidance, we argue that it is useful for individual group members with special influence to encourage task conflict and discourage relationship conflict. This function is especially critical if the group is unwilling or unable to manage its conflict collectively. A powerful individual (or subset of group members) may thus be able to control the timing and nature of conflict to the benefit of the group. Indeed, internal group members (rather than outside "supervisors") are uniquely suited to do so. Members of the team are more likely to have continuous access to the group's process as well as direct knowledge of the underlying causes of particular conflicts; they are thus able to intervene in a knowledgeable and well-timed fashion. A powerful team member also is likely to have the "idiosyncrasy credits" (Hollander 1958) to both influence the group to open discussion of task approaches and to persuade the group to shelve interpersonal disagreements in team interaction.

Proposition 3: Promoting well-timed task conflict is an appropriate use of individual power.

WORK VALUES, NORMS, AND GROUP PERFORMANCE

Norms are informal rules that groups adopt to regulate group members' behavior; they are among the least visible and most powerful forms of social control over human action (Hackman 1976; Sherif 1936). Although there has been a great deal of research on norms, most of it has focused on examining the impact norms have on other social phenomena (Feldman 1984). There has been relatively little attention to how norms actually form and who is responsible for the norms we see operating in groups. The classic research on norm formation comes from Sherif (1936) and his work on the autokinetic effect. Sherif argued that his results demonstrated the basic psychological processes involved in the establishment of social norms; our experience is organized around or modified by collectively produced frames of reference. Feldman (1984) has presented a task-oriented alternative to this concept of emergent norms. He proposes that norms form in one or more of four ways: explicit statements by supervisors or coworkers—that is, by fiat; critical events in the group's history; primacy—that is, based on early behavior patterns that set up group expectations; and carryover behaviors from past situations. Norms generated by fiat are similar to rules, in which a powerful individual explicitly expresses values, norms, or prescribed behaviors. The remaining three forms might be categorized as variations of collectively emergent norms.

In a relatively recent study of how norms form, Bettenhausen and Murnighan (1985) examined the formation of norms using a multi-round negotiation exercise played over several weeks. They found that group norms regarding resource allocation emerged from the interaction between each group members' definition of the situation and the scripts or schemas that group members used to frame the situation. When group members had similar scripts, the group's interaction proceeded smoothly—each interaction confirmed the meaning that group members attached to the action. When the scripts were not similar, however, conflict resulted that was not always easy to resolve. At times, group members made overt persuasion attempts to pull the group toward their interpretation through challenges to the implied norm.

Thus, newly formed groups may or may not have a high level of agreement, or consensus, on important work-related norms and values. When group members have a high level of value consensus, members will tend to agree on norms regarding work, in turn promoting harmony and coordination (Nemeth and Staw 1989). By contrast, when low-value consensus exists, members' core values and beliefs about their everyday work are challenged, causing friction and emotional upset (Bar-Tal 1989; Schein 1986). Differing values may cause group members to perceive situations and priorities differently, impeding the coordinated flow of work (Ravlin and Meglino 1987). In addition, value differences between a leader and the rest of the group can be a continuous source of tension for the team (Gray, Bougon, and Donnellon 1985).

Consensus, or the lack of it, on work-related norms has implications for the type and amount of conflict that a group experiences. Groups that agree too readily on work values and norms may be advantaged by low levels of relationship conflict but may be disadvantaged by similarly low levels of task conflict. Group members with divergent work values and norms may have the opposite problem—that is, high task conflict as well as high relationship conflict (Jehn 1994). The first case may be dealt with by an intervention from a powerful group member or team leader, as described previously. The second case, however, is somewhat more difficult. It requires that the group come to a workable arrangement on a variety of important work-related norms. This might be done by fiat—that is, by a powerful individual—or it might be arrived at by the collective.

We argue that the definition of work-related values and norms should be left to the group as a whole. By allowing the group to negotiate their own work norms, they have the opportunity to discover the true underlying differences, fully understand one another's viewpoints, and struggle toward agreement. The conflict this generates is likely to increase acceptance, understanding, and commitment to the final outcome (Maier 1967; Pruitt and Rubin 1986). In fact, the discussion of norms should be clearly and openly addressed by all newly formed groups and periodically reexamined. Like conflict, explicit discussion of norms tends to be a function in groups that is avoided by most team members. The role for a powerful individual is in influencing the group to address its norms directly as well as redirecting relationship conflict back to the task.

Proposition 4a: Influencing the group to address and evaluate its work values and norms is an appropriate use of individual power.

Proposition 4b: Dictating work values or norms by fiat is a misuse of individual power.

RELATIONS DOMAIN: EXTERNAL

Although task behaviors and internal relations have a long history in theory and research about group effectiveness, group external activity has only recently come to the attention of groups researchers (Ancona 1987). This oversight may in part be due to early focus on laboratory-based groups, which had no external clients nor an organizational context beyond the experiment itself. External relations may also have become more prominent because of recent changes in the kinds of organizational teams researchers have the opportunity to observe: As "empowerment" and self-directed work teams become more prevalent, many more teams have the authority to deal directly with clients, to manage resources, and to engage in other activities external to the team.

Evidence for the importance of external activities to team performance is mounting. For example, researchers have stressed that teams must match their information processing capability to the information processing demands of the task environment (Gresov 1989; Nadler and Tushman 1988). Those studying innovation have emphasized the importance of boundary-spanning activities (Katz and Tushman 1979), whereas theorists interested in power have focused on the importance of external constituents for political action and influence (Pfeffer 1992). Ancona and colleagues, however, truly developed this area of research by attempting to map out the full range of activities that groups use to cope with their environments (Ancona 1987, 1990). This work began with a study of 100 sales teams in the telecommunications industry (Gladstein 1984). Ancona found that group members saw the process aspects of their work as divided into an internal and an external component. In her study, internal processes were associated with team member satisfaction and team-rated performance; external process, however, was associated with sales revenue. In subsequent work, she concluded that teams enact a distinct set of activities and strategies toward their external environment (Ancona 1990; Ancona and Caldwell 1992). We draw from this research to identify and focus on two particular external team functions: managing an outside authority and managing a client. We speculate as to the effects on team outcomes of a powerful individual team member fulfilling these functions alone versus the team as a whole fulfilling these functions.

It has been found that one of the important external relations that teams attempt to manage involves the perceptions and support of outside authority; Ancona and Caldwell (1992) labeled this "ambassadorial activity." This external-relations activity typically involves presenting the team capabilities and needs to managers in the larger organization to persuade authority that the team deserves and will use effectively additional resources. Although researchers have recognized that teams carry on this function, they have not addressed who in the team is likely to enact the behavior. It can, theoretically, be done by any or several team members or be a role shared at different times by different team members. We argue that a powerful team member is uniquely suited to fulfill this team function to the benefit of group performance.

As discussed earlier, individuals with greater power within the team may have that power for a variety of reasons, including higher status in the organizational hierarchy, special competence or expertise, a broad network of relations, or even extraordinary verbal ability. Just as these power sources allow the individual to have special influence over the actions of team members, they also can enhance the credibility of that individual with external authorities. Network relations, in addition, enhance the range of access that the individual has to organizational members with the authority to provide needed resources to the team. Thus, the capability of powerful individuals to fulfill this function to the benefit of the team is greater than that of other team members.

Proposition 5: Managing the perceptions and support of outside authority is an effective use of individual power.

The second external activity we address is managing the relationship of the team with its client. Although not all teams have clients external to the organization, most teams do at least have a user of their product or service. Indeed, a definition of team effectiveness may include the degree to which the team product meets the standards of the people who receive or use the product (Hackman 1990). In many organizational teams, direct client contact is maintained exclusively by one individual who has greater power in the organization than do other members. In consulting teams, for example, the project manager is usually a team member with greater status in the organizational hierarchy. This team leader meets with the client to outline the nature of the project and produce a prospectus, interprets client needs, and keeps the client informed throughout the project. Only at project completion do other team members typically meet with the client, often simply to present the team's conclusions. What effect does this pattern of behavior have on team performance? In our view, exclusive contact between a high-status team member and the client is likely to undermine team performance relative to contact between the client and the team as a whole. The pattern cited previously is defended typically on the basis of "efficiency"—that is, minimizing the time involved in meetings with a client while still satisfying their requirements. This means of managing client relations, however, can be detrimental to group performance for two reasons. First, direct contact with users of the team's product or service is known to be an important source of task-based motivation (Hackman and Oldham 1980). Second, understanding the requirements of a client is an interpretive act, and determining the process of meeting those requirements is a creative one. Both activities can benefit from drawing on the unique perspectives and abilities of individual team members. When powerful individuals monopolize contact with the external client, both team-level motivation and the quality of work done for the client are compromised.

Proposition 6: Maintaining exclusive relations with the client is a misuse of individual power.

GENERAL DISCUSSION

The arguments presented in the preceding section allow us to develop some general propositions about the uses and misuses of power by individual members of task-performing teams. We previously argued that groups were better off if the group as a whole (a) collectively established its operating norms and (b) participated in managing relations with external clients. In each case, the benefit of the group's involvement in these functions derives from their effect on team members' motivation or their commitment to team outcomes. Acceptance of the group norms that promote high standards is likely to be greater when those norms have been discussed and established by consensus rather than by fiat. Similarly, direct contact with the group's client influences the overall level of engagement members feel with their task. Consequently, when a powerful individual engages in these behaviors, only that individual's motivation is maximized, to the detriment of that of other team members.

General Proposition I: Fulfilling behavioral functions that influence the collective motivation of the team is a misuse of individual power.

We also argued that certain features of team effectiveness will suffer when powerful individuals (a) assert team task strategies rather than allowing them to be developed by the group as a whole or (b) exclusively manage relations with the client.

Team task performance will improve when the team as a whole fulfills these functions because task performance is influenced directly by the use made of collective knowledge and skills. When powerful individuals assert particular task strategies, or when they maintain exclusive contact with the client, only that individual's talents are brought to bear on the team's approach to its work. By contrast, when all team members are engaged in fulfilling these functions, the team has the opportunity to draw on the full range of capabilities within the team.

General Proposition II: Fulfilling behavioral functions that are influenced by the collective capabilities of the team is a misuse of individual power.

An example of the negative consequences of General Propositions I and II can be seen in our project team examples from the beginning of this chapter. We labeled one pattern of individual power use as the overuse pattern. In this example, the powerful team member uses his or her special status in the group to exert influence over most aspects of group functioning. As we described, many of these teams perform quite poorly and are characterized by widespread member dissatisfaction and frustration. We suggest that the negative effects experienced by these teams are the result of an individual team member that has taken over group functions that are linked to team capabilities and motivation. By overusing power, that individual undermined the group's performance through reducing the level of talent that was brought to bear on task strategy and the unity of execution that comes from collective commitment. The widespread dissatisfaction may be a function of perceived poor performance, or it may be a result of team members feeling their authority usurped and their contributions underutilized.

On the positive side, however, at least these groups have fulfilled some of the important task and relationship functions. In contrast is the second pattern we described, which we labeled abdication. In this pattern, the powerful team member exerts no special influence over task or relations processes—not even to the extent of managing the team's entry into the client organization. Thus, a critical external function was inadequately addressed or addressed by members with less likelihood of doing so effectively. These abdicating individuals also missed important influence opportunities in other domains. By failing to recognize their special influence, they may have been especially complicit in allowing the group to avoid critical functions such as task conflict; hence the smooth interpersonal relations of these groups—but the subsequent poor performance.

Team performance is enhanced when appropriate performance strategies are invented to deal with changing task demands. Thus, the ability of the team to improve as a performing unit over time increases when performance feedback is drawn to the attention of the team, when the team needs are presented to higher authorities, and when its interpersonal conflicts are dealt with. In addition, the commitment of individual members within the team increases when values are articulated that appeal to team members and when its capabilities and successes are drawn to the attention of external entities. Those teams that fail to fulfill these functions do so to the detriment of team effectiveness. Measures to fill such gaps can be taken by a powerful individual team member with unique status in the group. Better still, if those missing functions are related to member motivation or collective capabilities, the powerful individual can influence the team to address issues that it has avoided or ignored.

> *General Proposition III:* Influencing the team to fulfill behavioral functions that the team has avoided or ignored is an effective use of individual power.

Thus, there is a role for a powerful team member to use his or her influence to the benefit of the group. Related to this notion is our third example of power use in project teams, labeled managing the resource. In this instance, the powerful member influences other team members only in the specific domain of his or her special resource—that is, smoothing and facilitating access to the client. Such individuals help the team interpret information and feedback from the client—although they do not assert strategies and interpretations without input from the group. On the basis of our observations, this appears to be a highly effective pattern of influence. In General Proposition III, we expand the range of this behavior to suggest that powerful team members also should encourage the team to address important task and relations functions, when and if they are being neglected or avoided.

In this [article], we attempted to open and explore an area of research that has thus far been neglected—that of who enacts important task and relational functions within teams. Our purpose has been to raise the issue of the uses and misuses of individual power within groups, and how it might be related to team effectiveness and performance.

We close by raising two issues about power use in teams that we believe call for further exploration—one relevant to structural influences on power dynamics in teams and one about individual differences.

The first, more structural issue has to do with sources of power. We noted at the beginning of the [article] that certain team members may come to the team with greater power than others for a variety of reasons, including networks of relations outside the group, special skills, and access to critical resources. These structural influences on who holds power in groups may also have implications for the effects of power use on team outcomes. We note that the effectiveness of powerholders in managing the relations of the team to outside authority may be influenced by the individuals' source of power. For example, those who derive power in the team from having powerful external allies or from having extraordinary verbal skills are more likely to fulfill this function effectively than are those who derive their power from a special skill visible only to the team and not to outside authority.

The second issue is that individual powerholders vary in their political tactics and the skill with which they exert influence on team behavior. Individual differences in influence skills will surely affect the impact of power uses on team effectiveness. For example, the potential positive impact of a powerholder encouraging task-related conflict depends on that individual's skill in eliciting diverse opinions about task strategy and helping the group to determine the best course of action. It is at least conceivable that unskilled attempts to raise task conflict could foment relational conflict that undermines team effectiveness. We thus acknowledge the potential importance of considering power sources and skill differences in the relationships we have proposed. These issues, and the propositions we have presented, are meant to stimulate new directions for research and thinking about groups that might prove of interest to the theorist and of importance to the practitioner.

REFERENCES

Alderfer, C.P., and Smith, K.K. (1982). Studying intergroup relations embedded in organizations. *Administrative Science Quarterly* 27: 35–65.

Amason, A. (1996). Distinguishing effects of functional and dysfunctional conflict on strategic decision making: Resolving a paradox for top management teams. *Academy of Management Journal* 39: 123–148.

Ancona, D. (1987). Groups in organizations: Extending laboratory models. In C. Hendrick (ed.), *Group Processes and Intergroup Relations*. Newbury Park, CA: Sage.

———. (1990). Outward bound: Strategies for team survival in an organization. *Academy of Management Journal* 33: 334–365.

Ancona, D., and Caldwell, D. (1992). Demography and design: Predictors of new product team performance. *Organization Science* 3(3), 321–341.

Ancona, D., Friedman, R., and Kolb, D. (1991). The group and what happens on the way to "yes." *Negotiation Journal* 7: 155–174.

Argote, L. (1989). Agreement about norms and work unit effectiveness: Evidence from the field. *Basic Applied Social Psychology* 10: 131–140.

Argyris, C. (1962). *Interpersonal Competence and Organizational Effectiveness*. Homewood, IL: Dorsey.

Baron, R. (1990). Countering the effects of destructive criticism: The relative efficacy of four interventions. *Journal of Applied Psychology* 75: 235–245.

Bar-Tal, D. (1989). *Group Beliefs: A Conception for Analyzing Group Structure, Processes, and Behavior*. New York: Springer-Verlag.

Bazerman, M.H., Mannix, E., and Thompson, L. (1988). Groups as mixed-motive negotiations. In E.J. Lawler and B. Markovsky (eds.), *Advances in Group Processes: Theory and Research*, 5. Greenwich CT: JAI.

Bettenhausen, K., and Murnighan, J.K. (1985). The emergence of norms in competitive decision-making groups. *Administrative Science Quarterly* 30: 350–372.

Boulding, K. (1963). *Conflict and Defense.* New York: Harper and Row.

Bourgeois, L.J. (1980). Performance and consensus. *Strategic Management Journal* 1, 227–248.

———. (1985). Strategic goals, environmental uncertainty, and economic performance in volatile environments. *Academy of Management Journal* 28: 548–573.

Brehmer, B. (1976). Social judgment theory and the analysis of interpersonal conflict. *Psychological Bulletin* 83: 985–1003.

Burt, R. (1992). *Structural Holes: The Social Structure of Competition.* Boston: Harvard University Press.

Cohen, S.G. (1994). Designing effective self-managing work teams. In M. Beyerlein and D. Johnson (eds.), *Advances in Interdisciplinary Studies of Work Teams* (pp. 67–102). Greenwich, CT: JAI.

Coser, L. (1970). *Continuities in the Study of Social Conflict.* New York: Free Press.

Crosier, R., and Rose, G. (1977). Cognitive conflict and goal conflict effects on task performance. *Organizational Behavior and Human Decision Processes* 19: 378–391.

Crowne, D., and Rosse, J. (1995). Yours, mine, and ours: Facilitating group productivity through the integration of individual and group goals. *Organizational Behavior and Human Decision Processes* 64: 138–150.

Dahl, R. (1957). The concept of power. *Behavioral Science* 2: 201–218.

Deutsch, M. (1969). Conflicts: Productive and destructive. *Journal of Social Issues* 25: 7–41.

Druskat, V.U. (1995). A team competency study of self-managed manufacturing teams. Unpublished doctoral dissertation, Boston University, Boston.

Eisenhardt, K., and Bourgeois, J. (1988). Politics of strategic decision making in high-velocity environments: Toward a midrange theory. *Academy of Management Journal* 31: 737–770.

Eisenhardt, K., and Schoonhoven, C. (1990). Organizational growth: Linking founding team, strategy, environment, and growth among U.S. semiconductor ventures 1978–1988. *Administrative Science Quarterly* 35: 504–529.

Eisenhardt, K., and Zbaracki, M. (1992). Strategic decision making. *Strategic Management Journal* 73: 17–37.

Emerson, R.M. (1964). Power-dependence relations: Two experiments. *Sociometry* 27, 282–298.

Evan, W. (1965). Conflict and performance in R and D organizations. *Industrial Management Review* 7: 37–46.

Feldman, D.C. (1984). The development and enforcement of group norms. *Academy of Management Review* 9: 47–53.

French, J.R.P, Jr., and Raven, B. (1959). The bases of social power. In D. Cartwright (ed.), *Studies in Social Power.* Ann Arbor: University of Michigan Press.

Gladstein, D. (1984). A model of task group effectiveness. *Administrative Science Quarterly* 29: 499–517.

Goodman, P., Ravlin, E., and Schminke, M. (1987). Understanding groups in organizations. In L. Cummings and B. Staw (eds.), *Research in Organizational Behavior* (vol. 9, pp. 121–173). Greenwich, CT: JAI.

Granovetter, M. (1973). The strength of weak ties. *American Journal of Sociology* 78: 1360–1379.

Gray, B., Bougon, M.G., and Donnellon, A. (1985). Organizations as constructions and destructions of meaning. *Journal of Management* 11: 83–98.

Gresov, C. (1989). Exploring fit and misfit with multiple contingencies. *Administrative Science Quarterly* 34: 431–453.

Guetzkow, H., and Gyr, J. (1954). An analysis of conflict in decision making groups. *Human Relations* 7: 367–381.

Guzzo, R. (ed.). (1982). *Improving Group Decision Making in Organizations: Approaches from Theory and Research.* New York: Academic Press.

Hackman, J.R. (1976). Group influences on individuals. In M. Dunnette (ed.), *Handbook of Industrial and Organizational Psychology.* Chicago: Rand McNally.

———. (1983). A normative model of work team effectiveness (Tech. Rep. No. 2, Group effectiveness research project). New Haven, CT: Yale University, School of Organization and Management.

———. (1987). The design of work teams. In J. Lorsch (ed.), *Handbook of Organizational Behavior* (pp. 315–342). Englewood Cliffs, NJ: Prentice Hall.

Hackman, J.R. (ed.). (1990). *Groups That Work (and Those That Don't): Creating Conditions for Effective Teamwork.* San Francisco: Jossey-Bass.

Hackman, J.R., and Oldham, G. (1980). *Work Redesign.* Reading, MA: Addison-Wesley.

Hare, A.P. (1976). *Handbook of Small Group Research* (2d ed.). New York: Free Press.

Hollander, E. (1958). Conformity, status and idiosyncrasy credit. *Psychological Bulletin* 65: 117–127.

Jackson, S., and Schuler, R. (1985). A meta-analysis and conceptual critique of research on role ambiguity and role conflict in work settings. *Organizational Behavior* 36: 16–78.

Janis, I.L. (1982). *Victims of Groupthink* (2d ed.). Boston: Houghton-Mifflin.

Jehn, K. (1994). Enhancing effectiveness: An investigation of advantages and disadvantages of value-based intragroup conflict. *International Journal of Conflict Management* 5: 223–238.

———. (1995). A multimethod examination of the benefits and detriments of intragroup conflict. *Administrative Science Quarterly* 40: 256–282.

Jehn, K., and Mannix, E.A. (1996, December). The dynamic nature of conflict: A longitudinal study of intragroup conflict and group performance. (Working paper.)

Katz, R., and Tushman, M. (1979). Communication patterns, project performance, and task characteristics: An empirical evaluation and integration in an R&D setting. *Organizational Behavior and Human Performance* 23: 139–162.

———. (1981). An investigation into the managerial roles and career paths of gatekeepers and project supervisors in a major R&D facility. *Administrative Science Quarterly* 27: 103–110.

Kelley, H.H. (1979). *Personal Relationships.* Hillsdale, NJ: Lawrence Erlbaum.

Kolodny, H.F., and Kiggundu, M.N. (1980). Towards the development of a sociotechnical systems model in woodlands mechanical harvesting. *Human Relations* 33: 623–645.

Kotter, J. (1979). *Power in Management.* New York: AMACOM.

Levine, J., and Moreland, R. (1990). Progress in small group research. *Annual Review of Psychology* 41: 585–634.

Lewicki, R., and Litterer, J.A. (1994). *Negotiation* (2d ed.). Homewood, IL: Irwin.

Liang, D.W., Moreland, R., and Argote, L. (1995). Group versus individual training and group performance: The mediating role of transactive memory. *Personality and Social Psychology Bulletin* 21(4): 384–393.

Maier, N.R.F. (1967). Assets and liabilities in group problem-solving: The need for an integrative function. *Psychological Review* 74: 239–249.

———. (1970). *Problem Solving and Creativity: In Individuals and Groups.* Monterey, CA: Brooks/Cole.

Mannix, E., Goins, S., and Carroll, S. (1996, June). Starting at the beginning: Team formation, process and performance. (Working paper.)

Marsden, P. (1983). Restricted access in networks and models of power. *American Journal of Sociology* 88: 686–717.

Mason, R.O., and Mitroff, I.I. (1981). *Challenging Strategic Planning Assumptions.* New York: Wiley.

McGrath, J. (1984). *Groups: Interaction and Performance.* Englewood Cliffs, NJ: Prentice-Hall.

McGrath, J., and Kravitz, D. (1982). Group research. *Annual Review of Psychology* 33: 195–230.

McIntyre, R.M., and Salas, E. (1995). Measuring and managing for team performance: Lessons from complex environments. In R. Guzzo and E. Salas (eds.), *Team Effectiveness and Decision Making in Complex Organizations.* San Francisco: Jossey-Bass.

Miller, C. (1989). The social psychological effects of group decision rules. In P. Paulus (ed.), *Psychology of Group Influence* (2d ed.). Hillsdale, NJ: Lawrence Erlbaum.

Mitchell, T.R., and Silver, W. (1990). Individual and group goals when workers are interdependent: Effects on task strategies and performance. *Journal of Applied Psychology* 75: 185–193.

Moreland, R. (1987). The formation of small groups. In C. Hendrick (ed.), *Group Process* (pp. 80–110). Newbury Park, CA: Sage.

Moreland, R., and Levine, J. (1982). Socialization in small groups: Temporal changes in individual-group relations. In L. Berkowitz (ed.), *Advances in Experimental Social Psychology* (vol. 15, pp. 137–192). New York: Academic Press.

Nadler, D. (1979). The effects of feedback on task group behavior: A review of the research. *Organizational Behavior and Human Decision Processes* 23: 309–338.

Nadler, D.A., and Tushman, M. (1988). *Strategic Organizational Design: Concepts, Tools, and Processes.* Glenview, IL: Scott Foresman.

Neale, M.A., and Bazerman, M.H. (1991). *Cognition and Rationality in Negotiation.* New York: Free Press.

Nemeth, C.J., and Staw, B. (1989). The tradeoffs of social control in groups and organizations. *Advances in Experimental Social Psychology* 22: 175–210.

O'Reilly, C., and Caldwell, D. (1985). The impact of normative social influence and cohesiveness on task perceptions and attitudes: A social information processing approach. *Journal of Occupational Psychology* 58: 193–206.

Pearce, J.A., and Ravlin, E.C. (1987). The design and activation of self-regulating work groups. *Human Relations* 40: 751–782.

Pfeffer, J. (1986). A resource dependence perspective on intercorporate relations. In M.S. Mizruchi and M. Schwartz (eds.), *Structural Analysis of Business* (pp. 117–132). New York: Academic Press.

———. (1992). *Managing with Power: Politics and Influence in Organizations.* Cambridge, MA: Harvard University Press.

Pfeffer, J., and Salancik, G. (1974). Organizational decision making: The case of a university budget. *Administrative Science Quarterly* 19: 135–151.

———. (1977). Organizational design: The case for a coalitional model of organizations. *Organizational Dynamics* 6: 15–29.

———. (1978). *The External Control of Organizations: A Resource Dependence Perspective.* New York: Harper and Row.

Pinkley, R. (1990). Dimensions of the conflict frame: Disputant interpretations of conflict. *Journal of Applied Psychology* 75: 117–128.

Pruitt, D.G. (1981). *Negotiation Behavior.* New York: Academic Press.

Pruitt, D.G., and Rubin, J.Z. (1986). *Social Conflict.* New York: Random House.

Ravlin, E.C., and Meglino, B.M. (1987). Effects of values on perception and decision making: A study of alternative work value measures. *Journal of Applied Psychology* 72: 666–673.

Roseman, L., Wiest, C., and Swartz, T. (1994). Phenomenology, behaviors and goals differentiate emotions. *Journal of Personality and Social Psychology* 67: 206–221.

Schein, E.H. (1986). What you need to know about organizational culture. *Training and Development Journal* 8(1), 30–33.

Schwarz, R. (1994). *Team Facilitation.* Englewood Cliffs, NJ: Prentice-Hall.

Schweiger, D., and Sandberg, W. (1989). The utilization of individual capabilities in group approaches to strategic decision making. *Strategic Management Journal* 10: 31–43.

Schweiger, D., Sandberg, W., and Ragan, J. (1986). Group approaches for improving strategic decision making: A comparative analysis of dialectical inquiry, devil's advocacy, and consensus approaches to strategic decision making. *Academy of Management Journal* 29: 51–71.

Schweiger, D., Sandberg, W., and Rechner, P. (1989). Experiential effects of dialectical inquiry, devil's advocacy, and consensus approaches to strategic decision making. *Academy of Management Journal* 32: 745–772.

Schwenk, C. (1990). Conflict in organizational decision making: An exploratory study of its effects in for-profit and not-for-profit organizations. *Management Science* 36: 436–448.

Schwenk, C., and Crosier, R. (1993). Effects of the expert, devil's advocate and dialectical inquiry methods on prediction performance. *Organizational Behavior and Human Decision Processes* 26: 409–424.

Shah, P., and Jehn, K. (1993). Do friends perform better than acquaintances? The interaction of friendship, conflict and task. *Group Decision and Negotiation* 2: 149–166.

Sherif, M. (1936). *The Psychology of Social Norms*. New York: Harper.

Stasser, G., Kerr, N., and Davis, J. (1989). Influence processes and consensus models in decision-making groups. In P. Paulus (ed.), *Psychology of Group Influence* (2d ed.). Hillsdale, NJ: Lawrence Erlbaum.

Staw, B.M., Sandelands, L., and Dutton, J. (1981). Threat-rigidity effects in organizational performance. *Administrative Science Quarterly* 28: 582–600.

Steiner, I. (1972). *Group Process and Productivity*. New York: Academic Press.

Thibaut, J.W., and Kelley, H.H. (1959). *The Social Psychology of Groups*. New York: Wiley.

Tjosvold, D. (1991). Rights and responsibilities of dissent: Cooperative conflict. *Employee Responsibilities and Rights Journal* 4: 13–23.

Turner, R., and Colomy, P. (1988). Role differentiation: Orienting principles. In E.J. Lawler and B. Markovsky (eds.), *Social Psychology of Groups: A reader*. Greenwich, CT: JAI.

Tushman, M. (1977). Special boundary roles in the innovation process. *Administrative Science Quarterly* 22: 587–605.

Wageman, R. (1995). Interdependence and group effectiveness. *Administrative Science Quarterly* 40: 145–180.

———. (1996, June). A field study of leadership of self-managing teams: The effects of team design and coaching. (Working paper.)

Wall, V., and Nolan, L. (1986). Perceptions of inequity, satisfaction, and conflict in task oriented groups. *Human Relations* 39: 1033–1052.

Weingart, L.R. (1992). Impact of group goals, task component complexity, effort, and planning on group performance. *Journal of Applied Psychology* 77: 33–54.

White, H.C. (1970). *Chains of Opportunity*. Cambridge, MA: Harvard University Press.

Zander, A. (1979). The psychology of group process. *Annual Review of Psychology* 30: 417–451.

22

Influence Without Authority: The Use of Alliances, Reciprocity, and Exchange to Accomplish Work

Allan R. Cohen and David L. Bradford

Bill Heatton is the director of research at a $250 million division of a large West Coast company. The division manufactures exotic telecommunications components and has many technical advancements to its credit. During the past several years, however, the division's performance has been spotty at best; multimillion dollar losses have been experienced in some years despite many efforts to make the division more profitable. Several large contracts have resulted in major financial losses, and in each instance the various parts of the division blamed the others for the problems. Listen to Bill's frustration as he talks about his efforts to influence Ted, a colleague who is marketing director, and Roland, the program manager who reports to Ted.

> Another program is about to come through. Roland is a nice guy, but he knows nothing and never will. He was responsible for our last big loss, and now he's in charge of this one. I've tried to convince Ted, his boss, to get Roland off the program, but I get nowhere. Although Ted doesn't argue that Roland is capable, he doesn't act to find someone else. Instead, he comes to me with worries about my area.
>
> I decided to respond by changing my staffing plan, assigning to Roland's program the people they wanted. I had to override my staff's best judgment about who should be assigned. Yet I'm not getting needed progress reports from Roland, and he's never available for planning. I get little argument from him, but there's no action to correct the problem. That's bad because I'm responding but not getting any response.
>
> There's no way to resolve this. If they disagree, that's it. I could go to a tit-for-tat strategy, saying that if they don't do what I want, well get even with them next time. But I don't know how to do that without hurting the organization, which would feel worse than getting even!

Ted, Roland's boss, is so much better than his predecessor that I hate to ask that he be removed. We could go together to our boss, the general manager, but I'm very reluctant to do that. You've failed in a matrix organization if you have to go to your boss. I have to try hard because I'd look bad if I had to throw it in his lap.

Meanwhile, I'm being forceful, but I'm afraid it's in a destructive way. I don't want to wait until the program has failed to be told it was all my fault.

Bill is clearly angry and frustrated, leading him to behave in ways that he does not feel good about. Like other managers who very much want to influence an uncooperative coworker whom they cannot control, Bill has begun to think of the intransigent employee as the enemy. Bill's anger is narrowing his sense of what is possible; he fantasizes revenge but is too dedicated to the organization to actually harm it. He is genuinely stuck.

Organizational members who want to make things happen often find themselves in this position. Irrespective of whether they are staff or line employees, professionals or managers, they find it increasingly necessary to influence colleagues and superiors. These critical others control needed resources, possess required information, set priorities on important activities, and have to agree and cooperate if plans are to be implemented. They cannot be ordered around because they are under another area's control and can legitimately say no because they have many other valid priorities. They respond only when they choose to. Despite the clear need and appropriateness of what is being asked for (certainly as seen by the person who is making the request), compliance may not be forthcoming.

All of this places a large burden on organizational members, who are expected not only to take initiatives but also to respond intelligently to requests made of them by others. Judgment is needed to sort out the value of the many requests made of anyone who has valuable resources to contribute. As Robert Kaplan argued in his article "Trade Routes: The Manager's Network of Relationships" (*Organizational Dynamics*, Spring 1984), managers must now develop the organizational equivalent of "trade routes" to get things done. Informal networks of mutual influence are needed. In her book *The Change Masters* (Simon and Schuster, 1983) Rosabeth Moss Kanter showed that developing and implementing all kinds of innovations requires coalitions to be built to shape and support new ways of doing business.

A key current problem, then, is finding ways to develop mutual influence without the formal authority to command. A peer cannot "order" a colleague to change priorities, modify an approach, or implement a grand new idea. A staff member cannot "command" his or her supervisor to back a proposal, fight top management for greater resources, or allow more autonomy. Even Bill Heatton, in dealing with Roland (who was a level below him in the hierarchy but in another department), could not dictate that Roland provide the progress reports that Bill so desperately wanted.

EXCHANGE AND THE LAW OF RECIPROCITY

The way influence is acquired without formal authority is through the "law of reciprocity"—the almost universal belief that people should be paid back for what they do, that one good (or bad) deed deserves another. This belief is held by people in primitive and not-so-primitive societies all around the world, and it serves as the grease that allows the organizational wheels to turn smoothly. Because people expect that their actions will be paid back in one form or another, influence is possible.

In the case of Bill Heatton, his inability to get what he wanted from Roland and Ted stemmed from his failure to understand fully how reciprocity works in organizations. He therefore was unable to set up mutually beneficial exchanges. Bill believed that he had gone out of his way to help the marketing department by changing his staffing patterns, and he expected Roland to reciprocate by providing regular progress reports. When Roland failed to provide the reports, Bill believed that Ted was obligated to remove Roland from the project. When Ted did not respond, Bill became angry and wanted to retaliate. Thus Bill recognized the appropriateness of exchange in making organizations work. However, he did not understand how exchange operates.

Before exploring in detail how exchange can work in dealing with colleagues and superiors, it is important to recognize that reciprocity is the basic principle behind all organizational transactions. For example, the basic employment contract is an exchange ("an honest day's work for an honest day's pay"). Even work that is above and beyond what is formally required involves exchange. The person who helps out may not necessarily get (or expect) immediate payment for the extra effort requested, but some eventual compensation is expected.

Think of the likely irritation an employee would feel if his or her boss asked him or her to work through several weekends, never so much as said thanks, and then claimed credit for the extra work. The employee might not say anything the first time this happened, expecting or hoping that the boss would make it up somehow. However, if the effort were never acknowledged in any way, the employee, like most people, would feel that something important had been violated.

The expectation of reciprocal exchanges occurs between an employee and his or her supervisor, among peers, with higher level managers in other parts of the organization, or all of the above. The exchange can be of tangible goods, such as a budget increase, new equipment, or more personnel; of tangible services, such as a faster response time, more information, or public support; or of sentiments, such as gratitude, admiration, or praise. Whatever form exchanges take, unless they are roughly equivalent over time, hard feelings will result.

Exchanges enable people to handle the give-and-take of working together without strong feelings of injustice arising. They are especially important during periods of rapid change because the number of requests that go far beyond the routine tends to escalate. In those situations, exchanges become less predictable, more free-floating, and spontaneous. Nevertheless, people still expect that somehow or other, sooner or later, they will be (roughly) equally compensated for the acts they do above and beyond those that are covered by the formal exchange agreements in their job. Consequently, some kind of "currency" equivalent needs to be worked out, implicitly if not explicitly, to keep the parties in the exchange feeling fairly treated.

CURRENCIES: THE SOURCE OF INFLUENCE

If the basis of organizational influence depends on mutually satisfactory exchanges, then people are influential only insofar as they can offer something that others need. Thus power comes from the ability to meet others' needs.

A useful way to think of how the process of exchange actually works in organizations is to use the metaphor of "currencies." This metaphor provides a powerful way to conceptualize what is important to the influencer and the person to be influenced. Just as many types of currencies are traded in the world financial market, many types are "traded" in organizational life. Too often people think only of money or promotion and status. Those "currencies," however, usually are available only to a manager in dealing with his or her employees. Peers who want to influence colleagues or employees who want to influence their supervisors often feel helpless. They need to recognize that many types of payments exist, broadening the range of what can be exchanged.

Some major currencies that are commonly valued and traded in organizations are listed in Table 22.1. Although not exhaustive, the list makes evident that a person does not have to be at the top of an organization or have hands on the formal levers of power to command multiple resources that others may value.

Part of the usefulness of currencies comes from their flexibility. For example, there are many ways to express gratitude and to give assistance. A manager who most values the currency of appreciation could be paid through verbal thanks, praise, a public statement at a meeting, informal comments to his peers, and/or a note to her boss. However, the same note of thanks seen by one person as a sign of appreciation may be seen by another person as an attempt to brownnose or by a third person as a cheap way to try to repay extensive favors and service. Thus currencies have value not in some abstract sense but as defined by the receiver.

Although we have stressed the interactive nature of exchange, "payments" do not always have to be made by the other person. They can be self-generated to fit beliefs about being virtuous, benevolent, or committed to the organization's welfare. Someone may respond to another persons request because it reinforces cherished values, a sense of identity, or feelings of self-worth. The exchange is interpersonally stimulated because the one who wants influence has set up conditions that allow this kind of self-payment to occur by asking for cooperation to accomplish organizational goals. However, the person who responds because "it is the right thing to do" and who feels good about being the "kind of person who does not act out of narrow self-interest" is printing currency (virtue) that is self-satisfying.

Of course, the five categories of currencies listed in Table 22.1 are not mutually

Table 22.1
Commonly Traded Organizational Currencies

Inspiration-Related Currencies	
Vision	Being involved in a task that has larger significance for the unit, organization, customers, or society.
Excellence	Having a chance to do important things really well.
Moral/Ethical Correctness	Doing what is "right" by a higher standard than efficiency.
Task-Related Currencies	
Resources	Lending or giving money, budget increases, personnel, space, and so forth.
Assistance	Helping with existing projects or undertaking unwanted tasks.
Cooperation	Giving task support, providing quicker response time, approving a project, or aiding implementation.
Information	Providing organizational as well as technical knowledge.
Position-Related Currencies	
Advancement	Giving a task or assignment that can aid in promotion.
Recognition	Acknowledging effort, accomplishment, or abilities.
Visibility	Providing chance to be known by higher-ups or significant others in the organization.
Reputation	Enhancing the way a person is seen.
Importance/Insiderness	Offering a sense of importance, of "belonging."
Network/Contacts	Providing opportunities for linking with others.
Relationship-Related Currencies	
Acceptance/Inclusion	Providing closeness and friendship.
Personal Support	Giving personal and emotional backing.
Understanding	Listening to others' concerns and issues.
Personal-Related Currencies	
Self-Concept	Affirming one's values, self-esteem, and identity.
Challenge/Learning	Sharing tasks that increase skills and abilities.
Ownership/Involvement	Letting others have ownership and influence.
Gratitude	Expressing appreciation or indebtedness.

exclusive. When the demand from the other person is high, people are likely to pay in several currencies across several categories. They may, for example, stress the organizational value of their request, promise to return the favor at a later time, imply that it will increase the other's prestige in the organization, and express their appreciation.

ESTABLISHING EXCHANGE RATES

What does it take to pay back in a currency that the other party in an exchange will perceive as equivalent? In impersonal markets, because everything is translated into a common monetary currency, it generally is easy to say what a fair payment is. Does a ton of steel equal a case of golfclubs? By translating both into dollar equivalents, a satisfactory deal can be worked out.

In interpersonal exchanges, however, the process becomes a bit more complicated. Just how does someone repay another person's willingness to help finish a report? Is a simple "thank you" enough? Does it also require the recipient to say something nice about the helper to his or her boss? Whose standard of fairness should be used? What if one person's idea of fair repayment is very different from the others?

Because of the natural differences in the way two parties can interpret the same activity, establishing exchanges that both parties will perceive as equitable can be problematic. Thus it is critical to understand what is important to the person to be influenced. Without a clear understanding of what that person experiences and values, it will be extremely difficult for anyone to thread a path through the minefield of creating mutually satisfactory exchanges.

Fortunately, the calibration of equivalent exchanges in the interpersonal and organizational worlds is facilitated by the fact that approximations will do in most cases. Occasionally, organizational members know exactly what they want in return for favors or help, but more often they will settle for very rough equivalents (providing that there is reasonable goodwill).

THE PROCESS OF EXCHANGE

To make the exchange process effective, the influencer needs to (1) think about the person to be influenced as a potential ally, not an adversary; (2) know the world of the potential ally, including the pressures as well as the person's needs and goals; (3) be aware of key goals and available resources that may be valued by the potential ally; and (4) understand the exchange transaction itself so that win-win outcomes are achieved. Each of these factors is discussed below.

Potential Ally, Not Adversary

A key to influence is thinking of the other person as a potential ally. Just as many contemporary organizations have discovered the importance of creating strategic alliances with suppliers and customers, employees who want influence within the organization need to create internal allies. Even though each party in an alliance continues to have freedom to pursue its own interests, the goal is to find areas of mutual benefit and develop trusting, sustainable relationships. Similarly, each person whose cooperation is needed inside the organization is a potential ally. Each still has self-interests to pursue, but those self-interests do not preclude searching for and building areas of mutual benefit.

Seeing other organizational members as potential allies decreases the chance that adversarial relationships will develop an all-too-frequent result (as in the case of Bill

Heatton) when the eager influencer does not quickly get the assistance or cooperation needed. Assuming that even a difficult person is a potential ally makes it easier to understand that person's world and thereby discover what that person values and needs.

The Potential Ally's World

We have stressed the importance of knowing the world of the potential ally. Without awareness of what the ally needs (what currencies are valued), attempts to influence that person can only be haphazard. Although this conclusion may seem self-evident, it is remarkable how often people attempt to influence without adequate information about what is important to the potential ally. Instead, they are driven by their own definition of "what should be" and "what is right" when they should be seeing the world from the other person's perspective.

For example, Bill Heatton never thought about the costs to Ted of removing Roland from the project. Did Ted believe he could coach Roland to perform better on this project? Did Ted even agree that Roland had done a poor job on the previous project, or did Ted think Roland had been hampered by other departments' shortcomings? Bill just did not know.

Several factors can keep the influencer from seeing the potential ally clearly. As with Bill Heatton, the frustration of meeting resistance from a potential ally can get in the way of really understanding the other person's world. The desire to influence is so strong that only the need for cooperation is visible to the influencer. As a result of not being understood, the potential ally digs in, making the influencer repeat an inappropriate strategy or back off in frustration.

When a potential ally's behavior is not understandable ("Why won't Roland send the needed progress reports?"), the influencer tends to stereotype that person. If early attempts to influence do not work, the influencer is tempted to write the person off as negative, stubborn, selfish, or "just another bean counter/whiz kid/sales-type" or whatever pejorative label is used in that organizational culture to dismiss those organizational members who are different.

Although some stereotypes may have a grain of truth, they generally conceal more than they reveal. The actuary who understands that judgment, not just numbers, is needed to make decisions disappears as an individual when the stereotype of "impersonal, detached number machine" is the filter through which he or she is seen. Once the stereotype is applied, the frustrated influencer is no longer likely to see what currencies that particular potential ally actually values.

Sometimes, the lack of clear understanding about a potential ally stems from the influencer's failure to appreciate the organizational forces acting on the potential ally. To a great extent, a person's behavior is a result of the situation in which that person works (and not just his or her personality). Potential allies are embedded in an organizational culture that shapes their interests and responses. For example, one of the key determinants of anyone's behavior is likely to be the way the person's performance is measured and rewarded. In many instances, what is mistaken for personal orneriness is merely the result of the person doing something that will be seen as good performance in his or her function.

The salesperson who is furious because the plant manager resists changing priorities for a rush order may not realize that part of the plant manager's bonus depends on holding unit costs down—a task made easier with long production runs. The plant manager's resistance does not necessarily reflect his or her inability to be flexible or lack of concern about pleasing customers or about the company's overall success.

Other organizational forces that can affect the potential ally's behavior include the daily time demands on that person's position; the amount of contact the person has with customers, suppliers, and other outsiders; the organization's information flow (or lack of it); the style of the potential ally's boss; the belief and assumptions held by that person's coworkers; and so forth. Although some of these factors cannot be changed by the influencer, understanding them can be useful in figuring out how to frame and time requests. It also helps the influencer resist the temptation to stereotype the noncooperator.

Self-Awareness of the Influencer

Unfortunately, people desiring influence are not always aware of precisely what they want. Often their requests contain a cluster of needs (a certain product, arranged in a certain way, delivered at a specified time). They fail to think through which aspects are more important and which can be jettisoned if necessary. Did Bill Heatton want Roland removed, or did he want the project effectively managed? Did he want overt concessions from Ted, or did he want better progress reports?

Further, there is a tendency to confuse and intermingle the desired end goal with the means of accomplishing it, leading to too many battles over the wrong things. In *The Change Masters,* Kanter reported that successful influencers in organizations were those who never lost sight of the ultimate objective but were willing to be flexible about means.

Sometimes influencers underestimate the range of currencies available for use. They may assume, for example, that just because they are low in the organization they have nothing that others want. Employees who want to influence their boss are especially likely not to realize all of the supervisor's needs that they can fulfill. They become so caught up with their feelings of powerlessness that they fail to see the many ways they can generate valuable currencies.

In other instances, influencers fail to be aware of their preferred style of interaction and its fit with the potential ally's preferred style. Everyone has a way of relating to others to get work done. However, like the fish who is unaware of the water, many people are oblivious of their own style of interaction or see it as the only way to be. Yet interaction style can cause problems with potential allies who are different.

For example, does the influencer tend to socialize first and work later? If so, that style of interaction will distress a potential ally who likes to dig right in to solve the problem at hand and only afterward chat about sports, family, or office politics. Does the potential ally want to be approached with answers, not problems? If so, a tendency to start influence attempts with open-ended, exploratory problem solving can lead to rejection despite good intentions.

Nature of the Exchange Transaction

Many of the problems that occur in the actual exchange negotiation have their roots in the failure to deal adequately with the first three factors outlined above. Failure to treat other people as potential allies, to understand a potential ally's world, and to be self-aware are all factors that interfere with successful exchange. In addition, some special problems commonly arise when both parties are in the process of working out a mutually satisfactory exchange agreement.

- *Not knowing how to use reciprocity.* Using reciprocity requires stating needs clearly without "crying wolf," being aware of the needs of an ally without being manipulative, and seeking mutual gain rather than playing "winner takes all." One trap that Bill Heatton fell into was not being able to "close on the exchange." That is, he assumed that if he acted in good faith and did his part, others would automatically reciprocate. Part of his failure was not understanding the other party's world; another part was not being able to negotiate clearly with Ted about what each of them wanted. It is not even clear that Ted realized Bill was altering his organization as per Ted's requests, that Ted got what he wanted, or that Ted knew Bill intended an exchange of responses.
- *Preferring to be right rather than effective.* This problem is especially endemic to professionals of all kinds. Because of their dedication to the "truth" (as their profession defines it), they stubbornly stick to their one right way when trying to line up potential allies instead of thinking about what will work given the audience and conditions. Organizational members with strong technical backgrounds often chorus the equivalent of "I'll be damned if I'm going to sell out and become a phony salesman, trying to get by on a shoeshine and smile." The failure to accommodate to the potential ally's needs and desires often kills otherwise sound ideas.
- *Overusing what has been successful.* When people find that a certain approach is effective in many situations, they often begin to use it in places where it does not fit. By overusing the approach, they block more appropriate methods. Just as a weight lifter becomes muscle-bound from overdeveloping particular muscles at the expense of others, people who have been reasonably successful at influencing other people can diminish that ability by overusing the same technique.

For example, John Brucker, the human resources director at a medium-size company, often cultivated support for new programs by taking people out to fancy restaurants for an evening of fine food and wine. He genuinely derived pleasure from entertaining, but at the same time he created subtle obligations. One time, a new program he wanted to introduce required the agreement of William Adams, head of engineering. Adams, an old-timer, perceived Brucker's proposal as an unnecessary frill, mainly because he did not perceive the real benefits to the overall organization. Brucker responded to Adams's negative comments as he always did in such cases—by becoming more friendly and insisting that they get together for dinner soon. After several of these invitations, Adams became furious. Insulted by what he considered to be Brucker's attempts to buy him off, he fought even harder to kill the proposal. Not only did the program die, but Brucker lost all possibility of influencing Adams in the future. Adams saw Brucker's attempts at socializing as a sleazy and crude way of trying to soften him up. For his part, Brucker was totally puzzled by Adams's frostiness and assumed that he was against all progress. He never realized that Adams had a deep sense of integrity and a real commitment to the good of the organization. Thus Brucker lost his opportunity to sell a program that, ironically, Adams would have found valuable had it been implemented.

As the case above illustrates, a broad repertoire of influence approaches is needed in modern organizations. Johnny-one-notes soon fall flat.

THE ROLE OF RELATIONSHIPS

All of the preceding discussion needs to be conditioned by one important variable: the nature of the relationship between both parties. The greater the extent to which the influencer has worked with the potential ally and created trust, the easier the exchange process will be. Each party will know the other's desired currencies and situational pressures, and each will have developed a mutually productive interaction style. With trust, less energy will be spent on figuring out the intentions of the ally, and there will be less suspicion about when and how the payback will occur.

A poor relationship (based on previous interactions, on the reputation each party has in the organization, and/or on stereotypes and animosities between the functions or departments that each party represents) will impede an otherwise easy exchange. Distrust of the goodwill, veracity, or reliability of the influencer can lead to the demand for "no credit; cash up front," which constrains the flexibility of both parties.

The nature of the interaction during the influencer process also affects the nature of the relationship between the influencer and the other party. The way that John Brucker attempted to relate to William Adams not only did not work but also irreparably damaged any future exchanges between them.

Few transactions within organizations are one-time deals. (Who knows when the other person may be needed again or even who may be working for him or her in the future?) Thus in most exchange situations two outcomes matter: success in achieving task goals and success in improving the relationship so that the next interaction will be even more productive. Too often, people who want to be influential focus only on the task and act as if there is no tomorrow. Although both task accomplishment and an improved relationship cannot always be realized at the same time, on some occasions the latter can be more important than the former. Winning the battle but losing the war is an expensive outcome.

INCONVERTIBLE CURRENCIES

We have spelled out ways organizational members operate to gain influence for achieving organizational goals. By effectively using exchange, organizational members can achieve their goals and at the same time help others achieve theirs. Exchange permits organizational members to be assertive without being antagonistic by keeping mutual benefit a central outcome.

In many cases, organizational members fail to acquire desired influence because they do not use all of their potential power. However, they sometimes fail because not all situations are amenable to even the best efforts at influencing. Not everything can be translated into compatible currencies. If there are fundamental differences in what is valued by two parties, it may not be possible to find common ground, as illustrated in the example below.

The founder and chairman of a high-technology company and the president he had hired five years previously were constantly displeased with one another. The president was committed to creating maximum shareholder value, the currency he valued most as a result of his M.B.A. training, his position, and his temperament. Accordingly, he had concluded that the company was in a perfect position to cash in by squeezing expenses to maximize profits and going public. He could see that the company's product line of exotic components was within a few years of saturating its market and would require massive, risky investment to move to sophisticated end-user products.

The president could not influence the chairman to adopt this direction, however, because the chairman valued a totally different currency, the fun of technological challenge. An independently wealthy man, the chairman had no interest in realizing the $10 million or so he would get if the company maximized profits by cutting research and selling out. He wanted a place to test his intuitive, creative research hunches, not a source of income.

Thus the president's and chairman's currencies were not convertible into one another at an acceptable exchange rate. After they explored various possibilities but failed to find common ground, they mutually agreed that the president should leave—on good terms and only after a more compatible replacement could be found. Although this example acknowledges that influence through alliance, currency conversion, and exchange is not always possible, it is hard to be certain that any situation is hopeless until the person desiring influence has fully applied all of the diagnostic and interpersonal skills we have described.

Influence is enhanced by using the model of strategic alliances to engage in mutually beneficial exchanges with potential allies. Even though it is not always possible to be successful, the chances of achieving success can be greatly increased. In a period of rapid competitive, technological, regulative, and consumer change, individuals and their organizations need all the help they can get.

23

Political Skill at Work

Gerald R. Ferris, Pamela L. Perrewe, William P. Anthony, and David C. Gilmore

POLITICAL SKILL AT WORK

"Only in America do we use the word 'politics' to describe the process so well; 'poli' in Latin meaning 'many' and 'tics' meaning 'blood-sucking creatures!'" Mention politics or political skill to many managers and their reaction may be, "Why play those unprofessional games?" Although political skill usually carries a negative connotation, we do not see it that way. In fact, we believe effective use of political skill will become increasingly important to a manager's career. Consider the following situation. You are recently assigned to work on a project management team that has an ineffective yet high-ranking leader. Furthermore, your team has a complex task to complete within a tight deadline. The successful completion of the project will have a direct effect on your career. What can you do to overcome the deficiencies of the ineffective leader and enhance team performance?

This situation calls for the effective use of political skill because you have no authority over the team leader. It also exemplifies a major trend—organizations are becoming increasingly more social in nature. Managers and employees don't spend their time at work toiling at individual tasks and duties that isolate them from others. Instead, they coordinate their efforts with others on teams, communicate directly with customers or clients, or reflect managerial skills aimed at negotiation, coordination, or facilitation of others. Such efforts require well-developed social or interpersonal skills, and indeed, such skills are in great demand for jobs at all levels of organizations. Reliance on traditional authority and hierarchical structures to accomplish work has given way to team-based management, and the social skills necessary to effectively facilitate, coach, and orchestrate interaction-based outcomes.

In this article, we refine and further develop the notion of "political skill," and suggest how it is absolutely critical to job and career success in organizations today. Political

Reprinted from *Organizational Dynamics*, vol. 28, no. 4, Gerald R. Ferris, Pamela L. Perrewe, William P. Anthony, and David C. Gilmore, "Political Skill at Work," pp. 25–37, copyright 2000, with permission from Elsevier Science.

skill is an interpersonal style that combines social awareness with the ability to communicate well. People who practice this skill behave in a disarmingly charming and engaging manner that inspires confidence, trust, and sincerity. We also discuss how political skill is related to and differentiated from a host of other social skill concepts. Industrial psychologists and management consultants have spent a lot of time trying to identify knowledge, skills, and abilities that are predictive of job performance. We argue that political skill, along with general mental ability (i.e., intelligence), represent compatible (yet distinct) sets of adaptability-enhancing abilities. These abilities combine to form a personal portfolio necessary for success in a broad array of jobs in what we are witnessing as highly dynamic organizational environments that require flexibility in their human resources.

DYNAMIC ORGANIZATIONAL ENVIRONMENTS

People interested in careers in human resources management used to respond to questions concerning their choice of occupation by saying, "I want to work with people." Implying that the only way we can work with people in organizations is to work in the human resources department is, of course, absurd. Organizations, by definition, are collections of people working collaboratively, often on interdependent tasks, but certainly under a common set of goals and objectives. However, it was more common decades ago to find people working on jobs whereby they interacted much more with machinery or data than with people. Think of the traditional automobile assembly line.

Work environments have changed dramatically, particularly within the past twenty years, as organizations have realized nothing short of monumental transformations. In efforts to increase their competitive positions, organizations have engaged in extensive downsizing and restructuring, resulting in flatter, more rectangular structures with coordination and control mechanisms operating more horizontally than vertically. In such structures, hierarchy has been replaced with information technology, team-based work structures, and norms and controls based on the organization's culture. Employees are expected to perform in fluid and changing sets of roles instead of the static and rigid boundaries formerly placed around jobs and job descriptions. Furthermore, the demise of the bureaucratic structure and adoption of more adaptable, flexible forms has removed the barriers top management enjoyed from the division of labor and chain of command.

Consider this example experienced by one of the authors. An electronics plant that produced high-tech radios for the military switched from a typical assembly line process to produce the radios to a team-based management approach. Instead of sitting at their individual work stations all day as the radio parts passed by, workers formed product assembly teams. Teams were not only assigned the responsibility of assembling component radio parts and the entire radio; they were also given the responsibility of managing their own quality control. Employees in these different work structures need to exercise not just job knowledge, but also social skills aimed at working effectively with and through others. Furthermore, the supervisor role in such contexts has changed from direct and immediate monitoring and control to one involving coaching and facilitation of the team's efforts. This scenario has been repeated countless times in numerous industries such as electronics, automotive, steel, and even health care.

We are indeed seeing the rise of the more open, "social organization," where management is expected to be more visible and in touch with what is going on, and employees are insisting on more "face time"—where they can interact directly with each other in teams and with those from whom they need decisions and action. With such increased interpersonal interaction in organizations, social skill and political skill, specifically, are being seen as increasingly important.

SOCIAL SKILL IN ORGANIZATIONS

For most jobs today, the very nature of effective performance is some combination of required tasks and duties, but also—and at least as important, if not more—the demonstration of extra-role or contextual performance. Although the interpersonal skill of communication has always been important, other social skills such as facilitating, coaching, influencing, and coordinating with others are now being recognized as important. Indeed, working with and through others is critical for most jobs, certainly for managers. In fact, recent research from the Center for Creative Leadership reports that one of the leading causes of "management derailment" is lack of good interpersonal skills. Executive coaches today, assigned to work with managers on skill deficiencies, report that most of their time is spent on the development of social and political skills.

Interest in social skill has been growing in recent years, and it has been presented under labels like social intelligence, emotional intelligence, ego resiliency, self-monitoring, and practical intelligence. Although each of these purports to assess something a little different from one another, it is fair to characterize all of them as part of this general category of social skill that indicates a facility in interactions with others. However, none of these forms of social skill was developed explicitly to address interpersonal interactions in organizational settings. Although much about the social skill exhibited in everyday life can be generalized to work environments, there are also some unique contextual dynamics in work organizations that suggest a type of social skill is needed which is developed in the context of organizational social and political realities. However, before explicitly considering the nature of political skill, we will examine some of these related forms of social skill.

Types of Social Skill

Social Intelligence

A concept dating back to 1920, social intelligence very simply refers to the ability to understand and manage people. Despite decades of failure to develop an acceptable way to measure social intelligence, the construct remains alive and well in theory, particularly in light of efforts to expand our views of intelligence beyond I.Q. This concept probably first introduced the notion that there is more than one way (i.e., I.Q.) to be intelligent and that social astuteness might contribute to success in aspects of life that extend beyond classroom learning contexts. We argue that general social intelligence plays a dominant role in political skill. Political skill is more specific to the work setting and deals with understanding and managing people in work or organizational settings. Furthermore, we see political skill as focusing on both the behaviors to exhibit, but at least if not more important, the style employed to make the behaviors convincing and effective.

Emotional Intelligence

Considerable interest has been generated in just the past few years in the concept of emotional intelligence, which generally refers to the ability to monitor one's own and others feelings and emotions, and to use this information in the demonstration and regulation of emotions. More specifically, emotional intelligence can be viewed as involving the ability to control impulses and delay gratification, to regulate one's moods, and to be able to empathize. Controlling and regulating emotions is, indeed, an important part of social skill; however, there are other aspects, such as building and leveraging social capital, which we discuss later as part of political skill.

Ego-Resiliency

Ego-resiliency is a form of social skill that fundamentally contributes to effective environmental adaptation through the capacity for self-regulation of behavior to different and changing environmental demands or cues. This concept includes the components of emotional self-regulation, adaptive impulse control, social intelligence, and a sense of self-efficacy (i.e., individuals' beliefs in their ability to execute courses of action required for successful performance). The ability to adapt well to different social situations is seen as contributing to political skill.

Social Self-Efficacy

Another type of social skill is social self-efficacy, which refers to judgments of personal capability in social interactions and contexts. People high in social self-efficacy believe they can control the outcomes of social interactions. Those low on this construct, on the other hand, believe they lack the ability to master social interactions, regardless of their actual level of social competence or knowledge of socially appropriate behavior. Thus, social self-efficacy is a basic belief or confidence in one's ability to control social situations, which contributes to an optimistic attitude and a positive demeanor, both of which contribute to effectiveness in social situations. Political skill mirrors the concept of social self-efficacy; however, political skill is concerned with the unique contexts and interactions within the organizational realm as well as effecting change in organizations.

Self-Monitoring

People high in self-monitoring are skilled at knowing what is socially appropriate in particular situations. They demonstrate the ability to control their emotional expression, and they are capable of using these abilities effectively to create desired impressions. Thus, self-monitoring represents a type of social skill that focuses on the effective demonstration of situation-appropriate social behavior, but also reflects the unique skill of being able to read, interpret, and understand social situations. High self-monitoring social style is one that attempts to present the appropriate type of person called for in every situation. People with this orientation are sensitive and responsive to interpersonal cues to situational appropriateness. Political skill differs from self-monitoring in that political skill is often used to effect change in the desired manner, whereas self-monitoring describes individuals' attempts to behave in a socially appropriate fashion.

Tacit Knowledge and Practical Intelligence

Tacit knowledge refers to action-oriented relevant knowledge that allows people to achieve goals they personally value. It is knowledge acquired without the help of others—in other words, learned on one's own. It is procedural in nature (how to), and it is directly related to goal attainment. Tacit knowledge is related to practical intelligence, or common sense, and it relies on the unspoken rules one finds in the workplace. Another word for this is "savvy." Tacit knowledge and practical intelligence are closely related to each other and to political skill. Simply, if one has this knowledge, one is more likely to be able to demonstrate political skill. Thus, political skill is largely based on one's tacit knowledge and practical intelligence.

To summarize, we conceptualize political skill as a distinct type of social skill. We also see other types of social skills as influencing political skill. Figure 23.1 graphically depicts our conceptualization of political skill and other social skill concepts. As can be seen, although the various types of social skills are related to and may influence political skill, we believe political skill is a distinct concept that warrants attention in organizations.

THE NATURE OF POLITICAL SKILL

Many subscribe to the belief that organizations are inherently political arenas—where competing interest groups, scarce resources, coalition building, and the exercise of power and influence best characterize such environments, and the way things get done. To succeed and be effective in such organizations, it seems that people must possess intuitive savvy concerning what behaviors to demonstrate in particular situations. Indeed, bookstore shelves are full of books that identify political influence tactics and behaviors designed to make one effective at office politics. Furthermore, an extensive

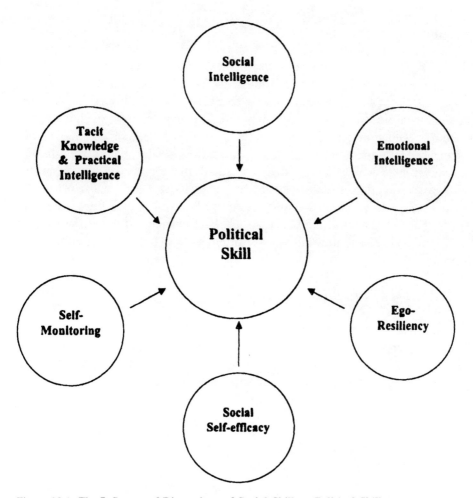

Figure 23.1. **The Influence of Dimensions of Social Skill on Political Skill**

body of work now exists showing that employment decisions such as personnel selection, performance evaluation, and promotions tend to be quite political in nature.

However, what has been missing is an understanding of how the interpersonal style with which the political influence attempts are carried out is absolutely essential to the success of such efforts. If an appreciation of which behaviors or tactics to exhibit were sufficient for effective influence attempts, we would see less management derailment and more effective supervisor-employee relationships. The style or execution of the influence behaviors in organizations is a critical missing piece, and it represents a special type of social competency and astuteness we refer to as political skill.

We define political skill as an interpersonal style construct that combines social astuteness with the ability to relate well, and otherwise demonstrate situationally appropriate behavior in a disarmingly charming and engaging manner that inspires confidence, trust, sincerity, and genuineness. We suggest that people high in political skill not only know precisely what to do in different social situations at work, but they know exactly how to do it in a sincere manner that disguises any potentially manipulative motives and renders the influence attempt successful. Political skill differs from other types of social skills in that political skill is specific to interactions aimed at achieving success in organizations. Clearly, these interactions may take place outside of the organizational context (e.g., a wedding reception), however, the goal is still organizational influence and success.

The use of political skill is not limited to "face-to-face" interactions. Technological advances have given impetus to a host of communication modes such as electronic mail and voice mail. People high in political skill are able to express emotion in a genuine and convincing manner via electronic forms of communication, through such means as tone of voice, as well as in their written communication. Thus, we are not simply referring to the ability to demonstrate particular behaviors that might be regarded as contributing to effective interpersonal interactions. Instead, political skill allows people to create synergy among discrete behaviors that transcends the simple sum of the parts to realize a set of interpersonal dynamics and effective execution that results in personal and career success.

Political skill, therefore, is not a single trait or skill. Rather, it reflects an integrated composite of internally consistent and mutually reinforcing and compatible skills and abilities that create a synergistic social dynamic that defies precise description. This is why we refer to it as a style-type of component, because the term style is defined in a manner that reflects best what we mean by political skill. The dictionary defines style as: (1) "a manner or mode of expression in language; way of putting thoughts into words," or (2) "specific or characteristic manner of expression, execution, construction, or design in art, period, work, employment, etc."

Additionally, we believe political skill is inherent in a person to some extent, but we also contend that it can be developed or shaped. This might sound as if we are hedging or trying to have it both ways. However, the integration of dispositional and situational perspectives on behavior reflects a more contemporary view, in contrast to the prior, mutually exclusive, trait-versus-situation approaches. So, we believe one is likely born with a predisposition toward political skill, but that without proper environmental stimuli or precipitants, this set of skills may never be fully realized. Furthermore, the very nature and effectiveness of political skill relies upon the ability to adjust one's behavior to the nuances and environmental demands of particular situations. In this sense, political skill contributes to the behavioral flexibility so important in today's dynamic organizational environments—similar to the way in which general mental ability or intelligence contributes to cognitive flexibility. We view both types of flexibility as critical to effectiveness, though cognitive flexibility seems less amenable to training. As we discuss later in this article, we see the development of political skill as a potentially new area of interest and activity in management development programs and in hiring and promotion decisions.

We believe that political skill has a direct effect on the reactions and evaluations of others because of its effective combination of social astuteness about what to do, but also the ability to do it in an appropriate way. More analytically, political skill can be seen to also play a facilitative role in the effective execution of a number of types of interpersonal behaviors. In this respect, we might characterize political skill as the "BASF of interpersonal relations." Like the advertisement for the large chemical company—"We don't make a lot of the products you buy. We make a lot of the products you buy better"—we would suggest that political skill doesn't make the interpersonal influence behavior, it makes the influence behavior better.

SOCIAL AND REPUTATIONAL CAPITAL

Our discussion of how political skill makes people more successful at work, to this point, has focused on the social savvy and astuteness one exhibits in face-to-face interactions. This is important, and a key aspect of how political skill leads to job and career success, but it does not tell the whole story. Another quite important feature of political skill dynamics relates to how people accumulate forms of personal, nonfinancial capital. Labor economists discuss the importance of human capital variables (e.g., education, skills, etc.) in understanding wage differentials among employees. Furthermore, organizations increasingly are attempting to develop sustained competitive advantage from the invisible assets of organizational knowledge and information commonly referred to as intellectual capital.

We now turn to two other forms of nonfinancial capital to illustrate our point about political skill dynamics. Charles Fombrun has done some interesting work on corporate reputation, and how organizations that enhance their reputations build "reputational capital"—the increased value realized by a firm that leads the consumer public to buy its products or services, leads investors to buy its stock, and talented job candidates to seek employment there. We believe these same attributes of companies also apply to individuals who are concerned about their reputations, make investments in the development of their reputations, and hope for a good return on such investments. Indeed, this perspective reflects the metaphor of the individual employee as a private enterprise (i.e., "Me, Inc."), which attempts to make sound investments in the creation of a diversified portfolio that can reap large returns in the form of job and career success. Another important element in this portfolio is the creation of what has been referred to as social capital, or the extensive networks of connections and alliances one forms with others. Personal reputation, we believe, both contributes to the accumulation of social capital, and it is also enhanced by it.

This personal, nonfinancial capital perspective on employees is useful for our understanding of political skill. We suggest that people high in political skill are quite shrewd and calculating about the personal investments they make and the social connections they form, inspiring trust and confidence in others that allows them to effectively leverage social and reputational capital to maximize job and career success. Reputation, indeed, has been appropriately characterized as more of a political than a scientific concept, and we argue that those who are successful at developing and maintaining high quality reputations do so with political skill.

JOB AND CAREER SUCCESS WITH POLITICAL SKILL

Political skill has been argued to be a critical factor in managerial effectiveness, and some research has provided support for these notions. Others have suggested that political skill is one of the most prominent differentiating qualities in women who succeed in managerial careers, thus breaking the glass ceiling. Yet other recent work has argued that "political skill deficiency" may be responsible for the failure of women and ethnic/racial minorities to make progress in organizations (e.g., salary progression, promotions, and career advancement), thus posing an alternative explanation for employment discrimination. These "intangibles" are important for long-term career success. However, this latter explanation characterized political skill as focusing on learning the informal rules of the game, which are passed on selectively by the dominant coalition in efforts to perpetuate the status quo. Therefore, although this explanation implicitly makes reference to the style of behavioral presentation, it tends to focus much more on the types of behavior or the content of interpersonal interactions including networking, mentor selection, and maintaining visibility.

However, we suggest that political skill is critical to performance and success in a broad array of jobs at all levels of organizations. Indeed, one study recently reported that supervisor political skill was an important predictor of permanency or placement rate for foster children in a statewide child welfare system. The political skill of supervisors of 100 foster care teams, along with social worker caseload, significantly predicted permanency rate, which included adoptions, children reunited with their families, and children placed with a guardian. Apparently, supervisors higher in political skill more effectively orchestrated foster-care team member talents and dynamics, thus leading to more success in placement rates by the foster-care team.

Furthermore, in a recent study, we found that political skill played a pivotal role in the job performance ratings supervisors made of employees in the job of computer programmer at a large bank—not a job that we would expect to involve much social interaction, and thus one in which political skill might not be expected to affect job performance. In this study, we investigated the effects of personality traits (i.e., Agreeableness, Conscientiousness, Emotional Stability, Extraversion, and Openness to Experience—referred to as the Big Five or Five-Factor Model), intelligence or general mental ability, and political skill on supervisor ratings of employee performance.

Past research has found that intelligence best predicted task performance and personality traits best predicted contextual performance (i.e., job dedication and interpersonal facilitation). We found political skill to be the single strongest predictor of ALL performance ratings, completely dominating personality traits and intelligence, which were not significant predictors of any performance ratings. However, political skill in conjunction with intelligence affected both job performance ratings and salary more than political skill alone.

Therefore, we see the potential to suggest in the future that political skill as well as intelligence might serve as two generally effective predictors of performance across a broad array of jobs. Jobs will continue to change to emphasize social skills, flexibility, and adaptability. We see political skill and intelligence as enhancing adaptability and flexibility, yet in compatible but not overlapping ways. Intelligence may well contribute to cognitive or mental flexibility, whereas political skill may enhance behavioral flexibility. Both of these characteristics are critical to effectiveness in dynamic work environments, which maximize the need to embrace change and "thrive on chaos."

DEVELOPING AND BUILDING POLITICAL SKILL

As we note above in our discussion of the nature of political skill, we see it as a set of skills that are partially inherent in the person, yet can also be developed or enhanced. That is, people are probably born with the capacity for political skill, but it may never be realized to its fullest extent unless they find themselves in situations that call upon them to exercise it, and thus further hone the skill to perfection, or unless they engage in active efforts to train or develop the skill through management development programs. Therefore, we suggest there are both personnel selection and training implications for political skill.

As we continue to refine our understanding of political skill, we eventually believe that trained assessors in simulations, interviews, and assessment center–type contexts can make more focused and behaviorally specific assessments and evaluations of this construct. We see this as becoming more important as organizations seek to make more comprehensive, informed assessments of candidates for selection and promotion in organizations, particularly for managerial jobs where political skill is seen as necessary for job performance and effectiveness.

Methods for Political Skill Development

We believe that an important new area for human resource development programs, particularly at managerial levels, is the training of political skill. Because political skill involves both a social astuteness about which behaviors to demonstrate in particular contexts, and the delivery, execution, or presentation style component, we see such development programs as involving some focus on both content (i.e., what behaviors to exhibit in which situations), and process issues. Such process issues are typically best addressed through development methods that require active involvement of trainees in the learning or skill-building process. The first step to developing political skill is self-awareness and understanding of oneself. Next, political skill can be shaped and developed through established learning methods such as experiential exercises, cases, vicarious learning, role-playing, and communication skill training. Finally, periodic evaluation and feedback is recommended. Individuals who are politically inept are often unaware that their behavior might be offensive, tactless, or viewed as crass by others. One of the first developmental activities, therefore, should include self-assessment and understanding, with a particular focus on self-awareness.

Self-Assessment and Understanding

Better self-awareness can take place by understanding one's personality and how one makes decisions. Well-established personality assessment questionnaires include the Five-Factor Model and the Sixteen Personality Factor Questionnaire (16 PF). Both of these popular instruments can provide insight into stable individual personality dimensions that are useful in determining how individuals will respond to various organizational situations. Another well-respected and established self-assessment measure is the Myers-Briggs Type Indicator (MBTI). This instrument provides information regarding how individuals solve problems, make decisions, and their preferred interaction style.

Self-assessment might also be facilitated through 360-degree feedback instruments that are becoming very commonplace in management circles. Essentially, this process involves the collection of others' perceptions of how a manager's persona or behavior is perceived in an organizational context. These are only examples of methods and instruments organizations might want to consider for self-assessment purposes. These instruments do not, however, measure political skill directly.

Methods for Learning and Developing Political Skill

Political skill can be learned or developed in a variety of ways. Experiential exercises involve participants in role-playing and scenario simulations. For example, participants might be asked to role-play a particularly difficult situation—such as telling a superior that you believe him or her to be wrong about a particular decision. A simulation could be developed that could extend the role-play over a longer time period, with new factors and situations introduced in a give-and-take situation. This play-acting of a scenario would allow participants to see how their actions produce consequences over a period of time. Case analyses involve examining a particular case situation and discussing it as a group. For example, participants could read a case or watch a video depicting a situation in which an individual practiced particularly poor or ineffective political skill.

This could be contrasted with a situation where effective political skill was practiced. Vicarious learning (i.e., learning by observing others' behavior) is another recommended method for developing political skill. Specifically, assigning a trainee to work closely with a mentor or coach who is a master at political skill can help build political skill. This can be accomplished by putting the individual in a task force or committee that the mentor leads or by assigning the individual to a project of which the politically skilled person is in charge.

Dramaturgy is the method of providing participants the opportunity to learn from theatrical training. This training teaches them how to emote well (i.e., strategically showing emotions) and otherwise effectively execute roles and staged performances. Indeed, we have seen executives in the past make use of acting or drama classes to hone their delivery of information in speeches, managing impressions of sincere and genuine intentions.

Communication skills training is another method recommended for shaping political skill. Managers are clearly interested not just in what they say, but how they say it, and thus how the audience perceives and interprets the message. As the focal representative of organizations, managers are very aware of and concerned about the image they convey. They devote considerable time to their political skill development as it is exhibited through carefully crafted speeches, effective orchestration of the media in press conferences, and the image management literary masterpiece known as the corporate annual report.

A good example of the marriage of political skill and communication can be see in President Clinton. We see the political skill and communication style of President Clinton discussed by supporters and detractors alike, who marvel at his amazing capacity to emerge from adversity relatively unscathed. Careful examination of President Clinton's behavioral style in televised speeches, interviews, and press conferences reveals strategic use of pauses for effect, and carefully calculated emotion control to convey proper images that are impactful and believable. Indeed, this is not unlike the self-presentation strategy and emotion control of the TV anchorman played by the actor William Hurt in the movie *Broadcast News*.

Evaluation and Feedback

From time to time, individuals will need to have an evaluation on their improvement and progression on political skill. Evaluations by others such as the individual's supervisor, clients, colleagues, and even spouse would provide the necessary feedback. Of course, based on this evaluation, adjustments and new learning opportunities can be undertaken.

CONCLUSION

The use of political skill is becoming increasingly important in organizations as team-based management and related programs are implemented. Organizations, whereas not explicitly recognizing it and labeling it as such, have been selecting and promoting people based upon political skill. Political skill serves as a catalyst to enhance communication and effectively orchestrate the collective interpersonal interactions necessary for team and organization performance. Ultimately, successful people in many jobs have the political savvy to know when, what, and how to say "the right thing," and to do so in a disarmingly, charming and engaging manner that inspires confidence and trust. Many believe organizations to be inherently "political arenas." That being the case, we desperately need to develop the requisite set of skills necessary for performance and career success in such contexts. We see political skill as fundamental to performing well in dynamic organizational environments, because it allows people to effectively navigate these turbulent waters by providing the flexibility and adaptability necessary to be successful.

PART 4

Upward Influence

This set of readings completes our examination of organizational influence processes. Part 4, Upward Influence, examines those influence attempts that are directed at a target who occupies a role that is higher in the formal hierarchy than the influence agent. Often the target of an upward influence attempt is one's immediate boss, but it can be anyone senior to the person exerting influence.

In this final section we will highlight the differences between upward influence and the influence directions that have been covered in the preceding sections. The readings will focus on how upward influence is different from downward or lateral influence, with emphasis on differences in effective influence strategies for lower-level organization members who lack the position power or formal authority that would be available to higher-level members. Two subthemes emerge from our analysis of this power imbalance: (1) upward influence is often "political" because influence methods that are not organizationally-sanctioned need to be resorted to; and (2) one type of influence that lower-level participants frequently resort to is *impression management,* that is, managing appearances and the attributions of others. Indeed, three of the seven articles in this section are on the topic of impression management.

HOW IS UPWARD INFLUENCE DIFFERENT?

One obvious way in which upward influence tends to differ from downward influence involves the means available to the agent of influence. Certain bases of power that organizations typically provide to supervisors and managers—such as the ability to give or withhold rewards, issue orders, make decisions, and if necessary take punitive action—are less often available to subordinates than to seniors. This limits the repertoire of influence methods or tactics that the subordinate can reasonably employ. This is not to say that the subordinate is powerless. It simply means that s/he may have little recourse to such *positional* bases of power as coercion, rewards, or formal authority. Instead, the individual may need to rely more often on such *personal* bases of power as expertise or charisma, or may need to resort to persuasion or even manipulation (i.e., influencing a person to do what is desired without the person's awareness that he or she is a target of influence). As indicated above, one influence tactic that is often useful for achieving upward influence is *impression management.*

Before proceeding, we should acknowledge that there *are* circumstances in which lower-level employees do possess some of the positional-power resources that are usually reserved for their bosses. As Pfeffer (1997) noted, changes in organizations have made lateral and upward influence more important than in past times, as many organizations have flattened their hierarchies, taking out entire levels of management. Of late, there have been a number of innovations in organizations aimed at increasing the formal power of lower-level members to influence decisions that were once the exclusive prerogative of higher-level management. These include employee committees of the kind that have been integral to such "gainsharing" efforts as the Scanlon Plan (Collins 1995). Similar employee participation committees have emerged under many different names, have assumed different forms, and have performed different functions. These range from employee job enrichment teams or quality circles that examine issues like productivity, efficiency, and morale to employee communications committees that serve as sounding boards for issues of concern in the organization (Martin 1993).

In a similar vein, self-managed work teams have proliferated in organizations under the banner of the so-called employee empowerment movement. In Europe, formal mechanisms for the exercise of upward influence in organizations have long existed under the rubric of "industrial democracy." Formally established *works councils,* in such countries as Germany or Sweden, often enjoy very broadly-based powers to influence fundamental decisions in the workplace.

That having been said, we do not intend to focus on such formally-sanctioned aspects of upward influence in this section. While these issues are interesting in their own right—and they are certainly gaining in importance in a rapidly changing, global workplace—they fall outside the scope of this section. Our interest is specifically on those upward influence processes that are not built-in to organizational systems but, instead, are informal and unofficial. Such processes represent discretionary (as opposed to prescribed) behavior, on the part of the influence agent.

It would appear, almost by definition, that our deliberate focus on the informal and unofficial aspects of upward influence would lead us to an organizational-politics perspective on upward influence. This supposition is generally accurate. Clearly, those attempts at upward influence that are primarily intended to promote or protect the self-interest of the influence agent are closely associated with many scholarly definitions of organizational politics.

Even so, it is important to avoid the trap of considering upward influence and organizational politics as one and the same thing. On the contrary, there are instances of political behavior that are lateral or peer-to-peer (Farrell and Peterson 1982; Cobb 1986). Turning the issue on its head, we also observe political behavior by seniors which is aimed at their juniors (Drory and Romm 1990). Furthermore, Mayes and Allen (1977) argued that there are upward influence processes that are *not* political, that is, those upward influence attempts that use organizationally sanctioned means to help attain organizationally sanctioned ends. (We'll expand upon this point, below.) With these caveats in mind, then, let us move on to a consideration of organizational politics, per se.

ORGANIZATIONAL POLITICS—STILL A NEGLECTED TOPIC

As we pointed out in Part 1, only recently has the subject of organizational politics found its way into the formal education of students interested in learning about behavior in organizations. Unlike leadership and group influence processes, organizational politics was largely ignored for many years, despite what appears to have been a tacit admission of its existence in most organizations. At the time the first edition of this book was published, there was clearly a deficit in published academic research on organizational politics. This is epitomized in the introduction to the (1981) reading by Porter, Allen and Angle in this section, which notes that, of more than 1,700 research articles that had been published over a sixteen-year period, fewer than a dozen were on organizational politics.

It appears that the situation has improved somewhat in the intervening twenty years or so. For example, Kacmar and Baron (1999) were able to identify more than fifty articles that examined the political process in organizations, which had been published since Porter et al. made their observation. Others (Falbe and Yukl 1992; Farmer and Maslyn 1999; Pfeffer 1992) have also observed that there has been a growing recognition that a political-influence perspective is a useful way to study management processes. Still, we adhere to the view that organizational politics does not receive the amount of attention warranted by its prevalence or its importance. We believe that understanding political processes in organizations is essential to the education of students interested in organizations and their management. Indeed, we consider politics to be a central aspect of organizational behavior—an aspect which is part and parcel of many, if not all, upward influence processes. The rationale for this view is set forth in the Porter et al. reading in this section:

> It appears reasonable to say that, while not all (or even most) upward influence involves political behavior, most political behavior (in organizations) does involve upward influence. . . . [This] is based on the assumption that the typical object of influence will be someone or some group possessing more formal, legitimate power than the would-be political actor. While it is possible to cite clear exceptions to this proposition, we would, nevertheless, contend that the vast majority of political attempts at influence are in the upward direction.

The focus in Part 4, then, will highlight organizational politics as an interesting and crucial aspect of many upward influence process in organizational settings.

WHAT IS ORGANIZATIONAL POLITICS?

We tend to agree with the observation offered by Kacmar and Baron (1999, p. 2) that "Over the last thirty years, virtually as many definitions of organizational politics have been offered as there are articles on the topic." Mayes and Allen (1977) observed that political activities are difficult to define because what is termed political by one observer may not be viewed as political by another. Thus, it would probably be useful, here, to attempt to synthesize some of the more compelling definitions that have been offered, in order to try to reduce the level of construct confusion on organizational politics, and so we may attempt to share a common frame of reference with the reader as s/he encounters the readings in this section.

Historically, definitions of politics have often been so broad that in encompassing everything they explain next to nothing. For example, Martin and Sims (1956) asserted that, as politics is concerned with relationships of control or influence, everyone who exercises power must be a politician. Robbins (1998) has argued that any self-serving behavior by a member of an organization is political. In fact, over the years, Robbins has taken the position that, because all behavior is self-serving, all organizational behavior is political.

Burns (1961, p. 257) was only slightly less all-inclusive when he claimed that behavior could be considered political if ". . . others are made use of as resources in competitive situations." The implication, here is that organizational politics is essentially self-serving, with the additional quality that it involves "using others" in pursuit of ones own objectives. As reviewed by Kacmar and Baron (1999) self-serving objectives recurred as a central theme in a large number of definitions of organizational politics over the past twenty years or so. In their own synthesis of the literature, Kacmar and Baron offered the following definition:

> Organizational politics involves actions by individuals which are directed toward the goal of furthering their own self-interests without regard for the well-being of others or their organization. (1999, p. 4)

Our own view is closer to that of Mayes and Allen (1977), who disavowed any tendency toward overgeneralization in defining organizational politics. They took specific issue with Burns' (1961) approach to defining politics (and would presumably have taken issue with Kacmar and Baron) because it relies upon determining the intent of the actor, and this would raise some very difficult empirical problems. As Drory and Romm (1990) later noted, intent cannot be measured objectively—instead, its determination involves a process of attribution on the part of the observer.

Apart from these obvious empirical difficulties, whether or not behavior is self-serving may not be a very useful criterion for defining organizational politics. Obviously, it is very often the case that upward influence is self-serving—for example, where the employee attempts to influence his or her boss to provide outcomes that will satisfy the employee's personal needs or self-interests. This can include anything from getting a more desirable workspace (such as an office with windows), getting selected for a promotion, or any number of similar examples. On the other hand, not all upward influence is strictly self-serving. Some of the upward influence that is attempted by subordinates takes place in the course of routine working relationships, and is at least in part directed toward accomplishing organizational goals and objectives. Examples might include: getting the immediate superior to approve the purchase of a new laser printer; obtaining upper management approval or support for proceeding with a new product design; or perhaps construction of a new facility.

Even the latter examples may contain a component of self-interest. Mayes and Allen (1977) noted that "self-serving intent" is an imprecise criterion, because almost any action ultimately serves some self-interest—even those actions that also serve the purposes of the larger system. They opted, therefore, for a more rigorous approach to defining organizational politics—one based on observable criteria, which do not rely upon any special knowledge of the actor's intent. A basic requirement for such a definition would have to be that it must clearly discriminate between political and nonpolitical behavior.

Mayes and Allen also argued that a useful definition of organizational politics would not focus on outcomes alone, but would instead be construed in terms of process—specifically the process of *influence*. This is important because, as Drory and Romm (1990) observed, a political event must involve at least two parties—an initiator or actor, and a target or object of influence. An influence episode is a social event. Briefly stated, Mayes and Allen's definition of organizational politics is: ". . . the management of influence to obtain ends not sanctioned by the organization or to obtain sanctioned ends through non-sanctioned influence means" (1977, p. 675).

This definition allows for the existence of functional, as well as dysfunctional, political behavior. It also allows for influence behavior that would not be considered political at all. This is laid out in the accompanying 2 × 2 table (see Table P4.1).

As Table P4.1 shows, the political nature of an influence attempt depends, jointly, upon both *means* used and *ends* sought. As the table also indicates, both means and ends can be partitioned into two subsets: "organizationally sanctioned" and "not sanctioned by the organization." In combination, the means-ends criteria define whether an act is political or apolitical and, if the former, whether it is a functional or dysfunctional version of organizational politics.

This serves as a useful point-of-departure for our examination of the readings included in Part 4. Although the term "politics" appears in the titles of only two of the seven readings, and although we have been careful to avoid claiming that all upward influence is political, none of the material in this section strays very far from the domain of organizational politics.

THE READINGS IN PART 4

Although the first reading in this section ("Sources of Power of Lower Participants in Complex Organizations") is roughly forty years old, it has been widely influential. David Mechanic dispels any idea that only people in lofty positions possess power. As with many other writers on the subject of power, he argues that power is closely related to dependence. He contends that individuals within organizations can make others dependent upon them and thereby acquire power if they control access to information,

Table P4.1
Mayes and Allen's (1977) Organizational Politics Framework

Influence Means	Influence Ends	
	Organizationally Sanctioned	Not Organizationally Sanctioned
Organizationally sanctioned	Nonpolitical	Dysfunctionally political
Not organizationally sanctioned	Functionally political	Dysfunctionally political

persons, or instrumentalities (e.g., resources). Mechanic discusses how such factors as expertise, effort and interest, attractiveness, rules, coalitions, and location and position serve to increase the power of lower-level participants in an organization. In turn, this enables the lower-level participants to exert considerable influence over other higher-ranking individuals within the organization. This influence can be directed toward the attainment of organizational goals and objectives, or it can be directed toward the attainment of personal goals and self-interests of the lower participant.

In the second reading in Part 4, Lyman W. Porter, Robert L. Allen, and Harold L. Angle discuss the politics of upward influence in organizations from a micro, or "one-on-one" perspective. The definition of organizational politics presented by these authors is generally consistent with definitions presented by many mainstream scholars. A social influence attempt is political if the behavior: (1) is *discretionary;* (2) is intended to *promote or protect self-interests;* and (3) *threatens the self-interests of others.* It is important to emphasize that all of these elements must be present in order for an influence attempt to be considered "political."

It should also be noted that, for the purposes of this definition, "discretionary" behaviors are those that are *neither* mandatory *nor* prohibited by formal policies of the organization. On the other hand, they may be, and often are, incorporated into the system of informal *norms.* Strong political norms may exist, even though the organization's formal policies are silent on such matters. Porter et al. emphasize the importance of such political norms which may either foster or suppress attempts at political influence in organizations. However, it is important to note that their definition of politics is not premised on norms; only on official policies. That is, an influence attempt may be "political" if it is consonant with a norm that promotes such activity, but it may also be political if it is perpetrated *despite* a strong normative prohibition of such behaviors.

This does not in any way imply that norms are somehow "weaker" than formal policies. Anyone who has spent very much time in any organization should harbor little doubt about the importance of norms, particularly those which Schein (1968) termed *pivotal* (Schein's article is included as a reading in Part 3). Political norms can be highly influential in shaping political behaviors in organizations, although Porter et al. observe that it may be difficult for an organizational newcomer to learn what the political norms are in any given organization—particularly those norms that condone rather than condemn political behaviors.

Porter et al. emphasize the importance of context in shaping the level and type of upward political influence. Ambiguity, resource scarcity, and personal stake in the outcome are among the situational elements that are conducive to political activity. Individual differences that the influence agent brings to the situation, such as needs, personality, and risk propensity, seem equally important. Whether upward influence will even be attempted with a given target person is a function of the influence agent's analysis of risks and costs, given the relative power of the parties and the nature of their preexisting relationship and interaction history. The reading concludes with a classification scheme for methods of upward political influence that separates positive or negative sanctions from such "informational" methods as persuasion. The inclusion of manipulative persuasion among the informational methods is an extension of earlier writing on social influence.

The third article in Part 4, by David Kipnis and Stuart M. Schmidt ("Upward-Influence Styles: Relationship with Performance Evaluations, Salary, and Stress") builds upon the work of Perrault and Miles (1978), as well as their own stream of research on patterns of influence strategies (e.g., Kipnis, Schmidt, Wilkinson 1980; Kipnis and Schmidt 1983). These scholars were among the first to recognize that influence methods are often used in predictable combinations, rather than singly.

Based upon six previously identified influence strategies (*reason, friendliness, assertiveness, coalition, higher authority* and *bargaining*), Kipnis and Schmidt identified four prototypical upward-influence patterns. Two patterns were essentially all or nothing; the *shotgun* style used all six methods (but emphasized assertiveness and appeal to higher authority), while the *bystander* style tended to avoid all six methods. The other two clusters were, arguably, single-method influencers—the *ingratiator* used friendliness more than any other method, while the *tactician* favored reason over all other methods.

The four upward-influence patterns were the basis for investigating the relationships between upward-influence methods and performance ratings by the influence target. While Kipnis and Schmidt's results do indicate differences in these relationships, it can be argued that their research raises as many questions as it answers. For one thing, it is not clear whether the differences in performance ratings associated with different influence styles are the result of influence methods or simply reflect the fact that "favored" employees are able to use different methods from those used by employees who are relatively "out of favor" (i.e., a favored employee might be able to get away with bolder tactics than would an employee who is less well regarded). It is also not clear whether the differences between *shotgun* and *bystander* employees are really a difference in influence patterns at all, or whether they simply represent two different gross levels of aggressiveness as influence agents. (Alternately, the differences may simply reflect a response-set bias—a possibility that Kipnis and Schmidt attempt to refute.) Finally, it is not unlikely that some of the results were sample-specific. The content-validity of the influence methods included in the research has been challenged (Schriesheim and Hinkin 1990; Yukl and Falbe 1990), with the suggestion that the source for item generation (students) contributed to an overly narrow range of tactics considered.

These cautions are not intended to invalidate the study. Kipnis and Schmidt were clearly pioneers in linking influence styles with personal outcomes of the influence agent. By bringing the complexity of the issues in upward-influence research into clearer focus, Kipnis and Schmidt have made an important contribution to research by offering several tentative findings which help to define a broad and rich research agenda for the field. Indeed, reading this report provides considerable insight into the complexity of the several interrelated issues that arise in any investigation of upward-influence dynamics, and thus provides a sort of road map for the researcher of the future. As an example, Farmer and Maslyn (1995) were able to identify and verify three of the four influence patterns proposed by Kipnis and Schmidt, even though they used different methods and measures. The influence of Kipnis and Schmidt's research is also evident in having guided Wayne, Liden, Graf, and Ferris (1997) in their research, which elaborated and extended the Kipnis/Schmidt notion that variations in patterns of subordinate influence attempts are related to differences in supervisory perceptions of subordinate competence. The Kipnis and Schmidt reading, then, is an important nodal point in a network of related research that is continuing to develop and extend our understanding of the dynamics of upward influence.

The next three readings in this section address the issue of *impression management,* which is defined very generally as the tactics people use to influence the way they are perceived by others (ostensibly favorably). As put by Schlenker (1980):

> Impression management is a form of social influence. People affect their own outcomes by attempting to influence the impressions that others form of them. Through words and deeds, we leave impressions on others that shape how they approach and treat us. Controlling these impressions is a means of controlling others' actions, which, in turn, affect our own outcomes for better or worse. (p. 22)

On the face of it, one might expect impression management to be a preferred tactic of the type of upward influencer Kipnis and Schmidt termed "ingratiator" in the reading that immediately precedes this set. Collectively, these three readings portray impression management as a complex phenomenon—one that is multidimensional with respect to tactics, goals, and outcomes. This complexity appears at odds with the conventional wisdom, that is, that people engage in impression management, simply out of a desire to be liked by others.

"Upward Impression Management: Goals, Influence Strategies, and Consequences," by Asha Rao, Stuart M. Schmidt, and Lynda H. Murray, suggests that people who use impression management as an upward-influence tactic are often pursuing multiple goals (which are not always obviously related), and they tend to select a mix of influence strategies to fit that mix of goals. For example, their strategies can include reason and assertiveness, in addition to ingratiation, in order to create an intended impression of competence, rather than simply one of likeability.

An interesting implication of this research is that the *actual* impressions formed by seniors are often at variance with the intentions of the influencer. This is largely due to such factors as selective attention on the part of the target and the distorting effects of context factors that the influence agent may not control—and in fact may not even take into consideration. The result can be that impression management "backfires" and thus results in a negative appraisal, rather than the intended positive assessment.

Mark C. Bolino's article, "Citizenship and Impression Management: Good Soldiers or Good Actors?" looks at *organizational citizenship behaviors* (OCB) through a new—and some might say cynical—lens. Since Smith, Organ, and Near (1983) introduced the construct, OCB has been a very thoroughly researched topic. OCBs are behaviors that are not explicitly rewarded if performed and are not specifically punished if not performed. They fall outside prescribed role behaviors (e.g., job descriptions), and are thus strictly discretionary and are usually seen as contributions that go "beyond the call of duty."

Interestingly, Bolino points out that OCBs may be very difficult to distinguish from impression management. He goes on to present a set of researchable propositions regarding conditions under which impression-management behavior is more or less likely and how impression-management behaviors relate systematically to OCBs. The article concludes with a caution for managers—that is, that they need to learn to make accurate attributions regarding the underlying motives for their subordinates' OCBs—as well as some useful suggestions to help managers distinguish between employees who are *looking* good and those who are actually *being* good.

One frequent goal of upward impression management is the attainment of good performance ratings. The third impression-management article, "Effects of Impression Management on Performance Ratings: A Longitudinal Study" addresses this issue. Here, Sandy J. Wayne and Robert C. Liden present results from a longitudinal study of supervisor-subordinate pairs over a six-week period. Two specific aspects of impression management—self-presentation and other enhancement—were the focus for this research. That is, the research design distinguished between self-focused impression management (creating a favorable self-image) and supervisor-focused impression management (typically the use of flattery and similar other-enhancement tactics).

The research results tended to support the notion that perceived-similarity is at the heart of "successful" impression management, that is, impression management that has a favorable impact on supervisors' performance ratings. More specifically, impression management that led to supervisors' perceiving their subordinates as similar to themselves tended to lead to supervisors' *liking* the subordinates more.

The delayed effect of this dynamic is that, in the future, the supervisor is apt to perceive the subordinate's performance through a somewhat biased set of lenses—biased, that is, in favor of the subordinate. The important implication is that, while impression management is often intended to have immediate impacts on the target person, the *delayed* impacts may be at least as important, or perhaps even more important. This epitomizes the power of *primacy*. Under the principle of primacy, early mind-sets are not easily dislodged by new data—what happens instead is that new information (which may be somewhat ambiguous) becomes interpreted against what is already "known." As an upward-influence strategy, then, impression management can be very powerful because it can leverage its efforts through a process of perceptual generalization on the part of the target person. In other words, it may be possible to establish a general mindset on the part of the influence target so that he or she is predisposed to interpret future, similar, observations of the influence agent in a manner favorable to that influence agent—even in the absence of any additional impression-management efforts by the latter.

The last article in Part 4, "Ethical Perceptions of Organizational Politics: A Comparative Evaluation of American and Hong Kong Managers," returns our attention to the area of organizational politics. As we reviewed the literature on organizational influence processes that had appeared since the first edition of this book was published, we were sorely disappointed at the dearth of work on cross-cultural or international aspects of the topic. This article is one of but very few which we were able to identify that raise the highly important issue of differences in influence dynamics that may exist across national or cultural boundaries. This article also raises, for our consideration, the issue of ethical implications of upward organizational influence tactics. As with the cross-cultural dimension, this is a highly important—but often neglected—aspect of organizational influence processes.

Using the "Strategies of Upward Influence" instrument, David A. Ralston, Robert A. Giacalone and Robert H. Terpstra compared U.S. and Hong Kong managers with respect to their evaluations of the ethics or morality of eight different strategies of upward influence. Hypothesized differences between U.S. and Chinese managers' ethical evaluations of the range of possible upward-influence tactics were purportedly based on Hofstede's (1980) famous characterization of cross-cultural contrasts. Specifically, U.S. managers were expected to be more individualistic and lower in power-distance than their more collectivist Chinese counterparts. This was expected to lead the U.S. managers to favor tactics that focus on self-promotion while the Chinese would tend to favor more private or circuitous tactics.

In general, the results were in alignment with the rationale—U.S. managers appeared to give higher ethical marks to tactics that resemble the impression management tactics described in the preceding triad of articles in this section. Chinese managers, on the other hand, tended to favor information control or coercion. While this study's findings can hardly be described as definitive, the research raises some very important cross-cultural issues regarding organizational influence processes that have, to date, been almost completely ignored in the research literature. This is a research gap that needs to be addressed by organizational scholars.

ONE MORE TIME . . .

In order to integrate the many parts of an organization successfully, and to channel behaviors efficiently so that individual, subunit, and organizational goals can all be achieved, a manager must make effective use of power and the means of organizational influence. Although they are "intendedly rational" (Porter, Lawler, and Hackman 1975, p. 69), organizations are often less than straightforward in their functioning. Indeed, an organization is essentially a negotiated relationship among many participants—a relationship that is dynamic and often rather subtle.

Nowhere is this more evident than in the study of organizational influence processes, which are often informal and tend to occur in all directions—downward, laterally, and upward. Regardless of their position or organizational level, all organizational members are both potential targets and potential sources of influence. For these important reasons, we believe that the study of organizational influence processes is essential to the education of anyone who is anticipating or continuing a career in organizational management.

REFERENCES

Burns, T. (1961). Micropolitics: Mechanism of institutional change. *Administrative Science Quarterly* 6: 257–281.

Cobb, A.T. (1986). Informal influence in the formal organization: Psychological and situational correlates. *Group and Organization Studies* 11(3): 229–253.

Collins, D. (1995). Death of a Gainsharing Plan: Power Politics and Participatory Management. *Organizational Dynamics* 24(1): 23–37.

Drory, A., and Romm, T. (1990). The Definition of Organizational Politics: A Review. *Human Relations* 43(11): 1133–1154.

Falbe, C.M., and Yukl, G. (1991). Consequences for managers of using single influence tactics and combinations of tactics. *Academy of Management Journal* 35(3): 638–652.

Farmer, S.M., and Maslyn, J.M. (1999). Why are styles of upward influence neglected? Making the case for a configurational approach to influences. *Journal of Management* 25(5): 653–682.

Farrell, D., and Petersen. (1982). Patterns of political behavior in organizations. *Academy of Management Review* 7(3): 403–412.

Frost, P.J., and Hayes, D.C. (1979). An exploration in two cultures of a model of political behavior in organizations. In George W. England, Anant R. Negandhi, Bernhard Wilpert (eds). *Organizational Functioning in a Cross-Cultural Perspective*. Kent, OH: Kent State University Press.

Hofstede, G. (1980). *Culture's Consequences*. Beverly Hills, CA: Sage.

Kacmar, K.M., and Baron, R.A. (1999). Organizational politics: The state of the field, links to related processes, and an agenda for future research. In G. Ferris (ed.), *Research in Personnel and Human Resource Management*. Greenwich, CT: JAI.

Kipnis, D., and Schmidt, S. (1983). An Influence Perspective on Bargaining within Organizations. In M. Bazerman and R.J. Lewicki (eds.), *Negotiating in Organizations*. Beverly Hills, CA: Sage.

Kipnis, D., Schmidt, S.M., and Wilkinson, I. (1980). Intraorganizational influence tactics: Explorations in getting one's way. *Journal of Applied Psychology* 65(4) (August): 440–452.

Martin, C. (1993). 'Electromation' and its aftermath. *Employee Relations Law Journal* 19(1): 133–140.

Martin, J., and Sims. (1956). Power tactics. *Harvard Business Review* (November–December): 25–29.

Mayes, B.T., and Allen, R.W. (1977). Toward a definition of organizational politics. *The Academy of Management Review* 2(4): 672–678.

Perreault, W.D., and Miles, R.H. (1978). Influence strategy mixes in complex organizations. *Behavioral Science* 23(2): 86–98.

Pfeffer, J. (1992). *Managing with Power*. Boston, MA: Harvard Business School Press.

———. (1997). Developing and exercising power and influence. In J. Pfeffer (ed.), *New Directions in Organization Theory: Problems and Prospects*. New York: Oxford Press.

Porter, L.W., Lawler, E.E., III, and Hackman, J.R. (1975). *Behavior in Organizations*. New York: McGraw-Hill.

Robbins, S.P. (1998). *Organizational Behavior: Concepts, Controversies, Applications* (8th ed.). Upper Saddle River, NJ: Prentice-Hall.

Schein, E. (1968). Organizational socialization and the profession of management. *Sloan Management Review* 9(2): 1–16.

Schlenker, B.R. (1980). *Impression Management: The Self-concept, Social Identity, and Interpersonal Relations.* Monterey, CA: Brooks-Cole.

Schriesheim, C.A., and Hinkin, T.R. (1990). Influence tactics used by subordinates: A theoretical and empirical analysis and refinement of the Kipnis, Schmidt, and Wilkinson subscales. *Journal of Applied Psychology* 75(3): 246–257.

Smith, C.A., Organ, D.W., and Near, J.P. (1983). Organizational citizenship behavior: Its nature and antecedents. *Journal of Applied Psychology* 68(4): 653–663.

Wayne, S.J., Liden, R.C., Graf, I.K., and Ferris, G.R. (1997). The role of upward influence tactics in human resource decisions. *Personnel Psychology* 50(4): 979–1006.

Yukl, G., and Falbe, C.M. (1990). Influence tactics and objectives in upward, downward, and lateral influence attempts. *Journal of Applied Psychology* 75(2) (April): 132–140.

24

Sources of Power of Lower Participants in Complex Organizations

David Mechanic

It is not unusual for lower participants[1] in complex organizations to assume and wield considerable power and influence not associated with their formally defined positions within these organizations. In sociological terms they have considerable personal power but no authority. Such personal power is often attained, for example, by executive secretaries and accountants in business firms, by attendants in mental hospitals, and even by inmates in prisons. The personal power achieved by these lower participants does not necessarily result from unique personal characteristics, although these may be relevant, but results rather from particular aspects of their location within their organizations.

INFORMAL VERSUS FORMAL POWER

Within organizations the distribution of authority (institutionalized power) is closely if not perfectly correlated with the prestige of positions. Those who have argued for the independence of these variables[2] have taken their examples from diverse organizations and do not deal with situations where power is clearly comparable.[3] Thus when Bierstedt argues that Einstein had prestige but no power, and the policeman power but no prestige, it is apparent that he is comparing categories that are not comparable. Generally persons occupying high-ranking positions within organizations have more authority than those holding low-ranking positions.

One might ask what characterizes high-ranking positions within organizations. What is most evident, perhaps, is that lower participants recognize the right of higher-ranking participants to exercise power, and yield without difficulty to demands they regard as legitimate. Moreover, persons in high-ranking positions tend to have considerable access and control over information and persons both within and outside the organization, and to instrumentalities or resources. Although higher supervisory personnel may be isolated from the task activities of lower participants, they maintain access to them through formally established intermediary positions and exercise control through intermediary participants. There appears, therefore, to be a clear correlation between the prestige of positions within organizations and the extent to which they offer access to information, persons, and instrumentalities.

Since formal organizations tend to structure lines of access and communication, access should be a clue to institutional prestige. Yet access depends on variables other than those controlled by the formal structure of an organization, and this often makes the informal power structure that develops within organizations somewhat incongruent with the formally intended plan. It is these variables that allow work groups to limit production through norms that contravene the goals of the larger organization, that allow hospital attendants to thwart changes in the structure of a hospital, and that allow prison inmates to exercise some control over prison guards. Organizations, in a sense, are continuously at the mercy of their lower participants, and it is this fact that makes organizational power structure especially interesting to the sociologist and social psychologist.

Clarification of Definitions

The purpose of this paper is to present some hypotheses explaining why lower participants in organizations can often assume and wield considerable power which is not associated with their positions as formally defined within these organizations. For the purposes of this analysis the concepts "influence," "power," and "control" will be used synonymously. Moreover, we shall not be concerned with type of power, that is, whether the power is based on reward, punishment, identification, power to veto, or whatever.[4] Power will be defined as any force that results in behavior that would not have occurred if the force had not been present. We have defined power as a force rather than a relationship because it appears that much of what we mean by power is encompassed by the normative framework of an organization, and thus any analysis of power must take into consideration the power of norms as well as persons.

I shall also argue, following Thibaut and Kelley,[5] that power is closely related to dependence. To the extent that a person is dependent on another, he is potentially subject to the other person's power. Within organizations one makes others dependent upon him by controlling access to information, persons, and instrumentalities, which I shall define as follows:

a. *Information* includes knowledge of the organization, knowledge about persons; knowledge of the norms, procedures, techniques, and so forth.
b. *Persons* include anyone within the organization or anyone outside the organization upon whom the organization is in some way dependent.
c. *Instrumentalities* include any aspect of the physical plant of the organization or its resources (equipment, machines, money, and so on).

Power is a function not only of the extent to which a person controls information, persons, and instrumentalities, but also of the importance of the various attributes he controls.[6]

Finally, following Dahl,[7] we shall agree that comparisons of power among persons should, as far as possible, utilize comparable units. Thus we shall strive for clarification by attempting to oversimplify organizational processes; the goal is to set up a number of hypothetical statements of the relationship between variables taken two at a time, "all other factors being assumed to remain constant."

A Classic Example

Like many other aspects of organizational theory, one can find a classic statement of our problem in Weber's discussion of the political bureaucracy. Weber indicated the extent to which bureaucrats may have considerable power over political incumbents, as a result, in part, of their permanence within the political bureaucracy, as contrasted to public officials, who are replaced rather frequently.[8] Weber noted how the low-ranking bureaucrat becomes familiar with the organization—its rules and operations, the work flow, and so on, which gives him considerable power over the new political incumbent, who might have higher rank but is not as familiar with the organization. While Weber does not directly state the point, his analysis suggests that bureaucratic permanence has some relationship to increased access to persons, information, and instrumentalities. To state the hypothesis suggested somewhat more formally:

> *Hypothesis 1:* Other factors remaining constant, organizational power is related to access to persons, information, and instrumentalities.
>
> *Hypothesis 2:* Other factors remaining constant, as a participant's length of time in an organization increases, he has increased access to persons, information, and instrumentalities.

While these hypotheses are obvious, they do suggest that a careful scrutiny of the organizational literature, especially that dealing with the power or counterpower of lower participants, might lead to further formalized statements, some considerably less obvious than the ones stated. This kind of hypothesis formation is treated later in the paper, but at this point I would like to place the discussion of power within a larger theoretical context and discuss the relevance of role theory to the study of power processes.

IMPLICATIONS OF ROLE THEORY FOR THE STUDY OF POWER

There are many points of departure for the study of power processes within organizations. An investigator might view influence in terms of its sources and strategies; he might undertake a study of the flow of influence; he might concentrate on the structure of organizations, seeing to what extent regularities in behavior might be explained through the study of norms, roles, and traditions; and, finally, more psychologically oriented investigators might concentrate on the recipients of influence and the factors affecting susceptibility to influence attempts. Each of these points of departure leads to different theoretical emphases. For our purposes the most important emphasis is that presented by role theorists.

Role theorists approach the question of influence and power in identities within specific social contexts like families, hospitals, and business firms. The underlying premise of most role theorists is that a large proportion of all behavior is brought about through socialization within specific organizations, and much behavior is routine and established through learning the traditional modes of adaptation in dealing with specific tasks. Thus the positions persons occupy in an organization account for much of their behavior. Norms and roles serve as mediating forces in influence processes.

While role theorists have argued much about vocabulary, the basic premises underlying their thought have been rather consistent. The argument is essentially that knowledge of one's identity or social position is a powerful index of the expectations such a person is likely to face in various social situations. Since behavior tends to be highly correlated with expectations, prediction of behavior is therefore possible. The approach of role theorists to the study of behavior within organizations is of particular merit in that it provides a consistent set of concepts which is useful analytically in describing recruitment, socialization, interaction, and personality, as well as the formal structure of organizations. Thus the concept of role is one of the few concepts clearly linking social structure, social process, and social character.

Many problems pertaining to role theory have been raised. At times it is not clear whether role is regarded as a real entity, a theoretical construct, or both. Moreover, Gross has raised the issue of role consensus, that is, the extent to which the expectations impinging upon a position are held in common by persons occupying reciprocal positions to the one in question.[9] Merton has attempted to deal with inevitable inconsistencies in expectations of role occupants by introducing the concept of role-set which treats differences in expectations as resulting, in part, from the fact that any position is differently related to a number of reciprocal positions.[10] Furthermore, Goffman has criticized role theory lot—its failure to deal adequately with commitment to roles[11]— a factor which Etzioni has found to be related intimately to the kind of power exercised in organizations.[12] Perhaps these various criticisms directed at role theory reflect its importance as well as its deficiencies, and despite the difficulties involved in role analysis, the concept of role may prove useful in various ways.

Role theory is useful in emphasizing the extent to which influence and power can be exercised without conflict. This occurs when power is integrated with a legitimate order, when sentiments are held in common, and when there are adequate mechanisms for introducing persons into the system and training them to recognize, accept, and value the legitimacy of control within the organization. By providing the conditions whereby participants within an organization may internalize the norms, these generalized rules, values, and sentiments serve as substitutes for interpersonal influence and make the workings of the organization more agreeable and pleasant for all.

It should be clear that lower participants will be more likely to circumvent higher authority, other factors remaining constant, when the mandates of those in power, if not the authority itself, are regarded as illegitimate. Thus as Etzioni points out, when lower participants become alienated from the organization, coercive power is likely to be required if its formal mandates are to be fulfilled.[13]

Moreover, all organizations must maintain control over lower participants. To the extent that lower participants fail to recognize the legitimacy of power, or believe that sanctions cannot or will not be exercised when violations occur, the organization loses, to some extent, its ability to control their behavior. Moreover, insofar as higher participants can create the impression that they can or will exert sanctions above their actual willingness to use such sanctions, control over lower participants will increase. It is usually to the advantage of an organization to externalize and impersonalize controls, however, and if possible to develop positive sentiments toward its rules.

In other words, an effective organization can control its participants in such a way as to make it hardly perceivable that it exercises the control that it does. It seeks commitment from lower participants, and when commitment is obtained, surveillance can be relaxed. On the other hand, when the power of lower participants in organizations is considered, it often appears to be clearly divorced from the traditions, norms, and goals and sentiments of the organization as a whole. Lower participants do not usually achieve control by using the role structure of the organization, but rather by circumventing, sabotaging, and manipulating it.

SOURCES OF POWER OF LOWER PARTICIPANTS

The most effective way for lower participants to achieve power is to obtain, maintain, and control access to persons, information, and instrumentalities. To the extent that this can be accomplished, lower participants make higher-ranking participants dependent upon them. Thus dependence together with the manipulation of the dependency relationship is the key to the power of lower participants.

A number of examples can be cited which illustrate the preceding point. Scheff, for example, reports on the failure of a state mental hospital to bring about intended reform because of the opposition of hospital attendants.[14] He noted that the power of hospital attendants was largely a result of the dependence of ward physicians on attendants. This dependence resulted from the physician's short tenure, his lack of interest in administration, and the large amount of administrative responsibility he had to assume. An implicit trading agreement developed between physicians and attendants, whereby attendants would take on some of the responsibilities and obligations of the ward physician in return for increased power in decision-making processes concerning patients. Failure of the ward physician to honor his part of the agreement resulted in information being withheld, disobedience, lack of cooperation, and unwillingness of the attendants to serve as a barrier between the physician and a ward full of patients demanding attention and recognition. When the attendant withheld cooperation, the physician had difficulty in making a graceful entrance and departure from the ward, in handling necessary paper work (officially his responsibility), and in obtaining information needed to deal adequately with daily treatment and behavior problems. When attendants opposed change, they could wield influence by refusing to assume responsibilities officially assigned to the physician.

Similarly, Sykes describes the dependence of prison guards on inmates and the power obtained by inmates over guards.[15] He suggests that although guards could report inmates for disobedience, frequent reports would give prison officials the impression that the guard was unable to command obedience. The guard, therefore, had some stake in ensuring the good behavior of prisoners without use of formal sanctions against them. The result was a trading agreement whereby the guard allowed violations of certain rules in return for cooperative behavior. A similar situation is found in respect to officers in the Armed Services or foremen in industry. To the extent that they require formal sanctions to bring about cooperation, they are usually perceived by their superiors as less valuable to the organization. For a good leader is expected to command obedience, at least, if not commitment.

FACTORS AFFECTING POWER

Expertise

Increasing specialization and organizational growth has made the expert or staff person important. The expert maintains power because high-ranking persons in the organization are dependent upon him for his special skills and access to certain kinds of information. One possible reason for lawyers obtaining many high governmental offices is that they are likely to have access to rather specialized but highly important means to organizational goals.[16] We can state these ideas in hypotheses, as follows:

> *Hypothesis 3:* Other factors remaining constant, to the extent that a low-ranking participant has important expert knowledge not available to high-ranking participants, he is likely to have power over them.

Power stemming from expertise, however, is likely to be limited unless it is difficult to replace the expert. This leads to two further hypotheses:

> *Hypothesis 4:* Other factors remaining constant, a person difficult to replace will have greater power than a person easily replaceable.
> *Hypothesis 5:* Other factors remaining constant, experts will be more difficult to replace than nonexperts.

While persons having expertise are likely to be fairly high-ranking participants in an organization, the same hypotheses that explain the power of lower participants are relevant in explaining the comparative power positions of intermediate- and high-ranking persons.

The application of our hypothesis about expertise is clearly relevant if we look at certain organizational issues. For example, the merits of medical versus lay hospital administrators are often debated. It should be clear, however, that all other factors remaining unchanged, the medical administrator has clear advantage over the lay administrator. Where lay administrators receive preference, there is an implicit assumption that the lay person is better at administrative duties. This may be empirically valid but is not necessarily so. The special expert knowledge of the medical administrator stems from his ability legitimately to oppose a physician who contests an administrative decision on the basis of medical necessity. Usually hospitals are viewed primarily as universalistic in orientation both by the general public and most of their participants. Thus medical necessity usually takes precedence over management policies, a factor contributing to the poor financial position of most hospitals. The lay administrator is not in a position to contest such claims independently, since he usually lacks the basis for evaluation of the medical problems involved and also lacks official recognition of his competence to make such decisions. If the lay administrator is to evaluate these claims adequately on the basis of professional necessity, he must have a group of medical consultants or a committee of medical men to serve as a buffer between medical staff and the lay administration.

As a result of growing specialization, expertise is increasingly important in organizations. As the complexity of organizational tasks increases, and as organizations grow in size, there is a limit to responsibility that can be efficiently exercised by one person. Delegation of responsibility occurs, experts and specialists are brought in to provide information and research, and the higher participants become dependent upon them. Experts have tremendous potentialities for power by withholding information, providing incorrect information, and so on, and to the extent that experts are dissatisfied, the probability of organizational sabotage increases.

Effort and Interest

The extent to which lower participants may exercise power depends in part on their willingness to exert effort in areas where higher-ranking participants are often reluctant to participate. Effort exerted is directly related to the degree of interest one has in an area.

> *Hypothesis 6:* Other factors remaining constant, there is a direct relationship between the amount of effort a person is willing to exert in an area and the power he can command.

For example, secretarial staffs in universities often have power to make decisions about the purchase and allocation of supplies, the allocation of their services, the scheduling of classes, and, at times, the disposition of student complaints. Such control may in some instances lead to sanctions against a professor by polite reluctance to furnish supplies, ignoring his preferences for the scheduling of classes, and giving others preference in the allocation of services. While the power to make such decisions may easily be removed from the jurisdiction of the lower participant, it can only be accomplished at a cost—the willingness to allocate time and effort to the decisions dealing with these matters. To the extent that responsibilities are delegated to lower participants, a certain degree of power is likely to accompany the responsibility. Also, should the lower participant see his perceived rights in jeopardy, he may sabotage the system in various ways.

Let us visualize a hypothetical situation where a department concludes that secretarial services are being allocated on a prejudicial basis as a result of complaints to the chairman of the department by several of the younger faculty. Let us also assume that, when the complaint is investigated, it is found to be substantially correct; that is, some of the younger faculty have difficulty obtaining secretarial services because of preferences among the secretarial staff. If in attempting to eliminate discretion by the secretarial staff, the chairman establishes a rule ordering the allocation of services on the basis of the order in which work appears, the rule can easily be made ineffective by complete conformity to it. Deadlines for papers, examinations, and the like will occur, and flexibility in the allocation of services is required if these deadlines are to be met. Thus the need for flexibility can be made to conflict with the rule by a staff usually not untalented in such operations.

When an organization gives discretion to lower participants, it is usually trading the power of discretion for needed flexibility. The cost of constant surveillance is too high, and the effort required too great; it is very often much easier for all concerned to allow the secretary discretion in return for cooperation and not too great an abuse of power.

Hypothesis 7: Other factors remaining constant, the less effort and interest higher-ranking participants are willing to devote to a task, the more likely are lower participants to obtain power relevant to this task.

Attractiveness

Another personal attribute associated with the power of low-ranking persons in an organization is attractiveness or what some call "personality." People who are viewed as attractive are more likely to obtain access to persons, and, once such access is gained, they may be more likely to succeed in promoting a cause. But once again dependence is the key to the power of attractiveness, for whether a person is dependent upon another for a service he provides, or for approval or affection, what is most relevant is the relational bond which is highly valued.

Hypothesis 8: Other factors remaining constant, the more attractive a person, the more likely he is to obtain access to persons and control over these persons.

Location and Position

In any organization the person's location in physical space and position in social space are important factors influencing access to persons, information, and instrumentalities.[17] Propinquity affects the opportunities for interaction, as well as one's position within a communication network. Although these are somewhat separate factors, we shall refer to their combined effect as centrality[18] within the organization.

> *Hypothesis 9:* Other factors remaining constant, the more central a person is in an organization, the greater is his access to persons, information, and instrumentalities.

Some low participants may have great centrality within an organization. An executive's or university president's secretary not only has access, but often controls access in making appointments and scheduling events. Although she may have no great formal authority, she may have considerable power.

Coalitions

It should be clear that the variables we are considering are at different levels of analysis; some of them define attributes of persons, while others define attributes of communication and organization. Power processes within organizations are particularly interesting in that there are many channels of power and ways of achieving it.

In complex organizations different occupational groups attend to different functions, each group often maintaining its own power structure within the organization. Thus hospitals have administrators, medical personnel, nursing personnel, attendants, maintenance personnel, laboratory personnel, and so on. Universities, similarly, have teaching personnel, research personnel, administrative personnel, maintenance personnel, and so on. Each of these functional tasks within organizations often becomes the sphere of a particular group that controls activities relating to the task. While these tasks usually are coordinated at the highest levels of the organization, they often are not coordinated at intermediate and lower levels. It is not unusual, however, for coalitions to form among lower participants in these multiple structures. A secretary may know the man who manages the supply of stores, or the person assigning parking stickers. Such acquaintances may give her the ability to handle informally certain needs that would be more time-consuming and difficult to handle formally. Her ability to provide services informally makes higher-ranking participants in some degree dependent upon her, thereby giving her power, which increases her ability to bargain on issues important to her.

Rules

In organizations with complex power structures lower participants can use their knowledge of the norms of the organization to thwart attempted change. In discussing the various functions of bureaucratic rules, Gouldner maintains that such rules serve as excellent substitutes for surveillance, since surveillance, in addition to being expensive in time and effort, arouses considerable hostility and antagonism.[19] Moreover, he argues, rules are a functional equivalent for direct, personally given orders, since they specify the obligations of workers to do things in specific ways. Standardized rules, in addition, allow simple screening of violations, facilitate remote control, and to some extent legitimize punishment when the rule is violated. The worker who violates a bureaucratic rule has little recourse to the excuse that he did not know what was expected, as he might claim for a direct order. Finally, Gouldner argues that rules are "the 'chips' to which the company staked the supervisors and which they could use to play the game"[20]; that is, rules established a punishment which could be withheld, and this facilitated the supervisors' bargaining power with lower participants.

While Gouldner emphasizes the functional characteristics of rules within an organization, it should be clear that full compliance to all the rules at all times will probably be dysfunctional for the organization. Complete and apathetic compliance may do everything but facilitate achievement of organizational goals. Lower participants who are familiar with an organization and its rules can often find rules to support their contention that they not do what they have been asked to do, and rules are also often a rationalization for inaction on their part. The following of rules becomes especially complex when associations and unions become involved, for there are then two sets of rules to which the participant can appeal.

What is suggested is that rules may be chips for everyone concerned in the game. Rules become the "chips" through which the bargaining process is maintained. Scheff, as noted earlier, observed that attendants in mental hospitals often took on responsibilities assigned legally to the ward physician, and when attendants refused to share these responsibilities the physician's position became extremely difficult.[21]

The ward physician is legally responsible for the care and treatment of each ward patient. This responsibility requires attention to a host of details. Medicine, seclusion, sedation and transfer orders, for example, require the doctor's signature. Tranquilizers are particularly troublesome in this regard since they require frequent adjustment of dosage in order to get the desired effects. The physician's order is required to each change in dosage. With 150 patients under his care on tranquilizers, and several changes of dosages a week desirable, the physician could spend a major portion of his ward time in dealing with this single detail.

Given the time-consuming formal chores of the physician, and his many other duties, he usually worked out an arrangement with the ward personnel, particularly the charge (supervisory attendant), to handle these duties. On several wards, the charge called specific problems to the doctor's attention, and the two of them, in effect, would have a consultation. The charge actually made most of the decisions concerning dosage change in the back wards. Since the doctor delegated portions of his formal responsibilities to the charge, he was dependent on her good will toward him. If she withheld her cooperation, the physician had absolutely no recourse but to do all the work himself.[22]

In a sense such delegation of responsibility involves a consideration of reward and cost, whereby the decision to be made involves a question of what is more valuable—to retain control over an area, or to delegate one's work to lower participants.

There are occasions, of course, when rules are regarded as illegitimate by lower participants, and they may disregard them. Gouldner observed that, in the mine, men felt they could resist authority in a situation involving danger to themselves.[23] They did not feel that they could legitimately be ordered to do anything that would endanger their lives. It is probably significant that in extremely dangerous situations organizations are more likely to rely on commitment to work than on authority. Even within non-voluntary groups dangerous tasks are regarded usually as requiring task commitment, and it is likely that commitment is a much more powerful organizational force than coercive authority.

SUMMARY

The preceding remarks are general ones, and they are assumed to be in part true of all types of organizations. But power relationships in organizations are likely to be molded by the type of organization being considered, the nature of organizational goals, the ideology of organizational decision making, the kind of commitment participants have to the organization, the formal structure of the organization, and so on. In short, we have attempted to discuss power processes within organizations in a manner somewhat divorced from other major organizational processes. We have emphasized variables affecting control of access to persons, information, and facilities within organizations. Normative definitions, perception of legitimacy, exchange, and coalitions have all been viewed in relation to power processes. Moreover, we have dealt with some attributes of persons related to power: commitment, effort, interest, willingness to use power, skills, attractiveness, and so on. And we have discussed some other variables: time, centrality, complexity of power structure, and replaceability of persons. It appears that these variables help to account in part for power exercised by lower participants in organizations.

NOTES

1. The term "lower participants" comes from Amitai Etzioni, *A Comparative Analysis of Complex Organizations* (New York: Harcourt Brace, 1961) and is used by him to designate persons in positions of lower rank: employees, rank-and-file, members, clients, customers, and inmates. We shall use the term in this paper in a relative sense denoting position vis-à-vis a higher-ranking participant.

2. Robert Bierstedt, An Analysis of Social Power, *American Sociological Review* 15 (1950): 730–738.

3. Robert A. Dahl, The Concept of Power, *Behavioral Science* 2 (1957): 201–215.

4. One might observe, for example, that the power of lower participants is based primarily on the ability to "veto" or punish. For a discussion of bases of power, see John R.P. French Jr., and Bertram

Raven, "The Bases of Social Power," in D. Cartwright and A. Zander, eds., *Group Dynamics* (Evanston, IL: Row, Peterson, 1960): pp. 607–623.

5. John Thibaut and Harold H. Kelley, *The Social Psychology of Groups* (New York: Wiley, 1959). For a similar emphasis on dependence, see Richard M. Emerson, Power-Dependence Relationships, *American Sociological Review* 27(1962): 31–41.

6. Although this paper will not attempt to explain how access may be measured, the author feels confident that the hypotheses concerned with access are clearly testable.

7. Dahl, Concept of Power.

8. Max Weber, "The Essentials of Bureaucratic Organization: An Ideal-Type Construction," in Robert Merton et al., *Reader in Bureaucracy* (Glencoe, IL: Free Press, 1952), pp. 15–27.

9. Neal Gross, Ward S. Mason, and Alexander W. McEachern, *Explorations in Role Analysis* (New York: Wiley 1958).

10. Robert Merton, The Role-Set: Problems in Sociological Theory, *British Journal of Sociology* 8 (1957): 106–120.

11. Erving Goffman, *Encounters* (Indianapolis, IN: Bobbs Merrill, 1961), pp. 85–152.

12. Etzioni, *Comparative Analysis.*

13. Ibid.

14. Thomas J. Scheff, Control over Policy by Attendants in a Mental Hospital, *Journal of Health and Human Behavior* 2 (1961): 93–105.

15. Gresham M. Sykes, "The Corruption of Authority and Rehabilitation," in A. Etzioni, ed., *Complex Organizations* (New York: Holt Rinehart, Winston, 1961), pp. 191–197.

16. As an example, it appears that 6 members of the cabinet, 30 important subcabinet officials, 63 senators, and 230 congressmen are lawyers (*New Yorker,* April 14, 1962, p. 62). Although one can cite many reasons for lawyers holding political posts, an important one appears to be their legal expertise.

17. There is considerable data showing the powerful effect of propinquity on communication. For summary, see Thibaut and Kelley, *The Social Psychology of Groups,* pp. 39–42.

18. The concept of centrality is generally used in a more technical sense in the work of Bavelas, Shaw, Gilchrist, and others. For example, Bavelas defines the central region of a structure as the class of all cells with the smallest distance between one cell and any other cell in the structure, with distance measured in link units. Thus the most central position in a pattern is the position closest to all others. Cf. Harold Leavitt, "Some Effects of Certain Communication Patterns on Group Performance," in E. Maccoby, T.N. Newcomb, and E.L. Hartley, eds., *Readings in Social Psychology* (New York: Holt, Rinehart and Winston, 1959), p. 559.

19. Alvin W. Gouldner, *Patterns of Industrial Bureaucracy* (Glencoe, IL: Free Press, 1954).

20. Ibid., p. 173.

21. Scheff, Control over Policy.

22. Ibid., p. 97.

23. Gouldner, *Patterns of Industrial Bureaucracy.*

25

The Politics of Upward Influence in Organizations

*Lyman W. Porter, Robert W. Allen, and
Harold L. Angle*

The existence of political processes in organizations has been well recognized in the
"popular" management press, yet a mid-1970s survey of more than seventy textbooks
in industrial-organizational psychology, management, and organizational behavior revealed only seventy pages in which the topic of organizational politics was addressed—
about 2/10 of one percent of the textbook content! A review of eight of the most
appropriate academic journals revealed less than a dozen articles on the topic, out of a
total of more than 1,700 articles over a sixteen-year period (Porter, 1976). In light of
this scarcity of serious attention to the topic, therefore, it is our contention that a joint
examination of organizational politics and upward influence may help point the way
toward some important issues in analyzing behavior processes in organizations.

It is worth noting that the two topics are not unrelated. It appears reasonable to say
that while not all (or even most) upward influence involves political behavior, most
political behavior (in organizations) does involve upward influence. Taking the first part
of this statement, much of upward influence involves, of course, the normal routine
reporting relationships that exist in all organizations. We would contend, however, that
there is a substantial segment of upward influence that involves what can be labeled as
"political behavior" (to be defined later). The other part of the statement about the
relationship between the two topics—that most political behavior in organizations involves upward influence—is based on the assumption that the typical object of influence
will be someone or some group possessing more formal, legitimate power than the
would-be political actor. While it is possible to cite clear exceptions to this proposition,
we would, nevertheless, contend that the vast majority of political attempts at influence
are in the upward direction.

In this paper, we intend to maintain a focus on political influence as an individual

Adapted from "The Politics of Upward Influence in Organizations," by Larry L. Cummings and Barry
M. Staw (eds.) *Research in Organizational Behavior,* vol. 3 (Greenwich, CT: JAI, 1980), pp. 109–
149. Copyright © 1981 by JAI Press, Inc.

phenomenon. This is not because we consider coalitional political processes in organizations either uninteresting or unimportant. On the contrary, the many-on-one (or many-on-several) influence event is a fairly common fact of organizational life. However, we believe that the one-on-one political influence situation is a particularly prevalent, albeit little-understood, organizational reality. In the ensuing analysis, therefore, the focus will be on gaining a better understanding of the decision logic of the individual "politician."

Before proceeding further, two definitional matters must be dealt with: (1) "upward influence"; and (2) "political behavior." The first is simple, the second complex. For our purposes, we will define upward influence as "attempts to influence someone higher in the *formal hierarchy* of authority in the organization." The fact that the person attempting to exercise influence cannot rely on formal authority results in a situation that is distinctly different from that of downward influence.

"Political behavior in organizations" or "organizational politics" is not an easy term to define. Despite this, a number of authors have recently offered definitions (e.g., Frost and Hayes 1977; Mayes and Allen 1977; Robbins 1976), and our definitional framework will be consistent generally with the thrust of these definitions. However, any one of them may not include all four of the elements contained in our definition. For the purposes of the present paper, *organizational political behavior* is defined as:

(1) Social influence attempts
(2) that are discretionary (i.e., that are outside the behavioral zones prescribed or prohibited by the formal organization),
(3) that are intended (designed) to promote or protect the self-interests of individuals and groups (units),
(4) and that threaten the self-interests of others (individuals, units).

A few brief comments seem in order about each of the four components of the definition. First, we take it as a given that regardless of what else it is, political behavior is behavior aimed at influencing others; behavior carried out in such a way that there are no intended direct effects on others would fall into the category of nonpolitical behavior. Second, any behavior that the organization ordinarily requires and expects is nonpolitical; for example, coming to work every day and carrying out the assignments and expectations of the formal role. Likewise, behavior forbidden by formal rules or commonly accepted standards of behavior (e.g., fighting, stealing, etc.) would be excluded. That leaves discretionary behavior relating to the work situation (and meeting the other definitional requirements) as that which would be labeled "political." Third, we believe that the intention of promoting or protecting self-interests is a necessary (though not sufficient) element of political behavior. Of course, attributions of intention often vary widely between those who are the source of the behavior and those who are observing or labeling the behavior. It is our contention that if the behavior is seen by organizational participants as intended to promote or protect self-interests then (meeting the other criteria) the label "political" is appropriate. Finally, we believe that unless the behavior threatens the self-interests of others, it is nonpolitical. This puts political be-havior squarely in the camp of competitive as opposed to collaborative behavior, and focuses on the zero-sum aspect of organizational resource allocation. In the words of Frost and Hayes (1977), this last part of the definition emphasizes that political behavior is "nonconsensus" behavior.

KEY CONSIDERATIONS

Certain considerations emerge as particularly salient when one considers the present state of knowledge (or gaps in our knowledge) of political influence in organizations. What (if any) political norms exist in organizations and how do organizational members learn about them? What situational factors influence the prevalence of political activity? Further, what kinds of individuals are prone to engage in organizational politics? Finally, what factors lead to selection of particular organizational members as political influence targets, and what methods are available, and preferred, for political influence?

Political Norms

Our definition of organizational politics has incorporated the notion that organizationally political behaviors fall outside the range of those either prescribed or prohibited by the organization. At first blush, the implication would seem to be that "political" behaviors in organizations take place outside the normative framework. No such conclusion, how-ever, is intended. It is very likely that strong norms do exist in organizations, relative to "political" activity. However, the basis for these norms will not be found in official prescriptions originated by the formal organization. Rather, the signals by which the organizational member pieces together a picture of "political reality" originate from the informal organization, and are apt to be sent in disguised format and against a noisy background.

The two basic issues appear salient with respect to the micro-political norms of upward influence. First, what norms exist? Do norms ever permit or prescribe upward political influence attempts, or are all such attempts acts of deviance? What are the contingent factors? Do political norms differ in different parts of the organization? How does the goal or purpose behind an influence attempt bear upon its acceptability? Do norms prescribe or proscribe particular influence tactics?

A second general issue relates to the way political norms are learned in organizations. How clear are the "norm messages" regarding upward political influence? Are they transmitted "in the clear," or are they buried in subtlety and innuendo? This raises the parallel issue of norm consensus. Is there sufficient exchange of unambiguous norm information to permit consensual validation? How accurate are individual perceptions of the extent to which upward influence is attempted and the purpose or intent of the actor when such attempts are perceived?

Political Norm Structure

There is ample reason to believe that informal "political" norms abound in organizations. Schein (1977) asserted that political processes "may be as endemic to organizational life as planning, organizing, directing and controlling" (p. 64). It is unlikely, however, that these political norms are invariant, either across all situations, or in all parts of the organization.

Political behavior that clearly would be considered "deviant" at certain times may be seen as less so at other times. For instance, it has been suggested that the process of allocating scarce organizational resources typically has two phases. In the earlier phase, conflict is clearly institutionalized. Interested parties are expected to maneuver and bargain, in order to clarify the organization's values, goals, and priorities (Frost and Hayes 1977). Later on, after values, goals, and priorities have been defined, *consensus* rather than conflict becomes institutionalized. "Political" behaviors, that may have been tolerated earlier, are now considered clearly inappropriate.

Not only will political norms vary over time, they may also differ with location in the organization. One study, for example, found that more than 90 percent of managers interviewed reported that organizational politics occurred more frequently at upper and middle levels of management than at lower managerial levels (Madison et al. 1980). A related study (Allen et al. 1979b) found that lower-level managers describe the traits of political actors in more pejorative terms than do upper-level managers, indicating perhaps that political activity is more often considered counter-normative at lower hierarchical levels. In addition, managers in the Madison et al. study reported political activity as more prevalent in staff, as opposed to line positions. Departments in which organizational politics was seen as most prevalent were marketing and sales, while accounting/finance and production were seen as lowest in political activity.

It appears, then, that the "politically active" functional areas are those in which uncertainty is most prevalent. Organizational members in such roles may need to rely on political skill to deal with the conflicting demands of intra- and extra-organizational associates. Thus, norms that favor political influence as a means of conducting the day's business may arise, out of necessity, in such subunits.

In summary, searching for "the" organization's political norms might be far too simplistic a pursuit. We should, instead, be prepared to discover a mosaic of political-norm subsystems embedded in organizations.

Learning the Norms of Upward Political Influence

The period of organizational entry is always especially stressful. The initiate is faced with an intrinsically ambiguous, yet crucial task—that of "learning the ropes." We believe that the learning of political norms will pose special difficulties. Unlike many organizational norms, these are exclusively the purview of the informal organization. Since the formal organization neither prescribes nor forbids political behaviors, such norms cannot be transmitted in the form of explicit organizational policy. Moreover, there are constraints on feasible modes of communication, even by the "informal" organization. Unlike the cues provided for other types of norms, political norm cues frequently will be implicit, requiring considerable sensitivity on the part of the receiver. In this respect, messages regarding norms that *condone* political behaviors may be more vague than those that *condemn* such behaviors.

A key aspect of our definition of organizational politics is the idea that "political" behavior is self-serving while at the same time not intended to serve others (or intended, in fact, to misserve others). Such behavior, then will be resisted, *if recognized* by others (Frost and Hayes 1977). The implication is that the actor often will take pains to conceal attempts at political influence, adding to the ambiguity encountered by observers.

In discussing the acquisition of organizational power, a pursuit closely related to political influence, Moberg (1977) asserted that societal norms require unobtrusiveness. The "politician" must take care to avoid having his/her behavior attributed, by others, to a self-serving intent. Creation of the impression that behavior is legitimate (or non-existent) may be accomplished by acting in ways that make reliable attributions difficult. Some of the "smokescreen" tactics aimed at manipulating observers' attributions might include making certain that there is a reasonably credible organizational rationale for one's actions, by acting so enigmatically that observers lose confidence in their attributions, or by publicly advocating a "version" or interpretation of organizational goals that actually serves personal objectives.

Such tactics can seriously undermine "political" social learning. An individual's ability to behave appropriately in a social situation is determined in part by the accuracy with which she or he perceives the existing system norms. It is commonly assumed that social system members both share and are aware of each others' norms for the behavior of all members (Biddle 1964). However, when either communication or behavior observation is restricted, a state of "pluralistic ignorance" can exist. In effect, members of a social group might come to share a wholly mistaken view of the group's norms. Furthermore, the false consensus concerning these norms may become self-perpetuating. In view of the particular problems that surround political norm learning, it would appear that political-influence norms in organizations constitute a prime candidate for "pluralistic ignorance."

Thus, a misleading consensus may come to exist with respect to which "political" behaviors the informal organization condemns, and which such behaviors are condoned. This, in turn, may lead political actors to overestimate the extent of their own deviancy, resulting in their taking great pains to disguise their behavior. The vicious circle thus created can perpetuate a situation in which discovery of the "real" political norms in an organization may pose serious problems for researchers and organization members, alike.

As we have seen, informal political norms are a critical contextual factor in the politics of upward influence. There are also other contextual considerations surrounding any potential political act. The following section discusses several such situational factors.

Situational Factors

There is some evidence that certain organizational situations tend to be intrinsically "political." Madison et al. (1980) reported that managers saw certain situations as characterized by relatively high levels of political activity. Examples of such situations included reorganization changes, personnel changes, and budget allocation. On the other hand, such organizational situations as rule and procedure changes, establishment of individual performance standards and the purchase of major items were characterized as relatively low in prevalence of political activity. These differences were discussed by Madison et al. in terms of three variables: (1) uncertainty; (2) importance of the activity to the larger organization; and (3) salience of the issue to the individual.

The situations in which political activity may be most prevalent seem to combine situational ambiguity with sufficient personal stake to activate the individual to consider actions that fall outside the boundaries of the formal organizational norm system. While lack of structure or situational ambiguity may provide recognition of opportunity to engage in upward political influence, it is personal stake that may provide the incentive to engage in political behavior, per se.

Another situational factor which appears particularly relevant to organizational politics is resource scarcity. The essence of the political process is the struggle over the allocation of scarce resources, that is, who gets what, where and when (Lasswell, 1951). The relative abundance of resources represented by various organizational issues may have a great deal of influence regarding the extent to which "political" means become employed in their resolution.

While the preceding discussion of norms and of situational factors has described some aspects of what the potential political actor finds in the way of contextual factors—factors that may influence his/her "political" activity in the organization—it is also necessary to consider what the individual *brings* to the situation. These actor characteristics will now be considered.

Actor Characteristics

Each potential agency of upward political influence brings to the scene a rich array of personal characteristics. Such individual factors could easily lead two different organizational members either to perceive an identical situation differently or, even if they share identical perceptions, to behave characteristically in different ways. This now leads us to consider some particular classes of individual differences that might help predict organizational members' relative propensities to engage in upward political influence.

Beliefs About Action-Outcome Relationships

The truism, "organizational behavior is a function of its perceived consequences," is certainly as applicable in the arena of organizational politics as it is in other spheres of organizational life. It is a basic psychological tenet that behavior that has been rewarded in the past becomes more probable in the future.

From the perspective of expectancy theory (Vroom 1964), organizational members are believed to behave in a manner that maximizes their net outcomes. This, in turn, suggests that organization members undertake a series of subjective cost-benefit analyses, using salient available information. Some of the more explicit information available is the political actor's knowledge of the results of past attempts at social influence. Thus, the individual's "expectancy set" regarding the efficacy of engaging in upward political influence will be at least in part determined by what has gone before.

Manifest Needs

Most substantive or content theories of human motivation are based on the premise that individuals harbor a relatively stable set of needs, and that these needs incite action directed toward need satisfaction. While the assumption base underlying the need-satisfaction paradigm has not gone unchallenged, the concept of manifest needs, stemming from Murray's (1938) pioneering work, continues to influence research.

Although Murray's taxonomy included as many as twenty needs, recent focus, particularly in organizational settings, seems to have settled on need for achievement (nAch) and need for power (nPow) (Atkinson and Feather 1966; McClelland 1965; McClelland and Burnham 1976). In particular, nPow appears to be a likely candidate for investigation as a correlate of political activity in organizations.

Researchers have found nPow to be widely distributed, particularly among successful managers, in organizations (McClelland and Burnham 1976). While power motivation, according to McClelland, can often be "socialized" (i.e., oriented toward organizational, rather than personal objectives), nPow can also center on the desire to further one's own goals. Shostrom (1967) characterized man as a manipulator, and set forth the view that, for many, control of others can become its own reward apart from any extrinsic accomplishment that might be the ostensible object of the maneuver. Among the individual differences that might influence the accuracy of Shostrom's characteristics, it would seem that nPow would be rather important.

Locus of Control

The theory (Rotter 1954, 1966) that highlights this variable holds that people differ systematically in their beliefs that their personal successes and failures are the result either of uncontrollable external forces, or of their own actions. "Internals" tend to view their outcomes as the result of ability or effort, while "externals" would attribute personal consequences as the result of innate task difficulty or to luck (Weiner 1974). Thus, when faced with a problem in which upward political influence might be within the feasible set of coping strategies, it might seem reasonable that an "internal" might arrive at a different expectancy computation than would an "external." For the average outcome, an "internal" will probably assume a higher expectancy of effort leading to attainment. This might, in turn, lead "internals" to favor political activism, while "externals" might be more prone toward political apathy.

Risk-Seeking Propensity

Decision makers differ in their psychological reaction to risk. While some exhibit a conservative bias, avoiding risk when possible, others appear to place a positive value on risk, per se. In the language of decision theory, the former are termed risk averters while the latter are called risk seekers (Keeney and Raiffa 1976). (There are also many people, of course, who are essentially "risk neutral.") To the extent that an organizational member is a risk seeker, it might be reasonable to expect that he/she would be tempted to engage in a political influence attempt (which can indeed be dangerous) that might be shunned by a risk averter.

Next, we turn to consideration of the other participant in the dyadic process of upward political influence—the influence target.

Target Selection

Importance of Power

Engaging in organizational politics necessitates the selection of a target(s) of influence. An essential ingredient that a chosen target must possess is the control of scarce resources, or the ability to influence scarce resource controllers. This is basically a question of who has either the *power* to allocate desired resources or the ability to *influence* other desired resource powerholders. Power is considered to be the capacity to influence, while influence is viewed as a process of producing behavioral or psychological (e.g., values, beliefs, attitudes) effects in a target person. The political actor is concerned with identifying and selecting as a target an individual(s) who possesses an appropriate base, or bases, of power that as indicated earlier is sufficiently high to do or get done what the political actor desires. This point was recognized by Tedeschi, Schlenker, and Lindskold (1972), when they indicated that individuals possessing relatively greater expertise, status, or prestige than the source will be prime candidates as targets of influence.

Costs of Approaching Target

It seems clear that the potential risks or costs to the political actor are also an important consideration in choosing among various powerholders in the organization, as potential targets of political influence. The target must possess sufficient power to accomplish the outcome desired by the source and at a minimal, or acceptable, cost to the political actor. By costs to the agent, we are referring to possible negative outcomes that may be experienced by the agent as a result of the influence attempt. These negative outcomes range from the agent's failure to promote or protect self-interests in the specific situation at hand, to loss of the ability to promote or protect self-interests in other future situations. Indeed, the ultimate cost could be loss of position within the organization.

Therefore, while especially powerful individuals may be able to do what the agent desires, these are the same individuals who can impose the greatest adverse effects (costs) upon the agent. The power that makes a person attractive as a target could be used, were the target so to choose, against the source. Tedeschi et al. (1972) clearly recognized this point when they proposed that the most probable influence target would be the weakest person who possesses sufficient power to enable the influencer to realize his or her goal. It was suggested that, with respect to target selection in organizations, "people have a 'natural' tendency to go through the channels of authority" (p. 314), that is, the most likely target of influence would be the immediate superior. Allen, Angle, and Porter (1979a) found that the immediate superior is, in fact, the most frequent target of attempted influence. About two-thirds of their respondents (143) selected their immediate superior as a first-choice target of influence.

Agent-Target Relationship

An important consideration concerning the potential costs in selecting a target from among various powerholders in the organization may be the concept of interpersonal attraction between the agent and the potential target(s). Ideally, the selected target will possess sufficient power to provide the outcomes desired by the political actor *and* sufficiently high interpersonal attraction to be willing to do so at minimal or acceptable costs to the agent.

In upward influence, the political actor does not enjoy a given target, or even a "natural" set of targets. The appropriateness of a particular individual as an influence target is situationally determined, that is, the target will vary according to the outcomes desired by the source. The common denominator of potential political targets is the possession of sufficient power to provide, or assist in providing, outcomes desired by the political actor. It is the political actor's task to identify, select, and induce these organizational influentials to comply, willingly or unwittingly, with the intent of the political actor.

Methods of Upward Influence

The one inescapable fact about upward influence—that the agent of influence possesses less formal authority than the target of influence—colors any examination of the selection of methods of upward political influence. The fact that the political actor cannot rely on formal authority, and most likely has considerably less power (compared to a downward situation) to wield positive and negative sanctions, means that the search for an effective method or methods of upward influence will be different from the search that takes place in downward attempts.

Before discussing a classification of possible methods of upward political influence and the factors that will affect the choice of methods, it is important to keep in mind another aspect of the situation; the methods can be utilized (as Allen et al. 1979b, have pointed out) to promote self-interests (usually in a proactive manner) or protect those interests (usually in a reactive manner). The former use refers to upward influence attempts designed to advance self-interests and move the agent from a current position (in terms of access to organizational resources and rewards) to a better position. Such upward-influence attempts typically require initiation by the agent. In the latter mode, ordinarily requiring a response by the agent, attempts are made to reduce or minimize potential damage to self-interests that would tend to move the agent from a current position to a less desirable position. It is clear that political attempts at upward influence can be exercised in either of these modes.

Classification of Methods

A categorization scheme that may be useful for the purposes of analyzing upward political influence is shown in Table 25.1. As can be seen, influence methods have been classified into two major categories: sanctions and informational. In turn, sanctions have been divided into the familiar sets, "positive" and "negative," while informational methods have been divided into three types: "persuasion" (both the actor's objective and the influence attempt are open); "manipulative persuasion" (the objective is concealed but the attempt is open); and "manipulation" (both the objective and the attempt are concealed).

Each of the five methods listed in Table 25.1 can be considered for possible use by individual political actors. As will be discussed below, and as shown in Table 25.1, we have indicated what we think is the relative frequency of use: namely, positive and negative sanctions are not likely, persuasion is low to medium in likelihood, and manipulative persuasion and manipulation are (relatively) highly likely.

Considering each of the five methods in turn:

Positive Sanctions. In upward political influence situations, it is unlikely (though certainly by no means impossible) that positive sanctions, that is, rewards and promises of rewards, will be a very widely utilized method by individuals. The apparent reason is that the individual vis-à-vis his/her upward target is unlikely to control a wide range of rewards. To put it simply, while the upward target can do a lot for the would-be political actor in the way of providing rewards, he/she is relatively limited in the rewards that can be administered upward. The source does have his/her own performance that can serve as a reward—it can, for example, help make the boss look good—but since relatively good performance is such an expected part of normal organizational behavior, it is not likely to serve as a frequent reward in an upward direction unless it is truly exceptional performance. Other types of rewards (e.g., favors) can be promised by the lower level individual attempting upward influence, but on balance they are likely to be of limited and circumscribed impact.

Table 25.1
Classification of Methods of Upward Political Influence

	Types of Methods	Predicted Relative Frequency of Use
I. Sanctions	A. Positive	Low
	B. Negative	Low
II. Informational	A. Persuasion	Low to Medium
	B. Manipulative Persuasion	High
	C. Manipulation	High

Negative Sanctions. As Mechanic (1962) noted, "secretaries . . . accountants . . . attendants in mental hospitals, and even . . . inmates in prisons" (p. 350) can individually, if they wish, "gum up the works" by various tactics. Whether this is a very prevalent method, however, is a function of the possible costs or penalties for doing so. In particular, when influence is being attempted hierarchically upward, there are normative restrictions on the use of negative sanctions. While both the superior and subordinate may fully understand that the subordinate is in a threatening posture, face-saving norms (Goffman 1955) may require that neither party openly acknowledge the subordinate's threat. Were the threat to become overt, the superior would likely be compelled to retaliate. Thus, upward threats seldom will be explicit; rather, to the extent they exist at all, upward negative sanctions will tend to take the form of what Berne (1964) termed "covert transactions." In general, it is our view that negative sanctions will not be selected often as a viable upward influence method.

Persuasion. The term "persuasion" is usually substituted as a shorthand term for open informational methods. It seems obvious that persuasion, or the open utilization of an informational base, is a frequent and common method of nonpolitical upward influence on the part of the individual agent. However, when the aim of such persuasion is the promotion or protection of the self-interests of the influence agent, and where the self-interests of others are threatened, its use becomes far more problematical. Since the intentions of the influence agent are open as well as the method (i.e., a direct attempt to convince), the response will be based directly on the target's evaluation of the message and the source of the message. The "costs," therefore, may be greatly increased because of the possibility of a negative reaction on the part of the target—as opposed to perhaps mere indifference in nonpolitical situations. For this reason, we would argue that the likelihood of persuasion being utilized in upward political influence situations would be low to moderate.

It should be noted that the nature of the arguments in persuasion can take many forms, including pointing out probable consequences to the target for complying or failing to comply with the agent's wishes. Tedeschi et al. (1972) refer to this type of argument as the use of "warnings and mendations" (as contrasted with such direct sanctions as threats, punishments, and promises of rewards). "The important distinction between threat and a warning is that the source controls the punishment in the first instance but not in the second" (p. 292).

Manipulative Persuasion. The essence of this method of upward influence involves the deliberate attempt of the agent to conceal or disguise his/her true objectives, *even though* the agent is open about the fact that an influence attempt is taking place—it is the objective, not the influence attempt, that is concealed. This is illustrated by the well-known "hidden agenda" phenomenon.

We contend that manipulative persuasion is a frequently utilized approach to upward influence of a political sort. The reason, of course, is the influence agent's belief that if the (higher level) target knew what the source was trying to accomplish, the target would reject or ignore the message and thus avoid being influenced, or might even penalize the source. In this method, the agent is openly attempting to influence but is simultaneously attempting to disguise his/her intentions. The effectiveness of the influence method, therefore, depends on how effective is the disguise of objectives. There is probably no message so ineffective as one that is labeled by the target: "He/she is only trying to get me to do that because it will advance his/her own self-interests."

Manipulation. This form of influence involves the concealment of both the intent of the political actor and the fact that an influence attempt is taking place. This obviously involves greater effort on the part of the influence agent, as both intentions and the attempt must be disguised. Despite the potential difficulties, this is a common method of upward political influence. For example, in a study of managerial perceptions of the utilization of political tactics, Allen et al. (1979b) found that "the instrumental use of information" was one of the three most commonly observed tactics mentioned by the managerial respondents from thirty small- to medium-sized industrial firms. As these authors pointed out, this category of tactics involved withholding, or distorting information (short of outright lying), or overwhelming the target with too much information. The other two tactics most frequently cited by the respondents in the Allen et al. study could also be interpreted as the utilization of pure manipulation: namely, "attacking or blaming others" and "image building/impression management." Obviously, the success of these and similar tactics, including ingratiation, would appear to depend largely on how effectively the influence agent's intentions and the attempt at influence are concealed. Attacking others, for example, is likely to be dismissed if it is regarded as being only, or primarily, in the service of the attacker's self-interests and/or as an influence attempt.

Factors in the Choice of Method

If we assume that someone (individual or group) in an organization has made a decision to attempt upward influence for the purpose of promoting or protecting self-interests, then that person or group faces the choice of what method to use. Since we are focusing on *upward* influence, that choice will be greatly affected by the knowledge that the target has more formal authority than the agent. A choice that might be effective in downward influence might not, as noted earlier, be equally effective in the upward direction.

The choice of method is likely to be affected by the agent's instrumental motivation—the attempt to obtain particular outcomes (with satisfaction deriving from the attainment of the outcomes rather than from the process of attaining them). The agent is presumed to have some notion of what values he or she places on certain outcomes, and some idea of the probability that a given action will lead to various outcomes. It is this latter factor, the calculation of the probability that a particular method will lead to valued outcomes, that would seem to be the key ingredient in the choice of methods of influence. Alternatively, this could be thought of as a calculation of cost/benefit ratios for various possible methods. Those methods would be chosen which would bring the greatest benefits for the lowest cost.

Such calculations can be presumed to be dependent on the agent's assessment of: (1) Agent (self) characteristics; (2) Target characteristics; (3) Characteristics of the situation; and (4) The characteristics of the method. Agent characteristics would include the agent's assessment of the various resources he/she possesses vis-à-vis the target: for example, degree of expertise, potential to provide the target with positive or negative outcomes, possession of exclusive information, ability to disguise true intentions, general persuasive ability, risk-taking propensity, and the like. Target characteristics would include such variables as: perceived susceptibility to persuasion, likelihood of attributing self-interest motivation to the agent, power to provide the desired outcome, and so forth. Finally, some assessment would be made of the characteristics (costs and benefits) of the method itself. For example, in deciding whether to use some form of manipulation such as withholding information or attempting ingratiation, the *perceived* costs involved in detection may or may not be viewed as greater than the potential gains of straightforward persuasion. It would appear, then, that the choice of methods of influence, particularly in an upward situation, is a complex process.

CONCLUDING OBSERVATIONS

Some years ago, Leavitt (1964) observed: "People perceive what they think will help satisfy needs; ignore what is disturbing; and again perceive disturbances that persist and increase" (p. 33). It is interesting to apply the selective-perception framework to the relative prominence given by the field of organizational behavior to downward and lateral influence processes, on the one hand, compared to the lack of attention given to upward influence processes and organizational politics, on the other. We believe there has been an overfocus on the former, and that the field needs to redress the imbalance by giving increased emphasis to the latter.

One can speculate as to why this imbalance has occurred. In part, at least, it has come about because those who run organizations traditionally have been interested in improving the performance of those being led or managed. Hence, they have pressed social and behavioral scientists to learn more about leadership and motivation. This has created a ready market for knowledge directed toward influencing subordinates to perform in a desired manner. Another factor shaping research, particularly with respect to both downward and lateral influence processes, has been the small group tradition in social psychology. When only small groups, as opposed to (large) formal organizations, are the object of study, it is likely that the focus will be strongly downward, or perhaps lateral—as in the case of group dynamics. Chains of authority exist only in organizations of some size, and thus if only groups are being researched, it is difficult to investigate the intricacies of upward influence linkages except for the limited case of the group's impact on the immediate leader (and, it should be stressed that even this circumscribed type of upward influence has only recently begun to be examined by organizational behavior researchers). Our point is not that upward influence is more important than lateral or downward influence, only that it should be studied as much as the other two types. And, when one gets into the topic of upward influence in organizations, one is inevitably drawn into the realm of organizational politics. This, in turn, is a subject that has long been regarded as somewhat "taboo" by both organizations and researchers because of its mildly disturbing negative connotations—clandestine, self-serving, dysfunctional, and so on.

Finally, we feel that a broadened influence perspective—one that incorporates the concept of organizational politics—can contribute significantly to an understanding of many facets of organizational behavior, such as decision making, organizational design, communication, motivation and organizational development.

REFERENCES

Allen, R.W., H.L. Angle, and L.W. Porter. (1979a). A study of upward influence in political situations in organizations, unpublished manuscript, University of California, Irvine.

Allen, R.W., D.L. Madison, L.W. Porter, P.A. Renwick, and B.T. Mayes. (1979b). Organizational politics: Tactics and personal characteristics of political actors. *California Management Review* 22 (4): 77–83.

Atkinson, J.W. and N.T. Feather (eds.). (1966). *A Theory of Achievement Motivation.* New York: Wiley.

Berne, E. (1964). *Games People Play.* New York: Grove Press.

Biddle, B.J. (1964). Roles, goals, and value structures in organizations, in W.W. Cooper, H.J. Leavitt, and M.W. Shelly, (eds.). *New Perspectives in Organization Research.* New York: Wiley.

Frost, P.J., and D.C. Hayes. (1977). "An exploration in two cultures of political behavior in organizations," paper presented at the Conference on Cross-Cultural Studies of Organizational Functioning, University of Hawaii, Honolulu, September.

Goffman, E. (1955). On facework. *Psychiatry* 18: 213–231.

Keeney, R.L., and H. Raiffa. (1976). *Decisions and Multiple Objectives: Preferences and Value Tradeoffs.* New York: Wiley.

Lasswell, H.D. (1951). Who gets what, when, how, in *The Political Writings of Harold D. Lasswell.* Glencoe, IL: Free Press.

Leavitt, H.J. (1964). *Managerial Psychology.* Revised edition. Chicago: University of Chicago Press.

Madison, D.L., R.W. Allen, L.W. Porter, P.A. Renwick, and B.T. Mayes. (1980). Organizational politics: An exploration of managers' perceptions. *Human Relations* 33: 79–100.

Mayes, B.T. and R.W. Allen. (1977). Toward a definition of organizational politics. *Academy of Management Review* 2: 672–678.

McClelland, D.C. (1965). Toward a theory of motive acquisition. *American Psychologist* 20: 321–333.

McClelland, D.C., and D.H. Burnham. (1976). Power is the great motivator. *Harvard Business Review* 54 (2): 100–110.

Mechanic, D. (1962). Sources of power of lower participants in complex organizations. *Administrative Science Quarterly* 7: 349–364.

Moberg, D.J. (1977). Organizational politics: Perspectives from attribution theory, paper presented to the 1977 Meeting of the American Institute for Decision Sciences, Chicago, IL.

Murray, H.A. (1938). *Explorations in Personality.* New York: Oxford University Press.

Porter, L.W. (1976). Organizations as political animals, Presidential address, Division of Industrial-Organizational Psychology, 84th annual meeting of the American Psychological Association, Washington, DC.

Robbins, S.P. (1976). *The Administrative Process: Integrating Theory and Practice.* Englewood Cliffs, NJ: Prentice-Hall.

Rotter, J.B. (1954). *Social Learning and Clinical Psychology.* Englewood Cliffs, NJ: Prentice-Hall.

———. (1966). Generalized expectancies for internal versus external locus of control. *Psychological Monographs* 80: 1–28.

Schein, E. (1977). Individual power and political behaviors in organizations: An inadequately explored reality. *Academy of Management Review* 2: 64–72.

Shostrom, Everett L. (1967). *Man, the Manipulator.* Nashville, TN: Abingdon Press.

Tedeschi, J.T., B.R. Schlenker, and S. Lindskold (1972). The exercise of power and influence: The source of influence, in J.T. Tedeschi (ed.), *The Social Influence Process.* Chicago: Aldine-Atherton.

Vroom, V.H. (1964). *Work and Motivation.* New York: Wiley.

Weiner, B. (1974). An attributional interpretation of expectancy-value theory, in B. Weiner (ed.), *Cognitive Views of Human Motivation.* New York: Academic Press.

26

Upward-Influence Styles: Relationship with Performance Evaluations, Salary, and Stress

David Kipnis and Stuart M. Schmidt

Within the past decade, organizational theory and research have made substantial contributions to our understanding of the upward-influence process in organizations by which participants attempt to gain compliance from those at higher levels in the formal organizational structure. It is generally recognized that exercising upward influence is an essential aspect of organizational behavior and contributes substantially to individual effectiveness (Pelz 1952; Kanter 1977; Mowday 1978; Schilit 1986).

Recent studies of upward influence have focused on two related questions. First, how can the tactics used to influence others at higher levels be described succinctly? (Kipnis, Schmidt, and Wilkinson 1980; Schilit and Locke 1982). Second, under which circumstances do organizational participants choose to use an influence style? (Mowday 1978; Porter, Allen and Angle 1981; Kipnis and Schmidt 1983; Schmidt and Kipnis 1984). Conspicuously missing from this research literature is information on the relationship between the use of upward-influence styles and other individual outcomes. This paper begins to address this deficiency in the organizational literature by reporting on three studies that examined the relationship between the style subordinates used to influence their organizational superiors and their subsequent performance evaluations by their superiors, their salaries, and stress symptoms they reported.

CLASSIFICATION OF UPWARD-INFLUENCE STYLES

Both popular writers about power and influence theorists, such as Kelly (1988), reasoned that individuals typically use upward-influence styles in combinations when attempting to gain compliance from individuals at higher organizational levels. Unfortunately, very little research has been designed to identify empirically these mixes of influence styles and their relation to subordinates' organizational outcomes. Such

Reprinted from *Administrative Science Quarterly,* vol. 33, no. 4, pp. 528–542. Copyright © 1988 by Administrative Science Quarterly. Reprinted with permission of the publisher.

information cannot be obtained from the correlational analyses typically reported in the research literature that describe the relation between dimensions of influence, considered one at a time, and personal or organizational variables. To fill this gap in the empirical literature, we first classified individuals according to their influence styles and then related each style to specific individual outcomes. Since this method of analysis departs from traditional correlational analysis, the rationale is briefly discussed here.

Influence styles. In a pioneering study about influencing peers, Perreault and Miles (1978) used cluster analysis to identify five clusters of employees, each composed of individuals who used influence tactics similarly. The first cluster, or influence style, consisted of individuals who used multiple influence strategies. The second cluster consisted of individuals who used their expert knowledge as a basis for influencing others. The third cluster consisted of individuals who used friendly tactics. The fourth cluster comprised individuals who used their positions in the organization, and the fifth cluster consisted of employees who did not use influence of any kind, i.e., were noninfluencers.

In an earlier study (Kipnis and Schmidt 1983), we adopted Perreault and Miles's (1978) procedures to identify combinations of managerial influence strategies. By using a hierarchical cluster analysis of six organizational influence strategies, we identified three styles that characterized the way managers influence subordinates. "Shotgun" managers used the most influence and emphasized assertiveness and bargaining; "Tactician" managers used an average amount of influence and emphasized reason; and "Bystander" managers used little influence with their superiors. These influence styles correspond to three influence "mixes" identified by Perreault and Miles (1978): multiple influence users, expertise users, and noninfluencers.

On the basis of an analysis of background data about supervisors in each of these clusters, Kipnis and Schmidt (1983) reported that Shotgun managers had less job tenure than the remaining supervisors and reported the most reasons for influencing and the greatest needs to obtain personal benefits and "sell" their ideas about how the work should be done. To this end, Shotgun managers attempted to obtain what they wanted by robustly using many different tactics.

Tactician managers directed organizational subunits involved in nonroutine work which, as has been found in other settings (Salancik and Pfeffer 1977), provided them with a skill and knowledge power base. Tacticians had considerable influence in their organizations over such areas as budgets, policy, and personnel. Tacticians relied on reason and logic to gain compliance.

Bystander managers directed organizational units doing routine work. They reported having little organizational power, that is, little control over budgets, policy, or personnel matters. They reported having few personal or organizational objectives that required compliance from others. Having few objectives, they reported exerting little influence.

In the research reported here, employee upward-influence styles were also identified through cluster analysis. Respondents consisted of subordinates from three separate studies of blue-collar and clerical workers (Study 1), supervisors (Study 2), and chief executive officers (CEOs) of hospitals (Study 3). Respondents used items from the Profile of Organizational Influence Strategies (POIS, Form M), available from University Associates, San Diego, CA, to describe how they influenced their immediate superiors. This version of the POIS measured six upward-influence strategies identified through factor analytic procedures as reported in Kipnis, Schmidt, and Wilkinson (1980): Reason, Friendliness, Assertiveness, Coalition, Higher Authority, and Bargaining. The items and scale reliabilities are described in Study 1, below. The six POIS scores of each study were subjected to a K means cluster analysis (Engelman and Hartigan 1981).

The cluster analyses yielded four meaningful clusters, shown in the Appendix, that described combinations of influence strategy use. These clusters mirror four of the clusters found by Perreault and Miles (1978) and were labeled as follows:

Cluster 1 corresponds to the previously identified Shotgun influence style (Kipnis and Schmidt 1983) and was so labeled. The respondents' high scores on all six influence strategy scales, particularly assertiveness, suggested a nonjudicious selection of strategies.

Cluster 2 respondents scored high on the friendliness strategy and had average scores on the remaining influence strategies. This cluster was labeled Ingratiator to reflect the dominant mode by which they exercised influence.

Cluster 3 corresponded to the previously identified Bystander style (Kipnis and Schmidt 1983) and was so labeled. These respondents had low scores, compared with the other respondents, on all of the influence strategies.

Cluster 4 corresponded to the previously identified Tactician style (Kipnis and Schmidt 1983) and was so labeled. These respondents scored high on the reason strategy and had average scores on the other influence strategies.

Figure 26.1 illustrates how respondents in each of these four clusters scored in their use of the six individual strategies of influence. Figure 26.1 is based on computations within each study of each strategy's corresponding z score, which were then averaged across the three studies.

We wanted to find out whether individuals in each cluster differed by organizational context and respondent demographics, as was found in previous research. A partial answer was provided from an analysis of the background and organizational information about the respondents in each study, which is summarized in Table 26.1. In the worker and supervisor studies, respondents were asked how frequently they tried to influence their superiors for personal and organizational reasons (Schmidt and Kipnis 1984). Personal reasons included (1) to obtain benefits such as more pay, (2) to obtain assistance on the job, (3) to receive favorable performance evaluations, and (4) to persuade their bosses to think well of them. Organizational reasons for influencing a superior were to gain acceptance for new ideas or for a change, such as a new work project or a new program.

As Kipnis and Schmidt (1983) found in the earlier analyses, subordinates classified as using a Shotgun upward-influence style expressed the greatest interest in securing personal benefits from superiors and gaining acceptance for their ideas (see Table 26.1). To the contrary, subordinates classified as Bystanders expressed the fewest personal or

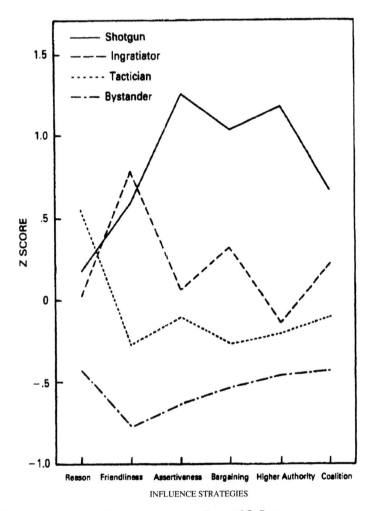

Figure 26.1. **Use of Six Influence Strategies by Four Types of Influencers**

organizational reasons for influencing their superiors. Thus Shotgun subordinates reported many reasons for influencing and Bystanders few.

Kipnis and Schmidt (1983) found that the Tacticians' base of power resided in their performance of nonroutine work. In the worker study reported here, we rated each respondent's description of his or her work in terms of individual skill levels, using a 3-point scale. A score of one described a job that required relatively little skill, such as a laborer or a production-line employee. A score of three described a skilled job such as a tool-and-die maker. As shown in Table 26.1, those classified as Tacticians had the highest skill ratings and those classified as Bystanders the lowest skill ratings ($p < .05$). These findings were similar to our earlier results; skill requirements of the work were associated with influence styles.

In the supervisor sample, Tacticians reported being in the highest job levels, as com-

Table 26.1
Organizational and Personal Characteristics of Respondents in the Four Influence Clusters

Characteristics	Study	Shotgun	Ingratiator	Bystander	Tactician	F
Reasons for influencing supervisors						
to obtain personal benefits	Workers	3.18	2.55	1.53	2.09	19.2[b]
	Supervisors	2.81	2.14	1.87	2.26	9.0[b]
to change the organization	Workers	3.32	2.55	2.26	2.59	4.2[b]
	Supervisors	3.29	2.91	2.74	3.01	2.8[a]
Skill level	Workers	2.2	1.9	1.6	2.5	3.5[a]
Job level	Supervisors	1.6	1.5	1.7	2.2	1.8
Number of physicians in hospital	CEOs	84.1	128.2	70.9	178.3	2.9[a]
Total employees	CEOs	415.9	494.6	319.3	532.5	1.9

Note: Frequency of influencing was rated on a five-point scale, on which 5 = Frequently and 1 = Never.
[a] $p < .05$.
[b] $p < .01$.

pared with the other three clusters, although this difference was not significant. Job level varied along a 3-point scale ranging from first-line supervisor (1), through middle management (2), to upper-middle management (3).

In the chief executive officer study, we also found evidence that Tacticians had positions that indicated they had greater power than respondents using the other three influence styles. As Table 26.1 shows, Tactician CEOs administered hospitals that employed an average of 178 doctors and 532 employees. In contrast, Bystander CEOs directed hospitals employing an average of 71 doctors and 319 employees. Thus, Tactician CEOs could be described as having more prestige and power than their peers, if organizational size is accepted as a measure of this factor.

There were no differences between clusters in the worker, supervisor, or CEO studies in terms of the respondents' ages, educational levels, or years of experience on the job.

The data thus suggested differences in influence style that were associated with organizational context and personal needs of the employees. Unfortunately, the questionnaires used were not designed to explore in depth the association between influence styles and these variables. Thus, we could not explain inconsistencies in the data, such as the finding that education and years on the job were not associated with influence style, although logically these variables should be associated. The present findings suggest only that both personal needs and wants, as well as organizational roles, contribute to influence style.

Research Questions

The following questions and the accompanying rationale guided our thinking about the kinds of data to be collected for this exploratory study. However, the questions and the findings should not be interpreted as implying a causal relation between using certain influence styles and other behaviors. In this exploratory study, we asked merely whether a relation exists.

Evaluations of Performance

There is general agreement that a relationship exists between impression management strategies and how people evaluate the person exercising influence (Schlenker 1980). The social psychological literature, for example, finds that people who use forceful and demanding tactics are disliked (French and Raven 1959). An implication for organizations is that subordinates who are persistent and demanding may be perceived by their superiors as acting outside of their expected roles. Such roles are characterized by compliance, passivity, and maintaining amiable relations with superiors. This leads to the following question:

Question 1 : Is there a relation between influence styles and measures of performance evaluation? More specifically, do subordinates who employ a Shotgun upward-influence style receive less favorable evaluations from superiors and receive lower salaries than those using other upward-influence styles?

We also wanted to discover if there is a relation between gender, influence style, and performance evaluations. Several researchers have suggested that male supervisors are threatened by demanding female subordinates (Costrich et al. 1975; Muehlenhard 1983; Powell 1988). This may mean that female subordinates employing an assertive and forceful upward-influence style would be evaluated less favorably than male counterparts using the same style of upward influence. We thus formulated the following question:

Question 2: Are there differences in performance evaluations given by male supervisors to male and female subordinates who employ a Shotgun upward-influence style?

The first two questions concern poor evaluations, but when we try to formulate questions about who will be evaluated most favorably, the literature contains contradictory information. On the one hand, considerable literature supports the view that persons who adopt an ingratiating influence style are evaluated favorably (Jones 1964; Wortman and Linsenmeier 1977), particularly when their superiors are experiencing organizational stress (Kipnis and Vanderveer 1971). This literature suggests that Ingratiators should receive the highest performance evaluations from their superiors. In other literature, however, it is argued that persons who rely on logic and reason best fit the organizational mold, which is based on rationality (Weber 1947; Koontz and O'Donnell 1968). If this is so, then Tacticians should receive the highest evaluations from their superiors. We formulated the following question:

Question 3: Is there a relation between influence styles and favorable evaluations? Are Ingratiator and Tactician influence styles associated with higher performance evaluations than Shotgun or Bystander styles?

Stress. The exercise or nonexercise of influence in organizations may be one of several causes of individual distress (Osipow and Spokane 1984; Deluga 1986; Ganster 1987). This suggestion is based on two separate areas of research. First, recent reviews suggest that a person with a stress-prone Type A personality is aggressively competitive, easily frustrated, anxious, or some combination of these (Booth-Kewley and Friedman 1987). Stress occurs when such persons are unable to get what they want, that is, control their environments.

A second area of research concerns the link between the exercise of influence and stress. From Thomas Hobbes in the seventeenth century (Hobbes 1968) to present-day social scientists (Wrong 1979; Pfeffer 1981), researchers have accepted the assumption that the more we want from other people or the more we perceive others as unwilling to provide what we want, the more likely we are to increase our attempts to influence. In the research presented here, we found that Shotguns wanted the most from their superiors and used all forms of influence to get what they wanted. These two areas of research suggest a link between influence styles and stress. May (1972) proposed that persons who fail to exercise influence suffer the most stress; therefore, Bystanders should report the highest levels of stress. However, Bystanders had given up wanting things from other people in the organization. Hence, issues of control were less important to this group than to Shotgun employees. Individuals characterized as Shotguns may be expected to experience more job tension and personal stress than their peers because they want much and use all forms of influence intensely to accomplish their objectives. While we had no direct personality measures, the behavior of Shotguns appeared consistent with Booth-Kewley and Friedman's (1987) description of the stress-prone personality as competitive, aggressive, and demanding much from others. This leads to the following question:

Question 4: Do subordinates employing a Shotgun upward-influence style report higher levels of job tension, and higher levels of physical and psychological stress, than subordinates using other influence styles?

The above research questions guided our analysis of three studies of upward influence. The first study, of workers, was done for an undergraduate Honor's thesis by Marge Pedrick, under the supervision of David Kipnis. While Pedrick's research was designed to examine research questions 1–3, she did not attempt to develop measures of upward-influence styles. We reanalyzed her data for this article. The second study, of supervisors, was undertaken to replicate the findings of the first study. The third study, of CEOs, was designed specifically to address question 4.

Study 1: Workers

Respondents and Procedure

Seventy-two first-line supervisors attending leadership training sessions were asked to designate one effective and one ineffective subordinate currently working for them. This designation was requested to increase the variability of reported performance evaluation of the designated subordinates. The subordinates were employed in nonmanagerial jobs ranging from production to clerical positions.

Using rating forms, supervisors evaluated the performances of these two subordinates. The supervisors were then asked to give each subordinate a packet that contained the Profile of Organizational Influence Strategies (POIS, Form M) and a stamped return envelope addressed to the first author. Both subordinates of 22 supervisors returned the POIS. An additional 15 returns were received from one of the subordinate pairs (10 effective and 5 ineffective). A total of 59 subordinates (37 male and 22 female) returned the questionnaires. Thirty-two returns were from subordinates rated as effective and 27 returns were from subordinates rated as ineffective. Through prior coding of the questionnaires, it was possible to match supervisors with their subordinates.

Some possible biases exist in this procedure for sampling employees. First, many of the supervisors may not have distributed the questionnaires to their subordinates, but we have no information on which to confirm or disconfirm this conjecture. Second, highly rated subordinates may have been more likely to return their questionnaires. The mean supervisory evaluation score for subordinates who returned the questionnaire was 30.6. The corresponding mean supervisory evaluation score of nonrespondents was 29.6 (n.s.). Third, it is possible that employees with low performance evaluations deliberately distorted their descriptions of their influence tactics. We had no evidence to confirm or disconfirm this point, although the reliability of influence scores of poorly rated employees was the same as that for highly rated employees.

Measures

Upward influence. POIS, Form M was used to measure the frequency with which respondents used the following six strategies to influence their immediate supervisors: Friendliness included six items, such as "acting humble" and "making my boss feel important" (alpha = .71); Assertiveness included five items, such as "demanding," "insisting," and "setting time deadlines" (alpha = .65); Reason included four items, such as "writing a detailed plan" and "explaining the reason for my request" (alpha = .70); Bargaining included five items, such as "offering an exchange" and "offering to make personal sacrifices" (alpha = .76); Higher Authority included four items, such as "making a formal appeal to higher levels" and "obtaining the informal support of higher-ups" (alpha = .65); Coalition included two items: "obtaining the support of coworkers" and "obtaining the support of subordinates" (alpha = .54).

Performance evaluations. Supervisors evaluated the performance of their subordinates on the following items: (1) ability to work independently, (2) ability to work cooperatively, (3) ability to solve problems, (4) motivation to work hard, (5) potential for promotion, and (6) overall performance. Each item was rated on a 7-point scale ranging from "Outstanding" (7) to "Very Poor" (1). A performance evaluation score was constructed by summing the six items (alpha = .78).

Study 2: Supervisors

Respondents and Procedures

This study essentially replicated Study 1 but used more skilled, career-oriented, and ambitious subordinates, who were themselves supervisors. These respondents consisted of 153 part-time M.B.A. students whose average age was 30 years. They had been employed for an average of three years in various entry-level managerial positions in such diverse fields as engineering, accounting, sales, computers, and personnel management. These respondents completed the POIS, Form M, in evening class, by describing how they influenced their immediate superiors. The respondents provided the names and addresses of their immediate superiors, and a packet consisting of a letter explaining the purpose of the research, a performance evaluation form, and a return envelope addressed to the authors, was sent to each superior. The immediate superiors of the respondents rated them with the same instrument that was used in Study 1.

A total of 113 superiors returned their questionnaires, which provided us with performance evaluations for 59 male subordinates and 54 female subordinates.

Results

As shown in Table 26.2, the findings from the studies of workers and supervisors were fairly consistent. In both studies, male and female subordinates classified as Shotguns received less favorable evaluations than those using other upward-influence styles. No support was found, however, for the suggested possibility that Shotgun women subordinates would be given lower evaluations than Shotgun men. Both male and female subordinates employing a Shotgun upward-influence style were given equally low ratings. It seems clear that forceful, assertive women in these studies were not evaluated less favorably than assertive men.

The research literature provides contradictory evidence about the link between influence styles and favorable evaluations. The findings in Table 26.2 illustrate why such contradictory evidence exists and allows us to determine who received the best performance evaluations.

Among the men, the highest performance evaluations were given to Tacticians in both studies. In contrast, among the women, the highest performance evaluations were given to Ingratiators in the worker study and to female Ingratiators and Bystanders in the supervisor study. One can only speculate whether the reverse of this pattern would occur if women were doing the evaluating. That is, would women supervisors give high evaluations to male Ingratiators and to female Tacticians?

Study 3: Chief Executive Officers

The first two studies showed that subordinates' upward-influence styles and superiors' performance evaluations were related. We next examined how upward-influence styles

Table 26.2
**Relation Between Subordinates' Upward-Influence Styles and Supervisors'
Performance Evaluations**

Influence Style	Study 1: Workers		Study 2: Supervisors[a]	
	Male (N = 37)	Female (N = 22)	Male (N = 59)	Female (N = 54)
Shotgun	24.0	32.3	30.1	32.1
Ingratiator	29.4	41.5	32.7	35.9
Bystander	30.1	30.2	34.7	36.2
Tactician	32.7	31.0	36.0	33.3
F-test	Style X Gender ($p < .05$)		Style ($p < .05$)	

Note: Higher scores denote more favorable evaluations.
[a]Based on the evaluations of male superiors.

were related to two other individual consequences. First, salary and, second, stress, which includes job tension, physical stress, and psychological stress.

Respondents

Respondents were obtained by sending a letter to each of 1,200 CEOs of profit and nonprofit hospitals with 300 or fewer beds. The letter asked them to participate in a study of administrative practices. Of the administrators contacted, 316 agreed to participate. These administrators were sent copies of the POIS, Form M, with directions to indicate how they influenced their board of directors, board of trustees, or, in the case of for-profit hospital chains, the person to whom the hospital CEO reported. One hundred and eight CEOs returned the questionnaires. Eight months later, they were sent second questionnaires, containing scales to measure job tension, physical stress, and psychological stress. Eighty-seven of the original 108 CEO respondents returned the second questionnaire.

Of the 108 respondents in this study, all but two were male. Their average age was 44; all had college degrees, and some had education beyond that, their salaries averaged $61,000; they had an average of four years experience as chief executive officer, an average of 100 doctors on their medical staffs, and an average of 400 employees.

Measures

Salary, used as an indicator of evaluation, was reported on a scale that increased in $10,000 increments from $25,000 to $100,000 or more. Since salary is known to be affected by demographic factors associated with the individual and his or her job, an attempt was made to control for these factors. Four control variables were used in the analysis: (1) the number of years the CEO had been in his or her present position; (2)

the size of the hospital as measured by the number of beds; (3) the number of physicians employed in the hospital; and (4) the total number of employees in the hospital. As Table 26.1 indicates, two of these control variables were related to the influence clusters. In addition, all four control factors correlated significantly with reported salary (years in current job, $r = .39$; number of hospital beds, $r = .62$; number of physicians, $r = .46$; number of employees, $r = .47$).

Job tension. Three subscales measuring work pressure, role ambiguity, and role conflict were included in the questionnaire completed by the CEOs. Items for the work pressure subscale were taken from the Work Environment Scale (Insel and Moos 1974). The subscales for role ambiguity and role conflict were drawn from the research described by Rizzo, House, and Lirtzman (1970). Each item was measured on a 4-point scale, ranging from "Greatly bothered me" (4) to "Hardly bothered me" (1). The intercorrelation between the three subscales of role ambiguity, work pressure, and role conflict averaged over .60. Because of these high intercorrelations the three subscales were combined into an index labeled job tension (alpha = .82).

Physical stress. Chief executive officers indicated how often they experienced each of the following health-related problems: severe headaches or migraines, difficulty in sleeping, exhaustion or severe fatigue at day's end, stomach pains or digestive problems, difficulty breathing, shortness of breath, and excessive coughing. Each item was answered on a 5-point scale ranging from "Almost every day" (5) to "Never" (1). Responses were summed over all items to provide a measure of physical stress (alpha = .67).

Psychological stress. CEOs indicated how frequently they experienced the following psychological symptoms of stress (Mayes, Sime, and Ganster 1984): tension, anxiety, general nervousness, periods of irritability or anger, periods of depression, feeling blue or helpless, periods of impatience, and feeling frustrated. Each item was answered on the same scale as that used to measure physical stress (alpha = .87).

Results

Average salaries were adjusted through an analysis of covariance to control for the number of hospital beds, number of physicians employed, total number of hospital employees, and years experience as a CEO. The four covariates accounted for 44 percent of the variance of salary ($p < .001$). Influence style accounted for significant variance (an additional 7 percent) in the CEOs' salaries after partialing out the variance attributable to the four control variables (df = 3 and 107, $F = 4.2$, p < .01). As Table 26.3 shows, Tacticians earned between $5,000 and $7,000 more per year than CEOs in the three other clusters after adjusting all salaries for the variance associated with the four control factors. Thus influence style was related to salary allocations.

Contrary to expectations, CEOs employing a Shotgun upward-influence style did not

Table 26.3
**Average Adjusted Salary of CEOs
by Upward-Influence Style**

Influence style	Salary
Shotgun ($N = 22$)	$57,000
Ingratiator ($N = 28$)	57,200
Bystander ($N = 43$)	60,000
Tactician ($N = 15$)	65,100

receive significantly lower salaries. Rather, Tactician CEOs had significantly higher salaries than CEOs classified as either Shotguns, Ingratiators, or Bystanders ($p < .05$). In this instance, then, emphasis on logic and reason was related to a recognized benchmark of being valued—money.

Stress and influence style. The relation between influence style and subjective reports of job and personal stress, is shown in Table 26.4. CEOs with an active, assertive, that is, Shotgun influence style reported the highest levels of stress. Shotguns reported the most job tension, as well as personal stress such as the inability to sleep, anger, and other psychological symptoms of stress. The same pattern was found for reports of physical stress symptoms, although not at a statistically significant level. CEOs who relied on reason and logic to influence, that is, Tacticians, reported the least amount of job tension and personal stress.

Here, then, is suggestive evidence linking influence style and stress. These findings suggest the interesting possibility that an individual's influence style may predict health status like direct measures of the Type A personality do (Booth-Kewley and Friedman 1987).

DISCUSSION

These studies were exploratory and although the findings exhibit a clear pattern of relationships, we need to consider whether the findings were based on response set. In the cluster analysis, it could be argued, Shotgun subordinates were "yeasayers" and Bystanders were "naysayers" when answering the POTS. Hence, these styles did not reflect meaningful classifications of patterns of influence. If response set accounted for the findings, however, then the most likely pattern of findings would be for Shotgun subordinates to have scores at one end of the continuum and Bystanders at the other. Instead, Bystanders have scores in the middle of the distribution, and Tacticians have extreme scores. That the classification of influence styles cannot be attributed to response set is also suggested by the significant relations between the four styles and superiors' evaluations. Apparently other people perceived differences in the influence activities of respondents that were consistent with their self-descriptions of how they got their way.

The findings show that upward-influence style plays a role in the performance eval-

Table 26.4

The Relation Between Upward-Influence Styles and Job Tension and Stress for Chief Executive Officers*

Influence style	Job tension	Physical stress	Psychological stress
Shotgun (N = 20)	44.45	11.25	12.65
Ingratiator (N = 20)	37.55	10.65	10.15
Bystander (N = 34)	35.26	11.00	10.71
Tactician (N = 11)	32.00	8.64	8.55
F-tests	Style ($p < .05$)	Style (n.s.)	Style ($p < .05$)

*High scores denote high levels of stress.

uations and salary achieved at work, as well as the work-related stress that people experience. How large a role is unknown. It is possible that influence styles were an epiphenomenon resulting from individual reactions to organizational success, or lack of it. It is clear that considerably more research is needed to evaluate the various alternative explanations of the present findings that can be offered. The suggestion that influence styles may moderate important individual outcomes from work, however, is of particular interest.

Among males, for example, a logical, reasoning, "Tactician" approach to influencing one's superiors was associated with more favorable individual outcomes than an assertive, forceful shotgun style. These results complement a previous report (Kipnis and Schmidt 1983) that Tacticians have power in their organizations based on their performance of nonroutine work. These findings bring to mind the classic Weberian grouping of authority (power) and rationality as the basis for organizational functioning and individual success.

This explanation, however, does not help us understand why female employees using a Tactician style did not also receive the most favorable performance evaluations. Perhaps Mainiero's (1986) explanations for gender differences in the use of influence at work can explain these findings. One possibility Mainiero suggested is that men and women are socialized to use different influence tactics and that this socialization process carries over to the work setting. A second possibility she discussed was that women and men vary in access to organizational power and hence vary in the influence tactics that they can use.

While Mainiero found little support for the socialization process explanation, its logic could be applied in the present study. That is, early learning socializes men to expect women to be passive or ingratiating and not to emphasize logic when seeking to influence. As a result, women employees who use little upward-influence, or use influence based on ingratiation, may be perceived by male superiors as effectively performing their roles. Alternatively, women subordinates using reason and logic may be perceived as acting "out of role" (Costrich et al. 1975) and therefore are evaluated less favorably than Ingratiators.

As this brief discussion indicates, the present findings raise many questions that require further study. For example, it is well documented that stress is caused by significant life events at work and at home. Based on the findings of this study, one wonders whether individuals experience added stress as a result of the influence styles they use.

The findings also raise questions about the number of styles that exist, as measured by cluster analysis. Perreault and Miles (1978) reported five styles when they measured the use of influence with peers. Kipnis and Schmidt (1983) reported three styles when they measured downward influence, and the present study reported four styles when upward influence was measured. At this time, we do not know whether these differences are due to differences associated with the target person or to instability in the technique of cluster analysis. It may be that an Ingratiator style only emerges in analyses of upward influence, where employees are influencing persons of greater power than themselves. A final research question concerns the role of the Bystander in organizational life. Between 30 and 40 percent of respondents in each of the three samples were classified as using little influence with their superiors. One possible explanation is that they had other ways to influence their superiors that were not measured here. If, however, 30–40 percent of organizational members are not, for whatever reasons, influencing upwards, then we should ask in what ways this lack of upward influence affects both subordinate-superior relations and organizational outcomes. Given the importance of upward influence to organizational functioning and individual effectiveness, further studies are essential to understand the social forces that restrain this substantial silent minority.

REFERENCES

Booth-Kewley, Stephanie, and Howard S. Friedman. 1987. Psychological predictors of heart disease: A quantitative review. *Psychological Bulletin* 101: 343–362.

Costrich, Norma, Jean Feinstein, Louise L. Kidder, and Jeanne Marecek. 1975. When stereotypes hurt: Three studies of penalties for sex-role reversals. *Journal of Experimental Social Psychology* 11: 520–530.

Deluga, Ron. 1986. Job tensions and the use of influence. Paper presented at the Eastern Psychological Association Annual Meeting, Boston.

Engelman, Lafzlo, and John Hartigan. 1981. K means clustering of cases. In Department of Biomathematics, University of California (eds.), *BMDP Statistical Software*: 464–473. Berkeley: University of California Press.

French, John R.P., and Bertram Raven. 1959. The bases of social power. In D. Cartwright (ed.), *Studies in Social Power*, 150–167. Ann Arbor, MI: Institute for Social Research

Ganster, Donald C. 1987. Type A behavior and occupational stress. *Journal of Behavioral Medicine* 10: 85–90.

Hobbes, Thomas. 1968. *Leviathan.* Harmondsworth, Middlesex: Penguin Books.

Insel, Paul, and R. Moos. 1974. *Work Environment Scale.* Monterey, CA: Consulting Psychologist Press.

Jones, Edward E. 1964. *Ingratiation.* New York: Appleton, Century.

Kanter, Rosabeth M. 1977. *Men and Women of the Corporation.* New York: Basic Books.

Kelly, Charles. 1988. *The Destructive Achiever.* Reading, MA: Addison-Wesley.

Kipnis, David, and Stuart Schmidt. 1983. An influence perspective on bargaining. In Max Bazerman and Roy Lewicki (eds.), *Negotiating in Organizations:* 303–319. Beverly Hills, CA: Sage.

Kipnis, David, Stuart Schmidt, and Ian Wilkinson. 1980. Intraorganizational influence tactics: Explorations in getting one's way *Journal of Applied Psychology* 65: 440–452.

Kipnis, David, and Richard Vanderveer. 1971. Ingratiation and the use of power. *Journal of Personality and Social Psychology* 17: 280–286.

Koontz, Harold, and Cyril O'Donnell. 1968. *Principles of Management.* New York: McGraw-Hill.

Mainiero, Lisa A. 1986. Coping with powerlessness: The relationship of gender and job dependency to empowerment-strategy usage. *Administrative Science Quarterly* 31: 633–653.

May, Rollo. 1972. *Power and Innocence.* New York: Norton.

Mayes, Bronston, Will Sime, and Donald Ganster. 1984. Convergent validity of Type A behavior pattern scales and their ability to predict physiological responsiveness in a sample of female public employees. *Journal of Behavioral Medicine* 7: 83–108.

Mowday, Richard. 1978. Leader characteristics, self-confidence and methods of upward influence in organizational decision-making. *Academy of Management Journal* 22: 709–725.

Muehlenhard, Charlotte L. 1983. Women's assertion and the feminine sex-role stereotype. In V. Franks and E.D. Rothblum (eds.), *The Stereotyping of Women:* 153–171. New York: Springer.

Osipow, Samuel, and Arnold Spokane. 1984. Measuring occupational stress, strain and coping. In S. Oskamp (ed.), *Applied Social Psychology Annual* 5: 67–86. Beverly Hills, CA: Sage.

Pelz, Donald. 1952. Influence: A key to effective leadership in the first line supervisor. *Personnel* 29: 3–11.

Perreault, William, and Robert Miles. 1978. Influence strategy mixes in complex organizations. *Behavioral Science* 23: 86–98.

Pfeffer, Jeffrey. 1981. *Power in Organizations.* Boston, MA: Pitman.

Porter, Lyman, Robert Allen, and Harold Angle. 1981. The politics of upward influence in organizations. In Larry L. Cummings and B.M. Staw (eds.), *Research in Organizational Behavior* 3: 109–149. Greenwich, CT: JAI.

Powell, Gary. 1988. *Women and Men in Management.* Newbury, CA: Sage.

Rizzo, John, Robert R. House, and Sidney I. Lirtzman. 1970. Role conflict and ambiguity in complex organizations. *Administrative Science Quarterly* 15: 155–163.

Salancik, Gerald R., and Jeffrey Pfeffer. 1977. Who gets power and how they hold it: A strategic contingency model of power. *Organizational Dynamics* (Winter): 3–21.

Schilit, Warren K. 1986. An examination of individual differences as a moderator of upward influence activities in strategic decisions. *Human Relations* 39: 933–953.

Schilit, Warren K., and Edwin Locke. 1982. A study of upward influence in organizations. *Administrative Science Quarterly* 27: 304–316.

Schlenker, Barry. 1980. *Impression Management.* Monterey, CA: Brooks/Cole.

Schmidt, Stuart M., and David Kipnis. 1984. Manager's pursuit of individual and organizational goals. *Human Relations,* 37: 781–794.

Weber, Max. 1947. *The Theory of Social and Economic Organizations.* A.M. Henderson and T. Parsons, trans. and eds. Glencoe, IL: Free Press.

Wortman, Camille, and Jane Linsenmeier. 1977. Interpersonal attraction and the techniques of ingratiation. In B. Staw and G. Salancik (eds.), *New Directions in Organizational Behavior:* 133–179. Chicago: St. Clair.

Wrong, Dennis. 1979. *Power: Its Forms and Uses.* New York: Harper and Row.

Appendix

Table 26A.1
Cluster Analysis of Upward-Influence Strategies in Three Studies

	Strategy					
Cluster	Friendliness	Reason	Assertiveness	Bargaining	Higher Authority	Coalition
Workers						
1 (*N* = 15)	18.1	13.8	18.5	12.4	9.7	5.7
2 (*N* = 9)	21.0	13.1	11.0	13.6	7.6	5.2
3 (*N* = 23)	12.7	11.0	7.9	5.7	5.2	3.3
4 (*N* = 12)	20.0	14.7	11.8	7.3	6.1	5.1
Mean	16.8	12.8	11.9	8.9	6.9	4.5
Supervisors						
1 (*N* = 19)	19.7	15.4	17.3	14.0	10.4	6.6
2 (*N* = 28)	20.6	14.7	10.8	8.4	5.9	5.1
3 (*N* = 35)	14.4	14.4	10.1	7.4	5.5	4.4
4 (*N* = 31)	18.2	16.3	14.8	9.3	6.8	5.4
Mean	17.9	15.2	12.8	9.3	6.8	5.2
Chief Executive Officers						
1 (*N* = 22)	22.3	17.9	14.0	12.2	8.5	6.4
2 (*N* = 28)	20.6	18.0	11.0	7.9	5.3	6.0
3 (*N* = 43)	15.0	16.7	10.0	6.7	5.2	5.0
4 (*N* = 15)	9.1	18.9	8.1	5.6	4.8	4.0
Mean	17.1	17.6	10.8	7.9	5.9	5.4

Upward Impression Management: Goals, Influence Strategies, and Consequences

Asha Rao, Stuart M. Schmidt, and Lynda H. Murray

INTRODUCTION

Impression management refers to the process by which people attempt to control or manipulate the reactions of others to images of themselves or their ideas (Leary and Kowalski 1990; Schlenker 1980; Tedeschi and Reiss 1981). The strategies that subordinates use to create favorable impressions with their managers has stimulated interest both in the popular press and in academic journals (Gardner and Martinko 1988a; Gilmore and Ferris 1989; Liden and Mitchell 1988; Ralston 1985; Wayne and Ferris 1990; Wayne and Kacmar 1991).

Our review of the impression management literature identified several deficiencies in the study of upward impression management. First, while theoretically acknowledging the existence of multiple goals such as appearing competent or pitiful (Gardner and Martinko 1988a; Godfrey, Jones, and Lord 1986), empirical research has usually assumed that people engage in impression management in order to be liked or appear attractive (Gilmore and Ferris 1989; Jones, Gergen, Gumpert, and Thibaut 1965; Liden and Mitchell 1988; Ralston 1985). Second, by limiting the range of goals in impression management, researchers have consequently limited the range of strategies studied. Most empirical studies emphasize the strategy of ingratiation (Ralston 1985; Wayne and Kacmar 1991). Third, with a few exceptions (Wayne and Ferris 1990), impression management research has been conducted in laboratories on students (Godfrey, Jones, and Lord 1986; Wayne and Kacmar 1991). Fourth, integrated frameworks of impression management in organizations provided by earlier researchers (Gardner and Martinko

---

1988a) have not been empirically examined. Finally, research cited to develop theoretical arguments of impression management in organizations was not usually conducted to explicitly examine impression management (Gardner and Martinko 1988a). We seek to remedy these deficiencies by studying impression management within organizations, integrating theoretical arguments developed by prior researchers.

Our study analyzes the relationships between subordinates' multiple goals in upward impression management, their influence strategies, and the impressions and appraisals reported by their managers. We adapt an integrated framework of impression management advocated by Gardner and Martinko (1988a) by incorporating research on social influence.

CONCEPTUAL FRAMEWORK

Applying Goffman's (1959) dramaturgical perspective of social interactions, Gardner and Martinko (1988a) developed a framework of impression management in organizations. In this framework, they described employees as actors upon an organizational stage, performing to create suitable images for their audience. Implicit in this framework is the belief that employees, as actors, consciously select specific impression management strategies to create images, within the constraints set by their organizations.

Four constructs are central to the impression management process. These are the motivation for managing impressions of oneself, the construction of impressions, the audience or target to whom the impression is addressed, and the organizational context in which impression management is enacted (Gardner and Martinko 1988a).

Motivation

Impression motivation describes why subordinates attempt to manipulate their managers' impressions. Specifically, impression motivation involves the goals people seek, the value of these goals, and the discrepancy between current and sought images (Leary and Kowalski 1990). Goals identified in impression management include appearing competent, pitiful, morally worthy, or dangerous (Jones and Pittman 1982). It is paradoxical that researchers describe the multiple nature of goals in impression management (Gardner and Martinko 1988a; Leary and Kowalski 1990; Schlenker 1980), yet assume in empirical research that a prime motive behind impression management is the desire to be liked (Gilmore and Ferris 1989; Liden and Mitchell 1988; Ralston 1985). We suggest that the goals identified by prior researchers are valued by subordinates because being liked, appearing competent, or even pitiful helps them achieve specific goals such as getting good appraisals or better job assignments.

Construction

Impression construction focuses on the strategies used to create impressions by altering the audience's perceptions. Prior research describes impression construction as the modification of one's own behavior, that is, self-presentation, to create the desired impression (Gardner and Martinko 1988b; Leary and Kowalski 1990). We expand the scope of impression construction to focus on the process of social influence which refers to strategies people use to alter the opinions or behavior of others to reach their goals (Kipnis, Schmidt, and Wilkinson 1980). Social influence strategies include not only ingratiation, but also reason, bargaining, assertiveness, coalitions, and appeals to higher authority (Kipnis et al. 1980).

Influence and impression management are related areas which were previously linked by Perreault and Miles (1978), who treated impression management as an influence strategy in getting compliance from others. We differ in our approach by viewing influence as part of the process of impression construction, where subordinates seek to alter their managers' perceptions of them. Both impression construction and influence are concerned with the behavioral strategies that people use to bring about a change in another's attitudes or opinions. Research on impression management has identified tactics such as supplication, intimidation, ingratiation, exemplification, and self-handicapping (Crant and Bateman 1993; Jones and Pittman 1982). Researchers in social influence have well-developed typologies of strategies which include many of the above tactics, and a wealth of organizational research that can be applied to the impression management context. By linking theoretical arguments in impression management with the empirical research on social influence we hope to enrich the study of these related fields.

Research on social influence in organizations indicates that subordinates' control over resources, goals in exercising influence, and contextual factors affect the strategies used (Kipnis and Schmidt 1983; Perrault and Miles 1978). For example, when subordinates have less power than the managers they are trying to influence, they emphasize ingratiation and reason (Kipnis and Schmidt 1983).

Audience

In Gardner and Martinko's (1988a) framework, the audience in impression management consists of the subordinates' immediate supervisors. Research on social influence indicates that subordinate performance appraisals are affected by their influence strategies (Kipnis and Schmidt 1988), and by managers' perceptions of who controls their subordinates' performance (Kipnis et al. 1981). A recent study highlights the connection between liking a subordinate, and giving that person a favorable evaluation (Judge and Ferris 1993). These findings indicate that it is necessary to relate the impressions formed by managers and their consequent appraisals to the impression management strategies used by their subordinates.

Context

Impression management strategies are also affected by the organizational context in which they are enacted (Gardner and Martinko 1988a; Kumar 1986; Perreault and Miles

1978; Schlenker 1980). These contextual factors include the opportunity for impression management, the existence of formal rules and procedures, task and role ambiguity, and scope for novelty in the organization (Gardner and Martinko 1988a). Prior empirical research in impression management has not taken into account the contextual factors affecting impression management.

AN INTEGRATED MODEL

Integrating the impression management and influence literatures led to the identification of three groups of factors affecting the choice of influence strategies in impression construction. As seen in Figure 27.1, these factors include individual factors related to impression management motivation, situational factors that form the context of impression management, and the subordinates' audience (Gardner and Martinko 1988a; Kipnis and Schmidt 1983; Perrault and Miles 1978). The consequences of subordinates using influence strategies in impression construction are the responses of their managerial audience, and include favorable performance appraisals, managerial perceptions of influence, and impressions of subordinates.

Individual Factors

Research on social influence identifies individual characteristics affecting influence strategies such as the need for power, attributional processes, the goals and relative power of the influencer, and level of work expertise (Ralston 1985; Kipnis et al. 1980). Because impression management has traditionally focused on being liked as a means to achieve goals such as good appraisals, we know little of the specific goals that subordinates seek in impression management. In this study, we identify seven goals from research on social influence. These goals include both individual goals such as seeking assistance on the job, favorable performance appraisals, and personal benefits, and organizational goals such as gaining acceptance of new ideas, getting more responsibility, assignment of work to managers, or convincing managers to work better (Kipnis and Schmidt 1984).

> *Proposition 1:* Influence behavior used in impression management varies with subordinates' goals.

Research on social influence indicates that in seeking personal goals such as a day off, or more pay, subordinates tend to rely on ingratiation and reason. Personal goals reflect the users' best interests, not necessarily that of their firm. Because ingratiation is a defensive strategy (Wood and Mitchell 1981), assertively demanding personal goals may not lead to the favorable impression sought by subordinates. But, in seeking organizational goals such as getting a project approved, subordinates may perceive greater legitimacy in their goals and use assertiveness, bargaining, and appeals to higher authority (Kipnis et al. 1984). We find some support for our argument of multiple goals

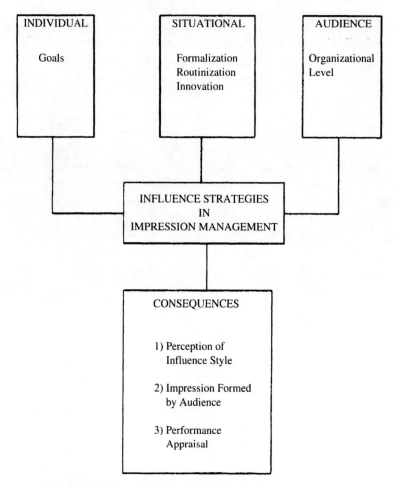

Figure 27.1. **Integrated Framework of Impression Management**

leading to multiple strategies in impression management in an experiment examining dual goals in selection interviews. The findings of this study indicated that subjects who sought to be liked used more ingratiation than when they wanted to be perceived as competent (Godfrey, Jones, and Lord 1986).

> *Hypothesis 1a:* The more subordinates seek to form impressions to fulfill personal goals, the more they use ingratiation.
>
> *Hypothesis 1b:* The more subordinates seek to form impressions to fulfill organizational goals, the more they use bargaining, reason, assertiveness, and higher authority.

Situational Factors

Situational factors include organizationally defined roles, management style, task ambiguity, resource scarcity, and information available to participants (Ralston 1985). In their framework of impression management in organizations, Gardner and Martinko (1988a) classified situational factors as the opportunity for positive impression, ambiguity, formality, and novelty. Based on Gardner and Martinko's (1988a) typology, we identify factors of routinization, formalization, and innovation.

Routine tasks rely on preestablished operations and plans, not allowing for much personal discretion or opportunity for positive impression. Formal organizations rely on a chain of command, documentation, and standard operating procedures, which, as in routine environments, restrict opportunities for accomplishing personal goals that are not in agreement with the organization (Gardner and Martinko 1988a). In routine situations that take place within formal organizations, we hypothesize that subordinates rely on ingratiation and reason to influence their managers' perceptions.

Low formalization leads to ambiguity of both the task and work responsibilities and causes uncertainty as to what successful performance entails. Innovation in the organization allows for more personal creativity, but, like ambiguity, is not clear on successful performance requirements. This uncertainty causes subordinates to resort to other methods of influencing their managers' perceptions and achieving desired outcomes. Greater freedom in performing tasks may lead to subordinates using assertiveness, bargaining, or invoking support from higher authorities to achieve desired outcomes.

Proposition 2: The degree of formalization and routinization inherent in an organization will affect the type of influence strategy used by subordinates.

Hypothesis 2a: The more formalized and routinized an organization's work operations, the more subordinates will use ingratiation to obtain desired outcomes.

Hypothesis 2b: The more innovative an organization's work operations, the more subordinates will use assertiveness and reasoning to obtain desired outcomes.

Audience Factors

In this study managers form their subordinates' audience. The audience's control of rewards that mediate individual goal achievement affect the subordinates' perception of the situation (Gardner and Martinko 1988a; Ralston 1985). Subordinates define the stimuli and select influence behaviors expected to make the most desirable impression on their audience (Gardner and Martinko 1988a; Schlenker 1980).

Interactions with a high status audience is more important than a low status audience (Gardner and Martinko 1988b). In impression management, subordinates exerting upward influence generally have low power and want to create an impression that will lead to desired outcomes. When trying to impress managers, ingratiation is a favored influence strategy (Liden and Mitchell 1988). In addition, research on social influence suggests that reason is also used by subordinates seeking to influence their managers (Kipnis et al. 1980).

> *Proposition 3:* Subordinates at different levels within an organization have different audiences which affects their choice of influence strategies.

> *Hypothesis 3:* The lower the subordinates' position within the organization, the more likely ingratiation and reason are used.

Consequences

Impressions formed by the audience lead to certain consequences for the actors (Gardner and Martinko 1988a). Managers' perceptions of their subordinates' influence strategies lead them to form specific impressions of their influence styles and general impressions of their subordinates (Wayne and Ferris 1990). Because managers have distinguished subordinates who want to be liked from those who want to appear competent from their behavior (Godfrey et al. 1986), we speculate that consequent performance appraisals are based on these impressions.

Managers may interpret their subordinates' influence styles as reasonable, tenacious, friendly, or negotiating. Managers also form holistic impressions of subordinates as being either amiable or disagreeable. These impressions can have a direct impact upon their appraisal of their subordinates. As stated earlier, a favorable performance appraisal is the most likely goal that subordinates seek in impression management. Impression management research, in general, tends to assume that ingratiation leads to liking or impressions of amiability, and hence to a favorable performance appraisal (Ralston 1985; Wayne and Ferris 1990). But, we speculate that ingratiation combined with reason leads to better appraisals than ingratiation alone because reason enhances perceptions of competence. We assume that competence is linked with performance on the job, and hence to good performance appraisals.

> *Proposition 4:* The influence strategies of subordinates affects the impression formed by their managers and their performance appraisals.

> *Hypothesis 4a:* The more managers perceive their subordinates as friendly or reasonable, the greater their impression of subordinate amiability.
> *Hypothesis 4b:* The more managers perceive their subordinates as tenacious or negotiating, the greater their impression of subordinate disagreeableness.
> *Hypothesis 4c:* The more managers perceive their subordinates as friendly or reasonable, the more favorable are the performance appraisals that subordinates receive.
> *Hypothesis 4d:* The more managers perceive their subordinates as tenacious or negotiating, the less favorable are the performance appraisals that subordinates receive.

METHODS

Sample

Subjects were recruited from management training seminars conducted at a British management training center. The participants were from several dozen manufacturing firms in the private sector as well as from municipal government and educational organizations in the public sector.

Procedure

A total of 156 questionnaire packets were distributed to volunteering managers. They were instructed to complete a questionnaire evaluating a subordinate whom they routinely evaluated. They were then given questionnaire packets to distribute to their designated subordinates who, in turn, were instructed to mail their completed questionnaires to the study headquarters.

Managers assessed their subordinates' performance, influence styles and provided their impression of these subordinates. Subordinates indicated their goals for influencing their managers, the influence strategies used, and provided general demographic and organization information.

Managers' questionnaires were matched with subordinates' questionnaires through a common code number. The data set consisted of 67 manager-subordinate pairs, that is, 134 responses, yielding a 43 percent response rate. The size of the employing organizations varied; 54 percent had under 500 employees, 27 percent had between 500 and 5,000 employees, and 18 percent had over 5,000 employees.

Of the responding subordinates, 75 percent were male and 25 percent female. Of their managers 90 percent were male and 10 percent female. Line positions accounted for 26 percent of the subordinates while 74 percent held staff positions. Overall, the responding subordinates had been in their positions 3.8 years and worked with their managers for 3.1 years. Given the opportunistic nature of the sample, we could not contact seminar participants who did not return the questionnaire. Hence, we were unable to test for response bias between the respondents and nonrespondents. This limits the generalizability of our findings to organizations and employees similar to our respondents. Despite this limitation, our study contributes to our knowledge of impression management by extending the arena of investigation from the laboratory to organizations.

Measures

The following measures were used to collect information on the individual, situational and audience factors in impression management. Subordinates indicated their goals in impression management, the degree of formalization, innovation, and routinization, and their influence strategies. All respondents indicated their level in the organization. Managers provided appraisals of their subordinates, overall impressions of their subordinates, and their perceptions of their subordinates' influence strategies.

Goals

Subordinates rated seven goals in influencing their managers on a 5-point response scale, ranging from (1) "never" to (5) "very often." The variables measured were personal goals of (a) assistance with own work, (b) receive personal benefits, (c) evaluate work favorably. We also included organizational goals of (a) convince managers to work better, (b) assign work to manager, (c) seek more responsibility, and (d) to accept ideas for change (Schmidt and Kipnis 1984).

Situational

Subordinates rated their situational circumstances which included formalization, routinization, and innovation. These situational variables were assessed on 5-point response scales ranging from (1) "almost none" to (5) "a great deal." Formalization included (a) clear objectives, (b) defined job responsibilities, (c) standard operating procedure, (d) procedures for dealing with new problems, (e) written work schedules, (f) written evaluation standards, (g) job duties well documented, and (h) written documents are an essential part of the job (alpha = .79).

Items for the routinization scale were (a) was work based on the same operations, and (b) the importance of planning (alpha = .40). Because of the low internal consistency in the scale, we retained the former item as a single item measure of routinization due to its face validity.

Items for innovation asked subordinates to indicate the degree to which there was (a) encouragement of alternative approaches, (b) novelty and variety, (c) the speed of policy changes, and (d) encouragement of creative activity (alpha = .60).

Audience

Subordinates identified their level in the organization as either (1) non-manager, (2) low manager, (3) mid-manager, or (4) upper manager. In all cases subordinates were seeking to manage impressions with a higher status audience, that is, their immediate supervisors.

Influence Strategies

Influence behaviors used by subordinates with their managers were assessed with the Profile of Organizational Influence Strategies-Form M (POIS) instrument (Kipnis and Schmidt 1982). This empirically derived instrument assesses upward influence usage along the subscales of Ingratiation, influencing by creating good feeling toward oneself (six items, alpha = .68); Bargaining, negotiating and offering an exchange of benefits or favors (five items, alpha = .72); Reason, using facts, data and logical arguments (four items, alpha = .72); Assertiveness, having a forceful manner, not taking no for an answer (six items, alpha = .64); Higher Authority, invoking the assistance of higher levels of management (four items, alpha = .66); and Coalition, mobilizing others as allies to apply social pressure (two items, alpha = .68). Emerging research indicates that the POIS instrument maintains its construct validity across an assortment of North American studies (Hinkin and Schriesheim 1990; Yukl and Falbe 1990).

Subordinates were asked to report how they typically behaved toward their immediate manager during the past 6 months. The response scale for indicating the frequency of using each influence tactic (item) ranged from (1) "never" to (5) "almost always."

Consequences

Managers reported on three consequences of subordinate influence which were, perceptions of influence style, impressions of subordinates and performance appraisals. On 7-point response scales ranging from (1) "very poor" to (7) "outstanding," managers evaluated their subordinates on the following dimensions of performance (Kipnis and Schmidt 1988): (a) independence, (b) cooperativeness, (c) creative approaches, (d) technical ability, (e) motivation, (f) potential for promotion, and (g) alternative problem-solving methods (alpha = .88). We also included a single-item measure of overall performance.

Managerial impressions of their subordinates were classified as either amiable (two items) or disagreeable (three items) on 5-point scales ranging from (1) "hardly ever" to (5) "usually." Amiable refers to perceptions of subordinates' cheerfulness and friendliness (alpha = .75). Disagreeable refers to the managers' perceptions of subordinates being irritable, tense, and helpless (alpha = .61).

Finally managers reported their impressions of how their subordinates normally attempted to influence their bosses. Subordinates were perceived as tenacious to the extent that they refused to take no for a answer, and engaged in confrontation (two items, alpha = .64). Reasonableness was the extent subordinates presented thoughtful ideas, and used logic and reasoning (two items, alpha = .77). Negotiation was the extent subordinates bargained and negotiated or haggled when communicating (two items, alpha = .77). Friendliness refers to how friendly and helpful subordinates were perceived when communicating with managers (two items, alpha = .71).

RESULTS

Hypothesis 1a, stating that subordinates pursue personal goals through ingratiation, was partially supported. Ingratiation was positively correlated with the personal goals of favorable appraisal ($r = .31$; $p < .01$) and personal benefits ($r = .29$; $p < .01$), but the correlations with assistance on the job and seeking more responsibility were not significant. Hypothesis 1b on the use of assertiveness, bargaining and higher authority by subordinates pursuing organizational goals was supported, as indicated in Table 27.1.

Table 27.1
Correlations of Subordinate Influence Strategies with Their Goals

	Personal goals (mean SD)		
Influence strategies	Assist work .77 (0.09)	Personal benefits 1.99 (0.91)	Favorable appraisals 2.96 (1.66)
Ingratiation	0.15	0.29**	0.31**
Bargaining	0.19	0.14	0.37***
Reason	0.00	0.30	0.02
Assertiveness	−0.10	−0.03	0.35***
Higher authority	0.14	0.03	0.31**
Coalition	0.12	−0.04	0.07

	Organizational goals (mean SD)		
Influence strategies	More responsibility 2.44 (1.04)	Manager's performance 1.99 (0.99)	Accept ideas 2.77 (0.79)	Assign work to manager 1.84 (0.99)
Ingratiation	0.19	0.10	0.17	0.17
Bargaining	0.15	0.31**	0.32***	0.20*
Reason	0.13	0.23*	0.48***	0.34**
Assertiveness	0.12	0.40***	0.44***	0.34**
Higher authority	0.11	0.35**	0.37**	0.31**
Coalition	−0.03	0.17	0.36**	0.03

Note: $N = 67$.
*$p < .05$. **$p < .01$. ***$p < .001$.

Hypothesis 2a regarding the relationship between ingratiation and formalized and routinized work conditions was not supported, as indicated in Table 27.2. Hypothesis 2b was also not supported. Subordinates' use of reason was negatively, and significantly, associated with innovative work environments, contrary to our hypothesis ($r = -.28$; $p < .05$). Furthermore, subordinate assertiveness was not associated with innovative work environments ($r = -.05$).

The third hypothesis, relating subordinates' level in their organizations to their using ingratiation and reason, was not supported by our findings. Rather than the negative relationship we expected, we found a positive correlation ($r = .24$; $p < .05$) between subordinates using reason and organizational level. Additionally, using coalitions was significantly and positively associated with the organizational level of subordinates ($r = .29$; $p < .05$).

The results of testing for the fourth set of hypotheses, relating managerial perceptions of their subordinates' influence styles (H4a and H4b), their impressions of subordinates (H4c), and performance appraisals (H4d) are presented in Table 27.3. As hypothesized in H4a, managers' impressions of subordinates as amiable was positively correlated with their perceptions of subordinate friendliness ($r = .55$; $p < .001$) and reason ($r = .20$; $p < .05$). In support of H4b, managers' impressions of their subordinates as dis-

Table 27.2
Correlations of Subordinate Influence Strategies with Situational and Audience Factors

Subordinate influence strategies	Mean (SD)	Situational factors			Audience factor level
		Formalization	Innovation	Routinization	
Ingratiation	2.16(0.64)	−0.16	−0.13	−0.03	−0.04
Bargaining	1.40(0.47)	−0.19	0.01	0.17	−0.08
Reason	3.25(0.70)	0.04	−0.28*	−0.01	0.24*
Assertiveness	1.76(0.53)	−0.14	−0.05	0.19	0.00
Higher authority	1.43(0.47)	−0.25*	0.18	0.01	0.12
Coalition	2.28(0.93)	0.10	−0.08	0.09	0.29*

Note: N = 67.
*p < .05.

Table 27.3
Correlations of Manager's Perceptions of Subordinate Influence Styles, Impressions of Subordinates, and Performance Appraisals

Manager's perception of influence	Impression of subordinate		Appraisal	
	Disagreeable	Amiable	Performance	Overall
Tenacious	0.47***	−0.24*	0.15	−0.05
Reasonable	−0.46***	0.20*	0.63***	0.46***
Negotiation	0.27*	0.08	−0.12	−0.12
Friendliness	−0.38**	0.55**	0.47***	0.21*
Impressions of subordinate				
Disagreeable			−0.42***	−0.26*
Amiable			0.31**	0.18

Note: N = .67.
*p < .05. **p < .01. ***p < .001.

agreeable was positively correlated with perceptions of style as tenacious ($r = .47$; $p < .001$), and negotiating ($r = .27$; $p < .01$). Subordinates perceived as using reason or friendliness were positively correlated with favorable performance appraisals ($r = .63$; $p < .001$; $r = .47$; $p < .001$) respectively, providing support for H4c. The relationships between perception of subordinates as negotiating or tenacious and performance appraisals was not significant, leading to the rejection of H4d.

DISCUSSION

In testing a theoretical model of impression management on a group of British managers and their subordinates we found some support for our model, along with some discrepancies.

Antecedents to Impression Construction

Previous empirical research has focused on the desire to be liked as the prime motive behind impression management (Gilmore and Ferris 1989; Liden and Mitchell 1988; Ralston 1985). But, we found that subordinates had many different goals such as assistance with their job, benefits, better appraisals, managerial performance, and acceptance of new ideas. These results support theoretical arguments that subordinates have multiple goals in impression management (Gardner and Martinko 1988a; Leary and Kowalski 1990; Jones and Pittman 1982).

In seeking favorable assessments, subordinates used multiple strategies of ingratiation, bargaining, and assertiveness. Subordinate ingratiation corroborated earlier research in impression management which indicated that ingratiation led to liking and perhaps to good appraisals (Wayne and Kacmar 1991). But, we see that assertiveness and bargaining were also used by subordinates who sought better appraisals. We find that reason was used more frequently than ingratiation by subordinates in pursuing their goals. Their reliance on reason confirms the importance of appearing competent to one's supervisor. We conclude that subordinates believe that merely being liked is not sufficient to achieve good appraisals.

There may be cultural differences in influence strategies in impression management. Managers in the United States use ingratiation, appeals to higher authority, and assertiveness to enhance their image with their immediate supervisor (Schmidt and Kipnis 1984). The British managers in this study did not use coalitions for achieving personal goals unlike their U.S. counterparts. In pursuing organizational goals, British managers used a wide range of strategies, all except ingratiation. In comparison, managers in the United States used a more limited range of strategies for each work goal, including ingratiation (Schmidt and Kipnis 1984). These cultural differences in influence strategies warrant further investigation of the cultural bases of tactics in impression management.

The subordinates' low managerial level (1.9) and tenure (3.8) indicated that they were lower level and relatively inexperienced managers. Subordinates appeared to use a full range of influence strategies to obtain their goals. Their approach is similar to the "shotgun" style of influence (Kipnis and Schmidt 1983). "Shotguns" are characterized as having less job tenure, many reasons for influencing others, and a greater need for personal benefits and promoting their work ideas (Kipnis and Schmidt 1983).

Contrary to our expectations, we found that subordinates in innovative organizations used less reason. Perhaps innovative organizations create an organizational climate where there is less emphasis on rational behavior. Because innovative organizations encourage their employees to be creative and different, employees may not believe that reason, a rather conventional strategy, is appropriate in their organization. The lack of support for the relationship between formalization, routinization, innovation, and influence strategies could also reflect the fact that the survey participants were from a wide range of organizations. Factors particular to their organizations may have affected respondents' strategies. By combining the different types of organizations from private industry, government, and education, we may have neutralized any differences due to organizational culture on impression management.

Consequences

Examining managerial impressions and appraisals, we find that subordinates perceived as friendly and reasonable were viewed as amiable people, and favorably evaluated. These results support the impression management literature which indicates that perceptions of subordinate friendliness leads to good impressions and appraisals. However, perceptions of rationality appear more important. While the impression management literature has not focused on negative impressions we discovered that subordinates appearing tenacious created unfavorable managerial impressions and received poor appraisals.

Two unanticipated findings emerged in cross-level analysis when we integrated the reports received from both managers and their subordinates. First, the link between influence strategies reported by subordinates with consequences initiated by managers was weak (Table 27.4). Subordinate reports of using reason and ingratiation were not associated with managerial impressions of amiability or disagreeability or performance appraisals. We also found that subordinates reporting being assertive, were perceived as rather disagreeable by their managers, and poorly evaluated. Apparently, assertive subordinates are not appreciated.

Second, in examining the relationship between reported subordinate influence strategies and managerial perceptions of their style, we find some anomalies which are presented in Table 27.4. Our comparisons are methodologically limited because we are attempting to link reported influence strategies with managerial perceptions of influence styles. But, operating within this limitation, our a priori expectations were that subordinate influence strategies of reason and ingratiation would be associated with managerial perceptions of reasonableness and friendliness; bargaining with negotiation; assertiveness with tenacity. In lieu of these relationships, we find that strategies of coalitions are associated with perceptions of friendliness; coalitions and bargaining with tenacity; coalitions and assertiveness with negotiation; and assertiveness is viewed as non-rational.

We offer some interpretations for inconsistencies between managerial perceptions and subordinate strategies by drawing upon Gardner and Martinko's (1988a) dramaturgical framework of impression management and research on social influence. One, subordinates, that is, actors, need to have greater self-awareness in enacting their impression management strategies. Second, managers or the audience in impression management, selectively attend and respond to subordinate influence. Situational and contextual factors may affect the selection of impressions and the audience's interpretation of actor's behavior. In our study, we expected these situational factors to affect the actors and did not anticipate their impact on the audience in impression management. Third, when behavior is perceived as incongruent within a certain context, impression management leads to consequences not intended by the actors. Gardner and

Table 27.4
Correlations of Subordinate Influence Strategies with Managerial Perceptions

Influence strategy reported	Managerial perceptions of subordinate influence style				Impressions of subordinates		Appraisals	
	Tenacious	Reason-able	Negotia-tion	Friendli-ness	Disagree-able	Amiable	Perfor-mance	Overall
Ingratiation	−0.06	0.07	0.05	0.11	−0.01	0.06	0.13	0.02
Bargaining	0.24*	−0.04	0.15	0.10	0.11	−0.02	0.02	0.05
Reason	0.01	0.18	0.06	0.06	−0.04	0.02	0.12	0.01
Assertive	0.16	−0.21*	0.26*	0.04	0.19	−0.02	−0.23*	−0.23*
Coalition	0.21*	−0.04	0.22*	0.22*	0.06	0.10	−0.06	−0.10
High authority	.016	−0.01	0.14	−0.08	0.17	−0.11	−0.04	−0.12

Note: $N = 67$.
*$p < .05$.

Martinko's (1988a) framework suggests that interpersonal factors we have not studied here, such as attraction and similarity, may play a part in the context of influence.

Recent research of social influence comparing reports of influence strategies provided by both actors and their audience concluded that attributional and judgment errors biased audience reports of influence strategies (Yukl and Falbe 1990). Assuming that subordinate reports were more accurate we looked for patterns in cross-level analysis. When subordinates reported being assertive, their managers perceived them as irrational and gave them poor performance appraisals. While our findings suggest that assertiveness leads to unfavorable impressions and evaluations, we interpret the results with caution. Our data are correlational and we cannot assess causality. Perhaps, poor past performance led to poor appraisals and resulted in subordinate assertiveness. We suggest that subordinates judiciously use assertiveness, and perhaps combine it with reason to avoid being perceived as irrational. Because coalitions are viewed in a favorable light, influencing their boss through peer pressure may serve their interest better than assertiveness. We also suggest that managers develop greater awareness of the association between their perceptions of assertiveness and performance appraisals.

The cross-level analysis also sheds light on the role of ingratiation in impression management. On the one hand, subordinates associate ingratiation with favorable appraisals, indicating the link between ingratiation and impression motivation and construction. On the other hand, managers appear to discount the value of ingratiation. The strategy is positively, yet not significantly, associated with managerial perceptions of subordinate friendliness, and performance appraisals. We speculate that managers either assume that a certain base level of ingratiation is acceptable, or consciously guard against letting these strategies affect their appraisals.

In summary, we find that subordinates reported using a range of influence strategies in seeking a number of goals in impression management. We also find that subordinates need to manage impressions that their managers form, because they are associated with their performance appraisals. Using the dramaturgical framework of Gardner and Martinko (1988a), we find that actors often do not create the images that they seek within their audience. Their managers react to the impressions constructed by subordinates based on their own perceptions of the images being conveyed.

Limitations

Our study has limitations which need to be remedied in future research. First, methodological artifacts, such as scales of measurement, may account for differences in strategies reported by subordinates and managerial perceptions of styles. By using the same units of measurement, stronger statistical techniques can be used to compare reports of influence by subordinates, and managerial perceptions of style. Second, we use retrospective, self-report data, which may account for some of the difference between manager and subordinate reports of influence. Using reports from other actors in the organization could provide an unbiased report of actual subordinate behavior. In defense of our approach, because subordinates' motivations may not be evident to others, and they consciously choose strategies in impression management, their perceptions are a necessary piece of the impression management puzzle. Incorporating perceptions of others guards against common method bias, but introduces perceptual biases of the other parties (Yukl and Falbe 1990). Also, Spector (1987) indicates that common method variance may not always bias questionnaire data when the scales of measurement are reliable. Third, while our study benefits from having data from manager-subordinate dyads, the limited number of dyads restricts our ability to use causal modeling techniques to examine the causal pattern in the process of impression management. Unfortunately, compromises and judgment calls have to be made in studying behavior in organizations (McGarth, Martin, and Kulka 1982). Asking managers to provide additional information on subordinate influence strategies, and the interpersonal context of influence would have increased the length of our questionnaire and reduced our response rate. Future researchers, by making other tradeoffs, can supplement the findings from this study.

Our contribution lies in the empirical examination of a theoretical framework of impression management. We find that subordinates have both multiple goals and influence strategies in impression management. By examining impression management within organizations, we have provided a stronger basis for further theoretical development and empirical exploration in the area of impression management.

CONCLUSION

Prior empirical research in impression management has had a limited perspective of the goals and influence strategies used, and their consequences. In this study we empirically investigated the relationship between subordinate goals in impression management, their upward influence behavior and the impressions formed by their managers. Our results indicate that individuals have multiple goals in impression management and use a variety of influence strategies to reach these goals. Our respondents report using reason more often than ingratiation.

Subordinate ingratiation was associated with their desire to secure better appraisals, but did not appear to lead to favorable impressions or appraisals. Managers' perceptions of their subordinates' influence styles were related to their impressions of subordinates and performance appraisals. Subordinates who were friendly and reasonable, were perceived as amiable, and favorably evaluated. Perceptions of tenacity and negotiation led to subordinates being perceived as disagreeable, but was not associated with unfavorable appraisals.

Assertiveness proved to be inappropriate in impression management, because it was associated with negative managerial perceptions and poor performance appraisals. We also found that managers' perceptions of influence were not in congruence with strategies reported by their subordinates. The relationship between influence strategies in impression management and managerial perception of these strategies needs to be further explored because of the consequences of these perceptions. In addition, the impact of organizational culture, which may be the missing link between organizational and individual variables in impression management needs further examination.

REFERENCES

Crant, M.J., and Bateman T.S. 1993. Assignment of credit and blame for performance outcomes. *Academy of Management Journal* 36(1), 7–27.

French, J.R.P., and Raven, B. 1959. The bases of social power. In D. Cartwright and A. Zander (Eds.), *Group Dynamics.* New York: Harper and Row.

Gardner, W.L., and Martinko, M.J. 1988a. Impression management in organizations. *Journal of Management* 14(2): 321–338.

———. 1988b. Impression management: An observational study linking audience characteristics with verbal self-presentation. *Academy of Management Journal* 31: 42–65.

Gilmore, D.C., and Ferris, G.R. 1989. The effects of applicant impression management tactics on interviewer judgments. *Journal of Management* 15(4): 557–564.

Godfrey, D.K., Jones, E.E., and Lord, C.G. 1986. Self-promotion is not ingratiating. *Journal of Personality and Social Psychology* 50(1): 1056–1115.

Hinkin, T.R., and Schriesheim, C.A. 1990. Relationships between subordinate perceptions of supervisor influence tactics and attributed bases of supervisory power. *Human Relations* 43(3): 221–237.

Jones, E.E., and Pittman, T.S. 1982. Towards a general theory of strategic self-presentation. In J. Suls (ed.), *Psychological Perspectives of the Self.* Hillsdale, NJ: Erlbaum, pp. 231–262.

Jones, E.E., Gergen, K.J., Gumpert, P., and Thibaut, J.W. 1965. Some conditions affecting the use of integration to influence performance evaluation. *Journal of Personality and Social Psychology* 1(6): 613–625.

Judge, T.A., and Ferris, G.R. 1993. Social context in performance evaluations. *Academy of Management Journal* 36(1): 80–105.

Kipnis, D. 1976. *The Powerholders.* Chicago: University of Chicago Press.

Kipnis, D., and Schmidt, S.M. 1982. *Profiles of Organizational Influence Strategies: Form M.* San Diego, CA: University Associates.

———. 1983. An influence perspective on bargaining within organizations. In M.H. Bazerman and R.J. Lewicki (eds.), *Negotiating in Organizations.* Beverly Hills, CA: Sage, pp. 303–319.

————. 1988. Upward-influence styles: Relationship with performance evaluations, salary, and stress. *Administrative Science Quarterly* 33: 528–542.

Kipnis, D., Schmidt, S., and Wilkinson, I. 1980. Intraorganizational influence tactics: Explorations in getting one's way. *Journal of Applied Psychology* 65(4): 440–452.

Kipnis, D., Schmidt, S., Price, K., and Stitt, C. 1981. Why do I like thee: Is it your performance or my orders? *Journal of Applied Psychology* 66(3): 324–328.

Kumar, P. 1986. Supervisor's authoritarianism and ingratiation among workers. *Psychological Studies* 31(2): 165–168.

Leary, M.R., and Kowalski, R.M. 1990. Impression management: A literature review and two-component model. *Psychology Bulletin* 107(1): 34–47.

Liden, R.C., and Mitchell, T.R. 1988. Ingratiatory behaviors in organizational settings. *Academy of Management Review* 13(4): 572–587.

McGarth, J.E., Martin, J., and Kulka, R.A. 1982. *Judgment Calls in Research.* Beverly Hills, CA: Sage.

Perreault, W.D., Jr., and Miles, R.H. 1978. Influence strategy mixes in complex organizations. *Behavioral Science* 23: 86–98.

Ralston, D.A. 1985. Employee ingratiation: The role of management. *Academy of Management Review* 10(3): 477–487.

Schlenker, B.R. 1980. *Impression management: The Self-concept, Social Identity, and Interpersonal Relations.* Monterey, CA: Brooks/Cole.

Schmidt, S.M., and Kipnis, D. 1984. Managers' pursuit of individual and organizational goals. *Human Relations* 37(10): 781–794.

Spector, P.E. 1987. Method variance as an artifact in self-reported affect and perception at work: Myth or significant problem? *Journal of Applied Psychology* 72(3): 438–443.

Tedeschi, J.T., and Reiss, M. 1981. Verbal tactics of impression management. In C. Antaki (ed.), *Ordinary Explanations of Social Behavior.* London Press, pp. 271–326.

Wayne, S.J., and Ferris, G.R. 1990. Influence tactics, affect, and exchange quality in supervisor-subordinate interactions: A laboratory experiment and field study. *Journal of Applied Psychology* 75(5): 487–499.

Wayne, S.J., and Kacmar, K.M. 1991. The effect of impression management on the performance appraisal process. *Organizational Behavior and Human Decision Processes* 48: 70–88.

Yukl, G., and Falbe, C. 1990. Influence tactics and subjectives in upward, downward, and lateral influence attempts. *Journal of Applied Psychology* 75(2): 132–140.

28

Citizenship and Impression Management: Good Soldiers or Good Actors?

Mark C. Bolino

In 1983 Bateman and Organ introduced the construct of organizational citizenship behavior (OCB), drawing upon concepts of suprarole behavior advanced by Katz and Kahn (1966). Organ describes OCB as "individual behavior that is discretionary, not directly or explicitly recognized by the formal reward system, and that in the aggregate promotes the effective functioning of the organization" (1988: 4). Since its introduction, the topic has received a great deal of research attention. A review of the literature on citizenship indicates that researchers generally maintain that OCBs stem from two motivational bases: (1) job attitudes and/or (2) disposition/personality (Organ 1990; Organ and Ryan 1995). The relationship between OCB and job attitudes is rooted in social exchange theory—that is, employees engage in OCBs in order to reciprocate the actions of their organizations. The second rationale holds that OCBs reflect an individual's predisposition to be helpful, cooperative, or conscientious.

Research on citizenship has almost exclusively concerned antecedents consistent with these theoretical bases. Examples of the antecedents examined by researchers include job attitudes (Bateman and Organ 1983), job cognitions (Organ and Konovsky 1989), dispositional factors (e.g., agreeableness, conscientiousness, and equity sensitivity; Konovsky and Organ 1996), positive affect (George 1991), positive mood states (Smith, Organ, and Near 1983), concern for others (McNeely and Meglino 1994), organizational justice (Niehoff and Moorman 1993), and collectivism (Moorman and Blakely 1995). The common denominator across these studies is the notion that citizenship stems from an individual's desire to help others or the organization because of disposition or a sense of obligation; describing such individuals as "good soldiers" or "good citizens" reinforces this idea.

Citizenship researchers argue that OCBs are critical to organizational functioning (Bateman and Organ 1983; Organ 1988)—an assertion based largely on the work of

Katz, who suggested that "an organization which depends solely upon its blueprints of prescribed behavior is a fragile social system" (1964: 132). However, in contrast to the numerous studies exploring the antecedents of OCB, there is a paucity of research examining the outcomes of citizenship behaviors in organizations (Organ and Ryan 1995).

Although researchers suggest that enhanced organizational functioning is the focal outcome variable of OCB, there have been few empirical studies addressing the topic. In addition, there are other products of citizenship that have not been examined. In particular, researchers have yet to look at the positive images likely to accrue to individuals who engage in citizenship behaviors. Several researchers recently have noted that engaging in citizenship behaviors might be quite impression enhancing and self-serving (e.g., Eastman 1994; Fandt and Ferris 1990; Ferris, Judge, Rowland, and Fitz-gibbons 1994). That is, people who engage in citizenship are likely to be favorably perceived by others (e.g., supervisors, coworkers, and so on) in their organizations.

Impression-management researchers have identified tactics that people use to enhance their images at work (Jones and Pittman 1982; Tedeschi and Melburg 1984). On the surface, many of these impression-management strategies are very similar—if not identical—to citizenship behaviors. For example, helping one's supervisor may be an act of citizenship or an act of impression management. In a finding unrelated to their primary research question, Wayne and Green (1993) noted that impression-management behaviors were correlated positively ($r = .49$) with altruistic citizenship behaviors. Thus, there is an empirical basis for linking these constructs. Moreover, Schnake (1991) points out that unless the motive behind citizenship is revealed, in some cases impression-management behaviors may mistakenly be coded as citizenship; likewise, OCB may sometimes be categorized as impression management. Thus, understanding motive is essential in order for research on citizenship to progress; moreover, the motives underlying citizenship may influence the effect that such behaviors have on individuals' images at work, as well as organization or work group effectiveness.

Given that image enhancement is likely to result from citizenship behaviors, impression-management concerns, in addition to reciprocity or personality/disposition to be helpful, may drive individuals' decisions to engage in such behaviors. My purpose in this article, then, is to explore the role of impression-management motivation in the context of citizenship. In exploring this issue, I seek to further the understanding of impression management and citizenship in three ways.

First, I review the relevant literature on citizenship and impression management, highlighting the conceptual overlap between citizenship and impression management. I then present a general model of citizenship that provides an overview of how motivational concerns, including impression management, influence acts of citizenship and the outcomes associated with them. Thus, in this model a more complex conceptualization of the motivational bases of organizational citizenship is proposed—an approach that seeks to improve our understanding of the intentionality of citizenship behaviors by examining how impression-management concerns interplay with motives of citizenship behaviors identified in past research.[1]

Second, based on Leary and Kowalski's (1990) impression-management motivation model, I outline specific antecedents of citizenship behaviors driven by impression-management concerns. Following their model, I propose that individuals will be motivated to engage in citizenship for impression-management reasons when (1) they believe that citizenship will facilitate the achievement of a "good organizational citizen" image, (2) they value being seen as good organizational citizens, and (3) there is a discrepancy between the good organizational citizen image that they believe others hold of them and how they wish to be viewed. I then detail the effects of citizenship behaviors, in turn, upon organization/work group effectiveness and an individual's image as a good organizational citizen. Thus, I seek not only to explore the impression-management motives underlying citizenship but also to examine the outcomes of citizenship in this context.

Third and finally, I offer recommendations for designing research aimed at empirically determining the motivational bases for citizenship behaviors, specifically addressing the means of developing research designs that will enable researchers to isolate the helping motivation from impression-management motives underlying OCBs. I also discuss implications for future theory development and practical implications.

CITIZENSHIP AND IMPRESSION MANAGEMENT: DOING GOOD— LOOKING GOOD

According to Organ (1988), OCBs are behaviors that employees (1) are not explicitly rewarded for exhibiting nor punished for not exhibiting, (2) are not part of an employee's job description, and (3) are behaviors for which employees do not receive training to perform.

Organ (1988) proffers five dimensions of organizational citizenship. Altruism represents behaviors directed at helping a specific person at work (e.g., a coworker or a supervisor). The label generalized compliance is used to describe general employee conscientiousness that surpasses enforceable work standards. Sportsmanship describes tolerance of nuisances on the job (i.e., when employees endure impositions or inconveniences without complaint). Courtesy refers to the act of "touching base" with others before taking actions or making decisions that would affect their work. Lastly, civic virtue behaviors describe the active participation and involvement of employees in company affairs, such as attending meetings, responding to mail, and keeping up with organizational issues. Most of the empirical work on citizenship is based on Organ's (1988) model, and empirical support has been found for his conceptualization[2] (MacKenzie, Podsakoff, and Fetter 1991).

By definition, OCBs are not necessarily selfless acts. Still, by and large, researchers have focused on motives that emphasize either prosocial or social exchange intent. For example, while Organ (1988) acknowledges that engaging in citizenship behaviors on a frequent basis might affect the impression that an individual makes on a supervisor or coworker, he maintains that such behavior is a consequence of other-serving rather than self-serving motivation. In fact, he suggests that to increase the prevalence of OCBs in the workplace, organizations should try to identify and recruit individuals prone to engage in OCBs and should avoid individuals who are egocentric. Similarly, while Podsakoff, MacKenzie, and Hui (1993) state that it may be interesting to understand how political motives affect employees' reasons for engaging in OCBs, they conclude that the intentions of employees are unimportant for understanding the impact that OCBs have on organizational functioning. Thus, although citizenship researchers have acknowledged that impression-management motives may explain citizenship behaviors, none has conducted theoretical or empirical research addressing this point.

Impression management refers to the process by which people attempt to influence the image others have of them (Rosenfeld, Giacalone, and Riordan 1995). Sociologists and social psychologists have studied such behavior for more than 30 years, but only more recently has the topic received the attention of organizational researchers. During this time, impression management has been documented as a common phenomenon in the workplace, and impression-management behaviors have been discussed in a variety of contexts. These include interviewing (Stevens and Kristof 1995), performance appraisal (Wayne and Ferris 1990; Wayne and Liden 1995), leadership (Wayne and Green 1993), careers (Feldman and Klich 1991), feedback seeking (Ashford and Northcraft 1992), and information seeking (Morrison and Bies 1991).

Impression-management theorists have identified many strategies that individuals may employ in organizational settings (e.g., Tedeschi and Melburg 1984). Jones and Pittman (1982) indicate that these tactics fall into five categories: (1) ingratiation, where individuals seek to be viewed as likable; (2) exemplification, in which people seek to be viewed as dedicated; (3) intimidation, where individuals seek to appear dangerous or threatening, (4) self-promotion, in which individuals hope to be seen as competent; and (5) supplication, where people seek to be viewed as needy or in need of assistance. Not only can achieving these desired images be facilitated by acts of citizenship, but many measures of impression management include specific behaviors that OCB researchers label as citizenship behaviors.

For example, exemplification strategies of impression management involve such behaviors as arriving to work early and leaving late. Rosenfeld et al. (1995) describe exemplifiers as employees who volunteer for tough assignments, suffer to help others in the organization, and "go beyond the call of duty." Likewise, Jones's (1964) typology of ingratiation tactics suggests that ingratiators engage in behaviors such as making others feel positive about themselves, rendering favors, and conformity. Wayne and Ferris's (1990) impression-management scale includes supervisor-focused ingratiation behaviors, such as agreeing with your supervisor, doing personal favors for your supervisor, and volunteering to help your supervisor on a task. Similarly, Kumar and Beyerlein's (1991) Measure of Ingratiatory Behaviors in Organizational Settings (MIBOS) measures the frequency of such behaviors as listening to others' problems, going out of one's way to run errands, volunteering one's help, and showing one's selflessness. On the surface, exemplification and ingratiation strategies of impression management appear to have much in common with citizenship behaviors.

Volunteering for special assignments and helping out others may provide workers with opportunities to show off their talents and knowledge. As such, these behaviors may be motivated by self-promotion strategies. Likewise, individuals may help out others in order to convey the message that they, too, need help at times. Such a strategy is consistent with research on supplication which suggests that individuals use such tactics to evoke feelings of social responsibility in others (Rosenfeld et al. 1995). Finally, it is conceivable that individuals might use OCBs as part of an intimidation strategy. For example, if employees are aware that their coworkers cannot stay at work late, they might stay late or threaten to do so. That is, because they can make their colleagues appear less dedicated in contrast, employees might use such tactics to intimidate or threaten their colleagues. Again, there is not only an overlap between impression-management behaviors themselves and several dimensions of citizenship, but OCBs may also prove instrumental in the achievement of an individual's impression-management goals.

Impression-management theorists suggest that a primary human motive, both inside and outside of organizations, is to be viewed by others in a favorable light and to avoid being viewed negatively (Rosenfeld et al. 1995). As indicated above, engaging in citizenship behaviors in organizational settings is a viable means of achieving favorable attributions. Although there is some disagreement among impression-management researchers regarding the authenticity of the impressions that people convey, Leary and Kowalski (1990) emphasize that impression-management theory does not imply that the impressions created by individuals are necessarily false. In other words, individuals who seek to be viewed as dedicated to their companies may, indeed, truly be committed to their organizations. Thus, I do not maintain here that employees engage in OCBs solely based on impression-management concerns; instead, I suggest that impression-management motives may motivate citizenship in addition to other motives, such as social exchange or personality/disposition.

Figure 28.1 illustrates the two motivational forces behind citizenship behavior. According to this model, one set of forces reflects the impression-management motive behind OCBs: citizenship behaviors result from an individual's desire to look like a good citizen. The second set of motivational forces encompasses those identified by previous research on this topic (Organ and Ryan 1995); here, citizenship behaviors result from an individual's genuine desire to help the organization or to help another individual at work based on social exchange or because of their personality/disposition. (Because these are the motives traditionally associated with citizenship behavior, I refer to them collectively as "traditional motives.")

The model indicates that impression-management motives have an additive effect on citizenship behaviors[3] (i.e., in addition to traditional motives). As I argue later, impression-management motives also moderate the relationship between traditional motives and citizenship behaviors (the relationship between traditional motives and OCB is weaker in the presence of impression-management motives). As in previous work, I show OCBs to positively impact organization/work group performance (Organ 1988). However, the model specifies that impression-management motives moderate the relationship between OCB and organization/work group effectiveness (the relationship be-

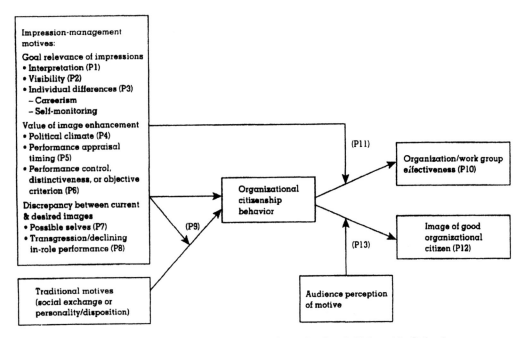

Figure 28.1. **An Impression-Management Model of Organizational Citizenship Behavior**

tween citizenship and effectiveness is weaker when OCBs are motivated by impression-management concerns). Lastly, the model suggests that although an employee who engages in citizenship behaviors generally will be viewed as a good organizational citizen, this outcome is moderated by the audience's perception of the employee's motive.

IMPRESSION-MANAGEMENT MOTIVES AND CITIZENSHIP BEHAVIORS

In a 1990 work, Leary and Kowalski reviewed over 30 years of social psychology research on impression management. The objective of their review was to reduce the many variables that affect impression management to the smallest set of theoretically meaningful factors. Based on their review of this literature, the authors developed an expectancy-value model of impression management. According to their theoretical model, three main factors determine the motivation to manage impressions: (1) the goal relevance of impressions, (2) the value of image enhancement, and (3) the discrepancy between current and desired images (Leary and Kowalski 1990). I discuss each set of factors in turn.

Goal Relevance of Impressions

Individuals are more motivated to manage impressions when they view such impressions as instrumental in achieving their goals (Leary and Kowalski 1990). In this article I propose that, in some cases, an individual's goal may be to be perceived as a good citizen. Individuals will be more likely to use citizenship behaviors to achieve such a goal when they believe OCBs will be instrumental in achieving this end. Three factors are likely to affect one's perception of the goal relevance of citizenship behaviors for impression management: (1) interpretation, (2) visibility, and (3) individual differences.

First, individuals are likely to view citizenship as image enhancing when such behavior will be interpreted in a positive manner by observers who influence outcomes that are valued by the individual. However, although it is typically assumed that citizenship is a desirable behavior and, therefore, seen in a favorable light, there are reasons that citizenship may not be viewed as such. For example, a corporate culture that disapproves of political behavior may diminish an employee's expectancy that citizenship behaviors will be viewed positively by others. Nonetheless, to the extent that citizenship is viewed favorably by important others, employees will be encouraged to engage in such behavior.

> *Proposition 1:* Individuals will be more likely to engage in OCBs when they believe that OCBs will be interpreted favorably by individuals who influence desired outcomes.

Second, citizenship behaviors that are visible are more likely to be relevant to the accomplishment of one's image goal than those that are private. That is, using citizenship as a form of impression management requires that the image-enhancing OCBs be recognized by those who influence desired outcomes—both tangible and intangible. Thus, citizenship behaviors are more likely to facilitate the accomplishment of one's goal to the extent that they are noticed by one's supervisor, coworkers, or other important targets. Individuals will be more likely to view citizenship as goal relevant and, therefore, carry out such behaviors when their expectancy is high that influential others will note their actions.

> *Proposition 2:* Individuals will be more likely to engage in OCBs when they believe that OCBs will be noticed by individuals who influence desired outcomes.

Third and finally, there is evidence that some individuals are more predisposed than others to believe that impression management is an important factor in accomplishing one's goals. Feldman and Weitz (1991) describe careerism as the tendency to pursue career advancement through non-performance-based means. Careerists believe that merit alone is not enough for achieving upward mobility in organizations and that appearances play an important role in career advancement (Feldman and Klich 1991). For this reason, individuals with such a disposition often focus more upon image building than hard work. Thus, careerists are more likely to view OCBs as relevant in achieving their image goals than those without a careerist orientation.

Self-monitors are individuals who are sensitive to the social appropriateness of their self-presentations and act like social chameleons, changing their attitudes, perspectives, and behaviors to suit a particular social setting (Snyder 1974). Fandt and Ferris (1990) have found that self-monitors use impression management in an opportunistic manner. Blakely, Fuller, and Smith (1996) have found that high self-monitors are also more likely to engage in citizenship behaviors. These authors assert that high self-monitors make better citizens because they are more likely to be sensitive to others' need for help and are able to adjust their behavior. Although the same relationship is postulated here, I suggest that self-monitors engage in OCBs because they believe such behaviors help them to "fit in" in a way that enhances their image.

Proposition 3: Careerism and self-monitoring will be positively associated with OCBs.

Value of Image Enhancement

Whereas the first set of factors addresses individuals' expectations that their acts of citizenship will prove successful in helping them achieve their image goals, the second set of factors related to impression-management motivation is the value of image enhancement itself. That is, individuals are more likely to engage in citizenship for impression-management reasons as the value they place on being seen as good organizational citizens increases. I suggest here that the value of such an image is salient in political climates; in periods of approaching performance appraisal deadlines; and in situations where in-role performance is constrained, where in-role performance is unlikely to be distinctive across employees, or where there is a lack of objective criteria for assessing in-role performance.

Researchers have described organizational politics as a social influence process in which behavior is strategically designed to maximize either short- or long-term self-interest at the expense of others' interests (Ferris, Russ, and Fandt 1989). When organizational processes such as rule enforcement, performance appraisal, and advancement decisions become politicized and subjective, rather than objective, an individual's image tends to become important. Consequently, as Ralston and Elsass (1989) suggest, individuals react to political environments by increasing their use of impression-management tactics. Therefore, in such an environment, employees are likely to place a premium on improving their personal image and to use acts of citizenship to achieve this end.

Proposition 4: The greater the level of organizational politics perceived by individuals, the more likely they will be to engage in OCBs.

Because performance appraisals typically affect the distribution of desirable outcomes (e.g., money and advancement), the value of being seen as a good organizational citizen is likely to increase as the evaluation date draws near. Indeed, Werner (1994) found that individuals who engage in OCBs receive higher performance ratings. Research suggests that individuals frequently increase their in-role performance as the performance appraisal period draws closer (Longenecker, Gioia, and Sims 1987); I suggest here that individuals in organizations will take advantage of rater recency biases by increasing extra-role behaviors as well.

Proposition 5: Individuals will be more likely to engage in OCBs as the perfor-mance appraisal deadline approaches.

Finally, the nature of the job is a factor likely to increase the value of one's image. Specifically, if employee control over in-role performance is limited, individuals may rely upon extra-role behaviors to enhance their image and distinguish themselves. For example, workers on an assembly line may have little opportunity to demonstrate su-perior performance and may therefore engage in citizenship behaviors, owing to their discretionary nature.

Similarly, situations in which employees have difficulty differentiating their perfor-mance from that of their peers may induce citizenship behaviors. For example, if an employee is competing with equally capable coworkers, that employee may be capable of distinguishing himself/herself via extra-role behaviors. Finally, individuals working in jobs with no formal or quantifiable performance criteria will be more likely to engage in OCBs. Ferris et al. (1989) suggest that individuals respond with impression-management behaviors when they are in situations where it is difficult for their perfor-mance to be assessed objectively. Thus, employees may use citizenship behaviors in such situations because OCBs become the primary indicator of their performance (i.e., by necessity, it is likely to be the criteria upon which most supervisors will base per-formance evaluations).

Proposition 6: Individuals will be more likely to engage in OCBs when their control over in-role performance is limited, when individual in-role performance is difficult to distinguish, or when objective cri-teria for assessing in-role performance are lacking.

Discrepancy Between Desired and Current Images

The final set of factors related to an individual's impression-management motivation is the discrepancy between one's desired image and the image one believes others may hold. Such discrepancies are likely to arise in at least two cases: (1) when individuals proactively seek to move to a more desirable self-conceptualization or (2) when they are reacting to a loss in their status that is due to transgressions or a decline in their in-role performance.

Research on the concept of possible selves suggests that individuals have ideas of what they would like to become and seek to achieve their ideal selves (Markus and Nurius 1986; Markus and Ruvolo 1989). Researchers have shown that impression man-agement can help people move closer to their desired selves or ideas of what they would like to be or become (Baumeister 1982). Thus, this research suggests that people may engage in citizenship behavior when they have a possible self of "the good organizational citizen." That is, the citizenship behaviors of some individuals may serve to facilitate the achievement of a goal that moves them from their present conceptualization of self to a more desirable image; citizenship behaviors may act to help individuals maintain this desired image as well.

Proposition 7: Individuals with a good organizational citizen possible self will be more likely to engage in OCBs.

Transgression is an act that violates a shared moral or legal code. Researchers in social psychology have established that transgression and subsequent prosocial behavior by the actor are positively related (Tedeschi and Riordan 1981). In other words, individuals often engage in prosocial acts in order to restore a positive image of themselves. This research suggests that employees will be likely to engage in citizenship behaviors when they have wronged their organization in some respect and are making amends for their transgression. For example, an employee may work overtime because of a damaged image after being caught using the office copier for personal purposes.

Similarly, a discrepancy between one's desired and current image is also likely to be created when an individual's in-role performance is suffering. That is, an employee trying to maintain a positive image may use citizenship behaviors in an effort to offset deteriorating in-role performance. For example, employees who cannot complete in-role assignments may step up their citizenship efforts—an approach that may maintain or increase their good-citizen image by offsetting their declining image or by providing justification for not properly managing their in-role work.

Proposition 8: Individuals will be more likely to engage in OCBs when their image has suffered because of transgressions against their organization or because of a decline in their in-role performance.

THE INTERACTION OF IMPRESSION-MANAGEMENT AND TRADITIONAL MOTIVES

According to Figure 28.1, citizenship may be a function of impression-management concerns or the genuine desire to help out—or both. Whereas Propositions 1–8 relate the additive effects that impression-management motives have on citizenship behaviors, Proposition 9 suggests that impression-management motives also moderate the relationship between traditional motives and citizenship behaviors. Specifically, the relationship between traditional motives and citizenship behaviors will be weaker in the presence of impression-management motives.

For example, consider the relationship between conscientiousness (a traditional motive) and citizenship in the context of an approaching performance appraisal (an impression-management motive). Employees who are highly conscientious generally engage in citizenship more frequently than those low in this trait (Organ and Ryan 1995). Therefore, in the absence of impression-management motives, highly conscientious employees will engage in a high degree of citizenship, whereas those low in conscientiousness will engage in a lower degree of citizenship. Similarly, as performance appraisals approach, those high in conscientiousness will exhibit a high degree of citizenship behaviors. However, because of their image-enhancing effects, when performance appraisals approach, even employees who are low in conscientiousness will engage in high levels of citizenship behaviors. That is, the impact of conscientiousness will be weaker when performance appraisals are near. Thus, in this example the presence of an approaching performance appraisal moderates the relationship between conscientiousness and citizenship behaviors.

Take the relationship between organizational justice (a traditional motive) and careerism (an impression-management motive) as another illustration. Among noncareerists, the relationship between organizational justice and citizenship should be fairly strong (Niehoff and Moorman 1993). However, among high careerists, one expects citizenship levels to be relatively high, even in instances where organizational justice is low. That is, in the presence of an impression-management motive such as careerism, the influence of organizational justice on citizenship behaviors is diminished. Therefore, I propose the following:

Proposition 9: The relationship between traditional motives and citizenship behaviors is moderated by impression-management motives; the relationship will be weaker when impression-management motives are present.

IMPRESSION MANAGEMENT AND THE CONSEQUENCES OF CITIZENSHIP

Organ and Ryan (1995) note that, since its introduction, most research on citizenship has examined it as a dependent variable. Although confirming empirical work is lacking, in theory, OCBs are thought to facilitate organization performance. Consistent with this perspective, I suggest that OCBs are positively related to organization and work group effectiveness. However, drawing upon impression-management theory, I propose that acts of citizenship also have important enhancement effects on an employee's image. In this section, then, I discuss the relationship between citizenship behaviors and organization/work group effectiveness and image enhancement.

Impression Management, Citizenship Behaviors, and Organization/Work Group Effectiveness

A primary assumption in previous work on OCB is that citizenship plays an important role in organization/work group functioning (Organ 1988). Researchers have offered several explanations for this assumption. First, citizenship is thought to increase organization performance by reducing the need to allocate scarce resources to maintenance functions within organizations, thereby freeing up these resources for more productive purposes. Second, citizenship can act to improve coordination within work groups, thus reducing friction within organizations and improving effectiveness. Finally, by making them attractive places to work, organizations where citizenship is prevalent may be better able to attract and retain the best employees, thereby improving their performance. Although researchers have little examined these specific processes, the extant studies, in general, appear to support the idea that citizenship and organization/work group effectiveness are positively related (Podsakoff, Ahearne, and MacKenzie 1997).

Proposition 10: OCBs are positively related to organization/work group effectiveness.

It is unclear how the motivation underlying citizenship behaviors is likely to impact organizational functioning. For example, Fandt and Ferris (1990) believe that acts of citizenship, regardless of their motive, are likely to facilitate organizational functioning. However, Schnake (1991) speculates that, in the long term, citizenship behavior motivated purely by self-interest will produce dysfunctional outcomes for organizations. Impression-management theorists, too, suggest that impression-management motives are likely to have deleterious effects on the relationship between citizenship behaviors and organization or work group effectiveness.

There are two reasons why impression-management motives are likely to reduce the impact citizenship behaviors have on organization/work group effectiveness. First, as Baumeister (1989) argues, when individuals undertake actions based upon impression-management concerns, they are less able to devote their full attention to the task at hand. Consequently, when employees are concerned with impression management, this concern frequently impairs their performance. For example, employees who volunteer to assist on a task may be so concerned with their image that they are unable to focus their attention on properly executing the task at hand. Moreover, in carrying out their citizenship behaviors, individuals whose primary goal is to increase the welfare of the organization or others are likely to outperform those whose goal is to look good. For this reason, when individuals undertake citizenship based on impression-management concerns, it is less likely that their OCBs will make as great a contribution to organization or work group functioning as will individuals' OCBs that stem from traditional motives.

Second, when citizenship behaviors are motivated by impression-management concerns, individuals may consciously invest less effort or expend less energy in carrying out the behavior. For example, compared with those motivated by traditional motives, employees who join a task force for impression-management reasons will be more likely to simply show up for meetings and do the minimum required of them. In other words, those volunteering because they sincerely desire to contribute to the organization will be likely to contribute to a greater extent than those who volunteer for impression-management reasons. Likewise, it is probable that employees who show up for work early or stay late as a result of impression-management motives will be more likely to spend some of their time socializing or reading the newspaper, thereby adding little to the performance of their work groups or organizations.

Nevertheless, even citizenship behaviors motivated by impression-management concerns are likely to facilitate organization/work group effectiveness to some extent. For example, even those who come to work early primarily to look dedicated may actually execute important tasks; likewise, although those engaging in citizenship owing to traditional motives may be more dedicated to or focused on their tasks and may execute them more effectively, those whose citizenship behaviors are motivated by impression management are likely to contribute as well, albeit to a lesser extent.

The extent to which motive is relevant in this regard may depend upon the type of citizenship behavior involved. For instance, for the more mundane forms of citizenship, motive may be less critical. However, given more complex acts of citizenship (i.e., those characterized by subtle quality contributions and extended efforts), motive may indeed play an important role. Further, because citizenship's impact on organizational functioning is frequently attributable to subtle contributions, to the extent that employees emphasize only the visible aspects of citizenship, it is less likely that the full value of citizenship will be realized.

Acts of citizenship are thought to enhance the effectiveness of organizations. Although it is unlikely that OCBs motivated by impression management will adversely affect organization/work group effectiveness, acts that are inferior or those that merely appear to be citizenship on the surface are less likely to greatly facilitate organization performance. Therefore:

> *Proposition 11:* Impression-management motives moderate the relationship between OCB and organization/work group effectiveness; the relationship will be weaker when impression-management concerns are present.

Citizenship Behaviors and Good Soldiers

The premise of this article is that engaging in OCBs can result in image enhancement. That is, employees who engage in such behaviors are more likely to be viewed as good organizational citizens by others. There is empirical support for this idea as well. For example, Werner (1994) found that supervisors use information regarding subordinate extra-role behaviors in determining performance appraisal ratings. Likewise, Podsakoff et al. (1993) indicate that citizenship behaviors affect managers' evaluations of subordinates' effectiveness over and above their objective productivity. Finally, Ferris et al. (1994) suggest that employees who engage in citizenship behaviors are likely to be viewed as better, more committed performers.

> *Proposition 12:* Individuals who engage in OCBs will be more likely to be viewed as good organizational citizens.

Although Proposition 12 suggests that OCBs are likely to foster an image of good organizational citizenship, audience attributions are an important moderator of this relationship. For example, Eastman (1994) found that employees labeled as good citizens received greater rewards from their supervisors than those labeled as ingratiators. Similarly, Jones's (1964) work on ingratiation indicates that impression-management tactics are successful only to the extent that they are perceived as authentic by observers. That is, employees may derive little benefit from engaging in OCBs if their motivation for doing so is perceived as insincere.

Some researchers speculate that engaging in behavior that is viewed purely as impression management may do more harm to one's image than abstaining from such behavior completely (e.g., Jones and Pittman 1982); however, Liden and Mitchell's (1988) work suggests that individuals will simply derive less benefit from their acts of citizenship when their behaviors are seen as stemming from impression-management motives. Because observers are likely to have difficulty discerning motive, they will most likely simply discount the credit given to those seen as impression managers.

Proposition 13: The relationship between citizenship behaviors and the image of a good organizational citizen is moderated by observer attributions of motive; the relationship will be weaker when observers view citizenship behaviors as motivated by impression-management concerns.

Impression-Management Motives and Other Characteristics of OCB

In studying organizational citizenship, researchers have primarily used measures tapping the frequency of OCB (e.g., Bateman and Organ 1983). Likewise, here I have centered on how impression-management motives drive the extent to which individuals will engage in citizenship. As Proposition 12 suggests, the more an individual engages in OCB, the more likely he or she is to be seen as a good soldier. For this reason, studying frequency of OCB is a logical starting point for investigating the relationship between impression management and citizenship; however, by focusing solely on the frequency of citizenship behaviors, researchers neglect other important features of citizenship, which, if examined, may help researchers better understand citizenship motives and aid them in designing research that identifies the likely motive underlying OCB. Table 28.1 describes five other characteristics—type, target, audience, timing, and magnitude— that might inform future research on citizenship, particularly research examining its underlying motives.

For example, there has been little attempt on the part of researchers to examine why individuals engage in certain types of citizenship behaviors to the exclusion of others (e.g., generalized compliance behaviors as opposed to altruism behaviors). This is unfortunate, because the type of citizenship demonstrated by an individual may affect its image-enhancing potential. In particular, impression-management researchers suggest that images are enhanced when they match the values and preferences of the target

Table 28.1
Impression-Management-Relevant Characteristics of OCB

Characteristic	Impression-Management Issue	Illustration
Type	Certain types of OCBs may be more image enhancing than others.	In organizations that value cooperation, *altruism* behaviors may be the most image enhancing.
Target	OCBs directed at certain individuals may be more instrumental in achieving one's image goals.	Helping a supervisor may be more image enhancing than helping a coworker.
Audience	Who the citizenship observers are, and how many there are, may affect OCBs' image-enhancing potential.	Citizenship witnessed by a large number of powerful people is likely to facilitate impression-management goals to a greater extent than if such behaviors are witnessed by a single unimportant individual.
Timing	Being a good citizen when it counts most may increase the image-enhancing potential of OCBs.	Staying late is likely to be highly valued in general; however, staying late before a critical assignment is due is likely to be more important for enhancing one's image.
Magnitude	The dramatic effect of OCBs is likely to influence their image-enhancing potential.	An act like coming to the office in severe weather is likely to facilitate image enhancement more so than an act like photocopying a document as a favor for someone.

(Goes and Tedeschi 1978). Thus, for example, if one's supervisor values conscientiousness, an employee's image is likely to be enhanced to the extent that he or she engages in generalized compliance behaviors; if helping teammates is considered paramount by a supervisor, acts of altruism should be of greater benefit to the actor's image.

Recent research has examined the issue of target, to the extent that this research considers the foci of employee citizenship behaviors (i.e., helping directed at another individual or helping directed at the organization). For example, McNeely and Meglino (1994) found that individuals high in concern and empathy for others were more likely to engage in citizenship directed at specific individuals, rather than the organization. However, researchers have not considered the issue of which particular person an individual chooses to help. Targeting one's citizenship behavior to coincide with the preferences of a powerful target is likely to heighten the degree of image enhancement achieved. For example, if a supervisor prefers that his or her subordinates assist their colleagues, altruism behaviors targeted at coworkers should be more image enhancing than those targeted at the supervisor.

The witnesses or audience to citizenship behaviors is potentially relevant as well with regard to image enhancement. Clearly, individuals who engage in citizenship for impression-management purposes should derive more image benefit from OCBs when there is an audience present. Further, the more powerful the audience or the larger the audience, the more image enhancing an act of citizenship is likely to be. Thus, the witnesses of employee citizenship behaviors—that is, coworkers, supervisors, or clients—may affect their image-enhancing potential.

Another relevant characteristic of citizenship is the timing of such behaviors. Citizenship behaviors may have stronger image-enhancing effects when they are timed strategically (i.e., executed at critical junctures). For example, working long hours to complete a critical assignment may be more image enhancing than staying late to complete regular assignments. In other words, being a good citizen when it counts most is likely to maximize image enhancement.

The final characteristic of citizenship behavior deals with the nature of the behavior in terms of its magnitude or its dramatic effect. Magnitude reflects how much effort or personal cost is required on the part of the individual engaging in citizenship. Image enhancement is likely to be greater when acts of citizenship are dramatic, costly, and appear to involve self-sacrifice. That is, certain acts of citizenship are more likely to elicit a positive reaction than others. Even within a particular class of citizenship behaviors, some behaviors are certain to be more noteworthy than others. For example, an employee may be helpful by making a fresh pot of coffee for his or her supervisor. That employee may also drive his supervisor to the airport at 5:00 A.M. Although both behaviors are forms of altruism, the second behavior would be considered to be of a greater magnitude than the first and, thus, more greatly enhance the employee's image.

I suggest here that these characteristics of citizenship are informative in gaining a more comprehensive understanding of OCB. Moreover, as with the frequency of citizenship behaviors, it is likely that impression-management motives influence the type, target, audience, timing, and magnitude of citizenship behaviors so that the acts are more image enhancing.

Proposition 14: Impression-management concerns will motivate individuals to engage in citizenship behaviors that (a) correspond with the type of OCBs preferred by an influential target, (b) are directed in the way that is most valued by an influential target, (c) are noticed by an audience of influential targets, (d) are timed so that their execution occurs at critical junctures, and (e) are of great magnitude in terms of their level of effort or personal cost.

IDENTIFYING IMPRESSION-MANAGEMENT MOTIVES

Identifying the motivation behind citizenship behaviors is an important undertaking. First, from a theory development perspective, gaining insight into employees' citizenship motives and the distinctions between organizational citizenship and impression management should produce a clearer understanding of both of these constructs. Second, it is valuable to understand impression-management motives because they are likely to influence the impact that OCBs have on organization and work group performance. Here, I address the means of identifying impression-management motives using a variety of research designs.

Because motivation cannot be observed (only behaviors can), many researchers maintain that identifying the motive underlying acts of altruism is impossible. Recently, however, researchers in social psychology have developed a research program aimed at distinguishing self-serving from other-serving motives (e.g., Batson 1991). Batson and Shaw (1991) state that the premise of this approach is based on three principles. First, motivation or intent cannot be observed directly; it can only be inferred from an individual's behavior. Second, the true motivation for a behavior cannot be ascertained by observing a single behavior that might be attributable to different motives. Third, if an individual's behavior can be observed in different situations that isolate the potential goals of the individual, its underlying motive reasonably can be inferred.

Based on these principles, these researchers outline two steps necessary to infer the nature of one's motive from that individual's behavior. First, the two goals must be identified. In the impression-management-OCB context, these goals are (1) looking like a good organizational citizen, and (2) contributing to the organization/work group. Second, the individual's behavior must be observed under circumstances that are varied systematically. That is, the situation must be manipulated in a manner that untangles the relationship between the two potential goals, enabling the individual to obtain one goal without obtaining the other. For example, a researcher could accomplish this by developing research designs whereby individuals can achieve their goals of enhancing their "good soldier" image without actually having to engage in the OCB. In contrast, if an individual engages in citizenship under conditions where he or she believes that a relevant audience will never know those OCBs had been performed (thereby negating the impression-management motive), a motive to help the organization reasonably can be inferred.

Again, the key is not to seek to identify the motivation behind a single behavior but, rather, to infer motivation based upon a pattern of behaviors across a series of systematically varied situations. Indeed, this methodology has already proven successful in research on altruism (Batson 1991; Batson and Shaw 1991). The approach described here is most easily implemented in laboratory studies—a research design commonly utilized in research on impression management (e.g., Fandt and Ferris 1990; Wayne and Ferris 1990), as well as organizational citizenship (e.g., Werner 1994; Wright, George, Farnsworth, and McMahan 1993). In addition to laboratory experiments, researchers might employ studies where individuals are asked to react to hypothetical vignettes in order to examine the role of motives. Ashford and Northcraft (1992) successfully used hypothetical scenarios in their work on impression management; Orr, Sackett, and Mercer (1989) have studied citizenship behavior using hypothetical accounts as well.

Propositions 1 through 8 suggest some key motives that might be varied using such designs. For example, performance appraisal deadline is a factor that could be studied using hypothetical vignettes. That is, subjects could be assigned to two conditions: (1) performance deadline close or (2) deadline far off. Likewise, subjects could be placed in conditions where they had transgressed/not transgressed against their organizations. In such studies researchers could explore how these conditions affect individuals' propensity to engage in citizenship behaviors.

In addition to OCB frequency, such studies might also examine the other character-istics of citizenship (i.e., type, target, audience, timing, and magnitude). For example, subjects could be placed in a situation where they must choose between engaging in an altruism behavior that, they are informed, will help the organization greatly but will be minimally image enhancing (e.g., helping a colleague finish an important project) or a civic virtue behavior that will only moderately help the organization but will provide them with a great deal of image enhancement (e.g., attending an optional work function, but one that their boss would like them to attend). If an employee's true motive is to help the organization, he or she should opt for the type of OCB that will help the organization most. Such designs could be expanded further to see if certain situational variables influence this decision; for example, subjects could be given the same general choice scenario, but subjects in one condition could be placed in a situation where their performance is based on a highly subjective (as opposed to objective) criterion.

The approach recommended here could also be applied in field-based settings. How-ever, because simply knowing the type of citizenship in which an employee engages is not particularly revealing in terms of motive, such studies must necessarily entail mea-suring individuals' citizenship behaviors longitudinally. For instance, impression-management researchers suggest that individuals will tend to derive more benefit from citizenship if they tailor the type of citizenship they use to the preferences of a relevant target. Still, there may be a traditional motive underlying the choice of this type of citizenship (i.e., it may happen to be the most image-enhancing type of OCB, as well as the one that contributes most to the organization). Therefore, in order to infer motive in the field, one must observe a change or deviation in the pattern of citizenship char-acteristics in the presence of impression-management motives.

For example, in future research scholars might examine citizenship characteristics like type in terms of the specific mix of citizenship behaviors that individuals undertake at various points in time. That is, individuals might rate low in altruism, high in gen-eralized compliance, low in civic virtue, and so on. One might then observe or record, for example, how such behaviors change as performance appraisals approach. Using a survey or observational approach, researchers gathering longitudinal data on employee citizenship behaviors that capture how patterns of these characteristics or others, such as frequency and timing, may change in the presence of impression-management mo-tives may help reveal employees' motives. Similarly, measures of how employees' pre-ferred targets, audiences, and the magnitude of citizenship acts deviate in a more image-enhancing direction can aid researchers in identifying whose behavior is designed to help others or the organization and whose behavior is aimed largely at image enhancement.

Consider two illustrations of how OCBs might look when impression-management motives are absent and how they might appear when impression-management motives are present. First, consider a case in which an employee recently has transgressed against a group of junior colleagues (e.g., by violating a work group norm). In order to make amends for this transgression, the employee has stepped up citizenship behav-iors directed at these junior colleagues (assuming here that, typically, the junior col-leagues are the least likely target of the employee's OCBs). Thus, a shift in the target of the employee's citizenship behavior can be identified. Consider now a case where the overall pattern of an individual's OCBs changes in a more image-enhancing direction when performance appraisals are close. Specifically, when appraisals are close, this individual increases the frequency of OCBs, engages in the OCBs most valued by influential targets, directs OCBs at influential others, executes OCBs in front of large numbers of influential others, performs OCBs when they are most valued, and performs them at greatest personal cost. This example, too, illustrates how the profile of an individual's citizenship behavior might be analyzed.

Finally, qualitative research that investigates the issue of motive is likely to prove useful. For example, Becker and Martin (1995) used a qualitative methodology to examine why employees might try to intentionally look hard at work (i.e., manage poor or unfavorable images). Using a qualitative approach that asks for workers' opinions about their citizenship and impression-management behaviors, as well as that of their coworkers, researchers may be able to obtain richer, more honest, and more telling data than might be obtained using other research designs. Like Becker and Martin's (1995) study, such research would need to be executed in a manner that mitigates against the social desirability and demand effects that may be problematic in qualitative research on this topic.

IMPLICATIONS AND DIRECTIONS FOR FUTURE RESEARCH

In this article I have contended that impression management is an important motivational force underlying OCB. I have offered a framework for understanding (1) how concerns about one's image may drive individuals' citizenship behavior, (2) the good citizen image that results from OCBs, and (3) the moderating effects of impression-management concerns upon organization/work group functioning. Understanding the underlying motivation for citizenship is important in advancing research on this topic, for several reasons.

First, Organ and Ryan's (1995) meta-analysis highlights the generally weak and inconsistent predictive power of dispositional antecedents in accounting for citizenship. Likewise, job attitudes explain only small amounts of variance in OCB. A possible explanation for these disappointing results is the overlap between impression management and citizenship. By separating good soldiers from good actors, researchers may be better able to predict true acts of citizenship. Second, because motivation is likely to adversely affect the impact of OCBs on organization/work group effectiveness, gaining a better understanding of these effects is relevant for researchers and practitioners alike.

This article enhances our understanding of impression management as well. It provides a framework for examining the role of image concerns in the context of organizational citizenship—a widely studied and important context. Further, this article suggests that, like citizenship researchers, researchers of organizational politics and impression management need to examine their key constructs and ensure that they are theoretically and empirically sound. Last, work on impression management mainly has been aimed at studying the effects that such behaviors have for individuals. In contrast, this article suggests that impression-management behaviors ultimately have organizational implications as well. Thus, in future research on impression management, researchers should consider the consequences such behaviors pose for organization functioning and performance.

In addition to methodological issues, I have raised some theoretical questions that must be dealt with in the future. First, what is the nature of the relationship between. impression-management and traditional motives of OCB? While I have highlighted the interaction of impression-management and traditional motives of OCBs, further exploration of the interplay of these motives would enhance our knowledge of citizenship, as well as impression management. For example, uncovering those instances where one motive is dominant and the other is subordinate is an endeavor deserving future research attention.

Second, what is the role of observer attributions regarding acts of citizenship? Eastman's (1994) results indicate that judging behavior as citizenship or impression management is a subjective process. More theoretical work is necessary to explain how attributions regarding citizenship are formed. Situational factors, individual factors, and other determinants may affect such attributions. For example, a person's status as a peer or supervisor may influence how that person interprets motives, or situational factors—for example, political climate—may bias one's attribution. Because attributions of authenticity are likely to impact the instrumentality of citizenship's image-enhancing effects, an improved understanding of these issues is necessary.

The introduction of additional characteristics of OCB is likely to be relevant for research beyond the impression-management question. For instance, understanding the impact of traditional citizenship motives on the various dimensions of citizenship (e.g., type or timing) might improve our understanding of these extra-role behaviors. This is particularly important because it is likely that certain types of OCBs, the directing of OCBs at certain targets, or the timing of OCBs may affect their contribution to organization functioning. For example, altruism behaviors may be more valuable in certain organizational settings than sportsmanship or generalized compliance behaviors.

Also, work that further integrates the impression-management and citizenship research streams would improve our understanding of both topics. In particular, specific impression-management strategies, such as self-promotion or ingratiation, may affect the character of citizenship behaviors. For example, ingratiators may be more sensitive to the target of their citizenship behaviors than the type or timing of their OCBs. Likewise, different impression-management motives may differentially affect patterns of citizenship behavior. For example, if gaining visibility is a person's motive, such a motive may affect the audience of OCBs; however, if the performance appraisal deadline is close, employees may be more concerned with the target or magnitude of their behaviors than with frequency. Thus, while I have offered a general framework explaining the relationship between impression management and citizenship, it is possible that a more micro-level understanding might be achieved in future work.

Finally, if the propositions in this article are true, there are important implications for practicing managers. First, the article illustrates why managers must be careful in assessing the citizenship behavior of their subordinates. Toward that end, I have suggested some key characteristics that might help practicing managers identify employee motives. Likewise, if OCBs motivated by impression management are less likely to facilitate organization performance, organizations should be cautious in how they promote such behavior. Last, impression managers should be wary that certain factors may reveal their true intent and that such revelations are likely to reduce the odds that they will be seen as one of the good soldiers.

NOTES

1. Although it is likely that individuals' motives generally are mixed, in the interest of clearly contrasting such motives, I at times discuss citizenship behaviors as stemming mainly from impression-management motives or from motives previously identified by researchers.

2. There is support for Organ's (1988) conceptualization, although researchers have proposed alternative models. For example, Van Dyne, Graham, and Dienesch (1994) identified—both theoretically and empirically—five dimensions of OCB: (1) loyalty (commitment to and promotion of one's organization), (2) obedience (adherence to rules and policies), (3) advocacy participation (innovative behavior/willingness to be controversial and engage one's coworkers), (4) functional participation (self-development and volunteering), and (5) social participation (attending meetings and group activities). Although their model overlaps greatly with Organ's, their dimensions are based on geopolitical theory and, thus, include behaviors that are more change oriented and controversial than the more affiliative and promotive behaviors proposed by Organ (1988).

In addition, Moorman and Blakely (1995) developed a four-dimension scale aimed at integrating the Organ (1988) and Van Dyne et al. (1994) models. The dimensions of their model include (1) interpersonal helping (altruism behaviors), (2) individual initiative (civic virtue and advocacy behaviors), (3) personal industry (conscientiousness and functional participation behaviors), and (4) loyal boosterism (loyalty behaviors).

Recently, Van Dyne, Cummings, and McLean Parks (1995) suggested that, in the interest of construct clarity, future research should focus on citizenship behaviors that are affiliative and promotive and should not address more challenging and change-oriented behaviors as part of the OCB construct. Based on this recommendation, then, I use here Organ's (1988) model of organizational citizenship, focusing on affiliative and promotive behaviors.

3. Citizenship behaviors are conceptualized here as merely the observable behaviors themselves. That is, I do not consider motivation as part of the citizenship construct itself; thus, OCBs refer to acts of altruism, generalized compliance, sportsmanship, courtesy, and civic virtue, but not motive.

REFERENCES

Ashford, S.J., and Northcraft, G.B. 1992. Conveying more (or less) than we realize: The role of impression-management in feedback-seeking. *Organizational Behavior and Human Decision Processes* 53: 310–334.

Bateman, T.S., and Organ, D.W. 1983. Job satisfaction and the good soldier: The relationship between affect and employee "citizenship." *Academy of Management Journal* 26: 587–595.

Batson, C.D. 1991. *The Altruism Question: Toward a Social-Psychological Answer*. Hillsdale, NJ: Lawrence Erlbaum.

Batson, C.D., and Shaw, L.L. 1991. Evidence for altruism: Toward a pluralism of prosocial motives. *Psychological Inquiry* 2: 107–122.

Baumeister, R.F. 1982. A self-presentational view of social phenomena. *Psychological Bulletin* 91: 3–26.

———. 1989. Motives and costs of self-presentation in organizations. In R.A. Giacalone and P. Rosenfeld (eds.), *Impression Management in the Organization*, 57–71. Hillsdale, NJ: Lawrence Erlbaum.

Becker, T.E., and Martin, S.L. 1995. Trying to look bad at work: Methods and motives for managing poor impressions in organizations. *Academy of Management Journal* 38: 174–199.

Blakely, G.L., Fuller, J., and Smith, D. 1996. Are chameleons good citizens? The relationship between self-monitoring and organizational citizenship behavior. Paper presented at the annual meeting of the Southern Management Association, New Orleans.

Eastman, K.K. 1994. In the eyes of the beholder: An attributional approach to ingratiation and organizational citizenship behavior. *Academy of Management Journal* 37: 1379–1391.

Fandt, P.M., and Ferris, G.R. 1990. The management of information and impressions: When employees behave opportunistically. *Organizational Behavior and Human Decision Processes* 45: 140–158.

Feldman, D.C., and Klich, N.R. 1991. Impression management and career strategies. In R.A. Giacalone and P. Rosenfeld (eds.), *Applied Impression Management: How Imagemaking Affects Managerial Decisions*, 67–80. Newbury Park, CA: Sage.

Feldman, D.C., and Weitz, B.A. 1991. From the invisible hand to the gladhand: Understanding a careerist orientation to work. *Human Resource Management* 30: 237–257.

Ferris, G.R., Judge, T.A., Rowland, K.M., and Fitzgibbons, D.E. 1994. Subordinate influence and the performance evaluation process: Test of a model. *Organizational Behavior and Human Decision Processes* 58: 101–135.

Ferris, G.R., Russ, G.S., and Fandt, P.M. 1989. Politics in organizations. In R.A. Giacalone and P. Rosenfeld (eds.), *Impression Management in the Organization*, 143–170. Hillsdale, NJ: Lawrence Erlbaum.

Gaes, G.G., and Tedeschi, J.T. 1978. An evaluation of self-esteem and impression management theories of anticipatory belief change. *Journal of Experimental Social Psychology* 14: 579–587.

George, J.M. 1991. State or trait: Effects of positive mood on prosocial behaviors at work. *Journal of Applied Psychology* 76: 299–307.

Jones, E.E. 1964. *Ingratiation*. New York: Appleton-Century-Crofts.

Jones, E.E., and Pittman, T.S. 1982. Toward a general theory of strategic self-presentation. In J. Suls (ed.), *Psychological Perspectives on the Self*, 231–263. Hillsdale, NJ: Lawrence Erlbaum.

Katz, D. 1964. The motivational basis of organizational behavior. *Behavioral Science* 9: 131–133.

Katz, D., and Kahn, R. 1966. *The Social Psychology of Organizations*. New York: Wiley.

Konovsky, M.A., and Organ, D.W. 1996. Dispositional and contextual determinants of organizational citizenship behavior. *Journal of Organizational Behavior* 17: 253–266.

Kumar, K., and Beyerlein, M. 1991. Construction and validation of an instrument for measuring ingratiatory behaviors in organizational settings. *Journal of Applied Psychology* 76: 619–627.

Leary, M.R., and Kowalski, R.M. 1990. Impression management: A literature review and two-component model. *Psychological Bulletin* 107: 34–47.

Liden, R.C., and Mitchell, T.R. 1988. Ingratiatory behaviors in organizational settings. *Academy of Management Review* 13: 572–587.

Longenecker, C.O., Gioia, D.A., and Sims, H.P. 1987. Behind the mask: The politics of employee appraisal. *Academy of Management Executive* 1: 163–193.

MacKenzie, S.B., Podsakoff, P.M., and Fetter, R. 1991. Organizational citizenship behavior and objective productivity as determinants of managerial evaluations of salespersons' performance. *Organizational Behavior and Human Decision Processes* 50: 123–150.

Markus, H., and Nurius, P. 1986. Possible selves. *American Psychologist* 41: 954–969.

Markus, H., and Ruvolo, A. 1989. Possible selves: Personalized representations of goals. In L.A. Pervin (ed.), *Goal Concepts in Personality and Social Psychology*, 211–241. Hillsdale, NJ: Lawrence Erlbaum.

McNeely, B.L., and Meglino, B.M. 1994. The role of dispositional and situational antecedents in prosocial organizational behavior: An examination of the intended beneficiaries of prosocial behavior. *Journal of Applied Psychology* 79: 836–844.

Moorman, R.H., and Blakely, G.L. 1995. Individualism-collectivism as an individual difference predictor of organization citizenship behavior. *Journal of Organizational Behavior* 16: 127–142.

Morrison, E.W., and Bies, R.J. 1991. Impression management in the feedback-seeking process: A literature review and research agenda. *Academy of Management Review* 16: 522–541.

Niehoff, B.P., and Moorman, R.H. 1993. Justice as a mediator of the relationship between methods of monitoring and organizational citizenship behavior. *Academy of Management Journal* 36: 527–556.

Organ, D.W. 1988. *Organizational Citizenship Behavior: The Good Soldier Syndrome*. Lexington, MA: Lexington Books.

———. 1990. The motivational basis of organizational citizenship behavior. In B.M. Staw and L.L. Cummings (eds.), *Research in Organizational Behavior* 12: 43–72. Greenwich, CT: JAI Press.

Organ, D.W., and Konovsky, M.A. 1989. Cognitive versus affective determinants of organizational citizenship behavior. *Journal of Applied Psychology* 74: 157–164.

Organ, D.W., and Ryan, K. 1995. A meta-analytic review of attitudinal and dispositional predictors of organizational citizenship behavior. *Personnel Psychology* 48: 775–802.

Orr, J.M., Sackett, P.R., and Mercer, M. 1989. The role of prescribed and nonprescribed behaviors in estimating the dollar value of performance. *Journal of Applied Psychology* 74: 34–40.

Podsakoff, P.M., Ahearne, M., and MacKenzie, S.B. 1997. Organizational citizenship behavior and the quantity and quality of work group performance. *Journal of Applied Psychology* 82: 262–270.

Podsakoff, P.M., MacKenzie, S.B., and Hui, C. 1993. Organizational citizenship behaviors and managerial evaluations of employee performance: A review and suggestions for future research. In G.R. Ferris (ed.), *Research in Personnel and Human Resources Management* 11: 1–40. Greenwich, CT: JAI.

Ralston, D.A., and Elsass, P.M. 1989. Ingratiation and impression management in the organization. In R.A. Giacalone and P. Rosenfeld (eds.), *Impression Management in the Organization,* 235–249. Hillsdale, NJ: Lawrence Erlbaum.

Rosenfeld, P.R., Giacalone, R.A., and Riordan, C.A. 1995. *Impression Management in Organizations: Theory, Measurement, and Practice.* New York: Routledge.

Schnake, M. 1991. Organizational citizenship: A review, proposed model, and research agenda. *Human Relations* 44: 735–759.

Smith, C.A., Organ, D.W., and Near, J.P. 1983. Organizational citizenship behavior: Its nature and antecedents. *Journal of Applied Psychology* 68: 653–663.

Snyder, M. 1974. Self-monitoring of expressive behavior. *Journal of Personality and Social Psychology* 30: 526–537.

Stevens, C.K., and Kristof, A.L. 1995. Making the right impression: A field study of applicant impression management during job interviews. *Journal of Applied Psychology* 80: 587–606.

Tedeschi, J.T., and Melburg, V. 1984. Impression management and influence in the organization. In S.B. Bacharach and E.J. Lawler (eds.), *Research in the Sociology of Organizations* 3: 31–58. Greenwich, CT: JAI.

Tedeschi, J.T., and Riordan, C.A. 1981. Impression management and prosocial behavior following transgression. In J. Tedeschi (ed.), *Impression Management Theory and Social Psychological Research,* 223–244. New York: Academic Press.

Van Dyne, L., Cummings, L.L., and McLean Parks, J. 1995. Extra-role behaviors: In pursuit of construct and definitional clarity (a bridge over muddied waters). In B.M. Staw and L.L. Cummings (eds.), *Research in Organizational Behavior,* vol. 17: 215–285. Greenwich, CT: JAI.

Van Dyne, L., Graham, J.W., and Dienesch, R.M. 1994. Organizational citizenship behavior: Construct redefinition, measurement, and validation. *Academy of Management Journal* 37: 765–802.

Wayne, S.J., and Ferris, G.R. 1990. Influence tactics, affect, and exchange quality in supervisor-subordinate interactions: A laboratory experiment and field study. *Journal of Applied Psychology* 75: 487–499.

Wayne, S.J., and Green, S.A. 1993. The effects of leader-member exchange on employee citizenship and impression management behavior. *Human Relations* 46:1431–1440.

Wayne, S.J., and Liden, R.C. 1995. Effects of impression management on performance ratings: A longitudinal study. *Academy of Management Journal* 38: 232–260.

Werner, J.M. 1994. Dimensions that make a difference: Examining the impact of in-role and extrarole behaviors on supervisory ratings. *Journal of Applied Psychology* 79: 98–107.

Wright, P.M., George, J.M., Farnsworth, S.R., and McMahan, G.C. 1993. Productivity and extra-role behavior: The effects of goals and incentives on spontaneous helping. *Journal of Applied Psychology* 78: 374–381.

29

Effects of Impression Management on Performance Ratings: A Longitudinal Study

Sandy J. Wayne and Robert C. Liden

Over the past 30 years, social psychologists have devoted much research attention to impression management and the related topics of self-presentation and ingratiation (Jones 1964; Leary and Kowalski 1990; Schlenker and Weigold 1992). Drawing on Schlenker (1980), we defined impression management as those behaviors individuals employ to protect their self-images, influence the way they are perceived by significant others, or both. Most impression management research has been conducted at the dyadic level and has focused on the types of strategies employed (Buss, Gomes, Higgins, and Lauterbach 1987), motivations behind the use of each strategy (Arkin, Appleman, and Berger 1980), individual characteristics of agents and targets related to the use of impression management (Baumeister and Jones 1978; Schlenker and Leary 1982a), and reactions of targets to impression management behaviors (Schlenker and Leary 1982b).

Following Wortman and Linsenmeier's (1977) suggestion that impression management findings in social psychology research may generalize to organizational settings, organizational researchers began to study impression management (e.g., Ansari and Kapoor 1987; Ashford and Northcraft 1992; Baron 1983; Bohra and Pandey 1984; Caldwell and O'Reilly 1982; Fandt and Ferris 1990; Giacalone 1985; Hinkin and Schriesheim 1990; Judge and Ferris 1993; Kipnis and Schmidt 1988; Kipnis, Schmidt, and Wilkinson 1980; Mowday 1979; Schriesheim and Hinkin 1990; Vecchio and Sussmann 1991; Wayne and Ferris 1990; Wayne and Kacmar 1991; Yukl and Falbe 1990; Yukl and Tracey 1992). Most of this research has focused on identifying impression management tactics or developing theoretical models of the impression management process. Although much has been accomplished within this stream of research, only a few studies have empirically examined the relationship between impression management and performance ratings (Ferris, Judge, Rowland, and Fitzgibbons 1994; Kipnis and Schmidt 1988; Wayne and Ferris 1990; Wayne and Kacmar 1991).

To date, impression management studies in the performance appraisal area have either been conducted in a laboratory setting or have employed cross-sectional designs with established supervisor-subordinate dyads. Whereas much can be learned from these studies, longitudinal research with newly formed supervisor-subordinate dyads is needed in order to determine whether subordinate impression management behavior affects performance ratings over time. Liden and Mitchell (1988) and Tedeschi and Melburg (1984) argued that impression management can be used for either short-term or long-term purposes. Tedeschi and Melburg made a clear distinction between tactical impression management behaviors, targeted at obtaining immediate gratification, and strategic impression management behaviors, geared for influencing future outcomes. The lack of longitudinal research in the area has precluded the possibility of investigating the long-term or strategic uses of impression management. One purpose of the current study was to develop a theoretical model for understanding the long-term effects of subordinate impression management behavior on supervisor performance ratings and to empirically examine hypotheses based on this model with a longitudinal research design.

Few studies have examined the process by which impression management influences performance ratings, and they have not investigated alternative explanations for apparent impression management effects. Thus, a second purpose of the current study was to examine the processes surrounding the influence of impression management on performance ratings. In particular, we examined supervisors' liking of and perceived similarity to subordinates as intervening variables in the relationship between impression management and performance ratings. In addition, we explored the impact of demographic similarity on performance ratings through its effect on perceived similarity and liking.

HYPOTHESIZED MODEL OF THE EFFECTS OF IMPRESSION MANAGEMENT ON PERFORMANCE RATINGS

In the theoretical model guiding our research (Figure 29.1), we propose that subordinates' impression management behaviors influence supervisors' liking of the subordinates as well as the supervisors' perceptions of similarity to the subordinates. Liking and perceived similarity assessed at an initial point in time in turn relate to supervisory ratings of the subordinates' performance made later. The model is not intended to be a comprehensive model of social influence processes in performance appraisal. Other models, such as Ilgen and Feldman's (1983) and Villanova and Bernardin's (1989, 1991), are more inclusive.

Impression Management Strategies

A vast array of impression management strategies have been reported in the relevant literature. Many of these focus on defensive tactics (Tedeschi and Melburg 1984; Tedeschi and Norman 1985) typically used in response to poor performance (Liden and Mitchell 1988), such as accounts, excuses, apologies, self-handicapping, learned helplessness, self-deprecation, alcoholism, and drug abuse. Because the current investigation

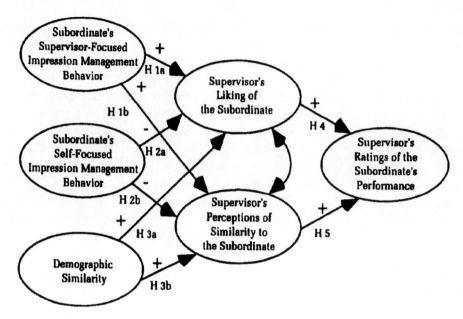

Figure 29.1. **Hypothesized Model of the Effects of Impression Management on Performance Ratings**

did not focus on subordinate poor performance, defensive strategies were not of interest. In contrast to those strategies, assertive impression management tactics are used by individuals to establish a particular identity for an audience and are not merely a reaction to situational demands (Tedeschi and Melburg 1984).

Self-presentation and other-enhancement, two main types of impression management, provided the focus for the current study. Self-presentation strategies, intended by an individual, or agent, to make himself or herself more appealing to a target (Jones 1964), are accomplished either verbally or with nonverbal cues such as smiling, eye contact, and touching (DePaulo 1992; Drake and Moberg 1986). Other-enhancement refers to the favorable evaluation of, or agreement with, the target. Flattery, favor-doing, and opinion conformity are common forms of other-enhancement that have been shown to positively influence target individuals (Ralston and Elsass 1989; Tedeschi and Melburg 1984).

The agent's objective in the use of all impression management strategies is to favorably influence attributions made by the target (Jones and Wortman 1973). Because prior research has shown that lower-status agents frequently use impression management in attempts to influence higher-status targets (Gardner and Martinko 1988; Leary and Kowalski 1990; Pandey 1981; Ralston 1985; Yukl and Tracey 1992), subordinate impression management targeted at supervisors represents an especially rich setting for research on impression management (Bohra and Pandey 1984).

Several studies have examined the effects of subordinate impression management behavior on performance ratings. In particular, Kipnis and Schmidt (1988), Wayne and Ferris (1990), Wayne and Kacmar (1991), and Ferris and colleagues (1994) found support for the relationship between subordinate impression management behavior and supervisor performance ratings. Although these studies have provided useful results, they have a number of limitations. Specifically, the prior studies have been conducted either in laboratory settings in which students were used as subjects or in field settings with established supervisor-subordinate dyads and cross-sectional designs. Thus, although significant relationships between impression management and performance ratings have emerged, the causal relationship is unclear, the intervening processes are not well understood, and the impact of impression management behavior on performance ratings over time is unknown.

Individuals can use many impression management behaviors to accomplish either short- or long-term goals (Tedeschi and Melburg 1984). For example, a subordinate may do a favor for a supervisor in the morning because the former plans to ask for the afternoon off. In contrast, the subordinate may do favors for the supervisor over time in the hope of getting a good annual performance appraisal. To influence salient outcomes such as performance ratings, compensation, and promotions, individuals would seem to need to use impression management behaviors strategically over time.

Cognitive Information Processing

Cognitive information processing approaches provide a theoretical framework for explaining how supervisors translate their perceptions of subordinate impression management into initial impressions, encode them into memory, and later retrieve and decode them when rating the subordinates' performance (Lord 1985; Schneider 1991).[1] Successful subordinate impression management behaviors favorably alter supervisor attributions of a subordinate (Jones and Wortman 1973; Wood and Mitchell 1981). Attributions in turn provide information the supervisor uses in categorizing or recategorizing the subordinate (Schneider 1991).

Subordinate impression management may have the most salient influence on supervisors when the relationship between the two is developing. This time is when initial categorization of the subordinate occurs (Feldman 1986). In many cases, supervisors begin to process information about a new subordinate before the individual's first day on the job, or even before interviewing the prospective employee. It has been found that interviewers, who are often the applicants' future supervisors, form impressions of applicants before interviews on the basis of preemployment information, such as résumés (Phillips and Dipboye 1989). Thus, the categorization of information based on schemata may occur prior to an interview (Dipboye 1989). However, even at this early stage, applicants may use impression management to manipulate the information presented in their résumés and cover letters announcing job candidacy (Liden and Mitchell 1989). Impression management during actual interviews may further influence the interviewers' information processing, either positively (Fletcher 1989; Gilmore and Ferris 1989) or negatively (Baron 1989).

Although initial impressions may be formed before the first day a supervisor and subordinate work together, we suspect that in most cases, supervisors continue to engage in a controlled processing mode when observing new subordinates' behavior on the job for the first time (Feldman 1981). In most cases, assimilation of a new subordinate should be sufficiently unique to trigger a controlled categorization process[2] (Dienesch and Liden 1986). Supervisors who have categorized a new subordinate as, for example, lazy may interpret the subordinate's use of impression management behaviors (such as doing favors) as schema-inconsistent information. This interpretation may in turn trigger an episode of controlled information processing (Fiske, Neuberg, Beattie, and Milberg 1987; Srull and Wyer 1989). Using this new positive information, the supervisor may revise the initial categorization of the subordinate.

Because such controlled processing involves making attributions for the new subordinates' behavior (Feldman 1981; Green and Mitchell 1979), the supervisors become vulnerable to subordinate impression management strategies designed to manipulate their attributions (Jones and Wortman 1973). For example, in part on the basis of the subordinates' impression management behavior, the supervisors may categorize the new employees as friendly, hard-working, and similar to themselves. This categorization may compare favorably with the supervisors' prototype of ideal subordinate behaviors. A match between prototype and processed information based on the subordinates' impression management may positively influence the task assignments, feedback, resources, and support the supervisors provide to the subordinates. This favorable treatment may cause the subordinates' actual performance to be higher than that of others, and rating biases may also occur (Feldman 1986; Ilgen and Feldman 1983).

Supervisor-Focused Impression Management

Greenwald (1980) and Steele (1988) argued that people strive to affirm their self-concepts. They may accomplish this goal through the use of impression management, attempting to control or manage the impressions that other people form so that those impressions are consistent with their desired self-images (Schlenker and Leary 1982). Often exerting such control translates into an attempt to behave in a way that will result in liking by a target. Research evidence shows that other-enhancement is often effective in provoking a favorable target impression. Jones and Wortman noted that "people find it hard not to like those who think highly of them" (1973: 4).

Because of our focus on subordinates' use of impression management in attempts to influence their immediate superiors, we refer to other-enhancement tactics as supervisor-focused impression management strategies. These include such strategies as flattery, which involves a subordinate's communicating feelings of liking and admiration to a supervisor, and doing favors for the supervisor. A supervisor who feels liked and admired by a subordinate will be more attracted to that subordinate. In fact, a target's attraction to and liking of an agent has been the dependent variable in the majority of the social psychology experiments on impression management. In nearly all those studies, researchers found agent use of flattery and favors to be related to target affect for and attraction to the agent (Jones 1964; Jones and Wortman 1973; Schlenker 1980; Wortman and Linsenmeier 1977). The handful of studies specifically designed to assess the use of other-enhancement in organizational situations has revealed similar results. For example, subordinate use of supervisor-focused impression management has been found to be related to supervisors' attraction to subordinates (Kipnis and Vanderveer 1971) and liking of the subordinates (Wayne and Ferris 1990).

> *Hypothesis 1a:* A subordinate's use of supervisor-focused impression management behaviors will have a positive effect on his or her supervisor's liking of the subordinate.

In an effort to maintain positive self-images, individuals may be especially attentive to positive things that are said about them and to favors done for them (cf. Markus 1980). According to self-verification theory, people tend to be attracted to and to identify with those who confirm the perceptions they have of themselves (Swann, Stein-Seroussi, and Giesler 1992). Individuals tend to perceive themselves as similar to those who display attractive behaviors, such as giving compliments (Byrne 1971; Lewicki 1983). It follows that supervisors will see themselves as being more similar to subordinates who compliment them and do favors for them than to subordinates who do not engage in these behaviors.

> *Hypothesis 1b:* A subordinate's use of supervisor-focused impression management behaviors will have a positive effect on his or her supervisor's perceptions of similarity to the subordinate.

Self-Focused Impression Management

There are many assertive self-presentation strategies, including false modesty, boasting, and a host of nonverbal behaviors such as smiling, making eye contact, and touching (Cialdini 1989; Ralston and Elsass 1989; Schlenker 1980; Tedeschi and Melburg 1984; Tedeschi and Norman 1985). We measured self-presentation in terms of two strategies, self-enhancement and exemplification, or acting as an exemplar. We refer to these strategies as self-focused impression management. With these strategies, a subordinate attempts to convey the impression that he or she is a friendly, hard-working, model employee.

A subordinate's goal with these self-focused strategies is to create an image that a supervisor will perceive favorably. An agent must be willing to assume risk when using self-focused strategies (Liden and Mitchell 1988) because the influence attempt will backfire if the target interprets the self-presentation as insincere (Wortman and Linsenmeier 1977). Subordinates who are consumed by presenting themselves favorably may fail to devote enough effort to job duties (Baumeister 1989), which results in negative supervisor reactions. As Cialdini and DeNicholas wrote, "If there is an overarching lesson to be learned from the large body of work on impression management, it is that favorable self-presentation is a tricky business" (1989: 626). Research results indicate that agents often do not succeed in the use of self-focused strategies, as is evidenced by neutral (Wayne and Ferris 1990) or negative (Baron 1986; Powers and Zuroff 1988) target reactions. For example, in Powers and Zuroff's research, agents who used self-focused impression management were less liked than were individuals who did not use impression management. Given the extreme skill that appears to be needed in the use of self-focused impression management tactics, we expect that most subordinates will not succeed in conveying a positive image with such tactics.

Hypothesis 2a: A subordinate's self-focused impression management behaviors will have a negative effect on his or her supervisor's liking of the subordinate.

A very consistent finding in the social psychology and organizational literatures is the strong association between perceived similarity and liking. It follows that if supervisors do not like subordinates who promote themselves, the supervisors will not perceive themselves as similar to the self-promoting subordinates. Psychologically healthy individuals tend not to identify with or perceive themselves as similar to those they consider undesirable (Byrne 1971; cf. Cialdini and DeNicholas 1989; Lewicki 1983; Swann et al. 1992).

Hypothesis 2b: A subordinate's self-focused impression management behaviors will have a negative effect on his or her supervisor's perceptions of similarity to the subordinate.

Demographic Similarity

A recent extension to the study of demography and individual differences has involved examining similarity between individuals at both dyadic and group levels. This new approach, termed relational demography, relies on the similarity-attraction paradigm (Byrne 1971) for its theoretical foundation. According to this theory, individuals who possess similar individual characteristics and attitudes will perceive one another as similar and will be attracted to each other. Experiments in social psychology have provided support for the theory (Berscheid and Walster 1969; Byrne 1971; Jamieson, Lydon, and Zanna 1987). Field research in organizational settings has demonstrated effects that explain variance in dependent variables beyond that explained by main effects for individual differences. For example, demographic similarity between supervisor and subordinate has been found to be positively related to a supervisor's liking of a subordinate (Judge and Ferris 1993; Tsui and O'Reilly 1989) and negatively related to role ambiguity (Tsui and O'Reilly 1989).

Hypothesis 3a: Demographic similarity between a supervisor and a subordinate will have a positive effect on the supervisor's liking of the subordinate.

Hypothesis 3b: Demographic similarity between a supervisor and a subordinate will have a positive effect on the supervisor's perceptions of his or her similarity to the subordinate.

Supervisor Liking and Ratings of Subordinate Performance

Zajonc (1980) argued for the primacy of affect, suggesting that it dominates interactions between people. An especially important interpersonal interaction in organizations is that between subordinate and supervisor. Empirical support has been found for Liden and Mitchell's (1989) proposition that affect plays a critical role in the type of exchange that develops between supervisor and subordinate (Liden, Wayne, and Stilwell 1993; Wayne and Ferris 1990). One implication of the importance of affect in subordinate-supervisor interactions is that it may cause bias in a supervisor's treatment (Feldman 1986) and evaluation of subordinates (Dipboye 1985; Villanova and Bernardin 1989).

Responding to calls by Landy and Farr (1980) and Mitchell (1983) for research on the social context of performance ratings, researchers have conducted studies in which they found social factors to be related to performance ratings (e.g., Mitchell and Liden 1982). Specifically, a supervisor's liking of a subordinate has been shown to be positively related to supervisory performance ratings (Judge and Ferris 1993; Tsui and Barry 1986; Wayne and Ferris 1990). These studies are also important because they were among the first to integrate cognitive information processing with the social context of performance rating (cf. Schneider 1991). However, the research reported in each of these studies was either conducted in a laboratory or in the field, with a cross-sectional design. Thus, common method variance is a concern because supervisors assessed their liking for and the performance of the subordinates at the same time. And even if common method variance did not influence the results, it is not known if liking at one time influences ratings made later.

Although the research that has appeared on the association between liking and performance appraisal has been cross-sectional, theory supports the argument that liking will have an enduring effect that will influence later performance ratings. French and Raven (1959) described being liked as "referent power" that provides the liked individual with influence. Tedeschi and Melburg noted that "on a long term basis there are many potential gains for the liked person" (1984: 45), including better communication, trust, and ability to influence. Specifically, liking may influence supervisors' observation and storage of information over time as well as their recall at the time they actually rate a subordinate's performance (Cardy and Dobbins 1986; DeNisi and Williams 1988; Srull and Wyer 1989). Supervisory liking of a subordinate may reflect job behaviors associated with good job performance, such as the subordinate's friendliness toward customers and working well with other employees (Ashforth and Humphrey 1993). However, liking may also mask performance deficiencies and lead to biased performance ratings. At least three biases resulting from liking or disliking a subordinate may influence a supervisor's performance ratings. First, the supervisor may provide liked subordinates with more resources and support than disliked subordinates, which may influence actual performance (Feldman 1986). Second, supervisors may be selectively attentive to subordinates' work behaviors over time, noticing and storing information concerning the positive work behaviors of liked subordinates and the negative work behaviors of disliked subordinates. Finally, when actually rating subordinates, supervisors will tend to recall the positive work behaviors of liked subordinates and the negative work behaviors of disliked subordinates.

> *Hypothesis 4:* A supervisor's liking of a subordinate will be positively related to the supervisor's ratings of the subordinate's performance.

Supervisor Perceptions of Similarity and Ratings of Subordinate Performance

Perceived similarity has also been shown to have a direct effect on performance ratings (Pulakos and Wexley 1983; Senger 1971; Turban and Jones 1988; Wexley, Alexander, Greenwalt, and Couch 1980; Zalesny and Highhouse 1992; Zalesny and Kirsch 1989). Zalesny and Highhouse suggested that research in social cognitive information processing might explain correlations between perceived similarity and performance ratings. Specifically, substantial support has been found for the idea that people develop self-schemata for organizing perceptions of themselves (Markus, Smith, and Moreland 1985; Srull and Gaelick 1983). Research findings of self-serving attributional biases (Ross 1977) and tendencies to protect self-image (Schlenker 1980; Steele 1988; Swann 1982) imply that most people evaluate themselves positively (DeNisi and Shaw 1977; Shore, Shore, and Thornton 1992). These findings also suggest that supervisors' self-schemata should approximate the prototypes of desired characteristics and behaviors they use in the process of rating performance. Thus, a supervisor, comparing his or her self-schema with information remembered about a similar subordinate, should rate that subordinate more positively than a dissimilar subordinate (Lewicki 1983).

> *Hypothesis 5:* A supervisor's perceptions of similarity to a subordinate will be positively related to the supervisor's ratings of the subordinate's performance.

Long-Term Effects of Impression Management

To our knowledge, researchers have not used longitudinal research designs in the investigation of impression management and its effects on performance ratings. It is not clear if the results found in previous cross-sectional research will also be found in longitudinal studies. However, drawing on a cognitive information processing model, we predict that impression management will influence later performance ratings.

METHODS

Respondents

The study was conducted at two major universities located in the Midwest and Southeast. We collected complete data from 111 pairs of subordinates and their immediate supervisors. The respondents held a wide range of non-academic positions, such as that of secretary, electrician, librarian, admissions counselor, research scientist, and computer programmer. The average age of the subordinates was 33 and the average age of the supervisors was 41. The subordinate group included 47 men and 64 women, and the supervisor group included 51 men and 60 women. Of the subordinates, 73 were Caucasian, 27 were African-American, and 11 indicated they were of another race. Of the supervisors, 98 were Caucasian, 8 were African-American, and 5 marked "other." The average educational levels were an associate's degree for the subordinates and a bachelor's degree for the supervisors. Supervisors had held their positions for an average five years.

Procedures

Recently hired subordinates at both sites were required to attend a one-day orientation session. The orientation sessions were held biweekly with small groups of new subordinates. Over a one-year period, a member of our research team at each location attended every orientation session in order to describe the study and to elicit participation. It was necessary to attend orientation sessions over an entire year because of the fairly low number of new hires at any single session. Over the course of the entire data collection period, approximately 35 percent of all individuals attending orientation sessions at one site and about 70 percent of all attendees at the other site agreed to participate in the study. These percentages should be interpreted as the lower bounds for response rates as many individuals did not participate because they were not eligible. For example, employees who held academic appointments, had worked with the supervisors previously, or had worked with their supervisors for more than 28 days were not eligible for the study. The personnel directors at both sites also informed us that some of the new employees attending orientation sessions were illiterate or functionally illiterate. For ethical reasons, we did not attempt to identify employees who were eligible for the study but who elected not to participate. Thus, 35 and 70 percent are conservative estimates of the response rates. The difference in the response rates at the two sites resulted from one of the organizations having a large temporary work program. Thus, many orientation attendees were ineligible for the study because they had been working with their supervisors as temporary employees.

   The measures from which the data used in this study are drawn were part of a larger organizational survey of supervisor-subordinate relationships (Liden et al. 1993). We intended to have all respondents complete four surveys at the following times: within five days of starting employment, after two weeks, after six weeks, and after six months. The demographic items were included in the initial survey. Although the personnel departments at both sites encouraged all new employees to attend the orientation within the first five days of their employment, many employees worked with their supervisors for a couple of weeks before attending the session. As a result, we modified the study so that new employees who had been working with their supervisors for more than five days completed the two-week, six-week, and six-month surveys. For these respondents, the demographic items were included in the two-week survey.

New employees who agreed to participate completed either three or four surveys, depending on how many days it had been since they first started working with their new supervisors. Those who said it had been five days or less completed the zero-to-five-day questionnaire immediately. They received another three questionnaires via campus mail after two weeks, six weeks, and six months from their hiring date. Employees volunteering to participate in the study who indicated that it had been between 6 and 28 days since they started working with their new supervisors were provided with the two-week survey and asked to complete it immediately and return it by mail to us. They received the six-week and six-month surveys through campus mail. Except for the variation noted in regard to demographic items, all subordinates completed the same surveys after two weeks, six weeks, and six months from their hiring dates.

We asked all respondents for their direct supervisors' phone numbers and contacted the latter immediately after the orientation to ask them to participate in the study. A supervisor who agreed to participate completed either three or four surveys, depending on how many days it had been since the focal subordinate first started working with the supervisor. Again, the demographic items were included either in the zero-to-five-day survey or in the two-week survey. Except in regard to the demographic items, all supervisors completed the same surveys after two weeks, six weeks, and six months from the subordinate's hiring date.

As in any longitudinal study, it was necessary to identify respondents so that responses at each time could be compared. Identification was also necessary for matching supervisor and subordinate responses. A code number on each questionnaire served this purpose. We told all employees that their responses would be held in strict confidence and provided envelopes in which they were to return the surveys by mail.

Given the longitudinal design, some subject mortality occurred during the study. A total of 160 supervisor-subordinate dyads completed the two-week survey; 149 of these completed the six-week survey; and 111 dyads completed all three surveys. All analyses are based on the 111 supervisor-subordinate dyads.

Measures

Subordinates reported their impression management behavior in the two-week and six-week surveys. Supervisors also reported their subordinates' impression management behavior at those points. Supervisors completed measures of perceived similarity and liking of the subordinate in the six-week survey and evaluated their subordinate's performance at six months.

Subordinate Impression Management Behavior

Wayne and Ferris (1990) developed a 24-item scale to measure a number of assertive impression management behaviors, including self-enhancement, other enhancement, opinion conformity, favor-doing, and exemplification. Results of their principal components analysis indicated three types of impression management: job-focused, supervisor-focused, and self-focused. The reliabilities for these scales in their study were .87 for job-focused, .78 for supervisor-focused, and .71 for self-focused impression management. We used a shortened version of the 24-item Wayne and Ferris scale to assess impression management behavior, assessing two of the three types of tactics, supervisor-focused and self-focused impression management. Subordinates reported how often during the past six weeks they had engaged in 12 impression-management behaviors on a seven-point scale ("never," 1, to "always," 7). Using the same response scale, supervisors also reported how often their subordinates had engaged in the 12 impression management behaviors during the past six weeks.

Demographic Similarity

Drawing on research by Turban and Jones (1988), we created a measure of demographic similarity including gender, race, and age. Educational level was not included because some data for this variable were missing. Respondents indicated their race as white, African-American, or other. For the other category, respondents were asked to specify their race. Subordinates and supervisors who both checked the other category but did not specify their race were not included in the analyses because we could not determine similarity in terms of race. Gender and race were coded as "the same" (0) or as "different" (1). Age was measured in years. Age discrepancy was the absolute difference between supervisors and subordinates. We divided the discrepancy values by their respective standard deviations, summed them, and then reverse-scored them so that the larger the score, the greater the demographic similarity.

Supervisor Liking

Three items were used to measure liking. Two items, developed by Wayne and Ferris (1990), were: "I like my subordinate very much as a person" and "I think my subordinate would make a good friend." Each item was scaled from "strongly disagree," 1, to "strongly agree," 7. For the third item, developed for this study, the following instructions were provided: "Liking refers to the mutual affection the supervisor and subordinate have for each other. Please rate each of your subordinates on the degree to which you like each other" (1 = dislike each other very much, 4 = indifferent about each other, 7 = like each other very much). The response scale was designed in such a way that a supervisor's response on the liking item for a new subordinate could be identified from among the responses concerning his or her other subordinates. We summed ratings on the three items to create the liking measure (α = .79).

Supervisor Perceptions of Similarity

We used three items developed by Turban and Jones (1988) to measure perceived similarity: "My subordinate and I are similar in terms of our outlook, perspective, and values," "My subordinate and I see things in much the same way," and "My subordinate and I are alike in a number of areas." Supervisors responded on a seven-point scale ranging from "strongly disagree" to "strongly agree." The items were summed to create the measure (α = .89).

Performance Ratings

We developed the following four items: (1) "This subordinate is superior (so far) to other new subordinates that I've supervised before," ("strongly disagree" to "strongly agree"), (2) "Rate the overall level of performance that you observe for this subordinate" ("unacceptable," "poor," "below average," "average," "above average," "excellent," and "outstanding"), (3) "What is your personal view of your subordinate in terms of his or her overall effectiveness?" ("very ineffective" to "very effective"), (4) "Overall, to what extent do you feel your subordinate has been effectively fulfilling his or her roles and responsibilities?" ("not effectively at all" to "very effectively"). In addition, we used three items developed by Tsui (1984) that measure the extent to which a supervisor feels a subordinate is meeting the demands of his or her roles. Responses for all seven items were made on seven-point scales and were summed (α = .94).

RESULTS

Because data were collected at two organizations, we examined differences between the sites on all variables. A moderated hierarchical regression analysis was conducted with site entered first, followed by the independent variables and the interactions between site and each independent variable. The results revealed no significant main effect for site and no significant interaction terms. Therefore, we merged data from the two organizations for all analyses.

Before testing the proposed model, we conducted a series of principal components analyses with the variables of interest. First, principal components analysis with varimax rotation was used to examine the 12-item impression management scale administered to the subordinates and supervisors at two weeks. The resulting factor structures were ambiguous and unreliable, perhaps because employees had not had an adequate opportunity to engage in impression management behaviors. Thus, impression management behavior at two weeks was not included in this study.

Table 29.1
Rotated Factors and Loadings for the Impression Management Items

Items	Factor 1	Factor 2
To what extent do you		
1. Do personal favors for your supervisor (for example, getting him or her a cup of coffee or a coke, etc.)	.83	−.02
2. Offer to do something for your supervisor which you were not required to do; that is, you did it as a personal favor for him or her	.76	.08
3. Compliment your immediate supervisor on his or her dress or appearance	.73	.13
4. Praise your immediate supervisor on his or her accomplishments	.65	.14
5. Take an interest in your supervisor's personal life	.62	−.06
6. Try to be polite when interacting with your supervisor	−.13	.83
7. Try to be a friendly person when interacting with your supervisor	−.17	.74
8. Try to act as a "model" employee by, for example, never taking longer than the established time for lunch	.20	.72
9. Work hard when you know the results will be seen by your supervisor	.13	.60
10. Let your supervisor know that you try to do a good job in your work	.20	.59

Note: N = 111.

We examined the factor structure of the 12-item impression management scale completed by subordinates at six weeks by conducting a principal components analysis with varimax rotation. First, a three-factor solution was examined. Three factors emerged with eigenvalues greater than 1.0; however, only one item loaded above .40 on factor 3. Because these results did not support a three-factor solution and because prior research has found support for a two-factor solution (Wayne and Ferris 1990), we conducted a principal components analysis in which we set the number of factors to two. One item with a cross-loading and a second item that did not load above .40 on either factor were omitted. Analysis of the remaining ten items yielded two eigenvalues greater than 1.0 (2.94 for factor 1 and 2.30 for factor 2), and the factors explained 52.4 percent of the variance. The Cronbach alpha estimate for the supervisor-focused impression management scale (factor 1) was .78, and for the self-focused impression management scale (factor 2), it was .71. As Table 29.1 shows, the factor matrix indicated that all items loaded on the intended factors had acceptable loadings. Because subordinates may have responded in a socially desirable way to the impression management items, we included the Crowne-Marlowe measure of social desirability (Crowne and Marlowe 1960) in the initial subordinate survey (zero-to-five days). Forty-three subordinates completed this survey. The social desirability scale, which had a Cronbach alpha estimate of .84, was not significantly correlated with supervisor-focused impression management ($r = .13$, n.s.) nor self-focused impression management ($r = .06$, n.s.). These results suggest that subordinates did not respond in a socially desirable way to the impression management items.

Table 29.2
Rotated Factors and Loadings for Performance, Perceived Similarity, and Liking Items

Items	Factors		
	1	2	3
1. Overall, to what extent do you feel your subordinate is performing his or her job the way you would like it to be performed?	.92	.06	.11
2. To what extent has your subordinate's performance met your own expectations?	.90	.05	.14
3. Overall, to what extent do you feel your subordinate has been effectively fulfilling his or her roles and responsibilities?	.90	.14	.21
4. Rate the overall level of performance that you observe for this subordinate.	.87	.24	.16
5. This subordinate is superior (after 6 months) to other new subordinates that I've supervised before.	.83	.14	.14
6. What is your personal view of your subordinate in terms of his or her overall effectiveness?	.82	.20	.29
7. If you entirely had your way, to what extent would you change the manner in which your subordinate is doing his or her job?	.75	.29	−.11
8. My subordinate and I are similar in terms of our outlook, perspective, and values.	.13	.87	.24
9. My subordinate and I are alike in a number of areas.	.16	.83	.32
10. My subordinate and I see things in much the same way.	.30	.82	.22
11. I like my subordinate very much as a person.	.12	.21	.88
12. I think my subordinate would make a good friend.	.19	.23	.80
13. Please rate your subordinate on the degree to which you like each other.	.14	.40	.61

Note: N = 111.

The factor structure of the supervisor reports of subordinate impression management (ten items) measured at six weeks was also examined with principal components analysis with varimax rotation and the number of factors set to two. The factor structure was consistent with the results for the factor structure based on subordinates' reports. The correlations between supervisor and subordinate reports of impression management were significant for supervisor-focused impression management ($r = .51$, $p < .001$) and nonsignificant for self-focused impression management ($r = .08$, n.s.). We did not include supervisor reports of impression management in the analyses for three reasons: the number of observations would have been reduced because of missing data; common method problems may have arisen because liking, perceived similarity, and performance ratings were assessed from the supervisor's perspective; and supervisors may have been unaware of impression management behaviors when subordinates engaged in those behaviors effectively.

Table 29.3

Descriptive Statistics and Correlations

Variables	Mean	S.D.	1	2	3	4	5
1. Subordinate's supervisor-focused impression management behavior	2.97	1.08					
2. Subordinate's self-focused impression management behavior	5.53	0.88	.16				
3. Demographic similarity	5.53	1.79	.11	.06			
4. Supervisor's liking of the subordinate	5.39	0.97	.34***	.07	.31**		
5. Supervisor's perceptions of similarity	4.84	0.97	.28**	−.09	.31**	.59***	
6. Supervisor's ratings of the subordinate's performance	5.59	1.04	.18	.01	.17	.36***	.42***

Note: N = 111. **p* < .01. ****p* < .001.

A principal components analysis with varimax rotation was also conducted for the supervisor responses to the perceived similarity, liking, and performance rating items. The number of factors was set to three. The eigenvalues were 6.76 for factor 1 (performance), 2.41 for factor 2 (perceived similarity), and 1.01 for factor 3 (liking). A total of 78.3 percent of the variance was explained. The results, shown in Table 29.2, indicated that all the items loaded on the intended factors and had acceptable loadings.

Table 29.3 gives means, standard deviations, and correlations among the variables. The subordinates' reports of supervisor-focused impression management behavior were positively related to the supervisors' liking of the subordinates and perceptions of similarity. Demographic similarity was also positively related to the supervisors' liking and perceptions of similarity. Supervisors' liking of subordinates was strongly and positively correlated with perceptions of similarity. Further, supervisors' liking of the subordinates and perceptions of similarity measured at six weeks were positively related to supervisors' ratings of the subordinates' performance measured at six months.

Structural Equations Modeling

To test the hypothesized model presented in Figure 29.1, we used structural equations modeling, taking this approach because the model specifies causality rather than mere empirical association. In addition, structural equations modeling allows the correction of structural estimates for measurement error. Finally, structural equations modeling can be used to examine the overall fit of a model and to examine alternative models (Jöreskog and Sörbom 1989). Scale values for each variable were calculated and the covariance matrix was used as input to LISREL 8.03 (Jöreskog and Sörbom 1993). To adjust for measurement error in the scale values, we set the path from the latent variable to the indicator equal to the square root of the scale reliability. The error variance was set equal to the variance of the scale value multiplied by 1.0 minus the reliability

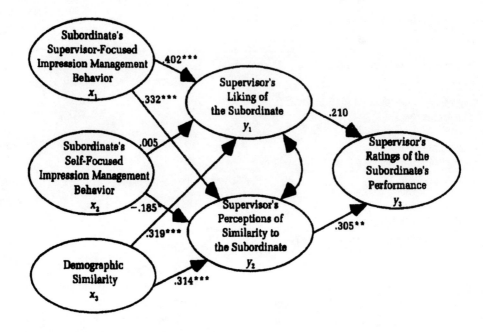

Note: Standardized path coefficients; $N = 111$.
*$p < .05$, one-tailed test. **$p < .01$, one-tailed test. ***$p < .001$, one-tailed test.

Figure 29.2. **Structural Estimates of the Hypothesized Model**

(Jöreskog and Sörbom 1989; Williams and Hazer 1986). The reliability of the demographic similarity variable was estimated at .95 (Hayduk 1987).

Figure 29.2 presents the maximum likelihood parameter estimates of the proposed model. Because supervisor liking of a subordinate and perceived similarity were both measured at the same time (six weeks), causality could not be determined. Thus, the model depicts the relationship between liking and perceived similarity as noncausal. Six of the eight predicted links were statistically significant. Hypothesis 1a was supported; the parameter estimate for the relationship between supervisor-focused impression management behavior and supervisor liking of a subordinate was significant. However, Hypothesis 2a was not supported; self-focused impression management was not significantly related to a supervisor's liking a subordinate. The significant parameter estimate for the relationship between supervisor-focused impression management behavior and supervisor's perceptions of similarity indicated support for Hypothesis 1b. For the relationship between self-focused impression management behavior and supervisor's perceptions of similarity, the parameter estimate was negative and significant,

Table 29.4
Results of the LISREL Analyses

Models	df	χ^2	Goodness-of-fit index	Adjusted goodness-of-fit index	Root-mean-square residual
1	14	60.08***	.839	.759	.252
2	6	4.46	.986	.952	.066
3	9	11.90	.964	.917	.074

*$p < .05$. **$p < .01$. ***$p < .001$.

providing support for Hypothesis 2b. Findings also supported Hypotheses 3a and 3b; demographic similarity was significantly related to a supervisor's liking a subordinate and to perceptions of similarity. In terms of the predictors of performance ratings, the parameter estimate for the path linking a supervisor's liking a subordinate to performance ratings was not significant. However, the parameter estimate was significant for the link between perceptions of similarity and performance ratings. Thus, Hypothesis 4 was not supported and Hypothesis 5 was supported. In addition, a subordinate's report of supervisor-focused impression management behavior exerted a significant, indirect effect on the supervisor's ratings of the subordinate's performance ($t = 3.02$, $p < .01$) via perceptions of similarity. Demographic similarity also had a significant, indirect effect on performance ratings through perceptions of similarity ($t = 3.06$, $p < .01$).

The results for the overall model (model 2, Table 29.4) indicate that the data fit the proposed model very well. Results were as follows: chi-square, with 6 degrees of freedom, 4.46 ($p = .615$); goodness-of-fit (GFI) index, .986; adjusted goodness-of-fit index (AGFI), .952; and root-mean-square residual (RMSR), .066. The Rz for the ratings of the subordinate's performance was .23.

The overall fit indexes for the proposed model were compared to those of a null model (model 1) in which no relationships among the variables are posited. The results for this model were chi-square, with 14 degrees of freedom, 60.08 ($p < .001$); GFI, .839; AGFI, .759; and RMSR, .252. The change in chi-square between models 1 and 2 was 55.62, with 8 degrees of freedom, a significant change ($p < .001$). These results indicate that the proposed model is superior to the null model specifying no causal paths among the variables.

It may be that the two impression management behaviors and demographic similarity directly influence perceptions of similarity, which in turn influence liking. Further, liking a subordinate may have a direct impact on ratings of the subordinate's performance. We examined this alternative model, in which the causal path from perceptions of similarity to ratings of the subordinate's performance was not included and the impression management behaviors and demographic similarity were not directly linked to liking. The fit indexes for this model, model 3, had lower values than those for the hypothesized model: chi-square, with 9 degrees of freedom, 11.90 ($p = .22$); GFI, .964;

AGFI, .917; and RMSR, .074. The change in chi-square between models 2 and 3 was 7.44, with 3 degrees of freedom, a significant value ($p < .05$). These results indicate that the hypothesized model was superior to model 3.

DISCUSSION

Overall, the results of this study provide strong support for the hypothesized model. Demographic similarity and subordinate impression management behavior influenced supervisory performance ratings through their impact on supervisors' perceptions of similarity to subordinates. The fit of the data to the full model and parameters for six of the eight hypothesized links in the model were significant. The current study extends knowledge on impression management by demonstrating that a subordinate's use of impression management early in the relationship with a supervisor induces liking and perceptions of similarity, which in turn influence performance ratings made later. Another addition to current knowledge was the independent effect of demographic similarity on performance ratings through perceived similarity.

Supporting the hypotheses, supervisor-focused impression management was positively related to a supervisor's perceived similarity to a subordinate. Also, as predicted, self-focused impression management was negatively related to perceptions of similarity. The predictions of a negative path between self-focused impression management and liking and of a path between liking and performance ratings were not supported. The results suggest that agents are more successful in the use of other-enhancement (supervisor-focused) strategies than in the use of self-focused strategies. With supervisor-focused impression management, it appears that supervisors do not suspect that subordinates have ulterior motives. In other words, the supervisors may believe and accept positive statements and compliments about themselves made by the subordinates, but not accept positive statements concerning the subordinates' qualities. However, although self-presentation strategies often fail (Cialdini and DeNicholas 1989), targets may have positive reactions to agents' use of self-presentation (Ashforth and Humphrey 1993; Schlenker 1980). Future research is needed to determine what differentiates favorable target reactions to agent self-presentation from unfavorable ones (Baron 1989; Godfrey, Jones, and Lord 1986).

Demographic similarity was also found to affect perceived similarity. Supervisors perceived themselves to be more similar to subordinates whose demographic profiles were similar to the supervisors' than to those with dissimilar demographic profiles. Interestingly, the paths between demographic similarity and perceived similarity and between impression management and perceived similarity were both significant. Thus, demographic similarity and subordinate impression management uniquely influence performance ratings through a supervisor's perceptions of similarity to a subordinate.

Although the self-focused impression management behaviors were quite subtle, they resulted in lowering the supervisors' perceptions of their own similarity to subordinates. Despite this effect, these behaviors did not influence supervisor liking. This finding suggests that even when targets do not interpret self-focused impression management as bragging or conceit, they may find such self-promotional behaviors to be boring and tiresome (Leary, Rogers, Canfield, and Coe 1986). In a controlled laboratory setting, Leary and colleagues (1986) found self-focused impression management led neither to like nor dislike on the part of subjects. An alternative explanation is that when a subordinate uses self-focused tactics, especially those of acting as an exemplar or model employee, supervisors may form expectations that the subordinate does not or cannot live up to over time, causing performance ratings to suffer (Baumeister 1989). Further research is needed to examine the underlying reasons for the different effects of supervisor-focused and self-focused impression management on supervisory reactions.

As the current model suggests, supervisors' perceptions of their own similarity to subordinates were significantly related to liking the subordinates, a finding that provides support in an organizational setting for Byrne's similarity-attraction hypothesis. Previous research testing this hypothesis has either been conducted in laboratory experiments or in field studies involving nonorganizational samples, such as teenagers (Kandel 1978). Organizational researchers have assumed the validity of the similarity-attraction association, but the current results provide the first evidence of generalizability to organizational settings.

Strong support emerged for the predicted effect of supervisor-perceived similarity to a subordinate and ratings of the subordinate's performance. Although substantial evidence for similarity-performance rating effects has accumulated in the organizational literature (Pulakos and Wexley 1983; Senger 1971; Turban and Jones 1988; Wexley et al. 1980; Zalesny and Highhouse 1992; Zalesny and Kirsch 1989), our results demonstrate that performance ratings can be predicted from similarity perceptions assessed 20 weeks before performance is rated. In cross-sectional designs, causality cannot be demonstrated, even with LISREL analysis (Jöreskog and Sörbom 1989); the time separation between the similarity measurement and the performance rating featured in our design supports the plausibility of causality from similarity to performance rating. However, because supervisors may informally evaluate subordinates' performance prior to formally appraising it, there may be a reciprocal interdependence between perceived similarity and performance ratings.

Although prior studies have found strong support for the path between a supervisor's liking a subordinate and the supervisor's ratings of the subordinate's performance, no support for the relationship emerged in the current investigation. One explanation may be that, unlike previous studies, this study measured liking and performance 20 weeks apart, substantially reducing the effect of common method variance occurring when the two are assessed simultaneously. Another explanation is that although liking and perceived similarity were both significantly correlated with performance ratings, perceived similarity dominated liking when tested using LISREL, a multivariate technique. Previous studies demonstrating significant effects for liking on performance ratings (e.g., Judge and Ferris 1993; Tsui and Barry 1986) have not included a measure of perceived similarity.

The time-lagged effects are theoretically important because they provide support for the assertion that impression management behaviors have long-term effects. Although we cannot determine whether the respondents in our study consciously or unconsciously engaged in impression management with the intent of influencing future performance ratings, our results are consistent with such an interpretation. Supervisor-focused impression management measured at six weeks had a significant, indirect effect on performance ratings made at six months, but self-focused impression management did not. Impression management's long-term effect on performance ratings provides support for Tedeschi and Melburg's (1984) thesis that impression management can be used strategically to influence future outcomes with important organizational implications. Although short-term tactical impression management behaviors may affect such outcomes as getting the day off, outcomes of lasting importance, such as performance ratings and compensation, are most likely influenced by strategic, not tactical, uses of impression management.

Although not directly tested in the current research, the effect of the long-term outcomes of strategic impression management can be explained with a cognitive information processing approach. Subordinates' supervisor focused impression management may favorably influence their supervisors' impressions and categorizations of them, and the latter are "encoded into memory." Months later, when the supervisors evaluate the subordinates' performance, the favorable categorization is "retrieved," resulting in a biased rating. Alternatively, the initially favorable categorization may have influenced the supervisors' behavior toward the subordinates in terms of task assignments, feedback, and support so that the subordinates' actual performance is higher than that of others (Feldman 1986; Ilgen and Feldman 1983). Studies that include objective measures of performance are needed if researchers are to examine these alternative processes. However, in response to Ilgen, Barnes-Farrell, and McKellin's (1993) call for research on work group and organizational variables that influence supervisors' cognitive information processing, results of the current study suggest that impression management behavior may be an important factor.

Just as supervisors develop categorizations, they may develop expectations about subordinates' performance during the job interview process rather than after working with the subordinates. Thus, supervisor performance expectations and impressions of a subordinate formed during an interview may influence subsequent performance ratings to a greater extent than impression management behavior that occurs on the job.[3] Future research integrating the study of employment recruiting and selection with work on the early interactions between supervisors and subordinates is needed. To what extent do impression management and the expectations formed prior to an individual's employment influence the initial work interactions between supervisor and subordinate and performance ratings?

A number of weaknesses of the current study should be acknowledged. One potential weakness is that, as in most longitudinal studies, some subject mortality occurred over the duration of the study. In addition, because supervisors responded to the six-week and six-month surveys, there may have been a testing effect in which the responses at six weeks influenced the subsequent responses. Also, although not a problem for the model as a whole, common method bias may have influenced the reported correlation between supervisors' liking of and perceived similarity to the subordinates as both were measured from the supervisors' point of view at six weeks. Another limitation is that we examined only two impression management tactics, and use of both tactics was reported by the same source, the subordinates. The subordinates' report of impression management was considered preferable to the supervisors' report because supervisors may not detect successful use of impression management. Additional sources that might be used in future research to assess impression management include independent observers and coworkers.

A problem with existing, cross-sectional impression management research is that the history of subordinates' prior behavior, from well before data are collected, may influence supervisor reactions to subordinate use of impression management (cf. Green, Fairhurst, and Snavely 1986). The current research included only newly formed supervisor-subordinate dyads, thus controlling for potential history effects. Another strength of the current investigation was the reduction of the common method variance explanations that have been characteristic of some impression management studies. It is possible that when all data are collected from the same source, mood or response tendencies may influence relations between variables (Mitchell 1985; Schmitt and Klimoski 1991; Wagner and Gooding 1987). In the current investigation, impression management was measured from the agent's (subordinate's) perspective and reactions to impression management were assessed from the target's (supervisor's) perspective. In addition to having advantages inherent in longitudinal designs, this study was unique for its examination of the intervening processes involved in the link between impression management behavior and performance ratings.

Suggestions for future research include examining the relative impacts of subordinate impression management behavior and performance-related behavior on performance ratings and outcomes such as pay and promotion decisions. For example, to what extent can supervisor-focused impression management compensate for unsatisfactory performance? This question may be difficult to examine because the objective performance measures used in a given setting are problematic or nonexistent, as was the case in the current investigation. Independent raters should be employed in lieu of, or in addition, to objective measures.

The performance appraisal literature would also benefit from research integrating a full range of social context variables with the cognitive processes of supervisors in observing, storing, and recalling data about subordinates. How does impression management and degree of demographic similarity affect a supervisor's cognitive processing of information? How do situational variables such as organizational level, work group size, technology, and task interdependence influence the processing of information as altered by impression management behavior?

Additional longitudinal studies on impression management are needed so that its uses can be more fully understood. A substantial body of research on the short-term tactical use of impression management has accumulated, but long-term strategic uses have been virtually ignored. One question that needs to be addressed is whether agents deliberately use strategic impression management in an attempt to influence future outcomes. It would also be useful to examine more time periods than were covered here to determine how far into the future impression management behaviors can continue to influence outcomes.

In summary, results of the current investigation point to the importance of examining aspects of social contexts, including demographic similarity and impression management behavior, in relation to performance appraisal. Demographic similarity and impression management are topics worthy of additional investigation, given their implications for fairness in performance evaluations and personnel decisions based on these evaluations.

NOTES

1. Encoding involves the translation of perceived social information into existing schema or categories in one's memory. For example, if we notice on several occasions that an individual is quiet and avoids interaction with others, we may encode the person as fitting our introvert category. Retrieval occurs at a later time when information is accessed from memory and used in forming judgments, such as performance ratings.

2. Controlled processing of information involves conscious thought in the interpretation and encoding of information into memory. Unlike the processing of routine information or stimuli that is handled automatically, controlled processes are invoked when individuals are confronted with novel stimuli or information that is inconsistent with existing schema.

3. Data collected on a small portion of the study group (40 dyads) shed light on this issue. Supervisors' expectations of the subordinates' performance assessed within five days of the start of the working relationship were not significantly correlated with performance ratings at six months ($r = .02$, n.s.).

REFERENCES

Ansari, M.A., and Kapoor, A. 1987. Organizational context and upward influence tactics. *Organizational Behavior and Human Decision Processes* 40: 39–49.

Arkin, R.M., Appleman, A.J., and Berger, J.M. 1980. Social anxiety, self-presentation, and the self-serving bias in causal attribution. *Journal of Personality and Social Psychology* 38: 23–35.

Ashford, S.J., and Northcraft, G.B. 1992. Conveying more (or less) than we realize: The role of impression management in feedback seeking. *Organizational Behavior and Human Decision Processes* 53: 310–334.

Ashforth, B.E., and Humphrey, R.H. 1993. Emotional labor in service roles: The influence of identity. *Academy of Management Review* 18: 88–115.

Baron, R.A. 1983. "Sweet smell of success"? The impact of pleasant artificial scents on evaluations on job applicants, *Journal of Applied Psychology* 68: 709–713.

———. 1986. Self-presentation in job interviews: When there can be "too much of a good thing." *Journal of Applied Social Psychology* 16: 16–28.

———. 1989. Impression management by applicants during employment interviews: The "too much of a good thing" effect. In R.W. Eder and G.R. Ferris (eds.), *The Employment Interview: Theory, Research and Practice*, 204–215. Newbury Park, CA: Sage.

Baumeister, R.F. 1989. Motives and costs of self-presentation in organizations. In R.A. Giacalone and P. Rosenfeld (eds.), *Impression Management in the Organization*, 57–71. Hillsdale, NJ: Erlbaum.

Baumeister, R.F., and Jones, E.E. 1978. When self-presentation is constrained by the target's knowledge: Consistency and compensation. *Journal of Personality and Social Psychology* 36: 608–618.

Berscheid, E., and Walster, E.H. 1969. *Interpersonal Attraction.* Reading, MA: Addison-Wesley.

Bohra, K.A., and Pandey, J. 1984. Ingratiation of strangers, friends, and bosses. *Journal of Social Psychology* 122: 217–222.

Buss, D.M., Gomes, M., Higgins, D.S., and Lauterbach, K. 1987. Tactics of manipulation. *Journal of Personality and Social Psychology* 52: 1219–1229.

Byrne, D. 1971. *The Attraction Paradigm.* New York: Academic Press.

Caldwell, D.F., and O'Reilly, C.A. 1982. Responses to failure: The effects of choice and responsibility on impression management. *Academy of Management Journal* 25: 121–136.

Cardy, R.L., and Dobbins, G.H. 1986. Affect and appraisal accuracy: Liking as an integral dimension in evaluating performance. *Journal of Applied Psychology* 71: 672–678.

Cialdini, R.B. 1989. Indirect tactics of image management: Beyond basking. In R.A. Giacalone and P. Rosenfeld (eds.), *Impression Management in the Organization,* 45–56. Hillsdale, NJ: Erlbaum.

Cialdini, R.B., and DeNicholas, M.E. 1989. Self-presentation by association. *Journal of Personality and Social Psychology* 57: 626–631.

Crowne, D.P., and Marlowe, D.A. 1960. A new scale of social desirability independent of psychopathology. *Journal of Consulting Psychology* 24: 349–354.

DeNisi, A.S., and Shaw, J.B. 1977. Investigation of the uses of self-reports of abilities. *Journal of Applied Psychology* 62: 641–644.

DeNisi, A.S., and Williams, K.J. 1988. Cognitive approaches to performance appraisal. In G.R. Ferris and K.M. Rowland (eds.), *Research in Personnel and Human Resources Management,* vol. 6, 109–155, Greenwich, CT: JAI.

DePaulo, B.M. 1992. Nonverbal behavior and self-presentation. *Psychological Bulletin* 111: 203–243.

Dienesch, R.M., and Liden, R.C. 1986. Leader-member exchange model of leadership: A critique and further development. *Academy of Management Review* 11: 618–634.

Dipboye, R.L. 1985. Some neglected variables in research on discrimination in appraisals. *Academy of Management Review* 10: 116–127.

———. 1989. Threats to the incremental validity of interviewer judgments. In R.W. Eder and G.R. Ferris (eds.), *The Employment Interview: Theory, Research, and Practice,* 45–60. Newbury Park, CA: Sage.

Drake, B.H., and Moberg, D.J. 1986. Communicating influence attempts in dyads: Linguistic sedatives and palliatives. *Academy of Management Review* 11: 567–584.

Fandt, P.M., and Ferris, G.R. 1990. The management of information and impressions: When employees behave opportunistically. *Organizational Behavior and Human Decision Processes* 45: 140–158.

Feldman, J.M. 1981. Beyond attribution theory: Cognitive processes in performance appraisal. *Journal of Applied Psychology* 66: 127–148.

———. 1986. A note on the statistical correction of halo error. *Journal of Applied Psychology* 71: 173–176.

Ferris, G.R., Judge, T.A., Rowland, K.M., and Fitzgibbons, D.E. 1994. Subordinate influence and the performance evaluation process: Test of a model. *Organizational Behavior and Human Decision Processes* 58: 101–135.

Fiske, S.T., Neuberg, S.L., Beattie, A.E., and Milberg, S.J. 1987. Category-based and attribute-based reactions to others: Some informational conditions of stereotyping and individuating processes. *Journal of Experimental and Social Psychology* 23: 399–407.

Fletcher, C. 1989. Impression management in the employment interview. In R.A. Giacalone and P. Rosenfeld (eds.), *Impression Management in the Organization,* 269–281. Hillsdale, NJ: Erlbaum.

French, J.R.P., and Raven, B.H. 1959. The bases of social power. In D. Cartwright (ed.), *Studies in Social Power,* 150–167. Ann Arbor: University of Michigan Press.

Gardner, W.L., and Martinko, M.J. 1988. Impression management in organizations. *Journal of Management* 14: 321–338.

Giacalone, R.A. 1985. On slipping when you thought you had put your best foot forward: Self-promotion, self-destruction, and entitlements. *Group and Organization Studies* 10: 61–80.

Gilmore, D.C., and Ferris, G.R. 1989. The politics of the employment interview. In R.W. Eder and G.R. Ferris (eds.), *The Employment Interview: Theory, Research, and Practice,* 195–203. Newbury Park, CA: Sage.

Godfrey, D.K., Jones, E.E., and Lord, C.G. 1986. Self-promotion is not ingratiating. *Journal of Personality and Social Psychology* 50: 106–115.

Green, S.G., Fairhurst, G.T., and Snavely, B.K. 1986. Chains of poor performance and supervisory control. *Organizational Behavior and Human Decision Processes* 38: 7–27.

Green, S.G., and Mitchell, T.R. 1979. Attributional processes of leaders in leader-member interactions. *Organizational Behavior and Human Performance* 23: 429–458.

Greenwald, A.G. 1980. The totalitarian ego: Fabrication and revision of personal history. *American Psychologist* 35: 603–618.

Hayduk, L.A. 1987. *Structural Equation Modeling with LISREL.* Baltimore: Johns Hopkins University Press.

Hinkin, T.R., and Schriesheim, C.A. 1990. Relationships between subordinate perceptions of supervisor influence and attributed bases of supervisory power. *Human Relations* 43: 221–237.

Ilgen, D.R., Barnes-Farrell, J.L., and McKellin, D.B. 1993. Performance appraisal process research in the 1980s: What has it contributed to appraisals in use? *Organizational Behavior and Human Decision Processes* 54: 321–368.

Ilgen, D.R., and Feldman, J.M. 1983. Performance appraisal: A process focus. In L.L. Cummings and B.M. Staw (eds.), *Research in Organizational Behavior,* vol. 5, 141–197, Greenwich, CT: JAI.

Jamieson, D.W., Lydon, J.E., and Zanna, M.P. 1987. Attitude and activity preference similarity: Differential bases of interpersonal attraction for low and high self-monitors. *Journal of Personality and Social Psychology* 53: 1052–1060.

Jones, E.E. 1964. *Ingratiation.* New York: Appleton-Century-Crofts.

Jones, E.E., and Wortman, C.B. 1973. *Ingratiation: An Attributional Approach.* Morristown, NJ: General Learning Press.

Jöreskog, K.G., and Sörbom, D. 1989. LISREL 7. A guide to the program and applications. Chicago: SPSSX.

———. 1993. LISREL 8: User's reference guide. Chicago: Scientific Software International.

Judge, T.A., and Ferris, G.R. 1993. Social context of performance evaluation decisions. *Academy of Management Journal* 36: 80–105.

Kandel, D.B. 1978. Similarity in real-life adolescent friendship pairs. *Journal of Personality and Social Psychology* 36: 306–312.

Kipnis, D., and Schmidt, S.M. 1988. Upward influence styles: Relationship with performance evaluations, salary, and stress. *Administrative Science Quarterly* 33: 528–542.

Kipnis, D., Schmidt, S.M., and Wilkinson, I. 1980. Intraorganizational influence tactics: Exploration of getting one's way. *Journal of Applied Psychology* 65: 440–452.

Kipnis, D., and Vanderveer, R. 1971. Ingratiation and the use of power. *Journal of Personality and Social Psychology* 17: 280–286.

Landy, F.J., and Farr, J.L. 1980. Performance ratings. *Psychological Bulletin* 87: 72–107.

Leary, M.R., and Kowalski, R.M. 1990. Impression management: A literature review and two-component model. *Psychological Bulletin* 107: 34–47.

Leary, M.R., Rogers, P.A., Canfield, R.W., and Coe, C. 1986. Boredom in interpersonal encounters: Antecedents and social implications. *Journal of Personality and Social Psychology* 51: 968–975.

Lewicki, P. 1983. Self-image bias in person perception. *Journal of Personality and Social Psychology* 45: 384–393.

Liden, R.C., and Mitchell, T.R. 1988. Ingratiatory behaviors in organizational settings. *Academy of Management Review* 13: 572–587.

———. 1989. Ingratiation in the development of leader-member exchanges. In R.A. Giacalone and P. Rosenfeld (eds.), *Impression Management in the Organization,* 343–361. Hillsdale, NJ: Erlbaum.

Liden, R.C., Wayne, S.J., and Stilwell, D. 1993. A longitudinal study on the early development of leader-member exchanges. *Journal of Applied Psychology* 78: 662–674.

Lord, R.G. 1985. An information processing approach to social perceptions, leadership and behavioral measurement in organizations. In L.L. Cummings and B.M. Staw (eds.), *Research in organizational behavior,* vol. 7, 87–128. Greenwich, CT: JAI.

Markus, H. 1980. The self in thought and memory. In D.M. Wegner and R.R. Vallacher (eds.), *The Self in Social Psychology,* 102–130. New York: Oxford University Press.

Markus, H., Smith, J., and Moreland, R.L. 1985. Role of the self-concept in the perception of others. *Journal of Personality and Social Psychology* 49: 1494–1512.

Mitchell, T.R. 1983. The effects of social, task, and situational factors on motivation, performance, and appraisal. In F. Landy, S. Zedeck, and J. Cleveland (eds.), *Performance Measurement and Theory,* 39–59. Hillsdale, NJ: Erlbaum.

———. 1985. An evaluation of the validity of correlational research conducted in organizations. *Academy of Management Review* 10: 192–205.

Mitchell, T.R., and Liden, R.C. 1982. The effects of the social context on performance evaluations. *Organizational Behavior and Human Performance* 29: 241–256.

Mowday, R.T. 1979. Leader characteristics, self-confidence, and methods of upward influence in organizational decision situations. *Academy of Management Journal* 22: 709–725.

Pandey, J. 1981. A note on social power through ingratiation among workers. *Journal of Occupational Psychology* 52: 379–385.

Phillips, A.P., and Dipboye, R.L. 1989. Correlational tests of predictions from a process model of the interview. *Journal of Applied Psychology* 74: 41–52.

Powers, T.A., and Zuroff, D.C. 1988. Interpersonal consequences of overt self-criticism: A comparison with neutral and self-enhancing presentations of self. *Journal of Personality and Social Psychology* 54: 1054–1062.

Pulakos, E.D., and Wexley, K.N. 1983. The relationship among perceptual similarity, sex, and performance ratings in manager-subordinate dyads. *Academy of Management Journal* 26: 129–139.

Ralston, D.A. 1985. Employee ingratiation: The role of management. *Academy of Management Review* 10: 477–487.

Ralston, D.A., and Elsass, P.M. 1989. Ingratiation and impression management in the organization. In R.A. Giacalone and P. Rosenfeld (eds.), *Impression Management in the Organization,* 235–247. Hillsdale, NJ: Erlbaum.

Ross, L. 1977. The intuitive psychologist and his shortcomings: Distortions in the attribution process. In L. Berkowitz (ed.), *Advances in Experimental Social Psychology,* vol. 10: 174–220. New York: Academic Press.

Schlenker, B.R. 1980. *Impression management: The Self-Concept, Social Identity and Interpersonal Relations.* Monterey, CA: Brooks/Cole.

Schlenker, B.R., and Leary, M.R. 1982a. Social anxiety and self-presentations: A conceptualization and model. *Psychological Bulletin* 92: 641–669.

———. 1982b. Audiences' reactions to self-enhancing, self-denigrating, and accurate self-presentations. *Journal of Experimental Social Psychology* 18: 89–104.

Schlenker, B.R., and Weigold, M.F. 1992. Interpersonal processes involving impression regulation and management. In M.R. Rosenzweig and L.W. Porter (eds.), *Annual review of psychology,* 133–168. Palo Alto, CA: Annual Reviews.

Schmitt, N.W., and Klimoski, R.J. 1991. *Research Methods in Human Resources Management.* Cincinnati: South-Western.

Schneider, D.J. 1991. Social cognition. In M.R. Rosenzweig and L.W. Porter (eds.), *Annual Review of Psychology,* 527–561. Palo Alto, CA: Annual Reviews.

Schriesheim, C.A., and Hinkin, T.R. 1990. Influence tactics used by subordinates: A theoretical and empirical analysis and refinement of the Kipnis, Schmidt, and Wilkinson subscales. *Journal of Applied Psychology* 75: 246–257.

Senger, J. 1971. Manager's perceptions of subordinates' competencies as a function of personal value orientations. *Academy of Management Journal* 14: 415–424.

Shore, T.H., Shore, L.M., and Thornton, G.C. 1992. Construct validity of self- and peer evaluations of performance dimensions in an assessment center. *Journal of Applied Psychology* 77: 42–54.

Srull, T.K., and Gaelick, L. 1983. General principles and individual differences in the self as a habitual reference point: An examination of self-other judgments of similarity. *Social Cognition* 2: 108–121.

Srull, T.K., and Wyer, R.S. 1989. Person memory and judgment. *Psychological Review* 96: 58–83.

Steele, C.M. 1988. The psychology of self-affirmation: Sustaining the integrity of the self. In L. Berkowitz (ed.), *Advances in Experimental Social Psychology,* vol. 21, 261–302. San Diego: Academic Press.

Swann, W.B. 1982. Self-verification: Bringing social reality into harmony with the self. In J. Suls (ed.), *Psychological Perspectives on the Self,* vol. 2, 33–66. Hillside, NJ: Erlbaum.

Swann, W.B., Stein-Seroussi, A., and Giesler, R.B. 1992. Why people self-verify. *Journal of Personality and Social Psychology* 62: 392–401.

Tedeschi, J.T., and Melburg, V. 1984. Impression management and influence in the organization. In S.B. Bacharach and E.J. Lawler (eds.), *Research in the Sociology of Organizations,* vol. 3: 31–58. Greenwich, CT: JAI.

Tedeschi, J.T., and Norman, N. 1985. Social power, self-presentation, and the self. In B.R. Schlenker (ed.), *The Self and Social Life,* 293–322. New York: McGraw-Hill.

Tsui, A.S. 1984. A role set analysis of managerial reputation. *Organizational Behavior and Human Performance* 34: 64–96.

Tsui, A.S., and Barry, B. 1986. Interpersonal affect and rating errors. *Academy of Management Journal* 29: 586–599.

Tsui, A.S., and O'Reilly, C.A. 1989. Beyond simple demographic effects: The importance of relational demography in superior-subordinate dyads. *Academy of Management Journal* 32: 402–423.

Turban, D.B., and Jones, A.P. 1988. Supervisor-subordinate similarity: Types, effects, and mechanisms. *Journal of Applied Psychology* 73: 228–234.

Vecchio, R.P., and Sussmann, M. 1991. Choice of influence tactics: Individual and organizational determinants. *Journal of Occupational Behaviour* 12: 73–80.

Villanova, P., and Bernardin, H.J. 1989. Impression management in the context of performance appraisal. In R.A. Giacalone and P. Rosenfeld (eds.), *Impression Management in the Organization,* 235–247. Hillsdale, NJ: Erlbaum.

———. 1991. Performance appraisal: The means, motive, and opportunity to manage impression. In R.A. Giacalone and P. Rosenfeld (eds.), *Applied Impression Management,* 81–96. Newbury Park, CA: Sage.

Wagner, J.A., III, and Gooding, R.Z. 1987. Shared influence and organizational behavior: A meta-analysis of situational variables expected to moderate participation-outcome relationships. *Academy of Management Journal* 30: 524–541.

Wayne, S.J., and Ferris, G.R. 1990. Influence tactics, affect, and exchange quality in supervisor-subordinate interactions: A laboratory experiment and field study. *Journal of Applied Psychology* 75: 487–499.

Wayne, S.J., and Kacmar, M.K. 1991. The effects of impression management on the performance appraisal process. *Organizational Behavior and Human Decision Processes* 48: 70–88.

Wexley, K.N., Alexander, R.A, Greenwalt, J.P., and Couch, M.A. 1980. Attitudinal congruence and similarity as related to interpersonal evaluations in manager-subordinate dyads. *Academy of Management Journal* 23: 320–330.

Williams, L.J., and Hazer, J.T. 1986. Antecedents and consequences of satisfaction and commitment in turnover models: A reanalysis using latent variable structural equation methods. *Journal of Applied Psychology* 71: 219–231.

Wood, R.E., and Mitchell, T.R. 1981. Manager behavior in a social context: The impact of impression management on attributions and disciplinary actions. *Organizational Behavior and Human Performance* 28: 356–378.

Wortman, C.B., and Linsenmeier, J.A. 1977. Interpersonal attraction and techniques of ingratiation in organizational settings. In B.M. Staw and G.R. Salancik (eds.), *New Directions in Organizational Behavior,* 133–178. Chicago: St. Clair Press.

Yukl, G., and Falbe, C.M. 1990. Influence tactics and objectives in upward, downward, and lateral influence attempts. *Journal of Applied Psychology* 75: 132–140.

Yukl, G., and Tracey, J.B. 1992. Consequences of influence tactics used with subordinates, peers, and the boss. *Journal of Applied Psychology* 77: 525–535.

Zajonc, R.B. 1980. Feeling and thinking: Preferences need no inferences. *American Psychologist* 35: 151–175.

Zalesny, M.D., and Highhouse, S. 1992. Accuracy in performance evaluations. *Organizational Behavior and Human Decision Processes* 51: 22–50.

Zalesny, M.D., and Kirsch, M.P. 1989. The effect of similarity on performance ratings and interrater agreement. *Human Relations* 42: 81–96.

30

Ethical Perceptions of Organizational Politics: A Comparative Evaluation of American and Hong Kong Managers

David A. Ralston, Robert A. Giacalone, and Robert H. Terpstra

Business ethics are applied ethics (Velasquez 1992). More specifically, business ethics are what is perceived as appropriate in the organizational setting. The growing body of literature in this area provides evidence that business ethics is playing a growing part in the concern of management from the vantage point of both practitioners and academics. Indeed, the recent literature has been characterized by theoretical advances as well as issue-specific treatments in areas such as affirmative action (Berne and Freeman 1992), environmental impact (Singh and Lakhan 1989), and insider trading (Salbu 1992). However, to date, there has been limited scientific investigation into the differences in ethical behavior across cultures.

While it is commonly acknowledged that different cultures interpret ethical behavior differently, and while anecdotal information leads to the conclusion that the ethical climates of businesses across cultures differ substantially from each other (see Sethi, et al. 1984; Shenkar and Ronen 1987; Weiss 1994), relatively little empirical research has focused on cross-cultural ethical differences in business behavior. More specifically, there has been virtually no research that has empirically tested the cross-cultural differences in ethical perception of the political behaviors of individuals.

The objective of this paper is first to identify previous cross-cultural research on the ethics of political behavior, and second to combine this research with findings from previous cross-cultural values research in order to develop hypotheses that test the dimensions of the Strategies of Upward Influence instrument used with our sample of American and Hong Kong managers.

THE ISSUE OF ETHICS IN BUSINESS

While everyone seems to know what is meant by ethics, actually defining what is ethical has long proved to be problematic for both practitioners and researchers (Brenner and Molander 1977). Scholars have proposed a number of definitions of business ethics. For example, Ferrell and Fraederich (1991) note that "... business ethics comprise moral principles and standards that guide behavior in the world of business." Their definition is perhaps as good as any, and it certainly captures that essence of this issue— determining what "good behavior" is in the business world. Likewise, business ethics research has focused upon what is morally right and good in aspects of business ranging from affirmative action to insider trading.

The Evolution of the Ethics Research

The evolution of the business ethics field has been characterized by investigations of ethics-related phenomena from distinctively different perspectives. Some investigations have taken a philosophical approach, examining ethically relevant topic areas from traditional philosophical vantages (see Velasquez, et al. 1983). Others have taken a more descriptive, illustrative approach, focusing on examples of questionable business practices (see Lutz 1983; Olasky 1985). And another group has taken a methodological stance, based on behavioral science methodology, using questionnaires (e.g., Newstrom and Ruch 1975) or experimentation (e.g., Trevino and Ball 1992). Yet without a doubt, the driving force behind the critical thought and theory of the field has been the philosophical literature.

Still, while the primary literature in business ethics has emanated from, and is focused on a more philosophical base, a more recent objective has been to integrate organizational behavior issues, methods, and theory with traditional areas of ethical concern in business. The work of Trevino (1986) and Payne and Giacalone (1990), as well as a recent special issue in the 1992 *Journal of Business Ethics* focusing on behavior, attests to a growing integration and interpolation between behavioral science literature and business ethics literature. Since business ethics literature has traditionally been entrenched in a more philosophical base, the increasingly popular behavioral approach addresses many unexplored theoretical, research, and practitioner issues.

One of these under-explored areas of particular relevance in today's global economy is the issue of differences in ethics across cultures. The ethical relativists, while sometimes criticized for condoning any ethical code as long as a society accepts it, do accurately point out that different cultures have different ethical beliefs. More importantly, perhaps, is that these differences cannot be dismissed simply because the beliefs in other cultures do not coincide with our own (Velasquez 1992). Dismissing differences in ethical standards can have serious repercussions from both an ethical and business vantage. From an ethical perspective alone, for example, while we condemn the use of child labor in the United States as morally questionable, this position clearly ignores the fact that in some third world countries the money made by a child may be an indispensable source of income without which the family could not survive. Ignoring this critical fact could result in various ethically driven political and/or business decisions designed to pressure the end of these child labor practices, ultimately hurting the very child it was meant to help by eliminating a crucial source of income. Additionally, from a more narrow business perspective, to be insensitive to the ethical values of other cultures would be folly for a multinational company that wants to function effectively in a global economy. Such insensitivity could undermine business relationships by displaying a basic contempt for the values, moral standards and needs of others which would result in long-lasting resentment.

The Emerging Issue of Cross-Cultural Ethics Differences

Despite the growing concern with issues of multiculturalism and international management within the business world, the expanding base of behavioral research in business ethics has not provided much insight into the arena of cross-cultural ethics. The existing literature on cross-cultural ethics involves topic areas such as corporate codes of ethics (Langlois and Schlegelmilch 1990), managerial values (Becker and Fritzche 1987), ethical belief structures (Abratt, et al. 1992; Israeli 1988), judgments (Whipple and Swords 1992), bribery (e.g. Tsalikis and Nwachukwu 1991), and ethical perceptions (McDonald and Zepp 1988). In addition, there has been some theoretical discussion on generic ethical issues in international business (Scholhammer 1977), basic models (Wines and Napier 1992), and approaches to reconciling international norms (Donaldson 1985). However, virtually ignored in the business ethics literature has been the ethical perceptions of organizational politics, especially cross-cultural politics (see Zahra 1989).

Organizational politics, while a fact of life, has remained an illusive concept to define (Drory and Romm 1990; Ferris and Kacmar 1992). However, based upon contributions previously made in describing political behavior in organizations, we may define organizational politics as self-serving, informal behavior that requires at least two parties: an initiator—the individual trying to exert influence—and a target—the object of the influence attempt (Goffman 1959; Porter, et al. 1981). This informal behavior is self-serving in that the initiator attempts to use politics to gain control over the target in order to obtain resources or other goals that are not sanctioned by the organization (Mayes and Allen 1977; Pfeffer 1981). Porter et al. (1981) further extend the description of political behavior by noting that it is frequently used as an upward influence strategy to promote the self-interests of the initiator (e.g., a raise or promotion).

Our focus in this paper is upon the ethical perceptions across cultures of the upward influence political strategies used by organizational members. The dearth of research in this area is particularly unfortunate for two reasons. First, the literature has shown a serious concern with ethics and its impact on the organization (Mayes and Allen 1977; Zahra 1984). Such concern would indicate a need to explore the ethical ramifications and constraints inherent to organizational politics. Second, since the exercise of influence in culturally diverse groups is no doubt an important skill (see Ferguson 1988; Smith and Peterson 1988) and may even be a determinant of managerial success (Chacko 1990; Kotter 1985), the understanding of how such behaviors are viewed ethically across cultures is no doubt of consequence to the individuals exercising them.

Most research in ethics and organizational politics has been done from a U.S. perspective. Cavanagh, et al. (1981) and Velasquez, et al. (1983) took a primarily philosophical approach toward the ethics of organizational politics. They argue that because there is nothing inherently unethical regarding organizational behavior, the assessment of any political tactic should involve three distinct criteria: the utility of the political act to all of the involved constituencies, the rights of the individuals involved, and the extent to which the political tactic adheres to accepted canons of justice.

From a more behavioral approach, Zahra (1985) investigated the impact of various demographic and organizational factors on perceptions of organizational politics. In his sampling of managers, he found that while age, gender, and race were significantly associated with ethical perceptions of organizational politics, functional area, job level, and years of work experience were not associated with such perceptions. Using personality and attitudinal variables in another study, Zahra (1989) showed that executives having high scores on measures of concern with status, anomie, and external locus of control, or having a low acceptance of others, tended to view organizational politics as ethical.

From a cross-cultural standpoint, we identified only two studies which have investigated the ethical perceptions of organizational politics. Romm and Drory (1988), in comparing Canadian and Israeli samples, found that Canadians had a greater tendency to view some aspects of political behavior as less moral, but that both groups were generally in agreement that illegal influence attempts were less moral than formal or informal attempts. Dolecheck and Dolecheck's (1987) comparison of U.S. and Hong Kong managers, while not testing for statistical significance, did indicate that differences appear to exist. Specifically, they conclude that in Hong Kong ethics appear to be tied simply to "that which is allowed by law," whereas the Western view of ethics suggests that what is allowed by law is the lowest acceptable behavior and that ethical behavior transcends legality (Laczniak 1983).

As implied by the dearth of empirical, cross-cultural research on the ethics of organizational politics, studying this phenomenon can be challenging. Likewise, identifying a suitable measure proved problematic. A review of the literature and available instruments did not yield any cross-culturally developed measures of upward influence strategy.

THE "STRATEGIES OF UPWARD INFLUENCE" INSTRUMENT

Due to no cross-culturally developed measures of upward influence being available, the Strategies of Upward Influence [SUI] instrument was developed by Ralston and Gustafson. Our goal was to develop a suitable cross-cultural measure of upward influence.

Therefore, we felt that simply trying to modify existing Western measures might constrain the developmental process. Thus, relying heavily upon practitioner input as well as previous theoretical research for the foundation, the SUI instrument was created. The instrument development process identified two separate taxonomies for measuring upward influence.

One taxonomy identified seven "Job Tactics" dimensions. These tactics dimensions are similar to the influence strategies identified in previous studies of American subjects (Kipnis et al. 1980; Yukl and Falbe 1990; Yukl and Falbe 1991; Yukl and Tracey 1992). The other taxonomy, which is less traditional, identified the "Western Values" dimensions of ethics. The actual development procedure, analysis, and testing of this instrument are presented in another paper. However, an overview of the dimensions of the instrument is presented in the subsequent paragraphs.

THE JOB TACTICS TAXONOMY

The dimensions of the "Job Tactics" taxonomy are: Good Soldier (getting ahead through hard work that benefits the organization), Rational Persuasion (demonstrating, with facts and skills related accomplishments, that one should be given consideration), Ingratiation (using subtle, indirect tactics to make oneself appear interpersonally attractive to someone at the superior level), Image Management (actively presenting oneself in a positive manner across the entire organization), Personal Networking (developing and utilizing an informal organizational social structure for one's own benefit), Information Control (controlling information that is restricted from others in order to benefit oneself), and Strong-Arm Coercion (using illegal tactics, such as blackmail, to achieve personal goals).

THE WESTERN VALUES TAXONOMY

The other taxonomy identifies four hierarchical dimensions of "Western values." The purpose of this taxonomy was to create a baseline for comparing acceptable and unacceptable behavior using an American perspective. This taxonomy is unique from those used with other influence research instruments. The dimensions of this taxonomy are: Organizationally Sanctioned Behaviors (behaviors, such as working hard, that are usually prescribed and sanctioned for employees in organizations), Non-Destructive, Legal Behaviors (behaviors that do not directly hurt another person but are self-serving for the individual within the organization), Destructive, Legal Behaviors (self-serving behaviors, such as spreading rumors, that directly hurt others but are not extreme enough to be illegal), Destructive, Illegal Behaviors (extreme self-serving behaviors that directly hurt others and are illegal, such as stealing business documents).

HYPOTHESES

While the two cross-cultural studies identified contribute to our understanding of culturally different views on the ethics of organizational politics, they do not provide a significant basis upon which we could formulate hypotheses for our study. More specifically, only one of these studies focused on an East-West culture comparison, and it did not utilize hypothesis-testing statistics (Dolecheck and Dolecheck 1987). Therefore, to formulate our hypotheses, we relied heavily on the more general cross-cultural values research literature (Hofstede 1980; Ralston, et al. 1993; Tung 1988).

Hypotheses for the Job Tactics Dimensions

Recent research supports Hofstede's (1980) findings that the United States can be categorized as individualistic and low in power distance, while the Hong Kong culture can be categorized as collectivistic and high in power distance (Ralston et al. 1993). Previous ethics research (McDonald and Zepp 1988) has noted that these value differences are key distinguishing issues in one's orientation toward what is considered ethical behavior.

Therefore, we predicted that U.S. mangers will find tactics that tend to focus on public self-definition and self-promotion as more acceptable, and thus more ethical, than the Hong Kong, managers who identify with a collectivist image and eschew public displays of self-promotion. Specifically, we hypothesize that American managers will find the tactics of good soldier, rational persuasion, ingratiation, and image management, to be more ethical than their Hong Kong counterparts. Conversely, we believe that the Hong Kong managers, whose cultural orientation is to work quietly behind the scenes, will find the more private and circuitous tactics to be more ethical than the American managers. As such, we hypothesize that the Hong Kong managers will find personal networking, information control, and strong-arm coercion to be more acceptable—thus more ethical—than the American managers.

Hypothesis 1a: American managers will find good solider more ethical than will Hong Kong managers.

Hypothesis 1b: American managers will find rational persuasion more ethical than will Hong Kong managers.

Hypothesis 1c: American managers will find ingratiation more ethical than will Hong Kong managers.

Hypothesis 1d: American managers will find image management more ethical than will Hong Kong managers.

Hypothesis 1e: Hong Kong managers will find personal networking more ethical than will American managers.

Hypothesis 1f: Hong Kong managers will find information control more ethical than will American managers.

Hypothesis 1g: Hong Kong managers will find strong-arm coercion more ethical than will American managers.

Hypotheses for the Western Values Dimensions

As noted, previous cross-cultural ethics research (Dolecheck and Dolecheck 1987) found Hong Kong managers to equate ethics with acting within the law, while American managers were found to view ethical behavior as something that goes beyond mere adherence to the law. However, we believe that the actual explanation may be more complex than this conclusion. For example, Lee Ka-Shing, after being convicted in Hong Kong of insider trading, was selected as Hong Kong's "Man of the Year," and was praised by his associates as one of the most trustworthy people in Hong Kong.

Therefore, to attempt to understand this apparent disparity from a Western point of view, let us begin by noting that the Chinese translation of the word ethics, "dao de," means "the path to virtue." The *Chinese Culture Connection* (1987) has identified the Chinese society's search for virtue as Confucian work dynamism. This concept reflects the teachings of Confucius, which emphasize a social hierarchy or structure (Hofstede and Bond 1988; Louie 1980). It is characterized by a respect for tradition with a strong desire to save "face." Confucian work dynamism also implies a need to order relationships by status and to respect the order of that status. Thus, the Chinese view of ethical behavior appears to be very pragmatic (Bedding 1990). What is ethical is relative, and as long as "face" is not lost or is not a concern, "dao de" is intact. In contrast to this relative view of ethics, the Western view of ethics tends to be based upon an absolute ideal of "good behavior" (Velasquez 1992).

Thus, since the Western Values taxonomy is based upon the absolute of ideally good behavior, we would expect Hong Kong managers to be more willing to accept as ethical those things that American managers find less ethical, and vice versa, depending on how pragmatically those things fit the situation. Therefore, we hypothesize that American managers will find the Organizationally Sanctioned behaviors and the Legal/Nondestructive behaviors as more ethical than will the Hong Kong managers because these behaviors consistently fit the Western ideal of "good behavior." Conversely, we hypothesize that the Hong Kong managers will find the Legal/Destructive and Illegal behaviors to be more ethical than the American managers because these may be seen by the Hong Kong managers as pragmatically appropriate in some situations, and therefore more ethically acceptable. These following hypotheses represent morally acceptable strategies that fit within the cultural orientations of each country.

Hypothesis 2a: American managers will find organizationally sanctioned behavior more ethical than will Hong Kong managers.

Hypothesis 2b: American managers will find legal/nondestructive behavior more ethical than will Hong Kong managers.

Hypothesis 2c: Hong Kong managers will find legal/destructive behavior more ethical than will American managers.

Hypothesis 2d: Hong Kong managers will find illegal behavior more ethical than will American managers.

METHOD

Subjects

The subjects were full-time professionals in the United States ($n = 161$) and Hong Kong ($n = 144$). The average age of the American subjects was 32.7 years, while the average age of the Hong Kong Chinese subjects was 33.5 years. Overall, the two groups were reasonably comparable. Table 30.1 presents the demographic data for these groups.

Procedure

Potential participants were identified and mailed a survey with cover letter and postage-paid return envelope. The instructions accompanying the instrument asked the subjects to think of their work experiences when responding to the questions. The instruction also told the subjects that there were no right or wrong answers, and that it was their perceptions that were important.

Instrument

The 38-item Strategies of Upward Influence (SUI) instrument was used to assess influence tactics. For each of the 38 scenario items, the subjects were asked to evaluate the ethics (morality) of using the strategy. The 38 scenarios were measured on a 4-point Likert scale. The response options ranged from "highly ethical" to "highly unethical." The higher the score, the more ethical a scenario was seen to be.

Design and Analysis

The first step of the analysis consisted of two one-way multivariate analysis of variance (MANOVA) tests for the Job Tactics Dimensions and the Western Values Dimensions. Each multivariate analysis had two levels (Americans working in the United States and Hong Kong Chinese working in Hong Kong). The dependent variables for the job Tactics Dimensions analysis were Good Soldier, Rational Persuasion, Ingratiation, Image Management, Personal Networking, Information Control, and Strong-Arm, Coercion. The dependent variables for the Western Values Dimensions were Sanctioned Behavior, Non-Destructive Behavior, Destructive-Legal Behavior, and Illegal Behavior. The multivariate technique was used in these analyses to control experiment-wise error rate with multiple dependent measures. If a significant effect was found in a multivariate analysis, then the second step was to calculate the univariate analyses (ANOVAs) for each of its dimensions (Kirk 1982).

Table 30.1
Demographic Data for the Two Groups

	Americans working in the U.S.	H.K. Chinese working in Hong Kong
Age		
Mean	32.7	33.5
SD	5.8	6.7
Gender		
% male	64	59
Marital status		
% married	52	58
Years employed		
Mean	8.4	10.0
SD	5.4	6.1
Number of employees in the company		
Under 100	25%	30%
100 or more	75%	70%

RESULTS

Job Tactics

A MANOVA analysis indicated a significant effect for differences between U.S. managers and Hong Kong Chinese managers (lambda = 0.651, df = 6, 2, 456, $p < 0.001$).

Since the multivariate effect was significant for the job Tactics dimensions, univariate ANOVAs were used to ascertain which of the seven job tactics were different for the U.S. and Hong Kong managers. As Table 30.2 shows, all but the Personal Networking tactic showed significant differences.

The means for the significantly different tactic dimensions indicate that the U.S. managers rated the tactics of Good Soldier, Rational Persuasion, Image Management, and Ingratiation as more ethical, while their Hong Kong counterparts reported Informational Control and Strong-Arm Coercion as more ethical.

Western Values Hierarchy

A MANOVA analysis indicated a significant effect for differences among U.S. managers and Hong Kong Chinese managers (lambda = 0.632, df = 3, 2, 459, $p < 0.001$).

Again, because the multivariate effect was significant for the Western Values measures, univariate ANOVAs were used to determine on which of the four dimensions there were differences. As Table 30.3 shows, significant differences were found for the Sanctioned Behavior, Destructive-Legal Behavior, and Illegal Behavior dimensions.

The pattern of means for these dimensions showed that the Organizationally Sanctioned dimension was rated as more ethical by American managers, while the Destruc-

Table 30.2
Means, Standard Deviations, and *F*-Test Results for the Seven Job Tactics Dimensions

Dimension	Nationality	Location	Mean	SD	F
Good Soldier	American	U.S.	3.71	0.30	20.77***
	HK Chinese	Hong Kong	3.52	0.34	
Rational persuasion	American	U.S.	3.52	0.29	7.36***
	HK Chinese	Hong Kong	3.41	0.33	
Image management	American	U.S.	3.01	0.33	5.24**
	HK Chinese	Hong Kong	2.94	0.32	
Ingratiation	American	U.S.	3.10	0.39	11.65***
	HK Chinese	Hong Kong	2.99	0.38	
Personal networking	American	U.S.	2.64	0.37	0.63
	HK Chinese	Hong Kong	2.68	0.33	
Information control	American	U.S.	1.48	0.28	33.86***
	HK Chinese	Hong Kong	1.70	0.30	
Strong-arm coercion	American	U.S.	1.28	0.26	31.71***
	HK Chinese	Hong Kong	1.51	0.31	

**$p < 0.01$. ***$p < 0.001$.

tive/Legal and Illegal dimensions were rated as more acceptable by Hong Kong managers.

DISCUSSION

The results demonstrate that there were a number of cultural differences between the U.S. and Hong Kong managers in their perceptions of ethical behavior. Also, as shown in Tables 30.2 and 30.3, all dimensions showing significant differences followed the hypothesized direction.

Job Tactics

On the job tactics dimensions, as hypothesized, U.S. managers saw Good Soldier, Rational Persuasion, Image Management, and Ingratiation as being more ethical alternatives than did their Hong Kong counterparts. Likewise, as hypothesized, Information Control and Strong-Arm Coercion tactics were evaluated as more acceptable by the Hong Kong managers. The use of Personal Networking tactics was not reported as significantly different by the managers in our study. These findings are consistent with the cross-cultural values research that find Americans to be individualistic and openly aggressive, while finding Hong Kong Chinese as more collectivistic, preferring behind-the scenes strategies.

Western Values

Similarly, U.S. managers found Organizationally Sanctioned behavior as more ethically justifiable than did their Hong Kong counterparts. However, there was no difference

Table 30.3
Means, Standard Deviations, and F-Test Results for the Four Western Values Dimensions

Dimension	Nationality	Location	Mean	SD	F
Sanctioned	American	U.S.	3.71	0.30	20.33***
	HK Chinese	Hong Kong	3.52	0.34	
Non-destructive	American	U.S.	3.52	0.29	2.31
	HK Chinese	Hong Kong	3.41	0.33	
Destructive/legal	American	U.S.	3.01	0.33	26.06***
	HK Chinese	Hong Kong	2.94	0.32	
Illegal	American	U.S.	3.10	0.39	42.55***
	HK Chinese	Hong Kong	2.99	0.38	

***$p < 0.001$.

between U.S. and Hong Kong managers regarding Non-Destructive/Legal behavior. Also, as hypothesized, the Hong Kong managers reported the Destructive/Legal and Illegal behaviors as more acceptable. These findings are consistent with the view that in the West, ethical behavior is an absolute that applies universally, while in the East, "face" and ethical behavior depend on the situation.

CONCLUSIONS

These findings offer practitioners several avenues for consideration. For example, from a training standpoint, cross-cultural managers will need to consider the varying cultural perception of appropriate influence strategies as they train expatriates. Giacalone and Beard (in press) note that individuals who go abroad may succeed or fail largely on their ability to present themselves in socially appropriate ways, since foreign hosts tend to interact with expatriates from the host's cultural perspective. When there are substantive differences in the ethical perceptions of influence strategies between cultures (as this study demonstrates), expatriates will need to be sensitive to those differences, if they hope to attain their objectives of gaining influence.

Likewise, multinational corporations will need to consider the strategies they use to influence external stakeholder. Using strategies viewed as unethical by members of the other culture may backfire and result in negative perceptions of the individual attempting the influence strategy. This scenario has been proven in previous studies (see, for example, Giacalone 1985).

Future research potential can be drawn from two particular issues that this study did not address. First, the ethical climate within a given multinational organization may moderate the extent to which a particular influence strategy is seen as more or less appropriate (Victor and Cullen 1988). That is, there may be company cultures that vary across organizations influencing what organizational members perceive as ethical. For example, a company's culture may be influenced by the home office location of that company. This would be especially likely if many of the top executives come from the home office country, and as such have a common national culture which, in turn, would help to shape the company culture.

Additionally, the situational context may alter the ethical appropriateness perceived in various influence strategies. The cultural relationship between the person attempting the influence and the person over whom the influence is attempted may have an important effect on what is perceived as ethical (Ansari and Kapoor 1987). For example, a subordinate relating to a superior from his/her own culture may perceive what is acceptable behavior differently from what he/she would when relating to a superior from another culture.

In summary, the present study provides two things: information relevant to the hands-on operation of an organization doing business in a multicultural environment, and research avenues for further investigation. Further research may help to determine the degree to which our understanding of the ethical perceptions of organizational politics can be expanded. While our data should be applied cautiously within other cultural contexts, these findings offer global organizations some cogent considerations in their attempts to become more effective by increasing their awareness of the differences in ethical values between cultures.

REFERENCES

Abratt, R., D. Nel, and N.S. Higgs. 1992. An examination of the ethical beliefs of managers using selected scenarios in a cross-cultural environment. *Journal of Business Ethics* 11: 29–35.

Allen, R.L., and L.W. Porter. 1983. *Organizational Influence Processes* (Glenview, IL: Scott, Foresman).

Ansari, M.A., and A. Kapoor. 1987. Organizational context and upward influence tactics. *Organizational Behaviour and Human Decision Processes* 40(1): 39–49.

Becker, H., and D.J. Fritzche. 1987. Business ethics: A Cross-cultural comparison of managers' attitudes. *Journal of Business Ethics* 6: 289–295.

Berne, R.W., and R.E. Freeman. 1992. Ethics and affirmative action—A managerial approach, in R.W. McGee (ed.), *Business Ethics and Common Sense* (Westport, CT: Quorum).

Brenner, S.N. and E.A. Molander. 1977. Is the ethics of business changing? *Harvard Business Review* 55(1): 57–71.

Cavanagh, G.F., D.J. Moberg, and M. Velasquez. 1981. The ethics of organizational politics. *Academy of Management Review* 6: 363–374.

Chacko, H.E. 1990. Methods of upward influence, motivational needs and administrators' perceptions of their supervisors' leadership styles. *Group and Organizational Studies* 15: 253–265.

Chinese Culture Connection. 1987. Chinese values and the search for culture-free dimensions of culture. *Journal of Cross-Cultural Psychology* 18: 143–164.

Dolecheck, M., and C. Dolecheck. 1987. Business Ethics: A comparison of attitudes of managers in Hong Kong and the United States. *Hong Kong Manager* 1: 28–43.

Donaldson, T. 1985. Multinational decision-making: Reconciling international norms. *Journal of Business Ethics* 4: 357–366.

Drory A., and T. Romm. 1990. The definition of organizational politics: A review. *Human Relations* 43: 1133–1154.

Ferguson, H. 1988. *Tomorrow's Global Executive* (Homewood, IL: Dow Jones Irwin).

Ferrell, O.C., and J. Fraederich. 1991. *Business Ethics* (Boston: Houghton Mifflin).

Ferris, G.R., and K.M. Kacmar. 1992. Perceptions of organizational politics. *Journal of Management* 18: 93–116.

Giacalone, R.A. 1985. On slipping when you thought you had put your best foot forward: Self-promotion, self-destruction, and entitlements. *Group and Organization Studies* 10: 61–80.

Giacalone, R.A., and J.W. Beard. (in press). Reconceptualizing interactional problems between foreign nationals and expatriates as dysfunctional impression management. *American Behavioral Scientist.*

Giacalone, R.A., and H.G. Pollard. 1987. The efficacy of accounts for a breach of confidentiality by management. *Journal of Business Ethics* 6: 19–23.

Giacalone, R.A., and P. Rosenfeld (eds.). 1991. *Applied Impression Management* (Newbury Park, CA: Sage).

Goffman, E. 1959. *The Presentation of Self in Everyday Life* (Garden City, NY: Doubleday Anchor).

Hofstede, G. 1980. *Culture's Consequences* (Beverly Hills: Sage).

Izraeli, D. 1988. Ethical beliefs and behavior among managers: A cross-cultural perspective. *Journal of Business Ethics* 7: 263–271.

Kipnis, D., S.M. Schmidt, and I. Wilkinson. 1980. Intraorganizational influence tactics: Exploration in getting one's way. *Journal of Applied Psychology* 65: 440–452.

Kotter, J.P. 1985. *Power and Influence* (New York: Free Press).

Laczniak, G. (1983). Business ethics: A manager's primer. *Business* (January–March): 4.

Langlois, C.C., and B.B. Schlegelmilch. 1990. Do corporate codes reflect national character? Evidence from Europe and the United States. *Journal of International Business Studies* 21: 519–539.

Louie, Kam. 1980. *Critiques of Confucius in Contemporary China* (Hong Kong: Chinese University Press).

Lutz, W.D. 1983. Corporate doublespeak: Making bad news look good. *Business and Society Review* 44: 19–22.

Mayes, B.T., and B.W. Allen. 1977. Toward a definition of organizational politics. *Academy of Management Review* 2: 672–678.

McDonald, G.M., and R.A. Zepp. 1988. Ethical perceptions of Hong Kong Chinese business managers. *Journal of Business Ethics* 7: 835–845.

Newstrom, J.W., and W.A. Ruch. 1975. The ethics of management and the management of ethics. *MSU Business Topics* 23: 29–37.

Olasky, M.N. 1985. Inside the amoral world of public relations: Truth molded for corporate gain. *Business and Society Review* 52: 41–44.

Payne, S.L., and R.A. Giacalone. 1990. Social psychological approaches to the perception of ethical dilemmas. *Human Relations* 43: 649–665.

Pfeffer, J. 1981. *Power in Organizations* (Marshfield, MA: Pitman).

Porter, L.W., R.W. Allen, and H.L. Angle. 1981. The politics of upward influence in organizations, in L.L. Cummings and B.M. Staw (eds.), *Research in Organizational Behavior,* vol. 3 (Greenwich, CT: JAI), pp. 109–149.

Ralston, D.A., D.J. Gustafson, F. Cheung, and R.H. Terpstra. 1992. Eastern values: A comparison of U.S., Hong Kong and PRC managers. *Journal of Applied Psychology* 77: 664–671.

———. 1993. Differences in managerial values: A study of U.S., Hong Kong and PRC managers. *Journal of International Business Studies* 24: 249–275.

Redding, S.G. 1990. *The Spirit of Chinese Capitalism* (Berlin: Walter de Gruyter).

Romm, T., and A. Drory. 1988. Political behavior in organizations: A cross-cultural comparison. *International Journal of Value Based Management* 1: 97–113.

Salbu, S.R. 1992. A legal and economic analysis of insider trading: Establishing an appropriate sphere of regulation. *Business and Professional Ethics Journal* 8: 21–33.

Scholhammer, H. 1977. Ethics in an international business context. *MSU Business Topics* 25: 54–63.

Sethi, S., N. Namiki, and C. Swanson. 1984. *The False Promise of the Japanese Miradi: Illusions and Realities of the Japanese Management System* (Boston: Pitman).

Shenkar, O., and S. Ronen. 1987. Structure and importance of work goals among managers in the PRC. *Academy of Management Journal* 30: 564–576.

Singh, J.B., and V.C. Lakhan. 1989. Business ethics and the international trade in hazardous wastes. *Journal of Business Ethics* 8: 889–899.

Smith, P.B., and M.F. Peterson. 1988. *Leadership, Organizations, and Culture: An Event Management Model* (London: Sage).

Trevino, L.K., and G.A. Ball. 1992. The social implications of punishing unethical behavior: Observers' cognitive and affective reactions. *Journal of Management* 18: 751–768.

Tsalikis, J., and O. Nwachukwu. 1991. A comparison of Nigerian to American views of bribery and extortion in international commerce. *Journal of Business Ethics* 10: 85–98.

Tung, R.L. 1988. People's Republic of China, in R. Nath (ed.), *Comparative Management: A Regional View* (Cambridge, MA: Ballinger), pp. 139–168.

Velasquez, M.G. 1992. *Business Ethics: Concepts and Cases* (Englewood Cliffs, NJ: Prentice-Hall).

Velasquez, M.G., D.J. Moberg, and G.E. Cavanagh. 1983. Organizational Statesmanship and Dirty Politics: Ethical Guidelines for the Organizational Politician. *Organizational Dynamics* 12: 65–80.

Weiss, J.W. 1994. *Business Ethics: A Managerial Stakeholder Approach* (Belmont, CA: Wadsworth).

Wines, W.A., and N.K. Napier. 1992. Business ethics judgments: A Cross-cultural comparison. *Journal of Business Ethics* 11: 671–678.

———. 1992. Toward an understanding of cross-cultural ethics: A tentative model. *Journal of Business Ethics* 11: 831–841.

Wong, S. 1983. Ideology of Chinese industrial managers in Hong Kong. *Journal of the Royal Asiatic Society* 23: 136–171.

Yukl, G., and C.M. Falbe. 1990. Influence tactics in upward, downward and lateral influence attempts. *Journal of Applied Psychology* 75: 132–140.

———. 1991. Importance of different power sources in downward and lateral relations. *Journal of Applied Psychology* 76: 416–423.

Yukl, G., and J.B. Tracey. 1992. Consequences of influence tactics used with subordinates, peers, and the boss. *Journal of Applied Psychology* 77: 525–535.

Zahra, S.A. 1984. Managerial views of organizational politics. *Management Quarterly* 25: 31–37.

———. 1985. Background and work experience correlates of the ethics and effect of organizational politics. *Journal of Business Ethics* 4: 419–423.

———. 1989. Executive values and the ethics of company politics: Some preliminary findings. *Journal of Business Ethics* 8: 15–29.

INDEX

ABOUT THE EDITORS

Lyman W. Porter is professor emeritus in the Graduate School of Management at the University of California, Irvine, where he has been a member of the faculty since 1967. He was the president of the Academy of Management in 1974 and the Society of Industrial-Organizational Psychology in 1976, and he has received Distinguished Scientific Contributions Awards from both organizations. His major fields of interest are management and organizational behavior.

Harold L. Angle, who earned his Ph.D. in organizational behavior at the University of California, Irvine, is professor emeritus of management at the University of Cincinnati. His books and articles have emphasized such topics as influence dynamics, the member-organization relationship, work-family stresses, strategic human resource management, labor-management relations, and the management of innovation. Before entering academic life, he was a career officer in the United States Marine Corps and was the Director of the Marine Corps Office of Manpower Utilization.

The late **Robert W. Allen** was, at the time of his death, professor of management at California State Polytechnic University, Pomona. He received his Ph.D. from the University of California, Irvine, and during his professional career held several high-level management positions in business organizations. His areas of concentration were human resources, management, and organizational behavior.